Criminal Behavior
Second Edition

Criminal Behavior

Second Edition

Elaine Cassel

Lord Fairfax Community College

Douglas A. Bernstein

University of South Florida
University of Southampton, UK

LEA

LAWRENCE ERLBAUM ASSOCIATES, PUBLISHERS

2007   Mahwah, New Jersey   London

Pearson Education, Inc. previously published this work

Lawrence Erlbaum Associates, Inc., Publishers
10 Industrial Avenue
Mahwah, New Jersey 07430
www.erlbaum.com

Cover design by Tomai Maridou

Library of Congress Cataloging-in-Publication Data

Cassel, Elaine.
Criminal behavior / Elaine Cassel, Douglas A. Bernstein. — 2nd ed.
    p. cm.
Includes bibliographical references and index.
ISBN 0-8058-4892-4 (cloth : alk. paper) 1. Criminal behavior—United
States. 2. Criminal psychology—United States. 3. Criminal justice,
Administration of—United States. 4. Juvenile justice, Administration
of—United States. I. Bernstein, Douglas A. II. Title.
  HV6105.C37 2006
  364.3—dc22   2006011746

To my students, teachers, and clients, who have taught me about
psychology and the law—EC
To my sister, Ann Bernstein Harris—DB

Table of Contents

Preface

As this book went into production, a jury in Mississippi convicted 80-year-old former Ku Klux Klansman Edgar Roy Killen of manslaughter in the death of three civil rights workers 41 years to the day after the three men disappeared while investigating the burning of a Black church and helping local Blacks register to vote. The prosecutors had hoped for a murder conviction, but the trial was still notable because it marked the first time a state court had tried anyone for the crimes. When the victims' beaten bodies were found buried in an earthen dam, it was the 1960s, when the racial climate in Mississippi was explosive and when prosecutors were much more likely to prosecute Black rather than White defendants.

What caused Killen and his fellow Klansmen to hate these young men so intensely that they would perpetrate such a gruesome murder? Today, we call it hate crime, and in the book you are about to read, we discuss its roots and the origins of other types of crime, too.

Crime has always been of intense interest to the public and no less so today. Just turn on your television any night and pay attention to the number of crime-related series, documentaries, and movies. Students of psychology, sociology, law, and of course, criminology and criminal justice are interested in many aspects of crime. It is primarily for students of all disciplines who are studying criminal behavior that we wrote this book, although we hope it will also be of interest to others who want to understand the biological, social, and psychological origins of criminal behavior.

We try to answer the following questions:

- What biological, genetic, developmental, familial, social, educational, cultural, political, and economic factors contribute to crime?
- Why do some individuals internalize inhibitions against crime whereas others do not?
- Why do some weigh the risks of committing crime and chose to desist whereas others forge recklessly ahead?
- What motivates one person to settle differences with homicide and another with conciliation? Many criminals are motivated by what Western society encourages in all of everyone—self-interest, competitiveness, and the acquisition of power. However, most people do not cross the line and behave in ways that society condemns.
- What is the difference between criminals and the rest of society?
- What are the differences and similarities between and among criminals?
- Is the difference between a serial murderer and a spouse murderer merely a matter of degree?
- How about the difference between an armed robber and a shoplifter?

The answers are varied and complex, but research reveals some answers and many more clues.

Organization

The book is organized around five dimensions related to the causes, characteristics, and consequences of crime. They are

- The criminal and juvenile justice systems.
- The biological, psychological, social, and environmental roots of crime.
- The nature of the crimes themselves.
- The victims of crime.
- The punishment of crime.

A recurring theme of the book is to be found in its depiction of criminal behavior as developmental pathology that begins in childhood, takes roots in adolescence, and all too often, flourishes in adulthood. We took this developmental perspective on crime that echoes psychologist Erik Erikson's (1957) view that

> Potentialities for goodness and badness are inborn in all; they grow to probabilities during childhood. But the certainty of a man's or a woman's measure is not established before the end of his or her adolescence, and not without some kind of confirmation by the adult world. (p. 22)

Accordingly, we present the phenomenon of crime as a developmental process occurring in social, political, and individual contexts. In addition, we address the ways in which mental illness, the criminal and juvenile justice systems, methods of punishment, and the victims' rights movement affect criminal behavior and its consequences for perpetrators, individual victims, and society as a whole. We have attempted to include the latest criminal statistics available as well as the most current research on the causes and correlates of crime and violence. You will learn that although the last few years witnessed an explosion of multidisciplinary research into the causes of crime, little attention was paid as to how to "treat" crime and criminals. Seemingly at a loss for anything else to try, authorities in the United States have turned back the clock on its treatment of juvenile delinquents and adult criminals alike. Many states have lowered the age for trying juveniles as adults; the United States has the unflattering distinction of incarcerating more people for more crimes than any civilized country in the world, and it is alone among Western countries in imposing the ultimate punishment—the death penalty. Proponents of the U.S. approach point out that current statistics show that violent crime is decreasing, but these reductions must be viewed in comparison to the staggeringly high crime rates of the 1970s and 1980s when crack cocaine, poverty, and violent gangs contributed to skyrocketing violent crime that had some large U.S. cities in a virtual state of siege.

As you will learn from this book, much is known about the roots of crime and the pathways that lead to various patterns of criminal behavior. Much less is known, unfortunately, about how to prevent crime. We summarize programs that researchers suggest offer the best hope for doing a better job of dealing with crime in the 21st century than the country did in the 20th century. Most of these programs aim at intervening early in the lives of at-risk populations before the roots of crime have a chance to take hold. Whether such programs will be widely adopted and whether they will ultimately be successful is still in doubt. Time will tell, but we hope that reading this book will help you to recognize the importance of early experience on crime and will inspire you to consider what you might do—as a parent, a teacher, a policymaker, a law enforcement agent, a corrections officer, a voter, or simply as a concerned citizen—to become a part of the solution to the problem of crime.

Text Features

This edition has several new features. At various places in the margins you will find a gavel icon (ed: add it in paren) indicating the location of legal cases dealing with the topic under discussion. In addition, key terms are highlighted in boldface font and also listed at the end of each chapter. These key terms and their definitions also appear in the Glossary at the end of the book. Each chapter now includes a summary section, followed by a list of "Questions for Review" that reinforce the main concepts presented in the chapter.

Each chapter ends with a feature we call "Track It Down," a list of URLs for websites related to chapter content. The first URL listed in each "Track it Down" section is this book's own website, which will be frequently updated with new research, case decisions, and current events related to criminal behavior.

Acknowledgments

We wish to express our appreciation to Debra Riegert, the acquisitions editor who encouraged us and supported us in revising the manuscript for this second edition. Our gratitude to our production assistant, Lisa Ochoa, cannot be overstated. She is responsible for the creation of the figures and tables and for putting the thousands of references into acceptable format. We also want to thank Sarah Wright and all others at LEA for their expertise in bringing this second edition to you.

About the Authors

Elaine Cassel is an attorney. She also teaches criminal behavior and psychology at Lord Fairfax Community College (Virginia) and teaches law at other institutions. She is a frequent contributor to *FindLaw's Writ,* a Thomson-West online publication, where she writes about many of the issues related to crime and human behavior that are discussed in this book. She is often interviewed about psychological and legal issues on U.S. and international public radio programs.

Douglas Bernstein, a clinical psychologist, is Professor Emeritus at the University of Illinois, Courtesy Professor of Psychology at the University of South Florida, and Visiting Professor of Psychology at Southampton University. Among the other books he has coauthored or coedited are *Introduction to Clinical Psychology, Abnormal Psychology, Psychology, Essentials of Psychology,* and *Lifespan Development in Context.*

1

What Is Crime?

Crime as a Legal Concept
The Sociology of Crime
The Politics of Crime
The Morality of Crime

The Classification of Crimes
The Statistics of Crime
Methods for Studying Criminal Behavior
Criminals and Criminal Behavior

In Florida, a 12-year-old boy kills a 9-year-old girl with moves he learned from watching wrestling on television; 19 men hijack four airplanes and use them as flying bombs to damage the Pentagon building and destroy the World Trade Center, killing almost 3,000 people; a brilliant Harvard-educated scientist, Theodore Kaczynski (who became known as the "Unabomber") kills and maims victims by sending explosives through the mail; a man and a teenage boy terrorize the Washington, DC area by killing people at random with a high-powered rifle fired from the trunk of a car; someone sends anthrax in the mail, causing the death of several postal workers and sickening many more; a man in Washington State admits to killing more than 30 women; a doctor performs a late-term abortion on a woman whose life is in danger; a nurse gradually ups the dosage of morphine given to a dying patient to relieve her pain; a man who knows he is infected with the HIV virus has unprotected sex with many women; a woman consumes enough drugs and alcohol during her pregnancy to give her newborn a cocaine addiction and fetal alcohol syndrome; gay and lesbian couples engage in consensual sex; a pedophile uses Internet chat rooms to entice young boys to sexual encounters; a chemical company dumps carcinogenic waste on its property, contaminating groundwater for miles around and contributing to the development of leukemia in dozens of nearby residents; media mogul and homemaking queen Martha Stewart sells certain shares of stock after receiving inside information that the price is about to fall; executives manipulate energy markets and falsify corporate accounts for personal gain, ultimately bankrupting their company and costing its employees and stockholders their jobs and their money; tobacco company scientists make cigarettes more addictive by increasing their nicotine content; bank officers knowingly make bad loans that cause the failure of financial institutions; and high-level employees at Wall Street firms manipulate stock prices, costing investors billions and shaking public confidence in equity markets.

Which of these events do you consider the most loathsome? Before you answer, keep in mind that some of them are crimes and some are not. Some things that most of us would consider morally reprehensible are neither prohibited nor punishable by law. Why are certain acts crimes, whereas others—as at least as horrible—are not?

Also, how many perpetrators of the criminal acts just listed do you think could have been identified as likely criminals at birth? At the age of 2 years old? At 5 or 8? At 15? At 21? There are few, if any, parents who think that their babe in arms, their toddler, their school-aged child, or their teenager will become a serial killer, a terrorist, a child molester, or a stock manipulator. Yet with the benefit of hindsight, some parents of criminals are

1

able to look back on the lives of their children and recall acts and attitudes that could have been seen as predictors of trouble ahead.

This was certainly the case for Ted Kaczynski's mother. At the time of his arrest, a psychology professor we know assigned her introductory psychology class to follow the Unabomber story as it developed and to watch especially for information about Kaczynski's childhood that might provide clues as to factors that might have contributed to the development of his criminal behavior. At first, it appeared that the Unabomber was a brilliant young man from a normal middle-class family, but a less flattering picture soon emerged. The more Kaczynski's mother looked back on her son's childhood, the more she began to recall unusual behaviors that could have been warning signs of maladaptive development. Of course some of her memories may have been distorted by the lens of time and by learning of her son's criminal acts, but her recollections fit a pattern seen in the childhoods and upbringings of many notorious serial killers we describe in chapter 8. Characteristic patterns also appear in the psychological development, social history, and symptoms of maladjustment seen in many sex offenders and other types of criminals.

In fact, we organized this book as we have because we believe that the origins and emergence of criminal behavior can be best understood by looking at the psychology of individual criminals as well as at the biological, family, social, cultural, and political systems in which those criminals develop. We begin, in chapters 1, 2, and 3, by defining crime in its legal, social, political, and moral contexts and by discussing the role of the criminal justice system as part of the solution to crime and as part of the problem of crime. In chapters 4 through 9, we explore the biological, psychological, and social roots of crime, emphasizing the development of criminal personalities and behaviors from childhood. In chapters 10 and 11, we describe the characteristics of some specific forms of crime; and finally, in chapters 12, 13, and 14, we look at the consequences of crime for its victims, its perpetrators, and for society, and we consider the likely future role of crime in shaping our social and political landscapes.

Crime as a Legal Concept

Before we discuss criminal behavior, we must define crime. In the most general terms, crime is defined as acts, or failures to act, that a society has decided it wants to punish. This is the society's way of prohibiting conduct deemed to be in opposition to the interests of its citizens, their property, and the society itself. Criminal laws are enacted to protect people, property, and political and social institutions. These laws define prohibited acts from homicide to reckless driving and a myriad of other actions, establish procedures for law enforcement, and dictate methods and degrees of punishment for law violations. In theory, at least, punishment is imposed to provide a penalty, to protect society by temporarily or permanently incarcerating wrongdoers, to deter future wrongdoing, and to rehabilitate offenders.

In thinking about what constitutes punishable crimes, it is important to remember that acts that may be a crime in one situation are not a crime in another. For instance, sexual intercourse is legal behavior between married individuals and, in most states, between consenting unmarried adults. Yet sexual intercourse is a crime if it is with a child, with a close relative, by means of force, and, in some states, between unmarried people, either heterosexual or homosexual. In other words, in many cases, criminal behavior is the same as noncriminal behavior but for the social and/or situational context in which it occurs. The same law that mandates punishment for killing a stranger also excuses that killing if it was done in self-defense.

Legal Definitions of Crime

In more specific legal terms, **crime** is an intentional act or failure to act that is in violation of criminal law, committed without defense or excuse, and penalized by the state as a felony or misdemeanor. A **misdemeanor** is an offense typically punishable by incarceration for a year or less in a local jail and a fine of up to several thousand dollars. A **felony** is an offense punishable by commitment to the state penitentiary or other correctional institution for a period of one year to life. A **capital felony** is an offense that is potentially punishable by death. In addition to possible confinement in a penitentiary, being convicted of a felony in most states deprives the convict of several basic civil liberties including the right to vote, to serve as a juror, and to possess a firearm. Felons are not eligible for many types of jobs, including positions in law enforcement or government and military service, and they are ineligible for licensure in many professions.

Driving-related offenses such as speeding and violations of licensing and equipment requirements are not generally criminal. Although fines may be assessed, if there is no threat of punishment by incarceration, the offense is not a crime. However, driving while intoxicated, some types of reckless driving, and vehicular manslaughter are crimes. In a few instances, failure to act may constitute a crime. For instance, not stopping and rendering assistance to others if you have been involved in a motor vehicle accident may be a crime.

Even acts or omissions that are prohibited by law generally will not rise to the level of criminal conduct unless the accused person possesses **mens rea**, the mental element of culpability. This means that the offender must have had either the express or implied intent to act contrary to law. Striking out at someone with the intent to harm them is express *mens rea* and may be sufficient to constitute the crime of battery (an unlawful touching of another). However, if while flailing your arms during an animated conversation you accidentally harm someone, you may be forced to pay for the injuries you cause someone, but you will not be charged with a crime.

The law will presume *mens rea* even if you harm someone other than your intended victim. In one recent case, for example, a man fired into a vehicle in an effort to shoot the driver, a rival drug dealer. The bullet struck and killed the driver's son, who was also in the vehicle, but the man was still charged with first-degree (pre-meditated) murder because implied *mens rea* is embodied in the felony murder rule. If you accidentally and unintentionally kill someone while in the process of committing certain other serious felonies such as arson, rape, robbery, burglary, or abduction, you can be charged with first-degree felony murder. Thus, when some-one commits a serious felony in a manner such that death could result (e.g., holding up someone with a hand-gun that accidentally goes off), the law will presume that the criminal intended the accidental outcome. However, neither of these murderous situations would constitute capital murder (which is willful and deliber-ate) because there was no actual intent to murder the victim.

In most cases, it is not difficult for criminal prosecutors to prove *mens rea*. Even if you commit an illegal act while you were so drunk that you could not have formed a conscious intent to do wrong, you will proba-bly still be found to have *mens rea*. Why? Because your inability to form intent was caused by your intentional ingestion of alcohol; and because being drunk was a foreseeable result of your drinking, you bear responsibil-ity for the consequences—including the fact that drunkenness interfered with your ability to consciously choose *not* to commit the wrongful act. Hence, your actions will be treated as criminal.

Some laws are designed to punish actions even when express and implied intent is absent. The law desig-nates these acts as *malum in se,* meaning that they are so bad that society wants to punish them even if there was no knowledge of or intent to do harm. For example, having consensual sex with someone under a certain age may be punishable as statutory rape even if you did not know that the person was under age. In fact, even if you asked the person how old he or she is and were given false information, you could still be convicted of the crime. Similarly, some state and federal antipollution laws make no exception for persons who dispose of toxic substances without awareness that the substance is hazardous. If you dump the toxin in a river, you and your employer may be held criminally liable.

However, the law will not hold an individual responsible for conduct normally defined as criminal if the following justifications and defenses can be proven: (1) self-defense, (2) insanity at the time of the offense, (3) entrapment, and (4) infancy (being under a certain age). We discuss these justifications and defenses in more detail in later chapters.

Who Defines Crime?

The U.S. Constitution guarantees that there can be no punishment without laws, a principle derived from ancient Roman law (*Nulla poena sine lege*) by way of English common law. Yet where do criminal laws come from? Philosophers speak of two kinds of law: positivist law and natural law. *Positivist law* is reflected in leg-islative actions and court rulings. *Natural law* is manifest in a society's belief systems and norms of conduct that are outside—some say above—written laws. As we discuss later in relation to the morality of crime, there is often tension between positivist law and natural law.

In the United States, the three sources of positivist criminal law are (1) statutes enacted by legislative bodies and published as criminal codes; (2) case decisions made by courts of appeal; and (3) administrative laws that govern the licensing of professionals, the conduct of business, and the limits on air and water pollution, to name a few. Definitions of criminal behavior appear in local (county or city), state, and federal laws, all of which may govern the same actions and that may or may not be consistent with one another.

All citizens are presumed to know all the laws governing their actions, thus justifying the well-known maxim that "ignorance of the law is no defense." However, the Constitution's ban against *ex post facto* ("after the fact") laws requires that an act or omission must have been codified as a crime at the time of the offense. A law enacted after an act or omission took place cannot be used as the basis for a criminal prosecution of that act or omission.

Criminal Versus Civil Trials

It is important to note the difference between criminal prosecutions and civil lawsuits. Once crimes are defined, those who are alleged to have committed criminal acts are prosecuted by local, state, or federal governments because these acts are considered to be not only wrongs against the victim(s) but against the interests of the city, county, state, or federal government (also known as the "sovereign" body) in maintaining public morals, health, safety and order. In a criminal trial, the **plaintiff** (the party instigating the action) is the government or state, and the **defendant** (the party against whom the action is brought) is the alleged perpetrator of the crime.

In civil trials, the plaintiffs and defendants are individuals or business entities pitted against each other. A civil suit is based on laws or precedents requiring payment of money for acting wrongly or inappropriately in certain circumstances. For instance, if you fail to pay attention to your driving and damage someone's car and/or injure its occupants, you could be sued to pay for the damages to the car and for the medical expenses and pain and suffering of the occupants. If you sign a contract with a swimming pool company to have a swimming pool installed, and the pool has cracks or leaks, you could sue the company for money to repair the damage or to get your payment back.

Defendants have a right to a jury in felony criminal trials, but this right is not guaranteed in all types of civil cases. In almost all states, the verdict of a 12-member jury must be unanimous in criminal trials, but in most cases, only a majority vote of a panel of 6 jurors is required for a judgment in a civil case (see chapter 2). The state punishes guilty criminal defendants. As already noted, punishment usually consists of imprisonment for periods ranging from a few days to life; for some offenses in some jurisdictions, the death penalty can be imposed. In contrast, defendants in civil courts can only be found liable for wrongdoing and are punished only by being required to pay money, called damages, to those who brought the lawsuit. In some cases, a criminal act may not only be prosecuted in criminal court but also result in a civil suit for damages associated with the crime. In one famous example, O. J. Simpson was found not guilty of murdering his ex-wife and a friend of hers, but after the estates of both victims sued him in a civil court, he was found liable for damages in the amount of $33.1 million. We discuss the criminal justice process in more detail in chapter 2.

The Sociology of Crime

Given that the criminal codes in the United States and other democracies are enacted by elected legislative bodies, the laws that prohibit, or, in some cases, require certain acts, are considered to be "the will of the people." So behind every *legal* judgment defining some act as a crime is a *social* judgment that the prohibited activity deserves to be outlawed and punished. Thus, criminal law serves as a means of social control. In his social history of the criminal justice system in the United States, Lawrence Friedman (1993) put it this way: "Law is a fabric of norms and practices in a particular society; the norms and practices are social judgments made concrete: the living, breathing embodiment of society's attitudes, prejudices, and values" (p. 101). Thus, the body of criminal law appearing in a given jurisdiction is not a random collection of statutory enactments. A country's legal history is mainly a reflection of its social and political history.

The enormous impact of social values and political forces in relation to crime can be seen in the U.S. Supreme Court's ruling that "crimes in the United States are what the laws of the individual States make them, subject to constitutional limitations" (*Rochin v. California,* 342 U.S. 165, 168, 1952). As a result, acts that are prohibited in some states may not be prohibited in others. Such interstate inconsistency is relatively rare, but criminal codes (and prosecution policies) do change as the will of the people changes in particular jurisdictions. For example, most states have struck down laws forbidding fornication (sexual acts between unmarried heterosexual individuals) and adultery (sexual intercourse in which one participant is married to someone else). Yet 19 states have laws prohibiting sodomy (anal or oral sex) between consenting adults. In some states, such as Virginia, undercover police officers set up "sting" operations in locations known to be frequented by homosexuals and target them for arrest.

The U.S. Supreme Court supported at least one state sodomy law as a legitimate manifestation of the will of the people when, in 1986, it upheld convictions for sodomy between consenting homosexual partners under a Georgia statute (*Bowers v. Hardwick,* 1986). However, in November 1998, the Georgia Supreme Court ruled that same statute to be a violation of privacy and overturned the conviction of a man who engaged in consensual heterosexual oral sex with his niece. The social values communicated by this decision are clear in that the statute was struck down when it resulted in the prosecution of heterosexuals. Texas's sodomy law was struck down by the U.S. Supreme Court in 2003 because it applied only to homosexuals (*Lawrence v. Texas,* 2003). Yet sodomy laws that forbid consensual sex between gays and straights are still on the books in many states.

The U.S. Supreme Court has also overridden the "will" of some states, reflecting a federal policy that restrictions on certain types of behavior violate individual rights guaranteed by the U.S. Constitution. For example, in 1967, the Court ruled that it was unconstitutional for Virginia and 16 other states to have laws prohibiting marriage between Blacks and Whites. The case arose from the conviction of an interracial couple who had been lawfully married in Washington, DC, then moved to Virginia, where interracial marriage was a crime. In its ruling, the Court said that "under our Constitution, the freedom to marry or not marry a person of another race resides with the individual and cannot be infringed by the State" (*Loving v. Virginia,* 388 U.S. 1, 1967).

Other examples of criminal laws reflecting changes in social values include U.S. statutes that, during the Prohibition era, outlawed the manufacture, purchase, and consumption of alcohol and current laws against the manufacture, sale, and possession of drugs such as cocaine and heroin. Heroin was developed for use as a painkiller for soldiers suffering battle wounds. Only when its addictive properties became apparent was it outlawed. The same can be said for LSD and other psychedelic drugs, which were not legislated against until their harmful effects became generally known. Also, strange as it seems in these days of multistate lotteries, it was not very long ago that gambling was prohibited in most states. Then, in the 1980s, cash-strapped state legislatures decided that it would be acceptable to fill the public coffers (without raising taxes) by legalizing what had once been considered a threat to public decency and morals. As a result, many states passed laws that allow gambling in certain formats, notably state-controlled lottery systems and other state-sanctioned betting activities. Today, however, faced with growing evidence that gambling can become compulsive and that those who gamble the most are those who can least afford to do so, some states (such as Maryland) are again outlawing certain gambling activities.

Advances in technology have also changed laws. We now have criminal statutes concerning behaviors that did not exist even 30 years ago—everything from theft using ATMs, to unapproved efforts at human cloning and genetic engineering, to offenses committed on the Internet and crimes of terror. In other words, as people continue to find new ways to subvert and misuse technology, new criminal laws will continue to appear as a reflection of the will of the people.

The fact that the definition of criminal conduct changes with changes in societal values, economic conditions, and political climates has been raised by critics as a major philosophical problem with the legal concept of crime. No matter how you look at it, they say, the law represents the coercive threat of punishment over those who violate it. In short, say these critics, the law protects power and those in power. Consider, for example, the 19th century "slave codes" that prohibited slaves in the United States from engaging in everything from insubordination, insurrection, and running away to conducting commerce, administering medicine, meeting with other slaves, or playing musical instruments. Slaves who violated these laws were subject to summary punishment by their masters, usually by whipping, branding, or being pinned by the ears to posts for many hours. Slaves accused of slave code violations were not granted trials unless they were accused of raping a White woman. Such cases could result in the death penalty, but the trials tended to be summary proceedings that typically ended in a guilty verdict, especially because the slave codes also made it a crime for slaves to testify against White people (Friedman, 1993).

American legal history contains many other examples in which the will of the people reflected social values that worked against ethnic minorities and the poor. When American Indians resisted the settlement of their lands in the 18th and 19th centuries, their behavior was defined as criminal and they were prosecuted for murder, rape, and robbery. In the 1870s, California enacted laws that severely limited the rights of Chinese residents. Until the advent of the civil rights laws of the 1960s, the laws of some states not only prohibited interracial marriages but also forbade Blacks from attending "White" schools. "Jim Crow" laws made it a crime for them to frequent "White establishments," drink from "White fountains," or sit in those areas of buses, movie theaters, and other public places that were reserved for White patrons. The "poor laws" of the 19th century allowed people who owed money to be confined in prisons, whereas vagrancy laws allowed the arrest of people who were deemed to be "undesirable" and a public nuisance because they lived on the streets or on "Skid Row." Even today, homeless citizens in many U.S. cities tend to receive special scrutiny by the legal system, and social critics suggest that it is no accident that the weight of criminal law continues to fall most heavily on the lower socioeconomic classes.

Critics of law as a means of social control see criminal law as part of the process of maintaining the social *status quo*, especially the stratification of various classes of citizens. They predict that when changing social conditions create a need for legal changes, the criminal statutes will be revised to meet the needs of new vested interests (Chambliss, 1964). This concept has been described as the politicalization of law. Today, efforts to prohibit marriage between homosexuals, including a movement to pass an amendment to the U.S. Constitution prohibiting gay marriage, are an example laws as an effort at social control. The gay and lesbian rights movement of the past 30 years has led to increasing numbers of gays and lesbians "coming out" and demanding treatment equal to that received by heterosexuals including privileges afforded to married persons. The law is now trying to play "catch-up" as same-sex marriage becomes a hot political issue.

The Politics of Crime

As we already noted, in democratic countries, criminal laws are supposed to represent the will of the people because those laws were enacted by elected representatives. When judges are elected to the bench, the common law rulings they hand down might also be seen as reflecting the people's will. In this sense then, criminal laws are designed to protect political power systems as well as people and property. Criminal laws also regulate businesses, determine public versus private ownership of property, and raise revenue (it is a crime not to pay one's taxes). Virtually every country has at one time or another utilized criminal laws for social and political control, to punish acts or people repugnant to those in power; and because all laws are creations of governing individuals and institutions, all laws are political to some degree.

Critical criminologists highlight the ways in which criminal laws are used as a mechanism of social control. They believe that social and political institutions make, create, and enforce criminal laws as a method of punishing those who do not conform to the needs of the powerful (L. J. Siegal, 1998; Sykes, 1974). Max Weber (1864–1920), a German economist and social historian whose ideas developed from the economic and political theories of Karl Marx, founded this line of thought known as social conflict theory. The major tenet of **social conflict theory** is that capitalist systems insure constant competition between social and political groups wishing to control the government and the economy. From this perspective, legal and judicial systems mainly serve the interests of the "power elite" (M. Schwartz & DeKeseredy, 1991), and crime is the result of unequal distributions of wealth and power. Followers of social conflict theory view capitalist criminal justice systems as instruments for controlling the behavior of the powerless.

Marxist feminism theory applies this line of reasoning to the origins of female criminality. Proponents of this theory believe that female criminals are victims of a system designed to exploit them and that much criminal behavior by women stems directly from their victimization by men, especially through physical and sexual abuse and sexual harassment. In short, they maintain that the roots of female criminality lie in the patterns and practices of male supremacy, aggression, and sexual dominance (Messerschmidt, 1986; Schwendinger & Schwendinger, 1983; Simpson, 1989).

Although proponents of social conflict theory are on the fringes of social, political, and legal thinking about crime, there is evidence that power structures in democratic societies do use criminal law to serve their political purposes. Consider situations in which government agencies in democratic countries engage in overt and covert activities that would be considered crimes were they to occur in nonpolitical contexts. For example, the U.S. Central Intelligence Agency (CIA) has a long history of involvement in foreign assassinations and has often given support in the form of money and arms to foreign governments whose actions most Americans would consider abhorrent and even criminal. To take just one case, the CIA played a clear role in the rise and fall of President Mobutu Seko Sese of Zaire. With the support of the United States and other Western governments, Mobutu came to power in 1965 following the Congo's independence from Belgium. The CIA was implicated in the assassination of Mobutu's predecessor, Patrice Lumumba, and because Zaire was a way station for covert CIA operations in support of anticommunist rebels in Angola, the CIA made direct cash payments to Mobutu and provided other forms of assistance when he was in political trouble. Yet Mobutu was a tyrannical despot who sent Zaire into virtual bankruptcy even as he stole hundreds of millions of dollars from the proceeds of his mineral-rich country's exports. He threw out existing laws and replaced them with a new body of law, called "Mobutuism," which he enforced with ruthless disregard for the rights of his citizens. Few would disagree that Mobutu's actions were crimes, and it can be argued that the U.S. government's support of him was, itself, an abetting of crime. Yet Mobutu's actions were not crimes in the legal sense because Mobutuism sanctioned them, and the CIA's activities were merely an implementation of U.S. foreign policy. (Mobutu left office in May of 1997 under military pressure from rebel armies and political pressure from the United States, whose government had brought him to power 32 years earlier.)

A more recent example is the case of Iraq's now-deposed dictator Saddam Hussein. When Iran and Iraq were at war in the 1980s, the United States backed Hussein's government but at the turn of the 21st century decided that his long history of killing political opponents, his campaigns of mass murder against certain Iraqi religious groups, and his flaunting of United Nations sanctions following his invasion of Kuwait made him a criminal, a threat to peace in the region, and possibly an ally of Islamic terrorists. In 2003, after he refused to step down on his own, the United States led a coalition of countries in a controversial invasion of Iraq that removed Hussein from power and ultimately took him into custody.

Other examples of the politicalization of crime include prosecutorial discretion (chapter 2) and selective punishment (chapter 13). These politically driven facts of legal life are reflected in the U.S. legal system's relatively lenient treatment of banking swindles, illegal stock trading, various political shenanigans, violations of environmental pollution laws, and other white-collar and corporate crimes. Although these crimes cause far greater financial and personal losses to far more people than do drug possession, burglary, car theft, and other nonviolent crimes against property, the perpetrators of these latter crimes make up the largest segment of U.S. prison populations.

Yet another example of the politicization of crime is seen in the success of demands made by citizens' groups that their legislators "do something" about crime by enacting laws that make it a federal as well as a state offense to engage in car jacking, drive-by shooting, domestic violence, bombings, and certain other actions. It was through such laws that Timothy McVeigh and Terry Nichols faced both federal and state prosecution for the bombing of the Oklahoma City federal building in 1995. Indeed, 40% of federal crime laws enacted since 1865 have been passed since 1970. In his 1998 annual report to Congress, then Supreme Court Chief Justice William H. Rehnquist cautioned that federalizing crimes has rarely, if ever, reduced such crimes significantly because without dramatic increases in federal police and prosecutors, the federal government is able to deal with only a small percentage of these crimes. Other legal experts note that federal prosecution of crimes normally handled by the states tend to distract federal law enforcement personnel from fighting broader crimes such as violations of antitrust, civil rights, and food and drug laws.

Yet public pressure for the "federalization" of crime is hard to resist—especially when it is driven by sensational news stories. For example, in the wake of the brutal slaying of Matthew Shepard, a homosexual man, in Wyoming in 1998, there was an initiative to make it a federal crime to murder a gay person. When the law failed to pass, gay rights activists accused the U.S. Congress of callousness about such crimes despite the fact that the two men arrested for Shepard's murder were prosecuted and ultimately given life sentences under the state's murder law. After the September 11, 2001 terrorist attacks on this country, the U.S. Congress created many new crimes under the heading of "terrorism" (see chapter 8). Many states have not only followed the federal laws but created their own terrorism crimes.

The Morality of Crime

Given that morality is a belief system that determines right from wrong, by now it should be apparent that morality and law are not necessarily synonymous. The 18th-century philosopher Immanuel Kant noted this dichotomy in making the distinction between the universal law of morals representing value and belief systems (what some call natural law) and positivist or human-made laws. U.S. slave codes, anti-Chinese statutes, summary trials of American Indians, and the U.S. government's support for the Mobutu regime demonstrate that acts that are morally repugnant under most value systems may not be illegal in certain social or political climates. Yet, in each of these examples, once social thought evolved to recognize their immorality, the laws relating to them were changed. So in a sense, immoral laws may be the precursors to social change. It has been suggested that the Athenian government's trial and punishment of Socrates for his independent thinking so shocked the average citizen of Athens that the way was prepared for a new morality and a new social order.

A more recent example of this process in U.S. history was the enactment of civil rights laws in the 1960s that eradicated Jim Crow and other statutes that had limited the rights and opportunities of African Americans. In leading the social and political revolution that led to the passage of civil rights legislation, Dr. Martin Luther King Jr. advocated "civil disobedience," a doctrine in which protesters deliberately disobeyed discriminatory laws on the grounds that they are immoral. In his "Letter from the Birmingham Jail" (King, 1963), Dr. King stated his belief that there are two types of laws: just and unjust. King said that people have a duty to disobey unjust laws. King believed that just laws were moral laws, what the philosophers called natural laws, and that unjust laws, although positivist laws enacted by sovereign powers, were immoral laws. King (1963) wrote that an unjust law is not "rooted in eternal law and natural law. Any law that uplifts human personality is just. Any law that degrades human personality is unjust. ... I would agree with St. Augustine that 'an unjust law is no law at all'" (pp. 8.27–8.29). Earlier, sociologist Durkheim (1938/1997) noted that

> It would never have been possible to establish the freedom of thought we now enjoy if the regulations prohibiting it had not been violated before being solemnly abrogated. At that time, however, the violation was a crime, since it was an offense against sentiments still very keen in the average conscience. And yet this crime was useful as a prelude to reforms which daily became more necessary. (p. 18)

Psychologist Lawrence Kohlberg (1984) made a similar distinction between law and morality in his theory of moral development. He believed that achievement of a sense of morality, of right and wrong, proceeds in developmental stages. In the earliest, or "preconventional," stage, a child's sense of right and wrong, Kohlberg (1984) said, derives from the threat of punishment. Thus, when a 4-year-old refrains from some prohibited act, it is typically because of fear of "getting in trouble." Kohlberg believed that most adults enter and remain in a second, or "conventional," developmental stage governed by positivist law. That is, most of us behave in accordance with the law simply because "it is the law." In this stage, morality (rightness) is synonymous with what the code of law says. Kohlberg believed that only a few adults consistently achieve a third, or "postconventional," stage of moral development in which morality is defined by general, universal principles that are above and beyond positivist laws and represent universal moral principles. The actions of people at this stage are seen as reflecting a "higher" law that they believe governs what is right and wrong. Dr. King's exhortation to disobey unjust laws is a notable example of postconventional morality. We discuss the significance of Kohlberg's theory further in chapter 7.

The Classification of Crimes

Most criminal codes classify crimes into eight major categories:

1. Crimes against persons: These include homicide and manslaughter, kidnapping, assault and battery, robbery, extortion, and criminal sexual assaults (rape, sexual battery).
2. Crimes against property: Included here are arson, burglary, larceny, embezzlement, and trespass.

3. Crimes involving fraud: Forgery, impersonation, false pretense, writing bad checks, and illegally using a credit card are the main examples.
4. Crimes involving health and safety: These involve possession, manufacture, and distribution of illicit drugs; driving while intoxicated; and violations of gun laws or other weapon statutes.
5. Crimes involving morals and decency: These include gambling; prostitution; cruelty to animals: and sexual offenses such as fornication, cohabitation, incest, and obscenity.
6. Crimes against peace and order: Examples are riot, unlawful assembly, and disorderly conduct.
7. Crimes against the administration of justice: This category refers to perjury (lying under oath), bribery of officials, contempt of court, resisting arrest, and obstruction of justice.
8. Offenses against the sovereign: The main crime here is treason.

Each of these crimes has its own standard legal definition. For instance, *criminal homicide* is the willful killing of one human being by another (excluding attempted killing, negligent killing, accidental death, and justifiable homicide). *Forcible rape* is the carnal knowledge of a female forcibly against her will (note that male victims are not included). *Robbery* is taking, or attempting to take, anything of value from the care, custody, or control of a person by force or threat of force or violence and/or by putting the victim in fear. *Aggravated assault* is an unlawful attack by one person on another for inflicting severe or aggravated bodily injury, usually by means of a weapon or by means likely to produce death or great bodily harm. *Theft* involves the unlawful taking of money or property without force or threat of force. *Arson* is the destruction of property by fire, and its victims may be subjected to force. Although not yet a formal category, a wide range of offenses are now considered crimes of terror in the United States. They include, for example, contributing money to a terrorist organization, and using or threatening to use force against civilians for political purposes. We discuss these crime categories in more detail in chapters 10 and 11.

The Statistics of Crime

Do you ever wonder where the news media get the information that tells us that crime is decreasing, that most criminals are male, or that most violent offenders know their victims? Usually, news accounts about crime, criminals, and crime rates in the United States come from the *Uniform Crime Reporting* (UCR) Program, a nationwide cooperative effort by more than 16,000 city, county, and state law enforcement agencies that send information to the Federal Bureau of Investigation (FBI) in Washington, DC, about crimes brought to their attention in their respective jurisdictions. The primary objective of the UCR Program is to generate reliable statistics for use in law enforcement management, administration, and operation. However, it is also a leading indicator of social conditions in the United States and as such, is important to researchers and scholars in the fields of psychology, criminology, sociology, and political science.

Presently, official UCR statistics are confined to data for seven specific offenses that are "indexed," or categorized, as either violent crimes or property crimes. These two categories were chosen to serve as an index for gauging fluctuations in the overall volume and rate of crime. Thus, the UCR statistics are compiled and reported as the number of reports for index crimes per 100,000 of population, although other information—such as age and ethnicity of criminal and victim—are also reported when known.

Violent crimes, called "Index 1" crimes, include murder and nonnegligent manslaughter, forcible rape, robbery, and aggravated assault. Property crimes, known as "Index 2" crimes, include burglary, larceny theft, motor vehicle theft, and arson. In 2002, 12.0% of the reported index offenses were violent crimes and 88.0% were property crimes. Larceny theft showed the highest volume, representing 59.4% of all 2002 index offenses; murder, representing only one-tenth of a percent, accounted for the fewest offenses. Data such as these are standard features of an annual volume called *Crime in the United States.* Each year's edition contains many different types of statistical information on crime, including its distribution across age, gender, and ethnicity, and changes in its prevalence. The report's "Crime Clock" depicts the regularity of the commission of nonviolent crime as compared to violent crime. Figure 1.1 is from 2003.

Before the FBI conducts its statistical analyses of UCR data, program staff thoroughly examine each crime report for deviations from standard reporting criteria and requirements. Indeed, the accuracy of UCR data and

CRIME CLOCK

Every 22.8 seconds	One Violent Crime

Every 31.8 minutes	One Murder
Every 5.6 minutes	One Forcible Rape
Every 1.3 minutes	One Robbery
Every 36.8 seconds	One Aggravated Assault

Every 3.0 seconds	One Property Crime

Every 14.6 seconds	One Burglary
Every 4.5 seconds	One Larceny-theft
Every 25.0 seconds	One Motor Vehicle Theft

FIGURE 1.1   *Crime clock.* From *Crime in the United States–2003* (p. 7), by Federal Bureau of Investigation, 2004, Washington, DC: Government Printing Office.

the statistics derived from them depend primarily on the care with which each reporting agency collects and reports crime within its jurisdiction. Those data can be affected by a staff member's decision not to report incidents or to downgrade the seriousness of incidents. So if the victim of domestic violence does not want to prosecute his or her partner for assault, the case may not be reported as a criminal incident. Similarly, stolen property is sometimes logged as missing property.

The UCR has several other limitations as well. For example, the data are based only on the number of crimes reported, not on the number of arrests made. Arrests are reported separately in terms of *clearance rates*.[1] Further, when more than one crime occurs in a single incident, the UCR includes only the most serious offense. Thus, if rape and murder occur during a car theft, only the murder will become a part of the UCR index data. Finally, given its reliance on victim and witness reports, the UCR system probably seriously underestimates violent crime statistics because fewer than half of all violent crimes may actually be reported (Bastian, 1993)[2]

The UCR program is currently switching to a "full incident reporting" system that is designed to address some of these problems and limitations. When this new *National Incident-Based Reporting System* is fully operational, law enforcement agencies will report data on each crime incident and arrest falling into 22 specific categories such as criminal homicide (murder and nonnegligent manslaughter), forcible rape, robbery,

---

[1] Crimes can be cleared by arrest or by decision not to bring charges. The arrest of one person may clear several crimes, or several persons may be arrested in connection with the clearance of one offense.

[2] The most common reasons for not reporting such crimes are beliefs that (a) the offense involved a matter that should be kept private, and (b) making a report is pointless because the criminal justice system is not responsive to victims' needs.

aggravated assault, burglary, larceny theft, arson, forgery, fraud, embezzlement, vandalism, prostitution, drug abuse violations, and hate crimes.

Another major database for crime statistics comes from the Bureau of Justice Statistics (BJS), an agency within the U.S. Department of Justice. Congress established the BJS in 1981 to furnish objective and independent data on crime using information provided by law enforcement agencies, communities, perpetrators, and victims. BJS staff study crime trends, analyze data, and issue a variety of reports on a continuing basis. Their recent publications have included *Alcohol and Crime* (1998), *HIV in Prisons* (2004), *Incarcerated Parents and Their Children* (2000) and *Sexual Victimization of College Women* (2000). Current publication lists can be obtained by mail from the BJS or through its Web site at www.ncjrs.org.

Finally, there is the National Crime Victimization Survey (NCVS) conducted by the U.S. Bureau of the Census in cooperation with the BJS. In this survey, about 66,000 households consisting of about 110,000 individuals (age 12 years or older) are surveyed about crime victimizations suffered in the preceding 6 months. The crimes surveyed are virtually the same as those included in the UCR indexes. Unfortunately, a number of methodological problems with this survey have raised concerns about the credibility of respondents' reports and thus about the possibility that its results overreport or underreport crime.

Methods for Studying Criminal Behavior

Like scientists in other fields, those who evaluate theories about the causes and correlates of criminal behavior collect empirical data in accordance with the basic rules of scientific research methods. Typically, they start with a *hypothesis,* usually a proposition that two or more variables are causally related. Consider, for example, the much-researched topic of the relationship between children's exposure to violent television programs and the display of violent behavior. It has been hypothesized that watching violence causes children to behave aggressively and violently.

How do scientists test such hypotheses? First they must clearly define the phenomena they are studying. In our example, they must define and establish procedures for measuring (1) the acts displayed on television that are "violent," (2) the age range of the children to be observed and tested, (3) the television shows to be viewed, (4) the number of hours of violent television to be viewed, (5) what child behaviors will meet the criteria for being "aggressive and violent," and (6) where and how aggressive and violent behaviors are to be assessed. Once these operational definitions are in place, the researcher would ideally conduct a controlled experiment designed to assess whether there is a cause–effect relationship between watching violent television and behaving violently.

The experimental method requires that one factor, or variable, in the study—such as the amount of exposure to violent television—be manipulated or controlled by the researcher. This manipulated variable is called the *independent variable.* Thus, the experimenter might randomly assign half the children to an experimental group whose members watch 10 violent shows each week for a year and the rest to a control group whose members watch no televised violence. The effect of this manipulation on a second variable—the children's subsequent behavior—would then be measured. This second variable is known as the *dependent variable* because it depends on the impact of the independent variable.

If children in the experimental group later display more violent behavior than those in the control group, televised violence could have been the cause. We say "could have been" because differences between the two groups in terms of initial violent tendencies, examples set for them by peers or family members, and many other uncontrolled factors known as *confounding variables* might have been wholly or partly responsible for the observed relationship. Ideally, the random assignment process will have equalized the groups on most of these uncontrolled factors, but as in any experiment, to draw cause–effect conclusions, the researcher must show that the effects of all variables besides violent television that could plausibly account for observed differences in violent behavior between groups have been ruled out or controlled for.

The ethical and practical limits on doing controlled experiments of this kind (would you want your child to spend a year in the violent-television group?) force crime researchers to employ other research designs. These alternative designs—which include quasi-experiments, correlational research, and case studies—are not as powerful as controlled experiments in terms of establishing cause–effect relationships, but they are far more likely to be "doable."

In *quasi-experiments* (the name means "experiment like"), researchers are usually not able to randomly assign participants to differing conditions that they manipulate as an independent variable. Instead, they take advantage of naturally occurring differences in that variable and then look for its effects on some other variable. For example, they might compare the amount of violent behavior occurring among inmates who live in crowded prisons with those living in less crowded facilities. Because the researchers are not able to randomly assign prisoners to facilities, there might be important differences in inmate characteristics (such as history of violence) from one kind of prison to the other. Still, the researchers can draw some tentative conclusions about the effects of prison crowding on inmate violence. If the same results appear when such quasi-experiments are repeated, or replicated, in many different prisons, some crowded and some not crowded, the researchers can have greater confidence that a cause–effect relationship between crowding and violence has been identified.

Correlational research usually involves even less control over the variables of interest, but it may offer the only way to study those variables. In a correlational study of televised violence, for example, scientists would not attempt to manipulate how much violence children see but would instead measure the strength of the correlation, or observed relationship, between violent behavior in children and the amount of violent television they are reported to have watched. However, even finding a strong positive *correlation coefficient* (i.e., the more violent television children watch, the more violent their behavior) only allows the researchers to describe the relationship between the two variables.[3] They cannot conclude that violent television caused violent behavior because too many confounding factors (such as parental influences) were left uncontrolled.

Case study methods are also commonly used in research on crime, especially when scientists are interested in relatively rare phenomena such as mass murderers and serial killers. Case studies are helpful in forming hypotheses about the causes of such phenomena because they examine in detail the specifics of a criminal's physical and mental health, family history, social and educational adjustment, and other factors that might provide clues as to what may have contributed to criminal behavior. Finding the same patterns in the case studies of numerous individuals who commit the same types of crimes tells researchers that they may be on the trail of important causal factors that can then be examined in more controlled research. Further, the more we know about experiences that are common in criminals' backgrounds, the more important it might be to work at preventing those conditions in the population at large. These conditions may not themselves cause crime, but they may contribute to it.

You will see numerous examples of experimental, quasi-experimental, correlational, case study, and other research methods throughout this book as we examine the efforts of scientists in psychology, sociology, criminology, and other fields to understand the roots of crime.

Criminals and Criminal Behavior

One day's edition of a major U.S. newspaper—*The Washington Post* for June 23, 2004—reported the following crime-related stories:

> "North Carolina Farmer Sentenced to Six Years in Prison for Parking Tractor in a Pond"
> "AOL Worker Arrested for Selling Customer List to Spammer"
> "House Oks More Jail Time for Identity Thieves"
> "Judge Wraps Up Hearing on Kobe Bryant Accuser's Sex Life"
> "US Anti-Doping Agency Notifies Sprinter Michelle Collins It Will Seek Life-Time Ban for Alleged Drug Violations"
> "Toxic Emissions Rising, EPA Says"
> "Ex-HUD Official To Pay Settlement, Accused of Scheme to File False Expense Reports"

---

[3]Correlation coefficients can be positive or negative and can range in strength from 0 (no correlation) to +1 or −1 (a perfect correlation). A negative correlation says that two variables tend to move in opposite directions. Thus, if our research example had yielded a negative correlation, it would mean that the more violent television children watched, the less violent behavior they displayed.

"NIH Scientists Broke Rules, Deals with Companies Went Unreported"
"Extremists Target Iraqi Prime Minister for Assassination"
"Lawyer's Terrorism Trial Opens in New York"
"Spain Sets Up Commission to Investigate Train Bombings"
"South Korean Beheaded in Iraq"
"Gunmen Kill Editor of Tijuana Newspaper"

If you created a composite picture of crime in your own community or the world at large by scanning local and regional newspapers for a day or a week, the list would probably be similar to this one because many other examples continue to appear virtually every day. Your list would include crimes that are common and crimes that are rare, each involving varying degrees of culpability and horror. There would surely be variety, for there seems to be no end to the ways people find to hurt each other. Our discussion of criminal behavior in the chapters to come focuses on many of the offenses represented in the headlines just listed. We discuss crimes ranging from serial murder to shoplifting, from rape to reckless driving, from pedophilia to prostitution, and many others as well. We also explore organized crime, white-collar crime, and environmental crimes, all of which have a profound impact on the physical, economic, and social well-being of almost everyone.

Our discussions are based on a definition of criminal behavior as the commission of acts that, in their situational and social setting, are considered crimes because they violate prevailing norms and codes of conduct regardless of whether the perpetrator is arrested or whether, if arrested and tried, he or she is convicted or acquitted. Thus, we adopt the behavioral scientist's "nonlegalistic" approach to the study of criminal behavior. We examine *why* people engage in behaviors that their society has criminally sanctioned, whether or not they have been identified, prosecuted, and punished. As you read, you will discover that the origins and development of criminal behavior are not easy to pinpoint because they usually involve complex, long-term interactions between people's psychological and biological characteristics and the economic, social, and cultural systems in which they are born, raised, and live. You will see also that although the story of every criminal, like that of every noncriminal, is somewhat unique, there are some personal characteristics and environmental risk factors that are seen again and again in these people's developmental histories. It is easy to see why some people who display these characteristics and face these risk factors become criminals, but it is also worth asking why others do not. A better understanding of the complex processes that contribute to criminality is likely to generate ever more effective programs for crime prevention, a goal that has never been of greater importance to human welfare.

Summary

Most people think of crime in strictly legal terms. Yet, the behaviors a society labels as criminal and what it does to deal with crime, take into account a people's social, political, and moral systems as well. The origins and emergence of criminal behavior can best be understood not just by looking at the psychology of the individual criminal but by taking into account the biological, family, social, cultural, and political systems in which criminals develop. The legal definition of crime is an act that is in violation of a criminal law enacted by state or federal legislatures. Sociologists think of criminal laws as a means of social control, not just in punishing bad conduct. The desire to control certain behaviors may vary by state, as one sees in variations in laws about consensual sexual conduct and gambling, for instance. What legislatures decide to make a crime is the result of a political process in which certain behaviors are singled out for prosecution and punishment as a political response to a demand from a certain constituency. Criminal laws and prosecutions do not necessarily comport with what all people think is the moral thing to do. For instance, laws making integration illegal were thought by many, including the great Dr. Martin Luther King, to be immoral. Eventually, these laws were struck down, and Dr. King's vision became more the norm of the American people.

To the phenomenon of crime itself, we use classification systems employed by legislative bodies and statistics collected by the federal government. The *Uniform Crime Reports,* published each year by the Federal Bureau of Investigation, is the most comprehensive picture of crime in the United States. Victimization surveys and special research reports focus on more specific demographics related to the commission of crime. Most research related to the causes and consequences of criminal behavior are correlational and quasi-experimental in method. This is because it would be illegal and unethical to conduct experimental research that would lead to illegal and harmful behavior. Because psychologists are so intensely interested in crime, we have a rich body of literature from which we draw to study criminal behavior.

Key Terms

Crime	*Plaintiff*
Misdemeanor	*Defendant*
Felony	*Critical criminologists*
Capital felony	*Social conflict theory*
Mens rea	*Marxist feminism theory*

Questions for Review

1. What are the three sources of criminal laws?
2. What are the two main sources of crime statistics, and what are the strengths and weaknesses of each?
3. What are the main methods for researching and studying criminal behavior?
4. How has the politics of crime led to longer prison terms and harsher policies toward juvenile offenders?
5. Give three examples of how criminal laws in the United States have reflected the social history of the times.

 ## Track It Down

Criminal Behavior Website
www.cassel2e.com
Federal Bureau of Investigations
www.fbi.gov
National Criminal Justice Reference Service
www.ncjrs.gov
U.S. Department of Justice Bureau of Justice Statistics
www.ojp.usdoj.gov/bjs/

2

The Criminal Justice System

The crimes we discussed in chapter 1 are dealt with by the processes and institutions of the U.S. criminal justice system through the work of law enforcement officers, prosecutors, defense attorneys, judges, and jurors. This system took shape early in the 19th century and is based on the English system of justice. It has worked well overall, but is far from perfect.

For example, the problems of police brutality and corruption and prison violence have a long history in America. In 1884, Illinois Governor Altgeld spoke of the failure of prisons to rehabilitate, saying that the inmates were "shoved downward instead of being helped by our penal machinery" (Altgeld, 1890, p. 163). Altgeld also asserted that the criminal justice system itself is criminogenic, meaning that it contributes to the problem of crime. Altgeld (1890) said "it seems, first, to make criminals out of many that are not naturally so; and, second, to render it difficult for those once convicted ever to be anything less than criminals" (p. 162). Altgeld's comments remain all too true today. Now, as then, America appears to have two crime-related problems: criminal behavior itself and the criminal justice system that is designed to deal with it.

In this chapter, we describe that system and consider how it affects criminal behavior in individual defendants and in society. We begin with an overview of the judicial process, including the special provisions it makes for dealing with defendants who are incompetent, insane, or dangerous. We then consider law enforcement officers and how they interact with offenders. Next, we focus on the roles played by prosecutors and defense attorneys and close with an examination of juries and judges. (Our exploration of the criminal justice system continues in chapter 3, where we discuss the juvenile justice system, and in chapter 13, where we discuss imprisonment and other forms of punishment.)

Overview of the Criminal Justice System

Although each state has its own rules governing the criminal justice system within its borders, we can generalize about the basics of criminal procedure, from arrest to trial to sentencing.

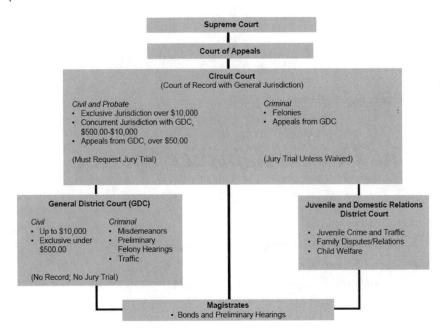

FIGURE 2.1 *Virginia Judicial System.*

Arrest

Recall from chapter 1 that there are two types of crimes: misdemeanors, which are punishable by less than a year in jail, and felonies, which can bring sentences from one year to life. Most arrests for misdemeanors and felonies occur when a law enforcement officer obtains an arrest warrant from a magistrate—a judicial officer appointed by the jurisdiction's highest level trial judge—on the basis of the officer's sworn complaint that probable cause exists to charge the defendant with a particular crime. Other arrests take place without a warrant, as when a crime is committed in the officer's presence. Once arrested, the defendant is brought before a magistrate who determines how to insure that the defendant will be present at any hearings and trials associated with the criminal charges. In misdemeanor cases, the magistrate may set **bond**, which can take the form of money paid (known as **bail**), property pledged, and/or conditions placed on the defendant's release from incarceration pending trial.

State Courts

Each state has a criminal court system and a judicial process designed to prosecute crimes committed inside its borders. Local jurisdictions within each state, usually called counties and cities, also have their own courts (see Figure 2.1). Most local jurisdictions have a lower level court, which conducts trials in misdemeanor criminal cases, handles traffic offenses, and deals with civil claims of up to a certain amount (perhaps $10,000). There are no juries in these lower courts; judges alone make all decisions about guilt, innocence, and punishment. It is in the lower courts, too, that prosecution of felony cases usually begins. In such cases, a lower court judge conducts a *preliminary* hearing to determine if the evidence justifies sending the matter to the *grand jury* for *indictment*.

A grand jury indictment is usually no more than a rubber-stamp sanctioning of the prosecutor's version of the case because grand jurors only hear testimony from prosecution witnesses. Neither the defendant nor the defense attorney is present. A typical indictment would read, "We the grand jurors of the County of Montgomery, sitting on December 15, 2003, find that on or about September 21, 2003, the defendant, John

Doe, did break and enter into the home of Jane Smith with the intent to commit larceny therein." On issuance of the indictment, the defendant appears in the highest court in the city or county, which is where felony cases are tried. That court will determine bail and set dates for pretrial hearings and the trial itself. State laws determine which felony defendants are eligible for bail; but generally, defendants granted bail must be perceived as not posing a danger to themselves or to the community and not likely to flee the court's jurisdiction or otherwise fail to appear in court.

Defendants in felony cases have the right to a trial by jury if they wish, or they can opt to have the case decided by the trial judge. Some states also give prosecutors the right to demand a jury trial even if the defendant does not want one.

Federal Courts

Trials for violations of federal law (i.e., laws enacted by the U.S. Congress) take place in *United States District Courts* located in 91 federal districts. Each state contains one or more of these districts, and defendants are tried in the one where their alleged crime took place. Federal crimes are serious offenses such as interstate drug trafficking, federal income tax fraud and evasion, hijacking, espionage, treason, and crimes against federal agents and federal buildings. Federal misdemeanors, which consist mainly of traffic and other petty offenses occurring on federal property, are tried without a jury in a *U.S. Magistrate's Court*.

Felony Trials

Before going to trial on felony charges, the defendant may be required to attend several pretrial hearings at which the date, location, and other details of the trial will be determined and at which he or she can raise objections to the use of certain evidence. If the defendant has chosen to be tried by a jury, its members—normally 12 local citizens—will be chosen from a panel of about 20 possible jurors. Two alternate jurors will also be chosen. They, too, hear all trial evidence and must be ready to join the jury if another juror cannot continue because of illness or misconduct.

In some jurisdictions, if the jury finds the defendant guilty, it must sit for a second hearing in the *sentencing phase* of the trial. At this hearing, prosecution and defense attorneys present evidence for and against various levels of punishment after which the jury makes its sentencing recommendation. Jurors can only recommend the length of prison terms and the size of fines; they cannot recommend options such as probation or community service. The judge will usually impose the sentence at a later date. If the crime is a serious felony, the defendant will probably have already been incarcerated immediately after conviction, pending the sentencing hearing.

Despite the images of trials portrayed by movies and television, the processes involved in prosecuting and defending criminal cases are tedious, technical, time consuming, and rarely dramatic. Except during the opening and closing arguments designed to sum up their cases, trial lawyers are not allowed to make pronouncements or arguments to the judge or jury. Rather, they must elicit the facts of their cases by asking questions of witnesses. No wonder trial attorneys (including one of your authors, Elaine Cassel) are amused by TV shows in which lawyer actors turn to the jury while questioning a witness and preach about how the case should be decided. In actuality, lawyers for each side try to bring out the "true facts" of the case—as each side sees them—by asking seemingly endless questions of witnesses. A criminal jury trial proceeds as follows:

1. The jury is chosen by questioning prospective jurors about any relevant biases they hold or other reasons they should not serve.
2. The prosecutor makes an opening statement to the jury.
3. The defense attorney makes an opening statement to the jury.
4. The prosecutor presents and questions witnesses for the prosecution.
5. The defense attorney cross-examines prosecution witnesses.
6. The defense attorney presents and questions witnesses for the defense.
7. The prosecutor cross-examines defense witnesses.
8. The defense attorney makes a closing statement to the jury.
9. The prosecutor makes a closing statement to the jury.

10. The judge instructs the jury on the laws governing the case, the evidence, and various standards of proof such as the factual elements that must exist to convict a person of a certain crime and the meaning of terms such as beyond a reasonable doubt.

11. The jury deliberates and returns verdict of guilty, not guilty, or, in rare cases we discuss later, not guilty by reason of insanity or guilty but mentally ill. The jury can also state that it is unable to reach a verdict (this outcome is referred to as a **hung jury**).

12. If punishment is to be recommended by the jury, jurors listen to evidence about sentencing, presented in the same order as was the trial evidence. The jury then deliberates and returns with a sentencing recommendation.

13. If sentencing is to be determined by the judge alone, he or she orders a presentence investigation to be prepared by probation officials and sets a sentencing date. On that date, the judge listens to evidence on sentencing presented in the same order as was the trial evidence. Both prosecuting and defense attorneys may call witnesses to testify on matters relevant to sentencing, and both present arguments for maximum punishment or leniency.

14. The judge imposes a sentence. At this point, the conviction is official and the clock governing time limits for filing appeals begins. If the defendant has been convicted of a violent crime and receives a prison sentence, he or she will most likely begin serving the sentence immediately, even if an appeal is planned. After conviction for nonviolent crimes such as fraud or embezzlement, the defendant may be freed on bail pending the outcome of the appeal.

New Trials and Appeals

Defendants convicted of misdemeanors in a lower court at the city or county level generally have the automatic right to request a new trial (or *trial de novo*) in the local jurisdiction's highest court where felonies are tried. In this court—which handles both civil and criminal trials of all kinds—the defendant "starts over" with a clean slate. In other words, the outcome of the previous trial is not mentioned and has no bearing on the outcome of the new trial.

Defendants convicted of a felony in the local jurisdiction may appeal their conviction to an appellate court by claiming that an error was made during their trial. The appellate court evaluates the defendant's claims to ascertain if there is reason to grant a full appeal, which would include preparation of briefs on the law and facts of the case and oral arguments by both sides. Usually, the defendant must present evidence, in the form of a petition and an accompanying trial transcript, to support the claim that the trial judge made a mistake of law that affected the outcome of the case—such as improperly selecting or instructing the jury or failing to recognize that there was insufficient evidence for a conviction. Mistakes that could not have affected the outcome of the case, called **harmless error**, cannot serve as the basis for an appeal. Further, a defendant can only appeal on the basis of matters that were objected to during the trial. For instance, if the judge made a mistake in instructing the jury, but the defense attorney did not raise an objection at the time, that error cannot be grounds for appeal. Finally, the defendant cannot appeal on the grounds that evidence that might have resulted in acquittal existed at the time of the trial but was not introduced by the defense attorney.

Appeals *are* justified, however, by newly discovered evidence, as when it can be shown that prosecutors failed to fulfill their legal obligation to provide a defendant's attorney with any exculpatory evidence they might have had. New forensic technology has led to a growing number of appeals based on the results of DNA evidence that had not been available when defendants were convicted.

At the federal level, defendants convicted in a U.S. District Court may, if their cases fall within strict statutory guidelines, enter an appeal to one of 11 *U.S. Circuit Courts of Appeal*. For instance, the U.S. Court of Appeals for the Fourth Circuit handles appeals from the states of Maryland, Virginia, and North Carolina. Defendants who are not satisfied with the outcome of this appeal may attempt a further appeal to the United States Supreme Court but again only if they can meet strict legal guidelines for doing so.

State court defendants, too, may ask the Supreme Court to review their case, but only if they have exhausted all their appeal rights in state courts and lower federal courts and only if they can claim that the state has acted contrary to their federally guaranteed constitutional rights. However, no state or federal defendant has an absolute right to an appeal or hearing before the Supreme Court, and the Court approves only a small number of the petitions for hearings that it receives every day.

Many of these petitions stem from cases in which defendants claim that a state's death penalty law, or its manner of application, is unconstitutional. Others involve claims that state law enforcement practices, such as traffic stops and searches of suspects and their homes, are unconstitutional.

Results of Appeals

Because the U.S. Constitution prohibits **double jeopardy**—that is, being retried for the same offense after having been acquitted—only the defendant has the right to ask for a new trial or to appeal an adverse outcome; the prosecution cannot appeal a defendant's acquittal. Depending on the nature of their crimes and their criminal records, convicted felons who wish to appeal their conviction may or may not be released on bail while awaiting the outcome of the appeal. Those who were convicted of violent crimes are rarely allowed to go free during the appeal process.

If a state or federal appellate court decides to hear a defendant's appeal and then finds that the trial judge or jury made an error or that the defendant's constitutional rights were violated at some stage, it may either (1) reverse the conviction and enter final judgment for the defendant, thus allowing release; (2) affirm the conviction of the trial court; or (3) return, or *remand*, the case to the trial court either for a new trial or for consideration of matters not heard during the trial that might have altered its outcome. Only a small percentage of convictions are overturned on appeal, and only a slightly larger percentage results in the case being remanded for additional hearings.

Dealing With Special Defendants

Our overview of the criminal justice system applies to the vast majority of defendants, but others are dealt with according to a special set of rules designed to protect them and to protect society from them. These special defendants are described, in legal terms, as *incompetent, insane, or dangerous.*

A person who steals someone's money to buy drugs is committing a crime and if caught, will no doubt be held responsible because mens rea, or criminal intent, was clearly there (see chapter 1). However, the person who stabs someone because he or she believed that the victim was a dangerous space alien would not be held criminally responsible for the act if mental disorder—in this case paranoid delusions—made mens rea impossible. Accordingly, as in most other democracies, the U.S. criminal justice system contains safeguards designed to protect mentally ill defendants from being punished for illegal acts. Instead, a jury can find such defendants **not guilty by reason of insanity** (**NGRI**) if they suffer from a serious mental disorder or defect that renders them unable to understand and appreciate the consequences of their actions and to control their behavior. Further, because the criminal justice system guarantees defendants a fair trial, those whose mental disorder renders them unable to understand the charges against them or to assist their attorney in preparing a defense may be found incompetent to even stand trial for an alleged crime.

Judgments about dangerousness, too, can affect many criminal justice decisions including whether a defendant should be (1) kept in jail pending trial or released on bond; (2) released pending appeal of a conviction; (3) released from a hospital after being found NGRI; (4) granted a suspended jail sentence (i.e., remaining free conditional on good behavior or other criteria); (5) given a short, long, or indeterminate (open-ended) prison sentence; (6) released on parole before completing a sentence; and (7) subject to civil commitment following release from prison for sexual offenses (American Bar Association, 1989).

Because incompetence, insanity, and dangerousness all refer to a defendant's state of mind, courts often call on psychiatrists, psychologists, and other mental health professionals to evaluate, report on, and testify about questions such as

1. Is the defendant mentally competent to stand trial?
2. Even if sane now, was the defendant insane at the time of the alleged crime?
3. Is the defendant too dangerous to be released from incarceration (if convicted) or hospitalization (if found NGRI)?
4. If sentenced to death, is the prisoner mentally competent to be executed?

We now consider how mental health professionals collect evidence about these questions and how the answers are used by the criminal justice system in dealing with special defendants.

Incompetent Defendants

In 1996, John DuPont, the 58-year-old heir to the DuPont chemical fortune, drove up to a house on his vast Pennsylvania estate where he had allowed David Schultz, a world-class wrestler, to live while using the training facility DuPont had provided to the U.S. Olympic wrestling team. DuPont approached Schultz, who was sitting in a car in the driveway, and killed him with three shots from a .44 magnum revolver. When DuPont appeared in court charged with first degree murder, his attorneys claimed that he was not mentally competent to stand trial. This argument was supported by testimony from psychologists who had examined him as well as from many of DuPont's friends and acquaintances who recalled his recent odd behavior, including asking an acquaintance to check the billiard balls in his recreation room for the eavesdropping devices he claimed were embedded in them. This pretrial testimony convinced the judge that DuPont was suffering from a mental illness (paranoid schizophrenia), and he sent DuPont to a state hospital for treatment.

A defendant who is **competent to stand trial** can understand the charges, participate in the legal proceedings associated with a trial in a meaningful way, and assist an attorney in preparing a defense. Competence is unrelated to the defendant's mental condition at the time of the alleged crime; it is instead a determination that the defendant "has sufficient present ability to consult with his lawyer with a reasonable degree of rational understanding and ... a factual understanding of the proceedings against him" (*Dusky v. United States*, 362 U.S. 401, 1960). A defendant must be competent at every stage of criminal proceedings, including when giving a confession to the police; when waiving the right to have an attorney; when pleading guilty or not guilty; when asking for or waiving a jury trial; when being tried; when sentenced; and if sentenced to death, when executed (Melton, Petrila, Poythress, & Slobogin, 1987).

Defendants must be competent at all these times to insure that they have a fair chance to defend themselves against the power of the government (Grisso & Siegel, 1986). The government, after all, controls much of the criminal justice process, from the gathering of evidence at the crime scene, to fashioning the charges, taking them before a grand jury, and in many other phases of the judicial process we discussed earlier in this chapter. As "officers of the court," prosecutors, judges, and defense attorneys are all obligated to protect the fairness and integrity of that process, so all of them can and should bring up the defendant's incompetence should it appear to be in question. In reality, however, the defense attorney is probably going to be the only person to actually do so because in most states, the law generally presumes defendants to be competent at all stages of legal proceedings.

When the defense attorney advises the judge that his or her client may be incompetent, the judge will usually order the defendant to be taken to a psychiatric hospital or other facility where a competency evaluation can be conducted. Even if declared competent at one point, a defendant's competency can be revisited, and reassessed, at any point in the criminal justice process.

Assessing Competency.   A defendant who has adequate financial resources and is not incarcerated may be examined by either a psychiatrist or psychologist without notice to the prosecutor or the court. The Supreme Court has ruled that indigent defendants too have the right to be examined by a mental health expert but not the right to the expert of their choice (*Ake v. Oklahoma*, 1985). Indigent defendants in state courts are usually evaluated by psychologists or psychiatrists employed by community mental health agencies. In federal courts, indigent defendants are usually evaluated by psychologists or psychiatrists who work in the federal correctional system (Heilbrun & Collins, 1995). In their initial assessment of competency, mental health experts focus on the defendant's ability to

1. Understand the charges filed.
2. Understand the nature and range of possible criminal penalties if convicted.
3. Understand the adversarial nature of the legal process (prosecution vs. defense).
4. Disclose to a defense attorney pertinent facts surrounding the alleged offense.
5. Communicate with a defense attorney.
6. Assist attorneys in planning a defense.

7. Realistically challenge the testimony of prosecution witnesses.
8. Behave appropriately in the courtroom.
9. Give relevant testimony in court.
10. Behave in self-beneficial ways in the legal process.
11. Cope with the stress of incarceration prior to trial.

Most mental health professionals assess competence using several standardized assessment instruments. By using the same set of methods in the same way, it is hoped that the same set of criteria will determine judgments about whether or not a defendant is competent. The competency assessment usually begins with a *mental status examination*, which is a brief focused interview designed to assess the defendant's memory, mood, orientation, thinking, and ability to concentrate. The assessor usually then administers one or more specialized instruments such as the *Competency Screening Test (CST)* (Lipsitt, Lelos, & McGarry, 1971), *the Competency Assessment Instrument (CAI)* (Young, Forquer, Tran, Starzynski, & Shatkin, 2000), or the *MacArthur Competence Assessment Tool–Criminal Adjudication (MacCAT-CA)* (Hoge, Bonnie, Poythress, & Monahan, 2004).

On completion of the assessment process, the mental health professional prepares a report and forwards it to the party who requested the competency evaluation. If the defendant is found to be competent, the defense attorney keeps the report confidential, thereby preserving the defendant's right to privacy. If the defendant is seen to be incompetent, however, copies of the report must be provided to the prosecutor and the judge. If the prosecution wants its own expert to evaluate the defendant's competency, the defendant must cooperate or lose the right to claim incompetence.

Incompetence need not be proven beyond a reasonable doubt, or even by "clear and convincing evidence." There must only be a *preponderance of the evidence*, meaning that it is at least 51% likely that the defendant is incompetent (*Cooper v. Oklahoma*, 1966). Even with this relatively low threshold of proof, it is estimated that of the nearly 40,000 criminal defendants evaluated for competency in the United States each year, 70% to 90% are found competent to stand trial. The more rigorous the evaluation, the more likely it is that the defendant will be found to be competent (Heilbrun & Collins, 1995).

Once a defendant is found to be competent, the judicial process begins or continues where it had left off, but there are several possible outcomes following a finding of incompetence. If the alleged crime is not serious, the charges may be dropped in exchange for an agreement whereby the defendant receives mental health treatment. If the charges are more serious, the defendant will be remanded to a psychiatric hospital for treatment designed to restore competency and thus allow a trial to take place later. For most defendants who are diagnosed with schizophrenia or other serious mental disorders, this treatment consists of antipsychotic or other medication. Once the symptoms have subsided, these defendants are given prescriptions for continued medication and returned to jail. John du Pont, for example, was found incompetent to stand trial, spent several months in a psychiatric hospital, and was then found to be "restored to competence."

Can a mentally ill defendant be forced to take medication solely to become competent to stand trial? If a serious felony is involved, the answer is yes. Consider the case of Russell Eugene Weston On July 24, 1998, Weston stormed the U.S. Capital building with a .38 caliber handgun to dismantle the "ruby satellite system" that he claimed was spreading a deadly disease. During the attack, he shot and killed two police officers. Weston had displayed symptoms of paranoid schizophrenia for many years and because he still suffered paranoid delusions, he was determined incompetent to stand trial (Miller, 1999). He was sent for treatment to the federal prison medical facility in Butner, North Carolina, but refused to take psychotropic medications. In September 1999, a federal judge ordered that he do so. As of this writing, Weston continues on medication but is still incompetent to stand trial.

Weston's case represents an exception to the general rule operating in most states and in the federal system, namely, that incompetent defendants cannot be hospitalized for more than 6 months (4 months in federal cases) without being either brought to trial or released[1]. If the state is intent on confining a defendant for a longer period while assuring that criminal charges remain pending, it can ask for a civil commitment that would allow

---

[1]Defendants found incompetent due to severe mental retardation may, if their condition warrants it, be placed in an institution. If restoration to competency is deemed unlikely, the length of their confinement would be governed by state mental health codes.

the person to be kept in the hospital indefinitely. To obtain a civil commitment, the state must convince a judge (or a jury, if the defendant requests one) that the defendant is both mentally *ill* and a danger to self or others or is incapable of self-care outside a hospital. In most states, people confined under a civil commitment are evaluated at least once each year and given a hearing to determine whether the condition that justified their confinement remains.

Insane Defendants

If Russell Weston is ever found competent to stand trial, he will undoubtedly enter a plea of NGRI. This is what Michael Laudor did in June 1998 after he was arrested and charged with stabbing to death his pregnant girlfriend in their apartment in an affluent New York City suburb. Laudor had earned an undergraduate degree from Yale in just 3 years, but paranoid schizophrenia was gradually taking control of his life. It was only after several hospitalizations that he became stable enough to attend and graduate from Yale Law School, gain admittance to the bar, and become an advocate for the mentally ill. Hollywood producer/director Ron Howard was planning a movie about his battle with mental disorder, but sources close to Laudor said that he seemed to have been "slipping" in the days before the murder (Span & Kastor, 1998). After three mental health experts found that Laudor was mentally incompetent to be tried for murder, he was committed to a New York State mental hospital. A year later, he was found competent to stand trial. At the trial, defense and prosecution mental health experts testified that he was suffering from a mental disease at the time of the murder and should not be held responsible for his actions. The judge accepted his plea of NGRI. Laudor was sent to a mental hospital, where he will remain as long as he is considered to be schizophrenic and dangerous.

The criteria for a successful insanity defense vary from state to state, but most laws require defendants to prove that at the time of their crime, they were suffering from a serious mental disease or defect and lacked substantial capacity either to appreciate the criminality or wrongfulness of their conduct or were unable to conform their behavior to the requirements of law. Further, unlike the 51% preponderance of the evidence required to demonstrate incompetence to stand trial, proving insanity takes *clear and convincing evidence*; the defense must convince a judge or jury that the probability of the defendant's insanity during the crime was at least 75%.

Success of the Insanity Plea.   No aspect of crime and mental illness frustrates the general public more than the idea that criminals might escape responsibility for their actions because they are judged to have been insane at the time of the offense. Critics complain that it is just one more example of the judicial system coddling criminals to the point of literally letting them get away with murder.

Publicity surrounding successful insanity plea cases—such as that of John Hinckley who attempted to assassinate President Ronald Reagan in 1982—leads many people to believe that criminals routinely evade punishment by claiming insanity. The fact is, however, that the insanity defense is seldom used and is rarely successful. Insanity pleas occur in only 1 out of every 200 criminal cases and are successful in only 2 of every 1,000 attempts (E. Silver, Cirincione, & Steadman, 1994). True, John Hinckley was found NGRI, but the law in Washington, DC, at the time required the prosecution to prove that Hinckley was *sane*, a very difficult task because Hinckley had a clear history of disordered behavior. What many people forget is that the insanity defense was *unsuccessful* in numerous other sensational trials including that of Jack Ruby, killer of presidential assassin Lee Harvey Oswald; Sirhan Sirhan who killed Robert Kennedy; mass murderers John Wayne Gacey and Jeffrey Dahmer; David Berkowitz (the "Son of Sam" who killed several women in New York City); Kenneth Bianchi (the "Hillside Strangler"), cult leader Charles Manson; Mark David Chapman, the man who shot John Lennon; and Andrea Yates, the young Texas mother who drowned her four children (Cassel, 2002a). Further, even in the rare cases in which a jury renders a verdict of NGRI, the defendant is not usually allowed to just walk away. A study in California showed that only 1% of insanity acquittees were released without any restriction, 4% were put on conditional release, and 95% were hospitalized (Steadman, 1993). Indeed, the typical NGRI defendant is committed to a state mental hospital until mental health professionals notify the court that the person is no longer mentally ill or a danger to society (Steadman, 1993). In most states, the defendant's mental status is reviewed annually for the first five years or so and then every two years thereafter. Defendants judged no longer mentally ill or dangerous cannot be confined further, but the fact is that most defendants found NGRI are hospitalized for two to nine times as long as they would have spent in prison had they been convicted— and they often face a lifetime of supervision after release (Perlin, 1994; Steadman, 1993). It is no surprise then that John Hinckley has been hospitalized in St. Elizabeth's Hospital Washington, DC, since 1982, and that in spite of his annual efforts to be released, he is unlikely to get out any time soon (B. Miller, 1998b). In 2004, a federal court judge approved Hinckley's requests to leave the hospital for visits with his parents, but he is bound by strict court-ordered regulations during the visits. His parents also are required to make detailed reports to the court about their son's behavior during the visits.

Reforming the Insanity Defense.   Lingering concerns that NGRI verdicts let criminals off too easy have prompted 12 states to allow juries to reach a new verdict: *guilty but mentally ill* (GBMI; Sales & Shuman, 1996). If defendants using the insanity defense are found GBMI, they usually receive the normal prison sentence for their offense, but they are to receive appropriate mental health treatment as well. Unfortunately, this treatment is rarely adequate because GBMI convicts have no special rights to a level of medical care beyond the minimum required by law for all convicts (Slobogin, 1985; Steadman, 1993). In states that allow both GBMI and NGRI, jurors usually require stronger proof of insanity before returning the NGRI verdict (Roberts, Sargent, & Chan, 1993). Research suggests that jurors tend to render GBMI verdicts when they believe defendants may not have been sane enough to be held *legally* responsible for their actions but that punishment is still called for (Sales & Shuman, 1996).

A few states, including Idaho and Montana, have abolished the insanity defense altogether. This step did not eliminate consideration of defendants' mental state, however, because the prosecution must still prove *mens rea*, the intent to commit a crime, and the defendant can introduce evidence that *mens rea* was lacking due to a mental disorder.

In yet another kind of reform, some states allow the defense to introduce evidence that is designed not to show insanity but merely that the defendant had "diminished capacity" to know right from wrong or to control behavior. This defense does not seek to absolve the defendant of responsibility but asks for a lighter than normal sentence because of the defendant's incapacity to form "meaningful premeditation."

For example, low IQ may be considered as evidence of diminished capacity and may mitigate punishment. In a 1997 Virginia case, a 54-year-old man with an IQ of only 69 entered a plea of *nolo contendere*[2] to a charge of second-degree murder. In light of the defendant's retardation, the judge imposed a shorter than average prison sentence (Finn, 1997). In 2002, in the case of *Atkins v. Virginia* (2003), the Supreme Court ruled that people with mental retardation who were convicted of capital crimes could not be executed.

Assessing Sanity.   The task of assessing a defendant's competence to stand trial is a relatively straightforward task of determining the person's present mental status. Assessing a defendant's mental condition during a criminal act that took place weeks, months, or even years earlier is a much tougher challenge for mental health professionals.

To accomplish this task, these professionals use a variety of methods beginning with a review of the defendant's social history—including family background, education, marital status, physical health, and work history—criminal record, history of mental disorder and psychiatric treatment, as well as the defendant's version of events surrounding the defendant's criminal act. Assessment also includes a *structured interview* (in which the defendant is asked a predetermined sequence of questions aimed at evaluating current mental condition) and a series of tests of intelligence, personality, and neurological functioning.

The intelligence tests typically include either the Weschler Adult Intelligence Scale™-Third Edition (WAIS-III, Weschler, 1997) or the Stanford–Binet Intelligence Scales, Fifth Edition (SB5, Roid, 2003). Commonly used objective personality tests are the Minnesota Multiphasic Personality Inventory (MMPI–2; Butcher, Dahlstrom, Graham, Tellegen, & Kaemmer, 1989), and the Hare Psychopathy Checklist–Revised (PCL–R; 2nd Ed., Hare, 2003, see chapter 5). Projective personality tests, such as the Rorschach Inkblot Test (Exner, 1986) and the Thematic Apperception Test (TAT; H. E. Murray, 1943), may also be used.

---

[2]This Latin term means, literally, "I do not contest." It is neither an admission nor denial of guilt. For all practical purposes, though, courts treat it as a guilty plea and sentence defendants as if they had pleaded guilty.

Defendants whose history, observed behavior, or IQ test results suggest the possibility of organic brain disorders may be given extensive tests—such as the Halstead–Reitan Neuropsychological Test Battery (HRNTB) (Reitan, 1993) or the Luria (Golden, Hammeke, & Purisch, 1979)–Nebraska Neuropsychological Battery (LNNB)—which measure abilities in areas such as information processing; attention; concentration; language; and perception of visual, auditory, and tactile stimulation. If there is a history of head trauma, brain injury, or recent change in personality or behavior, a neurologist or other physician may be called on to perform a medical examination and evaluate brain structure and function using various high-tech imaging procedures.

Given the stakes involved, it should not be too surprising that 20% to 25% of criminal defendants attempt to fake (or "malinger") mental illness during insanity evaluations to avoid punishment. Accordingly, psychologists have developed assessment methods designed to detect malingering, especially in cases of defendants who plead insanity (R. Rogers, Gillis, Dickens, & Bagby, 1991; Schretlen, Wilkins, Van Gorp, & Bobholz, 1992; Wetter, Baer, Berry, Smith, & Larsen, 1992).

Insanity Testimony.   After completing their interviews, tests, and other assessments, mental health professionals working on insanity cases prepare a written report summarizing the evaluation and offering an opinion about the defendant's sanity at the time of the offense. If the case goes to trial, the mental health professional can expect to be asked to testify, to be vigorously cross-examined by the opposing attorney, and perhaps directly contradicted by mental health experts hired by the opposition.[3]

Testimony by mental health experts is usually limited by law to descriptions of the defendant's symptoms, behaviors, and demeanor; explanations of the evaluation process and assessment instruments used; and opinions about the defendant's mental health including a diagnosis of mental disorder if appropriate. These experts are usually not allowed to state an opinion as to whether or not the defendant was insane at the time of the offense. Offering such "ultimate opinion testimony" would be drawing a legal conclusion, an act that is seen as usurping the prerogative of the judge and jury to apply the law to the facts and opinions given by the expert.

Several factors influence the impact on juries of evidence for a defendant's alleged insanity. First, jurors are unlikely to be influenced by mental health experts' testimony if they cannot understand it. Evidence presented by these experts tends to have more impact when the experts take the role of teachers, presenting complex concepts in simple terms and offering charts, videos, photographs, and models to help jurors visualize and comprehend the material.

Second, when the defense and the prosecution present contradictory mental health testimony, jurors tend to throw out both experts' opinions and base their decision on nonexpert testimony. This phenomenon was demonstrated in the 1998 case of Ruthann Aron, a wealthy Maryland real estate developer who pleaded NGRI after being charged with hiring a hit man to kill her husband (the police intervened before the plan was carried out). The prosecution expert testified that Aron was faking mental illness, whereas the defendant's expert said that she was psychotic. After five days of deliberation, the jury remained deadlocked at 11 to 1 in favor of conviction but not because of conflicting expert testimony. Jurors later told reporters that they did not even attempt to reconcile the two different versions of her mental condition. They relied instead on tape-recorded conversations she had with the hit man. The 11 jurors who voted for conviction said that if she had a mental disorder when she ordered the hit, it did not impair her thinking or excuse her actions (Ruane & Levine, 1998).[4]

Jurors' tendency to essentially ignore conflicting testimony by mental health experts challenges the belief that an adversarial process is the best way to get at the truth when the insanity defense is used. Yet the U.S. Supreme Court continues to rule that jurors should be capable of separating reliable from unreliable mental health evidence and opinion (Barefoot v. Estelle, 1983). Unfortunately, empirical research and anecdotal data do not support this view (Brekke, Enko, Claret, & Seesaw, 1991). Indeed, jurors' reluctance to declare a winner or loser in "the battle of the experts" is a major factor underlying the low rate of insanity acquittals. In other words, when in doubt about insanity, juries may convict out of caution.

---

[3]Each side's expert is allowed to remain in the courtroom while the other is testifying so that each can challenge the opinion of the other.

[4]This jury was eventually declared hung, but while the jury at her second trial was still deliberating, Aron ended the proceedings by entering a guilty plea.

Even uncontradicted mental health testimony does not always influence juries because many jurors perceive psychology and psychiatry to be "soft sciences" that are too dependent on subjective interpretations to be used as the basis for decisions about a defendant's guilt or innocence (e.g., Faust & Ziskin, 1988; Rohde, 1999).

Dangerous Defendants

As already mentioned, Russell Weston had been suffering from paranoid schizophrenia for many years before July 24, 1998, the day he killed two police officers at the U.S. Capitol Building. In fact, he had been involuntarily committed to a Montana mental hospital because of odd behavior, which included claims that both the Kennedy family and President Clinton were his close friends and that he was being spied on by the government through his neighbors' satellite TV dishes. Weston was released after 52 days because mental health professionals believed that he was not at risk for violent behavior as long as he took his prescribed medication.

Predicting Dangerousness.   How could psychologists have known in 1996 that Weston would kill people in 1998? Overly lenient judgments about dangerousness can be tragic for innocent victims, but being overly strict can impose needless hardships on harmless defendants and may violate the law. As noted earlier, NGRI defendants cannot be confined in a hospital just because their mental illness continues; they must also be found dangerous.

In one sense, the Weston case is typical: Mental health professionals' predictions about dangerousness are notoriously inaccurate. However, it is also an unusual case because judgment errors typically involve overpredicting dangerousness (R. P. Cooper & Werner, 1990; Dawes, Faust, & Meehl, 1989; Faust & Ziskin, 1988; Litwack & Schlesinger, 1999). One study (Lidz, Mulvey, & Gardiner, 1993) found that mental health professionals were wrong 47% of the time when they predicted that a mental patient would commit an act of violence within the next six months. In other words, they would not have done much worse by flipping a coin. Further, the predictions of highly trained and experienced mental health professionals are no better than those of laypersons or clinicians with little experience in risk prediction (Faust & Ziskin, 1988; Garb, 1989; L. R. Goldberg, 1968). The American Psychiatric Association (1983) itself has taken the position that psychiatrists have no special knowledge or ability that allows them to accurately predict dangerous behavior. Nevertheless, psychiatrists and psychologists are the only groups the courts deem qualified to make dangerousness assessments.

Why can't mental health professionals do a better job at this vital task? Aside from the difficulties inherent in accurately predicting *any* human behavior, especially in social situations in which actions are determined by complex interactions among numerous biological, psychological, and social factors (Litwack & Schlesinger, 1999), the prediction of dangerousness—especially long-term dangerousness—has been impaired by a lack of reliable and valid risk assessment methods. Other obstacles include the fact that (a) mental health professionals are being asked to forecast behavior that has a very low base rate (most people are not violent), (b) clinical assessments of future violence are usually conducted in hospitals or jails where drugs and situational restraints make it less likely to see signs of violent behavior, and (c) dangerousness assessments generally do not include lengthy interviews with the defendant and the family and friends who might be the best source of information about past behaviors and triggers for violence (Monahan, 1997; Rice, 1997).

Efforts are constantly being made to develop better methods and to use them more consistently (Monahan, 1997; Rice, 1997; Steadman et al., 1994), and research does hold some promise for improving the accuracy of dangerousness judgments. We now know, for example, that most forms of mental illness—including serious disorders such as schizophrenia—do not correlate strongly with dangerousness. We also know, however, that schizophrenic individuals are more likely to be dangerous if they abuse alcohol or other drugs, experience delusions or hallucinations that make them feel threatened by others, and perceive that others are trying to "control their mind" (Link & Steuve, 1994, 1995; Rice, 1997; Steadman et al., 1998; J. Swanson, Borum, Swartz, & Monahan, 1996). The same is true of people diagnosed as suffering from alcoholism or other substance-related disorders (Monahan, 1997).

Taking a cue from research showing that the accuracy of diagnostic judgments about mental disorders is improved by the systematic, often computer based, combination of clinical assessment information (Nietzel, Bernstein, Kramer, & Milich, 2003), researchers seeking to improve the prediction of dangerousness focus on systematically combining assessment evidence from four domains: (1) the defendant's dispositional tendencies such anger or impulsiveness; (2) clinical factors such as evidence of mental or personality disorders (see chapter 9); (3) historical factors, especially a record of violence; and (4) contextual factors such as the strength of social support from family and friends (Bjorkly, 1997; Steadman et al., 1994). Some researchers have suggested that this information be used in a way that emulates weather forecasters' estimates of the probability of rain—labeling people as posing a low, moderate, high, or very high risk for violence over somelimited period of time and in certain circumstances. The same information would be used as the basis formaking recommendations for actions and safeguards necessary to protect the public from these people much as meteorologists advise when to evacuate in the face of a major storm (Mohahan, 1997).

Law Enforcement Officers

Now that we have outlined the operation of the adult criminal justice system (we describe the juvenile justice system in chapter 3), it is time to consider the individuals who make that system work. We begin with those who are on the front lines in the fight against crime—law enforcement officers.

Federal law enforcement officers include FBI agents; agents of the Alcohol, Tobacco, and Firearms Division of the Treasury Department; Homeland Security agents and officers (including Transportation Security Agents who are responsible for airport security); and special officers such as U.S. Coast Guard Patrol, whose jurisdiction covers bays, coastal waters, and other waterways; and U.S. Border Patrols who have power over people entering the United States through Mexico and Canada. *State law* enforcement officers include elected local sheriffs and their appointed deputies, who have local arrest jurisdiction and are in charge of local jails and detention facilities, and state and local police. State and federal laws determine the limits of these various officers' jurisdictions and the type and extent of their involvement in criminal investigations.

When crime incidents are reported, law enforcement officers investigate to determine the identity of the offender and to decide whether to make an arrest. They usually have absolute discretion about whether or not to arrest people, and as we show, their arrest practices tend to reflect the political and social pressures operating within their community.

Effectiveness of Policing

It is reassuring to have police present and to have them busy arresting criminals, but their impact in terms of deterring crime is probably less significant than most people think. A 1997 report to the United States Congress (Sherman et al., 1997) analyzing crime prevention data concluded that the deterrent effect of making arrests in response to citizen complaints is "remarkably unencouraging." The report goes on to conclude that higher rates of arrest for particular types of crime do not lower the rate at which that crime occurs.

Why should this be? It appears that for some criminals, especially juveniles and unemployed adults, being arrested tends to intensify defiance of authority and tends to be followed by continued criminal activity, often of increasing severity (M. Klein, 1986; Sherman, 1993; Sherman et al., 1997). It is obviously not acceptable to abandon efforts to arrest criminals, but the long-term goal of reducing crime seems to be better served by police focusing their attention on certain categories of people (such as chronic serious offenders, potential robbery suspects, and drug dealers) and places known as criminal "hot spots" (drug marketplaces and locations and times associated with violence) rather than patrolling more widely and attempting to give equal attention to all categories of crime (Martin & Sherman, 1986; Sherman, 1999; Sherman et al., 1997; see chapter 6). In chapter 14, we discuss other important roles that police might play in crime prevention efforts in the community.

Police Behavior and Crime

Police officers are the only members of the criminal justice system with whom most members of the general public have direct contact. Highly visible because of their uniforms, patrol cars, weapons, and extraordinary powers, police officers' treatment of the public, whether average citizen or suspected offender—and the public's perception of that treatment—can have positive or negative effects on crime. If citizens see the police as sympathetic and protective allies, they are more likely to help officers catch criminals; if not, they may keep silent about what they know and may even become sympathetic toward criminals.

However, law enforcement officers have one of the toughest jobs imaginable, and it is often difficult for them to keep in mind how their behavior affects public perceptions and crime. Indeed, to expect perfection from the police is as unrealistic as it would be to expect it from people in any other occupation. The truth is that most police officers do their best carry out their difficult duties properly and with due regard for the rights and welfare of all citizens, but given the conditions of their work and the relatively small impact they have on the prevalence of crime, it is no wonder that many police officers feel frustrated and angry.

In some cases, these emotions lead to inappropriate behavior. One of the most shocking examples occurred on the evening of March 3, 1991, following a high-speed chase on a Los Angeles freeway. When the driver, a Black man named Rodney King, was finally stopped, four White Los Angeles police officers took turns beating him. When they were finished, King had a broken cheekbone, a broken collarbone, multiple fractures of his face, lacerations on his forehead, a fracture of his right leg, and various bruises, contusions, and abrasions. Images of this incident became etched in the public mind because a passing motorist captured most of it on videotape. A similar incident took place in August of 1997 in New York City when two White officers arrested a Haitian immigrant named Abner Louima for his alleged involvement in a fight at a nightclub. These officers beat him up in their squad car, and later, in the bathroom of the Brooklyn police station, they and three other White officers kicked Louima and sodomized him with a toilet plunger. Louima suffered a ruptured bladder and colon and several broken teeth. In February of 1998, one officer pled guilty and four others were tried on federal charges of violating Louima's civil rights (Russakoff, 1998). The jury convicted one officer, Charles Schwartz, but found the other three innocent.

In 1999, four New York City police officers looking for a rape suspect shot and killed Amadou Diallo, an unarmed 22-year-old African immigrant with no criminal record and no connection to the crime. An autopsy showed that he had been hit by 41 police bullets (K. Flynn, 1999). A civil jury found no wrongdoing on the part of the police officers and acquitted them (L. Duke, 2000). In January 2004, the City of New York paid Diallo's mother $3 million for the loss of her son but with no acknowledgment that the police had done anything wrong.

In 1999, widespread corruption was revealed in the Los Angeles Police Department's antigang unit including at least 100 incidents in which people were framed by officers for crimes they did not commit. In another case, officers shot an innocent man, rendering him quadriplegic, then made it look as if the victim had shot at them first. The victim was convicted of assaulting the police and sent to prison before being released when the truth eventually came out (R. Cohen, 2000). In 1999 in Tulia, Texas, an undercover drug agent single-handedly masterminded the false arrest and convictions of 38 Black residents—ten-percent of the town's Black population—on trumped up drug possession charges. It took several appeals, hundreds of dedicated defense attorneys, and four years of work to expose the fact that one deceitful law enforcement officer had managed to convince judges and juries that his uncorroborated testimony was the truth (Duggan, 2001).

Fortunately, such incidents are rare. A 1997 Justice Department survey (Greenfeld, Langan, & Smith, 1997) suggested that violence or threats of violence by law enforcement officers occurs in only about one-percent of the estimated 45 million cases in which citizens come in contact with the police each year—whether as witnesses, victims, crime suspects, or parties involved in traffic incidents. Still, this amounted to nearly half a million incidents, and worse, about half of those reporting such incidents were African Americans and Hispanic Americans who make up only about 20% of the population surveyed.

Police brutality appears to arise from a combination of aggressiveness and other personality characteristics, social influences (especially the police culture that reinforces authoritarianism, cynicism, isolation, secretiveness, and suspicion), situational stressors, and a variety of cognitive distortions (including stereotypes, prejudices, and faulty attributions) about suspects (Scriviner, 1994).

The use of excessive force may also reflect organizational characteristics including certain standard law enforcement practices. For instance, unlike in Great Britain where officers must have special permits to carry a gun, virtually all law enforcement officers in the United States are armed. Thus, like any other citizen who might ill-advisedly reach for a gun in moments of panic or tension, police officers can overreact with deadly force (Vrij, van der Steen, & Koppelarr, 1994).

In 1999, in response to public outrage over police brutality—especially in relation to minority groups—then U.S. Attorney General Janet Reno (1999) promised that the federal government would step up legal action against local police misconduct, stating that there is "no task more important to safe neighborhoods and civil rights than improving relationships and building greater trust between minority communities and law enforcement". Many police agree. Some New York City police officers, for example, are trying to divorce themselves from the image of brutality and reach out to citizens by conducting seminars at inner-city community centers to advise people on how to handle an encounter with the police whom many citizens fear more than crime (Grunwald, 1999).

Prosecutors

Once a crime has been investigated and an arrest made, the next player to come on the scene in the criminal justice process is the prosecutor, an attorney who represents the state or federal government in bringing charges against the defendant.

The federal government's prosecution team is led by the Attorney General of the United States, and each of the 91 Federal District Court jurisdictions has a *U.S. Attorney*, who is appointed by and serves at the discretion of the President of the United States. Working with each U.S. Attorney is a staff of *Assistant U.S. Attorneys* chosen by the U.S. Attorney. Prosecutors working for state governments can hold various titles, the most common of which are *District Attorney* (e.g., in Illinois and Maryland) and *Commonwealth's Attorney* (e.g., in Pennsylvania and Virginia). Unlike U.S. Attorneys, state prosecutors are elected officials chosen by voters in the jurisdictions they serve; but like U.S. Attorneys, they hire their own assistants.

Prosecutors perform several functions in bringing a defendant to trial. The first of these is to consult with the police who made the arrest to decide whether evidence against the defendant is strong enough to prosecute the case. If it is not, the charges will be dropped; with sufficient evidence, the prosecutor will either begin preparing for trial (in the case of misdemeanors) or take the case before a grand jury (if the offense is a felony).

The prosecutor also evaluates the appropriateness of plea bargaining—a process in which the defendant agrees to plead guilty in exchange for reduced charges (of manslaughter, say, instead of premeditated murder), a reduced number of charges, or the prosecutor's cooperation in asking the judge for leniency in sentencing. Although plea bargaining is a necessary component of the criminal justice process and reduces the number, length, risks, and cost of trials, the public generally sees it as giving undeserved gifts to the guilty. In truth, plea bargains work in favor of the prosecution. Without them, the criminal justice system in large jurisdictions would collapse under the strain of trials. (Texas outlawed plea bargaining for a time but reinstated it after so many defendants chose to go to trial that the system could not handle the caseload.) Prosecutors want to do the best they can for the public they serve, and that means convicting guilty people. Plea bargaining insures that the prosecutor will get those convictions; about 80% of all felony charges and 90% of misdemeanor cases are disposed of by plea-bargained guilty pleas (DeFrances & Steadman, 1998). Plea bargaining also allows prosecutors to devote more time to their most serious cases.

Particularly in federal jurisdictions, prosecutors may also consult with police officers in ongoing investigations, usually involving gang, drug, and organized crime activity. In this role, they advise the police about what investigative procedures are and are not legal, and they help obtain search and arrest warrants.

Prosecutorial Discretion

Prosecutors have considerable discretion about whether to conduct investigations, engage in plea bargains, or take particular cases to trial. Those who are elected to their posts will be held accountable for their actions when they seek reelection, and this political reality can affect the prosecutorial decisions they make. Two main considerations dictate prosecutors' decisions about pursuing investigations and trials: (1) the time and staff available to handle caseloads and (2) the likelihood of getting a conviction. Community standards and social pressure also affect some prosecutorial decisions. For instance, the political power of Mothers Against Drunk Drivers (MADD) is such that some elected state prosecutors will try drunk driving cases—even if the result is likely to be an acquittal—rather than risk incurring MADD's wrath.

Still, prosecutors have the legal duty to uncover the truth and to do justice for all citizens, not just special interest groups. Ethical guidelines for prosecutors mandate that their primary duty is to do justice, not convict. Yet, many feel that their job is to obtain a conviction and get a maximum sentence whatever the cost. Prosecutors with this attitude may go too far as illustrated by three Virginia cases. In the first, a trial court judge discovered that prosecutors were conducting illegal background checks on potential jurors. The prosecutors argued that such checks, although illegal, are necessary to insure exclusion of jurors with misdemeanor arrest records who might be biased in favor of criminal defendant (Glod, 1998). Because the checks were, indeed, illegal, the judge put a stop to it. In the second case, a judge in the trial of men with alleged connections to al-Qaeda and terrorism found that prosecutors had failed to give defense attorneys evidence that would have helped them prove that the government's star witness might have been lying. As mentioned earlier (p. 27), in 1999, Texas prosecutors conspired with local sheriffs to charge, convict, and imprison dozens of innocent Black residents of the tiny Texas town of Tulia who were charged with possession of drugs. All of the defendants, serving sentences ranging from 12 to 99 years, were released after an investigation led by *The New York Times* and the American Civil Liberties Union revealed the trumped-up drug "sting" (Duggan, 2001). Although rare, cases of prosecutor misconduct taint the criminal justice process and undermine the public's faith in the system (Cassel, 2004).

Defense Attorneys

All criminal defendants are entitled to have an attorney represent them if incarceration could result from conviction. Defendants who cannot afford to hire an attorney are provided with an attorney at government expense. In many federal and state courts, this attorney is a *public defender,* a government employee whose sole job is to represent indigent defendants. In smaller jurisdictions where there are not enough cases to justify paying a full-time public defender, local attorneys may be appointed by the court and paid a modest fee by the state to represent indigent defendants. Almost two thirds of all criminal defendants are indigent, and in large jurisdictions, public defenders or court appointed attorneys represent as many as 85% of defendants (G. F. Cole, 1992). For example, court-appointed attorneys represented Theodore Kaczynski (the Unabomber); Timothy McVeigh and Terry Nichols, defendants in the Oklahoma City Federal Building bombing trial; Russell Weston (see previous discussion); and defendants accused of terrorism such as Zacarias Moussaoui.

An indigent defendant's right to counsel is a relatively recent creation of law brought about by the case of Clarence Gideon (Lewis, 1964). In 1962, when Mr. Gideon was 51 years old, a Florida judge convicted and sentenced him to a jail term for breaking and entering with the intent to commit larceny. Gideon's request for a court-appointed attorney was denied because at that time, the U.S. Supreme Court had ruled that only defendants facing the death penalty had the right to court-appointed counsel. Gideon had to represent himself, but he was no match for the state's prosecutor. Later, he realized that being forced to represent himself left him essentially defenseless, so he filed a handwritten petition with the Supreme Court of the United States asking for a new trial. As it does in all such cases, the Court appointed an attorney to represent him in relation to his petition. That attorney, Abe Fortes, who would later become a Supreme Court Justice himself, convinced the Court to require states to provide counsel for all indigent defendants who face jail time if convicted. Gideon's case was remanded for retrial, and after his court-appointed attorney summoned witnesses who corroborated his alibi, it took a jury only 25 minutes to find Gideon not guilty. The Supreme Court's ruling in *Gideon v. Wainwright* (1963) was made retroactive, so it applied to all indigent defendants incarcerated at the time. The states either had to give them new trials, with court-appointed attorneys, or set them free.

Role of the Defense Attorney

Although we all have the right to a defense attorney—and few of us would be foolish enough to try to defend ourselves—these attorneys are often unpopular figures because they are perceived as slowing the wheels of justice and shielding criminals from the punishment they deserve. Still, it is the defense attorney's legal and ethical obligation to—within the bounds of law—zealously represent the defendant's interests, see to it that the defendant's constitutional rights are honored, and that the prosecution does its job by proving every element of the defendant's guilt.

Ideally, defense attorneys should not be necessary because prosecutors and juries should assure that justice is done in every case. However, this does not happen because, as already noted, prosecutors tend to be concerned mainly with getting convictions (K. Flynn, 1998), and many jurors believe that defendants must be guilty of "something" or they would not be in court. Indeed, if defendants do not have an ironclad alibi or a legal justification or excuse (such as self-defense or insanity), they are likely to be convicted; 85% of all criminal trials end in convictions (DeFrances & Steadman, 1998). Without defense attorneys, trials might become little more than exercises in finding guilt and imposing sentence.

Priscilla Chenoweth, a 68-year-old grandmother and retired defense attorney, took it on herself to prove the injustice of the 1991 murder conviction of Luis Kevin Rojas. After reading about his case in a New Jersey newspaper, Chenoweth concluded that the testimony linking Rojas to the murder was not credible and that Rojas's alibi was valid. Over a period of 7 years, while Rojas remained in prison, Chenoweth worked with other criminal defense attorneys (Flynn, 1998) to obtain a new trial for him. That trial finally took place in 1998 and led to Rojas's acquittal and release. Also, in an act of sisterly devotion, Betty Anne Waters put herself through law school to prove the innocence of her brother, Kenny, who was serving a life sentence for a murder he did not commit (Hewitt & Longley, 2001).

Juries

As we already noted, the U.S. Constitution gives all defendants in felony trials the right to trial by jury. Jury trials first appeared in ancient Greece around 600 B.C. to 500 B.C. In those days, there were no judges, and the size of the jury varied with the importance of the case. Socrates was sentenced to death by 501 jurors; the treason trial of Alcibiades involved 1,501 jurors (Abraham, 1994). Norman conquerors brought the jury trial to England in the 12th century where, under the rule of King Henry II (1154–1189), a jury system took shape that is similar to the one in the United States today. It consisted of a grand jury to hear evidence of the prosecutor (the King's counselors) and issue indictments and the *petit jury*, which determined guilt or innocence. The *Magna Carta* (1215), the British constitutional document guaranteeing certain rights and privileges to the King's subjects, secured the right to jury trials in perpetuity. The requirement that a jury's verdict be unanimous also has its origins in England, appearing in the 14th century. There was much about England's legal system that 18th century American colonists wanted to change, but the jury system was not one of them. Jurors could, and did, shield revolutionaries from the arbitrary justice of their English King.

Jury Composition

Why the English settled on 12-person juries is a matter of speculation. Some suggest it is based on the number of Christ's apostles. In the United States today, the 12-member jury and the requirement of a unanimous verdict in criminal trials are still the norm, although the Supreme Court has approved some modifications. For example, in *Williams v. Florida* (1970), the Court approved the use of 6-member criminal juries but 8 years later ruled that 5-person juries are too small (*Ballew v. Georgia*, 1978). In *Apodaca, Cooper, and Madden v. Oregon* (1972) and *Johnson v. Louisiana* (1972), the Supreme Court also agreed that it is constitutional for a jury verdict to be based on a 9 to 3 majority, but only Oregon, Oklahoma, and Louisiana have adopted this provision. In fact, Louisiana and Oklahoma have a multi-tier jury system in criminal cases. Only capital (death penalty) crimes require 12-person unanimous verdicts: Serious felony cases require 12-member juries but only a 9 to 3 vote for conviction, and trials of less serious felonies require a unanimous verdict but only a 6-member jury. From the criminal defendant's point of view, it is desirable to have a larger jury that must reach a unanimous verdict because larger juries spend more time deliberating, have better collective recall of testimony, generate more arguments, and try harder to agree.

Selecting a Jury

Potential jurors are drawn from a list of all registered voters (and in some jurisdictions, all those with motor vehicle licenses) who reside in the jurisdiction of the trial court. Noncitizens and convicted felons are ineligible for jury service. The Clerk of the Court sends notices to a group of qualified citizens, asking them to be available for duty for a period of 30 to 90 days (often called a term of court). Many of these people will receive exemptions from service, usually on grounds of hardship (such as personal or family illness, being the sole support of a family, business necessity, and even vacation plans). Some states automatically give exemptions to members of certain professions—including teachers, law enforcement officers, fire fighters, physicians, and attorneys.

The group of potential jurors from which a trial jury will be selected is called a **venire**, a term taken from the Latin term for the writ, or order, given by a judge to a sheriff to summons people to serve on a jury (venire facias). In an ordinary criminal trial, attorneys may start with a venire, of about 20 potential jurors; but if pretrial publicity is expected to limit the number of available unbiased jurors, the venire, may consist of several hundred. Members of the venire are summoned to a courtroom and questioned by attorneys and judges in a process known as *voir dire*, a French word meaning "to tell the truth." The purpose of *voir dire* is to obtain an impartial panel. The questions are designed to (1) determine whether the prospective juror meets statutory requirements for jury service; (2) discover any grounds to challenge the juror "for cause," such as prejudice arising from the type of case or the identity or characteristics of the trial participants (e.g., believing that police officers always tell the truth or that rape victims have only themselves to blame); and (3) uncover other information that might disqualify a person from serving on the jury. Attorneys can also ask that a potential juror be disqualified without saying why—as long as the reason does not involve ethnicity or gender (*Batson v. Kentucky*, 1986; *J.E.B. ex Rel v. T. B.*, 1994). Once all the jurors are chosen, they take an oath to faithfully execute their duties under the law.

Impact of Juror Characteristics

There is no empirical evidence that juror demographics—such as ethnicity, age, gender, income, education, marital status, religious affiliation, and occupation—consistently predict jury verdicts (Hastie, Penrod, & Pennington, 1983), but in certain situations, jurors may tend to favor defendants with whom they share certain characteristics. This tendency is described in the *similarity-leniency hypothesis* (Kerr, Hymes, Anderson, & Weathers, 1995). However, there is also evidence that similarity between juror and defendant can work against the defendant. In this so-called *black sheep effect*, jurors are harder on defendants who are similar to themselves because they perceive the defendant as reflecting badly on them. In one study (Kerr, Hymes, Anderson, & Weathers, 1995), when evidence against a defendant was weak, defendant–juror similarity in religion increased leniency; when evidence was strong, religious similarity went against the defendant.

Overall, jurors from higher income brackets are more likely to vote to convict (F. Adler, 1973; R. J. Simon, 1967) as are jurors with more education (Moran, Cutler, & Loftus, 1990). Research on ethnic influences have yielded no firm conclusions. For example, Black jurors are more inclined to convict a White defendant if the crime victim is Black, and White jurors are more inclined to acquit a White defendant if the crime victim is Black. However, higher income Black jurors may be harsher than White jurors are toward Black defendants charged with violent crimes (Nietzel & Dillehay, 1986). Jurors' personality characteristics—especially authoritarianism, locus of control, and belief in a just world (i.e., that people, including victims and defendants, get what they deserve)—may also influence their votes (Wrightsman, Nietzel, & Fortune, 1998).

Trial Consultants. A jury is supposed to be an unbiased, representative sample of the community from which its members were selected. This is rarely the case, though, because attorneys for both the prosecution and defense do all they can to insure that the voir dire results in a panel whose members are as favorably disposed as possible toward their own side of the case. Most attorneys have developed hypotheses about which juror characteristics they want and which they want to avoid. These hypotheses are based partly on psychological research with mock juries. In these studies, a group of 6 or 12 people with known characteristics are given evidence in hypothetical cases, asked to reach a verdict, and then questioned about why they voted as they did. Attorneys also take note of research regarding the influence on jurors of the gender, ethnicity, age, physical appearance, attractiveness, and personal style of defendants, witnesses, and attorneys (Kassin &

Studebaker, 1997; Zebrowitz & McDonald, 1991). There is even a Juror Bias Scale (Kassin & Wrightsman, 1983) that was designed to predict characteristics that may make some jurors prone to favor the prosecution or the defense.

Jury research has led to some rough guidelines about what kinds of people are likely to vote for acquittal or conviction in certain kinds of cases, but attorneys' decisions to "strike" or eliminate some jurors and accept others are also shaped by stereotypes based on their personal experiences with jurors and with people in general. Like all stereotypes, these are based partly on false assumptions, gross generalizations, and oversimplifications that can result in faulty decisions. Still, trial attorneys have faith in their ability to "read" potential jurors and to "slant" the jury in a favorable way. Clarence Darrow (as cited in Sutherland & Cressy, 1974), who became perhaps America's most famous trial attorney of the 1920s, described the type of jury he wanted when defending an accused criminal:

> I try to get a jury with little education but with much human emotion. The Irish are always the best jurymen for the defense. I don't want a Scotsman, for he has too little human feelings; I don't want a Scandinavian, for he has too strong a respect for law as law. In general, I don't want a religious person, for he believes in sin and punishment. The defense should avoid rich men who have a high regard for the law, as they make and use it. The smug and ultra-respectable think they are the guardians of society, and they believe the law is for them. (p. 417)

Gerry Spence, a successful contemporary litigator, has been quoted as preferring to avoid female jurors in criminal trials because he believes that they are "more punitive than men by a score of about five to one" (as cited in Franklin, 1994, A25). Women have had to "toe the line" more, whereas men "had more experience hell-raising and are more forgiving of it" (as cited in S. J. Adler, 1994, p. 55). Spence likes obese people because they lack self-control and do not demand as much self-control from others. Yuppies, Spence says, make the worst jurors because they "love property and haven't suffered enough to be sympathetic to the accused" (as cited in S. J. Adler, 1994, p. 55).

Although some attorneys make decisions about potential jurors solely on the basis of experienced-based hunches, superstitions, and stereotypes, many others seek the help of trial consultants, especially in high-profile cases. Usually, these consultants are psychologists who employ "scientific" jury selection techniques designed to identify jurors who are most likely to vote for or against acquittal, depending on which side hires the consultant. Trial consultants also help attorneys shape their cases. By asking questions of focus groups made up of people from the potential juror pool and by helping to conduct mock trials, jury consultants make it easier for attorneys to identify the strengths and weaknesses of their cases. On the basis of this information, the attorneys may rethink their trial strategy or how they structure the case. Trial consultants may have some impact on the outcome of a given trial, but their presence or absence does not exert enough influence to create a statistically significant difference in the overall pattern of trial verdicts (I. A. Horowitz, 1980). The effect of using jury selection consultants appears to be greatest in cases in which the evidence against a defendant is ambiguous and thus open to varying interpretations, for it is in these types of cases that juror characteristics have an influence on their attitudes. In "open and shut" cases in which there is little doubt about what happened or who did what, the correct verdict may be so obvious that juror characteristics may not matter much (Nietzel & Dillehay, 1986).

As was demonstrated in the O. J. Simpson criminal trial, though, attorneys must be careful about being overconfident in open and shut cases. Prosecutor Marcia Clark was sure she had evidence that would convince *any* jury to convict Simpson for the murder of his former wife, Nicole Brown, and her friend, Ron Goldman. So she ignored a prestigious jury selection consultant's warning against selecting Black women as jurors. She insisted that such women would be outraged about Simpson's history of abusing his wife (C. B. Murray, Kaiser, & Taylor, 1997). The defense attorneys listened to *their* consultants, however, and got a virtually hand-picked jury consisting of eight Black women, two White women, one Hispanic American man, and one Black man. All were Democrats, five said that they or a family member had a negative experience with law enforcement, five thought that using physical force on a family member was sometimes justified, and nine thought that Simpson was unlikely to have committed the murders because he excelled at football (Toobin, 1996). Despite hearing about DNA matches and other evidence linking the Simpson to the crimes, that jury took less than four hours to acquit him.[5] In a later trial for civil damages, an all-White jury selected with more influence from the plaintiffs' side found Simpson responsible for the murders and awarded the Brown and Goldman families $33.1 million.

The services of trial consultants are available only to defendants who are wealthy enough to pay for them, but all attorneys can be guided in their jury selection efforts by the results of research into the psychological, social, cognitive, and linguistic principles that underlie juror decision making.

Jury Instructions and Admonishments

After both sides have completed their closing arguments and before jurors are sent off to deliberate their verdict, the judge reads to them a set of instructions. Some of these instructions pertain to specific aspects of the case at hand, but judges also inform jurors about the defendant's rights. For instance, citing the Fifth Amendment to the Constitution, which guarantees that defendants do not have to testify against themselves, the judge will instruct jurors not to draw unfavorable conclusions if the defendant did not testify at the trial. Jurors are also instructed on the meaning of beyond a reasonable doubt, the legal standard of proof in a criminal case. Finally, the judge's instructions (1) set forth the legal requirements for reaching a verdict to convict, (2) outline all possible verdicts (including, perhaps, NGRI or GBMI), and (3) caution against paying attention to any evidence that was declared inadmissible.

Reaching a Verdict

In the classic 1957 movie *Twelve Angry Men* (Lumet, 1957), all but one member of a jury are prepared to convict a young Hispanic man of murder without any deliberation. The lone dissenter, played by Henry Fonda, shames the rest into carefully considering the evidence, and bit by bit, discussion of that evidence raises reasonable doubt about the defendant's guilt. In the process, the jurors struggle with the prejudices that had made them so eager to convict an innocent man. How often such things happen in the jury room we cannot know because no one is allowed to listen in on jury deliberations, and although some jurors are willing to talk about how a verdict was reached, they are not required to do so. These incomplete first-hand accounts, along with mock jury research, are the only sources of information we have to go on in trying to understand how juries make their decisions.

The jury's first task is to elect a *foreperson* who will conduct the voting process, record the verdict, and read it in court. It is also the foreperson who speaks for the jury if its members wish to ask the judge to clarify issues or allow them to review exhibits or other evidence. Reports from real jurors indicate that selection of a foreperson is a quick and casual process that follows a predictable pattern (Stasser, Kerr, & Bray, 1982). Often, the foreperson is the first person to speak once the jury gets settled in the jury room (Strodtbeck, James, & Hawkins, 1957) or one of those who sits at either end of the rectangular table (Bray & Noble, 1978; Strodtbeck & Hook, 1961). Forepersons are not just figureheads, however. Research suggests that they are more influential than most other members in shaping a verdict (Foley & Piggott, 1997).

The fact that men are more likely than women to become forepersons may be due in part to their tendency to speak first and to take the seats at the head of the table (Nemeth & Sosis, 1973). One study of 179 jury trials in California found that although 50% of the juries were female, 90% of the forepersons were male (Stasser et al., 1982). Forepersons also tend to be older and to have higher status jobs (Dillehay & Nietzel, 1985; Stasser et al., 1982).

---

[5]This verdict may not have been due entirely to the work of the jury selection consultants because any panel of jurors could have had reasonable doubt about the case, including the way White police investigators handled evidence (Dershowitz, 1996). Still, the grounds for doubt probably had more impact on these particular jurors because it appeared that they wanted to acquit Simpson.

Jury Deliberations.   Once the deliberation process begins, jurors are expected to put aside any preconceptions about a defendant's guilt or innocence and make an utterly unbiased assessment of the physical evidence and witness testimony presented in the courtroom. They are also expected to accurately remember (sometimes without taking notes) and focus on the facts of the case alone while ignoring any personal knowledge or experience related to it—including that coming from pretrial publicity. Finally, they are expected to ignore any evidence or testimony that the judge told them was improper and then flawlessly process all the information with which they were bombarded, ascertain the "truth" about what really happened, and reflect it in a just verdict. As you might expect, jurors often fall short of these ideals.

What really happens during jury deliberations? From the limited information that is available, it appears that jurors spend about 25% of their time discussing how to proceed, about 10% discussing the judge's instructions, and as little as 15% actually discussing trial testimony and evidence. In other words, up to half of the jurors' time is apparently spent on recounting personal experiences or expressing personal opinions about the case (James, 1959). Indeed, jurors gradually ease into the deliberative process by first talking in open-ended terms, raising questions, exploring facts, and perhaps taking a first ballot to see if there is an early consensus (Hastie et al., 1983; Stasser et al., 1982).

In an article about his experience while serving on a New York City criminal jury, writer Finnegan (1994) told how, once deliberations began, the jury immediately began to disobey the judge's instructions that they must not consider anything outside of the evidence or engage in guesswork or speculation:

> The impossibility of considering only 'the evidence' was so obvious it was hardly mentioned. As jurors, we had been kept firmly in the dark throughout the trial, allowed to hear only what the judge deemed fit for our ears. ... It was frustrating, and the disputed facts before us would make sense only if we could imagine the worlds around them. And so we told each other stories. ... [We] guessed and speculated about the lives and motives of the alibi witnesses, trying to put 'the evidence' into some narrative context that made sense. Those with more experience of the East Village [where the crime occurred] tried to evoke the neighborhood's street life for those with less. Odd details got passed over. (p. 51)

No doubt countless juries behave in a similar fashion. That they should want to do so is supported by psychological research into how jurors try to make sense of a case (J. H. Davis, Au, Hulbert, Chen, & Zarnoth, 1997; Kalven & Zeisel, 1966; Kaplan & Scherching, 1981; Lingle & Ostrom, 1981). However, if it comes to light that the jury deliberated over facts that were not put into evidence in court, a mistrial may be declared, which means that the case has to be tried all over again with a new jury. In a 2003 case in Virginia, a federal jury convicted Jay Lentz of kidnapping and murdering his estranged wife, but the judge threw out the case after learning that evidence he had ruled inadmissible had made its way into the jury room. Nonetheless, because the jurors testified that the forbidden evidence had significantly impacted their guilty verdict, the judge ordered a new trial (Cassel, 2004).

Mock jury research has indicated that when a roll call vote or a show of hands indicates that a large majority favors a particular verdict, the "holdouts" feel pressured to conform with the majority view (e.g., J. H. Davis et al., 1997). This research has also suggested that verdicts tend to be consistent with the majority view on the first ballot (Kerr, 1981; Sandys & Dillehay, 1995). Interviews studies have suggested that the same thing happens in real juries too (e.g., Kalven & Zeisel, 1966).

If a jury remains deadlocked, the judge can invoke the **Allen charge**, which encourages the jurors to try harder to reach a verdict by considering their own views and those of others with a mind open to being convinced (*Allen v. United States*, 1896). Invoking the Allen charge in criminal cases usually speeds the jury's verdict if the majority is in favor of conviction (V. L. Smith & Kassin, 1993). If, in spite of the Allen charge, jurors still cannot reach a verdict, the jury is declared to be *hung*, and a mistrial is declared. When this happens, it is as if there had been no trial, so the constitutional guarantee against double jeopardy does not apply and the defendant can be tried again. In fact, there is no limit on the number of times a defendant can be retried if successive juries cannot reach a verdict.

Jury Nullification

Jurors may sometimes render a verdict that flies in the face of the facts of the case. Their decision arises not out of confusion or ignorance but from a desire to disregard or protest the law. If this **jury nullification** of the law results in a defendant's acquittal in a criminal trial, the double jeopardy rule prevents that defendant from ever being tried again for the same offense.

In Colonial America, jury nullification provided a way for jurors to express their resentment toward British law and British-appointed judges (Rembar, 1980). For example, when John Peter Zenger, a New York printer, was tried in 1735 for publishing an anti-British tract, his attorney, Andrew Hamilton, convinced the jury to demonstrate their contempt for the British law by acquitting Zenger (J. Alexander, 1963). Jury nullification did not again become a significant issue until the 20th century when it arose in relation to Vietnam-era trials of antiwar activists and draft evaders. In 1968, the Supreme Court upheld the right of juries to decide cases as a matter of conscience, even if it means nullifying the law (*Duncan v. Louisiana*, 1968). This ruling said, in effect, that juries have the right, through nullification, to be the social conscience of the community (Becker, 1980).

Juries today continue to nullify the law but only when they feel that a defendant does not deserve to be blamed or punished (Wiener, Habert, Shkodriani, & Staebler, 1991). In these cases, the jury perceives that (1) the defendant's actions were morally right, although legally wrong; (2) the offense is petty; (3) the offense is a "victimless crime" (such as prostitution or gambling); (4) the defendant has already lost enough or been punished enough; or (5) acquittal will make an important social or political statement. In recent years, jury nullification may have been at work in the acquittal of Dr. Jack Kevorkian (who was ultimately convicted of new offenses after Michigan's laws were changed) and of law enforcement officers who beat Rodney King. In another case, a District of Columbia jury acquitted Tomar Locker even though he murdered a cancer patient named Reuben Bell in front of several witnesses and in full view of a hospital security camera (Tucker, 2000). Locker pleaded insanity, claiming that he had "snapped" due to rage over Bell's acquittal in the murder of Locker's girlfriend several years earlier. Locker had been seriously wounded in that attack, and although jurors initially said they acquitted him by reason of insanity, some of them later conceded that the verdict stemmed from their belief that he had "suffered enough". We'll never know exactly why O. J. Simpson was acquitted at his murder trial, but one factor might have been defense attorney Johnny Cochran's suggestion that the jury should send a message to the Los Angeles Police Department about their alleged misconduct in the case. (Cochran could not have directly argued for jury nullification, for to do so would have been to admit that his client was guilty.)

It has been suggested that jurors are more likely than ever to vote for acquittal as a means of social protest and that they will not be persuaded to vote for conviction because they believe the law, or its manner of enforcement, is unfair. Those who hold this view see evidence for it in a 1999 public opinion poll that found that three out of four Americans said they would act on their own beliefs regardless of instructions from a judge to follow the letter of the law (Biskupic, 1999). They point also to the increasing frequency of hung juries. For decades, hung juries could be expected in only about 5% of all trials (Kalven & Zeisel, 1966), but in recent years, that figure has grown considerably. Some California courts report a rate as high as 20%, whereas Washington, DC, averages 15%. It is not known how many of these juries hung because of genuine disagreement about evidence, but the possibility that they reflect nullification—at least by some jurors—is suggested by the fact that hung juries are particularly likely in drug possession cases, in cases when jurors know that a conviction will result in a life sentence (e.g., under "three strikes and you're out" laws), and in cases when jurors perceive that prosecutors are politically motivated. There were hung juries, for example, in the 1999 trials of Susan McDougal and Julie Hiatt Steele, each of whom was charged by Special Prosecutor Kenneth Starr with obstructing justice in cases involving then-President Bill Clinton.

Some Conclusions About Juries

Jurors and juries are far from perfect arbiters of justice, but even the harshest critics of the jury system agree that the unanimous decision of 12 jurors is about as close to justice as can be expected of human beings. Far more often than not, juries employ common sense, wisdom, and fairness in their deliberations, and they render just decisions. Also, despite occasional high-profile, controversial, or complex cases in which the process seems to go awry, jurors overwhelmingly render decisions that are appropriate to the law and the facts of the case (Visher, 1987). Accordingly, few criminal defendants are willing to give up their right to a trial by jury, nor should they. Although there is room for reform, this ancient institution is likely to be the foundation of the criminal justice process for a long time to come.

Judges

Our discussion of the criminal justice process has repeatedly alluded to the role of judges. We now focus more specifically on who they are and what they do. When the United States was founded in the 18th century, many judges were mostly laymen, but today, they are all attorneys.

State judges are either elected or serve at the discretion of the legislature for a fixed number of years. Although it is rare for a judge appointed by the legislature not to be reappointed, judges who are elected must run for reelection every few years if they wish to continue on the bench. Accordingly, political considerations account for some of the variation within a given state in judicial decisions about everything from the specifics of trial procedures to the severity of sentences for a given crime.

Many state and local judges reach the bench after having served as prosecutors, a role that, as we mentioned earlier, can be somewhat political in nature. Federal judges are nominated by the President of the United States and if confirmed by the Senate, are appointed for life. Nominations of individuals for federal judgeships usually represent repayment of political debts. However, the U.S. Senate has a duty under the Constitution to examine presidential judicial nominees and to approve, or vote down, the president's choices. Federal judges may once have been federal prosecutors, state judges, or members of politically well-connected law firms. Although presidents may select judges on the assumption that they will rule in certain ways on certain issues, in only a few instances has it been possible to correctly predict the voting patterns of federal judges, including Supreme Court justices.

The Judge's Duties

Judges are the "managers" of criminal trials. They participate in the *voir dire*, rule on objections to evidence, tell the jury to disregard any evidence that they deem irrelevant or inadmissible, and, of course, keep order in the court. Trial judges also instruct juries about what they should and should not do during their deliberations, take questions from jurors while they are deliberating, and urge the jury to reach a decision if they are deadlocked.

Trial judges are supposed to be impartial arbiters of fact and to follow the laws of the jurisdiction in determining matters of law both before and during the trial. However, like other human beings, judges are imperfect. The way a judge behaves during a trial can play a significant role in the conduct of the proceedings. Competent, authoritative, even-handed judges help trials run smoothly, whereas rude, brusque, overly officious, or erratic judges can make the proceedings difficult for attorneys and defendants alike. For example, judges who interpret laws and issues in a haphazard and inconsistent manner make it difficult or impossible for attorneys to anticipate the outcomes of hearings.

A judge's demeanor can also affect the outcome of a trial. If jurors perceive the judge to be biased in favor or against the defendant, they might be more likely to reach a verdict consistent with that bias than if the judge had not "telegraphed" an opinion. When judges do communicate their bias, it is more likely to favor the prosecution; very few are biased toward the defense.

In contrast to the vast literature available on police officers and jurors, there is almost no research on the personality and decision-making processes of judges. Although this lack of attention to judicial psychology is regrettable from a scientific standpoint, optimists see it as a reflection of how rare it is that judges are unfair or abuse their power. Indeed, judges best serve the process by not becoming issues in the trial themselves and by carrying out their duties firmly, fairly, and discretely.

In chapter 13, we discuss the role of judges in punishing crime, and in the next chapter (chapter 3), we consider their crucial role in the administration of juvenile justice.

Summary

Crimes are prosecuted through the processes and institutions of local, state, and federal criminal justice systems. The main participants are law enforcement officers, prosecutors, defense attorneys, judges, and jurors. Although each state and the federal government has its own rules governing its criminal justice system, most prosecutions proceed in a similar fashion from arrest to sentencing. Serious crimes, known as felonies, may be appealed to higher courts, which may affirm the decision of the trial court, remand the case (send it back) to the trial court to redo all or part of the trial, or reverse a conviction. Because of the U.S. Constitution's protection from being tried twice for the same offense, if a defendant is acquitted, the government cannot retry him.

The criminal justice system must deal differently with special defendants, specifically, those who are incompetent, insane, or dangerous. Mental health professionals play a critical role in cases involving these individuals, including assessing competency to be tried, giving an opinion about a defendant's ability to know what he or she was doing at the time an offense was committed, and helping a judge to decide if someone is too dangerous to be let out among the general population. Mental health professionals are most visible when a defendant pleads NGRI. An insanity plea is not as common as people believe it to be, and it is rarely successful. Contrary to the misconception that being found not guilty by reason of insanity is literally "getting away with murder," people who are successful in such a plea usually spend more time in a hospital than they would have served in jail if convicted of the crime. Predicting whether a person will be dangerous in the future is risky business, and few psychologists feel qualified to make that determination. However, using meteorological principles of predictions that are short-term in nature, psychologists can offer some guidance to judges who must balance the public's right to be safe with the defendant's right not to be locked up unnecessarily.

The criminal justice system depends on all its participants behaving with integrity and fairness. Psychologists help us understand how juries deliberate and make decisions, and they contribute their expertise as trial consultants who assist attorneys in shaping the trial to maximize their clients' chances of being acquitted. Psychology makes many contributions to the area of law enforcement. Law enforcement officers may use psychology to profile crimes and criminals in an aid to helping solve crimes. Psychologists study police behavior and the effectiveness of police practices on the community.

In addition to law enforcement officers, other important players in the criminal justice system include prosecutors who protect the public interest by bringing criminals to justice; defense attorneys who try to protect defendant's constitutional rights; and judges who act as referees at trials, decide legal issues, and impose sentences. Juries and jurors are of great interest to social scientists, including psychologists.

Key Terms

Bond (bail)	*Competent to stand trial*
Hung jury	*Venire*
Harmless error	*Voir dire*
Double jeopardy	*Allen charge*
Not guilty by reason of insanity (NGRI)	*Jury nullification*

Questions for Review

1. What takes place in the criminal justice process from arrest to sentencing?
2. What does it mean to be incompetent to stand trial?
3. What is the policy behind the insanity defense, how often is it used, and what disorders might result in a successful insanity defense?
4. Why are psychologists so poor at predicting which defendant will be dangerous?
5. What is jury nullification and when and why do jurors nullify?

Track It Down

Criminal Behavior Website
www.cassel2e.com
Learn about the Federal court system
www.uscourts.gov
National Association of Criminal Defense Attorneys
www.criminaljustice.org/public.nsf/freeform/publicwelcome?opendocument
National District Attorneys Association
www.ndaa-apri.org/
The MacArthur Research Network on Mental Health and the Law
macarthur.virginia.edu/violence.html
Psychology in the Courtroom
jonathan.mueller.faculty.noctrl.edu/crow/topiccourtroom.htm
Police Psychology Online
www.policepsych.com/

3

The Juvenile Justice System

The Juvenile Justice Process · *Juvenile Justice Applied: The Case of Ronald*

The Psycholegal Status of Juvenile Offenders · *The Future of Juvenile Justice*

On July 28, 1999, in Miami, Florida, 12-year-old Lionel Tate was playing with a 6-year-old girl, Tiffany Eunick, whom his mother, Kathleen Tate, was babysitting. Kathleen decided to take a nap in her upstairs bedroom, leaving Lionel and Tiffany downstairs. Mrs. Tate was awakened by noise from downstairs, where she found Tiffany unconscious. Lionel had been demonstrating with Tiffany some wrestling moves he had seen on television. The girl died of her injuries, and after being tried as an adult in criminal court, Lionel was sentenced to life in prison. In 2004, his sentence was commuted (reduced) by Florida's governor, Jeb Bush, to correspond to the nearly 5 years he had already served, but he was subsequently convicted of gun charges in connection with a robbery, sentenced to 30 years, and still faces life in prison on the robbery charge (*USA Today*, May 20, 2006).

In 2001, 13-year-old Nathaniel Brazill of West Palm Beach, Florida, was tried as an adult for murdering his teacher with a handgun. He was sentenced to 28 years in prison (Spencer-Wendel, 2005). That same year, Alex and Derek King, 12 and 13 years old, respectively, were also tried and convicted as adults for bludgeoning their father to death with a baseball bat (Colb, 2002).

These cases reflect a growing tendency to treat juveniles as adults when they are accused of serious crimes. This trend had been gathering steam since the 1980s and was hastened in the late 1990s by a series of school-yard shootings in Jonesboro, Arkansas; Bethel, Alaska; Pearl, Mississippi; West Paducah, Kentucky; Edinboro, Pennsylvania; and Springfield, Oregon. The killers in these cases were all under the age of 16. On February 29, 2000, a boy of only 6 pulled a .32 caliber handgun from his pants pocket and killed Kayla Rolland, another 6-year-old, in their first-grade classroom in Flint, Michigan. Also, of course, there was Columbine High School in Littleton, Colorado, where on April 20, 1999, 18-year-old Eric Harris and 17-year-old Dylan Klebold—members of an outcast White supremacist group known as the "Trenchcoat Mafia"—wore their trademark long black coats to school and over several hours killed 12 students and a teacher before turning their guns on themselves.

In short, juvenile crime is not what it used to be—petty thefts, stealing cars for joy rides, and underage drinking.

Fortunately, juvenile arrests have been declining overall since 1997 (Snyder, 2004). For instance, in 2001, only 10% of high school boys reported carrying a gun to school one day in the past 30 compared to almost 20% in 1993 (DeVoe et al., 2003). Also, in 2001, the number of juvenile arrests was 20% below its 1997 level. Unfortunately, even the drop in juvenile violence leaves a serious situation because the current decrease was

TABLE 3.1 *Minimum Age at Which Juveniles Can be Tried as Adults for Serious Crimes*

Minimum Age	State(s)
15	New Mexico
14	Alabama, Arkansas, California, Connecticut, Iowa, Kentucky, Louisiana, Massachusetts, Michigan, Minnesota, New Jersey, North Dakota, Ohio, Texas, Utah, Virginia
13	Illinois, Mississippi, New Hampshire, New York, North Carolina, Wyoming
12	Colorado, Missouri, Montana
10	Kansas, Vermont
No age specified	Alaska, Arizona, Delaware, District of Columbia, Florida, Georgia, Hawaii, Idaho, Indiana, Maine, Maryland, Nebraska, Nevada, Oklahoma, Oregon, Pennsylvania, Rhode Island, South Carolina, South Dakota, Tennessee, Washington, West Virginia, Wisconsin

Source: Adapted from Griffin, P., Torbet, P., and Szymanski, L. 1998. *Trying Juveniles as Adults in Criminal Court: An Analysis of State Transfer Provisions.* Washington, DC: U.S. Department of Justice, Office of Justice Programs, Office of Juvenile Justice and Delinquency Prevention.

preceded by a substantial growth in violent crimes by juveniles beginning in the late 1980s, as crack cocaine made its presence felt in inner-city neighborhoods. The combination of crack, gangs, and the increasing availability of handguns was associated with a 60% increase in juvenile arrests for rape, robbery, and murder between 1987 and 1993 (Blumstein, 1995; National Institute of Justice, 1996b). Between 1992 and 1996, juvenile arrests for drug abuse violations increased by 120%, and as of October 1999, almost 109,000 juveniles were in custody after being charged with a crime (Sickmund, 2002).

Concern over juvenile crime, especially violent juvenile crime, began to drive legislative and political agendas at every level of government. Many people believe that society should take juvenile crime more seriously including by dealing with young criminals in the adult justice system rather than in the juvenile justice system. For years, all states had laws allowing juveniles to be tried as adults if they commit serious violent crimes (particularly murder), but in most states, these provisions applied only to those who were at least 16 years old. In the 1990s, states began to lower the minimum age at which juveniles could be tried as adults and to extend the range of crimes for which this step is justified to include nonviolent crimes. In many states, the minimum age in murder cases was set at 14, and although a few set it lower (10 in Vermont and Kansas), many states specify no fixed age, allowing violent juveniles to be dealt with on a case-by-case basis (see Table 3.1). Because the minimum age in Arkansas for trying juveniles as adults is 14, the Jonesboro killers were sentenced to confinement but only in a juvenile facility and only until they are 18. Given the horrendous nature of their crimes, it is no wonder that many people in Arkansas and other states with similar laws began to call for a further lowering of the age at which children can be tried as adults.

The "get tough on juvenile crime" trend was the product of horrendous incidents of juvenile violence combined with warnings by experts that the 21st century could witness a new tidal wave of juvenile crime, as increasing numbers of children reached the age range during which their risk of primal activity is highest (F. Butterfield, 1995; Fox, 1996). Indeed, if the events of the late 1990s are any indication, violent crimes committed by juveniles may continue to decrease, but the age at which children commit violent crimes, especially murders and aggravated assaults, will be decreasing.

What is to be done with criminal children? In this chapter, we consider juvenile justice, a system of law enforcement, prosecution, and punishment designed specifically for children and adolescents who commit crimes. We will contrast this "junior" system with the adult system we described in chapter 2 and explore what the future holds for what many regard as a system that is not only out of touch with the violent tendencies of today's young people, but seems to serve as a contributing factor to juvenile crime.

The Juvenile Justice Process

The U.S. juvenile justice system is a product of the 20th century. Prior to 1899, children who violated criminal laws were held responsible for their actions in the same manner as adults. Those who wanted to reform this arrangement reasoned that delinquent juveniles were the product of their decaying environment, including the loosening of the nuclear family structure that came about as the U.S. population began to shift from its mainly rural, agricultural, family-oriented roots toward a life of work in big city factories. In the city, parents no longer could work side by side at home. Fathers, and to a lesser extent, mothers, were away at work for many hours each day.

Efforts by social reformers to assist children who were neglected, abused, or ended up committing crimes took various forms including removing them from their homes and placing them in newly created institutions for juveniles (known as "houses of refuge"). This "child saver" movement was based on the application of the legal principle of **parens patriae**, the power of the government to act as parents to endangered juveniles. Invocation of this principle protected these juveniles not only from abusive or neglectful parents and other negative environmental influences but also shielded them from the harsh processes and penalties of adult criminal courts. Little by little, the states began to institute judicial reforms designed to further this trend.

The first Juvenile Court Act in the United States was passed in Illinois in 1899. Its principles survive today as the foundation of the juvenile justice system nationwide. These include the beliefs that (1) children should not be held accountable for their actions in the same way as adults are; (2) the goal of the juvenile justice system is to aid, rehabilitate, and reform juveniles, not to punish them; (3) disposition of juveniles' cases should be tailored to their individual circumstances and needs; and (4) the system should avoid the formal, adversarial, and punitive procedures seen in adult criminal courts. On the basis of these beliefs, the states created separate juvenile courts governed by special rules of procedure.[1]

Juvenile Court Procedures

Juvenile court procedures differ from adult criminal court procedures in several respects including the terminology employed. Juveniles charged with an offense are either "detained" (i.e., held in a locked juvenile facility pending a speedy hearing) or placed in their parents' custody pending a hearing to adjudicate the charges. In 2000, about 20% of delinquency cases resulted in juveniles being held in detention facilities at some point after being referred to the court (Puzzanchera, Stahl, Finnegan, Tierney, & Snyder, 2003).

An adjudicatory hearing is synonymous with a trial in adult court, but it takes place before a judge only; there is no jury. The juvenile is adjudicated as either "innocent" or "not innocent" rather than guilty or not guilty. Juveniles found not innocent officially become *delinquents*. Juveniles adjudicated not innocent are not sentenced as in adult court. Instead, there is a "dispositional" hearing at which the judge decides whether to mandate mental health treatment, release on probation, or order confinement in a secure facility or juvenile training school. First-time nonviolent offenders are often placed on probation, whereas those who have committed serious or repeated offenses are often confined. As in adult criminal court, not all juvenile cases are formally adjudicated. In 2000, 39% of all juvenile defendants were adjudicated delinquent or sent to adult criminal court (Stahl, Finnegan, & Kang, 2002). Of these, approximately 63% were placed on probation, 24% were placed in a residential facility for delinquents (and for older juveniles, in adult jails), and the remaining disposed of in other ways such as referral to an outside agency or imposition of community service or restitution requirements (Stahl et al., 2002).

In some states, juvenile court proceedings are public, but most are open only to the juvenile offenders, their parents, attorneys, and court officers. Records of the proceedings, including the judge's findings and disposition of the case, are not available to outsiders other than court officers. Many people assume that these records are destroyed when the juvenile reaches legal adulthood, but actually they are kept for a number of years (the

---

[1]However, beginning in the 1960s, the U.S. Supreme Court extended procedural protections to juveniles that are similar to those enjoyed by adult criminals, including Miranda warnings and the right to counsel.

limit varies from state to state) and can be reviewed by adult courts should the juvenile be charged with criminal offenses as an adult.[2]

According to the latest figures available, for 2000, juvenile courts in the United States processed an estimated 1.7 million delinquency cases, an increase of 43% since 1985 (Stahl et al., 2002). These cases were brought not only for violations of criminal laws but for a set of offenses that only apply if juveniles commit them. These **status offenses** include disobeying parents, running away from home, truancy, violating curfews imposed on young people, possessing alcohol or cigarettes, and engaging in sex. These laws and statutes, enacted and enforced under the states' power of *parens patriae*, were designed to protect the best interests of children and teenagers. The intended purpose of bringing young people who violate these laws before a juvenile court is to provide children and their families with the social and psychological services they need. Too often, however, "status offenders" are dealt with harshly; in some cases, they are confined to secure detention facilities for skipping school, having sex, possessing alcohol, or disobeying their parents. Some juvenile justice experts believe that status offenses should be eliminated (Feld, 1993; I. Schwartz, 1989), but proponents believe that hard-line treatment of status offenders, especially repeat offenders, is an important part of delinquency prevention (Krisberg, Currie, & Onek, 1994; Shelden, Horvath, & Tracy, 1989; Snyder, 1988).

Trying Juveniles as Adults

Juvenile court judges decide whether to transfer or *waive* juvenile cases to adult criminal court after hearing evidence from prosecution and defense attorneys about (1) the seriousness of the alleged offense and the need to protect the community; (2) whether the offense was committed in an aggressive, violent, premeditated, or willful manner; (3) whether the offense was against a person or against property; (4) the juvenile's sophistication, maturity, record of achievement, and criminal history; and (5) the likelihood of rehabilitation (N. Miller, 1996). Most states have more than one mechanism for transferring cases to criminal court. In an increasing number of states, cases that meet certain age and offense criteria are excluded by statute from juvenile court jurisdiction and are thus filed directly in criminal court. In some states, statutes give prosecutors discretion to file certain juvenile cases directly in criminal court under concurrent jurisdiction provisions. The number of delinquency cases judicially waived to criminal court grew by 70% between 1985 and 1994 and then declined by 54% through 2000. However, trends varied across offense categories, with the most waivers occurring for violent crimes against persons (Stahl et al., 2002).

Ethnicity appears to play a role in whether cases are waived to adult criminal court. Black defendants are more likely than others to be waived for drug offenses, whereas White juveniles are more likely to be waived for crimes against people (Butts, 1997). Yamagata & Jones (2000) found that in every offense category (person, property, drug, and public order), a substantially greater percentage of Black youths were detained than White youths; Blacks were more likely to be formally charged than Whites, even when referred for the same offense; minority youth were more likely to be waived to adult criminal court than White offenders; and young people of color were more likely to be incarcerated.

Even when juveniles are tried and convicted as adults, the adult criminal court judge has flexibility in sentencing. Juveniles may receive a typical juvenile sentence (probation, confinement, and/or court-ordered services), a standard adult sentence, or some combination of the two. If sentenced to confinement, juveniles may be ordered to serve their time in a juvenile correctional facility or in an adult prison. In Florida, Minnesota, Texas, and other states whose laws provide for "blended sentencing," juveniles might serve time in a juvenile facility until the age of 18 or 21, after which they are either transferred to an adult prison to serve the remainder of their sentence or returned to court for further disposition (which may involve release or continued imprisonment).

Given that the goal of trying juveniles as adults is to get tough on them, most people assume that young criminals will be treated more harshly in adult court than in juvenile court. This is not necessarily the case. Regardless of their juvenile court history, juveniles may be treated as first-time offenders by adult court judges

---

[2]Federal courts have no juvenile system, so juveniles who have committed federal crimes are tried by the states. However, a proposed law would allow federal prosecution of juveniles over 13 who commit certain federal crimes.

and thus receive probation rather than incarceration or, if incarcerated, receive sentences comparable to those imposed in juvenile court (Brown, 1998).

It is mainly in murder cases that judges in adult courts have given stiff sentences to young defendants. For example, 16-year-old Barry Loukaitis was sentenced in Washington State to two consecutive life terms without the possibility of parole plus an additional 205 years after his conviction for killing two fellow students and a math teacher, assaulting another student and teacher, and kidnapping 15 students in his junior high school classroom when he was 14 (P. Anderson, 1997). In Florida, a 17-year-old boy known as the "vampire murderer" because he and his girlfriend drank each other's blood before they killed her parents was sentenced to death for the crime, which he committed at the age of 16 (D. Baker, 1998b). However, in 2005, the U.S. Supreme Court ruled that it is unconstitutional to impose the death penalty on someone who was under the age of 18 when the capital offense was committed (*Roper v. Simmons*). Thus, the vampire killer's sentence was reduced to life in prison.

Impact of Trying Juveniles as Adults

Juvenile transfer and waiver provisions have a significant impact on a young person's life. They establish a permanent criminal record that brings a lifelong stigma and deprivation of certain rights (including, in some states, the right to vote). Unfortunately, there is little reason to believe that these provisions have deterred juvenile crime.

For one thing, given that juvenile offenders often receive probation in adult criminal court, society is not protected should they decide to continue their criminal careers. Many do. In fact, juveniles tried as adults have higher recidivism rates overall than do those who were tried in juvenile courts (Redding, 2000). The only exception is for property crimes in which case juveniles are less likely to reoffend (D. M. Bishop, Frazier, Lanza-Kaduce, & Winner, 1996). When property offenders tried as adults do reoffend, however, they do so sooner and more often than those who had gone through the juvenile justice system. (Also, the more offenses juveniles commit, the more likely they are to become violent adult criminals; Pan, 1998.) This tendency may be due in part to the fact that these youngsters may eventually be incarcerated in overcrowded and dangerous adult institutions where—because they are not segregated from the adult inmate population—they are five times more likely to be sexually assaulted, twice as likely to be beaten by staff, and 50% more likely to be attacked with a weapon than their counterparts in juvenile facilities (Office of Juvenile Justice & Delinquency Prevention [OJJDP], 1999). (Unfortunately, the same criminogenic conditions also exist in some juvenile facilities; Allen-Hagen, 1993.) In adult confinement facilities, juveniles soon learn that to survive, they must adopt the abusive and violent ways of their fellow inmates and jailers. They become stigmatized and humiliated by the experience; some adopt a criminal self-concept (Redding, 2000) and many have great difficulty in finding employment after being released (Freed, 1992).

The Psycho-Legal Status of Juvenile Offenders

Like adult defendants, juveniles cannot be tried or punished for their crimes unless they are capable of forming criminal intent (*mens rea*) and mentally competent to stand trial. If deciding about these matters is difficult in adult cases, it can be downright confounding in the case of children, especially when they are to be tried as adults.

Criminal Intent in Juveniles

Before there were juvenile courts, common-law tradition held that children under the age of 7 years were incapable of forming the criminal intent necessary to raise an act from the level of "misconduct" to that of a crime punishable by the state. In the case of children between the ages of 7 and 14, there was no presumption that they either had or lacked criminal intent; the prosecution had the duty to prove the child's capacity for *mens rea* beyond a reasonable doubt. Only juveniles over the age of 14 were presumed to have the capacity for criminal intent and, like adults charged with crime, had the burden to prove lack of *mens rea* by clear and convincing evidence. With the establishment of juvenile courts, these common-law rules and presumptions were de-emphasized or eliminated because these courts existed to protect young children from exposure to the adult criminal system and to provide rehabilitation and treatment.

Today, however, as younger and younger juvenile defendants appear before juvenile and adult criminal courts, legislators are being pressured to reconsider the age at which criminal intent can be presumed. In what is perhaps a hint of things to come, the May 11, 1998, issue of *The Washington Post* ("Angry 5-Year-Old," 1998) carried a story about a Memphis, Tennessee, juvenile court judge who heard the case of a 5-year-old boy who had brought a loaded semiautomatic pistol to school so that he could kill the kindergarten teacher who had punished him with a "time-out." The judge dismissed the gun charges because "a five-year-old is not capable of forming criminal intent" (p. A5), but given the child's conduct, there are those who would strongly disagree with that view.

Juvenile Competence

Another question about juvenile offenders relates to their psychological competence during all stages of judicial proceedings—from police questioning to sentencing. As we mentioned in chapter 2, defendants are considered competent only if they are capable of understanding the nature of the charges against them and are able to assist their attorneys in preparing a defense.

If the defendant raises a question of competency at any stage, the judge may order a mental status evaluation and suspend proceedings until the defendant becomes competent. When tried as adults, defendants as young as 10 or 11 are presumed by the law to have an adult's understanding of their constitutional rights and the judicial process. This presumption may be incorrect in many cases and may reflect a misunderstanding of the cognitive and intellectual development of juveniles and adolescents. Accordingly, not all juvenile court judges are guided by a strict interpretation of the law. For example, a California judge found a 6-year-old boy to be incompetent to stand trial for the attempted murder of a 1-month-old baby (Frost & Shepherd, 1996).

Whereas the question of an adult's competency usually arises in relation to the presence of a serious mental disorder or significant mental retardation, juveniles may be declared incompetent by virtue of the mental and emotional immaturity associated with their young age. At what age *can* a juvenile realistically be presumed competent to stand trial? A recent study (Grisso et al., 2003) of 1,400 people aged 11 to 24 concluded that when competence is defined legally as the ability to understand the nature of criminal proceedings and the ability to assist an attorney in defending them, a significant proportion of juveniles who are 15 or younger are probably not competent to stand trial in a criminal proceeding. They concluded that states that transfer under 15-year-old juveniles to adult court are subjecting them to proceedings in which they are not competent to participate. To illustrate their point, in 1998, a judge in Pontiac, Michigan, would not allow into evidence the confession of an 11-year-old who was accused of shooting an 18-year-old boy. The evidence was disallowed because—although the youngster had waived his Miranda rights to have an attorney present before making a statement to police—a pretrial hearing revealed that the boy thought the "right to remain silent" meant that he could not go anywhere. His mother, who was present during the police interrogation, said that she did not understand that she could stop the questioning of her son ("Boy's Murder Conviction," 1998). In this instance, the judge essentially found the boy functionally incompetent.

Data from the Grisso and colleagues' study is consistent with the results of an earlier government-funded study of young offenders' understanding of Miranda warnings. In that study (Grisso, 1997), 400 juveniles in detention facilities were asked what various Miranda warnings mean. Even at ages 14 to 16, only about one fourth of these youngsters correctly described a "right" as a legal entitlement that cannot be revoked but that can be voluntarily relinquished (Grisso, 1980). When asked what it means when police say, "You do not have to make a statement and have the right to remain silent," many gave a conditional view of their legal rights such as "You can be silent unless you are told to talk," "You have to be quiet unless you are spoken to," or even "They might send me home tonight if I said I did it" (Grisso, 1997).

Setting age limits for competence is a tricky business then, partly because simply reaching a certain age does not guarantee an understanding of abstract legal principles and what is taking place in the courtroom. Older juveniles with limited mental abilities, learning disabilities, or emotional and mental disorders may be especially unlikely to meet standards for competence (Shepherd & Zaremba, 1995). In the Miranda study mentioned previously (Grisso,

1997), delinquents aged 15 to 17 with low IQ scores showed a poorer understanding of their legal rights than the average 12-year-old. Further, adolescents with relatively low intelligence test scores showed a poorer comprehension of legal matters than adults of similarly low intelligence.

Few adolescents, let alone preadolescents, are able to assist their defense attorneys by collaborating on decisions about pleas and other trial decisions. So even though a juvenile's attorney is obligated to advise the young client on trial strategy and honor the client's decisions regarding matters such as whether to testify, which witnesses to call, and whether to plead guilty, preadolescent juveniles are less capable of imagining the long-term consequences of these decisions than are older adolescents and adults (Peterson-Badali & Abramovitch, 1993). Indeed, the ability to think hypothetically only begins to develop in early adolescence and takes several years to mature. Studies show that, at least until late adolescence, juveniles minimize risks and are less likely than adults to focus on the long-range consequences of their decisions (Cohn, 1995). In one study (Grisso et al., 2003), for instance, 50% of 11- to 13-year-olds elected to confess to a crime rather than to remain silent during a police interrogation, whereas only 20% of young adults chose to confess. Similarly, 74% of 11- to 13-year-olds recommended accepting a plea agreement, whereas only 50% of young adults did. Overall, between 80% and 90% of adults referred for competency evaluations are considered competent to stand trial compared to only about 20% of juveniles under 13; only half of those 13 and older are found competent (Grisso, 1997). These limitations on competence-related mental abilities have led some researchers to recommend that juveniles under the age of 15 should not be tried in adult court for any crime (Grisso et al., 2003). In fact, some go even further by suggesting that regardless of age, children should never be tried as adults if they cannot meet the legal standards for adult competence.

Juvenile Justice Applied: The Case of Ronald

The juvenile justice system was created with good intentions, but like the adult criminal justice system, it is flawed, and it can sometimes inadvertently contribute to the development of juvenile delinquency. This was certainly true in the case of a 15-year-old Black youngster whom we call "Ronald." The story begins in 1994 when a juvenile court clerk summoned one of us (Elaine Cassel), a lawyer, to interview Ronald. When Elaine asked why Ronald, who had never been in trouble before, received a 10-day sentence in a juvenile facility simply for not attending school, the court clerk said that "the probation officer asked for it to 'get Ronald's attention.'" She also said that he has another court date in 10 days and the judge wants you to do something for him."

Ronald probably needed court-ordered psychological services, but he seemed a long way from being delinquent. He almost never spoke, and when he did, it was always in a soft voice. In the fifth grade, when he was 10, he had been labeled mentally retarded by a Virginia school district, and although he was placed in "retarded track" classes, he received no individualized special education services. Neither had he ever been given a psychological or educational test; the diagnosis of retardation was apparently given because he rarely spoke.

What his teachers did not know was that Ronald's reluctance to speak began at the age of 9 after he witnessed his sister being stoned to death in front of their home in an act of senseless violence. After his sister's death, Ronald's older brother and mother were convicted of drug dealing and sent to prison. He never knew his father. Until the recent incident of truancy, his record of school attendance and conduct had been exemplary. Unfortunately, though, he had been promoted from grade to grade without doing any work or making any academic progress. It was only when he began eighth grade at the county's large junior high school that his attendance became spotty. His grandmother and a maternal aunt said that they had a hard time waking him up and getting him out of bed. It never occurred to anyone that Ronald might be suffering from posttraumatic stress disorder (PTSD) and/or serious depression.[3]

---

[3]Mental health professionals later determined that Ronald was indeed suffering from posttraumatic stress disorder, and they recommended that he receive psychotherapy as well as medication for depression.

Elaine asked the judge presiding over Ronald's case to order a physical examination, a battery of neurological tests, several psychological tests, and a complete social and family history. When a psychologist administered the first of these assessments, an intelligence test, he reported as follows:

> Ronald is certainly not retarded. I cannot score the [verbal portion of the] test because he is so slow to verbalize that he can't pass the timed portion of the verbal tests. However, his answers, when he gets them out, are totally appropriate. And he ranks in the superior range on the performance tests. I can only guess that he was labeled retarded because he does not readily speak. And considering he was put in the "retarded classes," it is understandable why he did not want to go to school.

When Elainel reported the results of the intelligence test to the judge and advised him of Ronald's home situation, he said, "I want you to find a placement for him." She got him released from detention and placed with his grandmother while she contacted a social worker about finding a residential placement. Eventually, a 30-day probationary placement was found for Ronald at a wilderness program in the southwestern part of the state. It was agreed that if he did well during the probationary period, he would receive continued help there for a year.

Just before the end of the 30-day period, the director of the wilderness facility called Elaine to say that Ronald had been with a group of fellow residents who stole a car and took it for a short "joy ride" before running it off the road. Ronald had been arrested and charged with felony unauthorized use of an automobile. Elaine worked out an agreement with the prosecutor by which Ronald would plead guilty and receive a 90-day sentence in detention, which would be suspended if he continued to do well in the wilderness program. Would he? Ronald was a young man with virtually no family resources, suffering obvious psychological and emotional distress, in a strange place far from home with boys who had been in serious trouble and who were obviously capable of influencing him. He was now only one mistake away from the juvenile version of state prison. Yet the juvenile justice system held Ronald fully accountable for his actions. He was expected to do what he was told and "stay out of trouble" even though there were social forces pushing him in the opposite direction.

For the next 60 days, Ronald did indeed stay out of trouble. The staff liked his good manners, kind ways, and pleasant disposition. Although he was sometimes difficult to awaken in the mornings, when he was reminded of his obligations, he cheerfully complied. Then, on a family visitation day that, as usual, brought him no visitors, Ronald walked away from the facility and was found wandering around in a town seven miles away. The wilderness program had a "zero-tolerance" policy on runaways, and when Ronald left the grounds without permission, he violated that policy.

He was dismissed from the program, which meant that he would have to serve the previously suspended sentence for his felony conviction. The program director later discovered that Ronald's mother, a career criminal who had just been released from prison after serving time for drug offenses, was supposed to have visited Ronald on the day he ran away. He had waited all day for her, but she never showed up. The director understood that he might have left to avoid the embarrassment of once again having no visitors, but said that "rules are rules," and the decision was final.

After serving his felony sentence, Ronald was to be returned to his grandmother, but now his mother said she wanted him back. His grandmother and aunt could have sought a court order to keep her away from him, but they did not want to get into a family conflict; and truth to tell, they were worn out from dealing with Ronald. A little more than two years later, at the age of 17, Ronald and a group of other boys were arrested for breaking into houses. He was tried as an adult, convicted, and sentenced to five years in jail. However, the judge suspended all but one year of this sentence and ordered that Ronald be placed on supervised probation for two years upon release.

Although he had been a child without a home, and a schoolboy without an education, he will not be a man without a place; Ronald will likely join the society of career criminals. Given his personality, he will probably not be a violent criminal, but he will likely abuse drugs and alcohol, commit property crimes, and become part of a large and growing fraternity of Black, male, repeat offenders.

Truly, this is a sad tale. By bringing Elaine into the case, the juvenile justice system made an effort to establish an informed diagnosis of a youngster's problems and to bring beneficial services to bear. However, as so often happens, that same system demanded retribution for juvenile offenses, and as offenders seek to cope with their punishment as best they can given their limited cognitive and behavioral resources, they often end up taking the path of least resistance. In Ronald's case, his mother and brother had shown him the way. What long-term hope is there for him and others like him whom juvenile authorities poignantly label as "throwaway" kids—children nobody wants? Elaine will remember him as a sweet, kind boy; a witness to violent crime; and a victim of parental neglect and of failures in the educational, social, and judicial systems that were supposed to first protect and later rehabilitate him.

The Future of Juvenile Justice

We presented Ronald's case in some detail because it exemplifies how a well-intentioned juvenile justice system, in partnership with educational and social institutions, can actually contribute to the development and perpetuation of crime. Ronald's social, educational, and family background included many of the risks for criminality that we discuss in the next six chapters. His entry into the criminal justice system began when he was locked up for a trivial first offense. Within two years, he had an adult criminal record, but had he had more social and family support, it might all have been different.

More than 100 years after the birth of the juvenile justice system, there are those who support the idea of letting the pendulum of juvenile justice swing back toward the traditions that were prevalent when it began, namely, treating juvenile offenders as adults in spite of their immature cognitive, intellectual, and emotional development.[4] However, many researchers in the juvenile justice field believe that adult trials and stiff sentences in adult or juvenile facilities should be reserved only for the most violent juveniles—rapists, armed robbers, and murderers—who are least likely to reform (Pan, 1998). In such cases, they say, the primary goal should be to protect society from these people's predatory tendencies—even if a serious crime was their first offense. These researchers also believe that juveniles who are *not* violent offenders should receive the benefit of the best educational and rehabilitation programs available, including in-home and in-school interventions as soon as they commit a status offense or a petty crime. Many of those programs include parental responsibility components (in which parents can be fined for their children's lawbreaking), graduated sanctions (e.g., intensive supervision and services following a first offense; incarceration if offenses are repeated), cash incentives for high-school graduation, training in social and conflict-resolution skills, individual therapy aimed at enhancing self-esteem, and family therapy (Krisberg et al., 1994). It is also suggested that the best way to prevent serious crimes in the long run is to take a "zero tolerance" approach to youngsters who stay out late, break family rules, run away, skip school, have promiscuous sex, engage in vandalism, and use drugs and alcohol. These behaviors, which typically begin in late childhood or the early teens, are predictive of future, and more serious, delinquent behavior (National Conference on State Legislatures, 1996).

In other words, abandoning today's rehabilitative model for yesteryear's retributive model may not solve the problems of juvenile crime, enhance juvenile justice, or ensure public safety. Accordingly, in 1992, the U.S. Justice Department's Office of Juvenile Justice and Delinquency Prevention (OJJDP) set out to design a model of juvenile justice that can be adopted by state and local governments. Known as the "Balanced and Restorative Justice Project," its guiding principle is the implementation of restorative offender sanctions or penalties that include community service, victim involvement in sanctions, and making restitution to victims.

Where retributive justice is focused on vengeance, deterrence, and punishment through an adversarial process, **restorative justice** is concerned with repairing the harm done to victims and the community through negotiation, mediation, victim empowerment, and reparation (see Table 3.2). In contrast to the rehabilitative approach, which focuses on providing limited services to offenders, restorative justice is concerned with providing services to offenders, victims, and the community (Lawrence, 1991; Zehr, 1990). Thus, the focus of restorative justice is neither utterly punitive nor overly lenient; as such, it provides a clear alternative to both the retributive and rehabilitative models.

---

[4]Critics find this position ironic given that the same offender who is considered an adult at 12 cannot legally drink alcohol, smoke tobacco, or walk local streets after hours until the age of 18 or 21.

TABLE 3.2   *Retributive and Restorative Assumptions*

Retributive Justice	*Restorative Justice*
Crime is an act against the State, a violation of a law, an abstract idea.	Crime is an act against another person or the community.
The criminal justice system controls crime.	Crime control lies primarily in the community.
Offender accountability defined as taking punishment.	Accountability defined as assuming responsibility and taking action to repair harm.
Crime is an individual act with individual responsibility	Crime has both individual and social dimensions of responsibility.

Punishment is effective.
   a.   Threat of punishment deters crime.
   b.   Punishment changes behavior.
	Punishment alone is not effective in changing behavior and is disruptive to community harmony and good relationships.

Victims are peripheral to the process.	Victims are central to the process of resolving a crime.
The offender is defined by deficits.	The offender is defined by capacity to make reparation.
Focus on establishing blame, on guilt, on past (did he/she do it?).	Focus on problem solving, on liabilities/obligations, on future (what should be done?).
Emphasis on adversarial relationship.	Emphasis on dialogue and negotiation.
Imposition of pain to punish and deter/prevent.	Restitution as a means of restoring both parties; goal of reconciliation/restoration.
Community on sideline, represented abstractly by State.	Community as facilitator in restorative process.
Response focused on offender's past behavior.	Response focused on harmful consequences of offender's behavior; emphasis on the future.
Dependence on proxy professionals.	Direct involvement by participants.

Source: Office of Juvenile Justice and Delinquency Prevention. (1996). *Balanced and Restorative Justice: Program Summary*. Washington, DC: Author.

Balanced juvenile justice systems based on the restorative model place equal emphasis on (1) offender accountability to victims and the community, (2) development of more adaptive competencies in offenders, and (3) protection of citizens in the community (OJJDP, 1996). These systems are seen to be successful only when the following performance goals are met:

1. *Accountability*: When an offense occurs, the offender incurs an obligation to the victim and the community to restore what has been lost, stolen, damaged, or destroyed. Offenders are expected to make these reparations including payment for damage and return of or repayment for stolen goods. Victims are involved in determining the nature of these reparations, which often include community service.
2. *Competency development*: Juvenile offenders who come within the jurisdiction of the court should leave the system behaving in a manner that is better than when they entered it. Rather than simply receiving treatment and services aimed at suppressing problem behavior, offenders should display measurable improvements in their ability to function as productive, responsible citizens. Work, education, and community service requirements are imposed to help offenders develop skills and to create opportunities for them to earn money, engage in positive interactions with law-abiding adults, and demonstrate that they are capable of productive behavior.

3. Community protection: The juvenile justice system should provide a range of intervention alternatives geared to the varying risks presented by juvenile offenders under its supervision. These offenders should be under community-based surveillance and sanctions that channel their free time and energy into productive activities during nonschool, nonworking hours. There should be a system of graduated sanctions providing increasingly severe consequences for noncompliance with supervision requirements. Compliant offenders should be given rewards to reinforce their progress.

If a balanced juvenile justice system is successful, victims, communities, and offenders should receive equal attention, and all three should receive tangible benefits. Further, juvenile court dispositions based on this balanced approach must be individualized in accordance with the nature and circumstances of each offense and the offender's needs and risks. The roles of juvenile justice professionals, offenders, and local citizens in a balanced juvenile justice system are presented in Table 3.3. Note that the balanced approach relies strongly on local community support, which means that it must be adapted to the needs and resources of individual communities.

The concept of restorative justice began to gain momentum in the United States in the 1980s, partly because of the rise of the victims' rights movement (see chapter 12) and partly because of a growing trend toward informal neighborhood justice and dispute resolution programs (Galaway & Hudson, 1990; Schneider, 1985). So far, though, whereas many states and jurisdictions have expressed interest in the balanced restorative justice model, relatively few courts and probation departments have implemented the practical and policy changes it requires; and few jurisdictions have been successful in convincing citizens that their community's ability to supervise—rather than confine—offenders is adequate to ensure public safety. It is all too rare, also, to see juvenile justice agencies collaborating with communities on prevention efforts and involving victims in a meaningful way (OJJDP, 1996).

Still, the OJJDP's Balanced and Restorative Justice program is being piloted, with the assistance of government funds, in 10 states (a total of 291 programs). Jurisdictions in Oregon and Texas have become models for implementing the balanced approach and will provide training and assistance to other jurisdictions. If these programs succeed according to the criteria listed in Table 3.4, and if the concept of balanced restorative justice can be sold to a punishment-minded public and to politicians for whom "getting tough on juveniles" is sure-fire, vote-getting rhetoric, restorative justice could be the first real reform of the juvenile justice system since its inception more than 100 years ago. Studies that assess the impact of restorative justice programs on the overall juvenile justice system are ongoing (Umbreit, 1998).

Indeed, juvenile justice experts believe that—with a properly implemented, comprehensive approach to early intervention and prevention backed up by the balanced approach to sanctions and rehabilitation found in the restorative justice model—something can be done about juvenile crime and violence. In 1995, the OJJDP published a guide for the future that outlines a comprehensive strategy for dealing with serious, violent, and chronic juvenile offenders (OJJDP, 1995). Recognizing the important role of crime-related risk factors (such as childhood abuse and neglect) and behavior problems (such as conduct disorder and early alcohol use) that we discuss in chapters 7 and 8, this comprehensive strategy emphasizes five main components:

1. **Strengthen the family.** The goal here is to help families carry out their responsibility to instill moral values and provide guidance and support to children. Children whose families fail to provide adequate supervision are more likely to become delinquent. Lacking proper role models, children develop their own norms based largely on their undisciplined desires. Although children are the first victims of the deterioration of family life, society suffers as well. Thus, strengthening the ability of families to raise healthy children must become a national priority (Cantelon, 1994). Where there is no functional family unit, there should be a surrogate family to guide and nurture the child. A family-strengthening program is any intervention that works with at least one target child and either that child's parent/caregiver or some other member of the family with the goal of reducing the risk or increasing protective factors for problem behavior. These interventions must be tailored to the needs of the family (Cantelon, 1994).
2. **Support core social institutions.** Society must support schools, religious organizations, community organizations, and other social institutions in fulfilling their role of helping to develop capable, mature, and responsible young people. A nurturing community environment consists of public and private youth-serving agencies, neighborhood groups, and business and commercial organizations providing employment training, recreational, and other meaningful opportunities for youth.

TABLE 3.3 *Roles in the Balanced Approach*

Accountability—When a crime occurs, a debt incurs. Justice requires that every effort be made by offenders to restore losses suffered by victims.

Juvenile justice system role: Direct juvenile justice resources to ensure that offenders repay victims and complete other relevant restorative requirements as a top system priority.	**Offender role**: Actively work to restore victims' losses and participate in activities that increase empathy with the victim and victims generally.	**Community role**: Assist in the process by providing paid work opportunities for offenders, helping to develop community service work projects, and supporting victim awareness education.
Intended outcome: Efficient, fair, and meaningful restorative justice practices; increased responsiveness to victims' needs	*Intended outcome*: Understanding of consequences of offense behavior; increased empathy; feeling of fairness in justice process.	*Intended outcome*: More participation in and support for the juvenile justice system; message that victims receive priority

Competency Development—Offenders should leave the juvenile justice system more capable of productive participation in conventional society than when they entered.

Juvenile justice system role: Assess youths' strengths and interests and identify community resources to build on those strengths in a way that demonstrates competency. Engage youth in these activities and provide necessary supports for successful completion. Build prevention capacity through productivity partnerships with employers, educators, and other community agencies.	**Offender role**: Become actively involved in activities that make a positive contribution to the community while building life skills; make continuous progress in improving educational skills while using existing skills to help others.	**Community role**: Become partner with juvenile justice system in developing opportunities for youth to make productive contributions to the community while learning positive civic and other values.
Intended outcome: More opportunities for youth competency development; improved image of juvenile justice; increased competency.	*Intended outcome*: Increased sense of competency and self-esteem; exposure to and interaction with positive adult role models; improved public image of youth.	*Intended outcome*: Increased community involvement in and ownership of delinquency problem; new attitudes toward youth; completion of positive work in communities. Improved quality of life in the community.

Community Protection—The public has a right to a safe and secure community; juvenile justice should develop a progressive response system to ensure offender control in the community and develop new ways to ensure public safety and respond to community concerns.

Juvenile justice system role: Ensure that offenders are carefully supervised by staff and a range of community guardians and that offenders' time is structured in productive activities; develop a range of supervision restrictiveness options and alternative responses to violations and incentives for progress.	**Offender role**: Become involved in competency building and restorative activities; avoid situations that may lead to further offenses.	**Community role**: Provide input to juvenile justice system regarding public safety concerns; share responsibility for offender control and reintegration.
Intended outcome: Increased public support for community supervision.	*Intended outcome*: No offenses while on supervision; reduced recidivism when the period of suspension is over.	*Intended outcome*: Increased feelings of safety in the community; increased confidence in juvenile community supervision.

Source: Office of Juvenile Justice and Delinquency Prevention. (1996). *Balanced and Restorative Justice: Program Summary*. Washington, DC: Author.

TABLE 3.4 *A Restorative Justice Yardstick*

Do victims experience justice?

Do victims have sufficient opportunities to tell their truth to relevant listeners?

Do victims receive needed compensation or restitution?

Is the injustice adequately acknowledged?

Are victims sufficiently protected against further violation?

Does the outcome adequately reflect the severity of the offense?

Do victims receive adequate information about the crime, the offender, and the legal process?

Do victims have a voice in the legal process?

Is the experience of justice adequately public?

Do victims receive adequate support from others?

Do victims' families receive adequate assistance and support?

Are other needs—material, psychological, and spiritual—being addressed?

Do offenders experience justice?

Are offenders encouraged to understand and take responsibility for what they have done?

Are misattributions challenged?

Are offenders given encouragement and opportunities to make things right?

Are offenders given opportunities to participate in the process?

Are offenders encouraged to change their behavior? Is there a mechanism for monitoring or verifying changes?

Are offenders' needs being addressed?
Do offenders' families receive support and assistance?

Is the victim-offender relationship addressed?

Is there an opportunity for victims and offenders to meet, if appropriate?

Is there an opportunity for victims and offenders to exchange information about the even and about one another?

Are community concerns taken into account?

Is the process and the outcome sufficiently public?

Is community protection being addressed?

Is there a need for restitution or a symbolic action for the community?

Is the community represented in some way in the legal process?

Is the future addressed?

Is there provision for solving the problems that led to this event?

Is there provision for solving problems caused by this event?

Have future intentions been addressed?

Are there provisions for monitoring and verifying outcomes and for problem solving?

Source: Office of Juvenile Justice and Delinquency Prevention. (1996). *Balanced and Restorative Justice: Program Summary*. Washington, DC: Author.

3. Promote delinquency prevention. This is seen as the most cost-effective approach to reducing juvenile delinquency. When children commit status offenses, the family and community, in concert with child welfare agencies, must respond with appropriate treatment and support services that address known risk factors (Foote, 1997).

4. Intervene immediately and effectively when delinquent behavior occurs. This component is seen as vital to keeping first-time juvenile offenders from becoming chronic offenders who commit progressively more serious and violent crimes. Appropriate responses by the family, the community, and the courts should come quickly and firmly in adjudicating and sanctioning each case. The OJJDP guidelines recommend use of the restorative justice model and the graduated sanctions we already discussed. It is never too early to intervene. The youngest children should receive services as soon as they are identified as being at risk for criminal behavior (Foote, 1997).

5. Identify and control the worst offenders. There is a relatively small group of violent and chronic juvenile offenders who have committed felony offenses or who have failed to respond to intervention and community-based treatment and rehabilitation services offered by the juvenile justice system. These offenders, who pose the most serious threat to community safety, should be placed in secure facilities or training schools. The most violent and chronic offenders should be tried as adults in the criminal justice system. However, it is never too late to attempt rehabilitative interventions. Programs should be established in secure facilities to help serious offenders reduce their risk of reoffending (Foote, 1997).

Conclusions

Together, the juvenile crime situation and the juvenile justice process present a rather grim picture. One can only hope that the federal government's comprehensive plan and the restorative justice model will eventually meet the public's need for protection from juvenile violence as well as the needs of the juveniles who run the risk of ruined lives when they are not protected from their own failings and those of family and social institutions. A number of innovative efforts that are consistent with the goals of this comprehensive plan are already evident, and some of them have come from the "grass roots."

For example, two attorneys in the District of Columbia are in charge of an alternative high school called "See Forever" that is funded by business and local charities as well as District of Columbia tax money for chartered schools (i.e., schools that are recognized and aided by local governments). This school is in session on a year-round basis, employs one teacher for every five students, and is open only to youngsters who have come in contact with the District of Columbia court system. Half of these students had been charged with crimes such as unauthorized use of a vehicle, fighting, or theft, whereas 30% were involved with more serious crimes such as armed robbery. The school's rules state that students must be in attendance on weekdays from 9:30 a.m. until 8 p.m., but many stay until the 11 p.m. closing time to work with community volunteers who serve as individual tutors. They eat two meals a day cooked by other students in a catering kitchen, which itself is a student-run business serving customers other than the school's students. Certified teachers are responsible for providing the District of Columbia government's required academic program, and members of the local community teach elective courses such as law, art, music, and public speaking. All students must also spend part of the year working at "internship" jobs for which they are paid $130 a week. The money goes into individual accounts that the students manage with the help of local investment professionals. The school provides this unique combination of educational, vocational, and social-skills training services because its administrators have recognized that such services are unlikely to reach most juvenile delinquents in the District of Columbia. As you might expect, there are strict rules for student conduct, academic performance, and dress. Some students drop out early, and those who won't comply with the rules are dismissed. A local juvenile judge remarked that the See Forever program is the only one for District of Columbia teenagers in which he has any faith. A 16-year-old female student at the school put it this way: "These streets are only going to lead you to getting locked up. Or you'll probably die. Today, I'm not all the way all right, but I'll be all right for the future. I know what I'm capable of doing" (Slevin, 1998, p. B8).

Another innovative program for juvenile delinquents across the country is called "America's Promise—The Alliance for Youth." Chaired by retired army general Colin Powell, the organization functions as a conduit through which targeted at-risk children receive five fundamental resources necessary for them to be successful citizens: (1) an ongoing relationship with a caring adult, (2) a safe place to live, (3) a healthy start in life, (4) an education that provides marketable skills, and (5) a chance to give back to the community. With the goal of creating a sense of community and family among schoolchildren, the organization chose to pilot its program in an inner city District of Columbia middle school where there was a history of tension between Black and Hispanic students (Gaines, 1998).

Unfortunately, evidence of efficacy of these programs in terms of reduced crime are only anecdotal; however, that does not diminish the good that the programs do in keeping young people in school and steering them away from the criminogenic influences in their environments.

Summary

The U.S. juvenile justice system is a product of the 20th century. Prior to 1899, children who violated criminal laws were treated much like adults. Social reformers set out to rehabilitate children and to ameliorate the conditions that led to juvenile crime including child abuse and neglect. Juvenile court procedures differ from adult criminal court procedures. Although traditionally the juvenile justice system has focused on reclaiming lives that have gone astray, increasingly juveniles who commit violent crimes are tried as adults. Research strongly suggests that trying juveniles as adults increases recidivism.

What is known about the cognitive processes of juveniles leads to the conclusion that most juveniles are not competent to be tried, meaning that they are not cognitively able to understand the nature of the criminal charges and to assist their attorneys in their defense. Resent research has suggested that most youths younger than 15 being tried in juvenile court are not competent to participate in these proceedings.

In the 1990s, a model of juvenile justice known as restorative justice gained the attention of some juvenile justice reformers and policymakers. The essence of restorative justice is a focus on rehabilitation of the individual offender, restitution to the victim, and reintegration of the offender into the community. Restorative justice blends components of the retributive justice approach—in which the focus is on vengeance, deterrence, and punishment—and the rehabilitation justice approach, which focuses on providing limited services to offenders. The focus of restorative justice is neither wholly punitive nor lenient. Sometimes referred to as balanced justice, restorative justice offers a reasonable alternative to a juvenile justice system that is in need of major overhauls if it is to meet the demands of the 21st century.

Key Terms

Parens patriae

Status offenses
Restorative justice

Questions for Review

1. How has the American system of juvenile justice evolved from 1899 to the present time?
2. What are some of the differences between the juvenile and adult criminal justice systems?
3. What is the procedure for trying a juvenile as an adult?
4. What evidence is there to suggest that most juveniles under the age of 15 years are not competent to be tried as adults?
5. Why is the model of restorative justice considered a balanced approach to juvenile justice?

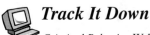

Track It Down

Criminal Behavior Website
www.cassel2e.com
Juvenile Justice Clearinghouse
www.fsu.edu/~crimdo/jjclearinghouse/jj16.html
Juvenile Competence to Stand Trial Policy Brief
www.jcpr.org/policybriefs/vol5_num1.html
Mental Health Issues in Juvenile Delinquency Proceedings
www.abanet.org/crimjust/juvjus/cjmental.html
Restorative Justice On-Line Notebook
www.ojp.usdoj.gov/nij/rest-just/

Biological Roots of Crime

Physical Appearance and Crime
Evolution and Crime
Genes and Crime

Crime and the Brain
Hormones and Crime
Alcohol, Drugs, and Crime

In this chapter, we begin our exploration of the roots of crime by considering theories that suggest that these roots lie partly in human biology, particularly in the genetic heritage we receive from our parents; in our evolution as a species; and in the unique characteristics of individual brains. Some of these theories are highly controversial and have stimulated intense debate.

Physical Appearance and Crime

There has been criminal behavior as long as there have been laws, but it was not until the 19th century that efforts were made to explain it in scientific terms. Scientists' earliest explanatory attempts focused on criminals' inherited physical characteristics.

The first of these attempts was undertaken by anatomist Franz Joseph Gall (1758–1828) whose name is most closely associated with the pseudoscience of phrenology. "Phrenologists" believed that by examining the contours of people's skulls, they could locate areas of overdevelopment and underdevelopment in parts of the brain associated with certain behavioral tendencies and personality characteristics (see Figure 4.1). After comparing the skulls of people confined in prisons and mental institutions with those of "normals," Gall claimed that certain bumps and irregularities—and therefore certain brain anatomies—were more common in criminals and "mental defectives."

An Italian physician named Cesare Lombroso (1836–1909) also claimed that criminal behavior was inborn and that along with their lawless nature, criminals also inherited a characteristic physical appearance. Criminals, he said, displayed an asymmetrical skull, large eyes, fat lips, huge jaws, high cheekbones, and slanted eyes (Savitz, 1972). It is worth noting, by the way, that Lombroso estimated that "born criminals" account for only about one third of the criminal population. The rest, he suggested, are led into crime as the result of being subjected to various environmental experiences of the kind we discuss in chapters 5 and 6.

The next significant attempt to relate crime to appearance was undertaken by William H. Sheldon (1942) as part of a larger research project on personality and physical characteristics. After collecting physical measurements on large numbers of people, Sheldon (1942) asserted that there were three basic body types: (1) the *endomorph* (fat and soft), (2) the *ectomorph* (thin and fragile), and (3) the *mesomorph* (muscular and hard). He believed that mesomorphs are likely to be aggressive, callous, and ruthless and supported this view with data

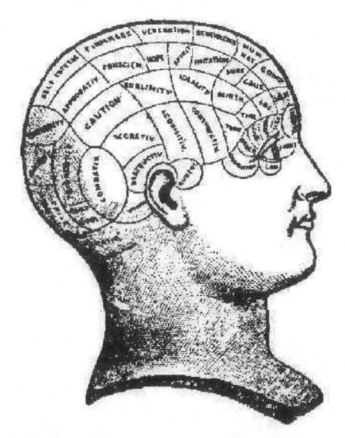

FIGURE 4.1 *Phrenological Map.* **From *Psychology* (4th ed.), by D. A. Bernstein, A. Clarke-Stewart, E. J. Roy, and C. D. Wickens, 1997, Boston: Houghton Mifflin. Copyright © 1997, by Houghton Mifflin Company. Reprinted with permission.**

showing that delinquent boys were more likely to be mesomorphic than were nondeliquent male college students. Several subsequent studies have also suggested a relation between mesomorphic characteristics and delinquent or antisocial behavior (Cortes & Gatti, 1972; Glueck & Glueck, 1950, 1956). Still other studies have reported adult criminals and juvenile delinquents to be "uglier" or at least "less attractive" than noncriminals (e.g., Cavior & Howard, 1978). However, flaws in the research methods that have been used in all of these studies seriously undermine the idea that criminal behavior is causally related to either body type or physical attractiveness.

The most recent effort to link physical features to criminality is found in research on minor physical anomalies, or MPAs (e.g., Halverson & Victor, 1976; Paulhus & Martin, 1986). These studies, which have focused on asymmetrical ears, curved fifth fingers, widely spaced eyes, and webbed toes, have found that these features are disproportionately common in school-aged boys who display risk factors for crime such as aggressiveness and impulsivity. However, the correlation between MPAs and risk factors for criminal behavior probably does not lie in the genes for the MPAs themselves but in more general abnormalities in the prenatal development of these children's nervous systems that lead to difficulties in socialization (Arseneault, Tremblay, Boulerice, Séruin, & Saucier, 2000). Many of these abnormalities appear due to environmental factors including prenatal exposure to drugs, alcohol, and other **teratogens** that adversely affect the developing fetus (see chapter 7).

In summary, then, the idea that physical appearance can serve as a biologically related marker of one's potential for criminal behavior has no serious support in the scientific community today.

Evolution and Crime

The search for more plausible biologically related explanations for the origins of crime began in earnest in the 1970s by scientists who, guided by Charles Darwin's (1809–1882) evolutionary theory, hypothesized that the aggression associated with criminal behavior is—like other forms of aggression—an innate characteristic of the human species.

Darwin asserted that at any given time, the characteristics of all life forms—from the tiniest microbes to the largest mammals and including human beings—are the result of changes brought about over many generations through the process of *"natural selection."* Natural selection occurs because, within a given species, there is a genetically influenced variability among individuals in terms of appearance and behavior. Those individuals whose inherited characteristics help them adapt to their environment by eluding predators, withstanding the elements, and finding food and water are the most likely to survive and successfully mate and procreate, thus passing on their genetic heritage to the next generation. The genes of those without those adaptive characteristics are more likely to die out along with the unfortunate individuals who carried them.

In looking for the evolutionary roots of crime, some psychologists have adopted the premise that people have inherited genetic propensities for aggression from their earliest ancestors and that aggressive behavior has helped the human species adapt and survive during thousands of years of changing environmental demands (E. O. Wilson, 1975). Some have suggested that aggression is still adaptive today, still necessary to insure the survival of the human species. Consider the fact that criminals more often tend to be males rather than females. Evolutionary theorists note that throughout most of human history, males have been more active than females in survival-related activities such as hunting for food, finding and fighting for a mate, and protecting close relatives and territory. So it is no accident, they say, that compared to females, human males are still more aggressive and still retain the physical and hormonal characteristics (including the stronger upper body and higher testosterone levels) that are important to displays of aggression. These aggression-related characteristics have survived because they "worked" (Wright, 1995).

Yet what about violence? It would not appear that acts of intentional violence—such as rape, murder, robbery, and other crimes—serve an evolutionary purpose. Indeed, they appear to be a maladaptive distortion of the aggressiveness that has long helped to insure human survival. Evolutionary theory suggests that interpersonal and intergroup violence probably originated from efforts to establish social stratification in animal groups including humans. For example, naturalist Jane Goodall (1991) found that chimpanzees—a species with whom humans share more than 95% of their genetic makeup—sometimes kill each other, not through competition for safety, food, or a mate but simply to be "on top" in the troop's social hierarchy. Perhaps the evolutionary origins of human violence relate to status and pride. As Samuel Johnson said (as cited in Wrangham & Peterson, 1996), "No two people can be half an hour together, but one shall acquire an evident superiority over the other" (p. 191). To some evolutionary psychologists, then, survival motivation may underlie certain types of homicide among humans, particularly interfamily murder (M. Daly & Wilson, 1997).

Wars between states and nations; hate crimes based on ethnic or religious differences; civil wars, acts of murder, rape, and destruction inflicted on inhabitants of conquered territory; family violence; gang wars; and terrorism by militia groups are all examples of violence arising from intergroup rivalry, from the need to be higher in status, to control, and/or to strike fear in the hearts of members of another group. Today, the age-old tendency in the human species to divide into status-differentiated groups—such as victors and vanquished or "haves" and "have-nots"—is less acceptable in civilized society. Still, acts of war, intergroup violence, and interpersonal violence continue, leading some to believe that in an era of weapons of mass destruction, the same genetically influenced behaviors that have long insured the survival of the human species may ultimately lead to its demise.

Given that violent behavior appears to be maladaptive for species survival, one is unlikely to find fully satisfactory explanations of crime in traditional evolutionary theory. Nevertheless, human behavior today is what it is partly because of our genes, so it is important to consider evidence for the roots of crime in that genetic heritage.

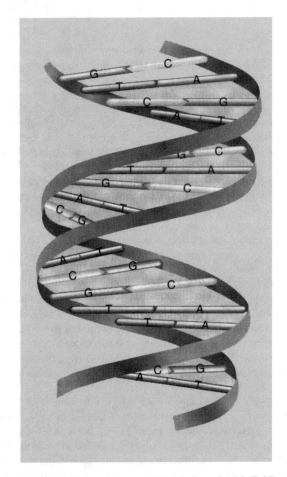

FIGURE 4.2   *The Structure of DNA.* **From *Abnormal Psychology*, by M. T. Nietzel, M. Speltz, E. McCauley, & D. A. Bernstein, 1998, Boston: Allyn & Bacon. Coyright © 1998 by Allyn & Bacon. Reprinted by permission of authors.**

Genes and Crime

Do genes influence criminal behavior? If so, how and to what extent? These are some of most hotly debated questions in psychology and criminology today. Now that the Human Genome Research Project has identified the 20,000 to 25,000 genes in human DNA, researchers are working to establish specific genetic factors that may be linked to various aspects of mental and physical health, illness, and behavior. Understanding the results of their work, including research on genetic influences on human aggression, requires an appreciation of the biological mechanisms of genetic inheritance.

What Are Genes and What Do They Do?

As shown in Figure 4.2, human genes consist of strands of **deoxyribonucleic acid**, or **DNA**. DNA consists of *nucleotides* that, in turn, consist of sugar, phosphate, and nitrogen bases. DNA is responsible for the complex series of biological commands that result in the assembly of amino acids into proteins. These proteins form and direct the structure of human cells. Thus, DNA contains the genetic code for the development and functioning of every cell in the human body.

Each gene is located at a specific place on one of the 23 pairs of *chromosomes* that reside in the nucleus of all human cells.[1] One member of each pair of chromosomes comes from our mother and one comes from our father. Not all genes are expressed in our behavior or appearance, however. Characteristics influenced by recessive genes will be evident only if we inherit the same gene from *both* parents. Characteristics influenced by a dominant gene, however, will be evident if it is inherited from *either* parent. For example, a single dominant gene causes a severe neurological disorder called Huntington's disease.

Faulty genes can cause a variety of dysfunctions. For instance, a single faulty gene is responsible for the appearance of *phenylketonuria* (PKU), a rare disorder that causes a deficiency in the enzyme that metabolizes phenylalanine, an amino acid in many foods. If PKU babies consume foods containing phenylalanine, they will suffer serious physical and mental problems; but if they are put on a phenylalanine-free diet, they will not display or express their inherited disorder.

The example of PKU illustrates a basic principle of genetics, namely, that genes alone are usually not "destiny." More often, genes act as risk factors that can cause a particular disorder or behavior to appear if certain environmental conditions are also present. Further, most characteristics and behaviors associated with genes are *polygenic,* meaning that many different genes influence them. Even the influence of sets of genes is affected by environmental factors. Consider, for example, the "breast cancer genes" that have been identified by researchers. A woman may carry one or more of these genes, but the likelihood of developing breast cancer depends on many other genetic and environmental factors, including whether and at what age the woman's mother or sisters had breast cancer, her ethnic background and race, her diet and exercise habits, whether or not she smokes and uses oral contraceptives, and her exposure to certain environmental toxins.

Genes, Crime, and Politics

The National Institutes of Health funded a national conference on the relation between crime and genes that was to have taken place in 1992 at the University of Maryland. Protests against it were so intense, however, that it had to be postponed. When the conference finally occurred in 1995, it was met with demonstrations and renunciations. Why is the search for genetic factors related to criminal behavior so controversial? One reason, say protestors, is that such research encourages the idea that high crime rates among certain ethnic groups are attributable to those groups' genes. They also worry that emphasizing genetic causes of criminal behavior will draw too much attention away from the social and environmental causes of crime and from efforts to prevent and deal with crime by changing those environmental causes. These concerns also reflect a more general feeling that research on genetics and human behavior is too reminiscent of Nazi Germany in the 1930s and 1940s when Adolph Hitler used the alleged genetic "inferiority" of certain groups to justify efforts to sterilize or kill them.

These criticisms are unfounded, however. For one thing, responsible scientists would never suggest that a particular gene causes criminal behavior. They recognize that genes alone do not cause a person to be violent any more than genes alone cause a person to be intelligent (Petrill et al., 1998). Indeed, no gene for violence or crime has ever been identified, nor is it likely to be. So why talk about the genetic roots of crime? Because a large body of research suggests that there is an *indirect link* between genetics and criminal behavior.

Methods for Studying Genetic Influences on Behavior

Some research has involved **family studies**, which look at whether the concordance (or shared appearance) of behavior is greater among family members who are more closely related (e.g., siblings vs. cousins). Families in which there are identical twins are of particular importance because identical twins share exactly the same genes. **Twin studies** are based on the following logic: If shared histories of violent or criminal behavior are more common in identical twin pairs compared to nonidentical pairs or other pairs of siblings (who share only about 50% of their genes), then genetic influences may be significant in such behavior. A problem with twin studies, though, is that twins usually grow up in the same environment, so any similarity in their criminal tendencies could be due to shared genes or to shared environmental influences. A pair of identical twins might

---

[1]The exception is sperm or egg cells, which contain 23 single chromosomes.

both be violent because they both associated with the same violent peer group or because a "bad" twin might have influenced a "good" twin to join in criminal ventures.

One way to separate genetic from environmental influences—nature from nurture—in twins is to study pairs who were separated at an early age and raised in different environments. In these studies, the traits of separated identical twins are compared with the traits of (a) identical twins raised together and (b) nonidentical twins raised apart. Finding similar traits in identical twins that were raised in different environments would provide strong evidence for a significant genetic influence on those traits. Indeed, such evidence has been found in relation to genetic influences on children's temperaments and personalities (N. Brody & Ehrlichmann, 1998; D. M. Buss, 1995a, 1995b; Loehlin, 1989; Saudino, 1998; Tellegen et al., 1988) and in mental disorders such as schizophrenia (Gottesman, 1991; Molden & Gottesman, 1997).

Adoption studies apply the same logic. Here, researchers study children (twins and nontwins alike) who were separated from their biological parents at birth and raised by an adoptive family. If these children's traits are more like those of their biological parents than their adopted parents, the role of genetic influence on those traits is supported. Adoption studies do in fact show that adopted children tend to share many kinds of traits with their biological parents. These traits include schizophrenia, substance abuse, and personality disorders (e.g., Weinberg, Scarr, & Waldman, 1992).

Family studies look for links between the degree of relationship among family members and various traits. For instance, researchers have found that having a parent or sibling who suffers from schizophrenia or alcoholism increases the risk of experiencing these disorders but with a lesser probability than in the case of identical twins. These findings indicate the importance of the environment even in the development of a disorder that has some genetic link.

Research on the Genetics of Crime

The "genetic school" of criminal behavior arose in the late 19th and early 20th centuries spurred by studies of families in which crime appeared to be a tradition passed on from one generation to the next. Prominent among these were studies of two families—the Kallikaks and the Jukes—whose criminality spanned several generations (Dugdale, 1910; Estabrook, 1916).[2]

Johannes Lange (1929), a German physician, completed the first study of twins and criminality in 1929. This study, based on 13 pairs of identical twins and 17 nonidentical pairs, found that 77% of identical twins shared criminal behavior patterns as opposed to 12% of nonidentical twins. In spite of the limitations imposed by his small sample size, Lange titled his resulting book *Crime and Destiny* (1929) to reflect his belief that criminal conduct is predestined by genetic inheritance. A. M. Legras (1932) found that 100% of identical twins shared criminal traits, but this study included only five twin pairs. Subsequent research on larger numbers of twins has found lower concordance rates for criminality. For example, Karl Christiansen (1977) found 35% concordance among 71 pairs of identical twins and 15% concordance among 120 nonidentical twin pairs. A summary of 13 twin studies concluded that, overall, there is a 51% concordance rate for criminal behavior among identical twins as opposed to a 20% rate for nonidentical twins (Raine, 1993). These figures are consistent with the conclusions of behavioral genetics research on the heritability of personality in general.

Another group of researchers (B. Coid, Lewis, & Reveley,1993) found a 25% concordance rate for criminal offending among 280 twin pairs but concluded that criminal behavior was significantly related to the presence of a psychiatric disorder rather than to a shared criminal gene. Indeed, this conclusion echoes a common theme in twin and adoption studies, namely, that genes do not directly cause criminal behavior but instead contribute to risk factors for certain behaviors that may lead to criminality. For instance, twin and adoption studies have strongly suggested that genetic factors contribute to the risk of antisocial personality disorder (APD), which is closely associated with criminal behavior (see chapter 5). In one such study (Mednick, Gabrielli, & Hutchings, 1987), children adopted away from biological parents who are criminals were arrested more frequently for antisocial conduct than children adopted away from noncriminal parents. The correlation between

---

[2]Recent research suggested that many members of the Jukes family were not criminal and that Dugdale (1910) distorted his analysis to support the eugenicist's notion that crime was hereditary (Christianson, 2003).

the criminal behavior of adoptees and their biological fathers appeared strongest among adoptees who were chronic offenders.

Research on the role of genetics in crime also says a lot about the role of the environment. The adoption study just mentioned (Mednick, Gabrielli, et al., 1987), for example, showed that how children are raised—including the quality of their parenting, communities, and peer groups—are important contributors to antisocial conduct. It was the adopted children whose biological parents had criminal backgrounds and whose adoptive parents were also criminal offenders who were at especially high risk for displaying criminal conduct themselves. Further, most adoptees do not become criminals even if their parents are criminals, and most members of identical twin pairs do not become criminals even if their sibling does. Thus, inheritance may play a role in criminality, but that role is not simple or straightforward.

How Might Genes Influence Criminal Behavior?

As already noted, no single gene directly causes people to be violent or to engage in criminal acts. It would appear instead that people can inherit more general characteristics that contribute to the appearance of criminal behavior. Research conducted so far suggests that the most important of these characteristics are related to (1) arousal systems in the central nervous system and the autonomic nervous system (ANS) and (2) intelligence and ethnicity. We briefly consider each of these potential pathways of inheritance.

Arousal Systems. **Arousal** is measured in terms of heart rate, blood pressure, respiration rate, skin temperature, galvanic skin response (GSR) and other sweat-related measures, urine production, brain wave activity, physical activation, and muscle tension (Bell, Green, Fisher, & Baum, 2001). Arousal can range from very low to very high, from sleep to intense excitement.

Research has suggested that some people inherit nervous systems that tend to operate at an unusually low level of arousal. This low base rate has several consequences including a tendency for these people to seek excitement and to be relatively insensitive to certain external events (Eysenck, 1964; Stoff, Breiling, & Maser, 1997). For example, studies of the brainwave activity of individuals diagnosed with antisocial personality disorder (APD) suggest that they are less aroused than other people when being hurt or when hurting others (Damasio, 2000; Raine, Lencz, Bihrle, LaCasse, & Colletti, 2000). These experiences do not upset them physiologically, so they tend to be less affected than other people are by punishment or by the distress of those they harm. Hans Eysenck (1964) suggested that their chronically low arousal makes it difficult for these so-called *criminal psychopaths* to learn through punishment, to delay gratification, or to experience genuine remorse over their crimes (see chapter 5).

The predictive value of low-arousal was demonstrated in a study (Raine, Venebles, & Williams, 1990) in England in which physiological arousal was measured in 101 fifteen-year-old boys. Ten years later, those who had been convicted of crimes had been the ones who had shown significantly lower heart rates and skin conductance levels when compared to nonoffenders. More recently, incarcerated male psychopaths were found to have lower GSRs to distressing stimuli than did nonpsychopathic male inmates (Blair, Jones, Clark, & Smith, 1997). Another study (Howard, Payamal, & Neo, 1997) of sensitivity to punishment among inmates in a Singapore prison concluded that psychopaths were the least affected by the threat of punishment. Lower skin conductance and heart rates have also been found in persons diagnosed with APD (Damasio, 2000; Raine et al., 2000).

Intelligence and Ethnicity. It has been suggested that criminal behavior is influenced by the genetics of intelligence and ethnicity. Studies conducted early in the 20th century by William Healey and Augusta Bronner (1931), Henry Goddard (1920), and others have found IQ scores of delinquent children to be lower than those of nondelinquents. Because in those days, intelligence was considered to be largely, if not totally, inherited, these studies have supported the belief that some of the same genetic characteristics that resulted in low intelligence also created an inherited predisposition to criminal behavior.

Although there were those who questioned the notion that intelligence is attributable solely to one's genes (Slawson, 1926), it was not until the 1950s and 1960s that scientists began to recognize that environment and upbringing accounts for at least 50% of the variability in what is called intelligence (Rosenthal & Jacobsen, 1968). The rest of that variability has to do with the social, educational, and other experiences people have as they grow from infancy into adulthood. Thus, when subsequent studies found positive correlations between IQ and criminal behavior (e.g., Hirschi & Hindelang, 1977; Lynam, Moffitt, & Stoughamer-Loeber, 1993; Moffitt, Gabrielli, Mednick, & Schulsinger, 1981; Yeudall, Fromm-Auch, & Davies, 1982), they led to more reasoned conclusions. For example, in their 1985 book, *Crime and Human Nature,* James Wilson and Richard Herrnstein presented the now widely held view that any link between intelligence and criminality is an indirect one mediated by factors other than intelligence per se. Lower intelligence, Wilson and Herrnstein noted, might be associated with crime because cognitive deficits—combined with social rejection and social skill deficits—can have a negative impact on school success (Denno, 1985). For example, a group of Swedish researchers found a link between late language development in childhood and later criminality (Stattin & Klackenberg-Larsson, 1993). Both cognitive and language deficits may lead to lack of educational success that, in turn, can lead to the kind of personal and social maladjustment that can motivate some youngsters to compensate by seeking out the company of other unsuccessful peers, some of whom might have criminal tendencies. Thus, for some less intellectually gifted people, entry into a criminal culture might not be caused by lack of intelligence itself but by its social and educational consequences.[3] In chapters 5 and 6, we discuss reasons why some people, but not others, display criminal behavior in reaction to school failure.

What about ethnicity and criminal behavior? The short answer is that there is no evidence for either a direct or indirect link between the two, even though individuals from certain ethnic groups engage in more criminal behavior than others. For instance, recent statistics show that Blacks are seven times more likely than Whites to commit homicide (FBI, 2004b). However, such differences between ethnic groups do not represent the role of ethnicity alone. They also reflect the effects of factors such as socioeconomic class, family history, and social conditions, all of which are themselves associated with differing rates of criminal behavior. Moreover, the fact that members of ethnic minority groups tend to be arrested and prosecuted at higher rates than nonminorities (FBI, 2004a) may exaggerate perceptions of the size of group differences in crime rates (Siegel, 1998).

Some Conclusions About Genes and Crime

As we noted earlier, no one has discovered a gene for crime, nor is it likely that anyone ever will. To the extent that genes are implicated in crime, several are probably involved, and their effects on behavior are indirect, affecting the appearance of traits that may make a person susceptible to criminal behavior (Rutter, 1997). Remember, too, that genes and the environment, nature and nurture, always interact. They never operate in isolation from each other (McGuffin, Riley, & Plomin, 2001). Accordingly, nature and nurture appear about equally important in influencing criminal behavior.

Crime and the Brain

In a 1931 movie, a scientist's assistant breaks into a medical school to steal a "normal" brain for use in creating a new living creature. When he drops the perfect brain his boss had requested, he takes another, which turns out to be that of a violent criminal. As a result, Dr. Frankenstein inadvertently creates an uncontrollable monster instead of the perfect being he had intended.

Brain Structures and Functions

We have shown that there are no criminal genes, but is there perhaps a criminal brain? If so, what is it like and how might its functioning differ from that of noncriminal brains? Before looking for the roots of crime in the brain, we briefly consider the brain's basic structure and normal functioning and the nervous system

---

[3]Genes might also be indirectly related to criminal behavior through their role in creating neuropsychological deficits that cause impairments in language abilities and a variety of symptoms associated with attention deficit hyperactivity disorder (ADHD)—such as inattention, impulse control problems, disruptiveness, and a general lack of social skills (Moffitt & Lynam, 1994; Rutter, 1997; see chapter 7).

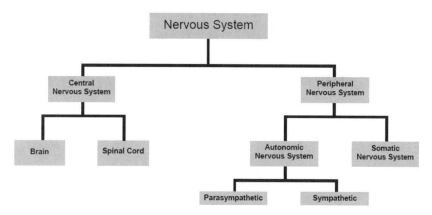

FIGURE 4.3 *Organization of the Nervous System.* **From *Abnormal Psychology*, by M. T. Nietzel, M. Speltz, E. McCauley, & D. A. Bernstein, 1998, Boston: Allyn & Bacon. Coyright © 1998 by Allyn & Bacon. Reprinted by permission of authors.**

of which it is a part. As shown in Figure 4.3, the brain and spinal cord are part of the bone-encased **central nervous system**. The other major division of the nervous system is the **peripheral nervous system**. It includes the *somatic nervous system,* which is largely concerned with voluntary control of the muscles, and the *autonomic nervous system* (ANS), which affects motivational, emotional, and other physical reactions. The ANS regulates the cardiovascular system, raises and lowers body temperature, and sends signals to other organs in the body. The ANS consists of sympathetic and parasympathetic divisions. Generally, the *sympathetic nervous system* prepares the body for action—for fighting or fleeing a threat, for example—by increasing arousal, stimulating heart rate, and increasing blood pressure. The *parasympathetic nervous system* decreases arousal, conserving the body's energy resources by slowing heart rate and decreasing blood pressure. All these systems work in concert to tell the brain what is happening in the outside world and within the body and to send instructions from the brain to the muscles and organs about how to respond.

The brain itself consists of three main parts: the hindbrain, the midbrain, and the forebrain (see Figure 4.4). The *hindbrain* includes structures that maintain activities essential for life. Here one finds the *medulla*—which regulates breathing, swallowing, heart rate, and blood pressure—and the *reticular formation,* which controls arousal, attention, sleep, and awakening. Here, too, is the *cerebellum,* which maintains balance and posture and controls locomotion and fine body movements such as threading a needle. Damage to hindbrain structures can lead to coma or death.

The *midbrain* helps coordinate head and eye movements and controls gross movements of the body and limbs. Midbrain structures are also involved in basic responses to visual, auditory, and tactile stimuli and regulate responsiveness to rewarding stimuli.

The *forebrain* is the largest part of the brain, and it is responsible for a wide variety of functions from interpreting sensory input to engaging in abstract thought. The thalamus, hypothalamus, and cerebrum are key structures in the forebrain. The *thalamus* is known as "the great relay station." It receives information from all of the senses (except smell) and then analyzes this information and sends it to higher areas of the brain for further interpretation and response. **The hypothalamus**, located just below the thalamus, is involved in the regulation of hunger, thirst, sex drive, and other motivated behavior. It is part of the **limbic system**, a group of forebrain structures—including the **hippocampus** and the **amygdala**—that play important roles in memory (the hippocampus) and emotion (the amygdala). The hypothalamus also maintains important connections with the ANS, receiving information about the functioning of internal organs and helping to regulate the activity of those organs. One of its most important functions in this regard is to assess the level of various hormones in the body and to transmit this information to the *pituitary gland*, which in turn directs the functioning of the other glands in the **endocrine system**. Because the endocrine system is involved in regulating our responses

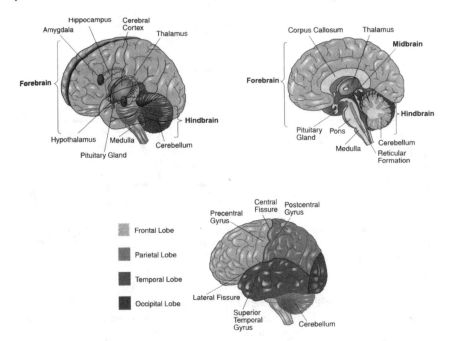

FIGURE 4.4 *The Human Brain.* From *Abnormal Psychology*, by M. T. Nietzel, M. Speltz, E. McCauley, & D. A. Bernstein, 1998, Boston: Allyn & Bacon. Copyright © 1998 by Allyn & Bacon. Reprinted by permission of authors.

to stressful events, scientists are looking at the hypothalamus as a brain structure that might influence whether or not people respond to stress with violence.

The outer surface of the *cerebrum,* known as the **cerebral cortex**, controls the brain's highest functions of thinking, planning, and decision making. The cerebrum is divided into left and right hemispheres. Because the sensory and motor nerves connecting the brain to the spinal cord and the rest of the body cross over as they enter and leave the brain, the left hemisphere receives information from and controls functions on the right side of the body, whereas the right hemisphere receives information from and controls functions on the left side of the body. The two hemispheres communicate with each other through a connecting band of millions of nerve fibers called the *corpus callosum.*

The cerebral cortex is divided into four sections, or lobes, each of which is somewhat specialized. For example, the *frontal lobe* is responsible for controlling bodily movement and for thinking, reasoning, and decision making. The *parietal lobe* processes information about touch and temperature. The *temporal lobes* process auditory information. The *occipital lobe* processes visual information.

Although the two hemispheres of the brain look almost exactly the same, they perform somewhat different functions. In general, the left hemisphere is more involved with logical and language abilities, whereas the right hemisphere is more involved in spatial, artistic, and musical abilities. The right hemisphere is also somewhat more involved in the expression of emotions (Vingerhoets, Berckmoes, & Stroobant, 2003). The precise nature and degree of this *hemispheric lateralization* varies among individuals, though, so it is important to remember that people are not "right-brained" or "left-brained" in the same way that they are right- or left-handed.

Neuropsychological Dysfunctions

In the early 1970s, neuropsychologists (who study the relation between the central nervous system and behavior) began to look to the brain for clues concerning the origins of aggression and violence. One review of research (Buikhuisen, 1987) with over 500 juvenile criminals indicated a high incidence of abnormal neuropsychological profiles in repeat offenders. These dysfunctions were mainly associated with the frontal and temporal lobes. Compared to nondelinquents, these youngsters showed greater deficits in their ability to comprehend, manipulate, and utilize abstract concepts; poorer performance on tasks requiring that things be performed in sequence; impaired processing of visual information; and poorer performance on tasks requiring sustained concentration (Yeudall et al., 1982). Such neuropsychological deficits may be due in part to scar tissue, or lesions, resulting from epilepsy or from concussions and other head traumas (Fishbein, 1990; Raine, 1993; Yeudall et al., 1982). Insensitivity to the possible consequences of one's actions and low arousal to anticipated negative outcomes have been found in people with damage in the frontal cortex (Damasio, 2000; Raine et al., 2000). One study (D. Lewis, Pinus, Feldan, Jackson, & Bard, 1986) found that a significant number of death row inmates had suffered head injuries as children.

Other studies have found abnormalities in the lateralization of criminals' cerebral hemispheres. For example, the right temporal lobe is usually more involved than the left in a person's responses to fear-provoking stimuli (Hare & Schalling, 1978). However, there is some evidence that in a large number of repeat violent offenders, the right hemisphere is not performing this function normally, thus rendering these people less likely to experience anxiety and the other negative emotions that are required to fear the consequences of unacceptable behavior (B. E. Wexler, 1980; Yeudall et al., 1982). As a result, these individuals may not be as likely to avoid engaging in behavior for which they might be sanctioned or punished (e.g., Raine, Buchsbaum, & LaCasse, 1997).

Researchers are also tracing the effects of environmental factors—such as expectant mothers' stress, nutritional habits, use of drugs and alcohol, and exposure to toxins—on babies' prenatal brain development. These environmental influences could relate to crime if they impair normal neurological development of brain systems related to temperament and mood (Kinsley & Svare, 1987). Several studies have found, for example, that children are more likely to be aggressive if their mothers had ingested lead from old house paint, inhaled gasoline fumes, smoke, drank alcohol, or used other drugs during pregnancy (Karr-Morse & Wiley, 1997).

Functional Abnormalities

By using EEG, CAT scans, PET scans, functional MRI (fMRI), single photon emission computed tomography (SPECT), and other high-tech imaging methods, neuroscientists have been able to obtain startlingly precise pictures of the brain's structure and activity. They have also sought to relate anomalies in brain structure and functioning to the appearance of criminal behavior.

EEG research has shown, for instance, that many criminals (a) have more abnormalities in brain waves than other people and (b) display lower levels of high-frequency brain waves and higher levels of low-frequency brain waves known as *theta waves* (Hare & McPherson, 1984b; Meloy, 1992). Indeed, this type of brain wave pattern—common in children but not in adults—is associated with immature and unregulated behavior, temper tantrums, hostility, and combativeness. In one study (Mednick, Volavka, Gabrielli, & Itil, 1981), Danish scientists examined the brain wave patterns of 265 children aged 11 to 13 and then, seven years later, classified these participants as noncriminals, one-time offenders, or multiple offenders. The multiple offenders were the ones who, when tested as children, had exhibited slower brain wave frequencies than either of the other two groups (Mednick et al., 1981). Other studies of violent offenders have shown that 25% to 50% of them exhibit EEG abnormalities, whereas only 5% to 20% of the normal population do so (Mednick, Pollock, Volavka, & Gabrielli, 1982; Meloy, 1992; Pillmann et al., 1999).

Neurotransmitter Systems

All human activity, from walking to thinking, depends on smooth and organized communication among the brain's nerve cells or neurons. Researchers have investigated how violence, aggression, and criminal behavior might be partially related to faulty communication patterns in these neural circuits.

Neural communication occurs when electrochemical activity in neurons causes them to "fire," thus releasing chemicals called **neurotransmitters** that affects neurons nearby. Neurons consist of a cell body, extending from which are long fibers, called *axons,* and branch-like structures called *dendrites.* As shown in Figure 4.5,

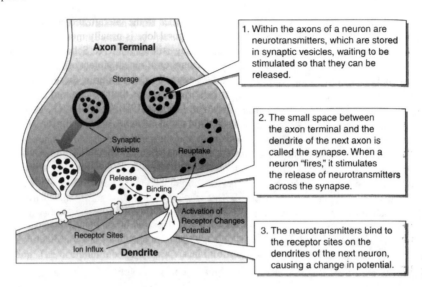

1. Within the axons of a neuron are neurotransmitters, which are stored in synaptic vesicles, waiting to be stimulated so that they can be released.

2. The small space between the axon terminal and the dendrite of the next axon is called the synapse. When a neuron "fires," it stimulates the release of neurotransmitters across the synapse.

3. The neurotransmitters bind to the receptor sites on the dendrites of the next neuron, causing a change in potential.

FIGURE 4.5   *The Synapse and Communication Between Neurons.* **From *Abnormal Psychology*, by M. T. Nietzel, M. Speltz, E. McCauley, & D. A. Bernstein, 1998, Boston: Allyn & Bacon. Copyright © 1998 by Allyn & Bacon. Reprinted by permission of authors.**

neurotransmitters are usually released from the end of one neuron's axon; flow across the *synapse,* a tiny gap between neurons; and come in contact with the next neuron's dendrites. The neurotransmitter stimulates receptor sites on the dendrite, thus sending a signal toward the cell body, which makes this neuron either more likely or less likely to fire. After affecting other neurons, neurotransmitters are either reabsorbed into the neurons that released them, through a process called *reuptake,* or are broken down by an enzyme.

Groups of brain cells that communicate through the action of neurotransmitters called *monoamines* (which include serotonin, dopamine, and norepinephrine) are involved in the regulation of mood, impulsiveness, aggressiveness, arousal, and risk taking (see Table 4.1). Low levels of some of these neurotransmitters, oversensitivity or undersensitivity of the receptors they normally affect, and overactivity of **monoamine oxidase** (MAO), an enzyme that metabolizes these transmitters, have been associated with violent and impulsive criminal behavior (Blackburn, 1993; Ellis, 1995; W. Gallagher, 1994; Kruesi et al., 1992; Lahey, McBurnett, Loeber, & Hart, 1995; Stalenheim, von Knorring, & Oreland, 1997). Two Swedish studies (Alm, Klinteberg, Humble, & Leppert, 1996; Stalenheim et al., 1997), for example, have found low monoamine levels in adult criminal psychopaths and in juvenile delinquents. Further, low levels of serotonin have been found in arsonists and violent male offenders (Virkkunen, Eggert, Rawlings, & Linnoila, 1996) as well as in impulsively violent alcoholics who have killed, or attempted to kill, when in a rage (Linnoila et al., 1983). Animal and human studies have also related low serotonin levels to aggression and violence arising from negative mood states (Eichelman, Ellis, & Barchas, 1981; Melloni, Delville, & Ferris, 1995; Valzelli, 1981).

Although surely biological in nature, crime-related problems in neurotransmitter systems may themselves be related to environmental factors. Research (Suomi, Higley, & Linnoila, 1997) with infant monkeys traced serotonin system problems to experiences in the early years of life. Suomi et al. showed that monkeys separated from their mothers and raised by peers had lower serotonin levels than those raised normally. Further, the peer-raised monkeys were more socially inept and excessively aggressive. Peer-raised monkeys also drank more alcohol than mother-reared monkeys (Suomi et al., 1997). In another study, this time with hamsters, Ferris and his colleagues (Delville, DeVries, Schwartz, & Ferris, 1998; Ferris & Grisso, 1998) placed adolescent hamsters in an older hamster's cage once a day for a week. Hamsters are highly territorial, so the older animals threatened and nipped at the adolescent intruders. When the adolescents reached maturity, they themselves not only displayed higher than

TABLE 4.1 *Characteristics Associated With Neurotransmitter System Activity*

	High	*Low*
Dopamine	Increased motor activity Extroverted Good motivation	Decreased motor activity Introverted Low motivation
Norephinephrine	Good concentration and attention High anxiety Inhibited	Poor attention Low anxiety Uninhibited
Serotonin	Good control of impulse Low aggression Positive mood states	Poor impulse control High aggression Negative mood states

normal aggression toward intruders into their territory, but an examination of their brains found an imbalance in their serotonin systems. The researchers concluded that changes in the serotonin system lowered the animal's threshold for responding aggressively to stress. These animal studies have suggested that early experiences can change the brain's neurochemistry, which in turn affects behavior (Azar, 1997).

Further research into the interdependence of biological and environmental factors that lead to antisocial and violent behavior will undoubtedly lead to a better understanding of the influence of the environment on the brain and vice versa (Raine, 2002).

Structural Anomalies

There is some evidence that criminal behavior may be related to abnormalities in the physical structure of the brain. These abnormalities are often diagnosed through EEGs or CAT scans in children who exhibit behavioral problems, deficits in motor functions, and impairments in visual and auditory processing abilities. Some of these abnormalities may be inherited, but others appear to stem from complications during delivery or from brain injuries during prenatal or perinatal development or in early childhood (Moffitt, 1993). These children are at risk for unsatisfactory achievement in school due to deficits in cognitive skills such as reasoning and problem solving, thus making them prone to delinquency (Seguin, Pihl, Harden, Tremblay, & Boulerice, 1995). One study (D. Lewis et al., 1986) found that a significant number of death row inmates had suffered head injuries as children.

Tumors, too, can apparently be related to the appearance of violent criminal behavior. One 65-year-old man who had no history of violence was arrested for strangling his wife to death after she scratched his face. Physical examination revealed a tumor in his left frontal lobe that may have impaired this man's ability to modulate his arousal and inhibit aggressive behavior (Paradis, Horn, Lazar, & Schwartz, 1994).

Nutrition

In 1979, Dan White killed San Francisco Mayor George Moscone and city councilman Harvey Milk. White was tried for first degree murder, but the jury convicted him of manslaughter, a lesser offense. The verdict reflected the impact of what became known as the "Twinkie defense." White's attorney claimed that White could not have the criminal intent required to justify a charge of first degree (premeditated) murder because the junk food to which he was allegedly "addicted" had created biochemical imbalances in White's brain that interfered with his thought processes (Sagon, 2005). (White served only 5 years in prison and committed suicide after his release.)

The success of the Twinkie defense was an aberration in the annals of law but blaming aggression and violence on diet is not. For example, diets high in sugar and carbohydrates have been linked to violence and aggression in a juvenile detention facility. It has also been claimed that when the staff in such facilities replace sweet drinks with fruit juices and eliminate high-sugar breakfast cereals, there is a dramatic reduction in the frequency of assaults, fights, and other rule violations (Schoenthaler, 1982).

There is general agreement that certain levels of vitamins and minerals are needed for healthy physical and mental functioning. When these minimum levels are not met for a period of time, people may display physical, mental, and behavioral problems. For example, deficiencies in vitamins B3, B6, and C have been related to aggression and violence (Hippchen, 1978). Also, foods such as cow's milk, wheat, corn, chocolate, citrus, and eggs can be allergens for some people, causing severe central nervous system reactions including depression, emotional outbursts, aggression, and violence (P. Marshall, 1993; Schauss & Simonsen, 1979; Wunderlich, 1978). Some researchers are also looking at the possibility that children born with minor physical anomalies in the mouth (such as cleft palate) may be more likely than other children to suffer feeding difficulties that lead to nutritional deficiencies and later aggression (Arseneault et al., 2000).

Data on diet and crime must be viewed with caution, however. Correlational studies show some relation between diet, metabolism, and antisocial behavior (Ferguson, Stoddarat, & Simeon, 1986; Gray, 1986), but the fact remains that most individuals with these deficiencies or problems do not act aggressively or violently. Those who do are likely to have been influenced by other factors as well.

Hormones and Crime

The endocrine system is made up of organs called glands, which, like the neurons in the nervous system, communicate with one another by secreting chemicals. However, whereas neurons in the brain release their chemicals into the synapses between nerve cells, endocrine glands secrete **hormones** into the bloodstream, which carries them to a wide variety of target organs throughout the body.

Recall that the hypothalamus influences the pituitary gland, which in turn controls all other endocrine glands. These glands include (a) the *thyroid* gland, which is responsible for regulating metabolism; (b) the sex glands (*ovaries* and *testes*), which influence physical development, the development of male and female reproductive organs, and sexual behavior; (c) the *pancreas,* which controls insulin and glucose levels and regulates sugar metabolism; and (d) the *adrenal* glands, which help prepare the body to fight or flee physical threats.

Are hormones related to criminal behavior? It is possible. Hormones secreted by the adrenal glands, the sex glands, and the pancreas have indirect relations to criminal behavior through the role they play in aggression and sexual motivation. To understand this role, it is important to understand the body's physical reactions to stress.

Threats posed by environmental events—whether a menacing stranger, a crucial job interview, or a big exam—set off an "alarm" in the hypothalamus. This alarm activates the sympathetic nervous system to stimulate the inner part of the adrenal glands. In response, the adrenals secrete two hormones, adrenaline and noradrenaline, which in turn activate the liver, kidneys, lungs, heart, and other organs to prepare the body to deal with the threat. The result is increased blood pressure, blood sugar, and muscle tension; dilation of the pupils; and other reactions known as the "fight-or-flight" syndrome. People typically experience this syndrome as a pounding heart, sweaty palms, and shakiness accompanied by negative emotions such as fear, anxiety, or panic.

At the same time, the hypothalamus sends a chemical message to the pituitary gland, which responds by secreting adrenocorticotropic hormone (ACTH). ACTH simulates the outer layer of the adrenal glands, which then secrete corticosteroids, also known as "stress hormones." These hormones stimulate release of the body's stored energy supply, thus providing extra energy for the physical exertion needed to deal with whatever threat is imminent.

It has long been suspected that there is an association between the male hormone testosterone and the appearance of aggression and violence (Dabbs, Carr, Frady, & Riad, 1995; Meloy, 1992), a link that to some appears obvious because about 90% of all adult violent crimes are committed by men (FBI, 2004a). Animal studies have shown relations between male hormones and aggression related to protection of territory, mates, and food (Valzelli, 1981). In humans, too, high testosterone levels have been associated with aggression, especially during adolescence and young adulthood (Archer, 1995; Olweus, 1988), although not all studies have found this relation (Coe & Levine, 1983). Note that this research does not establish the direction of the relation between aggression and testosterone. A burst of testosterone could trigger aggressive behavior, or aggressive impulses might generate a burst of testosterone. Still, removing the source of testosterone through castration has been shown to control violence in certain criminals (Bremer, 1959; H. Campbell, 1967). Treatment with antitestosterone drugs or female hormones (such as estrogen) may also reduce aggression (Chatz, 1972; Laschet, 1973; Meloy, 1992), but the relevance of all these findings is uncertain because a causal link between hormones and male criminal behavior has not been established. If there is a link, it may be indirect and may involve, for example, testosterone's effects on serotonin metabolism. As we noted earlier, low levels of serotonin are strongly correlated with aggression and violence (Lahey et al., 1995).

In women, increased testosterone levels occur during premenstrual and postpartum periods, which are often accompanied by increases in irritability and aggressiveness. In some women, this hormonal imbalance may trigger psychological and behavioral consequences including mood swings, depression, difficulty in concentration, and substance abuse (Haskett, 1987; Trunnel & Turner, 1988). A link between hormones and aggression has been found in female prisoners, many of whom committed aggressive criminal acts during a premenstrual phase (Ginsburg & Carter, 1987). The methodology of some of these studies has been challenged, however (Harry & Balcer, 1987), and as with testosterone in men, it is not clear whether hormonal changes trigger violence in women or whether aggressive behavior triggers hormonal changes (Horney, 1978).

Interestingly, no clear link has been found between sex hormones and sex crimes such as rape or pedophilia (sex with children). Some studies have found that testosterone levels are elevated in sex offenders; others have found that testosterone levels are lower. Indeed, there is no evidence to support a clear cause–effect relation between sex hormones and any form of criminal behavior.

There does seem to be a relation between violent behaviors and insulin, the hormone secreted by the pancreas that regulates metabolism of carbohydrates and sugars. When insulin imbalances occur, blood sugar can drop to the point of *hypoglycemia*. Hypoglycemic people suffer headaches, become irritable, confused, anxious, and, sometimes, aggressive. Several studies have linked hypoglycemia to antisocial behavior and violence in the general population (Benton, 1988), and research with prison populations has found severe hypoglycemia in violent and impulsive offenders (S. Cohen, 1980; J. Coid, 1979; Virkkunen & Narvanen, 1987; Virkkunen et al., 1996).

Alcohol, Drugs, and Crime

In Robert Lewis Stevenson's (1886/1991) classic story, *The Strange Case of Dr. Jekyll and Mr. Hyde,* Dr. Jekyll invents a drug that allows him to become another person who can act out his aggressive, evil impulses without harming his reputation as a scientist. Dr. Jekyll's description of this remarkable substance captures much of what we know about the relation between drugs, the brain, and crime:

> The drug had no discriminating action; it was neither diabolical nor divine; it but shook the doors of the prison house of my disposition; and, like the captives of Philippi, that which stood within ran forth. At that time my virtue slumbered; my evil, kept awake by ambition, was alert and swift to seize the occasion; and the thing that was projected was Edward Hyde.

In short, the drug released the evil within Dr. Jekyll—it did not create that evil. Similarly, it appears that alcohol and other **psychoactive drugs**—drugs that affect the brain and create psychological effects—do not directly cause aggression, violence, or criminal behavior. Their effects are indirect; they act on the brain to create changes that increase a person's propensity to act in an aggressive and violent manner.

Certain drugs, especially alcohol, appear to impair natural inhibitions against aggression and violence, particularly in those who have the tendency to behave aggressively and violently. For others, ingestion of alcohol or other drugs makes them behave more affectionately, not more aggressively. In other words, a psychoactive drug's effects on behavior depends on the interaction of its biochemical action with the characteristics of the person who uses it. These characteristics include the nature of the person's nervous system and body chemistry as well as the person's cultural background, learning history, stressors, expectations, motivation, and social conditions.

Psychoactive drugs are divided into four classes: sedatives, hallucinogens/psychedelics, opiate narcotics, and stimulants. We focus our attention on the drugs that are most commonly associated with criminal behavior, namely, alcohol, marijuana, phencyclidine (PCP), heroin, and cocaine. Many criminals, including most individuals who engage in crimes related to the possession and sale of drugs as well as many who engage in crimes of violence and property crimes, are found to be suffering from mental disorders involving substance abuse (excessive drug use) or substance dependence (addiction).

Alcohol. A recent U.S. Public Health Survey on Drug Abuse found that approximately 109 million persons over the age of 12—or about 48.3% of the total population—were current alcohol users, 20% were binge drinkers (consume five or more drinks on the same occasion at least once a month), and 5.7% were "heavy" drinkers (consume five or more drinks on the same occasion on at least five different days a month; United States Department of Health and Human Services [USDHHS], 2002). Alcohol's popularity is related to its perceived ability to lower social inhibitions, facilitate social interaction, and create pleasant feelings. The use of alcohol among teenagers is increasing at an alarming rate, with as many as 87% of high school seniors reporting its use in the past year (National Commission Against Drunk Driving [NCADD], 1999) and 47% of all students using alcohol in the past 30 days (Centers for Disease Control [CDC], 2002).

Alcohol can be dangerous for many reasons. For one thing, it is the largest single factor in fatal traffic accidents (NCADD, 1999) as well as in deaths due to fires, falls, and drowning. Alcohol is also involved in many suicides and in deaths from cirrhosis of the liver and other alcohol-related illnesses; the average life expectancy of people who abuse alcohol is at least 10 years shorter than those of nonabusers. The total loss of life due to the effects of alcohol may exceed that associated with cancer or heart disease.

Further, the National Institute on Alcohol Abuse and Alcoholism (NIAAA; 1998) reported that alcohol, more than any other drug, is linked to the appearance of violence and aggression. Almost 4 in 10 violent crimes—including homicides, robberies, and assaults—involve alcohol (Greenfeld, 1998). A 1996 survey of inmates in state and federal prisons showed that more than 40% of those convicted of homicide or assault and 38% of those convicted of robbery or other property crimes committed their offense while under the influence of alcohol or a combination of alcohol and illicit drugs (Greenfeld, 1998). The average amount of alcohol consumed before these offenses averaged nearly 9 ounces—about the equivalent of three 6-packs of beer or 2 quarts of wine. According to other reports, as many as half of all people, including teenagers, arrested for any crime were under the influence of alcohol at the time of their offense (Greenfeld, 1998). Three out of four reported incidents of domestic violence between spouses and two thirds of those between nonmarried partners involve alcohol use by the offender.

Among juveniles, the relation between alcohol and crime is especially strong. Alcohol use has been related not only to the release of aggressive tendencies, but to increased impulsivity, especially if handguns are present (Cornell, 1993). One Swiss study (Modestin, Berger, & Amman, 1996) compared the lifetime prevalence of criminal behavior in 18- to 78-year-old male psychiatric patients (360) diagnosed as alcohol dependent with that of 360 men from the general population living in the same area and matched for sex, age, marital status, and occupation. The alcoholic patients were nearly twice as likely to have a criminal record (68% vs. 37%) and also tended to commit violent crimes. Modestin and colleagues interpreted these data as suggesting that alcoholism is a contributory factor in criminal behavior.

The effect of alcohol on the brain may provide clues to how and why alcohol increases the likelihood of crime in some people at least. Alcohol depresses activity in the locus coeruleus, an area that helps activate the cerebral cortex. This reduced activity, in turn, tends to cause a reduction in culturally prescribed inhibitions and impairment of thinking, reasoning, and memory (Bernstein, Penner, Clarke-Stewart, & Roy, 2006). As a result, people may say or do things while under the influence of alcohol that they might not say or do when sober. In people who harbor but normally inhibit aggressive, angry, or violent tendencies, the disinhibitory effects of alcohol may prompt them to act on these tendencies in the form of criminal behavior (Hallman, Persson, & af Klinteberg, 2001; Ito, Miller, & Pollock, 1996). To take just one notable example, alcohol appears to have played a role in almost half of the alleged sexual assaults involving Air Force Academy cadets in the past decade (U.S. Air Force, 2003). In some people, the aggressiveness associated with intoxication appears in the form of brooding hostility often directed at spouses or other family members (K. E. Leonard, 1990).

The severity of alcohol's effects on behavior and personality depends on the drinker's age, education, drinking patterns, and accompanying medical complications.

Illicit Drugs. A 2001 National Institute on Drug Abuse (NIDA) survey estimated that 13.9 million Americans had used an illegal drug in the previous month. This figure represents 7.1% of the U.S. population who are at least 12 years old. Illicit drug use is related to crime in several ways. For one thing, by definition, it is a crime to use, possess, manufacture, or distribute drugs such as cocaine, heroin, marijuana, hallucinogens, and amphetamines, all of which are classified as having a potential for abuse. Illicit drugs are also related to crime through the effects they can have on increasing users' tendencies toward violence as well as by engendering violence and other illegal activity in connection with drug trafficking. We consider the relations between crime and drugs.

Marijuana—the dried, chopped leaves and stems of the hemp plant, cannabis sativa—is the most commonly used illicit drug in the United States (National Drug Intelligence Center [NDIC], 2001). About 60% of all illicit drug users have reported using marijuana only, whereas another 20% report marijuana use along with some other illicit drugs (USDHHS, 1997). In 2001, an estimated 5.4% of the population aged 12 and older had used marijuana at least once in the past month. Among high school seniors, the rate was 22.4% (Office of National Drug Control Policy [ONDCP], 2002). Other data put the numbers of current (past 30 days) users at 11 million, with 20 million using the substance in the past year (NDIC, 2001; NIDA, 2004).

Marijuana has a primarily sedating effect on the central nervous system (Makcie & Hille, 1992). Users report feelings of mild euphoria, well-being, and relaxation that begins within minutes after use and may last for 2 to 3 hr. At high doses, marijuana can produce hallucinations or other psychotic symptoms. Motor performance is impaired as are short-term memory, reaction times, and attention span (W. H. Wilson, Ellinwood, Mathew, & Johnson, 1994). Marijuana intoxication is frequently implicated in motor vehicle accidents (Soderstrom, Dischinger, Kerns, & Trifilli, 1995).

Marijuana is not generally considered to be an addictive drug, but prolonged frequent consumption does appear to create behavioral dependence including preoccupation with getting and using the drug, risk-taking behavior (such as driving while under the influence), interpersonal conflicts, and legal problems. Depression and a pattern of apathy and inability to meet personal and career goals have also been linked to long-term use (Cambor & Millman, 1991; Millman & Sbriglio, 1986; Musty & Kaback, 1995).

When marijuana first became popular in the United States in the 1930s, it was characterized as a cause of violent crime even though there was no scientific evidence to support this assertion. Direct causal evidence is still scanty, but one report (National Center for Justice, 1999) indicated that among persons arrested for various rimes in several cities during 1998, almost 39% of adult males, 28% of adult females, and 50% of juveniles tested positive for marijuana. These figures do not establish marijuana as the primary cause of criminal acts in these cases, partly because many of the arrestees used other illicit drugs as well. Nevertheless, opponents of marijuana legalization point to such statistics as supporting their view of cannabis as a dangerous drug. Canada and some states in the United States have "decrimininalized" possession and use of small amounts of marijuana. The medical benefits of marijuana are being increasingly accepted. California and nine other U.S. states have a medical marijuana law, allowing its use for medicinal purposes.

The main relation between marijuana and crime seems to be limited to trafficking in the drug. Perhaps because of its wide use and popularity, an enormous law enforcement effort is invested in prosecutions for marijuana trafficking [National Drug Information Center (NDIC), 2001].

Hallucinogens, also known as *psychedelics*, include *lysergic acid diethylamide (LSD), mescaline* (derived from the peyote cactus plant), and *psilocybin* (from mushrooms). According to the U.S. Public Health Service, about 1 million people in the United States currently use hallucinogens (NDIC, 2001) or about 0.7% of the population. Among people aged 12 to 17, the figure is about 1.7% (USDHHS, 1996). Hallucinogens can lead to serious perceptual distortions including depersonalization (feeling disconnected from your body), paranoid thinking (believing that others are trying to harm you), intense fear, and wild mood swings. The effects can begin within a hour after ingestion and last for several hours to a day.

The hallucinogen most commonly associated with criminal behavior is PCP, also known as "angel dust." In some users, PCP produces feelings of superhuman power and invulnerability, sometimes to the point of experiencing psychotic delusions (e.g., believing that you are someone you are not). The initial effects of PCP appear quickly, and because the drug stays in the bloodstream for a long time, continued use can lead to personality changes and confusion that may last for months. PCP users may become aggressive and injure or kill themselves or others (Sacks, 1990). Accordingly, PCP is one of the drugs commonly found in the bodies of people arrested for a variety of violent, often deadly, crimes (USDHHS Substance Abuse and Mental Health Services Administration, 2000).

Opioids, also called *narcotics*, come from the seed pods of the poppy plant, which grow in Asia and the Middle East. Opioids were used by the ancient Greeks and Romans to relieve pain and induce sleep. They are highly addictive, and discontinuing their use after physical dependence has set in can result in painful, even life-threatening withdrawal symptoms. Opioids were first outlawed in the United States by the Harrison Act of 1914; as controlled substances, they may be only be legally used when prescribed by physicians, usually as pain relievers and cough suppressants. Opioids exert their effects by interacting with the receptor sites used by the body's natural painkilling substances, which are known as endogenous opiates, or *endorphins*.

Heroin—a white odorless powder derived from morphine—is the most commonly used illegal opioid in the United States. (Other well-known opioids include morphine, codeine, and methadone.) Heroin can either be smoked or snorted, but the preferred delivery method is by intravenous injection ("mainlining") that produces an almost immediate, intense "rush" that lasts about a minute. The rush is followed by a sedated, dreamlike state marked by drowsy disconnection from the world that can last for up to 6 hr. Surveys suggest that there were 1.2 to 1.5 million heroin users in 1999, with 980,000 classified as "hard core addicts," an increase of 50% since 1992 (NDIC, 1999). The rise in heroin use is tied to its increasing purity and decreasing price (Nieves, 2001). The use of heroin is growing even among young people; 2% of 12th graders surveyed reported using heroin in the past 30 days (NDIC, 1999). One fourth of new users are under 18, and 47% are between the ages of 18 and 25 (Nieves, 2001). Although purer forms of heroin have attracted more affluent Euro-American users in recent years (Wren, 1999), heroin use has traditionally been most common among members of ethnic minorities who live in inner-city poverty and who rely heavily on crime for survival. Most crimes associated with heroin use appear to involve theft and other forms of property crime that are committed in the service of raising cash to buy the drug (NDIC, 2001; Nieves, 2001). As a general rule, heroin users do not commit rapes, aggravated assaults, or other violent crimes, but homicides may result when larceny or robbery efforts go awry.

Stimulants have an excitatory effect on the central nervous system. Common among these are *amphetamines*, also called "uppers" or "speed," 3, 4-methy-enedioxy-*methamphetamine* (also known as "Ecstasy"), and cocaine. Most stimulants create their effects by increasing the release of dopamine, a neurotransmitter associated with feelings of pleasure and reward.

Methamphetamine, referred to in its smokable form as "ice," "crystal," or "crystal-meth," crank," and "glass" is a powerfully addictive stimulant. It produces a brief, intense sensation or rush when smoked or injected. Taken orally or nasally it produces a long-lasting high. In addition to being at high risk for addiction, long-term users may experience depression, fatigue, paranoia, auditory hallucinations, mood disturbances, and delusions, all of which are more pronounced during withdrawal and are associated with aggression, rage, and extreme violence including homicide (NIDA, 1988). Methamphetamine has a direct relation to violent crime, particularly domestic violence, child abuse, aggravated assault, and murder (NDIC, 2001). Data from a recent National Household Survey on Drug Abuse found that 9.4 million people in the United States had tried methamphetamine at least once in their lifetime. Lifetime use among those aged 28 to 34 was 5.4% of the population (USDHHS Substance Abuse and Mental Health Services Administration, 2000).

Ecstasy, a synthetic cousin of amphetamine, first appeared in the early 1900s. As a stimulant, it suppresses appetite, creates increased energy, sex drive, and a sense of well-being. It also has hallucinogenic effects. About 10% of high school students say they have used Ecstasy in the prior 12 months (R. Weiss, 2002), often at all-night, heavy-metal band and dance parties known as "raves" (USDHHS Substance Abuse and Mental Health Services Administration, 2000). Although probably not addictive, Ecstasy can be extremely dangerous. Its effects are caused by its ability to stimulate dopamine-releasing and serotonin-releasing neurons, which results not only in pleasurable feelings but also visual hallucinations, dry mouth, hyperactivity, jaw muscle spasms that may result in "lockjaw," elevated blood pressure, fever, and dangerously abnormal heart rhythms. Some studies have suggested that continued use of Ecstacy can permanently impair the brain's ability to produce serotonin and may ultimately lead to impulsive and violent behavior. However, the Ecstasy-crime link appears mainly because the drug is illegal. Trafficking in Ecstasy is often accompanied by violence, including drive-by shootings and aggravated assaults (Leinwand, 2001).

Cocaine gained popularity as a recreational drug in the 1970s, especially among middle and upper income groups. By the 1980s, due to its high cost, it became a fashionable drug for the wealthy, the majority of whom snorted it in powder form. Heavy users either mixed cocaine powder with water and injected it intravenously or heated it with ether or ammonia and inhaled the vapor. In the late 1980s, a relatively cheap, fast-acting form of cocaine known as "crack" became popular among less affluent users. Crack is produced by combining cocaine powder with baking soda and heating the mixture until hard rocks of brownish crystals form. Its name refers to the noise the rocks make when lit in a pipe (Nietzel, Spelz, McCauley, & Bernstein, 1998). According to the U.S. Public Health Service, an estimated 2.5 million Americans were current cocaine users in 1995, representing 0.7% of the U.S. population aged 12 and older. Cocaine has highly pleasurable effects similar to those produced by amphetamine stimulants. However, cocaine also produces a more euphoric experience than amphetamines. The effect is faster, but does not last as long. A crack rush can last less than five minutes, so cocaine users must use the drug frequently to maintain a high and forestall the physical and emotional crash that follows disuse of the drug.

Because cocaine, especially crack, can lead to dependence in a very short period of time, people from all walks of life have suffered unemployment and ruined lives as they spend more and more of their time and money seeking and using this drug. Indeed, the main connection between cocaine and crime stems from individual users stealing to support their habit and from the violence associated with the world of cocaine sales and distribution. Law enforcement agencies have described crack cocaine as being more directly linked to crimes of violence than any other drug. Gang-related "drug wars" are primarily related to crack trafficking (NDIC, 2001).

Other crime-related drugs include rohypnol, ketamine, Gamma hydroxybutyrate (GHB), and OxyContin®. *Rohypnol*, also known as "roffies," "R2," "Roche," "rope," and "rib," is a powerful, commercially manufactured depressant. Ten times stronger than Valium®, it is not licensed or approved for medical use in the United States. Rohypnol is directly related to violent crime through its administration to women by men as part of a "date rape" scenario. *Ketamine*, or "Special K," which has a hallucinogenic effect, and GHB, a central nervous system depressant, are also associated with date rape. All three of these drugs are undetectable when added to the drink of an unsuspecting victim. The prescription pain-killing drug OxyContin® became popular as a recreational drug in the mid-1990s and soon was associated with criminal distribution rings. According to the 2000 National Survey on Drug Abuse, almost 1 million people reported using OxyContin® for nonprescription purposes at least once in their lifetimes. In 2002, 1.3% of 8th graders, 3.0% of 10th graders, and 4.0% of 12th graders reported using OxyContin® within the past year. The crimes associated with OxyContin are usually nonviolent and include burglary, larceny, and other property crimes undertaken to fund drug use (ONDCP, 2002). Several doctors, too, have been convicted for overprescribing OxyContin® and thus violating federal drug laws (Bradley, 2004).

In summary, U.S. government statistics have revealed several general facts about illicit drug use and crime (Beck, 2000; Mumola, 1999):

1. Drug users are six times more likely to commit a crime than nondrug users.
2. About half of state and federal prisoners said they committed their current offense while under the influence of drugs.
3. One in six of state and federal inmates committed their current offense to get money for drugs. Of convicted property and drug offenders, about one in four had committed their crimes to get money for drugs. A higher percentage of drug offenders in 1996 (24%) than in 1989 (14%) were in jail for a crime committed to raise money for drugs.
4. A total of 57% of state prisoners and 45% of federal prisoners surveyed in 1997 had used drugs in the month before their arrest. About 40% used marijuana and 25% cocaine or crack.
5. More than 80% of state prisoners and more than 70% of federal prisoners had used drugs in the past. A total of 20% of state prisoners and 12% of federal prisoners had used drugs intravenously.
6. About 60% of federal prisoners and 21% of state prisoners are in prison for a drug law violation. More than two thirds of state and federal drug offenders were trafficking in cocaine or crack during their current offense.
7. A total of 65% of mentally ill jail inmates and 57% of other jail inmates were under the influence of both drugs and alcohol at the time of their arrest.
8. The drug most closely linked to violent crime is alcohol.

Summary

The first effort to explore the roots of crime in human biology involved trying to link criminal behavior to physical appearance, mainly bodily type and minor physical anomalies. However, the idea that physical appearance is connected to criminal behavior found no empirical support. Looking for the roots of crime in evolutionary theory and especially in the principle of natural selection has also not been of much help in understanding the origins of crime, although some researchers believe that evolutionary theories can help explain certain types of interpersonal violence such an family homicides.

The mapping of the human genome is leading researchers to look for the origins of violence in our DNA. Genes are the foundation of all behavior, but the link between genes and crime is not direct. Rather, genes may provide the mechanisms or predispositions for certain traits and behaviors that may, in turn, lead to criminal offending. Behavioral genetics involves studying the relative effects of genes and environment on human behavior. Researchers use twin, adoption, and family studies to try to understand the contributions of nature and nurture to crime and violence.

Sophisticated techniques of brain imaging and advances in understanding neurochemistry are providing neuroscientists with tools to understand the role of the brain and neurotransmitters in crime. Neurotransmitters associated indirectly with aggression include serotonin, dopamine, and MAO. However, as with genes, the link between brain structure and function and criminal behavior is indirect except in the rare cases in which a brain-based problem, such as a brain tumor, may cause one to be violent.

Studying the endocrine system for links to criminal behavior shows that there is an indirect and relatively small connection between hormones and crime. The link is a complicated one, which sometimes involves interaction between the hormones, blood-borne messengers that travel throughout the body, and neurotransmitters, the brain's neural messengers. There appears to be a stronger link between insulin and violent behavior than there is with testosterone, the male hormone thought to be related to aggression. If there is a testosterone-aggression link, it appears to be indirect and probably lies in testosterone's effect on serotonin levels that in turn are associated with aggression.

Due to their effect on the central nervous system and brain, alcohol and other illicit drugs do influence criminal behavior. Sometimes the influence is direct, as when alcohol use releases inhibitions and causes one to act out aggression. At other times, the influence is indirect, as when addiction to drugs leads one to commit crimes to obtain money to buy the drugs. Without a doubt, alcohol—a legal drug—is associated with more crime than any illegal drug.

In short, aggression, violence, and crime are the result of a complex interaction of many factors. When looking for root causes of crime, biology is far from being destiny, but it may set the stage for traits and behaviors that, combined with social, psychological, economic, and cultural factors, lead to crime. Through the complex interaction of nature and nurture, one's biology and one's environment form complex systems within systems that reciprocally influence each other. As noted earlier, for example, neurotransmitter levels and activity can be influenced by events in childhood and by stressors in the environment. So, just as we shape and change our environments, our environments shape and change us. Still, learning more about the effects of genetics and biology on behavior may someday help researchers and clinicians to identify infants and children who are at high risk for later criminal behavior and perhaps to develop early treatment and prevention programs.

Key Terms

Teratogens	*Central nervous system*	*Endocrine system*
Deoxyribonucleic acid, DNA	*Peripheral nervous system*	*Cerebral cortex*
Family studies	*Hypothalamus*	*Neurotransmitters*
Twin studies	*Hippocampus*	*Monoamine oxidase (MAO)*
Adoption studies	*Limbic system*	*Hormones*
Arousal	*Amygdala*	*Psychoactive drugs*

Questions for Review

1. How do researchers study the genetic influences on criminal behavior?
2. What brain structures and functions are most associated with crimes of violence?
3. What neurotransmitters are most associated with criminal behavior, and what is the mechanism by which high and low levels lead to aggression and violence?
4. How do hormones set the stage for aggression?
5. How do psychoactive drugs (including alcohol) contribute to crime and violence?

Track It Down

Criminal Behavior Website
www.cassel2e.com
The Human Genome Science Project Information Site
http://www.ornl.gov/sci/techresources/Human_Genome/home.shtml
3D Tour of the Brain
http://www.pbs.org/wnet/brain/3d/
The Endocrine System
http://arbl.cvmbs.colostate.edu/hbooks/pathphys/endocrine/
National Institute on Alcohol Abuse and Alcoholism
http://www.niaaa.nih.gov/
Behavioral Effects of Alcohol
http://science.howstuffworks.com/alcohol.htm
National Institute on Drug Abuse
http://www.nida.nih.gov/
Adriane Raine Home Page
http://www.usc.edu/dept/nbio/ngp/Faculty/raine-a.shtml

5

Psychological Roots of Crime

Personality and Crime   *Learning and Crime*
Traits and Crime   *Cognition and Crime*
Psychodynamics and Crime   *Personality Disorders and Crime*

In chapter 4, we considered biological roots of crime, including the influence of genetic inheritance, the brain and central nervous system, and hormonal and other physiological mechanisms that influence aggression and violence. In this chapter, we introduce the psychological theories that attribute the roots of crime to mental processes that develop as people interact with their families and others. We focus on the major psychological theories of personality and personality development as well as on theories about how people process information, think, learn, and interact with others. We then apply these concepts as we trace the development of crime and mental disorders in chapters 7, 8, and 9.

Personality and Crime

We begin by looking at psychologists' efforts to develop theories about what personality is, how it can best be measured, how it develops, and how it might be changed.

In describing someone's personality, people usually employ adjectives such as "friendly," "kind," "warm," or perhaps "difficult," "hostile" or "insecure." In doing so, one is trying to summarize the essence of that person's behavior and attitudes, the characteristics that describe a particular individual. Most psychologists agree that **personality** consists of the unique patterns of thinking, feeling, and behaving that are relatively constant throughout one's life and through which one can be compared and contrasted with other people.

Where does personality come from? It begins with the biological predisposition to act and respond to the world in particular ways, which psychologists call **temperament** (Bernstein, Penner, Clarke-Stewart, & Roy, 2006). If you were to visit any hospital nursery and observe newborns for a while, you would soon be aware that they behave differently. Some are noisy, some are quiet; some are agitated, some are calm; some are easy to soothe, some are fussy. Because this temperamental foundation of future development is apparent from birth, psychologists see it as innate and inherited. It is the essence of what people are before other people and experiences have molded them.

Twin research supports the conclusion that temperament is inherited. For example, identical twins (who have exactly the same genes) appear to be more alike than nonidentical pairs (whose genes are no more similar than those of other siblings) in such aspects of temperament as activity and anxiety levels, emotional expressiveness, and sociability (Bernstein, Penner, Clarke-Stewart, & Roy, 2006). In addition, studies comparing identical twins raised together, identical twins raised apart, nonidentical twins raised together, and nonidentical twins raised apart indicate that identical twins tend to be more alike in personality than nonidentical twins, regardless of whether they are raised together or apart (Tellegen et al., 1988). Adoption studies have also highlighted the role of genetics in personality. The personalities of adopted children are more likely to resemble the personalities of their biological parents and siblings than those of the families in which they are raised (Raine, 1993). Indeed, research in behavioral genetics—the influence of genes on behavior—suggests that heredity accounts for about 30% to 60% of the variability that one sees in human personality (DiLalla & Gottesman, 1995). We return to the topic of temperament and its importance in influencing criminal behavior in chapter 7.

It is also clear, however, that each individual's personality is ultimately determined by an ever-shifting mix of biological and environmental factors, each of which influences the other. For example, people's experiences with the environment can make them more likely or less likely to express certain inborn characteristics and tendencies. At the same time, those inborn characteristics and tendencies influence the experiences people have or seek out.

Given this enormous complexity, it is no wonder that psychological theories characterize in many different ways the ongoing dance of nature and nurture that results in the development of human personality. These theories suggest that personality results as heredity and environment interact to create (a) stable psychological characteristics (trait theories); (b) conscious and unconscious mental conflicts (psychodynamic theories); (c) patterns of behavior and thinking shaped by reward, punishment, and the examples set by others (behavioral and cognitive-behavioral theories); and (d) unique perceptions of the world (humanistic or phenomenological theories).

Traits and Crime

Some psychologists have created theories about personality based on descriptors that they call *traits*. Personality traits describe people's typical or characteristic ways of thinking, feeling, and acting. Trait theories of personality make three basic assumptions: (1) that personality traits are relatively stable and predictable over time (if you are warm and friendly as a child, you are likely to be the same throughout your life), (2) that personality traits are relatively stable and predictable across diverse settings (if you are competitive at work, you will probably be competitive in a tennis game), and (3) that personality traits combine in a unique tapestry so as to result in the infinite variations people see in the people around them; no two people are exactly alike (Funder, 1997).

Sheldon and Eleanor Glueck (1950, 1968) were the first psychologists who have attempted to describe the "criminal personality" from the perspective of trait theory. Their longitudinal study followed more than 1,000 delinquent boys to adulthood in an effort to determine the factors that predicted chronic criminal behavior. Although they believed that family and social factors, body type, and intelligence all contributed to criminality, They also identified a set of traits that were commonly seen in chronic offenders from childhood onward. These traits included self-assertiveness, defiance, sadism, lack of concern for others, extroversion, feeling unappreciated, distrust of authority, impulsiveness, poor interpersonal skills, narcissism, mental instability, suspicion, hostility, destructiveness, and resentment (L. J. Siegel, 1998). These findings dovetail nicely with a broader trait theory of personality proposed by British psychologist Hans Eysenck (1964) that, although not originally designed to explain criminal behavior, has been used by others to do so.

Eysenck's Trait Theory of Personality

Eysenck (1967, 1987) described personality in terms of three basic factors or dimensions: *introversion–extraversion*, *neuroticism–stability*, and *psychoticism*. *Extroverts* are sociable, outgoing, and carefree. *Introverts* are thoughtful, controlled, and avoid social situations. People high on *neuroticism* (also called *emotionality*) are moody, restless, worried, and anxious, whereas those at the stable end of the emotionalism scale are likely to be calm, even tempered, and relaxed. People who score high on *psychoticism* are cruel, hostile, cold, and rejecting of social customs. Those low on psychoticism do not show these traits. Eysenck devised personality tests such as the Eysenck Personality Inventory (EPI; Eysenck & Rachman, 1965) to measure where individuals fall on each of these dimensions (see Figure 5.1).

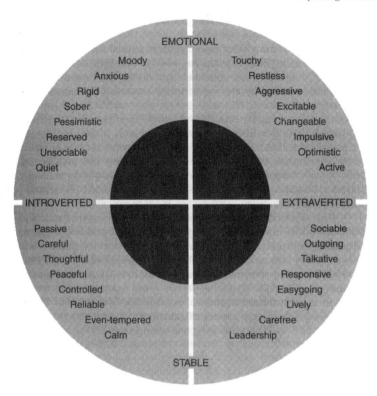

FIGURE 5.1   *Eysenck Personality Inventory Dimensions.* From *Psychology* (4th ed.), by
D. A. Bernstein, A. Clarke-Stewart, E. J. Roy, and C. D. Wickens, 1997, Boston: Houghton Mifflin.
Copyright © 1997 by Houghton Mifflin Company. Reprinted with permission.

Why do people differ on these dimensions? As we mentioned in chapter 4, Eysenck believed that people's personality traits are traceable to inherited differences in their central and autonomic nervous systems and in particular, to differences in their typical level of physiological arousal—an aspect of temperament. He argued, for example, that extroverts are people with low baseline levels of "resting" arousal (as measured by heart rate, brain waves, and other indexes). They seek stimulation and excitement to increase their arousal to an optimum level. Eysenck said that these people are also less affected by the consequences of their behavior, especially by punishment for misbehavior, so they may not as easily learn to change punished behavior. Introverts, on the other hand, have "overaroused" nervous systems, so they seek solitude and quiet as a way of reducing that arousal to an optimum level. In contrast to extroverts, introverts are quick to learn from experience, especially from punishment, and thus tend to become conforming, inhibited, and anxious (Eysenck, 1967, 1987).

Twin studies using the EPI support the idea that people's location on Eysenck's trait dimensions is influenced by genetics. There is evidence, for example, of higher concordance on the Extraversion and Neuroticism scales between identical twins—whether raised together or apart—than between nonidentical twins raised together (Shields, 1962). Eysenck (1967) found higher concordance on the Psychoticism scale for identical twins raised together than for nonidentical twins raised together.

Arousal, Traits, and Crime. When people score extremely high on both emotionality and extroversion, the stage may be set for criminal behavior. Many of these individuals are restless and moody as well as impulsive and aggressive. Persons high on the psychoticism scale might also have criminal tendencies because they are cold, unemotional, cruel, socially insensitive, and have no regard for others. Although Eysenck predicted that criminals as a group would be more extraverted, more neurotic, and more psychotic than noncriminals, he did not believe that all such individuals are destined to be criminals. If they have appropriate parenting and schooling, he said, they can learn to behave appropriately and to respect the law, but parents and teachers need to exercise special care using systematic rewards and punishments to socialize these individuals.

Eysenck and many other psychologists have used the EPI and the Eysenck Personality Questionnaire (EPQ) to assess the validity of Eysenck's hypotheses concerning the personality traits of criminals. Do criminals score higher than noncriminals on measures of extroversion, emotionality, and psychoticism? The results are equivocal (P. Feldman, 1993). Some studies of prisoners versus noncriminals have shown such differences, but it is possible that the criminals' personalities changed as a result of imprisonment; there is no way of knowing what their EPI or EPQ scores would have been at the time they committed their offenses. Further, there is no consistent association between crime in general and a particular combination of high extroversion, emotionality, and psychoticism. This makes sense because there are so many types of crime—from shoplifting to murder—and so many reasons for engaging in crime that it would be remarkable for all criminal perpetrators to share the same set of traits.

There is considerable support, however, for an association between high extroversion/emotionality and crimes committed by people displaying antisocial personality disorder (APD), also known as psychopathy. This type of chronic, violent criminal has been consistently shown to score high on the Extroversion scale (Eysenck & Eysenck, 1963). Indeed, extremely extroverted noncriminals, described by Eysenck as craving excitement, taking chances, acting impulsively and aggressively, and being quick tempered and unreliable, bear a strong resemblance to criminal psychopaths (Meloy, 1992). (We discuss APD in more detail later in this chapter when we consider the criminal personality and what trait and other personality theories have to say about its causes.)

Psychodynamics and Crime

Sigmund Freud (1856–1939) was the first to develop a unified theory of human psychology including mental processes and the structure of personality. Freud's (1938, 1948) theory is based on the idea that psychodynamic forces determine a persons' thoughts, feelings, and behaviors—a principle known as psychic determinism—and that the most important of these forces come from the unconscious and stem from sexual and aggressive instincts. Freud's psychodynamic theories of personality and psychotherapy are known collectively as *psychoanalysis*. From the time they were articulated in the late 1800s, these theories had an enormous influence in psychology, psychiatry, and many other fields including criminology. Their influence has waned considerably in recent decades, but from the 1920s through the 1950s, they did much to shape writing and thinking about criminal behavior in the United States.

Freud's Psychoanalysis

Freud (1938) believed that the sexual and aggressive instincts with which people are born drive the development of their personalities. All of people's other needs, he said—for love, security, achievement, and the like—are derived from these fundamental instincts. Personality develops as people seek to satisfy these instincts in a world that places restraints on their free expression. The first of these restraints comes from a person's caregivers, then siblings and peers, and ultimately from the broader society whose norms and laws people are expected to obey.

Personality Structure.   Freud (1948) described personality as having three parts: the id, the ego, and the superego (see Figure 5.2). The **id** is the unconscious part of the personality where sexual and aggressive instincts reside. Freud called the sexual instinct *Eros,* and he believed that it is manifest in positive psychic energy, called *libido,* which drives constructive behavior. The aggressive instinct, called *Thanatos,* is manifest in destructive psychic energy. Freud saw the id as operating on the "pleasure principle," meaning that it seeks immediate satisfaction regardless of society's rules or the rights and feelings of others. (It is easy to see how the concept of id might provide insight into some types of criminal behavior.) The **ego** develops as

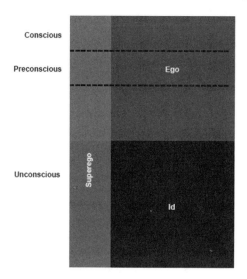

FIGURE 5.2 *Diagram of Freud's Personality Theory (Id, Ego, Superego).* **From** *Psychology* **(5th ed), by D. A. Bernstein, A. Clarke-Stewart, E. J. Roy, and C. D. Wickens, 2000, Boston: Houghton Mifflin. Copyright © 2000 by Houghton Mifflin Company. Adapted with permission.**

parents, teachers, and others place limits on the expression of id impulses. The **ego** operates on the "reality principle," meaning that it works out compromises between the desires of the id and the constraints imposed by the real world including society's laws. The **superego** develops as individuals adopt, or internalize, the rules, inhibitions, and values of their parents and their culture. The superego acts as people's conscience, telling them what they should and should not do. Thus, the superego seeks to control the impulses and instincts that come from the id.

Defense Mechanisms.   Freud believed that id, ego, and superego are constantly at odds with one another, creating struggles known as intrapsychic conflict. Because many of these conflicts involve a person's most threatening memories, thoughts, and impulses, they are usually kept out of consciousness by what Freud (1948) called psychological **defense mechanisms** (see Table 5.1). Defense mechanisms can be adaptive in helping people to function in society, but if people rely too heavily on them, they may result in problems. These problems can range from seemingly irrational symptoms of anxiety, worry, and guilt to substance abuse and interpersonal conflict, physical dysfunctions, and even schizophrenia or other severe mental disorders. Indeed, Freud saw the type, number, and intensity of intrapsychic conflicts—and the defense mechanisms required to deal with them—as shaping personality and mental disorders.

Personality Development.   Freud (1938) believed that psychological development occurs in five **psycho-sexual stages**, each of which is focused on the area of the body most associated with pleasure and unconscious conflict at the time. During the *oral* stage, from birth to about age 1 year, the child seeks gratification mainly through sucking and feeding. Weaning is a major source of conflict here. The *anal* stage occurs during the second year or so, as the focus of pleasure shifts to the anus and to stimuli associated with expelling or withholding feces. Here, conflict arises as the child is required to exert control over these bodily functions through toilet training. The *phallic* stage begins in the third or fourth years and lasts until age 5 or 6. At this stage, the genitals become a main source of pleasure, and children experience both sexual desire for the opposite-sex parent and fear of retribution from the same-sex parent. (These conflicts are called the "Oedipus complex" for boys and the "Electra complex" for girls. The names come from ancient Greek plays in which children unin-

TABLE 5.1 *Freudian Defense Mechanisms*

Repression	Unconsciously pushing threatening memories, urges, or ideas from conscious awareness: A person may experience loss of memory for unpleasant events.
Rationalization	Attempts to make actions or mistakes seem reasonable: The reason or excuses given (e.g., "I spank my children because it is good for them") have a rational ring to them, but they are not the real reasons for the behavior.
Projection	Unconsciously attributing one's own unacceptable thoughts or impulses to another person Instead of recognizing that "I hate him" a person may feel that "He hates me."
Reaction formation	Defending against unacceptable impulses by acting opposite to them: Sexual interest in a married friend might appear as strong dislike instead.
Sublimation	Converting unacceptable impulses into socially acceptable actions, and perhaps symbolically expressing them: Sexual or aggressive desires may appear as artistic creativity or devotion to athletic excellence.
Displacement	Deflecting an impulse from its original target to a less threatening one: Anger at one's boss may be expressed through hostility toward a clerk, a family member, or even the dog.
Denial	Simply discounting the existence of threatening impulses: A person may vehemently deny ever having had even the slightest degree of physical attraction to a person of the same sex.
Compensation	Striving to make up for unconscious impulses or fears: A business executive's extreme competitiveness might be aimed at compensating for unconscious feelings of inferiority.
Altruism	An unselfish concern for another's welfare.

The least mature defense mechanisms are repression, displacement, reaction formation, and denial. Psychodynamic theorists see them as involved in many cases of criminal behavior. More mature defense mechanisms, such as sublimation and altruism, are seen as channeling anxiety into productive, noncriminal outlets.

Source: D. A. Bernstein, A. Clarke-Stewart, E. J. Roy, and C. D. Wickens, 2000, Boston: Houghton Mifflin. Copyright © 2000 by Houghton Mifflin Company. Adapted with permission.

tentionally kill their opposite sex parents and marry their fathers or mothers.) Freud saw these conflicts being resolved as the child identifies with and imitates the same-sex parent (thus adopting a culturally expected gender role) and eventually seeks an opposite-sex mate. In the *latency* period, lasting from about age 6 to puberty, children enter school and become focused on academics, skill learning, and same-sex friendships. In adolescence, children enter the *genital* stage, and if all has gone well in earlier stages, they find intimacy and psychological stability in a relationship with an adult partner.

Failure to resolve the unconscious conflicts that occur at any given stage, said Freud, results in preoccupation or fixation with those conflicts and a tendency to show personality characteristics that signal one's continuing internal turmoil. For example, people fixated at the oral stage may show characteristics that unconsciously express their dissatisfaction with the nurturing they got from their caregivers. They may be either extremely independent, refusing assistance from anyone, or extremely dependent, always waiting for someone to do something for them. People with an anal personality display characteristics relating to self-control and exerting control over others. They may either be obsessively rigid, orderly, and conforming or messy, disorganized, and defiant of authority. People fixated at the phallic stage tend to have problems in sexual relations and intimate relationships in general. They may be sexually promiscuous or may shun sex and intimacy altogether. The genital personality represents ideal psychological adjustment and mental health. These people find it possible to balance career and family life and to maintain a healthy adult intimate relationship.

Psychodynamic Theory and Criminal Behavior

As noted earlier, Freud did not actually spend much time addressing the psychodynamic roots of criminal behavior. Freud (1938) did mention that there is a difference between the neurotic—whose unconscious conflicts result in anxiety, depression, and other self-damaging maladaptive behavior—and the criminal, whose symptoms result in damage to others. He (1901) also believed that many criminals are driven by the unconscious desire to be punished by society for behaviors that preceded their crimes, so that guilt comes not as the result of criminal behavior but is its unconscious cause.

It was left to a group of American psychiatrists to more actively apply psychoanalytic theory to criminal behavior (Abrahamsen, 1944, 1960; Aichorn, 1935; F. Alexander, 1935; Glueck & Glueck, 1950, 1968). Their analysis of crime began with the premise that the criminal has a weak ego, a weak or absent superego, and a strong id. Research on delinquent boys by August Aichorn (1935) typifies this view. He believed that repeat delinquent offenders had a predisposition for criminal behavior because of their inability to control the id's demands for immediate gratification and the failure of the superego to develop sufficient strength to generate respect for others and a sense of right and wrong. Psychoanalytic theorists (Redl & Toch, 1979) believe that juvenile criminals violate laws as a means of expressing unresolved unconscious conflicts. Their crimes, driven by uncontrolled ids, occur because they are unable to postpone gratification. The failure to develop healthy egos and superegos, say these theorists, is caused largely by failure to identify with parental figures or by the absence of law abiding, loving parental role models. Without such identification and the internalization of parental and societal norms, morals, and values, the superego will not develop properly. Other psychiatrists trained in psychoanalysis (e.g., Abrahamsen, 1960; Menninger, 1966) have elaborated on this theme and have described criminals in general as so dominated by id impulses that they are unable to control impulsive and aggressive tendencies. Having little or no superego development, criminals are said to lack a conscience and to have no empathy for others. They are also said to have weak egos that can be easily influenced toward criminal behavior by peer pressure and other social forces.

David Abrahamsen (1960), for example, used Freudian personality theory to explain sex crimes and murder. Sexual offenders are, Abrahamsen said, fixated at the phallic stage. Often, they have had sexual experiences involving their mothers either through incest or by watching her have sex. Abrahamsen said that these men were unable to identify with their fathers and thus developed confusion about their gender roles and sexual behavior. Abrahamsen claims that many of them were brought up by mothers who were cruel or sadistic and that they have weak egos and superegos. He saw murder, too, as motivated by unconscious conflicts and categorized murder as either symptomatic or manifest. *Symptomatic* murderers kill because of an unresolved conflict over hatred of the mother or some other important figure from childhood. Their murderous acts, often committed in a jealous rage when rejected or betrayed by a woman, are seen as retribution against the mother who rejected them in the phallic stage. In contrast, *manifest* murders are committed for profit or for other obvious reasons. Freudians believe that symptomatic murderers unconsciously want to be caught and punished, not so much for their killings as for childhood events about which they feel guilt or shame—most often for failing to win their parents' love and approval. In short, they murder to be punished.

Psychodynamic theorists claim that criminal behavior can also result from overuse of defense mechanisms. For example, although most individuals use *sublimation* to channel sexual and aggressive impulses into socially acceptable outlets—such as artistic creation or athletic competition—criminals may rely solely on *repression* or *denial* to hold these urges at bay until they explode when triggered by certain events or situations. Similarly, some psychodynamic theorists also invoke *displacement* to help explain some instances of child or spouse abuse. The abuser may be seen as too afraid to direct anger toward a boss or other authority figure and so may turn instead against a helpless child or submissive spouse. An abused spouse, in turn, may not be able to respond appropriately to the abuser's aggression and so may "take it out" on a child. Criminals are also said to use *rationalization*, claiming, for instance, that stealing from an employer is acceptable because "I don't get paid enough, and the company can afford it."

The essence of the **psychodynamic theory of crime**, then, is that "every element that prevents children from developing in a healthy way, both physically and emotionally, tends to bring about a pattern of emotional disturbances which is always at the root of antisocial or criminal behavior" (Abrahamsen, 1960, p. 56). Freudian theorists see criminal acts as reflecting (a) unbalanced psychic forces; (b) a form of neurosis expressed not through psychiatric symptoms but through overt aggressive acts; (c) the acting out of impulses that, if restrained, would result in mental illness; (d) fulfillment of a guilt-driven need for punishment and/or acceptance by a gang or other criminal group; (e) a substitute form of gratification for other unsatisfied needs; or (f) a means of compensating for repressed feelings of inadequacy (Barak, 1998; P. Feldman, 1993).

Jeffrey Dahmer's life and death typifies what Freudian theorists refer to as the desire for punishment. In 1994, while in a Wisconsin prison for the murder, dismemberment, and cannibalization of 16 young men, Dahmer was beaten to death by a psychotic fellow inmate. Apparently, Dahmer did not put up a fight; indeed, some claim that he wanted to die. At his sentencing in 1992, he had said, "Your honor, it is over now. This has never been a case of trying to get free. I didn't ever want freedom. Frankly, I wanted death for myself" (Gleick, 1994, p. 129).

Modern Variants on Psychodynamic Theory

Many of Freud's early followers eventually came to disagree with some of his ideas, especially about the importance of id impulses, internal conflicts, infantile sexuality, and other controversial aspects of orthodox psychoanalysis.

Erik Erikson.   Erik Erikson (1946), for example, assigned a larger role than Freud did to unconscious personality factors. He saw the ego as an autonomous force, not just a mediator of unconscious conflicts, and proposed eight stages of **psychosocial development**—rather than psychosexual development—that stress an individual's interactions with others rather than conflict over internal instincts. At each stage, the person faces a social crisis that is either resolved or left partly unsettled. Positive outcomes at each stage help the person deal with the crisis of the next stage; unsettled problems interfere with continued development. For example, if infants do not develop the feeling that parents can be trusted to take care of their needs, they will be unlikely to feel secure enough to try new behaviors on their own as is expected around the age of 2 years. In chapters 7 and 8, we trace the role of Erikson's theory in the development of crime.

Harry Stack Sullivan.   Harry Stack Sullivan (1953, 1965) emphasized the importance of social experiences for personality development. Sullivan believed that personality is not only shaped by the experiences we have with others, but that it is defined by how we relate to others. He believed, for example, that all mental disorders are the result of disturbed interpersonal experiences including failure to "connect" with and experience other people in a genuine way. Like Freud, Sullivan believed that personality develops in several stages. For him, though, the emphasis was on interpersonal, not psychosexual, development. Sullivan's first stage, *infancy,* lasts about 18 months and focuses on the child's interactions with its parents to obtain fulfillment of basic biological needs for nourishment and comfort. The infant gains an early sense of self on the basis of how these caregivers react to and meet those needs. Sullivan said that developing a healthy sense of self is necessary to feel secure. The second stage, *childhood,* lasts from about 18 months to 4 years of age and focuses on the development and use of language in relating to others. The *juvenile* era, from about 4 to 10 years of age, finds the child trying to relate to peers. The *preadolescent* learns to be psychologically intimate with a same sex friend, whereas the *adolescent* must learn to deal with hormonal urges and lustful impulses and integrate physical needs with psychological intimacy. In the final stage, *late adolescence,* the individual must learn to experience satisfying interpersonal relationships.

Object Relations Theories.   Erikson and Sullivan did much to modernize psychodynamic personality theory, but today, the most influential variants on Freud's ideas are to be found in the writings of **object relations** theorists, including Melanie Klein (1975), Otto Kernberg (1976), Heinz Kohut (1977), and Margaret Mahler (1968). *Object relations* are experiences with one's "love objects," the people to whom one becomes attached and with whom one seek closeness and intimacy. Peoples' first love objects are their parents (especially mothers) or other primary caregivers.

The relationship with people's first love object leads to their first "attachment" experience, their first "bonding" with another human being. This attachment can be secure—meaning that one feels that their basic needs for food and comfort will be met—or insecure, meaning that one is not sure whether or how consistently their needs will be met. Secure attachment to a caregiver gives the child a firm base from which to explore the world and develop as a person. Insecure attachment sets the stage for various kinds of problems including dysfunctional social relationships and even mental disorders.

Object relations theorists believe that people's experiences with their love objects during infancy and childhood are critical to personality development because they shape their thoughts, behaviors, and feelings toward all people. More specifically, they say that the attachment style people develop with primary caregivers will be reflected in the relationships they will have with "significant others" throughout their lives (K. D. Davis et al., 1994). If that attachment is insecure, the chance of success and satisfaction in romantic relationships is low (P. R. Shaver & Clark, 1994). According to some researchers, insecure attachment may also make criminal behavior more likely. For example, D. H. Stott (1980) concluded that the criminal acts of 102 English juvenile offenders were triggered by anxiety stemming from insecure attachment and resulting low self-esteem. Indeed, the reasons the boys gave for their crimes included (a) a search for excitement that would alleviate anxiety, (b) retaliation against parents, (c) getting attention from parents, (d) seeking removal from the home, and (e) obtaining peer respect for having flaunted the law (P. Feldman, 1993). Such retrospective reports may be biased and self-serving of course, but as we show later, object relations theories have nevertheless been invoked to explain various forms of juvenile and adult criminal behavior.

Learning and Crime

Give me a dozen healthy infants, well-formed, and my own specified world to bring them up in and I'll guarantee to take any one at random and train him to become any type of specialist I might select—doctor, lawyer, artist, merchant-chief, and yes, even beggar-man and thief, regardless of his talents, penchants, tendencies, abilities, vocations and race of his ancestors.

So said John Watson (1925), founder of **behaviorism** and the first American psychologist to advocate the idea that human behavior is shaped not by instincts or the unconscious but almost entirely by the environment and especially by learning. Psychologists define **learning** as a change in preexisting behavior or mental processes that occurs as a result of experience. There are two main categories of learning theories: those emphasizing classical conditioning and those emphasizing operant conditioning.

Classical Conditioning. The principles of classical conditioning arose from the work of Ivan Pavlov (1849–1936), a Russian physiologist who in the 1920s was studying salivation and other aspects of the digestive system in dogs. Pavlov knew that dogs salivate reflexively (an *unconditioned response*) when food (an *unconditioned stimulus*) is offered to them. What he found surprising was that the dogs also salivated when they saw the laboratory assistant who normally fed them, even if the assistant had no food to give at the moment. Apparently, the dogs had come to associate the unconditioned stimulus of food with a learned, or *conditioned,* stimulus—the laboratory assistant—and were thus making a learned, or conditioned, response when that conditioned stimulus appeared. Subsequent laboratory tests confirmed this idea. By repeatedly pairing food with a tone, Pavlov found that the animals soon began to salivate when the tone was presented without the food. Through classical conditioning, the dogs had associated the tone with food (see Fig. 5.3). When the bell was repeatedly sounded in the absence of food, the animals continued to salivate for a while but through a process known as extinction eventually ceased to do so.

Watson and his colleague, Rosalie Raynor, demonstrated that classical conditioning could also operate in humans. In one famous case (Watson & Raynor, 1920), they used conditioning to "teach" a young child known as "Little Albert" to fear a harmless white rat that had previously elicited no distress. Watson and Raynor did this by repeatedly pairing the sight of the rat (the conditioned stimulus) with an unconditioned stimulus—a loud noise—which reflexively caused the unconditioned response of fear. Eventually, the sight of the rat alone was enough to cause Albert to be afraid. Through a process known as *stimulus generalization*, the child also

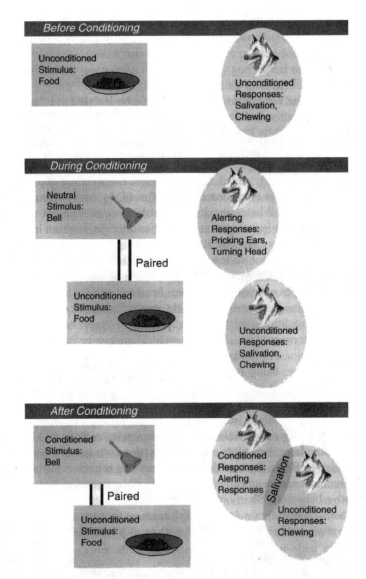

FIGURE 5.3   *Pavlovian Conditioning.* **From *Abnormal Psychology*, by M. T. Nietzel, M. Speltz, E. McCauley, & D. A. Bernstein, 1998, Boston: Allyn & Bacon. Copyright © 1998 by Allyn & Bacon. Reprinted by permission of authors.**

displayed some fear of other white furry objects such as rabbits and stuffed animals. A few years later, another learning-oriented psychologist, Mary Cover Jones (1924), used classical conditioning to reduce childhood fears by pairing feared stimuli with pleasant activities.

Operant Conditioning.   The principles of **operant conditioning** were described in the 1930s by Harvard psychologist B. F. Skinner (1904–1990). Skinner's work built on research by Edward L. Thorndike (1874–1949) who proposed that behavior is learned through the "law of effect" (1905). That law says that behaviors that bring about desirable effects (food, comfort, smiles, etc.) tend to occur again, whereas those that bring about undesirable effects (e.g., pain, loss, and the like) tend not to be repeated. Simply stated, the law of effect reflects the impact of reward and punishment. When behavior is rewarded or reinforced by environmental events that follow it, it becomes stronger. When behavior is punished or at least not rewarded, it is likely to cease. Suppose, for instance, that a child has a temper tantrum in a grocery store after a parent refuses to buy candy for the child. If the parent gives in and buys the candy, the child will be reinforced for having tantrums and is likely to do so again in similar situations.

Skinner (1938) referred to such learning as operant conditioning because behavior has its effects by "operating" on other people and the environment. Skinner emphasized three elements in operant learning: (1) antecedent conditions, the things that precede or trigger behaviors; (2) the behavior itself; and (3) the consequences of the behavior. There can be (and often are) many triggers for a given behavior. For instance, people who smoke find that certain situations prompt them to light up (e.g., being at a bar or party and sitting at the table after dinner). Skinner stressed that to change behavior, one may have to change the antecedent conditions that trigger the behavior. In our example, efforts to quit smoking would be eased by not going to bars or leaving the table immediately after a meal. The rewarding consequences of smoking may be relaxation or stimulation, so the would-be quitter might need to engage in alternative behaviors such as relaxation exercises or a brisk walk, which can bring about the same effects. Operant theory suggests that behaviors learned on the basis of operant reinforcement can be unlearned through a combination of extinction and reinforcement of alternative behaviors. So to stop a child's tantrums, the parent should stop giving in to them, thus discontinuing the reinforcement for tantrums. At the same time, the child should be rewarded (with praise or even with candy) for behaving properly in the grocery store.

The learning-theory-based idea that maladaptive, even criminal, behaviors can be unlearned has been influential in programs of prevention and rehabilitation, especially for children and juvenile offenders whose behavior patterns are still being formed.

Social Learning. Albert Bandura (1969, 1986) stressed the role of cognitive factors in learning. An early cognitive-behavioral theorist, he pointed out that people can learn even if they do not directly experience rewards or punishments. Often, people learn simply by watching other people, called *models,* and vicariously experiencing the consequences of their behavior. This process is known as **social learning**. Bandura noted that these phenomena, called *observational learning* and *vicarious conditioning,* depend heavily on cognitive processes—what people think about what they see and hear. Thus, if a child sees that a parent is afraid of going to the dentist, the child may learn to be afraid of the dentist too. If a coworker is praised for handling a task in a certain way, one may handle such tasks in the same way and expect the same praise.

Another social-learning theorist, Julian Rotter (1954), suggested in his expectancy theory of learning that the probability of a given behavior depends on (a) what the person has learned to expect will happen after the behavior and (b) the value they place on that outcome. Bandura (1977, 1982, 1986) amplified this notion by emphasizing the concept of *self-efficacy,* the idea that what one does and how well or persistently one does it depends on what one has learned to expect about the likelihood of achieving some desired outcome. The greater the self-efficacy, the greater will be the person's motivation and aspirations.

Other cognitive factors in learning have been emphasized by other cognitive-behavioral theorists. For example, *learned helplessness* is the tendency to give up trying to control one's environment after repeatedly experiencing failure to exert such control (Seligman, 1975). Learned helplessness was first demonstrated when dogs were placed in cages where they received electric shocks that they could not control or escape (Seligman & Maier, 1967). Following many experiences with inescapable shock, these dogs did not even try to get away from shocks that were delivered in a different cage where escape was possible. They had learned to be helpless. Research has suggested that the principle of learned helplessness applies to people as well (e.g., Hiroto & Seligman, 1975). When people's experiences lead them to believe that they can do nothing to change their lives, they generally stop trying (Dweck & Licht, 1980; Seligman, 1991).

Learning Theories and Criminal Behavior

Ideally, parental discipline (a combination of reward for good behavior and punishment for transgressions) teaches children to act in accordance with family rules and societal norms. Most children respond to such reward and punishment patterns by inhibiting impulses to do wrong and experience apprehension about punishment whenever they even think of misbehaving. As they come to anticipate and fear physical punishment, an "inner voice" (what Freud called superego and what others have called conscience) tells them what they should and should not do, even when no one is around to administer punishment. If these learning-based mechanisms do not operate normally, as appears to be the case in antisocial personality disorder (APD), for example, fear of punishment—even after observing the fate of punished criminals—would be less likely to inhibit criminal behavior. Eysenck's arousal theory of personality suggests that the operant, classical, and social learning processes that normally inhibit criminal behavior through punishment and conditioned anxiety might fail to operate as strongly in some individuals as they do in others.

The principles of classical conditioning, operant conditioning, and social learning can also help people to understand the role that parents, peers, and other environmental forces play in the development of childhood and adolescent behavior that may be disruptive, deviant, and eventually criminal. For example, some children may learn criminal skills—and that it is acceptable to use them—by watching admired criminal role models, by being rewarded for criminal behavior (crime often does pay, at least in the short run), and by associating excitement and peer acceptance with criminal activity. That children can learn to be aggressive from watching others was first demonstrated by Bandura and his colleagues (Bandura, Ross, & Ross, 1963) in research with an inflatable "Bobo doll" toy. In these experiments, children watched a film in which an adult model hit the doll and then was either punished or rewarded for doing so. When the children had an opportunity to play with the doll themselves, they imitated the aggressive model, especially if the model had been rewarded for aggression. The idea that some criminal behavior may be caused by watching violent television programs is based partly on the principles of observational learning.

In later chapters, we show how learned helplessness and other cognitive factors arising from learning theories help explain criminal behavior, particularly among young people living in poverty-stricken inner cities where gunfire is rampant and gangs control the neighborhood. Feeling helpless to escape their environment, these youngsters may embark on a life of crime as the path of least resistance. Feelings of powerlessness and helplessness are also one of the most common causes of violent crime in prisons (Silberman, 1995).

Cognition and Crime

Recognition by many behaviorists of the importance of cognitive factors in guiding behavior reflects the influence of a broader cognitive approach to psychology (R. W. Robins, Gosling, & Craik, 1999). Cognitive theories of psychology focus on how people take in, mentally represent, and store information; how they perceive and process that information; and how cognitive processes are related to the integrated patterns of behavior they can see. So according to cognitive theories, people learn not only as a result of operant and classical conditioning and observation but also through interpreting information about the world. These interpretations are guided, in turn, by what they attend to, perceive, think about, and remember. Two influential cognitive theories are particularly relevant to the understanding of criminal behavior: Jean Piaget's (1952) theory of cognitive development and the moral development theory of Lawrence Kohlberg (1964, 1976).

Jean Piaget's Theory of Cognitive Development

Jean Piaget was a Swiss scientist who became interested in understanding how children acquire information about themselves and their world. His (1952) theory of cognitive development is built around the concepts of schemas and adaptation. *Schemas* are the basic units of knowledge, the building blocks of intellectual development. A schema can be a mental image, a mental map, or a generalization about objects, events, and experiences that form one's world view. Schemas help people organize experiences and provide frameworks for what to expect in the future.

In infancy, schemas are simple. Consider a rattle, for example. The first thing babies do with a rattle is to put it in their mouths. They soon expand their schema of a rattle as they learn that they can also shake it, wave it, and throw it. The more they do with a rattle, the more their schema of a rattle changes. More complex schemas come later. In a violent inner-city neighborhood in Washington, DC, for example, children as young as 11 have been found carrying handguns to school because doing so is part of their schema of "things to take to school." These children are not surprised when they hear that a friend has been shot, because shootings are part of the schema of "life in my neighborhood."

Piaget noted that schemas change as the result of *adaptation,* or learning through experience, to adjust to the changing demands and conditions of the environment. He said that the process of adaptation involves two related processes: (a) assimilation and (b) accommodation. In *assimilation,* children take in new information and incorporate it into existing schemas. Thus, children learn that they can shake and wave the little doll they have been given just as they could do with the rattle they played with earlier. The schema that worked with one toy also works with another. *Accommodation,* on the other hand, means changing existing schemas on the basis of new information. Thus, a child's schema of toy will have to change when she or he tries to shake and wave a kitten or her or his mom's favorite crystal vase. Piaget believed that children's cognitive development proceeds in four stages: sensorimotor, preoperational, concrete operational, and formal operational.

In the first *sensorimotor* stage, which lasts about two years, the infant's mental activity is confined to sensory functions, such as seeing and hearing, and to motor skills, such as grasping and sucking. At this stage, schemas involve these simple sensory and motor functions. As motor skills develop and voluntary actions replace reflexes, babies elaborate these simple schemas into more complex ones. In the sensorimotor stage, infants can form schemas only of objects and actions that are present, things they can see or hear or touch. They cannot think about absent objects because they cannot act on them; thinking, for infants, is doing. In other words, they are not yet able to form mental representations of absent objects and actions.

It is in the first half of the *preoperational* stage (from about ages 2 to 4) that children begin to understand, create, and use symbols to represent things that are not present; they draw, pretend, and talk. In the second half of the preoperational stage, from about ages 4 to 7, thinking begins to involve intuitive guesses about the world. However, children still cannot distinguish between the seen and the unseen, between the physical and the mental. They tend to believe, for example, that dreams are real events. Thinking at this stage is so dominated by what children can see and touch that they also do not realize that something is the same if its appearance is changed. In one study (DeVries, 1969), for example, preoperational children thought that a cat wearing a dog mask was actually a dog because that's what it looked like. In short, they do not yet have what Piaget called *conservation,* the ability to recognize that important properties of a substance—including its volume, weight, and species—remain constant despite changes in its shape.

In the third, or *concrete operational* stage, about ages 7 to 11, children develop conservation and begin to use logical principles to categorize and count things. Still, they perform their logical operations only on real, concrete objects, not on abstract concepts like justice or freedom. They can reason, but only about what is, not about what is possible. It is in the fourth, or *formal operational,* stage, which appears around age 11, that children can begin to think about abstract concepts as opposed to concrete objects. They can now engage in hypothetical thinking including imagining the consequences of their behavior.

More recent research (e.g., Baillargeon, 1993, 1995; Wynn, 1992) has suggested that children's cognitive development actually occurs faster than Piaget described it. This research has also suggested that children do not move through the stages in linear fashion but in waves (Siegler, 1996) in which more, and then less, and then more advanced ways of thinking appear in the course of development. Nevertheless, once children reach an age where they can think about ideas (for some, this is as young as 6 or 7), they can start to reason and make decisions about what is right and wrong. Piaget's (1932) observations of children led him to suggest that those in the preoperational stage recognize that rules are made by others, whereas at the concrete operational stage, they learn that in some situations, rules can be invented and modified (as in games and in social play). By the time they reach the formal operational stage, youngsters are able to apply accepted rules and laws to particular situations (D. H. Feldman, 1994). Thus, Piaget (1932/1965) said that children learn to obey rules (a concept Piaget called "practical morality") before they understand why rules and laws should apply to them ("theoretical morality").

Lawrence Kohlberg's Theory of Moral Development

Lawrence Kohlberg's (1964) research on cognitive development focused more specifically on moral development. His, too, is a stage theory, and it is based on observations of how—beginning as children and continuing throughout the life span—people make decisions about what is right and wrong. Kohlberg was less concerned with what people's moral decisions are than with the reasons behind those decisions. He argued that there are three stages in the development of moral thinking and decision making: (1) preconventional, (2) conventional, and (3) postconventional.

In the *preconventional* stage, decisions about right and wrong are based on the threat of punishment. For instance, a child may refrain from taking money from mother's purse because if the child is caught, the behavior will be punished. Similarly, an adult may resist the temptation to exceed the speed limit for fear of being caught and fined. In the *conventional* stage, people see certain behaviors as wrong or right depending on whether prevailing conventions, in the form of laws, say they are wrong or right. People in the *postconventional* stage make moral decisions based not just on what customs or laws say but on a set of higher principles about right and justice to which they personally subscribe. In this sense, postconventional moral reasoning is above or beyond laws.

As in the more general case of cognitive development, people may not always move in simple steps from one stage of moral reasoning to the next. They may also show different kinds of reasoning in relation to different moral issues. For example, a teacher we know recently posed two dilemmas to college students in her criminal behavior class. She first asked how many believed that the law should allow doctors to assist terminally ill patients to commit suicide. Two-thirds of the class agreed that it should, although less than a third said that they would assist a loved one's suicide even if the law allowed it. Those who said they would not do so reasoned postconventionally, saying that they had no moral right to help take another's life even if the law would not punish them. The students were then asked if they were in favor of the death penalty, and if, as jurors, they would vote to impose it when the law allowed. More than two-thirds said they believed in the death penalty and would impose it. When these students were asked why they would help take a life in this situation when most of them had just said that they had no moral right to help take another's life, they invoked the law specifically allowing the death penalty and the duty of jurors to uphold the law. So in one situation, the students' moral reasoning was at the conventional level, whereas in the other, it was postconventional.

Kohlberg's model has been criticized by Carol Gilligan (1993), partly because his research participants were male and because Gilligan believed that North American women do not make moral decisions solely on the basis of abstract concepts such as justice and the higher good. Women, Gilligan argued, seek to maintain relationships, use empathy in making moral decisions, and are more caring than men. The difference between men and women in the "caring factor" has been borne out in some studies but not others (Miller & Bersoff, 1992; Rogers 1987). Kohlberg's theory has also been criticized for failing to include forms of moral reasoning that are sometimes seen in cultures outside North America (Shweder & Bourne, 1984). Still, evidence of Kohlberg's stages has been found in enough places around the world that it offers a useful framework for thinking about moral reasoning (Snarey, 1985).

Information-Processing Theories

Many cognitive scientists see human thought and reasoning as involving a multistage system of information processing that is analogous to the operation of a high-speed computer (Dodge, 1986; Siegler, 1996). First, they have said, people encode information about the world that comes to them through their senses. Next, people process that information using their powers of attention, perception, and memory and then decide what to do with the information (e.g., store it or act on it), and, if action is the choice, execute some response (see Figure 5.4).

Cognitive Theories and Criminal Behavior

Cognitive theories have a number of implications for criminal behavior. Consider, for example, the relation between moral reasoning and decisions about obeying laws. The development of moral reasoning does not take place in a vacuum. It depends on what is learned at home, from peers, and from society as a whole. To develop law-abiding tendencies, children need to see patterns of moral behavior in parents and peers that is at least at the conventional stage. Juveniles not grounded in moral values at home can more easily be affected by negative peer models, especially in social situations in which group influence is strong (Denton & Krebs, 1990).

Research on the moral reasoning of juveniles who are and are not criminal offenders has supported the applicability of Kohlberg's theory to an understanding of crime (Arbuthnot, Gordon, & Jurkovic, 1987;

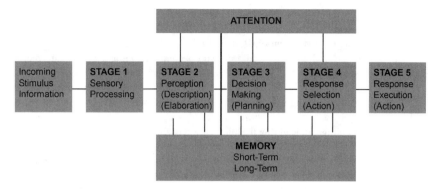

FIGURE 5.4 *Information-Processing Model. The first stage of this general information-processing model occurs without any attention on our part, as information reaches our brains by way of receptors in our eyes, ears, nose, tongue, and skin. In the second stage, we recognize, perceive, and interpret the information. This process requires that we attend to the incoming stimuli. In the third stage, we decide what to do with the information (e.g., store it in memory or act on it). If we decide we need to act, we plan that action in stage 4 and execute the action in stage 5.* From *Psychology* (**4th ed.**), by D. A. Bernstein, A. Clarke-Stewart, E. J. Roy, and C. D. Wickens, 1997, Boston: Houghton Mifflin. Copyright © 1997 by Houghton Mifflin Company. Reprinted with permission.

Jurkovic & Prentice, 1977). Most studies have shown that delinquents are operating at lower stages of moral development than nondelinquents (P. Feldman, 1993). Juveniles who commit crimes ranging from burglary to murder tend to see obedience to laws mainly as a way of avoiding jail, whereas their nondelinquent peers tend to believe that one should obey laws because they prevent chaos in society (Gregg, Gibbs, & Basinger, 1994). Studies of adult criminals have found that they, too, tend to operate at a significantly lower level of moral development than noncriminals from the same background (Henggeler, 1989; Kolhberg, Kufmann, Scharf, & Hickey, 1973). The reasons people do not commit crimes also appear to hinge on the stage of moral development at which they operate. People at the preconventional level are deterred by fear of punishment and fines, people at the conventional level wish to be perceived as law abiding and socially responsible, and people at the postconventional level refrain from crime because they believe that lawfulness is right and benefits society.

Accordingly, people who obey the law only to avoid punishment are more likely to commit crimes than those who view the law as something of value to society. Those at the postconventional stage are more likely to value ideals of honesty, generosity, and nonviolence, all of which are incompatible with criminal behavior (Henggeler, 1989). In addition, people who use postconventional reasoning are more likely to engage in productive behaviors that benefit society (L. J. Siegel, 1998).

There are several ways in which information-processing theories, too, relate to violation of criminal laws. For instance, we have shown that people's cognitive schemas influence how they interpret events, what they expect to happen in the world, how they should react to those events, and what the outcome of their behavior is likely to be. Depending on the nature of these schemas, people may tend to behave in a law abiding or criminal fashion (Dodge, Bates, & Petitt, 1990). For example, if a child's experiences at home include numerous episodes in which family members hit each other (or the child) when they disapprove of some behavior, the child may learn action sequences, or *scripts,* which establish interpersonal aggression as an acceptable way to try to influence another's behavior (Crick & Dodge, 1994). The child may also develop schemas in which hitting is an expected and acceptable response to frustration. Once children are accustomed to being threatened and perhaps physically attacked when they do something to displease a parent, they may learn to expect rejection and attack and may eventually learn to strike first to avoid being a victim. These expectations may also lead the child to interpret a wide range of social cues as threats and to be ready and willing to hit other children following the slightest provocation or no provocation. They may justify their aggression as a self-protective response to other people's aggressive intentions (Blair, 1997; M. K. Rothbart & Ahadi, 1994). According to information-processing theorists, then, many children who become known as "bullies" are merely acting in accordance with their experience-based schemas (Bosworth, Espelage, & Simon, 1999). Unfortunately, those schemas do not result in the restraint that society demands. These children's "preemptive strikes" cause them to be disliked by peers and teachers and usually lead to trouble in the neighborhood, in day care, or at school. If they are old enough, they may be charged with assault.

Faulty information processing can lead to a lifelong pattern of misinterpreting social cues and thus to inappropriate behavior including criminal acts. The schemas of people who are prone to violence may lead them to interpret the actions of others as more aggressive than they really are and thus prompt a "knee-jerk" aggressive response following "miscues" that involve little or no provocation. This reaction is especially likely in people who also have only a limited range of responses—such as aggression or indifference—to the actions and facial expressions of others (Lochman, 1987). So instead of taking time to carefully interpret the meaning of other people's actions, then considering the most appropriate of a range of possible responses, these individuals simply respond with aggression.

Faulty information processing may also help account for the crime of date rape (Lipton, McDonel, & McFall, 1987). Some date rapists claim that the women they raped "did not really mean it" when they said they did not want to have sex. Indeed, these men often say that their actions were based on one or more of the following schema-driven interpretations of a sexual situation (Sculley & Marolla, 1984): (1) the woman seduced them; (2) the woman meant "yes" even though she said "no"; (3) most women eventually enjoy forced sex; and (4) the victim's reputation or behavior—an unwed mother or a hitchhiker, for instance—made forced sex acceptable (it is sometimes claimed that "nice girls don't get raped"). These faulty schemas, which serve to promote sexual violence against women, have their roots in societal attitudes (Janoff-Bulman, Timko, & Carli, 1985), which prior to the advent of the feminist movement were generally accepted. In some circles, they still are (Littleton & Axsom, 2003).

In short, cognitive theories suggest that how people take in, process, and decide what to do with information is critical to acting in a law-abiding manner. Among individuals who are primed to disobey the law, faulty processing at one or more of the information-processing stages shown in Figure 5.4 can trigger criminal behavior.

Personality Disorders and Crime

To illustrate how various psychological theories have been applied to criminal behavior, we consider what they have to say about the development of antisocial personality disorder (APD), also sometimes called *criminal psychopathy* or the criminal personality.

The Nature of Personality Disorders

Personality disorders are consistent, lifelong patterns of thinking and acting that deviate substantially from cultural expectations and include actions that cause personal distress and/or discomfort for others and/or problems in interpersonal relationships. Personality disorders tend to first appear in late childhood and early adolescence as problematic behavior patterns, especially those involving interpersonal relationships, and to become fixed and inflexible by early adulthood. Individuals displaying personality disorders tend to repeat their habitual behavior patterns in spite of the fact that they bring consistently negative results. In many cases, these individuals are the last to see that they have a problem. In fact, most of them think that whatever problems they do have are caused by other people, not their own characteristics, and few of them see any need for treatment. Indeed, these individuals often suffer far less discomfort than do those who must live and work around them. The *Diagnostic and Statistical Manual of Mental Disorders* (4th ed., Text Revision [*DSM–IV–TR*]; American Psychiatric Association, 2000a) of the American Psychiatric Association arranges

TABLE 5.2   *Categories of Personality Disorders*

Cluster A *Odd/Eccentric*	*Cluster B* *Dramatic/Emotional/Erratic*	*Cluster C* *Anxious/Fearful*
Paranoid	Histrionic	Avoidant
Schizoid	Narcissistic	Dependent
Schizotypal	Borderline	Obsessive/Compulsive

Source: Based on information from American Psychiatric Association. (2000). *Diagnostic and Statistical Manual of Mental Disorders*. (4th ed., text revision). Washington, DC: Author.

personality disorders in three clusters that emphasize their most prominent traits or attributes: (a) odd/eccentric, (b) dramatic/ emotional/erratic, and (c) anxious/fearful (see Table 5.2).

The *anxious/fearful* cluster of personality disorders is not usually associated with criminal behavior; it includes avoidant personality disorder (characterized by anxiety and fearfulness in social situations and feelings of ineptitude and inadequacy), dependent personality disorder (featuring inability to make independent decisions, fear of being alone, and clinging to others), and obsessive–compulsive personality disorder (which involves overconscientiousness, inhibition, perfectionism, and preoccupation with control).

The *odd/eccentric* cluster includes paranoid, schizoid, and schizotypal personality disorders (see Table 5.3). People suffering from these disorders sometimes experience hallucinations (hearing or seeing nonexistent things) or delusions (false beliefs). If they do and if these misperceptions and misinterpretations lead them to feel threatened, they may engage in criminal behavior. For instance, people displaying paranoid personality disorder are suspicious, hostile, and prone to intense anger and jealousy. They may misinterpret a stranger at the door, an innocent action, or offhand remarks as threats or insults directed at them, and this misinterpretation might lead to a decision to act aggressively to prevent what is perceived as impending injury or death.

The *dramatic/emotional/erratic* cluster includes borderline, histrionic, narcissistic, and antisocial personality disorders. The last two of these are the personality disorders mostly closely linked to criminal behavior. The main feature of narcissistic personality disorder is inflated self-esteem and little or no empathy for others. Narcissists believe that they are entitled to special privileges and that they should not be bound by normal social constraints. The hallmarks of antisocial personality disorder (APD) are reckless disregard for the rights of others, callousness, lack of empathy for and manipulation of others, dishonesty, and lack of concern over wrongdoing. These characteristics are tailor made to support criminal behavior, so it is no wonder that theorists who seek the psychological roots of crime have focused their attention on APD.

Antisocial Personality Disorder

What the *DSM–IV–TR* (American Psychiatric Association, 2000a) refers to as **antisocial personality disorder** was first described 200 years ago by Phillipe Pinel (1801) in a group of patients who behaved in impulsive and self-destructive ways without any evidence of thought disorder or psychosis. He labeled their condition as *manie sans délire* (insanity without delirium). American physician Benjamin Rush (1812) characterized those with this disorder as morally reprehensible, and J. C. Prichard (1845) described them as suffering from *moral insanity*—a gross disturbance in social behavior without any impairment in mental functioning (Livesley, Schroeder, Jackson, & Jang, 1994). This label was meant to denote the fact that although these people are not legally insane, their lack of self-control and their propensity to harm others constitutes the moral equivalent of insanity. Later, Koch (1891) referred to these individuals as *psychopaths*. J. L. Koch and other German psychiatrists believed that there is a clear difference between mental disorders that are the result of a disease and those that are linked to disordered personality. They believed that personality disorders have a biological basis. Emile Kraepelin (1903–1904) suggested that psychopathy is both biologically and genetically based and also characterized by moral inferiority. Karl Birnbaum (1914) described these people as

TABLE 5.3   *The Odd/Eccentric Cluster of Personality Disorders*

DSM-IV Category	Primary Characteristics
Paranoid	Suspicious, hostile, aloof, controlling, rigid
Schizoid	Lack of emotional expression, poor social skills, few friendships
Schizotypal	Odd mannerisms, paranoia, problems with relating to others

Source: Based on information from American Psychiatric Association. (2000). *Diagnostic and Statistical Manual of Mental Disorders.* (4th ed., text revision). Washington, DC: Author.

sociopaths because he believed that their disorder is the product of social learning and deficient family environments.

In his 1941 book titled *The Mask of Sanity,* psychiatrist Hervey Cleckley described psychopathic personalities as being superficially charming and intelligent, unreliable, insincere, untruthful, unable to learn from experience, incapable of feeling guilt or remorse for misdeeds, and unable to feel genuine love for anyone. Few experience normal sexual relationships, and indeed, they virtually never have enduring relationships with anyone. Still, these people may be successful in business and amass great power and influence.

In his Psychopathy Checklist, Revised (PCL-R), Robert Hare (1980) sought to capture the behavioral characteristics seen in **psychopathy** including glibness/superficial charm; a grandiose sense of self-worth; need for stimulation and proneness to boredom; pathological lying; a conning/manipulative style; lack of remorse or guilt; shallow affect; callousness and lack of empathy; a parasitic lifestyle; poor behavioral control; sexual promiscuity and numerous short-term marriages; early behavior problems and juvenile delinquency; lack of realistic, long-term goals; impulsivity; irresponsibility; failure to accept responsibility for actions; violation of parole or probation (if convicted of crimes); and criminal versatility.

The terms *psychopathy* and *antisocial personality disorder* are often used interchangeably, as we do here, but some researchers view them as being somewhat different. The main distinction between the two terms is that criminal behavior is more common, and more serious, among those labeled as psychopaths than among those displaying antisocial personality. In the *DSM–IV–TR* (American Psychiatric Association, 2000a), though, APD is the main label for people who are chronically callous and manipulative, ignore laws and social customs, disregard the rights and feelings of others, behave dishonestly and impulsively, fail to learn from punishment, and lack remorse or guilt over crimes or hurting others. The most notorious of violent criminals fit both the *DSM–IV–TR* criteria for APD and Hare's criteria for psychopathy.

The prevalence of antisocial personality in the general population is estimated to be about 8% of men and 3% of women (American Psychiatric Association, 2000a; Barry, Fleming, & Maxwell, 1997).

Psychological Theories of Antisocial Personality Disorder

The causes of APD have been researched more than those of any other personality disorder (e.g., Andrews & Bonta, 1994). Psychodynamic, learning, and cognitive theories have all sought to offer insight into the mental processes that influence its development.

The psychodynamic theories include those of Freud, the neo-Freudians such as Erikson, and the object relations theorists. Freudian theorists believe that antisocial personality is the product of failure to proceed successfully through the five stages of psychosexual development. Freudians say that antisocial personalities are fixated at one stage or the other, mainly because id, ego, and superego have not reached a functional balance (Barak, 1998). Typically, the antisocial personality can be characterized by an inappropriately strong id.

Post-Freudian theories focus on the role of the family in the development of APD. Object relations theorists, for example, have emphasized that when children are 2 to 3 years old, they must achieve a secure attachment with a caregiver to develop self-esteem. Without self-esteem, these theorists have said, there will be no respect or empathy for others, a pattern that is common in individuals with APD. Indeed, as we discuss in chapters 7 and 8, many of these people failed to achieve a secure attachment and were raised by cold, dismissive parents (Buss, 1966; W. McCord & McCord, 1964; Oltman & Friedman, 1967).

More influential explanations of APD have come from theories that emphasize learning, social learning, and information processing. Cognitive theorists believe, for example, that faulty information processing, possibly caused by neuropsychological deficits, may be at the root of APD (Helfgott, 1997; af Klinteberg, 1996). Social learning theorists (Loeber, 1991; Loeber & Hay, 1997) have been more concerned with several specific family factors that appear to lead to antisocial personality. These factors include

1. A history of parental criminality (Loeber & Dishion, 1983). Parental criminality provides a role model for antisocial conduct and may also disrupt family life.
2. Chronic parental uninvolvement, erratic discipline, physical abuse, and poor supervision of children (Patterson, 1986). Any of these factors can make it more difficult for a child to learn the rules of society and be committed to obeying those rules. In addition, abusive relationships teach children that physical violence is an acceptable means of influencing others. One study (Weiler & Widom, 1996) of more than 1,100 young adults who were abused and neglected as children found a significant positive correlation between serious childhood abuse and the diagnosis of APD.
3. Exposure to deviant peers (Elliott, Huizinga, & Ageton, 1985b). Children who become habitually antisocial often learn some of this conduct from peers who model antisocial behavior and reinforce it by granting highest status to the most antisocial members in the group.

Terrie Moffit (1993) integrated numerous perspectives into a theory of "life-course-persistent offenders." She (1993) described them as a small group of people who engage in antisocial behavior of one sort or another at every stage of their lives: for instance, biting and hitting at 4, shoplifting and truancy at 10, drug dealing and car theft at 16, robbery and rape at 22, and fraud and child abuse at 30. Moffit believed that these behaviors begin with early neuropsychological problems caused by factors such as maternal drug and alcohol use or poor prenatal nutrition, birth complications resulting in brain damage, and deprivation of affection and abuse and neglect after birth. These biological and emotional factors, she said, are the foundation for the development of an impulsive personality style and poor self-control. These children's parents tend to have psychological deficiencies themselves and are often drug or alcohol abusers. They cannot discipline themselves, let alone their children; and if indeed they are present to raised the children, their faulty parenting tends to intensify the children's behavior problems. Those behavior problems lead to school failure, and school failure leads to early alcohol use, truancy, dropout, and crime (Moffitt, 1993).[1] Other researchers have reached similar conclusions (Caspi et al., 1994; Nagan & Land, 1993; Widom, 2000). In short, it appears that once children start down the developmental pathway leading to APD, the chances are great that they will develop into a lifetime offender (Loeber & Stouthamer-Loeber, 1998; Widom, 2000; see Figure 5.5).

This is hardly an optimistic assessment, but it shows how the application of psychological theories can help one to understand the constellation of factors that influence early development, to appreciate the gravity of the task of raising children well—especially in the critically important early years—and to devise better educational, intervention, and prevention strategies capable of combating the development of criminal behavior.

In the next chapter, we consider how families, schools, neighborhoods, socioeconomic class, and culture can sometimes provide fertile soil for the development of crime, especially when its psychological roots have already taken hold in the individual.

Summary

The psychological roots of criminal behavior lie in the mental processes and forces that arise in the course of the personality development and the person's interaction with others. Psychological development begins with the shaping of one's personality, the unique patterns of thinking, feeling, and behaving that develop early on and remain relatively constant throughout one's life. Personality development is a complex interaction of bio-

---

[1]More recently, Moffitt (2001) conducted research into gender differences in the development of criminal behavior, a topic we explore in chapter 8.

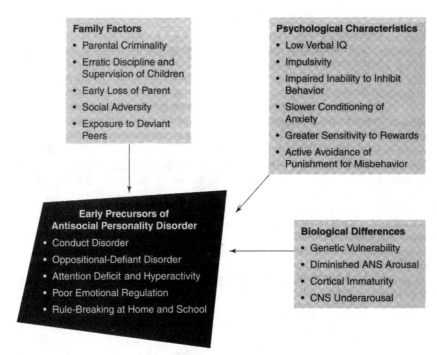

FIGURE 5.5 *Early Precursors of Antisocial Personality Disorder.* **From *Abnormal Psychology*, by M. T. Nietzel, M. Speltz, E. McCauley, & D. A. Bernstein, 1998, Boston: Allyn & Bacon. Copyright © 1998 by Allyn & Bacon. Reprinted by permission of authors.**

logical and environmental factors. Certain personality traits, for instance, extroversion, impulsiveness, and aggressiveness, are more associated with criminal behavior than are others.

The psychodynamic theories of Freud, Erikson, Sullivan, and the object relations theories explain crime and violence as the result of interpsychic forces. Freud's approach was more biological, whereas Erikson's and Sullivan's emphasized social interactions more. The object relations theories of Klein, Kohut, and Mahler, have focused on maladaptive relationships with caregivers as setting the stage for maladaptive behavior.

The learning theories of Skinner and Bandura are helpful in explaining how aggression and violence are acquired through rewards, reinforcement, and the modeling of others. Combinations of poor parenting in which children do not learn to behavior in law-abiding ways and observing aggression and violence in others may lead to criminal offending.

Piaget and Kohlberg have helped explain criminal behavior from a cognitive perspective. Piaget has helped us understand how people learn to think and reason generally through the development of cognitive schemas, whereas Kohlberg was concerned with how children and adults engage in moral reasoning and decision making. Other information-processing theorists such as Dodge and Siegler have examined how the development of schemas of behavior and decision making may lead to aggression and other types of criminal offending.

Sometimes personalities develop maladaptively, in which case the person may be said to have a personality disorder. The personality disorder most associated with criminal behavior is the antisocial personality disorder. Hare studied features of APD that may be associated with criminality and developed an assessment instrument, the PCL–R, which may predict a person's predisposition for criminal offending.

Moffitt integrated several psychological theories with biological factors to explain the life course of persistent criminal offenders. Her pioneering work has led others to explore the process of how a criminal is made; collectively, their findings have been useful in helping to fashion preventive and rehabilitative programs for juvenile and adult offenders.

Key Terms

Personality	*Object relations*
Temperament	*Behaviorism*
Id	*Learning*
Ego	*Classical conditioning*
Superego	*Operant conditioning*
Defense mechanisms	*Social learning*
Psychosexual stages	*Personality disorders*
Psychodynamic theory of crime	*Antisocial personality disorder*
Psychosocial development	*Psychopathy*

Questions for Review

1. How do some personality traits set the stage for crime?
2. How do you explain crime from the standpoints of the various psychodynamic theories?
3. What learning theories are most useful in explaining criminal behavior?
4. What cognitive and information-processing functions influence crime and violence?
5. What is antisocial personality disorder and how can it help explain the development of crime and violence according to the life-course model of offending?

 ## Track It Down

Criminal Behavior Website
www.cassel2e.com
Hans Eysenck
http://freespace.virgin.net/darrin.evans/
Sigmund Freud
http://www.iep.utm.edu/f/freud.htm
Erik Erikson
http://elvers.stjoe.udayton.edu/history/people/Erikson.html
B.F. Skinner
http://www.bfskinner.org/Operant.asp
Albert Bandura's Bobo doll experiment
http://psychclassics.yorku.ca/Bandura/bobo.htm
Jean Piaget
http://www.time.com/time/time100/scientist/profile/piaget.html
Lawrence Kohlberg
http://faculty.plts.edu/gpence/html/kohlberg.htm
Robert Hare
http://www.hare.org/

6

Social and Environmental Roots of Crime

Social Origins of Human Aggression and Violence
Social Cognition, Social Behavior, and Crime

The Environmental Roots of Crime
The Ecology of Crime

In chapter 3, we described a string of shootings by schoolchildren that, together, claimed the lives of 50 people. The worst of these horrific incidents was the one in Littleton, Colorado, when 18-year-old Eric Harris and 17-year-old Dylan Klebold used a variety of weapons to kill 12 of their classmates and a teacher before committing suicide. These troubled and rejected young men left behind more than 50 explosive devices apparently designed to destroy their school. They also left a nation asking itself once again what could be done about youthful killers and why so many young people are consumed with hatred and violent aggressiveness. More than any previous school violence incident, the tragedy at Littleton focused public attention on the need to do something to curtail the culture of violence in America, especially as reflected in easy access to guns and in the images of violence increasingly saturating television, movies, music, video games, and Internet Web sites. In short, Americans began to consider more carefully than ever the social and environmental roots of crime.

In this chapter, we examine the social and environmental forces that contribute to criminal behavior in people young and old—especially the impact of other people, living conditions, and cultural values. Understanding how these factors contribute to crime is critical in any effort to understand criminal behavior. Social factors are important not only because of the inherently social nature of the human species but because crime is itself a social—or, more properly, an antisocial—act. With few exceptions, crimes have victims. Sometimes, those victims are chosen at random, but more often, they are chosen for a reason, often because—as in the case of the minority students and athletes targeted by the Littleton killers—they are members of a particular group.

Groups are the basic unit of social interaction; they consist of two or more people who join together for a common purpose. All people belong to several groups. Some of them are formally recognized as in national citizenship, membership in political and religious organizations, or relationship to a family. Others are less formal as in peer groups or associations of people who share an interest in sports or books, for example. Still other, more general, groupings are based on demographic factors such as gender, ethnicity, regional background, or socioeconomic status.

The groups with which people are affiliated influence their behavior, and therein lies one of the roots of crime. Consider what the following violent and/or criminal events have in common: abuse of Iraqi prisoners at the Abu Ghraib prison, the massacre at the Vietnamese village of My Lai, the Holocaust, conflicts between Protestants and Catholics in Northern Ireland and between Arabs and Jews in the Middle East, lynchings by the Ku Klux Klan, standoffs between militant groups and government authorities at Waco and Ruby Ridge, the sexual harassment of female cadets at the U.S. Air Force Academy, assassinations of rival gang leaders, police brutality toward ethnic minority suspects, and terrorist acts by extremist Islamic groups.

In each case, the violence and/or crime is related to differences in group affiliations, and at the heart of each incident lies racism, elitism, or prejudice based on political, religious, or other differences between groups. Some of these crimes are perpetrated by groups and institutions cloaked in political and religious legitimacy. Others involve action by renegade groups, gangs, or cults. In almost all of these cases, the targets of violence are persons outside the group, and the violence is motivated by some combination of hatred, greed, and the need for power. However, criminals do not necessarily limit their attacks to those outside their group or sphere of influence. Indeed, the desire to dominate other people is a basic feature of human existence. As Merssault, the main character in Albert Camus's novel, *The Fall* (1956), put it, "We can't do without dominating others. ... Even the man on the bottom rung still has his wife, or his child. If he's a bachelor, his dog."

In examining the social roots of crime, we rely on theory and research in sociology and social and environmental psychology for clues to how criminal behavior is influenced by groups, institutions, cultural agents, and social and physical conditions. **Social psychology** is the branch of psychology that studies how people, and groups of people, influence the behavior of others. **Environmental psychology** studies the mutual impact of human behavior and the natural and built environment (e.g., climate, architectural space, and lighting). **Sociology** studies many kinds of groups—from the nuclear family to social, political, and religious institutions—and examines the relationships between individual behavior and membership in these groups. Sociologists typically hold individuals accountable for crime, but they tend to see criminal behavior as rooted in social institutions, not individuals. Accordingly, they suggest that effective solutions to the problems of crime must begin with changes in the structure, values, and functioning of society's most basic institutions—including the family and the legal, political, and educational systems.[1]

We begin our exploration of the social roots of crime with an examination of the social causes of aggression and violence, which are at the heart of what most people think of when they think of crime.

Social Origins of Human Aggression and Violence

All things considered, humans appear to be the most cruel and ruthless species that ever walked the earth (Storr, 1970). Yet research does not support Freud's theory that human aggressive tendencies are innate. The American Psychological Association and other international groups of psychologists issued a statement in 1991 rejecting the notion that violent aggression and war are genetically programmed or instinctual (Adams, 1991). If this conclusion is correct, where does human aggression come from?

There is strong evidence that people learn to be aggressive through their interactions and experiences with other people. Aggression in the service of certain goals is part of Western culture and central to the highly competitive culture of the United States where Vince Lombardi's famous motto is widely accepted: "Winning isn't everything, it's the only thing." Children in the United States are commonly taught to reach for the stars and never give up, and many learn that sometimes they may have to step on or run over others in the process.

Social Learning and Crime

As we noted in chapter 5, social learning theories have been invoked to explain how people learn aggressiveness of both the instrumental (goal oriented) and destructive, hostile (crime related) varieties. Albert Bandura (1969, 1986), was one of the first cognitive-behavioral theorists to have stressed that people can learn new behaviors and when to display or inhibit them without directly experiencing reward or punishment for engaging in those behaviors. Bandura (1969, 1986) went beyond classical and operant conditioning theories of learning to note that people often learn simply by watching what others do and what happens to them as a

---

[1]A detailed discussion of sociological theories of crime is beyond the scope of this book; for a comprehensive introduction, see Siegel, 2003.

result. Observational learning can be especially strong when the models people observe are those whom they admire and thus wish to emulate.

The idea that the violence portrayed in the mass media helps to cause violence and crime is based on the principles of observational learning (see the Bobo doll experiments we described in chapter 5). There are clearly correlations between exposure to media violence and real-life violence—for example, between violence-saturated prime time television in the United States and a per capita rate of violent crime that is the highest of any civilized nation. Do these correlations represent causal relations between media violence and criminal behavior?

Televised Violence. "Did TV make him do it?" This was the title of a story in the October 17, 1996 issue of *Time* magazine describing the murder of an elderly woman by Robert Zamora, her 15-year-old next door neighbor. Zamora's defense attorney argued that Robert was addicted to television violence and had learned to kill by watching it. In fact, his crime closely resembled a television episode he had seen shortly before the murder. The attorney also argued that Robert's viewing of a Dracula movie the night before the murder further "primed" him for violence. The defense claimed that Robert had watched so much television—as much as 6 hours a day—that he should be found not guilty by reason of insanity. The jury's decision to reject this defense and convict Robert of murder is in accord with the results of research on the effects of media violence on children and adults. Those results have shown that media violence, and television violence in particular, can contribute to violent behavior in some people but that for most people, its main effect is to make them less sensitive to seeing violence and the suffering it causes.

The role of media violence in causing, or at least triggering, violent crime is clearest in the case of "copycat" crimes in which people imitate what they see in a movie or on television. For example, in November of 1995 in New York City, thieves set on fire a subway token booth, seriously injuring the clerk inside. This callous act was almost identical to one in a film called *Money Train*, which the thieves had watched a few days before (*Boston Globe*, November 28, 1995). Nearly 2 years later, a 21-year-old man was arrested on charges of shooting to death a man at a high school running track (*Boston Globe*, August 15, 1997). The suspect confessed and said that this random killing had been aimed at emulating the hero of his favorite movie, *Natural Born Killers* (Oliver Stone, director, 1994). More recently, several murders have been committed by people who claim to have been trying to escape *The Matrix* (Andy Wachowski, director, 1999) as portrayed in a movie by the same name (Jackman, 2003). Also, when dramatic crimes are publicized—such as the case of contaminated Tylenol in the 1980s—several instances of similar crimes typically follow. It is not unreasonable to assume that mentally unstable individuals might be motivated to replicate a heinous act portrayed in a movie or that watching crime shows on television might give criminals new ideas. In fact, a 1977 *TV Guide* survey of 208 prison inmates found 90% of them reporting that they learned new criminal tricks by watching crime programs; 40% said they had later imitated the specific crimes they saw on television (Seppa, 1977).

Does watching television violence have similar effects on children? It is estimated that children and young people in the United States spend, on average, about two and one-half hours a day watching television (Woodard & Gridina, 2000), and much of what they see is violent (Gerbner, Gross, Morgan, & Signorielli, 1980; Potter et al., 1995; Signorielli, 1990). The National Television Violence Survey (B. J. Wilson et al., 1997), which examined the amount and content of violence on American television for three consecutive years, found that:

1. A total of 61% of television programs contain some violence.
2. A total of 44% of violent interactions on television involve perpetrators who display some engaging, attractive qualities.
3. A total of 43% of violent scenes involve humor either directed at the violence or used by characters involved in violence.
4. Nearly 75% of violent scenes on television feature no immediate punishment for, or condemnation of, violence.
5. Of all violent behavioral interactions on television, 58% depict no pain, 47% depict no harm, and 40% depict harm unrealistically.

As a result, the average child witnesses at least 8,000 murders and more than 100,000 other acts of televised violence before finishing elementary school and twice that number by age 18 (Annenberg Public Policy Center, 2000). Of course, media violence is not limited to entertainment programs. Television news also floods our homes with graphic images of violence and crime (van der Molen, 2004), which can have their own effects on some people. As with other spectacular crimes, the massively publicized Littleton, Colorado, school massacre was followed by arrests of students elsewhere in the United States and Canada for allegedly planning, attempting, or committing a similar crime.

Does watching violent television actually make children and young people violent? If so, how? Anecdotal evidence from teachers and parents has suggested that some children do become more aggressive after watching violent television. Parents, teachers, psychologists, and child advocacy media groups are especially concerned about programs such as *The Jerry Springer Show* that are popular with children, but feature adults reacting with physical aggression against those who offend them (Glod, 1998).[2]

It was once hypothesized that media violence was beneficial because watching provided catharsis, a release—through fantasy—of pent-up tendencies toward violent behavior. This idea can be traced to Aristotle (384–322 BC) who argued that people could release negative emotions by experiencing them in the course of viewing tragic plays (Butcher, 1951). Research has not supported the notion that watching violence deters violent actions, however. For example, one study (Phillips, 1986) in the United States found that homicides increase in the days following widely viewed televised championship prizefights, and that the more violent the fight, the greater the increase in homicides. There is also evidence that some people become more hostile after watching football, wrestling, or hockey games (Arms et al., 1979; Russell, 1983). A more recent evaluation (Bushman, Baumeister, & Stack, 1999) of the catharsis theory found that compared to a control group, people who were allowed to "vent" anger through physical aggression—in this case, hitting a punching bag—later displayed more anger and aggression during face-to-face contact with the person who had upset them.

Psychologists cannot ethically conduct experiments in which large numbers of children and adults are randomly assigned to watch excessive versus minimal amounts of violence for long periods to determine whether exposure to excessive violence causes violent behavior in the viewers. However, researchers have conducted extensive studies of the correlation between viewing violence and being violent (C. A. Anderson, Berkowitz, et al., 2003). One meta-analysis (Pail & Comstock, 1994) of 217 empirical studies on media violence and aggressive and violent behavior published between 1957 and 1990 indicates that brief exposure to violence in television and in films is associated with short-term increases in the aggressive behaviors of youths, including physically aggressive behavior.

Many correlational studies have been criticized because their data on childhood TV viewing habits came from parental reports, not from objective observations or self-reports by the children. Further, the association between watching televised aggression and engaging in aggressive behavior might be the result of factors other than television such as a biological predisposition toward violence, the effects of parental discipline and other child-rearing practices, and the influence of peers (Freedman, 2002). This latter concern remains even when measures of TV viewing and aggression are more objective. In one study (Singer & Singer, 1983), for example, the shows watched by preschool children were logged over 2-week periods several times a year for four years. At the same time, their play activity was monitored by observers who did not know anything about the children's viewing habits. The results indicated that aggression during play occurred more often in the children who watched more violent television. However, many of these children were subjected to harsh discipline and physical punishment, and this factor could have contributed to their aggressiveness.)

Experimental studies of institutionalized delinquent boys in the United States (Parke et al., 1977) and Belgium (Leyens et al., 1975) have yielded evidence that watching violent movies resulted in increased physical attacks. However, critics point out that it is unrealistic, and thus potentially misleading, to use research methods in which people watch aggressive films and are then immediately observed for signs of aggression.

Other studies have tried to assess the causal role of televised violence in aggression by taking advantage of "natural experiments" in which participants are not randomly chosen and assigned to experimental conditions

---

[2]This show often sets up angry confrontations—between women and their unfaithful partners, for example—and encourages the warring parties to "duke it out" in front of the cameras.

but are measured while engaging in what, for them, is normal television watching. These studies have tended to support earlier correlational results. For example, the initial introduction of television into a community has been followed by increased rates of violence, including homicide, in South Africa and playground violence in a Canadian town (Centerwall, 1989).

How might viewing violence contribute to violent behavior? For one thing, a steady diet of television violence may desensitize viewers and lead them to accept violent aggression as a normal part of modern life (Aronson, 2004). This desensitizing effect is supported by results of an experiment in which children watched either a violent police drama or a nonviolent show and then were observed responding to an aggressive encounter between other children. Those who had watched the police show responded less emotionally to the aggressive encounter than did children who had seen a nonviolent show (Thomas et al., 1977). Other studies have found that people accustomed to heavy doses of television violence display less physiological arousal when viewing such violence than those who are not as used to seeing it (American Psychological Association, 1993; Mueller, Donnerstein, & Hallam, 1983; Zillman, 1989).

Another explanation for how exposure to television violence might lead to aggressive behavior stems from the general affective aggression model (GAAM) proposed by C. A. Anderson and Dill (2000). In this model, aggression is seen as largely derived from observational learning and other social learning processes (e.g., Bandura, 1986). Through these processes, some people develop cognitive scripts and schemas that lead them to interpret social situations in threatening ways and to see aggression and violence as legitimate, even primary, responses to threat (e.g., C. A. Anderson, Anderson, & Deuser, 1996; see chapter 5). In the GAAM, exposure to violent television appears as an individual difference variable. It is a source of social information that can create more positive attitudes toward violence, hone viewers' aggression skills, and help to legitimize violent responses to threats. People with certain personality traits (such as hostility) are seen as especially likely to be influenced by this information and especially when emotionally aroused and threatened, to choose aggressive response alternatives (see Figure 6.1).

Taken together, research has suggested that the significant correlation between watching media violence and aggressive behavior might reflect a causal relation but mainly for aggressive children who watch a larger-than-average amount of violent television for children their age (American Psychological Association, 1993; J. Q. Wilson & Herrnstein, 1985). In other words, watching violence appears to trigger aggression mainly in youngsters who were already known to be aggressive (Josephson, 1987); further, the most aggressive children appear to be the ones most likely to watch violent television (American Psychological Association, 1993; Eron, 1982; Seppa, 1997). For less aggressive children, watching violent television appears to contribute to fear of becoming a victim of violence (American Psychological Association, 1993).

So the strongest effect of media violence appears to be on those who are otherwise predisposed to aggression and violence and those unstable enough to engage in copycat crimes. The effects on children can be especially significant if their parents do not counteract the influence of violent content by refraining from the use of physical punishment and by conveying the message that aggression and violence are not acceptable forms of social behavior (Signorelli, 1990; Singer & Singer, 1980). Such positive parental influences and other mediating factors appear responsible for the fact that millions of children (and adults) watch many hours of violence-filled television each day but do not themselves engage in aggressive, violent, or criminal behavior.

Violent Video Games and Internet Content.   As the "television of tomorrow," the Internet's effects on many aspects of behavior, including violence, deserve careful attention. One study (Kraut et al., 1998) concluded that the amount of time people spent on the Internet was positively correlated with increased levels of social isolation and depression, factors that are sometimes related to antisocial behavior. Following the Littleton, Colorado, school tragedy, it was suggested that killers Harris and Klebold had found a "recipe" for explosives online. They were also known to have enjoyed playing Doom, a violent video game used by the U.S. military to train soldiers in effective killing methods. Harris created a Web site with a customized version of the game in which two shooters were equipped with unlimited ammunition. As a class project, Harris and Klebold even videotaped themselves acting out a Doom scenario that was eerily similar to their later, real-life, massacre.

However, understanding the potential of violent video games and violence-oriented Internet content for directly causing aggression and violence will require much more research. That research has only recently

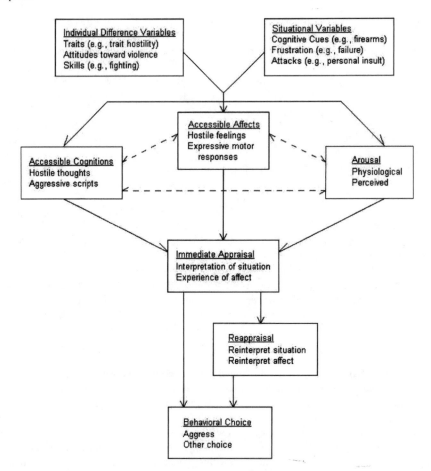

FIGURE 6.1 *General Affective Aggression Model (GAMM).* **From "Examining an Affective Aggression Framework: Weapon and Temperature Effects on Aggressive Thoughts, Affect, and Attitudes," by C. A. Anderson, K. B. Anderson, and W. E. Deuser, 1996,** *Personality and Social Psychology Bulletin, 2.* **Reprinted with permission of Sage Publications.**

gotten underway. In one experiment, for example, C. A. Anderson and Dill (2000) showed that college students who played a violent video game later behaved more aggressively toward an opponent in a subsequent game and some also engaged in more aggressive behavior. Using the GAAM as their guide, Anderson and Dill suggested that the short-term effects of playing a violent video game are to make aggressive thoughts more likely. The longer term effects of continued exposure to these games, they said, are to generate and solidify aggression-triggering cognitive scripts that become more and more likely to govern actions in real-life conflict situations.

Is the violence in video games more potentially harmful than the violent content of television and movies? Anderson and Dill (2000) thought so, for three reasons: (1) the interactive nature of video-game playing promotes an especially close identification with the aggressor; (2) in this interactive context, players are reinforced for choosing aggressive behavior, thus further supporting the adoption of aggressive cognitive habits (schemas and scripts); and (3) the realism and intensity of video games can make them virtually addictive. Given these concerns and the fact that there appears to be no limit to the popularity, graphic violence, and realism of these games, Anderson and Dill and others are seeking to warn players of violent video games (and their parents) of the potential risks involved.

Violent Lyrics. To many people, another aspect of today's culture of violence lies in popular music lyrics that depict, glorify, or encourage aggressive and violent behavior. Critics consider this music as potentially dangerous as televised violence, whereas its defenders argue that violent lyrics are no more than expressions of youthful alienation and parodies of mainstream culture and politics. Like slapstick comedy or blood-drenched fiction, they say, these lyrics are not intended to be taken as instructions about how to behave (Hunter, 1999). The question, of course, is whether, regardless of intent, the music of performers such as Marilyn Manson can cause violent behavior. Research by C. A. Anderson and his colleagues (e.g., C. A. Anderson, Carnagey, & Eubanks, 2003) suggested that listening to rock music lyrics that promote violence tends to arouse feelings of hostility and thoughts of aggression; listening to nonviolent rock music tends not to have these effects. In line with the GAAM, the researchers concluded that, as in the case of violent television or violent video games, lyric-inspired increases in aggressive thoughts and feelings can make people more likely to perceive threat in social interactions and lead them toward more aggressive responses in those situations.

Whether violent television, video games, internet sites, and music lyrics all pose unique and imminent danger for causing violent behavior, there is no question that they have added new elements to the social forces operating to trigger violent behavior, especially in the most disturbed, unstable, and aggressive people who are exposed to them. Still, it is important to keep in mind that young people were committing mass murders and other violent crimes long before the advent of Marilyn Manson, Doom, the Internet, or even televised violence. In 1951, 17-year-old Kenneth Skinner set fire to an apartment building in San Francisco, killing 8 people, none of whom he knew. In 1958, 19-year-old Charles Starkweather and 14-year-old Caril Fugate went on a week long shooting, stabbing, and strangling spree in which 11 people in Nebraska and Wyoming lost their lives. In July, 1966, 24 year-old Charles Whitman shot and killed 16 people from atop the clock tower at the University of Texas in Austin. Four months later, 18-year-old Robert Benjamin Smith took seven people hostage in a beauty salon in Mesa, Arizona, and killed five of them, including a 3-year-old girl (Lovinger, 1999). In short, the role of media violence in violent behavior is probably neither simple nor direct, so that even if it all disappeared tomorrow, there would probably still be violent crime–and plenty of it.

Pornography and Sexual Violence. In 1970, the National Commission on Obscenity and Pornography, a U.S. government-sponsored panel, set out to address the question of whether reading or viewing pornography causes sexual violence and aggression. After reviewing relevant research, the panel found no clear relation and recommended against blanket prohibition of the sale and possession of sexually explicit materials.

However, it does appear that sexually explicit material containing violent and sadistic sexual and physical assaults on women is correlated with, and may engender, sexually violent acts against women by some men who use such material (e.g., Donnerstein, Linz, & Penrod, 1987; Koop, 1987; U.S. Attorney General's Commission on Pornography, 1986). It appears that viewing violent pornography, which portrays degrading, sadistic sexual assaults on women (1) creates greater acceptance of the myth that women enjoy being raped and/or share the blame for their victimization, (2) has greater effects if the victim appears to enjoy being the target of sexual violence, (3) causes sexual arousal in criminal and noncriminal populations, and (4) causes sexual aggression against women in controlled laboratory experiments (Malamuth & Check, 1981; Siegel, 1998).

Pornography and the Internet. Pornography on the Internet is a multibillion dollar industry. The most troubling connection between Internet pornography and crime has to do with the victimization of children by pedophiles (see chapter 10) and others who exploit children sexually. Internet pornography that depicts real or digitized images of children engaging in sex acts is a crime. Part of the rationale for these laws is that children are victimized in the making of the pornography (although this is not the case if the images are created by digital technology); but the main rationale is that it leads pedophiles to seek out children and young teens as victims. In a sense, this is the same argument made with respect to traditional pornography—that it leads to sexual violence. As we have shown, there was no direct evidence for that, except as relates to sadistic, violent pornography.

At present, there are no studies that show a correlation (of course, there could be no experimental studies into this problem) between pedophilia and other sexual exploitation of children and Internet child pornography (Cass & Kovera, 2001). However, there is enough anecdotal evidence linking online child pornography with sexual exploitation of children that the law takes a hard-line position. The mere downloading of child pornography on your computer can land you in federal prison for years.

In summary, most researchers agree that "standard," nonviolent, adult pornography is not causally related to sexual aggression or other crimes but that sadistic, violent pornography and all forms of child pornography may indirectly influence sexually sadistic crimes against women and the sexual abuse of children. Violent adult pornography appears to have its effects by contributing to culturally based perceptions that women like to be forced to have sex, thus leading some young men to accept and act on these incorrect perceptions. Child pornography appears to stimulate the socially inappropriate sexual desires of pedophiles who may then seek out child victims.[3]

Social Cognition, Social Behavior, and Crime

Having discussed the notion that individuals learn how to behave by watching the behavior of people whom they admire or wish to emulate, we consider how violence and crime may develop in the broader context of society and culture. To do so, we must examine how the likelihood of committing crime can be influenced by the way people have learned to think about other people and by the way they have learned to act in the presence of others.

Attribution and Attributional Biases

Social psychologists use the term *attribution* to describe the processes people use to explain their own behavior and the behavior of others. These attributional processes are one example of **social cognition**, the ways in which people perceive, remember, and think about other people. Social cognition in general, and attributional processes in particular, are important in understanding crime because how people think about other people and the motives and characteristics they attribute to them can determine whether or not they will commit a crime against another person and may guide them toward or away from particular victims.

People tend to make either internal or external attributions about behavior. Internal attributions assume that the cause of behavior resides within the person (themselves or others), whereas external attributions see causes stemming from factors outside the person. Thus, attributing someone's lateness as due to their laziness reflects an internal attribution. Assuming they were late because of traffic would reflect an external attribution.

Often, people are correct in making attributions, but they also tend to make systematic errors in assigning responsibility for behavior, errors that reflect the operation of attributional biases. One of the most common of these biases results in the *fundamental attribution error* (Gilbert & Malone, 1995), a tendency to attribute the behavior of others to internal factors. Thus, when the car in front of a person is just poking along, that person is likely to assume that this is because the driver is a blithering fool, not because he or she is looking for an address. An extension of this phenomenon is seen in actor-observer bias (Baumeister, 1995)—the tendency to attribute other people's behavior to internal factors while attributing their own behaviors to external factors. Thus, people might see their classmates' failing test scores as due to their lack of mental ability, but a person's own low score as due to lack of study time. There is also a self-serving bias in which people tend to make external attributions about their failures ("I did poorly because the test was unfair") but make internal attributions about their successes ("I aced the test because I am smart"; Smith & Ellsworth, 1987). In other words, people tend to explain their own behavior in ways that make them look good. A final attributional bias is rooted in prejudice and stereotypes. Called the *ultimate attribution error*, it leads people to make external attributions about admirable behavior displayed by a member of a stereotyped group ("He got that scholarship because of favoritism") but attribute negative behaviors to internal factors ("She was speeding because she is irresponsible").

---

[3]Unfortunately, the Internet provides a means through which child molesters can "meet" and later try to have personal contact with children. One survey (Finkelhor, Mitchell, & Wolak, 2000) found that about 20% of 1,501 Internet users aged 10 to 17 had received a sexual solicitation or approach over the Internet in the previous year; in about 33% of these cases, the solicitation came from someone who asked to meet them in person, who called them, and/or sent money or gifts.

People's attributional habits and biases come from their experiences with others and from what they learn from their parents, peers, and other cultural influences.

To illustrate the effect of attributions on criminal behavior, we reconsider the research we described in chapter 5 in which convicted date rapists were interviewed about their crimes (Scully & Moralla, 1984). Many of these men justified the rape on the basis of attributions about their victims that made the victims, not themselves, blameworthy. For example, they tended to assume that women mean "yes" even when they say "no" and that most women eventually enjoy being raped. Scully and Moralla (1997) suggested that, like other attributions, these rape-justifying cognitions result from social learning:

> We view rape as behavior learned socially through interaction with others; convicted rapists have learned the attitudes and actions consistent with sexual aggression against women. Learning also includes the acquisition of culturally derived vocabularies of motive, which can be used to diminish responsibility and to negotiate a non-deviant identity. (p. 271)

Another example of faulty attributions leading to crime can be found in spouse abuse and other forms of domestic violence. In many cultures and subcultures, boys learn by watching their parents that it is not only acceptable to express displeasure with a partner through physical violence but that the partner expects such treatment. At the same time, girls may learn to accept being the target of domestic violence, often attributing the aggression to their having not done enough to please their husbands or boyfriends.

The crime-justifying attributions that remain prevalent among many men and women today appear to arise as part of what they learn about culturally approved gender roles. How men act and women act is strongly influenced by social learning, a process that begins at home when parents reward them for "gender-appropriate" behavior. For instance, when parents are always telling their little girl that she looks beautiful, she is likely to assume that her appearance is the most important dimension on which she is evaluated by others and especially by members of the opposite sex. When a little boy is praised for "sticking up for himself" during a playground dispute, he is learning to assume that adults value aggressiveness. Peers, teachers, toy manufacturers, and the media strongly reinforce these gender role messages, thus helping to solidify male- and female-appropriate patterns of behavior.

Understanding that gender-based behaviors are the result of social learning is important to understanding many aspects of crime. These roles help shape the types of crimes men and women commit and who is victimized by what crimes. For example, women are most likely to commit nonviolent crimes involving prostitution, drug offenses, and theft, whereas men are more likely to commit rape and other violent crimes. In fact, 83% of the people arrested for violent crimes and 70% of those arrested for property crimes are men (FBI, 2002).

Social Behavior and Social Influences

Attributions and other social-cognitive processes are not the only social sources of crime. The way people influence each other in social situations can play an important role as well. These social influences include frustration, deindividuation, conformity, compliance, and obedience to authority.

Frustration, Aggression, and Crime. On May 3, 1992, a jury acquitted four Los Angeles police officers who had been videotaped assaulting Black motorist Rodney King. Angered by what they saw as a miscarriage of justice, hundreds of Blacks in south central Los Angeles set fires, destroyed property, and looted businesses. In the end, 40 people were killed and damage totaled more than a billion dollars. Behavioral scientists attributed this outburst of violence to these people's intense and longstanding frustration over what they perceived to be continuing prejudice and discrimination against them as evidenced in decaying neighborhoods, poor schools, lack of economic opportunity, poverty, rampant crime, and an indifferent judicial system (Nietzel & Hartung, 1993).

Social psychologists define *frustration* as anything that blocks the achievement of a goal (Dollard, 1939). Frustration can result in aggression, and often the frustrated person's aggression is displaced onto a person or situation that is not the actual source of frustration. The classic example of displacement is seen in the case of a person who is frustrated by the boss but is hostile and aggressive toward a spouse, a child, or a pet. Frustration does not always result in aggression; it may lead instead to irritation or anxiety. Aggression is especially likely, though, when frustrating events are unexpected. For example, like the violence in Los Angeles in 1992, the riots that rocked several U.S. cities following the 1968 assassination of Dr. Martin Luther King, Jr. were reactions to a sudden and unexpected event, in this case, the loss of a great civil rights leader in whom Blacks had placed so much hope.

Another form of criminal behavior related to frustration is *road rage,* a term coined in the late 1990s to describe violent aggression by one driver against another. We consider just two cases: In May of 1998, a Florida motorist who did not have correct change at an automated highway toll booth was shot and killed by an angry motorist in the vehicle behind him (*Washington Post,* May 24, 1998). In November 1999, road rage between two women ended in death when one woman pulled a gun from the console of her car and shot the other driver after they had moved off the road to settle the score. The killer, Shirley Henson, was tried and convicted of manslaughter and sentenced to 13 years in prison (Sipress, 1999). More than 10,000 such incidents resulted in 218 deaths and 12,610 injuries in the United States from 1990 to 1996 alone, and the incidence of road rage appears to be increasing (AAA, 1999).

The link between frustration and aggression appears as a partial explanation for **terrorism**, which is defined by criminologists as the use of illegitimate force to target innocent civilians for political purposes or motives (Laqueur, 1999). The frustration associated with terrorism is seen to be based on the concept of relative deprivation (Kushner, 2003; Gurr, 1970) in which people perceive a discrepancy between what they have (especially in relation to others) and what they deserve. Put another way, relative deprivation appears when there is a gap between one's expectations and the satisfaction of those expectations. Indeed, Margolin (1977) argued that much terrorist behavior occurs as a response to the frustration of various political, economic, and personal needs or objectives. Relative deprivation can help to motivate terrorism (and other forms of violent aggression) in particular individuals, as in the case of Oklahoma City bomber Timothy McVeigh, or in whole groups, as seems to be the case with many young Palestinians who have grown up in occupied territories.[4]

Dov Cohen and colleagues (1996) studied a variation of the frustration-aggression phenomenon that they called "the pattern of insult and aggression in the culture of honor in the Southern states." They classified male undergraduates as Southerners (n = 41) or Northerners (n = 42) on the basis of whether or not the students had lived in a Southern state for more than 6 years. Then, as each of these students walked from one research room to another, he was "accidentally" bumped on the shoulder by a research assistant. Half of the students in each regional group were also insulted by the assistant, who called each of them an "asshole." The students' emotional reactions to this incident were assessed via observation of their facial expressions and by comparing levels of testosterone (a hormone associated with aggression) and the stress hormone cortisol in blood samples taken before and after the incident. They were also asked to complete two unfinished stories, one of which was emotionally neutral and one that was emotionally charged (involving another man "making a pass" at the student's girlfriend).

Northerners typically reacted to the bumping and name calling with amusement, Southerners with anger. Cortisol levels rose 79% for insulted Southerners compared to 33% for insulted Northerners. Similarly, testosterone levels rose 12% for insulted Southerners and only 6% for insulted Northerners. Further, 75% of the Southerners who had been insulted ended the girlfriend story with violence against the potential rival, whereas only 20% of the Northerners did so. However, Southerners were no more likely than Northerners to end the emotionally neutral story with aggression. This latter finding suggests that an insult made the Southern men angry, but that it took a subsequent affront to trigger an expression of aggression.

Cohen and colleagues' (1996) experiment was part of a larger body of research into the culture of the South that has found Southerners more reactive to insult than Northerners (Cohen, 1996; Cohen & Nisbett, 1994; Cohen et al., 1996). That research has consistently indicated that Southerners are more likely to believe that a child who is being bullied should fight back and a man should hit someone who insults him (Cohen & Nisbett, 1994). Southern states have more liberal gun laws and more liberal laws justifying homicide in self-defense

---

[4]Although frustration resulting from relative deprivation may help to trace the roots of terrorism, there is surely more to the story. Terrorism is a complex topic that cannot be understood without also taking into account the political and religious ideologies, beliefs, and lifestyles that provide a social context for the development of terrorist actions. We return to this topic later in this chapter.

than do Northern states, further laying the groundwork for violent response to insult (Cohen, 1996). The researchers have suggested that the origin of these attitudes lies in the slave system of the Old South, which legitimized violence to discipline, control, and punish and that, in turn, perpetuated systems, procedures, laws, and customs justifying the use force in everyday life (Cohen, 1996).

Although the relation between culture and individual behaviors is a complex one, research into subcultural attitudes, laws, and levels of violence represents an attempt to explain in social psychological terms why violent crime is more common in the U.S. Southern states than in any other region of the country (FBI, 2004).

Presence of Guns. Psychologists believe that frustration can be particularly likely to trigger aggression if the tools for releasing it are available. Leonard Berkowitz (1994) studied how the availability of guns can influence violence. He suggested that when people are looking for a way to release aggressive impulses brought on by frustration, a gun may not only permit violence but may actually help stimulate it by providing a "cue" for the release of tension. Guns, Berkowitz said, provide the literal trigger for aggression in such situations. For example, 66% of the 15,517 murders in the United States in 2000 were committed with guns. Firearms were also involved that year in 8% of the 6.3 million incidents of rape, sexual assault, robbery, and aggravated and simple assault (FBI, 2001).

The presence of firearms in the home—usually purchased for protection against crime—may be a key factor in the escalation of domestic violence from nonfatal injury to homicide. Having a gun at home makes it 12 times more likely that an assault involving family or intimate partners will result in a death (Saltzman, 1992) and three times more likely that someone in the home will be murdered by someone else who lives there (Kellerman, 1993). Indeed, despite their intended purposes, guns in homes are 22 times more likely to be used in a criminal, unintentional, or suicide-related shooting than in self-defense (Kellerman, 1998). So it is estimated that for every time someone at home uses a firearm to kill an armed intruder, 131 other lives are lost when protection weapons are used in murders, suicides, and accidents (Violence Policy Center, 1999). Only motor vehicles exceed guns as the cause of fatal injury stemming from a household or recreational product (Centers for Disease Control and Prevention [CDCP], 2001; Peters & Kochanek, 1998). To put the situation in international perspective, the overall rate of firearms deaths in the United States is eight times higher than in 25 other industrialized countries combined; for children, the rate is 12 times higher (CDCP, 1997; Krug & Powell, 1998). So although people everywhere experience frustration and anger, it is mainly in the United States that guns are so readily available to serve as the deadly expressions of these strong emotions.

Recognizing the dangers posed by the pervasive presence of firearms in a society, countries such as Britain have established strict national bans on the possession of handguns and automatic rifles. In the United States, though, the epidemic of gun deaths has not led to serious new efforts to reduce the number of guns on the street. In fact, in 2004, the U.S. Congress lifted the 10-year-old ban on the sale of assault weapons, considered by antigun activists to be of no value for any purpose other than mayhem. Gun advocates see the situation differently. They interpret the Second Amendment ("right to bear arms") to the U.S. Constitution as giving every American the right to limitless ownership and use of guns.

There is intense public and Congressional debate between gun control advocates and the progun lobby over whether to expand the relatively anemic gun laws now in force (Babington, 1999). The National Rifle Association, which stands at the head of the gun lobby, remains steadfast in its credo that "guns don't kill people, people kill people." This is true, of course, and it is also true that following the British example in banning most firearms would not necessarily eliminate violent crime. Gun crimes have shown a steady, upward increase in Britain from 1998 to 2002. Because few are authorized to own or carry a gun in England, the guns used in crimes are primarily illegal. Guns are used in 70% of robberies in Britain, and the murder rate in 2002 was the highest in the last 50 years (Travis, 2003).

Deindividuation. Another social factor that can shape crime is dramatically portrayed in Shirley Jackson's (1948) short story, "The Lottery." It tells of a small town's ritual in which the inhabitants meet periodically to stone to death one of their own, a victim chosen by lot. Once the unfortunate citizen is identified—a woman with several children, it turns out—the townspeople do not hesitate to begin throwing stones despite her protests.

Would real people do such a thing? It is not impossible. The fictional ritual was carried out in a group, and groups can create a phenomenon that social psychologists call **deindividuation**. It is defined as a psychological state in which individual identity merges with that of a group (a few other people, a political or religious organization, a gang, a cult, or the like), and people no longer feel personally responsible or accountable for their actions. They lose their moral compass and simply "follow the crowd" in doing things they would never do on their own (Prentice-Dunn & Rogers, 1989). Deindividuation is enhanced by uniforms, banners, songs, slogans, and other devices that amplify one's sense of affiliation with a group.

Deindividuation can result in criminal acts—such as those associated with urban riots—when individuals are swept away by the intensity of group behavior (Prentice-Dunn & Rogers, 1989). The larger the crowd, the greater the propensity to join in because as more people gather, emotional involvement with the group and the sense of anonymity increase. For example, an analysis of reports of lynchings over a 50-year period showed that the larger the crowd, the more savage the violence (Mullen, 1986). Deindividuation appears partly as the result of pressure for conformity, compliance, and obedience to authority (usually a group leader). We take a look at how these social processes, so vital to the smooth operation of civilized society, can also lead to criminal behavior.

Conformity, Compliance, and Obedience. Social psychologists define *conformity* as the tendency to behave in accordance with group norms or unspoken rules about what one should or should not do. For example, people who do not think that a concert was particularly good may conform to an unspoken, but highly influential group norm by standing and applauding when the people around them do so. Conformity tends to increase when (1) the individual's need for self-esteem creates a desire for group acceptance, (2) group members are important to the individual, (3) the individual strongly identifies with group members, and (4) the group members are experts (Aronson, 2004). In "The Lottery," individual townspeople joined in the stoning ritual because it was expected of them as citizens of their community and because doing so allowed them to be accepted by that community—even though they knew they could someday be the victim.

Compliance is defined as going along with an explicitly stated request as when someone asks a person to pass the salt or hold the door open. Obedience refers to following the demands or orders that come from some socially recognized authority figure such as a parent, a teacher, or a military commander.

Human history indicates that people conform, comply, and obey because they want to be approved and accepted, to be "in" with their groups and to identify themselves with power and authority. If those in power ask or tell people to commit criminal acts, the need to be accepted by one's group can lead those people to comply or obey by engaging in criminal activity—even if they would rather not do so. Thus, members of organized crime associations ("the mob,") and other criminal groups do as they are told partly to save themselves from being ostracized or punished for disobedience.

At Yale University in the 1960s, Stanley Milgram (1963) conducted a famous set of experiments on the extent and limits of people's obedience to authority. He recruited a group of adult male volunteers from the local community and told them that they would be part of a study on the effects of punishment on learning. Each volunteer became a "teacher" who was to read a list of word pairs to a "learner" seated in an adjoining room with electrodes attached to his arm. After reading the word-pair list once, the teacher read only the first word in each pair, and the learner was to say the word with which it had been paired. If the learner made a mistake, the teacher was told to punish him with an electric shock. Following each new mistake, the intensity of the shock was to be gradually increased from a mild 15 volts to a severe 450 volt jolt. In reality, the learner was working for Milgram, and although he did not actually receive any shocks, he portrayed increasingly intense reactions. As punishment appeared to increase, he begged to be let out of the experiment, complained of heart trouble, and then fell silent. As the teacher looked to the experimenter for guidance about what to do, he was told that "the experiment must continue," "proceed with the next word," and "you have no choice; you must continue."

Would you have continued to administer stronger and stronger shocks to a fellow human being who was crying out in pain? Milgram found that 65% of the participants did exactly that, stopping only when they had reached the maximum 450 volt level. He concluded that these people did so because the experimenter was an authority figure whom they felt they should obey, even though it upset them to behave in such an apparently cruel manner.

Although some critics argued that Milgram volunteers saw through the experiment and did as they were told only to be "good" research participants (Orne & Holland, 1968), the general consensus is that these experiments proved something horrifyingly true about human beings that is seen all too often outside the laboratory. It would appear that, especially under the influence of an authority figure, people are capable of committing unspeakable atrocities against other human beings. This has been demonstrated over the years in efforts to obliterate entire groups of people, from the Nazis' efforts to exterminate the Jews in the 1940s to campaigns of genocide against certain ethnic groups in Eastern Europe and Africa today.

The people who carry out these efforts need not be demented, cold-blooded murderers. Most of them are normal, everyday people who are influenced by socially recognized authority figures to behave like demons. For example, militant Islamic organizations in the Palestinian territories, Iraq, and a number of countries have been successful at influencing young men and women to become suicide bombers by promising them fame and glory in the afterlife as well as assuring reflected glory and monetary rewards to their relatives. Similarly, members of street gangs commonly carry out orders from gang leaders to execute rivals or even fellow gang members who have violated rules or codes of conduct. Obedience to authority can lead to crime in the world of business, too, when employees engage in criminal acts at the direction of their supervisors (see in chapter 11).

The Environmental Roots of Crime

Just as people create the social context of crime, numerous situational factors—such as physical location, time of day, weather, lighting, and other elements—create an environmental context that can influence criminal behavior. What kinds of environmental conditions have been found to contribute to crime? What causes some people to react to noxious environmental stimuli with violence, whereas others show no effects? **Environmental psychology** is a subdiscipline of psychology that studies the links between people's physical environment and their behavior (Sommer, 1999) including how factors such as location, temperature, and other situational variables affect aggression and crime (Bell, 1992).

Research by environmental psychologists is used by law enforcement organizations, correctional systems, legal systems, and urban planners as part of efforts to change or avoid creating physical conditions associated with violence and crime. For instance, a new approach to prison design called "direct supervision" arose as a result of environmental psychologists' research on the effects of prison overcrowding and of the location of prison inmates in relation to one another and to their guards (Wener, Frazier, & Farbstein, 1987). Environmental psychologists' research on the relation between crime and environmental conditions has also helped architects and urban planners to alter or create environments so as to make violence and crime less likely.

Environmental Contributions to Criminal Behavior

There are four main pathways through which environmental factors influence human behavior in general, and some or all of them may be involved in triggering violent or criminal behavior (Bell et al., 2001):

1. Specific, discrete environmental factors can create physiological arousal, which in turn alters behavior (the arousal model).
2. Environmental factors can act as more general stressors that accumulate over time and set off a pattern of physical, psychological, and behavioral responses (the environmental stress model). For instance, the typical prison environment, with its lack of privacy, overcrowding, uncomfortable temperatures, and unattractive cells requires that prisoners alter their schemas of day-to-day life and adapt to harsh new conditions. Failure to do so may impair their ability to succeed in other aspects of prison life including getting along with inmates and guards. The lack of control imposed by these environmental factors can also trigger criminal behavior (Rodin & Baum, 1978; Stokols, 1978; Zlutnick & Altman, 1972).
3. Environmental factors can affect behavior more directly by either prompting people to take action to control the environment or to give up efforts at control in the face of apparently overwhelming circumstances (the behavioral constraint model). For example, some people in crime-infested inner cities join with law enforcement officials in taking action to evict gangs and engage in neighborhood clean-up efforts, whereas others give up, give in, and let their environment continue to decay.

4. The actions people take in response to environmental factors may set in motion a continuing chain of events as their responses change the environment, prompting new responses, further environmental changes, further responses, and so on (we discuss this ecological model in more detail later). For example, prisoners who react with violence to overcrowding may be punished by being placed in even more restrictive conditions, thus amplifying their rage and making it more likely that further, even more violent outbursts will follow. Similarly, when community residents give up on their neighborhoods, those neighborhoods become even more conducive to crime, making it likely that residents and their families will be victims of crime or that their children will become part of the community's criminal element. However, successful efforts to reduce criminal activity and improve the physical environment tends to increase community pride and citizen involvement, leading to a new environment that is less likely to nurture crime.

The arousal and environmental stress models are particularly relevant for understanding crime. If environmental factors such as high temperature become stressors that create arousal and are perceived as a threat to one's physical, cognitive, and/or emotional balance (also known as "homeostasis"), aggressive or criminal behavior may result, especially in people who already have a tendency to react violently to stressors. The degree to which environmental stressors contribute to criminal behavior depends, however, on how individuals perceive them. If they are perceived as unimportant or as challenges to be overcome, environmental factors are less likely to result in violence.

Two types of environmental stressors are especially likely to trigger responses that may lead to criminal behavior: (1) traumatic events (e.g., hurricanes, tornadoes, floods, and other natural disasters; industrial accidents such as those at Three Mile Island and Chernobyl) and (2) so-called background stressors. There are two types of background stressors (Rotton, 1990): microstressors and ambient stressors. *Microstressors* are low-intensity problems—such as a clogged drain or a leaky pen—whereas *ambient stressors* are chronic environmental conditions such as crowding, heat, noise, traffic, and pollution. People tend to encounter both as a part of everyday life (Lazarus et al., 1985; Zika & Chamberlain, 1987), but ambient stressors are most likely to result in increased arousal and constant efforts to adapt to them. Aggressive, violent, and even criminal behavior may result when background stressors accumulate to a "critical mass." This behavior is seen mainly in people who already tend to act aggressively when under significant stress. Aside from prison conditions, one of the best examples of accumulated stress-induced crime is the cases of road rage we mentioned earlier.

We now consider some specific examples of environmental factors that are associated with violence and crime.

Criminal Places

A drug- and crime-infested area of Baltimore, Maryland, is the subject of a book called *The Corner: A Year in the Life of an Inner City Neighborhood* (Simon & Burn, 1998). In the center of this area is the notorious intersection of West Fayette and Monroe Street, an example of what criminologists refer to as criminal places. The location of criminal places can be in certain stores, homes, apartment buildings, street corners, subway stations, airports, and public transportation systems (Eck, 1997). In fact, most crime is highly concentrated in and around a relatively small number of such places. In the United States, for example, 10% of all places are consistently the site of about 60% of all crimes (Spelman, 1995; Spelman & Eck, 1989). Thus, most convenience stores are seldom if ever robbed, but a few are robbed again and again (Crow & Bull, 1975). Most residences are not burglarized, but some suffer repeated break-ins (Farrell, 1995). A few bars are the scenes of most tavern-related violence (Sherman, Schmidt, & Velke, 1992). Urban drug dealing is highly concentrated in relatively few locations (Eck, 1994; Sherman & Rogan, 1995).

Sociologists and criminologists explain these data on criminal places by focusing attention on the people inhabiting them (the offender search theory; Brantingham & Brantingham, 1981) and the activity going on there (the routine activity theory; Felson, 1994). These theories suggest that anticrime interventions will be most effective if police efforts are concentrated on keeping potential offenders away from criminal places and/or eliminating their opportunity to offend. Examples include closing off streets in neighborhoods where drug-dealing is rampant, installing closed circuit television in public establishments that are hot spots for burglaries, installing metal detectors in public transportation systems, and evicting violent tenants from apartment complexes known to harbor criminal occupants and criminal activity (Eck, 1997).

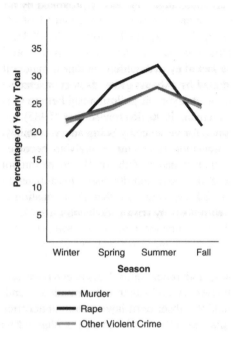

FIGURE 6.2 *Heat and Crime.* From *Psychology* (5th ed.), by D. A. Bernstein, A. Clarke-Stewart, E. J. Roy, and C. D. Wickens, 2000, Boston: Houghton Mifflin. Copyright © 2000 by Houghton Mifflin Company. Reprinted with permission.

Heat and Crime

The most studied of all environmental influences on violence and crime has been temperature (D. A. Anderson, 1989; R. A. Baron & Richardson, 1994). Researchers have found, for example, that all but one of the riots occurring in 79 U.S. cities in 1967 began on days when the temperature was at least in the 80s (United States Riot Commission, 1968). Other studies also supported the association between heat and street riots (Goranson & King, 1970; see Figure 6.2).

As shown in Figure 6.2, hot weather has also been associated with more general increases in crime (Cohn, 1993; FBI, 2004a); violent crime increases with each consecutive day of hot temperatures (Anderson, 1987; Harries & Stadler, 1988; Rotton & Frey, 1985). For example, the most violent crimes are committed in May, June, July, and August, and the fewest are committed in February (FBI, 2004a). Even intentionally misthrown baseball pitches are more common in hot weather than in cooler weather (Reifman, Larrick, & Fein, 1991). The frequency of aggressive family disturbances, too, increases along with heat-related increases in ozone levels (Rotton & Frey, 1985).

Noise and Crime

Noise, or "unwanted sound" (Bell et al., 2001) is an ambient stressor (Rotton, 1990) that, like other ambient stressors, generally do not in and of themselves cause or contribute to aggression or violence. When coupled with other stressors, however, noise can be the proverbial "straw that breaks the camel's back."

To the extent that noise increases arousal, it can increase aggressive behavior, especially in people who tend to react aggressively when overaroused (Bandura, 1973; Berkowitz, 1970; Zillman, 1987). In one experiment (Geen & O'Neal, 1969), for example, people watched either a nonviolent sports film or a violent prize fight and then had the opportunity to act aggressively by administering what they thought were electric shocks to other people. While watching the film, half the participants were exposed only to normal laboratory noise. The other half was subjected to a continuous stream of white noise. Seeing the violent film and hearing the added noise were each followed by an increase in the number of shocks delivered, but aggression was greatest following a combination of the two. It appears that viewing the violent film initiated arousal and that continuous noise intensified it. Subsequent research (Donnerstein & Wilson, 1976; Konecni et al., 1975) has also suggested that noise contributes to increased aggression only in people who are aroused to anger.

If it is true that noise intensifies aggression but does not necessarily provoke it unless people are already aggressive or angry (Bell et al., 2001; Cohen & Spacapan, 1984), the results of this research are of particular relevance in prisons, mental institutions, and other settings where the inhabitants are likely to be angry and easily provoked by noise.

Pollution and Crime

Like unwanted noise, air pollution is a fact of everyday life in and near major cities. It consists of toxic particles in the air generated by exhaust gases, factory discharges, cigarette smoke, and other sources. As an ambient stressor, air pollution can help to trigger aggressive behavior (Bell et al., 2001; Needleman, 1996; Rotton & Frey, 1985) by increasing arousal in people who are already primed for violence by being angry or annoyed. For example, laboratory studies showed that nonsmokers are more likely to become aggressive when breathing smoke-filled air rather than clean air (Zillman, Baron & Tamborini, 1981). There is also evidence that reports of child abuse and domestic quarrels tend to increase with increases in ozone levels (Rotton & Frey, 1985) and that a combination of air pollution and other stressors is associated with hostility (Evans & Jacob, 1981).

Natural Disasters and Crime

Earthquakes, fires, hurricanes, floods, and other natural disasters have an impact on crime by setting the stage for looting. Angry and frustrated individuals tend to use the resulting breakdown of social order and the absence of law enforcement officials to steal goods that they need to survive or plan to sell. The 2,706 adults charged with looting during the New York City blackout of 1977 tended to have stronger ties to their community and higher incomes than the average defendant in the criminal justice system, suggesting that deindividuation might have been operating in people who, as part of a crowd, felt that the blackout offered an opportunity to acquire goods in a way they might not normally pursue (Goodman, 2003).

Other observers see looting in the aftermath of natural disasters as a reaction to the chaos of the environment and as an attempt to exert some control over that environment (Brehm, 1996; Greenberger & Allen, 1980).

Personal Space and Crime

Personal space, the "portable, invisible boundary surrounding us, into which others may not trespass" (Bell, Fisher, Baum, & Greene, 1996, p. 275) has important implications for aggression, violence, and criminal behavior. Some psychologists suggest that people protect their personal space because of a need to control aggression against them, to preserve their individual autonomy, and thus reduce stress so that they can carry out tasks necessary for survival (Evans & Howard, 1973).

Although the sense of personal space may have evolved through natural selection, most researchers believe that it is also the result of culturally based learning that results in different-sized personal spaces in different countries, among different ethnic groups, and even across gender (Aiello & Thompson, 1980; Cappella & Greene, 1982; Bell et al., 2001). For example, in the United States, the "intimate distance" of 0 to 1.5 feet is usually reserved for intimate contact and physical sports; contacts between close friends and everyday interactions with acquaintances tend to occur at about 1.5 to 4 feet, whereas 4 to 12 feet is the appropriate range of distance for impersonal and businesslike contacts (Hall, 1963, 1966). Thus, personal space is violated when someone enters into the space inappropriate for the individual and the setting.

How does violation of personal space contribute to aggression and violence? For many people, the initial response to such a violation is emotional arousal. They may react aggressively to defend their space because they feel threatened and may fear for their safety. If people have reason to believe that they will suffer bodily harm at the hands of the violator of their space, they may perceive that any aggressive physical action they take can be considered as self-defense for which they will not be held accountable. Individuals who are not predisposed to react negatively to invasion of their personal space may perceive the invader as someone who wishes to establish closer proximity to enhance communication or assistance. However, those who are predisposed to anger or annoyance may react with physical force even if they do not feel that they will be attacked by the violator of their personal space. Prison inmates and mental hospital patients may be especially prone to react in this way (Ryden, Bossenmaier, & McLachlan, 1991). It is no wonder, then, that when opposing factions demonstrate simultaneously (e.g., at KKK rallies or abortion clinics), law enforcement officials routinely keep the two groups far enough from each other to prevent physical aggression (Hern, 1991).

Crowding and Crime

Invasion of personal space and the stressful arousal it can create become especially likely under crowded conditions. Research with animals and people has suggested that crowded settings increase the tendency for aggression. For example, high density living arrangements caused a disintegration in the existing social order among rats (Calhoun, 1962) and increased aggression among monkeys (Southwick, 1967). Ethical concerns limit similar experiments with humans, but correlational studies of cities, neighborhoods, and apartment buildings indicate that crowding is associated with increased aggression among both adults and juveniles (Bell et al., 2001; Paulus, 1988; Ray, Wandersman, Ellisor, & Huntington, 1982). Densely populated cities—those with more than 1 million inhabitants—have the highest violent crime rates, whereas the lowest crime rates are seen in those with 10,000 to 25,000 residents (FBI, 2004b). However, the relation between aggression and crowding is more significant for males than for females (Freedman et al., 1972; Schettino & Borden, 1976; Stokols et al., 1973).

As we noted earlier, the strongest correlations between crowding and aggression are seen in prisons. Some prison riots, such as the one staged in 1992 by 675 prisoners at the Montreal Detention Center in Canada, are motivated by protests against overcrowding. That riot alone caused $1.2 million in damage. Inmate assaults and murders, too, increase with prison population (Paulus, 1988) and decrease when crowding is relieved. In one study, a 20% increase in population was followed by a 30% increase in assaults; in another, a 30% decrease in a prison's population was followed by a 60% decrease in assaults (Ruback & Carr, 1984).

Territoriality and Crime

The effects of crowding on aggression may occur in part because they violate territoriality. Human territoriality consists of the behaviors and cognitions exhibited by persons and groups based on their perceived ownership of physical space (Bell, 2001).[5] Perhaps no environmental factor causes more large scale human violence than territoriality and violations of territorial boundaries. Territoriality is the expressed reason for most wars and for most acts of violence against neighbors or strangers. Also, to the extent that individuals feel that their romantic partners represent territory on which others are forbidden to "tread," even crimes of passion may be seen as the result of perceived territorial invasion. Evolutionary theories hold that claiming and defending territory (by marking boundaries and making threatening sounds and gestures) developed as an aid to survival. Animals of all species maintain territory to protect their food supplies, mates, and shelters and from which they fend off aggression by other members of their species (Bell et al., 2001). Although the origins of human territoriality, too, may be instinctual, the creation, extent, and defense of territory differs from culture to culture. Territoriality may serve several psychological functions for human beings. For example, defining spheres of perceived control and protection may reduce arousal and stress. If people only have to worry about protecting a limited territory and if others respect the boundaries of that territory, aggression and violence become less likely, and people can use their energy for

---

[5]Territoriality is similar to personal space, but unlike the boundaries of one's home territory, personal space is a "bubble" that stays with people as they move about.

activities other than defense. Research on territoriality and aggression has suggested that ill-defined territory—whether primary (one's home) or public (political boundaries or even bench space at a stadium)—is associated with aggression, whereas well-defined boundaries tend to be associated with peace. This idea is summed up in the phrase "good fences make good neighbors." Consider, for example, the ongoing conflicts between Arabs and Israelis in the Middle East. For more than 50 years, the location of Israel's "proper" boundaries have been a matter of debate, and the result has been a series of border skirmishes and wars. Recent wars among former Soviet states also illustrate the aggression associated with ill-defined territory. When the Soviet Union fell, its numerous states—especially those in the former Yugoslavia—attempted to regain their original borders as ethnic and religious groups tried to control the land and each other. By contrast, in the United States, where national boundaries have been undisputed for more than a century, border wars are unknown.

Violation of another's home territory is considered so unacceptable that such violations constitute the crime of trespassing. Indeed, depending on local laws, attacking or killing someone who is trespassing may be excusable because someone who threatens the sanctity of one's home may be considered a threat to one's life. Murdering the trespasser, then, becomes an act of self-defense. In 1996, for example, a Loudoun County, Virginia jury acquitted a man charged with murdering a neighbor with whom he had numerous disputes when the neighbor stepped onto the man's porch. In another Virginia case in the 1980s, a man was acquitted of murder when he shot a neighbor who was driving farm equipment across a property boundary. As in the first case, these men had a history of feuding over the location of the boundary, and the jury found that the shooter was justified in perceiving that his life was being threatened by his neighbor's intrusion on his property.

Homes and properties that display few "territorial markers" are more susceptible than others to being invaded or trespassed on (Brown, 1979). These markers include name and address signs, fences, rock borders, hedges, nighttime illumination, parked cars, and operating lawn sprinklers (Bell et al., 1996). Because residents of apartment buildings and group homes may not display as many territorial markers, vandalism and theft are especially common in these locations (Edney & Uhlig, 1977). Although burglars may see territorial markers as merely indicating the presence of valuables (MacDonald & Gifford, 1989), the point is that markers on home territories do exert some effect on criminal behavior.

By taking territorial factors into account, architects and others who design environments can help to reduce violence and crime. As we noted earlier, this trend has been demonstrated in a new form of prison design. In these direct supervision prisons, 12 or more inmates live in units of private cells surrounding a large common space. Giving inmates their own clearly defined primary territory decreases both opportunity and motive for aggression against each other.

Geography and Crime

The highest per capita crime rates in the United States are in the populous Southern states—Delaware, the District of Columbia, Florida, Georgia, Maryland, North Carolina, South Carolina, Virginia, West Virginia, Alabama, Kentucky, Mississippi, Tennessee, Arkansas, Louisiana, Oklahoma, and Texas. In 2003, for example, the South accounted for 41.6% of violent and nonviolent crimes in the United States including 39% of the murders and robberies. The lowest per capita rates were in the Northeast (Connecticut, Maine, Massachusetts, New Hampshire, Rhode Island, Vermont, New Jersey, New York, and Pennsylvania), which reported only 15.8% of violent crimes; followed by the Midwest (Illinois, Indiana, Michigan, Ohio, Wisconsin, Iowa, Kansas, Minnesota, Missouri, Nebraska, North Dakota, and South Dakota) with 22.5%; and the West (Arizona, Colorado, Idaho, Montana, Nevada, New Mexico, Utah, Wyoming, Alaska, California, Hawaii, Oregon, and Washington) reported 23.4% of violent crimes. (FBI, 2004b).

Why should crime be higher in the South than elsewhere? Environmental psychologists give as possible reasons higher temperatures, more poverty (the South is poorer than the rest of the country and poverty is associated with all types of crime including violent crime), and lower quality education and social services (Bell, et al., 2001; DeFronzo, 1984; Rotton, 1986). However, as we noted earlier, social psychologists suspect that the prevalence of crime in the South has more to do with culture than geography.

In summary, aggression and criminal behavior can be triggered or made more likely by a number of aversive environmental conditions, usually because those conditions act as stressors. Other people who share such conditions may respond to criminal behavior in ways that actually encourage further criminal acts as in the example of prison officials who enforce ever more stringent restraints following prison riots. The impact of stressors is just one example of the constant interaction that takes place between people and their environments, and it highlights the importance of understanding what might be called the ecology of crime.

The Ecology of Crime

Ecology has been defined as "the science of relations between the organism and the surrounding outer world" (Capra, 1996). In the 1920s, biologists who focused on these relations in plant and animal communities introduced the concept of food chains as an example of how the organization of biological communities involves interdependence among various species.

Crime has its own ecology. In fact, you might say that this entire book explores the ecology of crime because, in every chapter, we examine how criminal behavior develops through a complex pattern of relationships between people and their environments. We emphasize as well that to satisfactorily address the problem of crime, society must address all the personal and environmental factors responsible for it. Accordingly, psychologists who take an ecological approach to crime look not only at how people interact with their physical and built environment but also with their social, educational, military, political, legal, and other cultural systems. The importance of an ecological approach to crime lies in its emphasis on interdependence—the fact that societal systems influence individuals to act in certain ways and that these systems also change in response to people's actions.

Uri Bronfenbrenner's (1979) ecological theory of human development lists several kinds of systems that set the stage on which people play out their lives (see Figure 6.3). Microsystems are the immediate settings in which people live and work—their families, schools, and communities. Mesosystems involve relationships between microsystems that affect the individual such as interactions between family members and school officials and between individuals and peer groups. Exosystems are broader institutions that directly affect the individual including community organizations, government, and the legal system. Macrosystems include the educational, religious, political and social values of the culture in which an individual lives. Finally, the time, or era, in which an individual lives makes up the chronosystem.

We consider some examples of how crime develops through the mutually influential relationships between people and the systems in which they are immersed.

A Culture of Violence

It is easy to see how macrosystems and the chronosystem contributed to what has become known as the culture of violence in the United States. Born in the spirit of freedom and democracy, the United States cut its teeth on violence and bloodshed, thanks in part to the love of gunpowder. As the population spread westward in the 19th century, settlers, hunters, adventurers, and the U.S. military murdered, raped, pillaged, and ultimately displaced all the Native Americans they found. Also, as those unfortunate native inhabitants were brought under control, violence and anarchy took hold on the frontier. There was no codified law, so vigilantes and self-appointed lawmen determined what to punish and how. Outlaw gangs, bank and train robbers, horse thieves, cattle rustlers, and murderers flourished in the American West both before and after the Civil War of 1861 to 1865. The violence of that war was horrendous, even by today's military standards. As Americans fought each other, 617,000 of them died and another 375,000 were wounded. Before, and especially after the war, certain parts of the country, particularly the South, were engulfed in mob violence as the Ku Klux Klan and other hate organizations targeted members of minority groups, mostly Blacks and Asians. More than 3,200 lynchings of Blacks were recorded between 1889 and 1918.

As the United States became industrialized in the late 1800s and early 1900s, group violence became commonplace as labor unions organized strikes, attacked nonstrikers, and were themselves attacked by the police and company strike breakers. During the era of Prohibition (1920–1933), violence came in the form of murder and hijacking as bootleggers vied with each other to supply thirsty Americans with illegal alcoholic beverages.

During World War II, group violence and individual crime in the United States subsided, but all that changed in the 1960s as the country became involved in the agony of the Vietnam war. Countless veterans returned home addicted to drugs and alcohol while social unrest on college campuses and city streets was

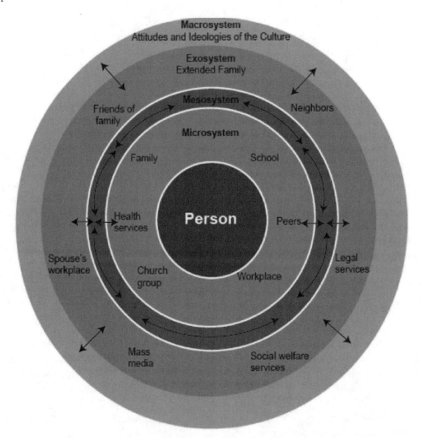

FIGURE 6.3 *Bronfenbrenner Systems.* From *Lifespan Development*, 2nd ed. (p. 9), by K. L. Seifert, 2000, Boston: Houghton Mifflin. Copyright © 2000 by Houghton Mifflin Company. Used with permission.

sparked by that seemingly endless war and the assassination of Dr. Martin Luther King, Jr. From the 1970s to the 1990s, violent crime rates soared, and juvenile crime flourished. Although the late 1990s have seen a slow but steady decrease in violent crime, it continues to be a major problem, and hate crimes against religious and ethnic groups and government itself are commonplace. In short, the U.S. is at once the most democratic and the most violent of civilized countries.

In the 1990s, the community macrosystem and the educational microsystem took on increasing significance in fostering criminality. It is now all too common for children to carry weapons to school and for students (and teachers) to be killed in school or on their way to or from school. Some schools, such as several in Washington, DC, have become virtual armed camps. In some states, such as Utah, teachers may carry weapons to protect themselves. Specially trained commercial airline pilots may now carry guns to protect themselves, their crews, and their passengers from armed and/or dangerous passengers who slip through airport security.

Ecological Niches for Crime

Within this general culture of violence, crime appears to be nurtured most in certain realms, or *ecological niches*, where it flourishes. Among the most prominent of these niches are (1) certain inner cities, (2) prisons, (3) the southern United States, and (4) the world of sports.

Life in the Big City.   Some American cities today provide places where it is all too easy to observe the complex and interconnecting forces that lead to crime. For example, during the week of April 20, 1997, the *Washington Post* printed a series of articles about a neighborhood in Washington, DC. where nine residents, eight of them between the ages of 12 and 19 years, had been murdered in the previous 6 months (Struck, 1997). Controlled by a gang known as "Crew," the neighborhood is so violent that fast-food restaurant owners had chosen to shut down rather than put their employees at risk for robbery and murder. There is so much gunfire at night that few residents venture out from their dreary government housing units. The neighborhood playground is given over to target practice and gun battles; in 1993, gang members opened fire on a community swimming pool filled with children, wounding six. The police, although present in force, seem powerless to make a change. There are many such communities in big U.S. cities where most children live in either single-parent (usually mother-only) homes or with relatives other than parents. Many of these children's parents have criminal records and may be in jail.

New Orleans, Louisiana, is another city that exemplifies the idea of an ecological niche for crime. It boasts a unique mix of history, drama, gentility, and excitement, but the murder rate in New Orleans is 10 times higher than that in other U.S. cities of its size (Pressley, 1997). Just north of the chic French Quarter live the desperately poor, and, as in Washington, DC, and many other cities, the sale and use of crack cocaine contributes to the crime rate as well as to the economy. People make a living selling what their neighbors have come to need to make life bearable in crowded, poverty-stricken, and crime-ridden conditions. New Orleans depends on tourism, and tourists, too, are at risk for being victimized. In fact, the night life and cultural values that bring tourists to New Orleans are also part of the ecology of crime there. Many tourists are drawn to the city by its reputation as a place where it is acceptable to party and drink alcohol—on the street if one wishes—all day and all night. Drunken and disoriented tourists make easy targets, not only for unscrupulous prostitutes but for armed robbers and murderers as well. It is ironic that some tourists, and even some local residents, say that the occasional need to dodge bullets is part of the charm of the place. Increasing police presence has been no more effective in New Orleans than it has been in Washington, DC.

So although violent crime rates have been falling in recent years, some cities remain in the grip of crime waves led by gangs and drug dealers. Baltimore, St. Louis, Houston, and Tampa are now at the top of the violent crime list, and though, according to the latest FBI (2004b) data, crime rates are still highest in the largest cities (over 1 million inhabitants), the greatest growth in violent crimes is being seen in cities of less than 10,000. This trend has been attributed to the migration of gangs to suburban and rural areas. It is in the small towns, too, where dealing in drugs such as Ecstasy and OxyContin® is growing and bringing violent crime with it (see chapter 4).

In short, the crime-infested streets of these and other big cities reflect the values, culture, and economic forces influencing inhabitants and visitors alike. If it were not for tourism, the French Quarter would not be the scene of so much violence. If certain residents of Washington, DC, did not have to rely on a street gang for their income or their self-prescribed stress-management medication, crime there would be reduced too. In the crime-supporting ecological niche provided by big cities, the community influences the development and lifestyle of its inhabitants, and their lifestyles, in turn, shape improvements in or deterioration of the community.

Life Behind Bars. ⎛ Prisons provide an example of how a closed institution can be an ecological niche for crime. As we discussed earlier, when prisons are crowded, inmates tend to behave more aggressively toward guards and each other (Paulus, 1988). Those aggressive and violent acts, in turn, prompt prison officials to further restrict inmates' freedom and privileges and to impose other increasingly harsh conditions. These steps may themselves cause the prisoners to react more violently against their guards. ⎞

This sequence was exemplified by the 1997 disturbances at the Maryland House of Corrections in Jessup. Because it houses a third more inmates than it was built for, the facility is what correctional officials refer to as a "powder keg." The sequence of events that caused it to explode began in May of 1997 when a fight broke out in the dining hall, resulting in injuries to several inmates and guards. The next day, in response to disciplinary actions associated with that incident, seven inmates serving life sentences attacked and injured guards and incited a riot. In response to these more serious infractions, prison officials put the facility on a 24-hr lockdown, meaning that all prisoners had to stay in their cells. After suffering harsh punishment and deprivations for their role in the riots, the inmates calmed down, and after a few days, the institution returned to normal. However, peace within overcrowded prisons tends to be short-lived. The inmates remain primed for violence when conditions again push them beyond the limits of their endurance.

As we describe in more detail in chapter 13, violence is a fact of prison life. Women may be raped by male guards (B. Miller, 1999), and men may be raped and beaten by guards and fellow inmates (Conover, 2001). Juveniles are brutalized by stuff who are supposed to protect them (Timberg, 1999). In March 2000, Maryland Governor Parris Glendenning virtually dismantled the Maryland Department of Juvenile Justice because of the physical abuse of youth by guards in juvenile facilities. The Texas juvenile justice system was under the supervision of the federal government for several years after a series of serious injuries and deaths suffered in that state.

Life in the South.   Studies we mentioned earlier by Dov Cohen and colleagues (Cohen, Nisbett, Bowdle, & Schwartz, 1996) have suggested that higher rates of violent crimes in the South stem from a deeply ingrained cultural response to insults and the need to protect one's honor. This culture of honor may have helped to establish an ecological niche for crime. For example, people in the South tend to be more approving of violence than people in the rest of the country and also more likely to endorse violence when used in the protection of one's personal safety, honor, home and property, and for social control—including the control of children and spouses and the punishment of criminals (Cohen & Nisbett, 1994). These attitudes are manifest in the contemporary laws of southern and western states that, more than other states, maintain and enforce laws that support capital punishment, allow aggressive self-defense, condone corporal punishment of children and laxity in arresting spouses for domestic violence, and establish little in the way of gun control.

The Sporting Life.   Football, hockey, boxing, basketball, soccer, rugby, and many other competitive sports are inherently violent. Unfortunately, there are many instances in which competitive violence becomes criminal violence and when sports stars engage in criminal behavior outside the competitive arena. In November 2004, during a professional basketball game with the Detroit Pistons, Indiana Pacers players Ron Artest, Jermaine O'Neal, and Stephen Jackson stormed the stands and started punching spectators after Pistons fans had been taunting them and throwing ice. The three were suspended for several future games and ordered to pay large fines. It was not the first time NBA players had been suspended or fined for violence. In 1997, Kermit Washington of the Los Angeles Lakers threw a punch that broke the jaw of Houston Rockets' Rudy Tomjanovich; the same year, Dennis Rodman was suspended for kicking a courtside cameraman in the groin. Still, attacking fans represented a new low in the annals of sports violence.

It has been suggested that the "culture of sports" is an ecological niche that supports crime as well as violence. It is difficult to know whether sports makes athletes prone to criminal violence or whether people prone to criminal violence are especially likely to become athletes, but whatever the case, certain athletes and the culture of their sport appear to influence each other in a feedback loop that offers a classic example of the ecology of human behavior.

For example, at a preseason practice in August of 1997, Michael Westbrook, a wide receiver for the Washington Redskins, wrestled running back Stephen Davis to the ground and repeatedly struck him in the face such that Davis required medical treatment. Westbrook had displayed enormous raw talent that had never quite coalesced into big time success on the field, and he had been known to display anger during games and practices. Perhaps he displaced frustration about his career by aggressing against his teammate. Westbrook was fined and forced to make a public apology, but no one is particularly shocked when football players do this sort of thing. It would have been a different matter had it been two college professors.

That same week, the training camp dormitory used by the Dallas Cowboys at a Texas college was trashed on their final night in residence. Team officials admitted that their players had ripped out security cameras and soaked the carpet with urine. Although college officials said they often experienced some trashing by pro athletes, that year's display was the worst ever. During that same training camp, several team members had to face criminal charges for offenses that included domestic assault and drunk driving. Perhaps their aggression, too, was frustration-based, but in any event, no one was particularly surprised by these events. Again, if the same behavior occurred among a group of college professors at a conference, imagine the outcry.

Consider also the case of Mike Tyson who, during a heavyweight boxing match with Evander Holyfield on June 28, 1997, bit off a piece of his opponent's ear, causing the bout to be suspended and Holyfield declared the winner. The Nevada Athletic Commission banned Tyson from boxing for a year and fined him 10% of his $30 million share of the purse. Restoration of Tyson's boxing license depended on the outcome of a psychiatric evaluation. That evaluation was positive, in spite of the fact that Tyson had recently been charged with assaulting two people following a minor traffic accident (K. Shaver, 1998). The Nevada Athletic Commission restored Tyson's boxing license, and in January of 1999, he successfully defended his heavyweight title. The following month, he began serving a one year jail sentence on the assault charges. During his first night in custody, he yanked a television set off the wall and threw it to the ground, hitting a correctional officer and earning several days in solitary confinement. Tyson's boxing talent made him a superstar, with all the money and notoriety that goes with that status. Yet his success has been based on the ability to excel in an arena that rewards skills that involve extreme aggression and violence. Obviously, he does not have these skills under control, either inside or outside the ring. He has been charged with assault on several occasions since the Holyfield incident and his wife has divorced him on grounds of physical and mental cruelty.

Mike Tyson did not kill anyone, but in 1999 Rae Carruth, a wide receiver for the NFL's Carolina Panthers, was charged with murder in the drive-by shooting murder of his pregnant girlfriend. He was convicted only of conspiracy to murder and is now serving a 19- to 24-year prison sentence. There are dozens of other incidents in recent years in which NFL players have been charged with domestic violence or spousal abuse.

Even though the crime rate among professional athletes is lower than among other males of the same age, economic, and demographic makeup (Heath, 2000), the high profile crimes committed by athletes have led to intense public debate about the connection between the culture of sports and violent behavior. Some say that hard-hitting sports breed violence in the players; others, that the players' aggression tips over into their personal lives. Most critics agree that overall, the owners and governing bodies (such as the National Football League) deny or minimize the problems of their players and write them off to individual, as opposed to ecological, factors. Then, too, the hero status of many sports' stars in the community make it less likely that they will be held accountable for their actions.

The world of sports seems to have created an ecological niche that supports violence and crime among fans, too. Hours before the Tyson–Holyfield fight, for example, violent conflicts broke out between their respective fans. After the Oakland Raiders' loss to the Tampa Bay Buccaneers in the 2003 Super Bowl, enraged Raiders' fans staged a miniriot in which dozens of people were injured and property was damaged. Also, when the University of Maryland lost a basketball championship in 2001, angry students went on a drunken rampage through the town, setting fires, smashing cars, and looting. Such problems are even more intense in other countries, especially in Europe and South America, where brawls and riots break out during and after soccer matches, often with fatal results. In 1994, a player on Columbia's soccer team was shot to death by fans after his team lost to the United States in a World Cup match. Indeed, the team played under constant death threats from fans (Sanchez-Bender, 1998).

Fan violence is nothing new. In 532 B.C., there was apparently a fan riot during a chariot race in Constantinople that resulted in the deaths of 30,000 people; and the Roman senate imposed a 10-year ban on gladiator fights in Pompeii in 59 A.D. because spectator violence was so prevalent during these contests (Guttmann, 1986).

Do fans fight each other because they are violent criminals or does the highly charged atmosphere surrounding many sporting events trigger their aggression? It is impossible to know for sure. The ecological perspective suggests that personal and situational factors affect each other and together result in crime. Simmons and Taylor (1992) proposed a psychosocial model of fan violence that takes into account several factors including those highlighted by some of the theories we discussed earlier in this chapter. Group-related contributions to fan violence include group solidarity, intergroup hostility, deindividuation, and dehumanization of the opposition. They suggested that the level of fan violence is related to the level of violence in the sport itself; aggressive behavior does, indeed, tend to be most intense at football and ice hockey games. Perhaps, then, fan violence is being stimulated by the violence modeled for them during the games they are watching. Other, more general, factors underlying fan violence may include frustration, the stress of high crowd density, and the effects of alcohol (Simmons & Taylor, 1992).

These and other factors are probably at work in yet another form of fan violence that occurs between parents of children involved in competitive sports. In July 2002, Thomas Junta was watching his son's hockey team practice when he exchanged words with the coach, Michael Costa (the father of a player), about the amount of violence among the players. Costa died of injuries sustained when the men got violent with each other. Junta was sentenced to 6 to 10 years in prison. In Canada in January 2005, a father reached over the glass separating the bleachers from the ice rink and began choking the coach. Spectators broke up the fight before the coach lost his life. Parent and coach interpersonal violence has gotten so bad—and so common—that children's sports teams now routinely adopt strict rules governing parental misbehavior.

Ecology, Ethnicity, and Crime

Sports-related violence is but one example of how social and environmental factors can converge to incline some people toward criminal behavior. The ecological approach to criminal behavior helps explain why criminals may be rich or poor, Black or White, gay or straight, or possessed of virtually any other set of attributes. However, anyone who is unfortunate enough to grow up in an ecological niche that strongly supports criminal behavior is at particular risk for engaging in such behavior. Further, if people who live in such circumstances share the same socioeconomic status, ethnicity, or other demographic characteristics, those characteristics will be especially frequent in the criminal population.

People from some ethnic backgrounds are indeed more likely than others to be exposed to a crime-risky ecology and are therefore more likely to be criminals. Members of certain ethnic minority groups, in particular, are involved in a disproportionate amount of crime in the United States. For example, although Blacks make up only about 13% of the general population, they represented 28% of all arrests for FBI Index offenses in 2000 (FBI, 2001). Of all those arrested for violent crimes in 2002, 40% were Blacks or Hispanic Americans (FBI, 2003). Part of this difference in ethnic representation among arrestees may be due to discriminatory law enforcement practices, but even when this factor is taken into account, Blacks do commit proportionally more crimes than Whites or other ethnic minorities (Currie & Sternbach, 1987; Silberman, 1979; Tonry, 1996; Wilson & Herrnstein, 1985). It is important to recognize, however, that these differences are not due to ethnicity per se but to differences the high-risk social and environmental conditions that certain ethnic groups tend to encounter more commonly than others.

Nevertheless, the very discussion of ethnic differences in criminal behavior is a highly charged matter in the United States today. To some, talking about ethnicity and crime in the same breath is politically incorrect and generates the specter of discrimination. Yet to not to talk about this issue means not talking about some problems that Black Americans—whether involved in crime or not—face more often than other people. For example:

1. A Black *New York Times* correspondent wrote of walking in his affluent Washington, DC neighborhood one spring day in 1999 when a police cruiser pulled alongside and the officer demanded that he produce identification and explain what he was doing there. When the author said that he lived there, a fact verified by his driver's license, the officer said that there had been a burglary in the area, and the author fit the description of the suspect. On returning home, the man called the police and was not surprised to learn that there had been no burglary; the officer's explanation was concocted to justify the random stop of a Black man in an area where he appeared not to belong (Holmes, 1999). In a similar incident a few months later, New York police arrested and strip searched Alton White, a Black Broadway star who they claimed fit the description of a Hispanic drug dealer they were seeking. Another Black actor, Danny Glover, missed a stage performance when New York City officers detained him in his own apartment building. Glover also allegedly resembled a suspect the police said they were looking for.

2. The fact is, Black men tend to be singled out for random police stops because they are allegedly suspicious when in fact they are merely conspicuous. Further, Blacks are more likely than Whites to be stopped by police for minor traffic infractions or for questioning about crimes simply because they fit criminal profiles. This fact has led some states to enact laws requiring law enforcement agencies to keep records about the ethnicity of people they stop.

2. Blacks are more likely than other groups to be prosecuted for drug crimes. Although they constitute only 13% of all drug users, Blacks represent 35% of arrests for drug possession, 55% of drug convictions, and 74% of prison sentences for drug-related crime (Bureau of Justice Statistics, 2003).

3. Blacks, and to a lesser extent other minorities, are more likely than other people to be the victims of violent crime, especially homicide. In 2001, Blacks made up only 13% of the U.S. adult population but were the victims in almost 50% of that year's homicides (FBI, 2002). Blacks are also disproportionally represented among the victims of police brutality (Nelson, 2000). Among the most prominent examples are the 1991 police beating of Rodney King in Los Angeles, the torture and sodomy of Haitian immigrant Abner Louima by Brooklyn police in 1997, and the 1999 murder by New York City police of Amadou Diallo, an unarmed African immigrant in the Bronx. These and many other cases contribute to minority citizens' distrust and resentment of law enforcement (Bruni, 1999; Greenfeld et al., 1997; Rudvosky, 1992).

4. Distrust and resentment is also fueled by the fact that there is often less vigorous prosecution of crimes against Black victims and less intense policing of predominantly Black neighborhoods. To take but one example, in rural St. Mary's County, Maryland, Black residents who make up 15% of the population demonstrated and called for hearings into the failure of local law enforcement to look for the killers of two Blacks murdered in separate incidents despite the fact that they had leads on suspects in both cases (Gowen, 1998). Even when those who murder Blacks are caught, prosecuted, and convicted, the odds of their being sentenced to death are more than four times less than if the victim had been White (Baldus, Woodworth, & Pulaski, 1990; Paternoster & Brame, 2003). Many Blacks view such inequality in law enforcement, prosecution, and punishment as a conspiracy against their welfare (Kennedy, 1998).

5. Efforts to exclude minority citizens from juries were once commonplace, and discriminatory practices may still haunt the jury selection process (Savage, 2002). This fact, when combined with the relatively small percentage of Blacks in the population, leads to underrepresentation of Blacks on criminal trial juries. This problem is especially troubling when Blacks are the defendants in those trials, as it may increase the likelihood of conviction and the severity of punishment (DiPerna, 1984; Nietzel, McCarthy, & Harris, 1999).

6. Blacks also tend to be discriminated against in sentencing. For example, they are more likely than Whites to receive the death penalty for murder, particularly for the murder of a White person (Baldus et al., 1990; Kennedy, 1998; Paternoster & Brame, 2003). Further, as part of a nationwide "war on drugs," new sentencing laws have created far harsher penalties for those caught with the crack cocaine popular in Black neighborhoods than for those caught with its pricier "uptown" cousin, powder cocaine (United States Sentencing Commission, 1995). Under the federal Anti-Drug Abuse Act of 1986, a person convicted of possession with intent to distribute 50 or more grams of crack cocaine must receive a sentence of no less than 10 years without possibility of parole. A defendant would have to possess, with intent to distribute, 5,000 grams of powder cocaine to be subject to a sentence that severe. There is even a mandatory minimum sentence of 5 years (with no parole) for the mere possession of 1 to 5 g of crack cocaine; it is the only drug for which there is a mandatory minimum penalty, even for a first offense.

Partly as a result of the previously mentioned racial disparities in the criminal justice system, 30% of Black men between the ages of 20 and 29 are incarcerated (Karberg & Beck, 2004). Given current incarceration rates, 28% of Black males will likely spend some part of their adult life in prison compared to16% of Hispanic males and 4.4% of White males (Bureau of Justice Statistics, 2003b). This high incarceration rate also means that sanctions on liberties and privileges after incarceration (a practice referred to as "invisible punishment"; see chapter 13) fall more heavily on the Black population than on other groups. These sanctions include loss of voting rights and ineligibility for student loans, food stamps, public housing, and even medical care. Disparity exists, too, in the treatment of Black juveniles. National data show that minority juvenile offenders are more likely than non-Hispanic White offenders to be placed in public (rather than private) custodial facilities (Snyder & Sickmund, 1999).

In a book that examines ethnicity and crime in the United States, Harvard Law School professor Kennedy (1998), himself Black, cautioned that if people do not thoughtfully examine the obvious fact that Blacks do commit more crimes—and have done so throughout most of the 20th century (Lane, 1989; Silberman, 1979)—and seriously consider the reasons why, then bigoted elements in America will control the debate just by reciting the numbers.

Prominent among the reasons underlying Blacks' disproportionate involvement in criminal activity is a two-century legacy of bigotry in the United States that led to economic, educational, social, and political discrimination against them. Criminologists point out, first, that slavery left an indelible scar on the Black psyche. Blacks were violently uprooted from their native countries, and after being brought to America as slaves, were subdued by their masters through violence, intimidation, and threats. Even after slavery was abolished in 1863, Blacks remained subject to danger from violent bigoted elements such as the Ku Klux Klan and to deprivations of every kind. Even today, Blacks are by no means fully integrated into America's social and political mainstream (Comer, 1985; Silberman, 1979).

That the Black experience in the United States and not ethnicity itself has a lot to do with Blacks' disproportionate involvement in crime is suggested by statistics that showed that crime rates among Blacks is much lower in other predominantly White cultures, such as Canada, as well as in predominantly Black cultures such as Nigeria (Siegel, 1998). Today, whether one likes it or not, ethnicity—and its consequences for members of particular ethnic groups—remain important factors in tracing the social and environmental roots of crime.

Summary

Social and environmental factors can contribute to criminal behavior in many ways—direct and indirect. For example, aggression and violence toward others is often learned from watching and listening to others—be they parents, friends, characters in violent movies and video games, or even musical performers. Psychologists studying the effects of media violence on young people believe that violence not only desensitizes many to violence but may also encourage violence by glorifying it and making it seem exciting. Interactive violent video games are particularly troublesome, as young people experience the "thrill" of "winning" that comes from committing virtual mayhem.

Crime can also be triggered by schemas, scripts, attributions, and other thought processes that lead some people to perceive the world as a threatening place and to believe that aggression and violence are the only, even primary, ways to deal with it. Frustration, deindividuation, conformity, compliance, and obedience to authority represent additional social factors that may lead some individuals to commit crimes in certain social situations.

Environmental factors trigger violence or crime in several ways, including by increasing physiological arousal, by acting as stressors, and by making it more likely that some people will behave aggressively. Research by environmental psychologists has suggested that heat, noise, air pollution, natural disasters, crowding, violation of personal space, and living in certain places can all raise the likelihood of crime and violence. For example, many cities, prisons, and sports are breeding grounds for violence, making it unsurprising that some people in those settings become violent.

Members of certain ethnic groups are more or less likely to be a perpetrator or victim of crime, not because of ethnicity itself but because of social, political, and legal forces that differ across ethnic groups.

Although an individual's interactions with other people, social systems, cultural forces, and the physical environment can contribute to crime, whether crime actually results from these interactions depends on each individual's response to these potentially powerful forces.

Key Terms

Groups	*Social cognition*
Social psychology	*Terrorism*
Environmental psychology	*Deindividuation*
Sociology	*Ecology*

Questions for Review

1. Describe how the disciplines of (a) social psychology, (b) environmental psychology, and (c) sociology study the social and environmental roots of crime.
2. Give an example of how Bronfenbrenner's microsystems, macrosystems, and exosystems contribute to crime.
3. How do faulty attributions and attributional biases help explain some rapes and incidents of spousal abuse?
4. What is the most reasonable conclusion to be made about the role of violent media to crime and violence?
5. What are the major environmental factors that contribute to crime, and what are the pathways through which they have their effect?

 ## *Track It Down*

Criminal Behavior Website
www.cassel2e.com
National Television Violence Study
www.ccsp.ucsb.edu/ntvs.htm
American Academy of Child and Adolescent Psychiatry Fact Sheets on Violent Lyrics and Other Media
www.findarticles.com/p/articles/mi_m1175/is_n6_v25/ai_12778347
Stanley Milgram's Obedience Experiment
http://en.wikipedia.org/wiki/Milgram_experiment
Redesigning Neighborhoods to Thwart Crime
www.ncjrs.org/txtfiles/164488.txt
Prison Violence
www.motherjones.com/news/special_reports/prisons/violence.html
Racial Disparity in U.S. Politics and Crime
www.solent.ac.uk/law/prcus.html

7

The Development of Crime From Early Childhood to Adolescence

Pathways to Crime

Biological Influences on the Development of Criminal Behavior

Developmental Disorders and Crime

Learning to Be—or Not to Be—a Criminal

Family Influences on Criminal Behavior

Putting It All in Perspective

The following case from Elaine Cassel's legal files provides an all-too-vivid example of how criminal potentialities in childhood are shaped by circumstances into criminal realities in adolescence. The names have been changed to protect confidentiality.

> "David" was 3 years old when I first met him. I was appointed to be his 3-month-old sister "Maria's" guardian *ad litem,* an attorney who protects the legal interests of children or adults unable to speak for themselves. She had been born 2 months prematurely, weighing 3 lb and addicted to cocaine. Maria was about to be discharged from the neonatal intensive care unit of a large suburban hospital where she had been since birth, and we were in court for a hearing to determine who would take custody of her. In the courtroom was David's and Maria's 23-year-old mother, "Debbie," who testified that she had consumed large amounts of cocaine and alcohol early in her pregnancy. Also present were Maria's father, "Danny," to whom Debbie was not married, and Danny's mother, who testified that she was willing to care for Maria in her home. The social worker who had brought Maria's case to the court's attention told the judge about David, who was still living with Debbie. Asked if David was at risk for abuse and neglect, the social worker said she had no reason to think so. When the judge ruled that Debbie could keep David, she sobbed with relief. She sobbed again, for a different reason, though, when the judge gave custody of Maria to Danny's mother.
>
> Social workers in the county where Debbie lived knew her well, for foster parents in the area had raised her. She had been a reasonably well-behaved child, but when she reached her teenage years, conflicts with foster parents led to Debbie being passed from home to home. When she was 17, she dropped out of high school and married a hard-working young man. The couple seemed happy, and the social workers recall thinking that her husband would give her the home she never had. She had a daughter when she was almost 19, and everyone thought that she was a good mother. About a year later, however, she met a man at a bar, had sex with him, and got pregnant with David. Ashamed and afraid to confess to her husband, she fled to another state with David's father. After a year with no word from Debbie, her

husband divorced her and was awarded sole custody of their daughter. A month before David was born; his father was killed in a car accident. Debbie eventually made her way back home, where she lived with friends and tried to support David. It was there that she met Maria's father, Danny, who introduced her to crack cocaine.

Three months after the custody hearing, Danny was murdered during a drug deal and, within a month of his death, Debbie had moved in with one of Danny's friends, "George." He did not use drugs, but drank a lot and physically abused Debbie and David. The child abuse came to light after police in a neighboring state where David, Debbie, and George had been camping notified social workers. The police were called after other campers heard David's screams, and he was taken to a hospital with injuries so severe that he remained there for a week. Debbie and George were charged with criminal child abuse. At their trial, George testified that he beat David to "teach him a lesson" after he had wet his pants. When David was released from the hospital, the same social worker who brought Maria's case before the court placed him temporarily in foster care. Because of my involvement with Maria's case, the judge asked me to serve as David's guardian *ad litem.*

A few months after their preliminary appearance on child abuse charges, Debbie and George were allowed to return to Virginia where they tried to get custody of David. Debbie asked the court for visitation rights, and the court granted them but only for an hour a week and only in the presence of Devon's foster mother. When David saw Debbie, he flew into a rage, literally tearing up everything he could get his hands on before being restrained. After a several such incidents, the judge suspended Debbie's visitations. Shortly thereafter, Debbie and George were convicted of child abuse and sentenced to 5 years in prison. David remained in foster care and had no further contact with either of them, but the damage had been done.

Whenever he saw a man whom he did not know, David would throw a tantrum, tearing up whatever was within reach. Eventually he began beating his toys and dolls, saying, "Bad Peter. Peter is bad." When asked who Peter was, he replied, "Peter is a bad boy." Psychiatrists diagnosed Peter as displaying dissociative identity disorder (formerly known as multiple personality disorder), noting that David had created Peter to be the bad boy who had been beaten by his mother's boyfriend. David's behavior eventually became so problematic that—like his own mother—he was moved from foster home to foster home. Each new set of foster parents had to take him to psychotherapy sessions and to learn how to deal with his violent outbursts.

By the time David was 8 years old, his violent outbursts were less frequent; his grades, although not particularly good, were passing; and he was manageable in the classroom. Teachers commented that he seemed sad, maybe even depressed. Considering what he had been through, though, this was not surprising. When David was 10, I was once again called to appear in court on his behalf. He had been playing with some older boys in the neighborhood and they had set a fire that burned several hundred feet of expensive wooden fencing. When I spoke with him, he was quiet and withdrawn, rarely making eye contact. He was unaffected by my warning that he would end up in juvenile jail if he continued to get into trouble. He said he did not care where he lived because "nobody wants me anyway." How could I argue with him? Actually, he was too young to be placed in juvenile detention, so a social worker found yet another foster home for him, this time with a couple who wanted to take David on as a challenge. Despite their efforts, before his 12th birthday, David was taken in by juvenile authorities for acting as a look-out man for older boys who were robbing a local pawn shop. This time, the judge rejected the idea of a new foster home placement and ordered that David be placed in an appropriate facility that might help "turn him around" before it was too late. I wondered if it was already too late.

At that point, my role in David's life ended, and I have no idea what happened to him. However, I would not be surprised to find that today, at about the age of 18, he is in jail somewhere—if he is alive. He is very likely to become a career criminal unless some miracle has saved him from this destiny. How can I be so sure? Because David's case illustrates that children are not born bad, nor do they just wake up one morning and become bad. David had been exposed to virtually every known risk factor for developing aggressive, violent behavior. His father died before he was born. The man his mother lived with during his earliest years was a criminal. He was the victim of almost deadly physical abuse from another of his mother's boyfriends. He moved from one foster home to another. He displayed signs of a psychiatric disorder. His mother had been in prison and was addicted to drugs and alcohol.

Yet David could have just as easily been born to different parents, with different genes, into a different environment. His parents could have been loving and law-abiding, and he could have spent his young life in a stable home, playing soccer, swimming, enjoying friends, and being cherished. Under those circumstances, how likely do you think it would have been for David to commit arson, larceny, and auto theft? What if he had had the same genes, but had been adopted at birth by a loving family? Answersto these questions involve the centuries-old debate about what has the greater influence over human development—genes (nature) or environment (nurture)?

In this chapter, we examine the influences of nature and nurture on the development of crime from childhood to adolescence. In doing so, we apply the theories and methods we mentioned in the previous three chapters to the facts and circumstances of David's life and to the lives of children who, like him, are at risk for antisocial conduct and criminal behavior. We explore the *"potentialities* for badness" that Erikson (1957, p. 15) and many other psychologists, sociologists, criminologists, and philosophers say reside within all human beings and how they develop into *probabilities* for badness through the circumstances of childhood.

Pathways to Crime

Aggressive behaviors are common in preschool children, but they tend to disappear in the years between preschool and elementary school, as toddlers are socialized by parents and teachers (Haapasalo & Tremblay, 1994; Tremblay et al., 1996). In some children, however, aggressive behaviors remain and may increase in intensity, becoming violent over time. Aggressive children may become violent, antisocial delinquent adolescents, and these adolescents in turn may become serious adult offenders.

Developmental psychologists speak of developmental pathways that lead to aggression, violence, and crime (Loeber, Keehan, & Zhang, 1997).[1] Loeber and Stouthamer-Loeber (1998) identified two such pathways: a life-course type and a limited duration type. Children following a *life-course* pathway develop persistent antisocial behavior in childhood that worsens in adolescence and adulthood. This type probably accounts for the highest number of adult violent offenders in the United States, although we do not know the exact proportion who meet this criterion (Loeber & Stouthamer-Loeber, 1998). Within the life-course type are two subtypes: a preschool subtype and a childhood-adolescent-onset subtype. Recent research has suggested that many children whose aggressive behavior begins in the preschool years may meet the diagnostic criteria for attention deficit disorder (ADHD); their aggression may escalate to symptoms of conduct disorder (CD; Barkley, 1998). Life-course offenders in the childhood-adolescent-onset subtype usually do not qualify for a diagnosis of ADHD; these boys generally show oppositional behaviors that may escalate into oppositional defiant disorder (ODD) and sometimes conduct disorder (CD) (Moffitt, Caspi, Harrington, & Milne, 2002; Patterson, Reid, & Dishion, 1992). (We discuss these disorders later in this chapter.) Children who follow a *limited duration* pathway become aggressive in childhood but "outgrow" it in late adolescence and early adulthood (Moffitt, 1993; Moffitt, Caspi, Dickson, Silva, & Stanton, 1996).

Only a minority of adult violent offenders follow a *late-onset* pathway to crime, meaning that they had no history of childhood or adolescent aggression (Farrington, 1994a; Windel & Windel, 1995).

Aggression and criminal behavior in childhood have been categorized in terms of overt versus covert acts. Overt acts cause direct physical harm to others. These tend to progress from bullying and annoying others in early childhood to fighting in middle childhood and to serious crime (rape, robbery, and murder) in adolescence. Covert acts progress from deceitful behaviors (e.g., shoplifting and lying), to property crimes (e.g., van-

---

[1]Because about 90% of violent offenders are men, researchers studying the developmental roots of juvenile and adult aggression generally concern themselves with boys.

dalism and fire setting), to more serious crimes such as fraud, burglary, and theft (Loeber & Stouthamer-Loeber, 1998).

The development of both overt and covert criminal behaviors in childhood has been linked to several conditions and disorders. These include biologically influenced problems in information processing, neurotransmitter and hormone activity, and temperament as well as a variety of developmental disorders. In the next two sections, we consider the most important of these conditions and disorders.

Biological Influences on the Development of Criminal Behavior

In one survey (Harlow, 1998), more than half of 567,000 male and female jail inmates said that at least one of their family members had been in jail or prison. Does this mean that criminal behavior is directly inherited? Probably not at all. As we noted in chapter 4, there is no direct link between genetics and criminal conduct. The fact that crime tends to "run in families" stems in large measure from environmental factors, especially from the fact that children often learn to be criminals from watching their relatives' examples. However, although scientists have not identified genes that cause or even directly contribute to violent or criminal behavior, they have identified several indirect pathways through which genes or groups of genes might increase the risk for criminal behavior. These pathways include genetic influences on many aspects of brain functioning and emotional expression (Comings, 1997; Rutter, Giller, & Hagell, 1998).

Neurological Disorders

Neurological dysfunctions—as measured by EEG, brain imaging, or performance tests (of motor abilities, visual processing, auditory-language functioning, and the like)—have been associated with impairment in abstract reasoning, problem-solving skills, and motor skills as well as with schizophrenia, depression, and other psychiatric disorders that may lead to aggression and violence in children (Raine et al., 2000; Seguin et al., 1995; Tibbits 1995; Voeller, 1986). These dysfunctions, often referred to as *"minimal brain dysfunctions,"* may be caused by low birth weight, brain injury, complications of delivery, fetal alcohol syndrome, or inherited abnormalities (Moffitt, 1993; Raine, Brennan, & Mednick, 1994) and can impair a child's ability to comply with expected norms of behavior (D. Lewis et al., 1986).

There is also evidence of a higher risk of conduct problems in children with learning disabilities involving impairments in listening, thinking, talking, reading, writing, or arithmetic (Heavey, Adelman, Nelson, & Smith, 1989; Rutter, Mayhood, & Howlin, 1992; R. J. Thompson & Kronenberger, 1990). One study (J. E. Porter & Rourke, 1985) found such disabilities in 40% of children with conduct problems. These learning disabilities have been linked to abnormalities in brain development that hinders information processing (Maughan & Yule, 1994; B. S. Peterson, 1995). The appearance of conduct problems in some children with learning disabilities may be related to social skills deficits—such as in interpersonal communication and the ability to accurately "read" the emotions of others—that result from their cognitive and perceptual problems (Rourke, 1988; H. L. Swanson, 1991). In several studies, children with learning disabilities have tended to be rated by peers as less popular than other children, and they were more likely to be rejected or neglected (e.g., Stone & LaGreca, 1990). When poor school performance and social rejection leads children with learning disabilities to experience frustration, anger, and low self-esteem, some of them react by displaying the kinds of aggressive and oppositional behaviors that can lead to delinquency (Moffitt, 1993). Several studies have suggested that there is indeed a link between some learning disabilities and delinquency (e.g., Winters, 1997). One of them (Brier, 1989) found that 36% of incarcerated juveniles had a learning disability and that youngsters with learning disabilities were more than twice as likely as other youths to commit a crime. A child with learning disabilities is especially likely to become delinquent if he or she also displays ADHD and low IQ.

Neurotransmitters and Hormones

The activity of certain neurotransmitter systems and hormones in the central, autonomic, and endocrine systems has been associated with some types of aggressive behavior. As we noted in chapter 4, for example, aggression in males is associated with high testosterone levels. Other research indicated that low levels of the neurotransmitter serotonin are correlated with violent behavior in children and adults (Moffitt & Lynam, 1994). Children's aggressive behavior has also been linked to high levels of the stress hormone cortisol (McBurnett, Lahey, Capasso, & Loeber, 1996; Sussman, Dorn, Inoff-Germain, Nottelmann, & Chrousos, 1997). Still, these data are correlational, so it is unclear whether the neurotransmitter and hormone levels observed in these studies are the cause or the effect of aggressive behavior.

Temperament

Temperament refers to each individual's way of expressing needs and emotions; responding to environmental stimuli, events, and people; and regulating those responses. Temperament is believed to be almost totally genetically based because it is evident in emotional expression from the moment of birth. For example, some infants appear happy and active as they gurgle, thrash, wiggle, and respond comfortably to attention and contact; others lie still, turn away, and fuss. Some cry and yell with gusto; others merely whine and whimper. As infants grow into children and children become adults, temperamental differences remain evident on many dimensions including energy level, communication style, risk-taking tendencies, and sociability. Indeed, temperament serves as the beginning of the personality that makes each person unique. The most prominent theories of temperamental types are those of Alexander Thomas and Stella Chess (1977) and of Jerome Kagan and his colleagues (Kagan, Snidman, Arcus, & Reznick, 1994).

Thomas and Chess (1977) asked parents to describe their infants' in terms of (1) general activity level; (2) regularity and predictability of sleeping, eating, and elimination; (3) initial reactions to people; (4) adaptation to new situations; (5) responsiveness to subtle stimulus events; (6) amount of energy associated with activity; (7) dominant mood; and (8) attention span and distractibility. In collating the responses, they found evidence for three types of infant temperament: easy, difficult, and slow to warm up. *Easy babies* were the most common, comprising 40% of the sample. These babies almost immediately get into regular schedules of feeding and sleeping, react to new situations cheerfully, and are rarely fussy. *Difficult babies* (10% of the sample) did not follow predictable schedules and were irritable. *Slow-to-warm-up babies* (15%) reacted cautiously to new situations and people but eventually came to enjoy them. (Characteristics of the remaining 35% of the sample did not fit into any of the three main types).

Thomas and Chess emphasized the importance of parent–child interactions in affecting the degree to which children express their inherited temperament and how such interactions can counteract temperamental tendencies toward certain traits such as shyness and irritability. From the moment of birth, interaction with caregivers begins to refine, and may to some extent reshape, a baby's temperament and personality development. Still, some temperamental features remain more or less constant throughout the life span, becoming a part of the child's personality. Easy infants usually tend to stay easy and become calm, confident, competent adults; difficult infants may become hard to get along with as adults; and slow-to-warm-up infants generally are timid toddlers, shy school-age children, and anxious teenagers and adults (Kagan & Snideman, 2004).

Recognizing the limitations of relying mainly on potentially biased parental reports about children's temperament, Kagan and his colleagues conducted laboratory observations of children; measured their brain-wave patterns, heart rates, and other physiological functions; and then stayed in contact over many years to assess the stability of children's early characteristics and whether they predicted behavior in later life. This research led Kagan to group children into one of two categories: inhibited or uninhibited. Compared to uninhibited children, inhibited children:

1. Are reluctant to initiate spontaneous comments in the presence of unfamiliar children or adults.
2. Do not smile spontaneously at unfamiliar people.
3. Need a long time to relax in new situations.
4. Show impaired memory of stressful events.
5. Are reluctant to take risks and cautious in making decisions.
6. Show disruptions in reading when confronted with threatening words.
7. Have unusual fears.
8. Show large increases in heart rate, diastolic blood pressure, and pupillary dilation in response to stressors or even to adopting a standing posture.

9. Display high muscle tension.
10. Have more brain activity in the right frontal lobe, an area associated with emotion and arousal (Kagan & Snideman, 2004).

Twin studies of 2-year-olds in each of the two temperament categories showed genetic influences to be particularly strong between children who are extremely inhibited or extremely uninhibited. Further, Kagan and his colleagues found that children's temperament type, as measured at age 2, was consistent with measures taken at ages 5 to 7. Children who did change over time were most likely to be those who had been in the middle range of the inhibited category—and they were more likely to become uninhibited. Children who were extremely inhibited at age 2 usually showed little change, unless it was to become even more inhibited. Overall, girls were more inhibited than boys, and their fear responses tended to increase over time. Of the the most fearful inhibited children, 86% were girls (Kagan, Snidman, Arcus, & Reznick, 1994).

Other researchers have attached different labels to temperament types, but all have been consistent with the inhibited/uninhibited distinction; they relate to the degree to which a child is extroverted or introverted, displays negative emotions, and shows self-control (e.g., M. D. Rothbart & Mauro, 1990).

The biologically-based characteristics associated with temperament influence a number of psychological dimensions that have been related to criminality—including learning experiences, regulation of emotional arousal, social and moral development, and attachment to caregivers (M. K. Rothbart & Ahadi, 1994).

Temperament and Learning Experiences. Temperament affects what and how children learn. For example, if children tend to react with fear to new people or situations, they are more likely to avoid or escape them. This tendency may also lead these children to lose confidence and come to believe that their inhibitions will insure their failure. Albert Bandura (1986) referred to this belief as a lack of self-efficacy. Thus, an inhibited child who has musical talent might also suffer stage fright and following mistakes at a recital, might lose so much confidence as to not even try to overcome the fear. Similarly, children who find social situations threatening may have a hard time developing social skills, which can cause them to be rejected by their peers and to feel anger and resentment as a result. Temperament can also affect a child's response to learning disabilities. As noted earlier, some children who feel frustrated, angry, rejected, and inferior as a result of academic and social failure might channel their desire for revenge into violent aggression. Indeed, vengeance has reportedly motivated many of the "outcast" students who have committed mass murder at U.S. schools in recent years.

Regulation of Arousal. Temperament can also affect emotional reactivity and the regulation of arousal. For example, as we described in chapter 4, an individual with a low tolerance for arousal is more likely to seek quiet pursuits and to try to keep the peace in interpersonal relationships. A person who can tolerate a lot of stimulation might seek excitement in life and in relationships. If the social and physical environment does not fit a person's temperament, there can be frustration and discontent. Quiet, shy people who work in a bustling and intensely social atmosphere may feel overstimulated and need to withdraw to reduce their arousal. Their withdrawal may cause others to feel suspicious or even offended. If individual temperaments are mismatched in personal and professional relationships, interpersonal conflicts may be more likely.

In England, Raine, Venables, and Mednick (1997) tested children's physiological arousal—as measured by heart rate and skin conductance—at age 3 and again at age 11. They found that lower arousal levels at age 3 predicted aggressive behaviors at 11. Other research has indicated that young adolescents with low resting heart rates are more likely than other youths to show aggression, instigate confrontations at school, and have criminal records 10 years later (Kindlon et al., 1995; Raine, 2002; Raine et al., 1990; see Figure 7.1). Low autonomic arousal is also associated with adult antisocial behavior (Farrington, 2006; Raine, 1993).

Social and Moral Development. Temperament exerts a strong influence on children's social and moral development, a critical factor in the appearance of prosocial and antisocial behavior. By the age of about 2, children should begin to learn that there are certain standards of acceptable conduct toward others (e.g., that grabbing other people's possessions or hitting others is unacceptable; Kagan, 1989). As their parents teach them these social and moral standards, children should also begin to understand that their behavior has an effect on others and that they must take others into account when deciding how to act. In other words, parents should be teaching empathy and stimulating development of the child's *conscience*.

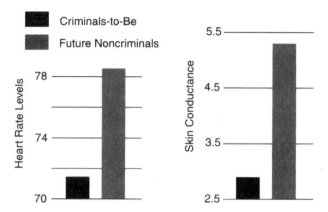

FIGURE 7.1 *Adolescent Underarousal and Adult Criminality.* **From *Abnormal Psychology*, by M. T. Nietzel, M. Speltz, E. McCauley, & D. A. Bernstein, 1998, Boston: Allyn & Bacon. Copyright © 1998 by Allyn & Bacon. Reprinted by permission of authors. Based on data from "Relationships Between Central and Automatic Measures of Arousal at Age 15 Years and Criminality at Age 24 Years," by A. Raine, P. H. Venables, & M. Williams, 1990, *Archives of General Psychiatry*, 47.**

Inhibited children are especially likely to experience anxiety, guilt, and shame when they do wrong and thus are more likely to avoid violating societal or family rules. Children who are fearful of violating rules are better able to regulate their behavior so as to avoid anxiety, guilt, or other negative emotions. Accordingly, it usually takes little or no punishment to socialize inhibited children. Often, just a warning about what is right and wrong and the prospect of punishment will suffice to promote prosocial behavior and avoid antisocial actions.

Just the opposite tends to be true of uninhibited children; they are likely to be slower than inhibited children in learning social skills and to have more difficulty in internalizing social values. Because their lower levels of arousal make them less reactive to punishment, they are not as easily shaped by their parents' efforts at social-ization. Some parents deal with this recalcitrance by using ever more coercive disciplinary tactics, thus making it more likely that there will be serious conflicts between parents and children. Even when such children con-form to avoid punishment, they may never fully internalize the parents' rules and values. If punishment becomes physical abuse, the uninhibited child is at risk for becoming aggressive toward others—partly because they expect aggression from others (Dodge, Bates, & Pettit, 1990). This aggressiveness tends to bring disap-proval and rejection by parents, peers, and teachers, which in turn can lead to loneliness, depression, and vul-nerability to gang involvement and drug and alcohol use. The inability of uninhibited children to self-regulate behavior and internalize societal rules and values can set the stage for the development of criminal behavior (Henry, Caspi, Moffit, & Silva, 1996).

Inhibited/introverted children are at much lower risk than uninhibited/extroverted children for engaging in criminal behavior. In fact, research by Farrington (1987) suggests that an inhibited temperament may protect even children living in high-risk criminal environments from becoming criminals themselves. They do not have aggressive tendencies, so they get along with others; they do not seek out social situations, so they avoid gangs; they are sensitive to punishment, so they avoid breaking rules.

Attachment. Infant temperament can influence the nature of the attachment that forms between babies and their caregivers. As we described in chapter 5, attachment refers to the deep, affectionate, close, and enduring relationships between infants and the "significant others" in their lives—especially the mother or other care-giver. In most cultures, 7- to 9-month-old children begin to show signs of distress when they are separated from their caregivers, thus signaling the presence of the attachment bond (Grossman & Grossman, 1990). This bond becomes more intense and pronounced between the ages of 14 and 24 months and sets the stage for the types of bonds that the child will form with significant others throughout life.

John Bowlby (1969) was among the first psychologists to study the importance of attachment. After observing infants and children orphaned during World War II, he concluded that their depression and other emotional scars,

TABLE 7.1   *Attachment Styles*

Secure	Avoidant	Ambivalent	Disorganized
Children view parents as the secure base from which to explore the world. They prefer the parent to a stranger, and may be temporarily upset when left. But upon return of the parent, the child actively seeks out contact with and welcomes the parent.	Children are not apparently concerned when the parent leaves and they are not particularly responsive when the parent returns. They do not generally cry when the parent leaves, nor do they cling when the parent returns.	These children may cling to the parent when the parent leaves but when the parent returns they may express angry or resistance behavior, such as hitting or pushing the parent. They may appear not to be soothed when the parent tries to comfort them.	These children exhibit confused and contradictory behaviors toward the parent, indicating detachment and a lack of emotional connection. They may, for instance, not look at the parent when being held or talked to, or they may show a flat affect.

such as inability to form close ties to substitute caregivers, was a result of the loss of their primary attachment object. Research by Mary Ainsworth (1973) identified two main types of attachment—secure and insecure—along with several subtypes (see Table 7.1). *Insecure attachment* can be either (a) ambivalent, (b) avoidant, or (c) disorganized. Employing the so-called strange situation, Ainsworth and her colleagues observed hundreds of children as they were left by their mothers in a room with only an adult stranger and some toys. The mothers returned a short time later. *Securely attached* children showed some initial distress when their mothers left but then quieted down and played-and greeted the mother warmly on her return. Children classified as having an *insecure-avoidant attachment* ignored the mother when she left and also when she returned. Those in the *insecure-ambivalent attachment* category were upset when the mother left but were angry or rejecting on her return. Children with an *insecure-disorganized attachment* showed inconsistent behavior such as crying on the mother's return but not responding to her efforts to soothe them or reaching out to her while looking away.

Children's temperament—and the goodness-of-fit between their temperament and their parents' personality—can affect the attachment process. For example, distress-prone children are more likely to develop insecure-avoidant and insecure-ambivalent attachments (M. K. Rothbart & Ahadi, 1994). Dymphna Van den Boom (1989) conducted two studies on the role of temperament in attachment. In the first, she related infants' distress proneness observed at 15 days of age to observations of parent and child interactions over the following year. Results indicated that most of the infants who had been distress prone as newborns exhibited insecure-avoidant attachment patterns later. Most of their mothers frequently ignored them and their pleas for attention and spent less time playing with them than did the mothers of other infants. Must a distress-prone temperament always lead to insecure attachment? In the second study, Van den Boom offered an attachment-enhancing training program to the mothers of a group of distress-prone 6-month-olds. Compared to infants whose mothers received no such training, infants whose mothers had learned how to soothe and play with them interacted more with their mothers and showed more positive emotions. By the age of 12 months, 68% of these infants were classified as securely attached compared to only 28% of infants whose mothers had not received training.

Studies such as these are important because they illustrate that attachment depends on the interaction of infants' temperament and parents' responses to that temperament. Indeed, studies of parental responses to crying and other signs of distress in difficult infants reveal increased physiological arousal (measured by skin conductance, heart rate, and blood pressure), negative psychological reactions, and a tendency to avoid the infants' distress (Bleichfeld & Moely, 1984; Boukydis & Burgess, 1982). In other words, it may be that insecurely attached children's avoidance of their mothers in the strange situation is a reaction to the mothers' tendency to avoid their children.

How might the temperament–attachment link lay the groundwork for crime? Research has suggested that infants whose temperaments facilitate the development of secure attachment tend to become children who are socially and emotionally competent, cooperative, enthusiastic, good at problem solving, compliant and controlled, popular,eee and playful (Clarke-Stewart, 1988; Elicker & Sroufe, 1993; Wartner, Grossman, Fremmer-Bombik, & Seuss, 1994). In fact, one report (Resnick et al., 1997) summarizing the survey and interview responses of more than 100,000 students in Grades 7 to12 concluded that connectedness to parents (defined as feelings of warmth, love, and caring from parents) is a significant factor in protecting adolescents from engaging in substance use and violence. Infants whose temperaments engender fussiness, overactivity, and a tendency not to respond to parents' attempts to comfort them are more likely to become children who conflict with and are rejected by their peers, thus leading to low self-esteem, truancy, and eventually delinquency (Rubin, LeMare, & Lollis, 1990). This outcome is not inevitable, of course, but inherited temperamental patterns that are associated with insecure attachment and are not altered by counteracting parental influences appear to at least increase the *probability* of child behaviors that set off the chain of negative reactions and further misbehavior that so often leads to aggressiveness, violence, and crime (Aytech, 1994; Rutter, 1990). As suggested by Van den Boom's (1989) research, however, parents can be taught how to respond to their infants to make secure attachment more likely. Similar programs that provide such mentoring for mothers living in disadvantaged environments have been effective in preventing crime among potentially high-risk children (Tremblay & Craig, 1995; Yoskikawa, 1994).

Developmental Disorders and Crime

The chain of events that leads to criminal behavior is especially likely to be forged when problems with attachment and other aspects of development become so extreme as to be classified as mental disorders by the criteria listed in the *DSM–IV–TR* (American Psychiatric Association, 2000a). These include reactive attachment disorder (RAD), attention deficit hyperactivity disorder (ADHD), oppositional defiant disorder (ODD), and conduct disorder (CD). We mentioned some of these disorders earlier in relation to pathways to crime. We now consider how the characteristics of these disorders might promote the development of criminal behavior.

Reactive Attachment Disorder

In 1996, Renee Polreis killed her 4-year-old Russian-born adopted son by beating him with a wooden spoon. She said she reacted to the boy's rages against her with rage of her own. In 2004, another woman beat to death her 6-year-old Russian-born adopted son. Indeed, between 1996 and 2005, 12 American adoptive mothers killed their Russian-born children. Some of these children, like many others raised in Eastern European orphanages, were said to have displayed reactive attachment disorder (RAD), (DeAngeles, 1997), a pattern often stemming from early abuse or neglect. According to the *DSM–IV–TR*, children displaying RAD are unable to form a bond with a caregiver, which impairs the development of their sense of self and their ability to develop appropriate social interaction skills. As shown in Table 7.2, the diagnostic criteria for this disorder focus on two inappropriate ways of relating to caregivers: The inhibited child is withdrawn, hypervigilant or ambivalent toward others, and resists being comforted; the uninhibited child exhibits indiscriminate friendliness, "clingyness," and a desire for attention from any adult.

When children fail to form a healthy, appropriate attachment to a caregiver, it is more difficult for that caregiver to teach these children to be empathic toward others. When children develop no sensitivity for the feelings and welfare of others, those children are less likely to develop a strong conscience, and children without a conscience are more likely to behave in antisocial and criminal ways. Many developmental psychologists believe that children who display RAD feel such distrust of, and rage toward, the world that they either become depressed or lash out against others. Publicity about RAD has led some adoption agencies to screen children for signs of the disorder and to inform prospective parents about the results before final decisions are made.

Attention Deficit Hyperactivity Disorder

The symptoms of attention deficit hyperactivity disorder (ADHD) include inattention, impulsivity, failure to stay on task, distractibility, impatience, disorganization, fidgeting, and difficulty getting along with other

TABLE 7.2   *Reactive Attachment Disorder*

The essential feature of reactive attachment disorder is inappropriate social relationships beginning before the age of 5 years that are not related to other developmental disorders or delays.

Reactive attachment disorder is presumed to be the result of pathological caregiving that involves:

(1) persistent disregard of the child's basic physical and/or emotional needs; and/or
(2) repeated changes of caregiver that interfere with the child's ability to form stable attachment relationships.

Children with reactive attachment disorder may fall into one of two main types;

(1) inhibited children fail to initiate or respond appropriately to social interaction, and may be hypervigilant, ambivalent, or contradictory in their interactions with others;
(2) uninhibited children may be very friendly to relative strangers and not show any selectivity or discrimination in their choice of attachment figures.

Source: Based on information from American Psychiatric Association. (2000). *Diagnostic and Statistical Manual of Mental Disorders* (4th ed. text revision). Washington, DC: Author.

children (see Table 7.3). Although ADHD is not a direct cause of delinquent behavior, it is associated with poor academic performance, oppositional and aggressive behaviors, rejection by peers, early substance use, and high dropout rates, all of which are correlated with delinquent behavior that may evolve into a life of crime (Wilens, Biederman, Spencer, & Frances, 1994).

One study (Satterfield, 1987) assessed the behavior of 110 boys with ADHD and 88 normal boys from as early as age 6 and followed them through adolescence. Satterfield found that compared to normals, the boys with ADHD were significantly more likely to have committed robbery, burglary, grand theft, assault with a deadly weapon, or other serious crimes in adolescence. They were six times more likely than normal boys to have committed a serious offense by the age of 18, were 28 times more likely to have committed two or more serious crimes, and were 25 times more likely to have been institutionalized. The likelihood of criminal behavior among hyperactive teenagers was many times higher for those in lower socioeconomic classes compared to those in middle or upper classes. This pattern reflects the fact that environmental factors such as poverty always interact with temperamental and other characteristics that children bring with them at birth.

A meta-analysis of more than 20 empirical studies (Pratt, Blevins, Daigle, Cullen, & Unnever, 2002) provided further support for a strong relationship between ADHD and crime. Indeed, more than 25% of then currently incarcerated inmates are diagnosed with ADHD, and as many as 80% display a variety of ADHD-like symptoms. However, the link between ADHD and crime is not simple and may not be direct. For example, ADHD children are difficult to discipline and difficult to teach, making subsequent behavioral and academic problems that much more likely.

Oppositional Defiant Disorder

The diagnosis of oppositional defiant disorder (ODD) is typically made between the ages of 3 and 7. These children usually display poor control over their emotions, are extremely noncompliant and argumentative with parents and teachers, have repeated conflicts with peers as a result of provocative and hostile interactions, blame others for their problems, and are easily angered (S. B. Campbell, 1990). Because many children engage in one or more of these behaviors at various times in their childhood, the *DSM–IV–TR* stipulates that the behaviors must impair social relations, school performance, or other aspects of adaptive functioning consistent with the child's age (see Table 7.4).

ODD is especially likely to appear in children with insecure attachments (Speltz, DeKlyen, Greenberg, & Dryden, 1995). About 80% of preschool boys referred to one mental health clinic for ODD showed evidence of insecure attachment as opposed to only 25% of boys that did not have ODD with equivalent family back-

TABLE 7.3 *Attention-Deficit/Hyperactivity Disorder*

The essential features of attention-deficit/hyperactivity disorder are a persistent pattern of inattention and/or hyperactivity and/or impulsivity than is typical for the age or social development of the individual.

Inattention: Six or more symptoms must persist for at least six months in at least two settings (e.g., home, school, social interactions). Some of the symptoms are:

1. Lack of attention to detail in school work, play, or other activities;
2. Lack of listening when spoken to;
3. Failure to complete homework, chores, or work duties;
4. Difficulty in organizing tasks and activities;
5. Easily distracted by extraneous stimuli.

Hyperactivity/Impulsivity: Six or more symptoms must persist for at least six months in at least two settings (e.g., home, school, social interactions). Some of the symptoms are:

1. Often fidgets or squirms or cannot remain seated when sitting still is expected;
2. May run or jump excessively when being still is expected or may (especially in older children or adults) show signs of restlessness;
3. Difficulty in sustaining play or leisure activities;
4. Often talks excessively;
5. Often interrupts or intrudes upon others' activities.

Source: Based on information from American Psychiatric Association. (2000). *Diagnostic and Statistical Manual of Mental Disorders* (4th ed. text revision). Washington, DC: Author.

grounds and learning abilities (M. T. Greenberg, Spelz, DeKlyen, & Endriga, 1991). As many as 50% of children referred for ODD continued to have difficulties through their early grade-school years. Another study (Fergusson, Horwood, & Lynskey, 1995) found that less than 14% of 905 New Zealand children who displayed ODD between the ages of 7 and 15 were considered to be improved within 2 years, suggesting that this disruptive behavior pattern is relatively stable from childhood through adolescence. Children who display ODD in kindergarten through third grade are more likely to develop depression, anxiety, or conduct disorder in adolescence (Egeland, Pianta, & Ogawa, 1996). Other studies have suggested that the majority of grade schoolers (particularly boys) referred for ODD will later show conduct problems, usually aggression and other antisocial behaviors during adolescence (Verhulst, Eussen, Berden, Sanders-Woudstra, & Van Der Ende, 1993). The likelihood that ODD in childhood will be followed by antisocial behaviors in adulthood seems highest when (1) the behavioral problems are seen both at home and at school; (2) aggression and hyperactivity accompany ODD features; (3) the child engages in covert activities, such as lying and stealing, as well as overt behaviors such as arguing and aggression; and (4) there is a high level of stress in the family (Ferguson et al., 1995).

Conduct Disorder

An even more severe pattern of childhood disruptiveness appears as conduct disorder (CD). This pattern consists of serious antisocial behaviors that substantially infringe on the rights of others; are potentially harmful to the child, to others, or to property; may violate laws relating to larceny, truancy, and vandalism; and persist over at least a 12-month period.

In the United States, 4% to 6% of children under the age of 18 meet the *DSM–IV–TR* criteria for CD (see Table 7.5), 75% to 80% of whom are boys. Of these children, about 25% will be diagnosed with antisocial personality disorder (APD) as adults (L. N. Robins, Tipp, & Pryzbeck, 1991). Several studies have suggested that children who manifest symptoms of CD before the age of 10 are most likely to develop adult antisocial behavior (Moffitt et al., 1996; White, Moffitt, Earls, Robins, & Silva, 1990). These children probably account for the

Table 7.4   *Oppositional Defiant Disorder*

The essential feature of oppositional defiant disorder is a recurrent pattern of negativistic, defiant, disobedient, and hostile behavior toward authority figures than is typical for he child's age or developmental level.

Four or more of the associated behaviors must persist for at least six months and must cause significant impairment in social, academic, or occupational functioning. Some of the symptoms are:

1. Frequent loss of temper;
2. Often argues with authority figures;
3. Frequently refuses to comply with adults' requests;
4. Blames others for mistakes or misbehaviors;
5. Often angry and resentful;
6. Frequently is spiteful or vindictive.

Source: Based on information from American Psychiatric Association. (2000). *Diagnostic and Statistical Manual of Mental Disorders* (4th ed. text revision). Washington, DC: Author.

---

largest proportion of violent adolescent and adult offenders (Loeber & Stouthamer-Loeber, 1998). Because the criteria for CD (e.g., aggressiveness, irresponsibility, deceitfulness) are essentially the same as those for APD, CD may be thought of as APD in people younger than 18. The *DSM–IV–TR* criteria for APD specifically state that it may not be given to a person who is younger than 18; however, to be diagnosed with APD, a person must have been diagnosable with CD prior to the age of 15. Adolescents who display CD are at higher than normal risk for substance abuse and emotional disorders (such as depression and anxiety) in adulthood (L. N. Robins, 1991), so it is no wonder that men who had been diagnosed with CD as children are quite likely to suffer mental disorders and/or have criminal records as adults (Kratzer & Hodgins, 1997).

Eric, a 14-year-old, typifies the progression from ODD to CD. Eric had a history of unusually violent temper tantrums at age 4, followed by a series of shoplifting incidents at age 8. In the eighth grade, he began to miss school regularly, either as a result of truancy or suspensions for the fights he started. Eric was known as a mean fighter who went out of his way to hurt his enemies. Prior to being brought to a psychological clinic, he had cut a classmate's arm with a knife. Eric claimed that the victim had started the fight, but then he admitted that he cut the boy because he did not like the way he looked at him (Nietzel et al., 1998).

A study of 6,449 males and 6,268 females who displayed conduct problems as children found that by the time these people reached the age of 30, 76% of the men and 30% of the women had either a criminal record, a mental disorder (typically a substance use disorder), or both (Mednick, Gabrielli, & Hutchings, 1987). Another study (Hamalainen & Pulkkinen, 1996) followed 196 boys and 173 girls from ages 8 to 14 through to age 27 and found that those who qualified for CD diagnoses as children and whose behavior problems persisted through adolescence had more extensive criminal records than if aggressive behavior first began in adolescence. Loeber and Stouthamer-Loeber (1998) cited similar data in support of their theory of life-course pathways to crime, which begins with childhood CD.

In short, there is little doubt that the appearance of CD in childhood is one of the most valid warnings of serious aggression and criminal behavior in adulthood. Even when CD does not lead to crime or psychological disorder, it is associated with divorce, joblessness, abusiveness toward children, and risky and self-destructive behaviors (Rydelius, 1988).

Multiple Developmental Disorders

About 10% of North American children are diagnosed with ODD or CD, and at least 5% are labeled as having ADHD. Boys are at least two to three times more likely than girls to be diagnosed with these problems (McDermott, 1996; Szatmari, Offord, & Boyle 1989).

Often, more than one of these disorders is seen in the same child. In one study (Hinshaw, 1987), for example, as many as 90% of children with CD were also diagnosed as having ADHD. In another study (Biederman et al., 1996b), all but one of 140 children with ADHD who had CD also had ODD that preceded the onset of

TABLE 7.5   *Conduct Disorder*

The essential feature of conduct disorder is a persistent pattern of behavior that involves violating the rights of others and age-appropriate social norms.

Three or more symptoms of the disorder must be present in the previous twelve months, with a least one of the symptoms present in the previous six months, and the behaviors must lead to impairment in social, academic, or occupational functioning. The symptoms are divided into these four categories:

1. Aggression to people and animals
   a. Bullying and threatening others
   b. Using weapons
   c. Physically cruel to people and animals
2. Destruction of property
   a. Firesetting
   b. Destruction of others' property
3. Deceitfulness or theft
   a. Lying
   b. Stealing
   c. Breaking and entering in another's car or home
4. Serious violations of the rules
   a. Stays out at night, after age of 13, despite parents' rules
   b. Run away from home at least twice
   c. Frequently truant from school

Source: Based on information from American Psychiatric Association. (2000). *Diagnostic and Statistical Manual of Mental Disorders* (4th ed. text revision). Washington, DC: Author.

CD by several years. Indeed, ODD is often thought of as an early version of CD (Rey et al., 1988), and as noted earlier, CD is often the precursor to APD.

Barkley (1998) suggested that ADHD can be a precursor common to ODD, CD, and APD (see also G. Weiss & Hechtman, 1993). Twenty to 50% of hyperactive children are likely to display CD by adolescence (Barkley, Fischer, Edelbrock, & Smallish, 1990; Biederman et al., 1996b; Mannuzza, Klein, Bessler, Malloy, & LaPadula, 1998). Further, 25% of hyperactive children display APD in young adulthood (Barkley, 1998; G. Weiss & Hechtman, 1993). Thus, the appearance of ADHD in childhood might enhance the risk of ODD, CD, and APD later. The risk seems especially high for females. Yet, there are gender differences in comorbidity of ADHD and other disruptive disorders. Compared to boys, only half as many girls diagnosed with ADHD also show evidence of CD or ODD (Bierderman, Faraone, & Mick, 1999).

Learning to Be—Or Not to Be—a Criminal

Richard Speck, killer of six Chicago nursing students in the 1960s, had a tattoo that read "Born to Raise Hell." We beg to differ. People are not born criminals. In fact, it would be safe to say that, although it does not necessarily take a long time for someone to become a criminal, it does take several ingredients. Biological and genetic factors set the stage, but research has suggested that children must learn to be oppositional, aggressive, and violent, and they most often do so in an environment that models and may even encourage such behavior. Consider the 6-year-old Flint, Michigan, boy we mentioned in chapter 3, who shot and killed his first-grade classmate. Even the city's hard-nosed prosecutor spoke of the boy as a victim of the deprived and depraved circumstances in which he lived, a "crack house" where the child's male role models threatened their drug customers with guns (Claiborne, 2000). The child's father was in prison, and his mother was living on the streets. The sheriff who took the boy into custody said that the child showed no awareness that what he did was any different from what he saw on television or for that matter, what he saw around him.

The learning theories we discussed in chapter 5 provide some insight into the development of antisocial behavior in childhood. For example, operant conditioning theory suggests that children learn how to behave partly on the basis of the feedback they get from parents and others who reward appropriate behavior and punish inappropriate behavior. Classical conditioning, too, helps children to associate certain situations with reward or punishment. If they have received consistent parental discipline and reacted to it as most children do, they are likely to develop a sense of right and wrong along with behavior patterns that are consistent with the values of their parents and society at large. This learning process is unlikely to go smoothly if children receive inconsistent parental discipline. Further, as we noted earlier, children born with an uninhibited/extroverted temperament tend to be chronically underaroused and less reactive to disapproval or punishment. These children are less likely to internalize the rules set for them by parents, teachers, and other authorities (Eysenck, 1962, 1967; Meloy, 1992). Accordingly, they may not develop a clear sense of right and wrong, sensitivity to the feelings of others, or a desire to abide by society's rules. Such children are more likely than others to be aggressive and violent in adolescence and adulthood (Raine, Venables, & Mednick, 1997).

Moral Development

Moral development is based on more than just reward and punishment, however. In discussing cognitive theories of crime in chapter 5, we pointed out that the ways in which people learn to perceive the world, interpret information, and make decisions can influence their propensity to engage in antisocial or criminal behavior. We now consider how these cognitive theories can help to understand the development of criminal behavior from childhood.

Recall that Piaget's (1932/1965) theory of cognitive development focused some attention on children's perception of rules of conduct. Piaget found that children in the preoperational stage recognized that rules are made by "all-powerful" others. At the concrete operational stage, they learn that in some situations, they can invent and modify rules (which often happens as children play games); and by the time they reach the formal operational stage, they are able to apply accepted rules and law to specific situations (Feldman, 1993). In short, Piaget said children develop practical morality by learning to obey rules before they understand why rules should apply to them (theoretical morality). Recall, too, that Kohlberg (1964) proposed three stages of moral reasoning: (1) preconventional (in which moral decisions are influenced mainly by a desire to avoid punishment), (2) conventional (in which behavior is guided by concern for obeying rules and laws), and (3) postconventional (in which moral decisions are based on a personal set of principles and sense of justice that may go beyond established laws).

So, moral development does not take place automatically or in a vacuum. It depends on what children learn from watching other people—family members, peers, and strangers—at home, at school, at play, on television, and in movies. If children do not see a pattern of law-abiding, moral behavior in their parents, they may be susceptible to breaking laws themselves. Juveniles not grounded in moral values at home are particularly vulnerable to influence by law-violating peers, especially in situations where group influence is strong (Denton & Krebs, 1990).

There are clear differences in the moral reasoning of delinquent and nondelinquent children (e.g., Arbuthnot, Gordon, & Jurkovic, 1987; Jurkovic & Prentice, 1977). Most studies show that delinquents are at lower stages of moral development than nondelinquents (D. H. Feldman, 1994). Studies of adult criminals, too, have found them to be at significantly lower levels of moral development than adult noncriminals from the same background (Henggeler, 1989; Kolhberg et al., 1973).

Information Processing

Faulty information processing can lead to inappropriate behavior that can start a child on the road to crime. For example, as we described in chapter 5, if children see people in their home hitting each other (or them) when they do not like what someone has done, they may develop cognitive schemas in which violent aggression becomes the expected and proper response to any displeasing situation. On the basis of those schemas, children may begin to hit other children (or even teachers) whom they perceive as frustrating or threatening them. It appears that when threatened, these children are unable to think of any actions other than aggression (Lochman & Dodge, 1994).

You have probably noticed a common theme underlying our discussion of how criminal behavior can be learned in childhood: the early and continuing influence of the family. That influence is so significant that we examine it in more detail.

Family Influences on Criminal Behavior

In July 1997, Malcolm Shabazz, the 12-year-old grandson of Malcolm X, pleaded guilty to setting a fire that killed his grandmother, Betty Shabazz. At his grandmother's funeral, poet Maya Angelou said of young Malcolm, "God created him, but we made him" (Swarns, 1997, p. 1). She was referring to Malcolm's family heritage, a background that contains a number of factors related to the development of criminal behavior.

Young Malcolm's grandfather, Malcolm X, was no stranger to violence. Born in 1925 as Michael Little, he was only 4 years old when his home was burned to the ground—allegedly by White men angry with his father's advocacy of Black nationalism. Malcolm X's father and five of his brothers died violently, and after his mother was confined to a mental institution when Malcolm X was 12 years old, he was raised by his sisters. After Malcolm X himself was assassinated in 1965, his wife, Betty Shabazz, raised their six daughters on her own. Of these, young Malcolm's mother, Quibilah, was the most troubled. After dropping out of Princeton University, she went to Paris and came home with baby Malcolm. Struggling with mood disorders and drug and alcohol abuse, she raised Malcolm mostly on her own (she never identified his father), although he also sometimes lived with relatives. Two years before Malcolm set the fire at his grandmother's apartment, Quibilah was arrested in connection with an alleged plot to kill Louis Farrakahn, her father's political rival. Child welfare authorities also charged Quibilah with child neglect, removed Malcolm from her custody, and placed him briefly in foster care before arranging for him to live with his grandmother.

Four months before he set the fire, Quibilah reported to police that he was acting erratically and attacking her. Malcolm told police that he was angry because his mother was drinking and would not take him to school. The investigating officer said that Malcolm was exhibiting psychotic symptoms and he took both mother and child to a psychiatric hospital for evaluation. Shortly thereafter, his behavior deteriorated further, and his grades plummeted. From April to June of 1997, Malcolm was shuttled between his mother's home in Texas and his grandmother's home in New York. Some say that Malcolm set fire to his grandmother's apartment to be able to go back and live with his mother. Whatever the reason, in August 1997, Malcolm was sentenced to a juvenile facility in Massachusetts, where, subject to annual reviews of progress, he may remain until he is 18 years old.

Families provide the most influential context for early child development, and this influence tends to remain preeminent at least until children are about 10, when the family's role in shaping development begins to be matched if not overshadowed by that of peers and nonfamily adults. In the family life of Malcolm Shabazz—as in the lives of thousands of other children today—one can see several major family-related risk factors for criminal behavior:

1. Maladaptive parenting styles and practices;
2. A family history of mental illness, substance use, teenage pregnancy, school dropout, and interpersonal conflict;
3. Parental attitudes that lead to tolerance or encouragement of children's problem behaviors;
4. Child abuse or neglect;
5. Domestic violence;
6. Criminal behavior by family members;
7. Frequent changes in custody (e.g., Harlow, 1998).

We now consider some of the ways in which family influences typically act to shape many aspects of personality—including emotional expression and self-control—and also how the risk factors we just listed can disrupt this process in ways that can lead to criminal behavior.

TABLE 7.6   *Erikson's Psychosocial Stages*

Stage	Adaptive Mode	Significant Events and Outcomes
Basic trust versus mistrust (birth to 1 year)	Incorporation—to take in (and give in return)	Babies must find consistency, predictability, and reliability in their caregivers' behaviors to gain a sense of trust and hope.
Autonomy versus shame and doubt (1–3 years)	Control—to hold on and to let go	The child begins to explore and make choices in order to understand what is manageable and socially acceptable.
Initiative versus guilt (3–6 years)	Intrusion—to go after	The child begins to make plans, set goals, and persist in both physical and social exchanges to gain a sense of purpose and remain enthusiastic even in the face of inevitable frustration.
Industry versus inferiority (6 years to puberty)	Construction—to build things and relationships	The child acquires skills and performs "work" in the form of becoming educated and supporting the family in order to feel competent and attain a sense of achievement.
Identity versus identity confusion (puberty to adulthood)	Integration—to be oneself (or not be oneself)	The adolescent attempts to discover his or her identity and place in society by trying out many roles in order to answer the question, "Who am I?"
Intimacy versus isolation (young adulthood)	Solidarity—to lose and find oneself in another	Having achieved a sense of identity, the young adult can now share himself or herself with another to avoid a sense of isolation, self-absorption, and the absence of love.
Generativity versus stagnation (middle adulthood)	Productivity—to make and to take care of	The adult produces things and ideas through work and creates and cares for the next generation to gain a sense of fulfillment and caring.
Integrity versus despair (old age)	Acceptance—to be (by having been) and to face not being	The older adult reviews and evaluates his or her life and accepts its worth, even if he or she has not reached all goals, to achieve a sense of wisdom.

Source: D. Bukatko & M. Daehler. *Child Development: A Thematic Approach* (5th ed.). Copyright © 2004 by Houghton Mifflin Company. Used with permission.

Family Influences on Personality Development

As mentioned in chapter 5, Erikson (1946) proposed a theory of psychological development in which people's personalities are seen as shaped mainly by their relationships with others. Early in life, those "others" are mainly family members or other caregivers. Erikson believed that during life's journey, each individual passes through eight stages of psychosocial development, in each of which a crisis must be resolved. Success or failure at resolving these crises, he said, has a major impact on personality and behavior (see Table 7.6).

Erikson's first stage occurs in the first year of life and centers around the crisis of *trust versus mistrust,* as children either learn to trust that caregivers will meet their basic needs (e.g., for food and comfort) or come to believe that the world is not a safe or dependable place. Mistrust is associated with insecure attachment. Erikson's second stage, in the 2nd year of life, focuses on the crisis of *autonomy versus shame and doubt,* as children learn to control bodily functions (e.g., toileting) and develop some mastery over physical activities (such as feeding) and their surroundings (such as by walking). This second stage of psychosocial development is important in relation to crime because it is during this stage that children learn that they have an existence separate from their caregivers and begin to show the first signs of a conscience. For example, as children learn that they can have some control and independence, they are increasingly subjected to parental evaluation of the rightness or wrongness of their behavior. Consistent, firm, but gentle parenting is important at this stage to ensure that the child accepts control over the things it can control while not feeling overly ashamed at mistakes relating to toilet training, spilled milk, broken toys, and the like.

The third of Erikson's stages, which normally occurs between the ages of 3 and 6, centers on the crisis of *initiative versus guilt*. It is here that children increasingly initiate their own activities and enjoy their accomplishments. If parents are too controlling and do not allow children to initiate action, the children may come to feel guilty about their efforts to be independent. The appearance of guilt over misbehavior is indicative of the continuing development of the child's conscience. It is at this stage, too, that some children begin to show the earliest signs of ODD.

The grade school years—from about age 6 through about age 12—constitute the fourth of Erikson's stages in which they face the crisis of *industry versus inferiority*. Here, children learn to be competent at school, whether through academics, sports, or other activities and in relationships with peers and teachers. If children resolve this crisis by developing industriousness, curiosity, and a love of learning, they are likely to experience self-esteem, a central component for mental health and prosocial behavior in Western cultures. Lack of success at school may lead to loss of self-esteem, feelings of inferiority, and perhaps a sense of learned helplessness that prompts the child to quit trying.

Children fail at school for many reasons, including deficient mental ability, learning disabilities, and physical and emotional problems. Those who are temperamentally extroverted may find it especially difficult to settle down to a school routine. School failure, in turn, often leads to truancy, dropping out, and committing crimes out of boredom, if for no other reason. Studies have linked school failures and behavioral problems (such as aggressiveness, impulsivity, and inability to pay attention) with later adult crime, substance abuse, and psychiatric disorders (e.g., Torestad & Magnusson, 1996). The industry versus inferiority crisis is a critical "fork in the road" for children, especially for those who may be predisposed by genetics or other factors toward antisocial behaviors that can lead to crime.

Family Influences on Emotional Expression and Self-Control

The development of control over emotions and their expression is a form of self-control that is vital for getting along in the social world. At birth and shortly thereafter, infants display a few *primary emotions*—joy, fear, anger, surprise, sadness, and disgust (M. Cole & Cole, 1996)—and by the time they are about 6 months old, babies have started learning to "read" their mothers' faces as guides to how they should feel and act in ambiguous situations, such as when a stranger appears. Between the ages of 18 and 24 months, children begin to develop *secondary emotions* such as embarrassment, pride, envy, shame, and guilt and to read a wider array of emotions in others.

Parents and other caregivers play an important role is this aspect of development. For example, one study (Malatesta, Grigoryev, Lamb, Albin, & Culver, 1986) of mother–infant interactions found that mothers frequently reinforce their babies' positive emotional expressions by imitating them but rarely imitate negative emotions. Later, parents use approval, disapproval, and modeling to teach their youngsters socially appropriate ways to express emotions, especially negative emotions such as anger, disappointment, or frustration. Through these forms of parental influence, most children can, by the age of 2, understand when they have hurt someone's feelings or otherwise upset them. For example, when shown pictures of typical childhood scenes—such as a birthday party, getting lost in the supermarket, or having a dog run away—they give appropriate answers to hypothetical questions about how the pictured children are likely to feel (Michalson & Lewis, 1985). Once children have reached this stage, they are developing both a conscience, which alerts them when they have done wrong, and a sense of empathy—the ability to anticipate, understand, or share another person's emotions. Between the ages of 6 and 9, children can not only understand another's emotions but can empathize with people in certain circumstances such as living in poverty or being sick. The development of empathy constitutes an important element in the development of prosocial behavior and in the discouragement of antisocial behavior (Eisenberg, 1992).

The influence of family caregivers not only helps children learn to read an ever widening array of emotions but also to develop the self-control necessary to express themselves in a socially acceptable manner. Children who fail to learn these self-control skills early in life are more likely than others to remain emotionally uncontrolled into adolescence and adulthood (Agnew, 1994; M. Gottfredson & Hirschi, 1993), thus placing themselves at risk for criminal behavior.

Aggression is perhaps the most problematic aspect of uncontrolled emotional expression and certainly the one most closely related to violent crime. If children learn that hurting someone can help them get what they want, they may start using instrumental aggression to do so. They may also use hostile aggression (Hartup, 1974) simply for the sake of dominating other children or as revenge for a perceived wrong done to them (Dunn, 1988; Hartup, 1974).

The sons of former Iraqi dictator Saddam Hussein are but two famous cases of children whose emotional expression was almost totally unchecked and who quickly learned to use both instrumental and hostile aggression. Uday and his younger brother, Qusay, were pampered by their tyrant father who also modeled for them the worst kind of cruelty and murderous aggression (Waxman, 2003). With no one to teach them to curb their own impulses, both boys learned from an early age how to inflict pain on others. Uday, for example, became a bully who, on a whim, would fire a gun simply to frighten his elementary school classmates. Both boys grew up with all the comforts and pleasures that money could buy, but they developed little or no empathy for other human beings. In adulthood, as head of Iraq's Olympic committee, Uday tortured athletes who failed to do as well as he thought they could and sometimes when their prowess threatened his own. Qusay was even worse. He sometimes ordered his guards to kill people he did not like, but he often simply shot his enemies himself. It was little wonder that there was rejoicing in the streets of Baghdad in 2003 when Uday and Qusay were killed by American forces (Waxman, 2003).

Parenting Style, Aggression, and Crime

The Hussein brothers' behavior illustrates that like prosocial behavior and self-control, hostile aggression—the foundation of antisocial behavior and violence—usually develops at home under parental influence. Diana Baumrind (1973) identified three main styles of parenting. *Authoritarian* parents tend to enforce rules rigidly without accompanying explanations or justification. These parents also typically do not show much affection, are not involved much in their children's lives, frequently show anger and displeasure toward their children, and employ harsh discipline that includes spankings and other corporal punishment. The children of authoritarian parents tend to grow up moody, unhappy, fearful, apprehensive, and to alternate between aggression and withdrawal. *Permissive* parents make few demands on their children, do not clearly communicate their rules, and are inconsistent in enforcing them. They are easily coerced and manipulated by their children's efforts to get their own way, are moderately warm, and tend not to express anger. Children of permissive parents tend to be resistant and noncompliant, low in self-esteem, aggressive and impulsive. *Authoritative* parents clearly communicate and justify their rules, enforce them fairly, give consistent feedback—showing displeasure in response to their children's misbehavior and encouragement and reward for good behavior. As a result, their children tend to learn that punishment follows disobedience and reward follows obedience. This parenting pattern appears important in helping children take responsibility for their behavior and for any punishment that results from it. Children of authoritative parents tend to do well academically, to get along well with peers and teachers, to be cooperative with adults, and to display high self-esteem and self-control.

Research on these parenting styles has suggested that when combined with other developmental risk factors, they may be related to the appearance of antisocial conduct in children. For example, when children's temperament makes them impulsive and difficult to discipline, parenting style can be a significant factor in turning them toward or away from antisocial behavior.

The relationship between parenting styles and children's tendencies toward antisocial behavior can be seen most clearly in relation to the use of physical punishment. Some studies have suggested that if physical punishment is used frequently with children who, due to family and temperamental factors, are predisposed to aggression, they are more likely to display aggression toward parents and peers (Berkowitz, 1973; Parke & Slaby, 1983; Straus, 1991). Other studies have found that it is overly harsh physical discipline combined with inconsistent discipline that enhances the risk of antisocial behavior (Broidy, 1995; Burton et al., 1995; Viemero, 1996).

Parental discipline involves more than punishment, however. It is a wider ranging effort to direct children's behavior toward patterns that parents or other caregivers find desirable. Discipline includes providing praise and other rewards for appropriate behavior, an often neglected element among parents who think of discipline mainly in terms of physical punishment. In an extensive series of home observations in which parents interacted with their antisocial children, Gerald Patterson and his colleagues (Patterson, 1976, 1986; Patterson, DeBaryshe, and Ramsey, 1989) found that these parents failed to consistently manage the children's propensity for aggression and other antisocial acts. They did not effectively monitor their children's activities inside or outside the home, failed to give adequate or appropriate negative feedback for antisocial behavior, and did not sufficiently reward prosocial conduct. Instead, these parents tended to respond aggressively to their children's antisocial and aggressive behavior, often to the point of engaging in physical abuse; and when their children became physically violent toward them during episodes of punishment, the parents often abandoned their efforts to provide discipline. In other words, the children learned that they could escape punishment by acting aggressively. Other studies have found that some parents actually reward aggression by allowing their children to get what they want through threats or assaults on siblings, peers, or the parents themselves (Berkowitz, 1993; McCord 1979). Such experiences tend to make children more aggressive in the future.

Some parents promote aggressiveness by encouraging children—usually boys—to respond to aggression with aggression, to "be a man," "get even," "stand up for themselves," and by providing praise for doing so. These parents tend to be well-intentioned and assume that they are teaching self-respect and pride. Although they may only want their children to be aggressive when attacked, legitimizing aggression in such situations may lead children to initiate it indiscriminately (Berkowitz, 1993). If children are not helped to understand that initiating hostile aggression is not appropriate and that responding to provocation with hostile aggression is not always desirable, male children, especially, may tend to behave aggressively in all too many situations. When boys who have been rewarded for aggression at home begin to play together, they encourage each other's aggressiveness. Some become bullies, continually intimidating others and thus solidifying their antisocial tendencies. Eventually, well-behaved peers avoid associating with these bullies, leaving them to band together and share their antisocial inclinations in gangs.

In summary, research evidence suggests that when parenting practices do not include clear expectations for behavior, fail to provide proper supervision of children, employ excessively harsh or inconsistent punishment and discipline, and directly encourage aggressiveness, children are at elevated risk for developing behavior problems that may escalate into violence and crime (Farrington, 1987; Kandel & Andrews, 1987; Patterson & Dishion, 1985; P. L. Peterson, Hawkins, Abbott, & Catalano, 1994; Thornberry, 1994). Recent studies have suggested, however, that parent-training programs designed to alter these problematic parenting practices can be effective in reducing aggressiveness among high-risk preschoolers (Hawkins, Catalano, Kosterman, Abbott, & Hill, 1999; Webster-Stratton, 1998).

Other Family Risk Factors for Crime

Children raised in a family with a history of addiction to alcohol or other drugs are at increased risk of having alcohol or other drug problems themselves (Goodwin, 1985), and children born or raised in a family with a history of criminal activity are at increased risk of delinquency (Bohman, 1978). Similarly, children born to teenage mothers are more likely to become teenage parents, and children of school dropouts are more likely to drop out, too (Slavin, 1990). Children raised in an environment of conflict also appear to be at risk for substance abuse, teen pregnancy, and school dropout (Krisberg & Onek, 1994). These patterns are important because drug and alcohol use by children and teenagers—and teenage pregnancy—are all related to the appearance of criminal behavior in juveniles.

Many family risk factors for delinquency have their effects through their negative impact on parenting. For example, the aggressiveness, delinquency, or other problems sometimes seen in children whose parents divorce (Doherty & Needle, 1991; Rutter & Giller, 1983; Wallerstein, Corbin, & Lewis, 1988) are related to relatively sudden changes in parenting style. On gaining custody of their children, some newly single mothers become overly permissive, but more often, they adopt an uncharacteristically authoritarian parenting style in which they are more demanding and express less affection (Hetherington, Cox, & Cox, 1982). This change may be especially likely if the father withdraws from his children's lives after the divorce. In such cases, the children, especially boys, tend to become less compliant, and their mothers become correspondingly more restrictive and punitive. Before long, parents and children can be caught in a spiral of conflict that leads to even more coercive parenting and increasingly serious child misbehavior.

Child Abuse or Neglect.   *Physical abuse* of a child is defined as intentional harm that exceeds acceptable standards of corporal punishment including beating, burning, choking, shaking, throwing, stabbing, punching, kicking, or threatening the child with a weapon. *Neglect* refers to refusal of, or delay in, care that seriously jeopardizes the child's life or health, abandonment, expulsion of the child from the home, and inadequate supervision (U.S. Department of Health and Human Services, 1997).

A confirmed case of child abuse or neglect is reported in the United States about every 35 seconds, and about every 6 hours in the United States, a child dies from abuse (Children's Defense Fund, 2004). In 2001, these trends translated into the deaths from abuse or neglect of more than 1,300 children, most of them under the age of 6 (Childhelp USA, 2003). Children living in certain kinds of family situations are especially vulnerable. The most potent risk factors for experiencing abuse are poverty, lack of social support, and having parents who are unemployed, engage in substance abuse, domestic violence, and who were themselves abused as children (U.S. Department of Health and Human Services, 2003).

What are these abused and neglected children like as they grow into adolescence and adulthood? Does their physical and mental suffering lead them to engage in antisocial and criminal acts against others? As mentioned earlier, the answer is probably "yes." According to U.S. government figures, children who have been physically abused or neglected by their parents are more likely to engage in antisocial and criminal behavior and to be arrested as juveniles or adults than nonabused children. In 1988, a longitudinal study (Widom & Maxfield, 2001) was begun that compared the arrest records of more than 1,500 individuals who were and were not maltreated as children. As of 2001, when the participants had reached an average age of 32.5, the researchers found the following:

1. Abused and neglected children were more likely to be arrested as juveniles (27% vs. 17%) and as adults (42% vs. 33%).
2. Those who were abused or neglected were younger at first arrest, committed twice as many offenses, and were arrested more frequently than those who had been not been abused or neglected.
3. Females who were abused or neglected in childhood were 73% more likely than nonmaltreated females to be arrested for property, alcohol, and drug offenses and for misdemeanor offenses such as disorderly conduct.
4. Despite the fact that, overall, females are less likely than males to be arrested for violent crimes, maltreated females were more likely than their nonabused peers to be arrested for such crimes. Abused and neglected males were no more likely to be arrested for crimes of violence than nonmaltreated males, but if they were arrested for such crimes, they *were* arrested more often than nonmaltreated males.
5. Compared to abused or neglected Whites, more Black adults who were abused or neglected as children were arrested for violent crimes.
6. Abused and neglected individuals were at higher risk of arrest at a younger age with more significant and repeated criminal involvement (Widom & Maxfield, 2001).

Further, children exposed to multiple forms of family violence (e.g., direct abuse, violence between parents or other adults in the home, and a climate of family hostility) are 50% more likely to engage in violence themselves than are children who grow up in nonviolent homes (Office of Juvenile Justice and Delinquency Prevention, 1994).

Children who are victims of *sexual abuse,* which is defined as oral, anal, or genital penile or digital penetration or molestation with or without genital contact (U.S. Department of Health & Human Services, 1997) are as likely to commit crimes as those who were physically abused, but sexually abused girls are more likely to become involved in prostitution than are physically abused girls (U.S. Department of Justice, 1995). Adults who commit rape and sodomy are more likely to have been physically, rather than sexually, abused as children. Overall, one third of male juvenile delinquents, 40% of sex offenders, and 76% of serial rapists have reported being sexually abused as youngsters (W. C. Holmes & Slap, 1998). Children subjected to both sexual and physical abuse are more likely to be involved in adolescent and adult crime than those who suffered only one type of abuse, but children who had suffered only sexual abuse were less likely to be arrested for a crime of violence than children who had been abused and neglected (Widom & Maxfield, 2001).

How does physical and sexual abuse increase the risk for criminal conduct? As suggested by learning theory, part of the story is that abusive parents act as models, providing examples of violent behavior that their children eventually come to imitate. This view helps account for the *transgenerational* nature of abuse in which parents who were abused as children are more likely than others to abuse their own children (Zaidi, Knutson, & Mehm, 1989). However, there is probably more to the story. Abuse can also cause children to develop the faulty and violence-justifying modes of information processing we discussed earlier and in chapter 5. Abused and neglected children are also more likely to have mental health problems (e.g., suicidality and PTSD), educational problems (e.g., reading difficulties), occupational problems (e.g., unemployment and/or employment in low-paying jobs), and substance abuse problems (Widom & Maxfield, 2001).

Domestic Violence.   Domestic violence in a family increases the likelihood that young people will engage in violent behavior (Loeber & Dishion, 1984; L. Walker, 2000). As has been suggested by research on observational learning, even children who are not subjected to abusive parenting can be influenced toward aggression and violence by seeing it in their homes. One study found that nonabused boys who witnessed their mothers being abused by their fathers (or by their mothers' boyfriends) were 10 times more likely to batter their female partners as adults than boys who did not live in a home where domestic violence took place (U.S. Department of Justice, 1995a). For men who were both abused as a child and witnessed the abuse of others in the home, the likelihood of abusing a female domestic partner can be 50% higher than if they had been exposed to only one kind of violence.

Observing violence in the home can have indirect effects as well. For example, one study (DePanfilis & Brooks, 1989) found that adults who grew up in a home where domestic violence was prevalent were 50% more likely to be depressed, to attempt suicide, and to abuse drugs and/or alcohol than if they had lived in nonabusive homes. Children living in homes where domestic abuse was common were also more likely than other children to fight with siblings, physically and verbally abuse their mothers, engage in self-destructive behavior, and otherwise act aggressively (DePanfilis & Brooks, 1989). Finally, like exposure to abuse, living around violence can generate violence-promoting, information-processing habits that leave children with the assumption that violent methods are the only ones available for dealing with conflict.

Family Criminality.   Parental attitudes toward drugs and crime influence the attitudes and behavior of their children (Brook, Whiteman, Gordon, & Brook, 1990; Hansen, Graham, Shelton, Flay, & Johnson, 1987). Children who are excused for breaking the law are more likely to become delinquent (Hawkins & Weis, 1985). If parents are tolerant of their children's drug and alcohol use—and especially if they encourage it by providing them with beer or cigarettes, for example—the children are more likely to become drug and alcohol users in adolescence (Ahmed, Bush, Davidson, & Iannotti, 1984), a major risk factor for delinquency.

Having family members who actually engage in criminal behavior may place children at risk for becoming criminals themselves. For example, the fathers of a significant number of delinquent boys have criminal records (Bohman, 1978; West & Farrington, 1977), and as many as 35% of the sons of repeat-offender fathers become repeat offenders themselves compared to only 8% of sons of noncriminals (Rowe & Gulley, 1992). Nearly half of all female prison inmates have close relatives who have been in prison (Snell, 1994). One 30-year study (Widom, 2000) recently concluded that children who were not abused or neglected but whose parents (either or both) had been arrested were two to three times more likely to engage in antisocial conduct as adults. This relation may be due to a number of factors including inherited characteristics that make the children of criminals more prone to antisocial conduct, imitation of criminal parents and siblings (Rowe & Gulley, 1992), psychological problems that result from exposure to a dysfunctional family, and the development of crime-justifying ways of thinking.

All in all, life in a dysfunctional, substance abusing, criminal family poses many risks that children in such families must overcome so as not to develop the sort of antisocial and violent behavior that may lead to a life of crime.

Putting It All in Perspective

In 1994, two boys, 10 and 11 years old, killed a 5-year-old child, Eric Morse, after he refused to steal candy for them. Their assumed names are Tony and Antoine (the law would not allow the disclosure of their real identities due to their youth), and at the time of the murder, they lived in the infamous Ida Wells public housing project on the South Side of Chicago. These boys had grown up fighting other kids with stones and chains, and they were already regular marijuana users. Both were addicted to drugs and alcohol. The older boy, Antoine, lived with a relative (his parents lived in a homeless shelter). Tony's father was serving a 4-year prison sentence for domestic assault of his then wife who was not the boy's mother. A juvenile court judge sentenced the boys to the Illinois Department of Corrections until they reached the age of 21. This was unprecedented, for prior to their cases, children under 13 were sentenced to probation and counseling.[2] The judge ordered that the boys receive maximum treatment in an effort to rehabilitate them (Marx, 1997).

After their convictions, Illinois changed its law to allow children as young as 10 to be tried and convicted as adults (see chapter 3). In 1998, Antoine (who was 10 at the time of the murder and at that time the youngest person in the United States to be charged with murder) was charged as an adult with sexually assaulting another young man in the prison. He pled guilty and was sentenced to 9 years in an adult prison (and his real name, Jessie Rankins, could now be disclosed because he was charged as an adult). Jessie had been caught sexually abusing younger boys in the first juvenile facility he was sent to and was transferred to the facility that held the most serious of juvenile offenders. The fate of Tony is unknown, but for Jessie, it seems, the cycle of violence continues.

What made Tony and Antoine become criminals? As we have described in this chapter, genetic or other biological factors might have been partly responsible, but these boys' families and neighborhood doubtlessly played a part as well by providing an environment that was conducive to and supportive of their development into violent people. The development of criminal behavior during adolescence and its evolution into adult criminality is the subject of our next chapter.

Summary

No child is born a criminal, but many developmental pathways that begin in childhood may lead to crime. These pathways include biological, cognitive, and social influences.

Biological markers for crime may be found in neurological disorders, imbalance in neurotransmitters and hormones, and in a child's temperament. Minimal brain dysfunctions, learning disabilities, and cognitive impairments may lead to academic and social maladjustment that in turn may lead to delinquency. Serotonin and testosterone levels may be linked to aggression. Temperament, an individual's innate way of expressing needs and emotions, is grounded in the person's biological makeup and may influence a number of psychological factors that are associated with crime—such as regulation of emotional arousal and social and moral development.

Several developmental disorders—those that arise in childhood and influence various domains of development—are associated with juvenile delinquency and sometimes adult crime. Reactive attachment disorder (RAD) (inability to form a bond with a care giver), may lead to an absence of empathy or concern for others. ADHD can impair social and academic development. Oppositional defiant disorder (ODD), disrespect for authority, may be lead a child to disrespect the law and law enforcement figures. Conduct disorder (CD)

---

[2]Also unprecedented was the conviction itself—Antoine was at the time the youngest person ever to be convicted of murder in the United States. Since then, several children between the ages of 10 and 13 have been convicted of murder.

may be a precursor to antisocial personality disorder (APD), a way of being that is characterized by lack of empathy, disregard for the rights of others, and perhaps aggression toward others.

A child may learn to be a criminal through several pathways. These include lapses in moral development that may leave a child without a fully developed sense of conscience and faulty parenting that leaves a child with poor impulse control and unhealthy patterns of emotional expression. Physical and/or sexual abuse and/or neglect of children are associated with higher rates of juvenile and adult offending, and domestic violence may leave a child thinking that interpersonal aggression is the best way to get what one wants in life.

Key Terms

Temperament

Reactive attachment disorder

Attention deficit-hyperactivity disorder

Oppositional defiant disorder

Conduct disorder

Questions for Review

1. Describe temperament and how it can impact on later aggression and criminality by way of its influence on (a) learning, (b) regulation of arousal, (c) social and moral development, and (d) attachment.
2. Discuss reactive attachment disorder, ADHD, oppositional defiant disorder, and conduct disorder and compare and contrast their respective influences on the development of criminal behavior.
3. Discuss how information processing and moral development might influence criminal behavior.
4. Discuss the family influences on a child's emotional expression and self-control.
5. How might child abuse and neglect impact on criminal behavior?

Track It Down

Criminal Behavior Website
www.cassel2e.com
Robert Sampson and John Laub's Life-Course Model of Crime
www.wjh.harvard.edu/soc/faculty/sampson/2004.2.pdf
ADHD and Crime
www.vathek.com/ijpsm/pdf/jpsm.4.4.344.pdf
Conduct Disorder and Crime
www.cs.mun.ca/~david12/papers/cd.html
Preventing Juvenile Delinquency Through Parenting
www.dsgonline.com/mpg_non_flash/parent_training.htm
Cathy Widom's Study on Effects of Child Abuse and Neglect
www.ncjrs.org/pdffiles1/jr000242b.pdf

8

The Development of Crime From Adolescence to Adulthood

They are fickle in their desires, which are violent while they last, but quickly over. ... They have exalted notions, because they have not yet been humbled by life or learnt its necessary limitations; moreover, their hopeful disposition makes them think themselves equal to great things—and that means exalted notions. ... All their mistakes are in the direction of doing things excessively and vehemently. ... They love too much and hate too much, and the same with everything else. They think they know everything; and are always quite sure about it; this in fact, is why they overdo everything.

Many people have probably had similar thoughts about adolescents themselves or perhaps know that their parents thought such things about them when they were teenagers. However, this typically negative description of adolescents came not from a disgruntled parent or teacher or from a psychology book but from Aristotle (trans. 1941) who wrote it in the 4th century B.C.E. (*Rhetorica*, Book II, Chapter 12). Aristotle's description is mostly a negative stereotype, and attitudes have not changed much since; one still rarely hears adults describe teenagers in a positive manner.

In this chapter, we focus on adolescent development and consider the main factors that contribute to the development of criminal behavior in adolescence and adulthood. Like adults, most adolescent criminals commit nonviolent offenses involving theft, burglary, destruction of property, and drugs (FBI, 2004a; L. Siegal & Walsh, 2006). Most of the adolescents who do commit violent crimes showed aggressiveness in childhood (Heide, 1998), but as noted in our discussion of pathways to crime in chapter 7, some do not display aggression and violence until they are teenagers (Loeber & Stouthaimer-Loeber, 1998). Only a small minority of adult offenders have no history of aggression or violence earlier in life (Farrington, 1994).

Adolescence: Challenges and Risks

The word *adolescence* comes from the Latin meaning "growing up" or "coming to maturity." Although adolescence normally refers to the teenage years, our discussion includes children who are a year or two younger than 13. Aristotle and Plato were the first to identify adolescence as a developmental stage distinct from childhood and adulthood, but it would be 2,500 years before anyone systematically studied it. In the Middle Ages, children and adolescents were regarded as miniature adults who had not yet been taught to behave like adults (Arnett, 2004). During the Industrial Revolution of the 19th century, teenagers were—like younger children—still being treated as immature versions of adults, and capable of working like adults. Eighteenth century philosophers John Locke and Jean-Jacques Rousseau were the first to consider people from a developmental perspective, but it was not until the early 20th century—when sociology appeared as a discipline and when child labor laws were enacted—that psychologists, sociologists, and anthropologists focused serious attention on adolescence as part of their efforts to understand the biological, psychological, and social development of individuals throughout the life span.

Psychologist G. Stanley Hall (1904) was the first to use the term *adolescence* to describe the teenage years. Hall saw these years as a critical stage of development, filled with the contradictory emotions and behaviors Aristotle had described and serving as a gateway to "rebirth" into adulthood. Other psychological theorists, too, wrote about adolescent development. Sigmund Freud (1905/1953) addressed teenagers' psychosexual crises, and Erik Erikson (1968) focused on their psychosocial development. Margaret Mead (1958) added an anthropological perspective by emphasizing the influence of societal values on adolescent thinking, values, and behaviors.

In one way or another, virtually all students of adolescence, past and present, regard its ultimate challenge as the establishment of psychological and social identity (Marcia, 1980). In facing this challenge, adolescents struggle with decisions about who and what they are—as men, women, romantic partners, and workers and members of families, ethnic groups, organizations, and other cultural institutions. Indeed, as we noted in chapter 7, Erikson (1968) saw adolescence as just the beginning of a period lasting throughout adulthood during which each person must resolve crises of (1) identity (choosing values, vocations, beliefs, family lifestyle, and gender roles), (2) intimacy (achieving closeness with a romantic partner), (3) generativity (having children and/or finding meaningful work or other productive activity), and (4) integrity (being able to look back on life with satisfaction). Although various psychological theories assume that most adolescents actually manage to establish their psychosocial identities, today's behavioral scientists (and parents) recognize that—in North America and Europe, at least—few adolescents achieve certainty about anything, let alone about their place in the world. Accordingly, many teenagers are no longer expected to make all their vocational, marital, and lifestyle choices by the time they are 20. Of those who go to college, many leave with a degree but with little or no certainty about what to do with it or about whether they have chosen the right career.

Identity confusion—including indecisiveness about what to do with one's life—can lead to many problems ranging from frequent changes of romantic partners and job hopping to criminal behavior. Some of the choices teenagers make about how to spend their time can increase the likelihood of becoming involved with criminal activity. This is especially true for those who enter adolescence burdened by the childhood risk factors for criminal behavior we discussed in chapter 7, including poverty, a weak conscience, and poor moral values; contact with criminal or drug-abusing family members; low self-esteem; school failure; poor social skills; parental abuse and/or neglect; conduct and/or attention deficit disorders; and early alcohol and drug use. The more of these risk factors children experience, the greater the likelihood that they will engage in antisocial behavior and criminal acts as adolescents and young adults. In other words, these risk factors can provide pathways to crime (see Table 8.1).

We begin our discussion of the development of crime in adolescence and early adulthood by dealing with the question of why some teenagers make choices—such as to ignore school or schoolwork, to associate with delinquent peers, and to use alcohol and drugs—that increase the likelihood of their engaging in criminal behavior.

TABLE 8.1 *Risk Factors for Health and Behavior Problems*

Risk Factors	Adolescent Problem Behaviors				
	Substance Abuse	Delinquency	Teenage Pregnancy	School Dropout	Violence
Community					
Availability of Drugs	X				
Availability of Firearms		X			X
Community Laws and Norms Favorable Toward Drug Use, Firearms, and Crime	X	X			X
Media Portrayals of Violence					X
Transitions and Mobility	X	X		X	
Low Neighborhood Attachment and Community Organization	X	X			X
Extreme Economic Deprivation	X	X	X	X	X
Family					
Family History of the Problem Behavior	X	X	X	X	
Family Management Problems	X	X	X	X	X
Family Conflict	X	X	X	X	X
Favorable Parental Attitudes Toward and Involvement in the Problem Behavior	X	X			X
School					
Early and Persistent Antisocial Behavior	X	X	X	X	X
Academic Failure Beginning in Elementary School	X	X	X	X	X
Lack of Commitment to School	X	X	X	X	
Individual/Peer					
Rebelliousness	X	X		X	
Friends Who Engage in the Problem Behavior	X	X	X	X	X
Favorable Attitudes Toward the Problem Behavior	X	X	X	X	
Early Initiation of the Problem Behavior	X	X	X	X	X
Constitutional Factors	X	X			X

Source: Office of Juvenile Justice and Delinquency Prevention. (1996). *Report to Congress: Title V Incentive Grants for Local Delinquency Prevention Programs*. Washington, D.C.: U.S. Department of Justice, Appendix, p. 3.

Choosing Crime: Moral Development and Social Influence

Recall from of our discussion of Kohlberg's (1964) theory of moral development in chapter 7 that young children tend to be in the preconventional stage of moral reasoning. This means that their decisions about whether or not to violate rules are driven by how likely they think it is that they will be punished for transgressions. In other words, preconventional children tend to obey rules to avoid punishment and not because there is anything inherently appealing about obedience. Then, in late childhood and early adolescence, decisions about how to behave tend to be based on respect for rules and laws and a belief that obeying them is a good thing to do. Youngsters reach this conventional stage of moral reasoning by internalizing the beliefs, values, rules, and laws established by respected people (e.g., parents, teachers) and institutions (the legal system). Once young people have adopted these rules and laws, special circumstances must usually be present before they will violate them. If by the time they reach adolescence, children have not developed respect for laws as laws—not simply as rules whose violation will lead to punishment—they may continue to refrain from criminal activity only because they fear punishment. Accordingly, they may engage in criminal activity when they think they can get away without incurring punishment.

Kohlberg' theory helps one understand how social learning normally promotes the conventional moral reasoning that keeps people from committing criminal acts, but it does not pay much attention to social influences that may *promote* criminal behavior. These influences include the words and deeds of deviant or criminal family members and peers as well as certain television and movie characters. Operating on the same principles of operant, classical, and observational learning through which most parents, teachers, and peers teach children to obey and adopt culturally approved rules of conduct, these negative social influences can dilute and even neutralize the deterrent effect of threatened punishment. For example, youngsters who associate with criminal peers may easily come to believe that "everybody breaks the rules," and this perception can lead them to conform by committing crimes, too. Daniel Kahan (1997a, 1997b) has suggested that the teenagers most likely to imitate the criminal behavior they see around them are the ones who have not internalized mainstream society's laws and who believe that other people are profiting from crime and are not being punished. Believing that everybody commits crimes and gets away with it (a) promotes the impression that "they can't catch everyone" (thus making the risks of committing a crime seem quite low, especially in relation to the potential rewards), (b) releases inhibitions against committing crime, and (c) removes concerns that criminal behavior will hurt one's social reputation or status.

A classic study in social psychology demonstrated both the effect of observing criminal acts and the power of the desire to imitate criminal models. In this study, Philip Zimbardo (1969) parked an abandoned automobile on the campus of Stanford University, where it remained for more than a week without being harmed in any way. Once he smashed the car's windshield with a sledgehammer, however, passersby immediately joined in, further damaging the car and stripping it of valuable parts. Zimbardo argued that it was the sight of someone damaging the car that released onlookers' inhibitions against vandalism and theft. Yet the effects were not universal. Some people merely watched others commit a crime. What determines who imitates criminal activity and who does not?

As we have shown in chapters 4, 5, and 6, whether or not a person engages in criminal behavior depends on the interaction of a whole range of biological, psychological, and sociocultural factors, many of which influence the appearance of aggressiveness, which is at the heart of violent crime (Heide, 1995). We encountered many of these factors in chapter 7 where we began to trace the development of aggression in childhood. We continue the story now by exploring how gender, psychological disorders, and substance abuse contribute to the further development of aggression and to its evolution into violent crime. Later, we examine the roles played by gangs and guns in solidifying violence and crime as a way of life for some teenagers.

Gender Differences in the Development of Criminal Behavior

It is generally assumed that males, as the traditional "warriors" in Western cultures, are inherently more aggressive than females. This gender difference is certainly apparent in adolescence, when far more aggression and violent crime is committed by adolescent boys than girls; we rarely see girls punching each other, for example. The fact is, though, that girls can be just as aggressive as boys; they just tend to express aggressiveness in different ways.

Until the age of about 3 years, boys and girls are equally physically aggressive, but between the ages of 3 and 6, sex-related differences in expressing aggression begin to appear (Fagot & Leinbach, 1989; Legault & Strayer, 1990). As parents and teachers discourage girls from displaying physical aggression, boys become more likely than girls to hit, push, and threaten to beat up other children. For their part, girls aggress by threatening to withhold friendship or to exclude others from their group if they fail to comply with their requests (Cairns, Cairns, Neckerman, Ferguson, & Gariepy, 1989; Crick & Grotpeter, 1995). Psychologists call this more typically female pattern *relational aggression*.

These gender differences in the childhood expression of aggression tend to remain in adulthood (Eagly & Steffen, 1986; Frodi, Maccaulay, & Thome, 1977), but this does not mean that women are not physically aggressive—especially in relation to intimate partners. A review (Archer, 1985) of dozens of studies of physical hostility in heterosexual relationships found that although women sustain more serious and visible injures than men during domestic disputes, women are just as likely as men to resort to physical aggression during an argument with a sexual partner. Younger women are particularly likely to use physical violence ranging from slapping, kicking and biting to choking and using a weapon (Zuger, 1998).

Anger, a common precursor to violence, is experienced by women as often as by men (Averil, 1982). In one study (Scherer, Wallbott, & Summerfield, 1986), 75% to 85% of participants, male and female alike, reported feeling anger within the previous one to four weeks. However, just as boys and girls learn to express aggression differently, men and women learn different ways of expressing anger as well as other emotions such as joy and sadness (Goleman, 1988). Men are more likely to display anger outwardly, whereas women are more likely to keep it in inside. This difference has been invoked to help explain the fact that women are far more likely than men to be depressed (Brannon, 2005).

Gender differences in the expression of aggression appear to underlie the fact that men commit 84% of violent crimes in the United States (FBI, 2004). This picture appears to be changing, however. Arrests of females for all types of crime—including murder, rape, robbery, aggravated assault, burglary, larceny-theft, motor vehicle theft, arson, forgery, counterfeiting, and embezzlement—are increasing (FBI, 2004). From 1993 to 1997, male arrests rose 6%, but female arrests were up 19%, and among females themselves, arrest rates for juveniles are increasing more than twice as fast as adults (FBI, 2004).

As adolescent criminals enter adulthood, the rates and patterns of male and female offenses tend to be related to factors such as marital and employment status. For example, married men are less likely than unmarried men to commit violent crime, and single women are more likely to commit theft and robbery than other crimes. Among female criminals, though, those who are married or previously married are more likely than single women to have murdered—usually their husbands or boyfriends. Employed women are more likely to commit nonviolent crime, whereas unemployed women are more likely to be involved with violent crime (Campbell & Robinson, 1997).

Girls' Pathways to Crime

In chapter 7, we focused on the pathways to crime that are typical of boys, but girls tend to follow a somewhat different route. How do girls grow up to be criminals? Some theorists have focused on girls' psychosexual development, including suggestions that their susceptibility to being dominated and manipulated by men can lead to low self-esteem. When combined with early sexual development, self-esteem problems can lead to early sexual contacts and affiliation with older adolescent boys who are themselves at high-risk for antisocial behavior (Caspi, Lyman, Moffitt, & Silvla, 1993). In other words, some see delinquency in females as having its roots in feelings of uncertainty and loneliness. For example, if a girl is rejected and/or abused by family and certain peers, she may seek social approval in promiscuous and potentially self-destructive sexual relationships (Konopka, 1966). Indeed, surveys of female prison inmates suggest that about a third of them had been physically or sexually abused before the age of 18 (Chesney-Lind, 1987; Snell, 1994). Other studies supported the idea that some women drift into crime after being victimized by men or adolescent boys through physical or sexual abuse or through other forms of exploitation (K. Daly & Chesney-Lind, 1988).

Other theorists have suggested that a dysfunctional home life has a more damaging effect on girls than on boys and that this difference puts girls in such homes at higher risk for criminal behavior (Calhoun, Jurgens, & Chen, 1993). Boys, they have said, become delinquent in the course of trying to gain social status with peers by demonstrating their masculinity, whereas girls drift into delinquency in the course of expressing hostility toward their parents and obtaining gratification and attention, especially from men (Baker & Adams, 1962; Heritage Foundation, 1995). This gender difference may be because girls tend to be more strongly influenced—

positively or negatively—by their relationships with their mothers and by their mother's own psychological well-being (Ensminger, Brown, & Kellam, 1982). For example, boys have been found to be less likely than girls to be controlled by their parents (e.g., J. Hagan & Kay, 1990).

Young female delinquents usually begin with nonviolent offenses such as shoplifting or prostitution, but this pattern changes when they start abusing drugs or alcohol (Biron, Brochu, & Desjardins, 1995). At that point, a girl's offenses may become more interpersonally violent (Sommers & Baskin, 1994).

Conduct Disorder and the Development of Criminal Behavior

Gender differences aside, the most potentially dangerous criminals, whether male or female, are those who display antisocial personality disorder (APD), which we described in chapter 5. To qualify for this diagnosis in adulthood, these people must have displayed conduct disorder (CD) before reaching the age of 15 (see chapter 7). We consider the processes through which some conduct-disordered children become emotionally cold, manipulative, adult criminals.

In September of 1997, in a posh suburb of Washington, DC, Samuel Sheinbein and Aaron Needle, 17-year-old high school dropouts from upper income homes, were charged with the gruesome slaying of an occasional companion, a 19-year-old boy from a single-parent, lower class Hispanic home. His death was caused by blunt force trauma to the head, cuts to the neck and chest, and strangulation. After the murder, the boys cut off their victim's arms and legs, burned his body parts almost beyond recognition, stuffed the charred remains into a garbage bag, and left them in a tarp-covered garden cart at one of their homes. The killers were privileged teenagers who had met at an exclusive private religious school but had a history of trouble with drugs and the law, strained family relations, and few close friends (Hockstader & Whitlock, 1999).

After breaking into cars and houses when he was in eighth grade, Sheinbein had been sent to juvenile boot camp, an alternative to incarceration that is designed to instill discipline and respect for authority. However, he was apparently so humiliated by the experience that its only effect was to motivate him to begin a bodybuilding program that he hoped would protect him from being bullied by stronger boys, a common occurrence at boot camp. Needle had a history of drug addiction and other behavior disorders that had led to his placement in special schools for emotionally disturbed children and a private military academy. His peers described him as volatile and prone to cursing and threatening people at the slightest provocation.

Both boys were released on bond pending their murder trial, but with the help of his attorney father, Sheinbein fled to Israel to avoid prosecution but was eventually sentenced by an Israeli judge to serve 24 years for his crimes. Needle's mental condition deteriorated to the extent that his attorney asked that state psychiatrists examine him, but the boy hanged himself on the day that the request was granted.

These cases illustrate once again the fact that the development of aggression and violence often begins with CD in childhood; adolescence provides a broader stage on which to act out and elaborate criminal impulses. The transition from childhood to adolescence can be difficult and challenging for anyone, but it becomes a battleground for children with CD. This is partly because adolescence is filled with new opportunities to test authority and try out newly found freedoms. Deficient in the development of conscience and empathy, these angry children turned adolescents are primed to act out aggressive impulses against others. It is no wonder, then, that these youngsters are as much as 16 times as likely to exhibit antisocial behaviors by the age of 15 as those who had not displayed CD in childhood (Fergusson & Horwood, 1996; Fergusson, Lynskey, & Horwood, 1996).

When, as is typically the case, adolescents with CD have trouble in school, they are often suspended or expelled, leaving them even more time for criminal activity. If they begin abusing alcohol and other drugs, their deviant and criminal lifestyle usually becomes entrenched and virtually impossible to change (Garnefski & Okma, 1996).

Substance Abuse and the Development of Criminal Behavior

The use of alcohol and other drugs is all too common among adolescents (U.S. Department of Health and Human Services, Substance Abuse and Mental Health Services Administration, 1998). Because of their age, this behavior is a crime in and of itself, but it is also strongly related to other forms of criminal activity. For example, a 1996 study (National Gang Crime Research Center, 1997) of 4,000 teenage boys arrested for various crimes in 23 metropolitan areas found that 52% of them tested positive for marijuana (up from 41% a year earlier) and 10% to 13% tested positive for cocaine. Not surprisingly, the same trends appear in adults. Among 21- to 30-year-olds arrested during 1996, 64% of men and 36% of women tested positive for marijuana (National Institute of Justice, 1996b). In 20 of 23 U.S. cities, more than 60% of all adult male arrestees tested positive for at least one illicit drug. Further, the prevalence of drug use among arrestees seems to be on the rise. In one large Virginia jurisdiction, 90% of the defendants in felony cases tested positive for drug and/or alcohol use ("Tough Talk," 1997).

For at least the last several decades, alcohol use has immediately preceded at least half of all violent crimes including murders (National Institute of Justice, 1997b). According to a government report (Mumola, 1999), about three fourths of all prisoners said they were alcohol or drug users during the time leading up to their arrest. In 1997, 33% of state and 22% of federal prisoners said they committed their latest offense while under the influence of drugs compared to 31% and 17% in 1991 (Bureau of Justice Statistics, 1998). Chronic drinkers are more likely than other people to have histories of violent behavior, and criminals who use illegal drugs commit robberies and assaults more frequently than do nonuser criminals. In the state of Washington, for example, 84% of prisoners released on probation or parole in 1990 were dependent on alcohol, and 75% were cocaine dependent. These figures approximate the national averages for prison populations (National Institute of Justice, 1997). A study (Modestin et al., 1996) that investigated the lifetime prevalence of criminal behavior concluded that male alcoholics were twice as likely as to have a criminal record than nonalcoholics and were more likely than nonalcoholics to commit violent crimes and property offenses. These people are especially likely to commit their crimes during periods of heavy drug use (National Institute of Justice, 1997). Because alcohol is by far the most significant psychoactive substance contributing to juvenile crime, we explore how teenagers come to abuse it.

Alcohol Abuse

The general public uses the term *alcoholic* to refer to people who drink heavily. Researchers, too, often use this term, but they are referring more specifically to a pattern of heavy drinking that steadily worsens until the person has lost control over drinking and become so dependent on alcohol that physical and mental health are jeopardized and social and occupational functioning are impaired (Nietzel et al., 1998). Many researchers believe that there are different forms of alcoholism associated with differing ages of onset, reasons for drinking, and social and psychological consequences (Babor et al., 1992; Hill, 1992; Zucker, 1987). One of the most widely accepted theories is that of Cloninger, Bohman, and Sigvardsson (1981) who described two types of alcoholism. *Type I* alcoholics start drinking in adulthood, are prone to binge drinking, often develop alcohol-related health problems, and do not generally engage in antisocial acts when they drink. *Type II* alcoholics begin drinking in adolescence, and even though they have fewer alcohol-related health problems, their drinking causes more social and occupational problems, and they tend to engage in antisocial behaviors when drinking.

There is considerable evidence that psychological and sociocultural factors both inside and outside the home interact with the biological factors we discussed in chapter 4 to elevate the risk of adolescents' problem drinking. For example, a youngster's motivation to drink might be related to the fact that some people find that alcohol helps reduce tension, anxiety, depression, and other unpleasant emotions (Conger, 1956). Experiencing tension-reducing effects in one stressful situation can, through operant conditioning, strengthen the tendency to use alcohol again. Adolescents' first use of alcohol is often related to expectations—usually based on observing parents, peers, or movie and TV characters—about its ability to reduce tension, enhance sexual performance, bolster confidence, and increase social competence (Marlatt, 1987; Zucker & Fitzgerald, 1991). Alcohol expectancy effects are strong enough that people who expect to get enjoyably drunk will do so, even if a drink contains little or no alcohol (Thombs, 1994). In one study (G. T. Smith, Goldman, Greenbaum, & Christiansen, 1995), positive expectancies for alcohol in 12- to 14-year-olds predicted higher levels of subsequent alcohol use 3 years later; and the more they drank, the more their positive expectancies about alcohol increased.

Temperament and personality are other important psychological factors in the development of problem drinking. For example, youngsters who score high on sensation seeking and novelty seeking in childhood are more prone to use alcohol in adolescence, perhaps as part of a more general pattern of impulsiveness, recklessness, and aggressiveness (Halikas, Meller, Morse, & Lyttle, 1990; Jessor & Jessor, 1977; Sher, Walitzer, Wood, & Brent, 1991).

A child's home environment can also help set the stage for problem drinking. Parents who are themselves problem drinkers not only provide maladaptive modeling, but their tendency toward marital conflict, domestic violence, and poor parenting skills can impair their children's performance at school and lead to aggressive, antisocial behaviors (Research Institute on Addictions, 1997). As adolescents, children usually emulate their parents' alcohol consumption whether the parents are nondrinkers, moderate drinkers, or nondrinkers (Berndt & Perry, 1986; Harburg, Davis, & Caplan, 1982). In general, the more the parents drink, the earlier their children begin to drink (Kandel, Kessler, & Marguiles, 1978). However, adolescent alcohol use is also sometimes inadvertently encouraged by nondrinking parents whose staunch opposition to alcohol leads their children to drink as a way of rebelling against parental authority (Lawson, Peterson, & Lawson, 1983), and parents who preach abstinence while using alcohol themselves may find that their children "do as they do, not as they say" (Brook et al., 1990).

More general aspects of parenting styles and the quality of parent–child relationships can also affect adolescent drinking. Parents who are nurturing and firm-but-fair disciplinarians are less likely than nonsupportive or inconsistent parents to have adolescents who drink (Barnes, Farrell, & Cairns, 1986; Tarter et al., 1993). Adolescents are less likely to drink if they feel close to their parents or are satisfied with the parent–child relationship (Kandel & Andrews, 1987; Tarter et al., 1993). The risks of adolescent alcohol abuse also appear to be lower in families that observe rituals such as a family dinner hour, family vacations, and organized celebrations of holidays and birthdays. Researchers have suggested that such family experiences foster feelings of mutual support and commitment that are incompatible with problem drinking (Bennet & Wolin, 1990; Research Institute on Addictions, 1997).

Peer influences, too, constitute an important social factor in the development of adolescent drinking. Most adolescents first drink with their peers, often through a desire to conform to peer group standards. Indeed, one study (Swaim, Oetting, Edwards, & Beauvais, 1989) of peer influence found that having friends who use alcohol (or other psychoactive drugs) was a better predictor of adolescent drug use than the presence of emotional problems. Another study (Wills, McNamara, Vaccaro, & Hirky, 1996) that measured alcohol use among more than 1,000 adolescents as they progressed through grades 7 to 9 found that the ones whose substance use increased were those who associated most with substance-using peers.

In short, alcohol abuse appears to stem from an interplay of biological, psychological, and social factors, all of which must be considered to fully appreciate the complexity of the causes of adolescent alcohol problems (Devor, 1994; E. E. Epstein & McCrady, 1994; Tarter & Vanyukov, 1994). Varying combinations of high-risk temperaments and environmental liabilities can create varying pathways to alcohol abuse. For example, children born with high emotional reactivity to parents who have poor parenting skills and high levels of stress are more likely to affiliate with drug-using peers in adolescence and more likely to use alcohol than are less emotional children born into more stable homes (Chassin, Pillow, Curran, Mollina, & Barrera, 1993).

Regardless of the source of problem drinking, it can lead to crime. After a drink or two, most people feel more talkative and relaxed but also prone to impairments in judgment and other thought processes. When blood alcohol content reaches 0.05% to 0.08%, there may be evidence of motor impairment and slurred speech. When it reaches 0.10%, there is lack of motor coordination, unsteady gait, drowsiness, and impaired perception.[1] At this point, the drinker may begin to display social, psychological, and behavioral changes such as lack of inhibition (becoming more aggressive, talkative, seductive, or the like—depending on what behaviors are normally inhibited) and a lessening of attentional and memory capabilities. Although the behavioral effects of alcohol are determined in large part by its chemical impact on the brain, these effects are also strongly influenced by such social and psychological factors as the situations in which people drink, their prior drinking experiences (especially their expectancies about what alcohol normally does to them), and what other nearby drinkers are doing. Thus, whereas the person drinking alone to cope with lost love may become sluggish, tearful, or angry, the person drinking with friends to celebrate a job promotion is likely to feel happy.

---

[1]In many jurisdictions, a blood alcohol content of 0.08 constitutes the legal definition of intoxication. In some jurisdictions, the criterion is 0.10.

For drinkers who build up a tolerance for alcohol, the physical manifestations of intoxication become less pronounced even as its effects on emotion and behavior become more evident. Some individuals become increasingly moody and hostile, leading to interpersonal conflicts with family and peers (M. K. Leonard, 1990). Chronic alcohol abusers show a gradual deterioration in thinking, judgment, problem solving, learning, memory, and social skills (Parsons, Butters, & Nathan, 1987; Steinglass, Bennett, Wolin, & Reiss, 1987), all of which can inspire a false sense of invulnerability and the courage to throw a punch, steal a car, or engage in other aggressive, violent, or criminal acts.

For many adolescents, the use of various substances, particularly alcohol, is yet another step along the pathway to crime on which they embarked in early childhood. Often, these drug and alcohol abusers reach adolescence alienated from their families and from the educational and other values of the larger society. They tend to do poorly in school and to drop out, thus virtually insuring a lifetime of drug use and often crime (Krohn, Thornberry, Collins-Hall, & Lizotte, 1995). The general pattern is for teenagers to begin by drinking alcohol and committing petty crimes and then go on to illicit drugs and more serious crimes (U.S. Department of Health and Human Services, Substance Abuse and Mental Health Services Administration, 1998). This pattern is especially common among youngsters who are members of the "underclass" who live in inner city poverty, who experience little or no success at school or on a job, and who have inadequate social skills or family support (Wish, 1990). In contrast, substance abuse and related criminal behavior are far less likely among adolescents who enjoy strong family ties including good relations with siblings, who do well at school, who are involved in religious activities, and who have access to non-substance-abusing role models (Brook et al., 1990: Hops, Tildesley, Lichtenstein, Ary, & Sherman, 1990).

Gangs, Guns, and the Development of Criminal Behavior

Unlike adult crime, most juvenile crime is committed in groups (Howell, 1994). Sometimes, these are groups of friends or acquaintances, but more often they are "groups of convenience" whose members just happen to be together for a particular criminal incident or two. However, many young people join juvenile gangs, which exist mainly for engaging in hostile aggression and that are both a cause and a result of today's epidemic of crimes committed by adolescents and young adults. In the United States, juvenile gangs are found in all 50 states, mainly in large and medium-size cities but also in smaller towns and suburban communities. They are creating increasing problems, not only on the street but in correctional institutions and schools as well. Compared with nongang offenders, gang members are responsible for a disproportionate percentage of serious and violent offenses and are more likely to engage in the sale and distribution of drugs.

What is a Gang?

Criminologists and law enforcement officials define a juvenile gang as a group of adolescents who (1) are generally perceived as a distinct aggregation by others in the neighborhood, (2) recognize themselves as a group (and have a name), and (3) have been involved in a sufficient number of delinquent incidents to bring a consistently negative response from neighborhood residents and/or law enforcement agencies (M. Klein, 1995). In some states, criminal statutes define gangs. For example, according to the California Penal Code, Section 186.22, a criminal street gang is "any organization, association, or group of three or more persons whether formal or informal … which has a common name or common identifying sign or symbol, where members individually or collectively engage in or have engaged in a pattern of criminal activity" including assault with a deadly weapon, robbery, homicide or manslaughter, and the manufacture and distribution of controlled substances. As certain gangs have gotten more organized and sophisticated in recent years, law enforcement is going after them with techniques it formerly used to attack organized criminal enterprises such as the mafia.

Gangs are organized under leaders, generally have territory (or "turf"), identifiable clothing or colors, symbols, and a language that may include distinctive graffiti and hand gestures. Only about 25% of gangs engage in group crimes such as drug trafficking or robbery, but they all use violent crimes to protect themselves, their honor, their territory, and their sources of income (Howell, 1994). Inner-city gangs are especially likely to have identifiable territories that rival gang members violate at their peril. One Washington, DC, gang marked the boundary between its territory and that of a rival gang by hanging on a power line the shoes of those killed by its members. Other gangs, such as motorcycle gangs and hate gangs (e.g., neo-Nazis), do not establish a geographic territory. In the past few years, gangs that move from the cities outward to the suburbs and even rural areas have become more common. Experts say that these gangs are following the demographic spread of jobs and housing much as businesses do (Weisheit & Wells, 1999). Some of these gangs consist of youths under 18, but many of the leaders are young adults.

A Brief History of Youth Gangs

Youth gangs are not unique to North America. Gang-related problems are also reported in most countries of Europe as well as in Kenya, South Africa, Australia, Mexico, Brazil, Peru, South Korea, Hong Kong, and mainland China (Spergel, 1995). Nor are gangs a new phenomenon. They have been around for centuries and tend to appear during times of rapid social change and political instability. As early as the 1600s, for example, London was terrorized by the Mims, the Hectors, the Bugles, and the Dead Boys, organized gangs whose members broke windows, demolished taverns, and assaulted guards. In fights between gangs, they wore identifiable colors and distinctive belts and pins. Youth gangs appeared in New York City before 1800, and by 1855, some gang members owed allegiance to gang leaders who, in turn, owed allegiance to various political factions. As early as the 1920s, gangs in Illinois prisons were engaged in violence and crime similar to that seen in prisons today—extortion, homosexual prostitution, murder, inciting riots, and illegitimate business enterprises (Yablonsky, 1996). The gang tradition has been particularly strong in the Southwestern United States. In Los Angeles, for example, where some gangs have a 60-year history, it is not uncommon to find fourth-generation Hispanic gang members.

In the early decades of the 20th century, gangs in the United States were made up of venturesome, unsupervised, immigrant children living in inner-city slums where they were seen more as nuisances than as threats. Even as recently as 1975, the federal government did not consider gangs to be a problem. In that year, a report by the President's Commission on Law Enforcement and Administration of Justice stated that

> Youth gangs are not and should not become a major object of concern. … Youth gang violence is not a major crime problem in the United States. What gang violence does exist can fairly readily be diverted into constructive channels through the provision of services by community agencies. (W. B. Miller, 1975)

Whether gangs were really not a problem in 1975 or whether the government simply failed to appreciate their impact, gangs did become a serious concern for law enforcement officials by the late 1980s when the appearance of crack cocaine on the streets of U.S. cities caused a proliferation of gangs whose members formed the distribution system for selling drugs on the street. More violent, and driven mainly by economic self-interest, these gangs were far different from the ones seen earlier in the 20th century.

The 2002 National Youth Gang Survey (Egley & Major, 2004) estimated that approximately 731,500 youth gang members and 21,500 gangs were active in the United States in 2002.[2] The estimated numbers of gang members between 1996 and 2002 decreased 14%, but 42% of jurisdictions responding to the survey reported that their youth gang problem was worsening. Most gang members are boys, but the number of girl gang members (placed somewhere between 11% and 8%) is growing. Gangs continue to spread from the inner cities to the suburbs and even rural areas, following the demographic shifts of population and jobs (Snyder & Sickmund, 1999).

---

[2]It is difficult to obtain precise figures on gang membership because there are no universally agreed on criteria for identifying gangs and gang members among respondent law enforcement agencies. The National Youth Gang Survey excludes motorcycle, prison, and adult gangs as well as hate or ideology groups.

The Gang–Crime Connection

The Uniform Crime Report for 2003 indicates that although the overall violent crime rate has remained level or fallen slightly since 2000, juvenile gang homicides have jumped 25% since 2000 (FBI, 2004). In major cities, gang-related homicides account for half of all homicides (Egley & Major, 2004), a figure that has remained steady for 10 years or more (Spergel, 1995). Most of these killings result from individual actions aimed at protecting gang honor or territory, including alarming, increasing trends of murdering witnesses of gang crime to keep them from testifying. ("Guns and Jeers," 2005). Like the Mafia, gangs have a "code of silence." In July 2003, in the rural and mountainous Shenandoah Valley of Virginia, 18-year-old Brenda Paz's badly decomposed body was found floating in a mountain stream. The girl was a member of a notorious Salvadoran gang, Mara Salvatrucha, or MS–13, which recruits immigrant children as young as 12 whose fam- ilies have come to the United States from Ecuador, Guatemala, Honduras, and Mexico. She was scheduled to testify in a federal criminal case involving the interstate drug trafficking of the gang. The MS–13 is a particu- larly intimidating gang—it has a signature form of intimidation slicing off their victims' hands, or slitting their throats with steel machetes. Members of a Baltimore, Maryland, gang sent gang members to court wearing T- shirts that warned against "snitching," and made a DVD waving guns and making violent threats against would-be witnesses ("Guns and Jeers," 2005). Prosecutors across the country cite witness intimidation as chal- lenging or impeding gang violence cases, and some federal courts are putting witnesses in the federal witness protection program, which gives witnesses new identities and relocates them to new parts of the country to live.

Saying that gangs are related to crime is to state the obvious. A 1998 U.S. Department of Justice study sum- marized the link between gang membership and juvenile crime by noting that (1) gang membership increases the likelihood that members will commit serious and violent crimes, (2) gang members are much more likely to sell drugs than nongang youths, (3) youngsters who join gangs earlier are arrested earlier, (4) gang members are much more likely than nongang members to possess powerful and lethal weapons, and (5) the criminal behavior of gang members is more extensive and serious than that of comparably at-risk nongang youths (Howell & Decker, 1999).

Studies indicate that youth gang members are responsible for a disproportionate share of all offenses, violence and nonviolent. In a survey of crime in Rochester, New York, youth gang members accounted for 69% of violent crimes, 68% of property crime, and 70% of drug sales reported in the interviews (Thornberry & Burch, 1997). Other surveys have yielded even more disproportionate results. Even when compared with similarly situated and comparably at-risk young people, gang members commit crimes at considerably higher rates than nonmembers. Also, individual gang members tend to be more deeply involved in crime while active in gangs than either before joining or after leaving (Snyder & Sickmund, 1999). These findings strongly suggest that a gang is much more than a mere association of criminally inclined young people and that the gang structure itself may encourage, facilitate, or even demand a heightened level of criminality among members.

The average age at which young people begin to associate with gangs is 13, and the median age for first arrest is 14. A study (Snyder & Sickmund, 1999) tracking the arrest histories of 83 gang members in Columbus, Ohio, found a clear progression in offense seriousness, beginning with property crimes and mov- ing to violent and drug crimes within two years. Forty-three percent of illegal drug sales in their jurisdictions were attributed to gang members.

Gang Ties to Organized Crime and Prisons.
Some law enforcement authorities believe that long-estab- lished Black, Asian, and motorcycle gangs have ties to organized crime, especially in the realm of drug distri- bution. Gang members and nongang drug dealers have developed a symbiotic relationship in some inner-city slum neighborhoods where the drug trade is rampant. Gang members provide protection for the drug dealers and are well paid for running errands. Younger gang members are recruited to deliver drugs. As we noted pre- viously, the trend is for law enforcement to treat gangs involved in drug distribution and other contraband not as having ties to organized crime but as epitomized by the main features of organized crime (see our discus- sion in chapter 11).

Prison gangs are usually branches of street gangs. A total of 61% of all correctional institutions reported that the gangs inside correctional institutions are basically the same gangs that exist on the street (National

Gang Crime Research Center, 1997). When prison gang members are released, they go back to the urban streets taking their hard-earned lessons about violence and crime with them. Unlike the prison gangs of 30 years ago, which arose to provide protection and obtain contraband in prison, today's prison gangs carry on illegitimate (usually drug-related) businesses. The criminal activities of prison gangs are highly organized and include not only drug sales but strong-arm robbery, homicide, gambling, and homosexual prostitution. Gang members obtain strategic prison work assignments, bribe prison officials, and abuse privileges (Camp & Camp, 1985). Gang members are more likely to assault prison guards and other inmates, smuggle drugs and contraband, and be involved in other prison disturbances (Gaes, Wallace, Gilman, Klein-Saffran, & Supa, 2001; Knox, 1999; National Gang Crime Research Center, 1997). Officials in Los Angeles have reported that gang members are responsible for 40% to 60% of all felonies committed in prison (Spergel, 1995; see chapter 12).

Who Joins Gangs?

As children enter adolescence, friends and peers typically replace family members as the primary social influence and source of attention. By early adolescence, most teens turn to their friends rather than their parents when they need emotional support and a confidant (Berndt & Perry, 1986). Teenagers form cliques of close friends, and they may attend concerts or football games or engage in other activities with those friends as well as with "crowds," which are groups of youngsters who happen to do things together. Teens may commit a crime in a group because they do not have the courage or desire to act alone or because they were talked into it by friends or acquaintances.

Some group adolescent activity is criminal, but these groups do not have the organizational structure and specialization at criminal activity that is associated with gangs. A 1997 survey (National Gang Crime Research Center, 1997) of 4,000 gang members was undertaken to try to understand who joins gangs. Results indicate that gang members are significantly more likely to:

- Be bullies in school.
- Come from a mother-only household.
- Have witnessed violence in the home.
- Have a family member in prison.
- Perceive themselves as part of the underclass.
- Sell crack cocaine.
- Have fired a gun at a police officer and to believe that shooting a police officer would improve their gang status and reputation.
- Have been in organized drug dealing.
- Have friends and associates who are gang members.
- Report that they get what they want "even if I have to take it from someone."

Gang members are also significantly less likely to:

- Have completed high school or completed a GED.
- Attend church or believe in God.
- Have reported having adequate parental supervision as children. (National Gang Crime Research Center, 1997)

The survey found no significant differences in male and female gang members on most of these measures.

Why do Adolescents Join Gangs?

Just as people commit crimes for many different reasons, there are many reasons why adolescents are motivated to join gangs. The typical gang member enters adolescence burdened with numerous psychosocial risk factors for crime including a history of oppositional defiant disorder or conduct disorder, truancy, school failure, and an absent father (Klein, 1995). Having failed to develop a strong conscience or empathy, they tend to have little regard for others, enabling them to manipulate, exploit, rape, and even kill without remorse. Many meet the diagnostic criteria for antisocial personality disorder (Yablonsky, 1996), and gang membership only solidifies their violent tendencies.

Still, joining a gang appears to be influenced not just by individual characteristics but also by social, economic, and other environmental factors. For example, living in a gang-infested neighborhood and having family members who are or were gang members seems to be a key factor in leading many youngsters into gang life. Gang membership is thus often transgenerational (Spergel & Curry, 1987). When gang members carrying guns and wearing bullet-proof vests take control of neighborhood streets, when playgrounds and other public areas become the site of gun battles, when the fear of being caught in the cross fire of intergang battles keeps residents in their homes at night, many youngsters do what seems most sensible and adaptive. Even if joining a gang had not been their main goal, it may appear to be the smartest thing to do because it allows them to identify and associate with the power and prestige in their neighborhoods. Indeed, where gangs rule a neighborhood, children have to go out of their way to reject gang life. So it may not be the desire to commit crimes but to seek protection while conforming to the behavior of powerful models that leads some juveniles into gangs. This tendency is encouraged, too, by young people's perceptions that gangs are revered by their peers and feared by their parents and teachers. Gang members increasingly cite economics as the justification for membership, with most saying they would give up membership if they could make at least $15 an hour in a legal job (Huff, 1998).

Girls who join gangs usually do so voluntarily rather than being recruited. Like their male counterparts, female gang members generally come from poverty-stricken homes, have low self-esteem, do poorly in school, and are rebellious. However, they are more likely than boys to use gang affiliation to shock their parents and peers (Campbell, 1994; Harris, 1988). They also join up and drop out in a more casual manner. The typical female gang member joins a gang between the ages of 12 and 14 and leaves between the ages of 16 and 18 (Molidor, 1996).

Martin Jankowski (1991), a sociologist who has studied why people join gangs, how gangs recruit members, and what happens to members when they leave gangs concluded that gang membership involves a mutual agreement between defiant individualists who want what a gang can offer and gang leaders who need followers. Jankowski (1991) said the most common reasons for joining a gang are:

1. The gang provides opportunities to consistently earn more money illegally than they could on their own and to have a better life than their parents, most of whom have low-paying, menial, dead-end jobs.
2. The gang provides members with entertainment much as does the neighborhood "Y" or a college fraternity house.
3. The gang provides members with anonymity, which lessens the chances that they will be arrested and charged with crimes.
4. The gang provides protection from the physical dangers of living in low-income, inner-city neighborhoods.
5. Where gangs have existed for generations and where family members may have been gang members, a gang unites individuals with the community tradition of gang membership.

Given these advantages, why would people in gang-infested neighborhoods *not* join gangs? Jankowski (1991) suggested that some youngsters stay away from gangs and resist being recruited by them either because they already have all the skills and opportunities they need to accomplish their goals–including illegal economic ventures—without gang involvement, or they view the risks of death and imprisonment as too high a price to pay for living the gang's defiant, deviant lifestyle (Jankowski, 1991).

Once in a gang, some members remain until they are well into their 30s, whereas others drop out sooner, either to pursue illegal economic ventures on their own or to join a smaller gang, an ethnic social club, or organized crime. Some leave the gang to take a job and adopt the kind of socially approved, conforming lifestyle they had wanted to avoid. Finally, all too many gang members "leave" when they die from a drug overdose or gang-related violence (Jankowski, 1991). The short, tragic life of Darryl Hall illustrates one pathway into gang membership that led to a common pathway out of gang life. In the fall of 1996 at the age of 12, Darryl returned to Simple City, a Washington, DC, public housing project, after having lived for several months with his grandmother in a nearby Maryland suburb. His parents had sent him there to protect him from the influence of local gangs, but Darryl was bored and wanted to come home. The home he returned to was a dreary tenement building whose walls were covered with spray-painted graffiti declaring gang war cries and the names of dead gang members. An illegal drug trade flourished on nearby corners, where groups of glaring young men guarded their gang's territory. Darryl was brash, even ambitious in a childlike way, and he was confident that he would thrive on the exciting streets of Southeast DC. More specifically, he wanted to join the neighborhood gang, Simple City Crew. In a display of bravado perhaps intended to be his initiation into the gang, Darryl ventured alone into "enemy territory," a basketball court on the other side of the street that divided his adopted gang's turf from that of a rival faction of Simple City Crew, and fired his pistol. In retaliation for this provocation, three of the rival gang members caught Darryl, threw him in a car, and drove him to a wooded ravine. There they dragged him to a streambed where, without a word, they shot him in the head (Struck, 1997). Darryl's death was the ninth that year attributed to infighting among warring factions of Simple City Crew.

The Role of Guns in Juvenile Crime

Gangs could not operate without the guns they depend on for protection in transporting drugs, holding territory, and "disciplining" straying members. Especially in inner city neighborhoods, even youngsters who are not directly involved in gangs or illegal drug sales may feel that they need guns to protect themselves from other juveniles, to impress their friends, or to intimidate people. A study (Lizotte & Sheppard, 2001) of 1,000 seventh- and eighth-grade boys in Rochester, New York, found that 5% to 10% had carried concealed guns in the past 30 days—some for protection, some for sport, respect, and some to engage in gang-related crime.[3] However, among boys who used guns while participating in gang-related drug sales, the percentage of gun carriers increased 35% (Lizotte & Sheppard, 2001). Another study focusing on juveniles arrested for crimes during the first 6 months of 1995 found that 20% of juveniles charged with a weapons offense said they carried a gun all or most of the time. Juvenile arrestees were twice as likely as all arrestees (juveniles and adults combined) to have stolen a gun (25% vs. 13%). Of all juvenile arrestees, 33% had used a gun in a crime, with the number higher for drug sellers (42%). Not surprisingly, 50% of all gang members arrested had used a gun in a crime (Lizotte & Sheppard, 2001), and young people between the ages of 12 and 17 who had symptoms of CD were eight times more likely to carry a gun than those without CD symptoms (Loeber, Burke, Mutchka, & Lahey, 2003).

Take the recklessness and bravado that often characterize teenage behavior, combine these tendencies with thinking and problem-solving skills that focus on aggression in dealing with conflict, add a generous measure of alcohol and drugs, make guns readily available, and what is the result? Situations that would have resulted in fist fights and bloody noses can easily be transformed into shooting incidents requiring body bags. Studies consistently show that as many as 80% of all juvenile homicide victims are killed with firearms (Office of Juvenile Justice & Delinquency Prevention, 1999). The tragic school killings we detailed in chapter 3 (this volume) would never have taken place were it not for young people wielding weapons and carrying them into the halls and classrooms. Psychologist Dewey Cornell (1999), expert in juvenile violence, testified before a congressional panel investigating the causes of these school-related tragedies. Cornell (1999) said

> Guns are a critical risk factor. When juvenile homicide tripled in this country in just ten years, all of the increase was in gun-related killing. There was no increase in juveniles stabbing or beating one another to death. Guns are not the cause of the violence, but they provide the means. (May 13, 1999, Testimony before the U.S. House of Representatives Judiciary Committee)

---

[3]In most states, gun possession by juveniles is illegal; moreover, gun possession in schools is prohibited by state and federal law.

Declining Family Influence and Criminal Behavior

In chapter 7, we listed several family influences on juvenile criminal behavior, including dysfunctional family structure and communication, parental crime and substance abuse, domestic violence, and child abuse and neglect. Children exposed to these risk factors for crime carry them into adolescence. However, even children who grow up in reasonably functional and well-managed homes may be at risk for engaging in criminal behavior if positive family influences decrease significantly. These influences tend to decline to some extent in the normal course of adolescent development as youngsters between the ages of 8 and 14 begin to confide less in parents and more in peers and to be more influenced by those peers for assistance in making decisions about what behaviors to adopt (Berndt & Perry, 1986; Paikoff & Brooks-Gunn, 1991). The risk of crime is greatest, though, for teenagers who become involved with deviant peers who may become a kind of surrogate family.

The extent to which young people turn to their peers tends to be influenced in part by the parenting style they have experienced because that style influences the quality of parent–child interactions. Teenagers exposed to authoritative as opposed to authoritarian parenting (see chapter 7) are generally less likely to turn peers for advice, for they have already established a history of open communication and self-disclosure with their parents (Fuligni & Eccles, 1993). They are also more likely to choose friends of whom their parents approve, which often means friends who do well in school (Fletcher, Darling, Steinberg, & Dornbusch, 1995). This kind of parental supervision along with expressions of warmth, connection, and caring appear to provide significant protection not only against the development of adolescent criminal behavior but also against emotional distress (including depression and suicide), teenage pregnancy, and substance abuse (Resnick et al., 1997).

Unfortunately, adolescents' access to these protective influences has declined in recent years, largely because parents are spending more and more time in the workplace. Children in the United States today spend, on average, 10 to 12 hours per week less time with their parents than children did in 1960 (Resnick et al., 1997; Stepp, 1999). Still, the alienation of adolescents from their parents is nothing new in North America or in most other Western cultures. Holden Caulfield, the 16-year-old misfit of Salinger's (1951/1999) Catcher in the Rye, typified this alienation, and there are probably no more alienated teens today than there were in the 1940s. The difference seems to be that alienated adolescents seem to be angrier now than ever before, and as exemplified in the tragic string of school shootings that began in the late 1990s and continue to this day, their anger appears to be exploding in more dramatic ways.

A study (National Gang Crime Research Center, 1997) of gang members found a strong and consistent relationship between gang members and dysfunctional families (characterized by parents who do not adequately supervise their children or participate in their school work and activities and who themselves had served time in prison). The more dysfunctional their families, the more likely gang members were to be committed to gang life. Those gang members from the more dysfunctional family environment are more likely to report having five or more close friends who are gang members, are less likely to have ever tried to quit gang life, and are more likely to remain active gang members (National Gang Crime Research Center, 1997). Gang members are more likely to have had a parent who had served time in prison, and having a family member serve time is a risk factor for crime. The ramifications of this are significant when one considers that parents held in U.S. prisons had an estimated 1.5 million minor children in 1999, an increase of over 500,000 since 1991. A majority of the parents in state prison were violent offenders (44%) or drug traffickers (13%), and 77% were incarcerated for a second or subsequent offense (Mumola, 2000).

School Failure and the Development of Criminal Behavior

Schools, like families, are a major socializing influence in the lives of most children. Many children begin some type of educational experience as early as 3 or 4 years of age. As we noted in chapter 7, success at school can counteract a number of the risk factors for juvenile crime, especially in children who come from broken or dysfunctional homes (Rutter, 1990).

Children who do not succeed in school tend to feel frustrated and rejected and, according to some researchers, experience a loss of self-esteem that can lead to a variety of psychological and behavioral dysfunctions. These children are likely to associate with similarly unsuccessful peers with whom they may begin to engage in antisocial behaviors (Siegel & Welsh, 2006). In short, school failure and delinquency go hand in hand. Studies have consistently found that the majority of imprisoned criminals had been failures in school (Devlin, 1996); as few as 40% of prison inmates have graduated from high school compared with 80% of the general population (Bureau of Justice Statistics, 1993; National Institute of Justice, 1997c).

Do schools themselves enhance the risk of school failure? Some observers suggest that they do, especially in relation to students with the weakest academic skills. In 1989, the Carnegie Council on Adolescent Development reported that (1) many American middle and high schools are too large and impersonal; (2) much of the high school curriculum is redundant and lacks focus; (3) learning opportunities are inequitable, with disadvantaged students getting too little help in improving their skills; (4) schools do not have enough health and social services to meet adolescents' physical and mental health needs; and (5) families and communities should be more involved in the schools.

In discussing what role, if any, that Columbine high school might have played in the anger and alienation of the two students who killed 12 classmates and a teacher there in 1999, some students noted that like many schools in affluent neighborhoods, Columbine caters mainly to successful students–be they "jocks" or "geeks," and that to be a mediocre student is to be ignored by teachers, administrators, and good students (Polycarpou, 1999; Stepp, 1999). Other common complaints among today's high school students are that their schools are too large and that their teachers do not respect or care about them personally, further fueling feelings of isolation and rejection (Stepp, 1999). Also, in too many schools, chaos, gang violence, drug dealing, and other crimes are commonplace (National Education Goals Panel, 1995). In these institutions, youngsters steal and vandalize school and student property and physically assault other students and teachers. According to the Centers for Disease Control and Prevention's 1997 Youth Risk Behavior Surveillance System, 9% of high school students had admitted taking a weapon onto school property in the past 30 days, and 15% of high school students had been in a physical fight on school property one or more times in the 12 months preceding the survey. One third said they had property such as a car, clothing, or books stolen or damaged on school property during the past 12 months, and 4% of high school students missed at least one day of school in the past 30 days because they felt unsafe at school or when traveling to or from school (Snyder & Sickmund, 1999).

Criminologists see chronic absenteeism as a stepping stone to juvenile crime partly because truant students are at higher risk of being drawn into alcohol and drug use and violence. A study by the U.S. Department of Justice's Drug Use Forecasting program reported that 53% of male and 51% of female juveniles arrested and taken into juvenile detention on school days tested positive for drug and alcohol use. In other words, many teenagers are out drinking or using drugs when they should be in school (National Institute of Justice, 1997b; Office of Juvenile Justice and Delinquency Prevention, 1999). Violent crimes by juveniles peak in the afternoon between 3 p.m. and 4 p.m. on school days (Mondays through Fridays); in fact, most violent crimes by juveniles (i.e., murder, forcible rape, robbery, and aggravated and simple assault) occur on school days (Snyder & Sickmund, 1999).

Teenagers are truant for many reasons including lack of interest or motivation in school, conflicts with peers, mental health and substance abuse problems, pregnancy, and the need to work (Snyder & Sickmund, 1999). Most parents of truant students do not themselves value education and may even keep their teenagers out of school to care for younger siblings or earn money.

Truancy leads to school dropout or expulsion, and once students are separated from educational opportunities, they tend to be increasingly exposed to opportunities and influences that encourage crime. One longitudinal study (Krohn et al., 1995) found that teenagers who drop out commit more crimes and experience more substance abuse and social problems than those who do not, and that persistent drug abusers are more likely to be school dropouts than nonabusers. A 1998 study (M. Cohen, 1998) estimated the external costs imposed on society by the average career criminal, heavy drug abuser, and high school dropout. The costs were based on the losses imposed on victims, expenses borne by the criminal justice and correctional systems, and loss of productively of the individual. The study concluded that allowing one youth to leave high school for a life of crime and drug abuse costs society $1.7 to $2.3 million (M. Cohen, 1998).

So although schools are often the setting for negative social influences—including exposure to disruptive and antisocial peers—and venues for drug dealing, violence, and crime, criminal justice statistics consistently suggest that not attending (and not succeeding in) school is even more dangerous in terms of increasing the risk of engaging in juvenile and adult crime. On balance, then, children and adolescents are better off in school than out of school. In fact, positive experiences in school can help to counteract the risk factors associated with growing up in dysfunctional homes (Rutter, 1990; Rutter, Maughan, Mortimore, & Ouston, 1979).

Pathways to Adult Crime

To round out our discussion of the development of crime from adolescence through adulthood, we consider the cases of Jimmy and Ted.

"Jimmy" was the youngest of two boys born to second-generation Eastern European parents, both of whom are certified public accountants. Like so many professionals who wanted the best of the city and the country, their tasteful and expensive home was in the Virginia countryside, 50 miles from the business they owned near Washington, DC. Accordingly, Jimmy's parents spent 2 hr or more a day commuting, and during the 5 months of the peak tax season, they were away from home from early morning until late at night. Both parents were heavy drinkers, and when Jimmy was 12, his mother died of an alcohol-related illness, leaving her husband to run the business and raise Jimmy and his 15 year-old brother. By the age of 14, Jimmy's criminal career was well underway, beginning with arrests for possession of alcohol, public drunkenness, disorderly conduct, and truancy and escalating to shoplifting, possession of marijuana, driving while intoxicated (for which he lost his driver's license), driving on a revoked license, probation violations, breaking and entering, and grand larceny. Eventually, Jimmy was sentenced to 10 years in prison for being an accessory in an attack on a young man who had been flirting with the girlfriend of one of his friends.

Jimmy is an example of what Loeber and Stouthamer-Loeber (1998) referred to as a **childhood-adolescent-onset offender** because his criminal career began so early (see chapter 7). Jimmy had probably been an alcoholic since the age of 12, perhaps younger. He began drinking beer with his maternal grandfather at about the age of 6 and remembers liking its taste immediately. He said that he began drinking alcohol regularly at about the age of 10 when he was at home alone after school. The extent to which alcoholism affected Jimmy's life and self-esteem is probably sufficient in itself to account for his criminal behavior, but he also suffered maternal neglect due to his mother's own alcohol problems and working habits. With little or no supervision at home most of the time, it was easy for him to skip school and drift into a bad crowd—for companionship if nothing else. In short, Jimmy followed the well-traveled road to prison shared by most male offenders, and he experienced virtually all of the biological, psychological, and social risk factors that mark the way. Jimmy's girlfriend gave birth to their son just before Jimmy went to prison. Will the child follow in his father's criminal footsteps? Perhaps, unless he is saved by individual resilience, protective factors provided by his mother, and societal interventions aimed at preventing psychological disorder, substance abuse, and crime.

Now consider Ted, who followed what Loeber and Stouthamer-Loeber (1998) called the **late-onset pathway to crime**. He was born in 1942, the first child of working class parents in a Chicago suburb. When Ted was 9 months old, he was hospitalized for several weeks because of an allergic reaction. Whenever his mother visited him, Ted did not make eye contact with her when she arrived or when she left. When he came home, his mother notes that he was limp and unresponsive, not the happy baby she had taken to the hospital. She wrote in her diary, "Baby home from hospital and is healthy but quite unresponsive after his experience. Hope his sudden removal to hospital and consequent unhappiness will not harm him" (Kovaleski, 1996, p. A-20). From that early age through his adulthood, Ted would sometimes "shut down" and seem not to be interested in anything around him. His nursery school teacher recalled that he did not want to play with other children, although he let them play alongside him. He never had any friends during his entire childhood and adolescence. As he reached his teenage years, he spent a lot of time at home, in the attic, telling his family that he did not want to be disturbed.

Some might say he was already disturbed, but certainly not in terms of intelligence. At the age of 10, his IQ was between 160 and 170, placing him far into the upper reaches of mental ability. Ted skipped a grade in elementary school and his junior year in high school. He played the trombone, read voraciously, and studied music. At 16, he entered Harvard University on a full scholarship and majored in mathematics. Students who shared his dormitory recall that he was reclusive, insisting on eating alone and spending his free time in a rocking chair in his room. Ted earned a PhD in mathematics at the University of Michigan in 1967. His professors there described his dissertation, which won a university prize, as brilliant and original. He was appointed

Assistant Professor of Mathematics at the University of California at Berkeley, where faculty colleagues described him as withdrawn and without a social life. His students complained that he was unapproachable, refused to answer their questions, and ignored them.

In 1969, Ted abruptly resigned his academic position and for two years drifted from town to town in Utah, Illinois, and Iowa. Then he and his brother David purchased some land in Montana, and Ted went there to live in a tiny shack with no electricity or running water. Except for occasional forays into Great Falls, he remained on his property, keeping in touch with his family only by letter. After seven years, Ted returned to Illinois where he took a job at the plant where his father and brother worked. Shortly after his arrival, Ted had two dates with a coworker at the plant, but when she expressed no further interest in him, he wrote insulting limericks about her and circulated them around the plant. David, who happened to be his supervisor, told him to stop this behavior or be fired, and when Ted refused, David fired him. Returning to Montana, Ted wrote letters to his family in which he raged against them and society.

On May 25, 1978, shortly after his return from Illinois, Ted committed his first act of terrorism, sending an explosive device to Northwestern University in Evanston, Illinois. The bomb exploded in a guard's hand. Over the next 18 years, the bombs that Ted constructed and mailed killed three people and injured 23 others. In 1995, after sending a bomb that killed a timber industry lobbyist, Ted submitted to the *New York Times* and the *Washington Post* a 35,000-word manifesto entitled *Society and Its Future*. This rambling political treatise was not only a diatribe against society but an autobiography and psychological road map containing clues to Ted's failure in emotional and psychosocial development. In April of 1996, with the help of Ted's brother, FBI agents went to the Montana shack and arrested Ted Kaczynski, who had become known as "The Unabomber." In 1998, Kaczynski was diagnosed as suffering from paranoid schizophrenia but chose to plead guilty to charges of murder, attempted murder, and manufacturing and mailing bombs through the U.S. mail. He was sentenced to life without parole in a federal maximum-security prison.

There is not much that families, schools, or mental health professionals can do to identify and help late-onset criminals like Ted Kaczynski, for although his childhood and adolescence were unusual, there were no glaring signs that he was a simmering volcano of terrorism. It is only in retrospect that some of his odd behaviors can be seen as reflections of the social and psychological problems that contributed to his violent adulthood. A retrospective study (Windel & Windel, 1995) of over 4,000 adult men in their 30s found that late-onset violent criminals had problems in childhood but that these were mostly unrelated to aggression. However, these men had been exposed to more significant life stressors and were more likely to suffer from psychiatric conditions than were those in a noncriminal control group (Windel & Windel, 1995). There is some support for the hypothesis that late-onset violence is highest among "overcontrolled" offenders—those who had strong inhibitions against expressing anger until provoked to a flashpoint (Blackburn, 1993; Megargee, 1966). This category might also include (1) adolescents who kill their parents after years of serious parental abuse but no history of adjustment problems outside the home (Cornell, 1990) and (2) adults who kill in the "heat of passion" (see chapter 10).

Jimmy's pathway to crime is by far the more familiar. His childhood was marked by obvious behavioral, substance abuse, and delinquent patterns that might have been remedied by timely and effective intervention. These problems significantly elevate the risk that the child will become a juvenile and/or adult criminal. Indeed, the age at which delinquent and antisocial behavior first appears is a good predictor of the persistence and seriousness of subsequent criminal behavior (Earls, 1994; Tolan & Thomas, 1995). Those whose antisocial behaviors begin in childhood (3% to 5% of the general population) are likely to continue displaying them through adolescence and adulthood (R. P. Cox, 1996; Greenfield & Weisner, 1995; Ouimet & Le Blanc, 1996; Wolfgang, 1995). Those for whom antisocial behavior does not appear until adolescence are less likely to continue such behavior into and through adulthood (Moffitt, 1993).

Summary

Adolescence is a time of challenge and risk. Even if young people do not go through the "storm and stress" that psychologist G. Stanley Hall suggested, the time is still one in which teens begin to seek out their identities across several domains—family, school, peers, and romantic relationships. During adolescence, peers are the most important influence on most young people's development. If, as youngsters, they have achieved a level of moral development that fosters respect for the law, they are less likely to be influenced by the negative influence of delinquent peers.

Girls' and boys' pathways to crime are somewhat different. Boys are naturally more aggressive and not surprisingly, grow up to commit 90% of all violent crimes. Girls are more likely to be involveed in violent crime with their boyfriends (and later, their husbands). Girls are more likely to get involved in crime as a result of low self-esteem and a dysfunctional home life. Boys are more likely to be diagnosable with conduct disorder and to have substance abuse problems, both of which are high-risk factors for crime. However, for both boys and girls, underage alcohol use is often the first crime they commit. Alcohol use loosens the normal inhibitions one may have to behave badly. Teens who do not enjoy strong family ties, good relations with their siblings, and school success are more likely to become substance abusers, even addicts.

Gangs are criminal organizations, so adolescents who are involved in gangs are leading lives of crime, for the most part. Those who join gangs are influenced by individual characteristics as well as social and economic factors. Gang members have generally failed to develop a conscience and failed at school; most come from dysfunctional families. The very presence of guns provides the opportunity for harm to others. When combined with drinking or drug use and gang affiliation, guns add the lethal component that set the stage for violent crime.

Dysfunctional schools can turn children away from the pursuit of an education to being dropouts. Truancy, expulsion, and dropping out expose teenagers to greater influences for crime including, having time on their hands. So, even if schools are not providing the optimal learning and social environment, staying in a bad school is, on balance, preferable to leaving school altogether.

In 2002, juveniles were involved in 1 in 10 arrests for murder, 1 in 8 arrests for a drug abuse violation, 1 in 5 arrests for a weapons violation, and 1 in 4 arrests for robbery (Snyder, 2004). Although the overall rate of juvenile violent crime was down from the 1990s, when rates had peaked, the number of female juvenile violent criminals increased. The arrest, punishment, and even imprisonment of adolescent offenders typically has no more effect on them than on adult criminals (see chapter 13). The overall lifetime rearrest rate in the United States is generally around 70%. In 1996, 4 of 10 convicted felons released on parole were reincarcerated for a new offense (many were technical parole or probation violations) within 1 year (Bureau of Justice Statistics, 1997). In short, the criminal justice system can rarely do what parents, teachers, friends, neighbors, clergy, and economic opportunities have failed to do.

As suggested by research on the importance of childhood risk factors for crime, the most effective interventions in the fight against juvenile crime appear to be those that provide early in-home monitoring and services for at-risk families and children (Greenwood, 1999). Until and unless such programs are widely implemented, it appears likely that chronic criminal activity among children and adolescents will continue and will probably remain concentrated in a relatively small number of serious offenders from high-risk backgrounds. We discuss these programs in more detail in chapter 14.

Unlike late-onset criminals, those who first start offending as adults, young people who show early risk factors for crime (i.e., truancy and alcohol and drug use) can be saved with early and appropriate intervention. Sadly, all too often warning signs are either not recognized or ignored, and today's problem teen becomes tomorrow's life-course offender.

Key Terms

Childhood-adolescent-onset offender

Late-onset pathway to crime

Questions for Review

1. What opportunities does adolescence present for children to become criminals?
2. How do boys' and girls' pathways to crime differ?
3. What are the roles of substance abuse and conduct disorder in the development of crime during adolescence?

4. What is the connection between gangs and crime?
5. How do Jimmy and Ted represent different pathways to crime?

 Track It Down

Criminal Behavior Website
www.cassel2e.com
Erik Erikson on Adolescent Identity
www.haverford.edu/psych/ddavis/p109g/erikson.identity.html
History of Research Disorder
assets.cambridge.org/052178/6398/sample/0521786398ws.pdf
The U.S. Department of Justice Office of Justice Programs Research on Drug and Alcohol Abuse and Crime
www.ojp.usdoj.gov/substanceabuse/whats_new.htm
The National Gang Crime Research Center
www.ngcrc.com/
Information on Youth Violence
www.familyeducation.com/topic/front/0,1156,66-24137,00.html
Radio Documentary of a young man who gave up a life of gangs and crime
www.soundportraits.org/on-air/blak's_story/

9

Mental Disorders and Crime

What Is Mental Disorder?	*Factors Contributing to Criminal Behavior*
Specific Mental Disorders and Crime	*Among the Mentally Ill*
Diagnostic Foundations for an Insanity Plea	*Mental Health Courts*

In the mistaken belief that she is romantically involved with a television celebrity, Margaret breaks into his empty house, camps out there, and makes use of his vehicle (Bruni, 1998). Rusty murders two policeman, thinking that they are keeping him from gaining access to an instrument that can save the world from cannibalism (B. Miller, 1999). After killing his 74-year-old brother by smashing a TV set over his head, 70-year-old James tells police that he has slain "the enemy" who had been disguised as his brother (Cazalas, 1998). On a subway train, John attacks a total stranger for no apparent reason. Margo puts her children to bed, walks into her bedroom, and shoots her husband in cold blood. After killing a teacher whom she claims had sexually abused her, Patty says she does not remember the crime and cannot explain the bloody clothing found in her laundry room; and on instructions from "voices," Andrea drowns her five children "to save them from the devil," then turns herself in to the police (Cassel, 2002a).

All of these people were suffering from a mental disorder at the time they committed their crimes. Rusty, James, and Margaret were diagnosed as schizophrenic. John was found to have epilepsy, and Patty displayed dissociative identity disorder; Margo was diagnosed with major depression and substance-related disorders involving alcohol and cocaine. Andrea was severely depressed and delusional.

In our discussion of the biological, psychological, and social roots of crime in chapters 4, 5, and 6, we noted that criminal behavior is associated with certain mental disorders. In this chapter, we address more specifically the relation between mental disorders and crime. Does having a mental disorder increase the risk that a person will engage in criminal and/or violent behavior? If so, which disorders create the greatest risk and for what types of crime?

Just as people are not usually "born bad," few are simply "born mad." Mental disorders, like crime, usually result from a complex interaction of biological, psychological, and social factors. **The biopsychosocial model** of mental illness suggests that genetic influences; abnormalities in brain structure and functioning; learned ways of thinking, behaving, and feeling; and families and other social systems within which people grow up and live all play a part in whether or not they will manifest a mental disorder. **The diathesis-stress model** of mental disorder suggests that people's genetic or biological predisposition (diathesis) for psychopathology interacts with environmental factors such that the disorder will not appear unless traumatic events, deprivations, or other stressors are sufficiently intense to trigger it.

Both of these models help to explain the relation between mental disorders and crime. We explore that relation by first considering major mental disorders and the symptoms that are most associated with violence and crime and then looking at individual and situational factors that make violent criminal behavior especially likely among some of those who display certain disorders.

What Is Mental Disorder?

Mental disorders are conditions that disrupt thinking, feeling, and other psychological processes such that a person behaves in a way that deviates from social expectations and causes significant impairment in occupational, interpersonal, and other important areas of daily functioning (Bernstein et al., 2006; Sue, Sue, & Sue, 2006). These disorders cause distress, either for the individual or for others. A more elaborate definition is given in the latest edition of the American Psychiatric Association's *Diagnostic and Statistical Manual of Mental Disorders*, (4th ed. text revision), (*DSM–IV–TR, 2000)* which contains the official list of mental disorders used by psychiatrists, psychologists, and other diagnosticians in North America, describes mental disorder as a

> Clinically significant behavioral or psychological syndrome or pattern that occurs in an individual and that is associated with present distress or disability or with a significantly increased risk of suffering death, pain, disability, or an important loss of freedom. In addition, this syndrome or pattern must not be merely an expectable or culturally sanctioned response to a particular event. ... Whatever its original cause, it must be currently considered a manifestation of a behavioral, psychological, or biological dysfunction in the individual. Neither deviant behavior ... nor conflicts that are primarily between individuals and society are mental disorders unless the deviance or conflict is a symptom of a dysfunction in the individual, as described above. (pp. xxi–xxii)

The *DSM–IV–TR* describes mental disorders on five dimensions or axes. Axis I contains major clinical disorders such as schizophrenia; anxiety, mood, and dissociative disorders; sexual, eating, and sleep disorders; cognitive disorders (such as delirium, dementia, and amnesia); and major childhood disorders other than mental retardation. Mental retardation and personality disorders are listed on Axis II, whereas on Axis III, diagnosticians note any medical conditions that could be relevant to understanding or treating a mental disorder. Psychosocial and environmental stressors that could affect diagnosis and treatment are listed on Axis IV, and Axis V provides a scale on which diagnosticians rate a person's overall level of functioning at the time of the evaluation. Together, the information provided on these axes summarizes the content and context of a person's diagnosed mental disorders. Table 9.1 lists the mental disorders and general medical conditions that are most closely associated with criminal behavior.[1]

The Link Between Crime and Mental Disorders

The link between mental disorders and crime is well illustrated in prison and jail populations. Consider the following data:

1. About 24% of male inmates and 36% of female inmates reported that they had been treated for mental or emotional problems, and more than 10% had been inpatients (Harlow, 1998).
2. On any given day, at least 16% of adult inmates at state and federal prisons and local jails are mentally ill (Conly, 1999), and about 5% of them display symptoms of severe forms of disorder such as schizophrenia, bipolar disorder, and major depression (American Psychiatric Association, 2000a; Human Rights Watch, 2003).
3. Rates of mental disorder among prisoners are up to four times higher than those found in the general population (Kanapaux, 2004).

---

[1]For more details on the nature and origins of all mental disorders and the processes through which they are diagnosed and treated, consult textbooks on abnormal psychology (e.g., Sue, Sue, & Sue, 2006.)

TABLE 9.1 *DSM-IV-TR Diagnoses Most Commonly Associated with Criminal Behavior.*

Axis I—Clinical Disorders

Disorders Usually First Diagnosed in Infancy, Childhood, or Adolescence
    Oppositional Defiant Disorder
    Conduct Disorder
    Attention-Deficit/Hyperactivity Disorder
Delirium, Dementia, and Amnestic and Other Cognitive Disorders
Mental Disorders Due to a General Medical Condition
    Delirium, Dementia, Amnesia, Psychosis, and Personality Change Due to Medical Conditions
Substance-Related Disorders
    Substance Intoxication
    Substance Abuse
    Substance Dependence
Schizophrenia and Other Psychotic Disorders
Mood Disorders
    Major Depressive Disorders
    Manic Episode
    Bipolar Disorder
Dissociative Disorders
    Dissociative Amnesia
    Dissociative Identity Disorder
Sexual and Gender Identity Disorders
    Pedophilia
    Sexual Sadism

Axis II—Personality Disorders and Mental Retardation

Paranoid Personality Disorder
Antisocial Personality Disorder
Borderline Personality Disorder
Narcissistic Personality Disorder
Mental Retardation

Source: Based on information from American Psychiatric Association. (2000a). *Diagnostic and Statistical Manual of Mental Disorders* (4th ed. revised). Washington, DC: Author.

Specific Mental Disorders and Crime

The mental disorders most closely associated with criminal behavior and violence are conduct disorder (CD), antisocial personality disorder (APD), schizophrenia, mood disorders (such as major depression and bipolar disorder), substance-related disorders, and, to a lesser extent, certain cognitive disorders. We discussed CD and APD in chapters 7 and 8. Here, we examine the other disorders associated with crime, how their symptoms may enhance the likelihood of criminal behavior, and their role in supporting an insanity defense at trial.

Schizophrenia

In November 1998, 46-year-old Margaret Ray—known as the "Letterman Stalker" because she had repeatedly broken into David Letterman's home and told people that she was married to him—knelt down in front of an oncoming coal train in a remote area of Colorado, ending a 20-year battle with schizophrenia that had been marked by repeated hospitalizations. She left a suicide note in which she expressed her exhaustion and her pessimism about the plight of the seriously and chronically mentally ill. Margaret's father and two older

TABLE 9.2   *Diagnostic Criteria for Schizophrenia*

The essential features of schizophrenia are a mixture of positive and negative symptoms associated with marked social or occupational dysfunctions that are present for between one to six months.

Positive symptoms, which reflect distortion of or excess in normal functioning, include:

(1)   Delusions
(2)   Hallucinations
(3)   Disorganized speech and behavior

Negative symptoms, which reflect a diminution in or loss of normal functioning, include:

(1)   Flat or absent emotional expression
(2)   Restricted language and thought processes
(3)   Absence of goal-directed behaviors

Source: Based on information from American Psychiatric Association. (2000a). *Diagnostic and Statistical Manual of Mental Disorders* (4th ed. text revision). Washington, DC: Author.

brothers had also been diagnosed as schizophrenic; both brothers had committed suicide some 20 years before Margaret took her life (Bruni, 1998).

Schizophrenia, a form of psychosis causing gross impairment in the perception of reality, is the most devastating of all mental disorders (APA, 2000a). It is marked by a fragmentation of the normally integrated psychological functions of attention, perception, thought, emotion, and behavior. People diagnosed as schizophrenic may see and hear things that do not exist (hallucinations), suffer confused thinking, and express inaccurate beliefs (delusions) about their own bodies as well as about the people and things around them (see Table 9.2).

The prevalence of schizophrenia is only about 1% in the general population, and although only a small number of schizophrenics commit crimes, some of the symptoms of this disorder—especially delusions and hallucinations—can lead to violent crime. In most cases, the schizophrenia patients who commit these crimes are those who harbor paranoid delusions involving the false belief that others are about to harm them or are already doing so. Others have delusions of grandeur such that they appoint themselves or believe they are appointed by God to save the world from evil forces. People who experience schizophrenic delusions have killed or seriously injured others in a misguided effort to protect themselves or the world from perceived dangers. Russell Weston, Jr.—the man we described in chapter 2 as having killed two police officers during his attack on the U.S. Capitol Building in 1998–said he was trying to gain access to the ruby satellite, a device he believed was kept in a Senate safe. This satellite, he claimed, was the key to ending cannibalism, which he saw as causing "Black Heva," an imaginary disease that Weston described as the "deadliest known to mankind." Weston believed that the police officers he killed were cannibals assigned to protect the satellite (B. Miller, 1999). A study of homicides committed by people diagnosed with schizophrenia found that 70% of them saw their victim as an enemy (Hafner & Boker, 1982).

Delusions are among the most common schizophrenia symptoms, and the potential for delusion-based violence appears to increase the longer a person suffers from the disorder (Humphreys, Johnstone, MacMillan, & Taylor, 1992; P. J. Taylor, 1993). This relation may be because delusions tend to become more entrenched and intense over time (Humphreys et al., 1992). The stronger the attachment to the delusions, the more likely it is that violence will result, particularly in the case of people who believe that their thoughts and actions are controlled by outside forces (P. J. Taylor et al., 1994).

The hallucinations commonly associated with schizophrenia (as well as with other mental disorders such as substance intoxication and some neurological conditions) may also trigger violent crime. Some schizophrenics report that voices tell them what to do. These auditory hallucinations may be especially likely to lead to violence in persons who are already suffering paranoid delusions that make them feel threatened by an enemy. Often, the voice tells them to kill the enemy. One study of these "command" hallucinations (McNeil,

TABLE 9.3 *Diagnostic Criteria for Major Depressive Episode*

The essential feature of major depressive episode is depressed mood or loss of interest or pleasure in major daily activities that lasts at least two consecutive weeks (for most of the day, nearly every day) and significantly impairs social or occupational functioning. Some of the symptoms are:

(1) Changes in appetite, weight, or sleep
(2) Decreased energy
(3) Feelings of guilt and/or worthlessness
(4) Difficulty thinking or concentrating
(5) Recurrent thoughts of death or suicide

Source: Based on information from American Psychiatric Association. (2000a). *Diagnostic and Statistical Manual of Mental Disorders* (4th ed. text revision). Washington, DC: Author.

1994) suggested that 51% of them involved urging the person to commit suicide, 12% instructed the person to injure someone, and 5% told the person to kill someone (Hellerstein, Frosch, & Koenigsberg, 1987).

The combination of delusional thoughts and command hallucinations has been called "*threat/control-override* symptoms" (Link & Stueve, 1994). People act on the commands because internal controls have been overridden by voices that imply a specific threat of harm from others (Link and Stueve, 1994).

Mood Disorders

Mood disorders involve extreme and relatively long-lasting emotional states that result in impairment in a person's ability to function in virtually every area of life, including work, social and family relations, enjoyment of pleasure, and the like. *Major depressive disorder* (periods of deep sadness and pessimism; see Table 9.3) and *bipolar disorder* (depression alternating with periods of overactivity and unrealistic optimism) are the most common mood disorders. They are also the ones that may be associated with violence and crime.

Major depressive disorder is strongly correlated with drug and alcohol use, a correlation that can be deadly because as with some schizophrenic symptoms, alcohol may reduce self-control to the point that severely depressed people may be more likely to act on their increasingly pessimistic outlook on life. Indeed, 15% of people suffering from a major depressive episode commit suicide, and sometimes they take a loved one with them. When you read about a person, usually a man, killing his estranged wife (and sometimes his children), it is a safe bet that the person was suffering severe depression and was probably drinking at the time.

People displaying bipolar disorder may also pose a risk for violent crime, especially if their manic phases include paranoid delusions and hallucinated voices telling them to kill an enemy or perform other illegal acts (American Psychiatric Association, 2000a). The danger of violence in such cases is further increased because as in major depression, people with bipolar disorder often abuse alcohol or other inhibition-reducing drugs.

A diagnosis of major depressive disorder or bipolar disorder can sometimes be used to justify an insanity defense, especially if the criminal exhibited delusional thinking as well as extremes of mood while committing a crime. In 1997, for example, a man who shot his elderly parents to death pleaded insanity based on evidence of bipolar symptoms at the time of the offense. Some time before the slayings, he had stopped taking the medica- tion that controlled his symptoms, and although the prosecution argued that he should not get the benefit of the insanity defense when his crime was caused by his own decision to discontinue medication, the verdict was not guilty by reason of insanity (Vogel, 1997). Defense attorneys for Andrea Yates claimed that postpartum depression, along with symptoms suggestive of schizophrenia, led her to drown her five children (Cassel, 2002a).

Substance-Related Disorders

The use of illicit drugs is, by definition, a crime; and in most states, it is also a crime for people under the age of 21 to drink alcohol. However, violations of these laws are just the beginning of the relation between crime and the use of alcohol and other drugs. Substance-related disorders (mainly substance abuse and dependence)

TABLE 9.4 *Diagnostic Criteria for Substance Abuse and Substance Dependence*

Substance abuse involves substance use that leads to the following occurring within a twelve-month period:

(1) Using the substance despite its negative impact on functioning at work, school or home
(2) Using the substance in situations that pose a danger to one's self, such as driving
(3) Experiencing legal problems related to the substance use, such as charges for driving while intoxicated or illegal possession of the substance
(4) Interpersonal or social problems caused by the effects of the substance, such as having arguments about the substance use

Substance dependence is the maladaptive use of the substance that causes significant impairment or distress manifest by three or more symptoms occurring at any time in the same twelve-month period. Some of the symptoms are:

(1) Tolerance for the substance marked by an increased need for more of the substance to achieve its desired effects
(2) Withdrawal, indicated by physical symptoms of withdrawal or using the substance to avoid withdrawal symptoms
(3) Persistent desire to decrease or control use of the substance
(4) Spending a great deal of time obtaining, using, or recovering from the effects of, the substance
(5) Giving up important social, occupational, or recreational activities because of using the substance
(6) Continuing to use the substance despite knowledge of the physical and psychological problems resulting from its use

Source: Based on information from American Psychiatric Association. (2000a). *Diagnostic and Statistical Manual of Mental Disorders* (4th ed. text revision). Washington, D.C.: Author.

are more strongly linked to the origin, expression, and persistence of violence and crime than any other DSM–IV diagnoses (Rasmussen & Levander, 1996). The diagnostic criteria for these disorders are listed in Table 9.4.

For example, 40% to 60% of incarcerated perpetrators of violent crimes reported that they were under the influence of alcohol, illicit drugs, or both, at the time of their offenses (Harlow, 1998); 65% to 75% of victims who suffered violence at the hands of a current or former spouse or intimate partner reported that alcohol had been a factor in the incident (Greenfeld, 1998). As we noted in chapters 5 and 6, drinking alcohol by the age of 12 is more strongly associated with the onset of criminal behavior than any other early adolescent risk factor. Also, when early alcohol use occurs in combination with other risk factors—including the use of substances such as marijuana and crack cocaine—the likelihood of engaging in crime is even greater (Harlow, 1998).

Other research on the role of substance abuse in violent crimes (Steadman et al., 1998) found that mental patients were no more likely than their community peers to commit an act of violence unless they also had a co-occurring substance abuse diagnoses. Specifically, 31% of patients diagnosed as displaying a major mental disorder (schizophrenia, major depression, bipolar disorder) *and* a substance abuse diagnosis committed violence within a year of discharge compared to only 18% of comparable patients without a substance abuse diagnosis. In fact, patients who did not carry a substance abuse diagnosis were no more violent than in a nonpatient control group who did not carry a substance abuse. However, substance abuse was significantly correlated with violence in both the patient and nonpatient samples (Steadman et al., 1998).

Alcohol is related to criminal behavior partly because it appears to lower inhibition of the strong impulses toward violence that exist in some people. In addition, substance abusers sometimes experience hallucinations and delusions that influence them to act violently (Assad, 1990; Surawicz, 1980). For example, chronic use of phencyclidine (PCP), a powerful hallucinogen, may directly trigger violent behavior but leave users with no memory for what they did while intoxicated (Aronow, 1980; Linder, Lerner, & Burn, 1981; D. E. Smith &

Wesson, 1980). PCP may also create a temporary psychosis or break with reality (Domino, 1978; Marrs-Simon, 1988). PCP-induced psychosis or amnesia has been used to support insanity pleas or claims of incompetence to stand trial (Sacks, 1990). In 1997, a man in Washington, DC, pleaded guilty to killing his girlfriend's 4-year-old child while suffering from a PCP-induced psychosis. He told the judge, "I didn't know how hard I was hitting her because of the drugs. I just tried to pop her so she would lay down and I could go to the bathroom and finish smoking my drugs." The prosecutor accepted a plea to manslaughter, recognizing that he might have a difficult time proving premeditated murder in light of the temporary psychosis (B. Miller, 1997). The use or abuse of drugs such as heroin and crack cocaine also tend to encourage crime, but less directly and usually in the context of getting quick money to buy drugs or settling conflicts over drug dealing.

Alcohol or drug intoxication generally will not absolve a defendant of criminal responsibility because getting drunk or "high" is a voluntary act. However, evidence of Korsakoff's syndrome, an irreversible brain disorder caused by long-term alcohol use, has been invoked as justifying an insanity defense or rendering one permanently incompetent to stand trial. Further, drug use resulting in total amnesia or temporary psychosis can sometimes mitigate criminal liability.

Cognitive Disorders

A 33-year-old Frenchman who had always been law-abiding suddenly began stealing cars and taking them on "joy rides." He was convicted and served jail time after each offense, but on release, he would commit the same crime again. Because the man's acts seemed so senseless, his wife persuaded neurologists to perform some tests. A CT scan found a small lesion in the right frontal lobe of his brain that had reduced blood flow in that area. His doctors won his release from prison by testifying that such lesions can trigger compulsive disorders in which affected people, although otherwise rational, are unaware of the consequences of their actions—in this case, "borrowing" 100 cars. (Colburn, 1999).

Cognitive disorders—also called organic brain syndromes—involve problems in the function and structure of the brain that impair judgment, memory, and other aspects of cognition. The disorders implicated in the appearance of criminal behavior include dementia, amnesia, and cognitive impairments caused by a variety of temporary conditions such as epileptic seizures, anoxia, hypoglycemia, involuntary intoxication, and adverse reactions to drugs.

Dementia is a severe deficit in memory, thinking, reasoning, and concentration. It significantly impairs daily functioning and tends to worsen with time. Many demented people forget their own names and the names and faces of even their closest relatives. The most common causes of dementia are Alzheimer's disease; stroke; infections; metabolic disturbances; drug reactions; tumors; AIDS; vitamin deficiencies; lung, kidney, or liver disease; and head injuries.

People suffering from dementia tend to experience depression and helplessness, personality changes, and impairment of social skills and judgment. They are prone to angry and aggressive outbursts. They may become highly suspicious and misinterpret the words and actions of others. Feeling threatened, the demented person may lash out self-protectively, and thus be more likely to commit simple assault rather than more serious violent acts. People with dementia are usually not found competent to stand trial or, if tried, are not held criminally responsible for their actions. It has been suggested that patients with dementia who become violent may have abnormally low levels of serotonin, a condition we discussed in chapter 4 as being associated with impulsivity and aggressiveness (Siever & Davis, 1991). Cases of dementia-related violent aggression can also be triggered by hallucinations (Lowenstein, Binder, & McNiel, 1990).

Amnesia involves loss of memory but no other cognitive deficits, and usually arises from organic causes, including a blow to the head, a stroke, a brain tumor, or long-term drug use. People who suffer *retrograde* amnesia have no memory for events prior to some trauma, whereas those with *anterograde* amnesia are unable to form new memories after the event. Anterograde amnesia is usually permanent and results from damage to the hippocampus, a brain area closely associated with placing new memories into permanent storage. Retrograde amnesia is usually temporary and often functional, meaning that it may have arisen in relation to a stressful situation and may have been a way to escape that situation. Like defendants with dementia, those who cannot recall anything about their crimes—especially if they have a brain tumor or have suffered a serious brain injury or dysfunction—may be found incompetent to stand trial. However, if amnesia is the result of psychosis brought on by the voluntary consumption of alcohol or other drugs or if defendants can remember any details leading up to the crime, they are likely to be found competent to be tried and probably found guilty.

Examples of crimes associated with cognitive disorders include those of (1) a man who drove to his mother-in-law's house, stabbed her death, and returned home, all while allegedly sleepwalking; (2) an agitated, head-injured accident victim who assaulted a police officer who arrived on the scene; (3) an elderly Alzheimer's patient who bit a nurse; (4) a woman in a hypoglycemic state who threatened to kill her husband with the knife she was using to cut vegetables; and (5) a person who, in the aftermath of an epileptic seizure, assaulted a fellow passenger on a commuter train. These people were all found to have been lacking in control over their actions as well as their thoughts and were either not charged or found not guilty.

Diagnostic Foundations for an Insanity Plea

As we described in chapter 2, some, but not all, of the mental disorders we have described here can serve as the basis for an insanity plea. Accordingly, the diagnoses that mentally ill defendants receive can determine whether they will be prosecuted, sent to a mental institution, or released; whether, if convicted, they are given a prison sentence, psychiatric treatment, or both; and whether the penalty for a capital crime will be life without parole or death.

To be considered insane during the commission of a crime, a defendant must have been suffering from a mental disease or defect that impaired cognitive and volitional abilities. Federal insanity law specifically requires that the mental disease or defect be severe. Similarly, the American Psychiatric Association (1982) recommended that the insanity defense be invoked only when defendants suffer conditions that grossly and demonstrably impair their perception or understanding of reality. This standard has been widely adopted. The insanity statute of New Mexico is typical, defining mental disorder as "the substantial disorder of the person's emotional processes, thought or recognition, which grossly impairs judgment, behavior or capacity to recognize reality" (NM. Stat. Ann. 1979 43–1–3(N)).

These criteria for severe mental illness disallow the use of some conditions as the foundation for an insanity defense. For example, the courts have generally followed the decision in the case of *United States v. Lyons* (1984) in which it was ruled that drug addiction is not a mental disease or defect for purposes of the insanity defense unless it causes a drug-induced psychosis or physical damage to the brain or nervous system. Case decisions are virtually unanimous in holding, too, that antisocial personality disorder does not fall within the legal definition of mental illness (*Johnson v. Noot,* 1982). In fact, some state laws specifically exclude all personality disorders from the definition of mental disease or defect (e.g., Ariz. Rev. Stat. 36–501(1)(c)). Even where it is not specifically excluded, testimony about a defendant's alleged antisocial personality disorder signals almost certain defeat for an insanity defense. In short, if a criminal defendant is to escape conviction on the grounds of insanity, the mental disease or defect involved must be severe indeed.

As illustrated in cases we described already, the diagnoses most often asserted as evidence of insanity include (1) schizophrenia or other forms of psychoses; (2) severe depression, mania, or bipolar disorder; (3) substance abuse disorders; and (4) cognitive disorders such as dementia or amnesia. In recent years, insanity claims have also been based on on alleged adverse reactions to antidepressant medications such as Zoloft®. These reactions are said to include mania and agitation leading to violent behavior, especially in teenagers.[2] The so-called Zoloft® defense was used, for example, in the case of Christopher Pittman who was 12 years old when he shot his grandparents to death. Just prior to the killings, his doctor had put him on Zoloft® for symptoms of depression, so at his murder trial, defense attorneys argued that his actions were due to a drug he had taken involuntarily—a variation on the involuntary intoxication defense. The jury did not agree and convicted Pittman, who was tried as an adult, and recommended a 30-year prison sentence (Cassel, 2005).

---

[2]In 2004, the Food and Drug Administration ordered the makers of Paxil™ and Zoloft® to place labels on these drugs warning that they might be associated with aggression.

Assessing Sanity

To accomplish the difficult task of assessing a defendant's mental condition during a criminal act that took place weeks, months, or even years earlier, mental health professionals use a variety of methods including structured interviews and tests of intelligence, personality, and neurological functioning.

The Structured Interview.   No assessment of a defendant's mental condition would be complete without a face-to-face interview. During this meeting, the assessor gathers information on the defendant's social history—including family background, education, marital status, physical health, and work history—criminal record, history of mental disorder and psychiatric treatment as well as the defendant's version of events surrounding the crime for which he or she is about to be tried.

The most important part of this session is a structured interview in which the defendant is asked a predetermined set of questions in a predetermined sequence. Structured interviews assure that all topics relevant to evaluating the defendant's mental condition will be covered in a standardized way. The content of some versions of these interviews is keyed to match *DSM–IV–TR* criteria for various disorders, thus making it easier for the interviewer to diagnose a mental disorder if appropriate.

Intelligence Tests.   In most cases, the assessor will administer an intelligence test (either the Wechsler Adult Intelligence Scale or the Stanford–Binet Intelligence Scale) to determine if there is evidence of mental retardation or other deficits in mental ability that may be consistent with impaired cognitive ability See chapter 2, page 23.

Personality Tests.   The assessor will also usually administer one or more personality tests. The one most commonly used with criminal defendants is the MMPI–2™. The MMPI–2™ consists of 567 true–false statements that are designed to (a) distinguish people who display mental disorders from those who do not and (b) distinguish among various forms of mental disorder. The rationale for the test is that particular groups of items (called *Clinical scales*) tend to be answered in particular ways by schizophrenics, depressed people, anxious people, and so on (see Table 9.5).[3] By comparing a person's profile of scores on all 10 clinical scales to that of thousands of people with known mental disorders, the tester can determine which disordered group the person most resembles. Of particular interest is evidence of high scores on the Clinical scales relating to paranoid thinking, schizophrenia, depression, and psychopathy antisocial personality disorder (APD).

Some psychologists also use one or more *projective tests* of personality—such as the Rorschach Inkblot Test or the Thematic Apperception Test—to help them assess a defendant's sanity. In contrast to *objective tests* of personality such as the MMPI–2 whose items are answered with "true" or "false" or say 1 to 5 ratings, projective tests present abstract patterns, ambiguous drawings, incomplete sentences, or other stimuli to which people can respond in any number of ways as they tell a story, complete a sentence, or draw a picture. These tests are called projective because it is assumed that people will project aspects of their own personality onto ambiguous stimuli, thus revealing important characteristics (Nietzel et al., 2003).

Neurological Examinations.   Interview data, observed behavior, or IQ test results sometimes indicate the need for assessment of neurological problems in the defendant's brain. This is particularly likely when there is a history of head trauma, brain injury, or recent changes in personality or behavior. Psychologists can shed light on the presence and nature of such problems by administering the Halstead–Reitan Battery or the Luria–Nebraska Neuropsychological Battery. These extensive tests measure the defendant's abilities in areas such as information processing; attention; concentration; language; and perception of visual, auditory, and tactile stimulation (see Table 9.6).

A neurologist or other physician may also be called on to perform a medical examination and evaluate brain structure and function using assessments such as the EEG, MRI (fMRI), PET, CT scan, and SPECT.

---

[3]There are also questions designed to detect faking or lying.

TABLE 9.5 *MMPI-2 Clinical Scales*

Clinical Scales	Description
1 or **H**s (Hypochondriasis)	Abnormal concern with bodily functions
2 or **D** (Depression)	Pessimism, hopelessness, loss of interest
3 or **H**y (Conversion Hysteria)	Using physical or mental symptoms to avoid conflicts or responsibilities
4 or **P**d (Psychopathic Deviate)	Disregard for social customs, emotional shallowness
5 or **M**f (Masculinity-Femininity)	Indications of homoeroticism and items differentiating traditional male and female roles
6 or **P**a (Paranoia)	Suspiciousness, delusions of grandeur or persecution
7 or **P**t (Psychasthenia)	Obsessions, compulsions, guilt, indecisiveness
8 or **S**c (Schizophrenia)	Bizarre or unusual thoughts Hallucinations, delusions
9 or **M**a (Mania)	Emotional excitement, over-activity Flight of ideas
0 or **S**i (Social Introversion)	Shyness, insecurity, little interest in people

Source: Based on information from the MMPI-2. "MMPI-2" and "Minnesota Multiphasic Personality Inventory-2" are trademarks owned by the University of Minnesota.

Faking Insanity

Given their generally dishonest tendencies, it should not be too surprising that 20% to 25% of criminal defendants attempt to avoid punishment by faking (or "malingering") mental illness during insanity evaluations. One of the cleverest examples of malingering occurred in the case of Kenneth Bianchi, the notorious "Hillside Strangler" who is believed to have murdered more than a dozen young women in California and Washington state in the 1970s. When he was charged with the murder of two coeds in Bellingham, Washington, Bianchi pleaded innocent and claimed to have no memory for the nights of the murders. His defense team hired a hypnotist to discover if he could remember details of any murder, and while apparently in a trance, Bianchi spoke as someone named "Steve." Steve said he had taken part in the killings of 10 women whose murders were still unsolved. On the basis of these hypnosis sessions, four expert witnesses testified that Steve was Bianchi's "alter" personality and that Bianchi suffered from multiple personality disorder (now known as dissociative identity disorder).

Did he suffer from this disorder? Not according to a hypnosis expert hired by the prosecution. When he, too, hypnotized the defendant and suggested that Bianchi might have yet another personality, Bianchi immediately adopted the persona of "Billy," a brand new alter. Bianchi's "con job" was revealed not only by his ability to produce alters on demand but also by the fact that, although he had denied knowing anything about multiple personality disorder, investigators found books on hypnosis and abnormal psychology among his personal effects. Bianchi eventually abandoned his insanity defense and pleaded guilty to murder in exchange for a guarantee that the prosecution would not seek the death penalty. It is no wonder that psychologists have developed assessment methods designed to detect malingering, especially in cases of defendants pleading insanity (Rogers et al., 1991; Schretlen et al., 1992; Wetter et al., 1992).

Factors Contributing to Criminal Behavior Among the Mentally Ill

A number of social and political factors have been identified as playing a role in criminal behavior among those diagnosed with serious mental disorders. Among the most significant of these factors are (1) a movement

TABLE 9.6   *Some Tests Used in the Halstead-Reitan Battery*

Test	Description
Categories test	Consists of 208 slides that require a subject to form correct categorizations of the visual stimuli in the slides. The test measures mental efficiency and the ability to form abstract concepts.
Tactual performance test	Consists of a board with spaces into which ten blocks of various shapes can be fitted, somewhat like a large jigsaw puzzle. The subject is blindfolded and then asked to fit the blocks into the spaces as quickly as possible. This test measures abilities such as motor speed, tactile and kinesthetic perception, and incidental memory.
Rhythm test	Presents thirty pairs of rhythmic beats. The subject says whether the rhythms are the same or different. It is a measure of nonverbal auditory perception, attention, and concentration.
Speech-sounds perception test	Requires that the subject match spoken nonsense words to words on written lists. Language processing, verbal auditory perception, attention, and concentration are measured by this task.
Finger tapping test	A simple test of motor speed in which the subject depresses a small lever with the index finger as fast as possible for ten seconds. Several trials with each hand are used, allowing comparison of lateralized motor speed.
Trail making test	A kind of "connect-the-dots" task involving a set of circles that are numbered or lettered. The circles must be connected in a consecutive sequence requiring speed, visual scanning, and the ability to use and integrate different sets.
Strength of grip test	A right-side versus left-side comparison of strength. The subject simply squeezes a dynamometer twice with each hand.
Sensory-perceptual exam	Assesses whether the subject can perceive tactile, auditory, and visual stimulation when presented on each side of the body.
Tactile perception tests	Various methods to assess the subject's ability to identify objects when they are placed in the right and left hand, to perceive touch in different fingers of both hands, and to decipher numbers when they are traced on the fingertips.
Aphasia screening test	A short test that measures several aspects of language usage and recognition, as well as abilities to reproduce geometric forms and pantomime simple actions.

Source: From *Abnormal Psychology*, by M. T. Nietzel, M. Speltz, E. McCauley, & D. A. Bernstein, 1998, Boston: Allyn & Bacon. Copyright © 1998 by Allyn and Bacon. Reprinted with permission of authors.

in the 1970s to release tens of thousands of the hospitalized mental patients into the community; (2) the failure of community mental health services to provide adequate treatment and prevention services to these people; (3) the lack of treatment, prevention, and discharge programs for mentally disordered jail inmates; (4) jail and prison conditions that exacerbate or even promote serious mental disorder among inmates; and (5) the lack of treatment and prevention services for children and adolescents with serious mental disorders, especially those who come in contact with the juvenile or criminal justice systems. We consider how each of these factors might increase the likelihood that disordered people will commit crimes.

Deinstitutionalization and Homelessness

In one study (Martell, 1991), nearly half of all individuals in New York City who had been found either not guilty of a crime by reason of insanity or unfit to stand trial were also classified as homeless at the time of their arrest. Data collected at several pretrial detention facilities in New York showed that 40% of detainees reported being homeless at some time during the previous 3 years; about 21% were homeless on the night prior to their arrest (Michaels, Zoloth, Alcabes, Braslow, & Safyer, 1992). Another study (Gellberg, Linn, & Leake, 1988) found that 75% of homeless persons with a history of hospitalization in a mental health facility had also had a history of being arrested; this was true for only 45% of the non-homeless population.

What accounts for the association between homelessness and crime? For centuries, people diagnosed with serious mental disorders were hospitalized for long periods and given a variety of essentially ineffective treatments ranging from bleedings and purges to cold baths and restraints (straitjackets). By the early 1960s, however, several events had set in motion a **deinstitutionalization** movement that led to the discharge of thousands of these patients. Among the most important of these was the discovery or development of the first psychoactive drugs that were capable of alleviating many of the symptoms of schizophrenia, severe depression, and bipolar disorder. The 1960s were also a time of turmoil, not only in relation to the Vietnam War but also to any and all examples of authoritarian control by the "establishment" over individuals including mental patients. Books such as Kesey's (1962) *One Flew Over the Cuckoo's Nest*, which publicized the dehumanizing conditions in many state mental hospitals, fueled an outcry for reform in the treatment of mental patients. In response, in 1963, a federal law was enacted directing the states to initiate policies designed to move people out of mental institutions and into less restrictive programs in the community such as day treatment centers, vocational rehabilitation facilities, and local community health centers.

After leaving the hospital, former mental patients were to be placed in halfway houses or other facilities where they were supposed to receive supervision of medication and learn the social skills needed to survive in their communities. In places where funding is adequate and where careful discharge planning, case management, and interagency cooperation is the rule, deinstitutionalization has worked reasonably well (Okin, 1995; Winerip, 1999). Unfortunately, success stories are the exception rather than the rule. Today, most observers agree that the community mental health system has failed to properly care for those with serious mental disorders mainly because of inadequate funding, poor planning, and political wrangling among those charged with administering and funding the system (Winerip, 1999). The legacy of deinstitutionalization is a "revolving door" through which patients are admitted to hospitals or other mental health facilities when they behave in ways that endanger themselves or others (often after arrest for a crime), given medication to reduce symptoms, and then released to relatives, a low-rent hotel, a homeless shelter, a halfway house, or, sometimes, a cardboard box on the street (Talbott, & Glick, 1986; Winerip, 1999). When they get into trouble again, they enter the mental health system again. The revolving door turns partly because space in treatment facilities is limited and partly because managed health care systems do not encourage long-term hospitalization. A schizophrenic patient with health insurance who might once have been hospitalized for several weeks or months is now likely to be released after a few days of stabilization on medication because the insurance company will not pay for further treatment (Karon, 1995). In short, whether or not seriously mentally disordered people have insurance, they are more likely than ever to become homeless.

When these people are discharged on medication, they are usually no longer dangerous. But many of the homeless mentally ill do not continue to take their medication, and when they return to their chaotic lives, they relapse, become even more disordered, and perhaps dangerous. One study (P. J. Taylor et al., 1994) of homeless schizophrenic men in New York City found that they displayed more paranoid delusions, hallucinations, impulsive behaviors, and substance abuse problems than nonhomeless mentally ill men. As we noted earlier, all of these are risk factors for violence. For example, Russell Weston Jr. had been hospitalized for paranoid schizophrenia off and on for many years, and just prior to his armed attack on the Capitol Building had been in a mental hospital for 52 days and released with a prescription for psychoactive drugs (see chapter 2). However, Weston did not go to his parents' home, where he was welcome, but to a tent in deserted area nearby. More importantly, he did not have his prescription filled.

Laws in several states now mandate outpatient treatment for persons believed to be noncompliant with psychiatric medication orders. New York, for example, enacted its law following the death of Kendra Webdale who died after being pushed in front of a train by Andrew Goldstein, a man who had been repeatedly hospitalized for schizophrenia but who had stopped taking his antipsychotic medication (Rohde, 1999).

Lack of Mental Health Services in Jails

We have shown that the homeless mentally ill are more likely than the general population to come in contact with the criminal justice system. Most of the mentally ill who are arrested are charged with relatively minor offenses such as prostitution, shoplifting, disorderly conduct, loitering, vagrancy, or disturbing the peace (Center on Crime, Communities and Culture, 1996; Haddad, 1993; Lamb & Shaner, 1993; McFarland & Blair, 1995). Often, these arrests are made by well-intentioned law enforcement officers in an effort to get the person into treatment (Janik, 1992; National Coalition for Jail Reform, 1984). Some family members have their seriously mentally ill relatives arrested for the same reason. Unfortunately, most of those convicted of minor offenses are simply kept in jail without treatment and then released when they have served their time (Conly, 1999).

As one of us (Elaine Cassel) discovered when working with mentally disordered defendants, even when a judge enters an order for inpatient evaluation and treatment, the options are limited. If the person has insurance (and some do because they receive Medicaid or other benefits in connection with Supplemental Social Security), private hospitals often refuse them because they are criminals or are perceived to be violent (F. Butterfield, 1998). If they are sent to a state hospital, they are given medication and after as little as 36 hours, sent to jail where they encounter guards who cannot or will not carry out the patient's medication orders (Steadman & Veysey, 1997).

As we noted earlier, the jail experience often intensifies depression, delusions, and other symptoms of mental disorder (F. Butterfield, 1998), and because judges are often reluctant to grant bail to the mentally ill, they tend to stay in jail longer than other inmates do. For example, the average inmate stays at Rikers Island (New York City's jail) for 42 days, but for the 15% of new inmates who have serious mental disorders, the average stay is 215 days (F. Butterfield, 1998). Mentally ill inmates are often the targets of taunting and mistreatment by other inmates. In some places, such as the Los Angeles Central Jail, the mentally ill are issued yellow jumpsuits to make them easily identifiable and are housed in isolation cells. Worse yet, it is standard practice that inmates who arrive with medication are not allowed to take it until a jail psychiatrist sees them, which can take days or even weeks (F. Butterfield, 1998). If the medication is controlling impulsive and violent urges, the now-unmedicated inmate is at greater risk for becoming violent.

The longer that mentally ill inmates remain in jail, the less tolerant they become of the rules restricting their behavior. Accordingly, these inmates are more likely than others to be disciplined for failing to stand in line or follow guards' commands or for assaulting other inmates or guards. If discipline includes solitary confinement, it can result in further deterioration of these inmates' mental condition (F. Butterfield, 1998).

The Conly (1999) Report, a government study of the chronically mentally ill in local jails, concluded that most of them had extremely limited access to mental health professionals, that jail medical staff were not usually trained to address the psychiatric needs of inmates, and that local community mental health systems were less than cooperative with jail officials who tried to obtain treatment for their mentally disordered inmates (Conly, 1999). What do these jail conditions have to do with crime? According to the Conly report:

1. Mentally ill inmates are especially likely to be rearrested following release, at least in part because of the lack of appropriate aftercare planning and services in the community.
2. Mentally ill offenders tend to pass through a variety of criminal justice settings, in part because of the lack of coordination among psychosocial service providers. Most mentally ill inmates are released with no plan for community-based care (Steadman & Veysey, 1997). They are not equipped to advocate for their own welfare. They face multiple challenges that put them at risk for continued mental illness and crime—homelessness, unemployment, estrangement from family and friends, and substance abuse. It is no surprise that they repeatedly run afoul of the criminal justice system. For some, being arrested and jailed provides a welcome respite from life on the streets. Margaret Ray, the "Letterman Stalker," spent her entire adult life in and out of jail, with an occasional admission to a hospital. Hers is a classic case of the chronically mentally ill petty criminal in the United States today.

Lack of Mental Health Services in Prisons

Like other criminals, many mentally ill people who commit serious violent crimes end up in a state or federal prison. There, access to mental health services is likely to be even more restricted than it is in local jails. Once within prison walls where the Department of Corrections and the local warden control every aspect of prison life, mentally ill convicts have no guarantee of any special treatment beyond the minimal standard required by federal law (see chapter 2). This situation continues because although the Supreme Court has affirmed the constitutional obligation to provide treatment to inmates suffering serious medical or mental health conditions (*DeShaney v. Winnebago Department of Social Services,* 1989; *Estelle v. Gamble,* 1976), federal courts have defined "serious conditions" as those that could "result in further significant injury," not as "routine discomfort that is part of the penalty that criminal offenders pay for their offenses against society" (*McGuckin v. Smith,* 1992, pp. 1059–1060). The Supreme Court itself has ruled that "mere depression" or behavioral and emotional problems alone do not qualify as serious mental illnesses mandating treatment, although treatment might be warranted for acute depression, paranoid schizophrenia, "nervous collapse," and suicidal tendencies (*Youngberg v. Romeo,* 1982). Accordingly, prison wardens are given great discretion in what services they authorize and for whom.

Guards and wardens tend to refuse treatment for prisoners whom they perceive as trying to manipulate them or to get special consideration (Ditton, 1999). With only a handful of prisoners receiving the mental health treatment they need (R. Johnson, 1996), most mentally ill prisoners will return to their communities more disordered, more dangerous, and perhaps more violent than they were when they were incarcerated. We return to this problem in chapter 13, where we discuss the social and political forces that have reduced the availability of all types of services to prisoners.

Lack of Services for Mentally Ill Delinquents

Of the more than one million children and adolescents who enter the U.S. juvenile justice system each year, at least 100,000 are detained in a juvenile facility. It is estimated that as many as 60% of these detainees display some form of psychiatric disorder, a rate three to four times higher than in the nondelinquent population (F. Butterfield, 1998; National Mental Health Association, 1993). A total of 20% have serious disorders, including major depression and schizophrenia, and many show signs of PTSD (Conly, 1999). As many as half have substance abuse disorders (Cocozza, 1992), and others suffer from less severe disorders such as conduct disorder and mild depression. Yet according to a national survey (National Mental Health Association, 1999), there are virtually no comprehensive screening, assessment, or treatment programs connected with juvenile court systems. When services are provided, it tends to occur in a haphazard and piecemeal manner.

This situation is particularly disturbing because some research suggested that if detained juveniles received adequate treatment, recidivism could be reduced by as much as 25% (Garfinkel, 1997).

Mental Health Courts

Some jurisdictions have created specialized *drug courts* to attempt to rehabilitate drug offenders. Recently, this paradigm has been applied to deal with mentally ill defendants who are charged with nonviolent crimes. These *mental health courts* require that defendants plead guilty to enter a treatment program. If they successfully complete that program, the criminal charges against them may be dismissed. Although some correctional officers and community health workers like the mental health court concept, some clinicians, attorneys, and civil rights advocates do not. They argue, first, that some of the people who come through mental health courts should not have been arrested in the first place and probably would not have been had they not been homeless. Second, critics claims that mental health courts are just another step in the criminalization of mental illness. Finally, they decry the fact that violent offenders are not eligible for mental health courts, when these offenders would benefit most from being diverted from a punishment model to a treatment model (Seltzer, 2005). We discuss mental health courts in more detail in chapter 13.

Summary

Like crime, mental disorders usually result from a complex interaction of biological, psychological, and social factors. Because the most serious mental disorders can disrupt thinking, emotion, and other psychological processes, it is no wonder that they are associated with behaviors that violate criminal laws. Mentally ill people are no more likely than the general population to be violent (unless they have a co-occurring substance abuse disorder), but they are more likely to be arrested for nonviolent, minor crimes because of their mental status. Among the mentally ill who are also homeless, the probability of arrest is especially high.

Schizophrenia, bipolar disorder, and substance-related disorders are the most prevalent disorders associated with criminal behavior. Each impair cognition and responsible behavior in different ways. People displaying paranoid schizophrenia, for example, may become so out of touch with reality as to not be in control of their behavior. The manic phase of bipolar disorder, too, may lead individuals to become aggressive or violent or to commit property crimes. Substance-related disorders, including those linked to alcohol and illicit drugs, are strongly related to criminal behavior. As many as 60% of state and federal inmates have reported being intoxicated at the time they committed crimes.

One of the most important and controversial intersections of law and psychology involves the assessment of whether defendants were insane at the time they committed a crime. Insanity is a legal term, not a medical one. Defendants judged to be insane are given special consideration that may result in their not being tried for a crime or not being held responsible for it. It is difficult for psychologists and psychiatrists to retrospectively determine a defendant's mental state during commission of a crime that occurred in the past, sometimes months or years earlier. Many types of psychological and neurological tests are employed to help these professionals advise the judges and juries who must determine whether to absolve a defendant of criminal responsibility.

The deinstitutionalization movement of the 1960s led to the closure of large numbers of mental hospitals. The promise of community-based treatment has not been realized, and today there may be more mentally ill people in jails and prisons than there are in mental health treatment facilities. In most jails and prisons, mental health treatment ranges from nonexistent to woefully inadequate, and the mental condition of most mentally ill inmates becomes worse during incarceration. These inmates are also more prone to being abused by guards and other inmates.

Mental health courts are a recent phenomenon and, to some, a misguided effort to divert the nonviolent mentally ill defendant from the criminal justice system into community treatment.

In this chapter, we have reinforced a theme sounded in several earlier chapters, namely, that understanding the role of mental disorders in criminal behavior is an essential part of understanding—and possibly eradicating—the roots of crime. Providing basic treatment services to people with schizophrenia and other serious mental disorders, housing the homeless mentally ill, educating young people about the dangers of substance abuse, treating existing substance abusers, and increasing public understanding of how mental disorders contribute to criminal behavior will go a long way toward reducing crime and the suffering and societal chaos that are its tragic consequences.

We have now completed our discussion of the roots of crime. In the next two chapters, we turn our attention to specific criminal acts, including violent crimes such as murder, rape, robbery, and aggravated assault; and property crimes such as larceny, arson, and fraud.

Key Terms

Bipsychosocial model of mental illness   *Mental disorders*
Diathesis-stress model of mental illness   *Deinstitutionalization*

Questions for Review

1. Which mental illnesses are most associated with crime?
2. What is the link between cognitive disorders and crime and violence?

3. What are the diagnostic foundations for an effective insanity plea?
4. What five factors contribute to criminal behavior among the mentally ill?
5. How does the lack of mental health services in jails and prisons lead to more violence among those who are incarcerated?

Track It down

Criminal Behavior Website
www.cassel2e.com
"Ill-Equipped: U.S. Prisons and Offenders with Mental Illness," a 2003 report by Human Rights Watch
www.hrw.org/reports/2003/usa1003/
The American Psychiatric Association's 2004 report on the high costs to society of criminalizing mental illness
www.psych.org/advocacy_policy/tapa01312005.pdf
Mental Illness and Violence: Truth or Stereotype
www.phac-aspc.gc.ca/mh-sm/mentalhealth/pubs/mental_illness/summary.htm
"Drawing a Clear Line Between the Criminals and the Criminally Insane" by Stephen Lally
www.washingtonpost.com/wp-srv/local/longterm/aron/expert1123.htm

10

Violent Crimes

Robbery   *Hate Crimes*
Murder and Nonnegligent Manslaughter   *Sex Crimes*
Aggravated Assault and Domestic Violence

In previous chapters, we have examined the biological, psychological, and social roots of crime; traced the development of crime from childhood; and identified the major risk factors for crime including the role of mental illness. Now it is time to examine the bitter fruit of these malignant roots and distorted developmental processes—crime itself. In the next chapter (chapter 11) we consider economic and property crimes. Here, we address violent crime: robbery, homicide, aggravated assault, violence against family members and intimate partners, hate crimes, and sex crimes. Most of these offenses constitute the Violent Crime Index of the FBI's *Uniform Crime Reports* we described in chapter 1.

Robbery

Silver-haired retiree Forrest Tucker was still working at the age of 78. He and his wife had moved to Florida to retire, but he still liked to make a little extra money. It was not the money, so much, as the fact that he enjoyed the work. So on a lovely spring day in 1999, while other retirees in Pompano Beach, Florida were playing golf or shopping, Tucker got all dressed up and left the house. Pausing in front of an ATM machine at a bank about 50 miles from his home, he reached into a bag, pulled out his gun, and charged into the bank. Flashing the gun, he ordered the tellers to put their money on the table. Tucker scooped up more than $5,000 and hurried to the door. A polite old man, he said to the tellers as he exited, "Thank you." Tucker ran to his car, which housed a veritable arsenal of guns, Mace, handcuffs, gloves, and duct tape and prepared for a fast getaway. However, the cops were hot on his tail, and as he got close to his home, Tucker lost control of the car, hit a palm tree, and waited to be rescued. The police were shocked to find that they had cornered a man described as one of the most notorious robbers in history. At the age of 83, he is back serving time, something he has done most of his life since he was a young boy. In fact, in telling his story, he says he has been in prison most of his life except for the times he broke out and robbed again. Most certainly, Tucker will die in prison (Grann, 2003).

Robbery is associated with some of the most romantic elements of American folklore. Our fascination with famous robbers and remarkable robberies, including the exploits of Robin Hood and Aladdin, the Dalton gang, Butch Cassidy, Bonnie and Clyde, John Dillinger, and Forrest Tucker (who has been profiled in *The New Yorker* magazine and in books), not to mention all sorts of fictional escapades, is reflected in countless books, films, and television specials. Robbery may be thrilling to read about, but few of us would leave our homes unlocked at night for fear of being robbed (J. Katz, 1995; Wright & Decker, 1997).

The FBI (2004) defines **robbery** as "the taking or attempting to take anything of value from the care, custody, or control of a person or persons by force of threat or violence and/or by putting the victim in fear." Robbery differs from burglary in that burglars take money or property without violence or threat, usually while the owner is asleep or away. During 2003, robbery accounted for almost 30% of all violent crime in the United States and resulted in property losses of $514 million (FBI, 2004). However, the cost of robbery cannot be counted in dollars alone. Although by definition, the object of robbery is to obtain money or property, this crime involves the use of force or the threat of force, and many victims suffer serious bodily injury. The weapons used in armed robberies during 2003 included firearms (42%), physical force ("strong-arm tactics," 40%), knives or other cutting instruments (9%), and other dangerous weapons (9%; FBI, 2004).

As with most other forms of violent crime, the highest percentage of robberies in the United States take place in the South (36%), followed by the West (23%), the Northeast (19%), and the Midwest (22%). Robberies tend to occur most often in January and August and least often in February and April. About 43% of all robberies in 2003 occurred on streets or highways; 14% took place in commercial and financial establishments and 14% in homes. The remainder were in miscellaneous locations including 6% in convenience stores (FBI, 2004).

Of all people arrested for robbery in 2003, 90% were males and 76% were over the age of 18 years. A total of 54% were Black, 44% White, and the rest were members of other racial groups (FBI, 2004). About 42% of robbers have prior felony arrests, and 60% have prior misdemeanor arrests, generally for other robberies, thefts, and frauds (Bureau of Justice Statistics, 2002b). Many robbers start their criminal activity in the early teenage years and "graduate" from simple theft (e.g., shoplifting), to auto theft, then to burglary and robbery (Gabor et al., 1987). Robberies typically involve some degree of planning and premeditation, sometimes with careful choice of individual victims or businesses, followed by detailed observations designed to insure success and escape.[1] By carrying a weapon, the robber has made the decision to use force, if necessary, either to commit the crime or to resist arrest.

At least 70% of robbers convicted in state court in 1994 (the last date for which figures are available) were rearrested for robbing again within 3 years of release. Half of them were convicted again (Bureau of Justice Statistics, 2002). The recidivism rate for robbery was only slightly less than that for car theft and other larceny crimes (79% and 75%, respectively).

Types of Robbers

Armed robbers have been classified as (1) chronic, (2) professional, (3) intensive, and (4) occasional (Gabor, 1987).

As the label implies, chronic armed robbers have the longest criminal histories. Their first criminal offense usually occurs between the ages of 12 and 14, with their first robbery coming at around age 17. In their careers as robbers, which typically last about 8 years before they start serving long prison sentences, they are involved in up to 25 armed robberies as well as in varying numbers of burglaries, drug offenses, and auto thefts. They are usually well armed, use disguises, and are prepared to harm or kill victims and to resist arrest (Gabor et al., 1987). Chronic robbers are potentially the most dangerous. They do not hesitate to use violence to get what they want and to gain the "respect" of their victims. They are often so successful at intimidating their victims that the victims may help them locate valuables and create escape paths (Katz, 1991).

Professional or career armed robbers, such as Forrest Tucker, are distinguished by their meticulous attention to detail, higher average "earnings" per robbery, and careers that begin a bit earlier than the chronic robber (usually their first armed robbery comes at about 16) and last 10 years or more. They, too, are usually well armed and often carrying automatic weapons, although they rarely use them. Robbery is their primary source of income. Professional robbers are not considered as dangerous as chronic robbers because they are more practical and businesslike in committing their crimes, and they do not engage in violence simply for the sake of being tough or asserting power (Katz, 1991).

---

[1]Without diminishing the seriousness of the crime of robbery, it is still entertaining to read collections of stories about less-than-brilliant robbers who find themselves locking their keys in their getaway car, handing bank tellers notes written on the back of their personalized deposit slips, or attempting to mug undercover police officers (e.g. Butler, Ray, & Gregory, 2000; Ray, Harris, & Butler, 1997).

Intensive armed robbers usually do little planning; they simply and suddenly commit a rash of 5 to 10 holdups in a short period of time, usually while they are in their mid-20s. Because they are inexperienced, though, they are often caught and incarcerated sooner than other types of robbers.

Occasional armed robbers are usually involved in less dangerous criminal pursuits such as drug dealing, auto theft, and fraud, committing robberies only if the opportunity or need arises (Gabor et al., 1987).

Not all robbers, of course, fit so easily into a category. The FBI and local authorities have been trying since 1998 to nab a "part-time bandit" who has hit on Washington DC banks, mostly within a 1 mile radius. Surveillance photos show a man wearing a topcoat and hat (even in August, when many of his heists have occurred), with his face fully visible. Tall, thin, and with a neatly trimmed beard, he fits more the profile of a professional robber, albeit a part-timer. Authorities call him the "Gentleman Bandit." He walks into the bank, asks about opening an account, then points his gun at the teller with an order to step aside. He calmly and slowly cleans out the vault, the cash drawer, and the ATM machine and vanishes without a trace, leaving law enforcement mystified yet again (Lengel, 2003).

Motivations for Robbery

What makes someone rob when he could commit burglary and not encounter the victim? The simple explanation is that robbery is almost sure to yield cash, not goods that must then be sold.

Overall, robbers tend to be committed to a life on the streets. Few have permanent homes, and most rob to avoid the need to hold a job or otherwise lead a conventional life. Most use the money obtained from robbery to buy high-status clothing, alcohol, and drugs (Wright & Decker, 1997). Indeed, many researchers argue that addiction to drugs or alcohol is a primary contributing factor to becoming and remaining an armed robber (P. Davis, 1995). Chronic robbers may display cycles of "earning and burning" in which they go on drinking, drugging, and spending sprees after a robbery and then, once their ill-gotten gains are gone, go out and rob again (Gabor et al., 1987). Only rarely are robbers' actions part of political efforts such as financing terrorism, protesting government policies, or trying to gain the release of imprisoned colleagues (Miethe & McCorkle, 1998).

Like Forrest Tucker, many armed robbers appear to become "addicted" to the thrill of the planning, the challenge of escaping arrest, and the power and control they wield over their victims (Katz, 1988). They come to believe that the potential gains far exceed the risks of getting caught, and this optimistic self-talk keeps them from thinking too much about the possibility of arrest. Among juveniles, economic motives for robbery may be less important than the desire to enhance their reputation among their friends or fellow gang members and/or to feel empowered by their victim's fear (Feeney, 1986; Katz, 1988).

Robbery Victims

According to the most recently available national victimization study, 74% of male victims of robbers and 42% of female victims were strangers to their assailants (Bureau of Justice Statistics, 2000). The remaining victims are robbed by family members involved in domestic disputes, by acquaintances who take property following an assault, by rival drug dealers or gang members, or by double-crossing accomplices in conspiracies to defraud insurance companies or financial institutions (MacDonald, 1975). As many as 6 out of 10 robbery victims are themselves involved in criminal activity (Wright & Decker, 1997), which accounts for the fact that many robberies go unreported. In fact, some robbers target drug dealers because they know they will have plenty of cash and, as criminals themselves, are unlikely to go to the police (Oliver, 1994). Drug-dealer victims may be armed, however, thus increasing the possibility that the robber will be killed or wounded. Most robbers prefer victims who are far less likely to resist, often choosing elderly or otherwise vulnerable people in their own neighborhoods (Wright & Decker, 1997).

Murder and Nonnegligent Manslaughter

There are many different types of murder, among them killing a passenger in a drive-by shooting, killing a spouse in the course of an argument, rival gang members killing each other to protect their economic turf, one mobster ordering the death of another, a robber killing a victim to protect the robber's identity, a mother killing her children while she is in the depths of depression, killing a family member to collect insurance money, killing a supervisor after being fired, killing fellow students in a school rampage, killing total strangers in a restaurant, and coolly plotting the death of a new victim after the thrill of the last killing has worn off. These are just a few examples of the many kinds of murders you can read about just about every day in the United States. Murder takes place in all kinds of settings under many different circumstances.

The FBI (2004a) defines **murder** as the willful, premeditated killing of another person without defense or justification. Nonnegligent manslaughter means willfully killing another without premeditation and without justification or excuse. In 2003, the latest year for which data are available, 16,503 people were murdered in the United States (FBI, 2004). Although this figure accounts for only .1% of all crime, the public is fascinated with murder. Perusing a week of prime time television suggests that nothing entertains more or more often than murder. How many movies do not have something to do with murder? The number of first-run movies dealing with mass murder or serial killings, for example, was 13 times higher in the 1990s than in the 1950s (Hickey, 1997).

We tend to be most fascinated by bizarre and horrific murders. Cannibal serial killers like Jeffrey Dahmer; handsome, bright, psychopathic killers like Ted Bundy; mass murderers like Oklahoma City bomber Timothy McVeigh; and deranged-yet-brilliant serial bombers like Theodore Kaczynski (the Unabomber) are inevitably the subject of intense media attention. Additionally, so are murders committed by the young, as when an 18-year-old boy abducted, raped, and strangled a 7-year-old girl in a Las Vegas casino; or when a pregnant teenager in New Jersey delivered a full term baby in the girl's room during her senior prom and then, before returning to the dance, wrapped it in a garbage bag and put it in a trash can to die. Fortunately, such cases are rare. Far more numerous, and therefore much less publicized, are the "everyday" murders of spouses and domestic partners, the murders of children by parents, and killings associated with drug dealing and gang-turf wars.

FBI (2004a) data for 2003 show that slightly more than 43% of U.S. murders occurred in the Southern states, 23% in the Western states, 20% in the Midwestern states, and 14% in the Northeastern states. From 1999 to 2003, the most murders occurred in July, August, and December (ranging from 9% to 9.4% of murders), whereas the fewest were committed in February (about 7%) and March and April (approximately 8%). As we discussed in chapter 6, these regional differences appear related both to sustained periods of heat and humidity and to the influence of Southern culture.Ninety percent of murderers were males, and 68% were under the age of 25. As between Black and White arrestees, the racial makeup was almost equal—51.3% were Black, 45.9% White, and the remaining from other racial groups. As for murder victims, 77% were male, 45% were aged 20 to 34, and almost equally represented Blacks (48.5%) and Whites (48.7%).

Murderers and their victims generally are of the same race. Data from single victim/single incident murders reported by the FBI for 2003 indicated that 92.4% of Black victims were slain by Black offenders, and 84.7% of White victims were slain by White offenders.

The relationship of the victim to the offender was unknown for 44.5% of the homicides reported to the FBI for 2003. An analysis of the 55.5% of the victims for whom the relationships to the offenders were known revealed that 77.6% knew their assailants, whereas 22.4% were slain by strangers. Of those who knew their assailants, 71% were killed by acquaintances and 29% by relatives. Husbands and boyfriends killed 32.3% of female victims, whereas wives and girlfriends murdered 2.5% of male victims (FBI, 2004). About 28% of the murders came about as the result of arguments. Juvenile gang killings, sniper attacks, and brawls were documented in slightly over 20% of murders (FBI, 2004).

Firearms are the typical murder weapons; they were used in 71% of all murders in 2003 (80% of guns were handguns). Knives or other cutting instruments were employed in 13.4% of murders, whereas fists, feet, and other body parts were used in 7%. Clubs, hammers, and other blunt objects were used in 4.8% of murders; the remaining cases involved weapons such as poison, arson, and narcotics (FBI, 2004).

The role of alcohol and other psychoactive substances in crime is nowhere more evident than in murders. One study (Leong & Silva, 1995) of murder defendants found that 61% met the *DSM–IV-TR* criteria for substance abuse, and 51% had used alcohol or drugs preceding the homicide. Another study (Yarvis, 1994) found that 50% of murderers were intoxicated by alcohol at the time of the murder. An interview study (Fendrich, Mackesy-Amiti, Goldstein, & Spunt, 1995) of juvenile murderers illustrates the familiar inhibition-releasing mechanism through which alcohol can facilitate homicide. These killers said that alcohol intensified their impulsiveness and violent reactions (Fendrich et al., 1995). Especially when guns are available, alcohol's dis-inhibition of a person's violent impulses can result in murder, even when murder was not the initial intent.

Types of Murderers

Criminologists have not developed a sophisticated or extensive typology of murderers who kill a single victim. They have, however, identified overcontrolled murderers and undercontrolled murderers (Megargee, 1966). *Overcontrolled* murderers are people who have never been in trouble with the law—they are often model citizens—but experience a burst of rage that results in an emotional "heat-of-passion" murder. Not only do these people usually have no history of violence, they tend to be introverted, to have low self-esteem, and to feel lonely and frustrated (Weiss, Lamberti, & Blackburn, 1960). In short, overcontrolled murderers tend to be mild-mannered, long-suffering individuals whose intense anger and resentment are kept under strict psycho-logical control until a "breaking point" is reached, allowing pent-up aggression to be expressed in a sudden murderous act. This appears to be what happened in Honolulu, Hawaii in November of 1999 when Byran Uyesugi walked into the copier repair center where he had been employed for 15 years and without a word, killed seven of his co-workers. There is some evidence that the sudden rage of the overcontrolled murderer may be especially likely to be triggered by depictions of violence in media reports, television shows, and movies (Conduit, 1995). There is also evidence that overcontrolled murderers are capable of more extreme acts of violence than those for whom anger, temper tantrums, and violence had been a more common experience (Lee, Zimbardo, & Bertholf, 1977).

Undercontrolled murderers tend to be emotionally reactive, violence prone, impulsive criminals (Berkowitz, 1993; Tupin, Mahar, & Smith, 1973; Wilson & Herrnstein, 1985). They usually have a history sug-gestive of antisocial personality disorder. Several studies have indicated that most juvenile killers fit the under-controlled murderer profile (Bailey, 1996; Hardwick & Rowton-Lee, 1996; R. C. Katz & Marquette, 1996). These people kill when aroused to the (relatively easily reached) point that they can no longer control the aggressive inclinations they have exhibited many times in the past. Later, they may say that they meant only to warn or injure their victims, not to kill.

A tragic example of this kind of murder occurred late one afternoon in a suburb of Washington, DC, when a 19-year-old driver gently bumped the back of a bicycle in heavy, slow-moving rush hour traffic. The cyclist fell from his bike, and the driver stopped her car to check on him. As she approached, the cyclist shouted curses at her and then drew a handgun and shot her in the head, killing her instantly (Pan & Thomas-Lester, 1997). The murderer had a history of arrests for assaulting police officers, once while being arrested for disorderly and threatening behavior in a bar. On the day of the murder, he was in violation of his probation (related to an assault conviction) because he recently failed three court-ordered drug tests. When arrested for murder, he had crack cocaine in his possession. He told police that he killed the woman because he felt she had endangered him and he wanted her to "know how it felt."

Multiple-Victim Murderers

Murderers who kill several people, either at once or over a period of time, have been classified in terms of the length of the interval between murders. Thus, there are spree murderers, mass murderers, and serial murderers (Douglas, Ressler, Burgess, & Hartman, 1986).

Spree Murderers.   Spree murderers kill several people in succession but at different locations, perhaps in one day or over several days, with little or no "cooling off" between incidents. For example, on August 19, 1997, Carl Drega shattered the quiet of Colebrook, New Hampshire, a small town 10 miles south of the Canadian border. Drega was a 62-year-old power-plant worker with a history of disputes with town officials and citizens over property rights. When he came out of a store that day to find state trooper Scott Philips putting a motor vehicle citation on his windshield, Drega took an AR–15 assault rifle from his truck, followed the officer to his cruiser and killed him. When another state trooper approached, Drega killed him, too. Drega then took Phillip's bulletproof vest and cruiser and drove to a downtown office building where he shot and killed Vickie Brunnel, an attorney and part-time judge who had angered Drega several years before when she was on the town council. As Dennis Joos, co-editor of the town's newspaper, attempted to tackle and disarm Drega, Drega killed him as well. Drega returned to his home and set it on fire before driving to Vermont where he abandoned his stolen cruiser in a rural area near Brunswick. Tipped off by a local farmer, several police officers were approaching the car when Drega began firing at them from nearby woods. He managed to wound a Vermont state trooper and a Canadian Border Patrol agent before being killed by a police bullet (Wulf, 1997).

Other examples of spree murders come to mind. On June 29, 1999, Mark Barton, a stock trader in Atlanta, Georgia, who was deeply in debt because of market losses, embarked on one of the deadliest murder sprees in U.S. history. After killing his wife and two children, he took the lives of nine employees at their day-trading firms. In Pittsburgh, Pennsylvania, on April 21, 2000, Richard Scott Baumhammers, a 34-year-old unemployed immigration lawyer with a history of mental illness, went on a rampage that began when he killed his neighbor, a 63-year-old Jewish woman. Then he killed two men from India at an Indian-owned grocery store, two Asian Americans at a Chinese restaurant, and a Black man at a karate school (Duke, 2000).

Mass Murderers. Mass murderers kill three or more people at a single location at the same time. For example, in July 1984, James Oliver Huberty killed 21 patrons at a McDonald's in San Ysidro, California, apparently selecting a fast-food restaurant in the Hispanic community because he disliked Hispanics and children (Zuniga, 2004). The school killings we discussed in chapter 8 are mass murders. In March 2005, native American Jeff Weise killed nine people—his grandfather who raised him, his grandfather's girlfriend, a school guard, a teacher, and five classmates—before turning his gun on himself and taking his own life (Hardin & Hedgpeth, 2005).

Mass murderers' motivation or choice of victims has led some researchers to put them into several subcategories including disciple murderers, family annihilators, pseudocommandos, disgruntled employees, and hit-and-run killers (Goldstein, 1995). The number of school killings in the past 10 years has led the FBI to study school killers as a distinct category (FBI, 2000).

The *disciple murderer* kills as directed by a charismatic leader such as Charles Manson who, in the late 1960s, lived with his 40 member "family" of runaways and petty criminals on a Southern California ranch. Manson's disciples stole, used hallucinogenic drugs, and armed themselves for "Helter Skelter," the nuclear and race war that Manson predicted was coming. In 1969, he and several of his followers killed a record producer whom Manson accused of hindering his musical career. A week later, acting on Manson's orders, his followers killed actress Sharon Tate and fours others at the home of film director Roman Polanski. Manson and eight of his disciples were convicted of murder and remain incarcerated.

As the name implies, *family annihilators* are mass murderers who kill their entire family. Usually, the killer is the family's senior male figure—typically the father—who is likely to have a serious drinking problem and is battling depression over money problems or domestic troubles involving the loss or impending loss of a wife or girlfriend. The annihilator almost always kills himself after murdering his family (Palmero, 1994). This was the case in September of 1998 in New York City when police officer Patrick Fitzgerald murdered his wife, his two children, and himself. The couple had long-standing marital difficulties and were considering a separation. Yet Fitzgerald was known to be a devoted father who coached his 7-year-old daughter Ashley's flag football team. It was Ashley who was on the phone with 911 dispatchers as Fitzgerald shot her younger brother, Shane. Within minutes, Fitzgerald had hung up the phone, killed Ashley, then phoned his precinct station and said, "I've shot my family. Now I'm going to kill myself" (Yardley & Herszenhorn, 1998).

The *pseudocommando* typically stockpiles arms and uses them in a mass murder event designed to gain attention or make a statement of protest. Colorado students Eric Harris and Dylan Klebold, who killed 12 fellow students and a teacher in a commando-style attack at Columbine High School in Littleton, Colorado in April 1999, would be considered pseudocommandos.

People who carry out politically motivated suicide bombings and other attacks that kill anywhere from a few victims to thousands in one attack, such as the September 11, 2001, hijackers who took over airplanes and drove them into the World Trade Center, the Pentagon, and a field in Pennsylvania; and the countless occurrences of suicide bombings in the Middle East and South Asia carried out by political and religious extremists are in a class all their own. They are known as *terrorists*. **Terrorism**, legally defined as targeting innocent civilians with violence for political purposes, is now being studied as a distinct type of violent crime (Kegley, 2003).

The *disgruntled employee* is a vengeful person, usually depressed and socially isolated, who retaliates for perceived mistreatment by a current or former employer by killing supervisors, fellow employees, customers, and then, in most cases, committing suicide. Most of these work-related mass murders take place within large, rule-bound organizations such as the U.S. Postal Service. For example, shortly after midnight on December 19, 1997, as 1,500 workers in the main Milwaukee, Wisconsin, post office were sorting mail, Anthony Deculit, a 37-year-old postal service employee, shot and wounded his supervisor who had recently placed him on probation for sleeping on the job. He then killed a man with whom he had frequent disagreements at work and wounded another worker before shooting himself to death. Between 1986 and 1993, 38 postal employees were murdered at their workplace by present or former employees (Solomon & King, 1993). The worst incident occurred in August of 1986, when a part-time letter carrier in Edmond, Oklahoma, killed 14 colleagues and then himself because he expected to be fired.

The postal service is not the only organization to be wracked by mass murder. In 1997 alone, employees killed fellow workers in a manufacturing plant in Aiken, South Carolina; at a plastics company in Los Angeles; and at an embroidery firm in Santa Fe Springs, California (Hardin, 1998d). In March 1998, a Connecticut state lottery accountant shot to death four senior executives (and then killed himself) because of a grievance about pay. Overall, about 20 people a week are killed in workplace violence in the United States ("Hostages Released," 1997), a tenfold increase since 1988.

Disgruntled-employee mass murderers are almost always individuals who have experienced such a profound sense of failure in other aspects of their lives that anything that threatens their job status gravely threatens their self-esteem (Hardin, 1998d). They see murder, and usually suicide, as the only way out. Murder serves as revenge against those who have wronged them, and suicide guarantees that they will not be wronged again.

Hit-and-run murderers typically mail or plant bombs or introduce poison into food or medicine that will be sold to an unsuspecting public. Those who tamper with products are usually motivated by thrill seeking, whereas bombers are usually making a political statement. For decades, the Irish Republican Army detonated bombs in public places to protest British rule in Northern Ireland, Timothy McVeigh's bombing of the Oklahoma City Federal Building was a protest against the U.S. government, and Unabomber Ted Kaczynski saw his bombs as protests against society in general and technology in particular (Glaberson, 1997). Suicide car bombings are one of the major forms of terrorism practiced today by extremists in the Middle East and South Asia.

Overall, most mass murderers tend to be social loners and outcasts with little social support from family or anyone else. They often have a history of substance abuse, especially alcohol abuse, and have many symptoms of severe mental illness (Fessenden, 2000a). Juvenile mass killers differ somewhat from this picture in that they are more likely than adults to have worked with peers in preparing for, if not in executing, their rampages (Fessenden, 2000b). Some attacks are meticulously planned and are often preceded by the stockpiling of weapons. Some mass murderers intend to die at the scene of their rampage, either at the hands of law enforcement officials or by suicide. Their violent outburst is seen as their opportunity to have a few moments of revenge, domination, recognition, and control before they die (Fessenden, 2000a; Hendin, 1994).

Serial Murderers.

Serial murderers kill three or more individuals, but each incident is separated by a cooling-off period of at least 30 days. For example, in April 2000, authorities in Spokane, Washington, arrested Robert Yates, a 47-year-old helicopter pilot and father of five who killed as many as 18 prostitutes over a 10-year period (Walter, 2000). Most serial killers fit the diagnostic criteria for antisocial personality disorder and psychopathy (see chapter 5). Most, like Yates, are White males who murder White females. An exception to this rule was Jeffrey Dahmer, a White male who killed at least nine Black males in 1991 and probably killed many more over a period of 10 years. Female serial killers are rare. Their victims are usually husbands or boyfriends, and they kill for insurance benefits or to gain control of money, property, or other resources. They prefer to kill using cyanide or other poisons, and about half of them have male accomplices (Hickey, 1997). Female killers may also be involved in serial killing by assisting boyfriends or spouses who are themselves serial killers. This was the case with Charlene Gallego, who helped her husband Gerald murder at least 10 people (S. T. Holmes, Hickey, & Holmes 1991). A notable exception to the typical profile of the female serial killer was Aileen Carol Wuornos who on her own shot to death six men after luring them with offers of prostitution. Depicted in the Oscar-winning movie, *Monster* (Patty Jenkins, director, 2003), she was executed in Florida in 1998.

The victims of serial killers are usually easy targets—unaccompanied women, prostitutes, runaways, solitary drifters, and the elderly (Hickey, 1997). Rarely do serial killers break into middle-class homes and kill occupants. There is no way of knowing exactly how many murders each year are the work of serial killers, partly because about 35% of all murders remain unsolved and partly because the deaths of drifters, prostitutes, and the elderly poor are the least likely to be reported promptly or to receive intense scrutiny by the police (Escobar, 1997b).

Criminologists classify serial killers as (a) visionary, (b) mission oriented, (c) hedonistic, and (d) power/control oriented (R. M. Holmes & DeBurger, 1988). The visionary type is generally psychotic and claims to be acting on instructions, from God or inner voices, to eliminate a certain group of people such as homosexuals or prostitutes. The mission-oriented type may not be psychotic but believes that it is his or her duty to destroy certain types of people such as doctors who perform abortions. For example, James Charles Kopp, a member of an extremist group called the Lambs of Christ, eluded federal law enforcement agents for several years before being captured and pleading guilty in May 2003 to killing Dr. Barnett Slepian, a New York doctor who was murdered in his home in October of 1998. John Salvi, another of this group's members had already been convicted of the murders of two abortion clinic workers. Eric Rudolph, who claimed membership in the Lambs of Christ, was also implicated in bombing of abortion clinics, gay night clubs, and bombing of an Atlanta, Georgia, Park during the 1996 Olympics in that city.

The hedonistic type kills for the thrill of it using grisly techniques to gain pleasure from the murder itself. Hannibel Lecter, the fiction character in the famous book *The Silence of the Lambs* (Harris, 1998) as well as Jeffrey Dahmer were famous for torturing and maiming their victims. Closely related is the *power/control* type who seeks satisfaction from having control over the life or death of his or her victims. Many hedonistic and power/control types display a measure of sadism, deriving sexual excitement from the psychological and/or physical suffering of their victims (American Psychiatric Association, 1994). Serial killers may beat, burn, cut, sexually mutilate, and torture their victims before killing them as a means of achieving sexual stimulation and release. Some experts on serial murder believe that even if there is no evidence of sexual sadism as defined in *DSM–IV–TR*, the physical torture that precedes the victim's death often provides the killer with sexual satisfaction (Abrahamsen, 1973). Serial killers almost never use a gun because the murders would be too quick and impersonal, thus depriving them of the "fun" of watching victims suffer.

How does someone become a serial killer? Some researchers blame the same factors we discussed in chapters 7 and 8 as being risks for the development of other kinds of violent crime (Hickey, 1997). For example, many of these killers have suffered some form of head injury or organic brain pathology, such as epilepsy, that compromises information processing and rational decision making. Most serial killers have also experienced severe childhood trauma, usually a combination of physical and psychological abuse and family dysfunction (Cleary & Luxenburg, 1993; Keeney & Heide, 1994). Most were rejected by parents; some witnessed murder, rape, or suicide; and some had sexual relationships with their mothers.

Hickey (1997) argued that in certain individuals, these experiences may lead not only to low self-esteem but to fantasies of violence, perhaps of violent retribution against those who had hurt them. Many report having fantasized about mutilating and killing people even as children (Keppel, 1995). Acting out these fantasies is usually triggered by some environmental cue, often something about the victim that brings back memories of and emotions about someone who once embarrassed or hurt the killer. The killer attacks the victim, said Hickey, in an attempt to remove the memory of the pain. However, because the victim is only a symbol of the hated person, the murder does not erase the traumatic memories or drain away the hatred, so the killer must eventually, and endlessly, kill another similar victim (Hale, 1994).

Hickey (1997) and others (e.g., Cline, 1990; McKenzie, 1995; Strauss & Baron, 1983) believe that substance abuse, particularly alcoholism, and compulsive consumption of pornography may facilitate the expression of the serial killer's murderous impulses. Compulsive attraction to pornography leads to a desire for more and more deviant, bizarre, and explicit material until the person becomes so desensitized to unthinkable acts against women that he begins to play out his fantasies in real life (Cline, 1990). Hickey suggested that, although not true in every case, pornography may stimulate the killer to act out his fantasies, whereas alcohol releases his remaining inhibitions against doing so. In other cases, the killer may simply lose control over rage. For instance, Henry Lucas, a confessed serial killer of dozens of victims, described how his "quick temper" led him to kill his 15-year-old girlfriend by repeatedly stabbing her after she slapped him during an argument (Hickey, 1997).

Many serial killers do indeed have traumatic, even bizarre childhoods. For example, Jeffrey Dahmer was born in Milwaukee in 1960 and grew up a quiet boy in a broken home, a loner who did poorly in school and was the victim of childhood sexual abuse (Matthews, 1992). Like most serial killers, he had a preference for a certain type of victim—in his case dark-skinned gay men. He picked up these men in bath houses and then lured them to his home where he slipped drugs into their drinks so that they would be unconscious and unable to resist his sexual advances. After killing the men, Dahmer mutilated some of them, sometimes removing skin, sometimes dismembering them. Henry Lee Lucas was born in 1936 in Virginia to a prostitute mother who beat him, forced him to watch her having sex with her customers, and made him wear a dress to school. Introduced to bestiality by one of his mother's lovers, he killed for the first time at 15 and ultimately killed his mother. Otis Toole was born in 1947 to a fundamentalist Christian mother who dressed him in skirts and female undergarments because she had hoped for a daughter. His grandmother called him "the devil's child," a term of endearment to her because she was a Satanist. Toole used satanic rituals in some of his murders, the first of which he committed when he was 14. Joseph Kallinger, born in 1936, was adopted by Austrian immigrants who beat him and threatened to castrate him. When he was 8, older boys sexually abused him at knife point. As an adolescent, he masturbated while holding a knife. Robert Joseph Long was born in 1953 with a genetic disorder that caused him to develop unnaturally large breasts. His mother slept with him until he was 13. He suffered a severe head injury in motorcycle accident before he started to kill people, mostly women, whom he first sexually assaulted (Hickey, 1997).

It is noteworthy that Aileen Wuornos, one of the rare females to show a true serial killing pattern, had a childhood similar to that of many male serial killers. Her parents were divorced by the time she was born and her mother left her to be raised by her maternal grandparents, both of whom were alcoholics. Her biological father hanged himself in prison where he was serving time for rape and kidnaping, and her adoptive grandfather committed suicide. By the age of 12, she exhibited hearing loss, vision problems, an IQ of 81, and poor performance in school. A family friend raped her when she was 14. Forced to have the baby, she gave it up for adoption and left home to begin a life of drug and alcohol abuse and prostitution.

Profiling Murderers

The movie *The Silence of the Lambs* (Jonathan Demme, director, 1991) was one of the first media vehicles to raise public awareness of the work of the FBI's Behavioral Science Unit at Quantico, Virginia. This unit is the major U.S. center for research on and the practice of **criminal profiling**, a process in which investigators study the characteristics of a known crime and then work backward to try to determine the characteristics of the person who might be responsible for the crime. Profiling, also known as "retroclassification" (Douglas, Burgess, Burgess, & Reseller, 1992), is used not only to track serial killers but also to characterize those who repeatedly rape, set fires, commit terrorist acts, or serve as drug couriers (Monahan & Walker, 1990).

Criminal profilers begin with information about the demographic, family, and personality characteristics of those who have previously been convicted of crimes similar to those currently under investigation. This information comes from law enforcement files as well as from personal interviews with known offenders—including Charles Manson, Richard Speck, David Berkowitz, and other notorious mass murderers and serial killers—to discover how each selects and approaches victims, how they react to their crimes, their reasons for killing, and the like (Ressler & Schachtman, 1992). Next, profilers consider information about evidence left at each crime scene that might serve as this killer's personal "signature" or "calling card" such as a particular sequence or method of torture. Experience-based guesses about the killer's characteristics solicited from psychologists, criminologists, crime investigators, and other experts also contribute to the pool of data analyzed by specially programmed computers. The resulting criminal profile offers a reasonably detailed description of the sort of person the police should be seeking. This profile is continuously revised as new information or updated theories become available.

Results of the profiling process have ranged from amazingly accurate to embarrassingly erroneous (B. Porter; 1983; Ressler, Burgess, & Douglas, 1988; Rider, 1980). One of the first examples of successful criminal profiling came in 1957 with the arrest of George Matesky, the so-called Mad Bomber of New York City. After trying for over a decade to identify the person responsible for more than 30 bombings in the New York area, the police consulted Dr. James Brussel, a local psychiatrist. Brussel examined pictures of the bomb scenes and analyzed letters sent to police by the bomber. Based on these data, Brussel advised the police to look for a heavyset, middle-aged, Eastern European, Catholic man who was single and lived with a sibling or an aunt. He predicted that when the man was found, he would be wearing a buttoned double-breasted suit. When the police arrested Matesky, the profile was uncannily correct, right down to the clothes he was wearing (Brussel, 1978).

Relying too heavily on criminal profiles can lead to errors, however. For example, after a bomb exploded at the 1996 Olympic Games in Atlanta, Georgia, police used an FBI profile to focus their search for suspects. It told them to look for a White, single, middle-class male who craved the spotlight and wanted to be in law enforcement. (The profilers recalled that a security guard who had "discovered" a bomb at the 1984 Olympics had actually planted it.) Richard Jewell, a security guard working at the Olympics, fit this profile and was arrested almost immediately. Subsequent investigation showed that he was innocent, however. It was not until September of 1998 that the FBI announced that it had linked the Olympic bombing to Eric Robert Rudolph, the antiabortion extremist we mentioned earlier in this chapter (Sack, 1998).

Indeed, one of the main problems with criminal profiling is that often too many suspects fit the profile, leading the police to focus on the wrong one or leaving them uncertain about whom to arrest. For example, in September 1988, after several women disappeared in Poughkeepsie, New York, police there began observing a number of men, including Kendall "Stinky" Francois, who fit an FBI serial killer profile. However, they did not know whether to arrest any of them until a woman reported having escaped from Francois after he abducted her at knifepoint. In his house they found the bodies of three women (Belluck, 1999).

Despite the problems associated with retrospective profiling, behavioral scientists and law enforcement officers work together in an effort to predict who might be a murderer. A recent successful collaboration resulted in the FBI's publication on how school teachers and administrators, parents, and others can recognize the warning signs of young people who may be potential school killers (FBI, 2000). The downside is that innocent young people who are not threats may be wrongly singled out (Forrest, 1999).

Aggravated Assault and Domestic Violence

Under English common law, a system that remains the basis for some U.S. states' criminal codes, assault and battery are different offenses. **Assault** does not require actually touching a victim, only attempting to do so or even just leading someone to believe that they are about to be attacked. **Battery** means unwanted (often called offensive) touching of another by means of pushing, hitting, punching, kicking, or other bodily contact. The criminal codes of many states also recognize an offense called simple assault, which is battery without intent to do serious bodily harm. **Simple assault** is a misdemeanor, meaning that the maximum punishment is only a year in jail and a fine.

In contrast to simple assault, **aggravated assault** is an unlawful attack by one person on another for inflicting severe bodily injury (FBI, 2004a). This type of assault is usually perpetrated with a weapon or by other means (such as the use of fists or feet) likely to produce death or great bodily harm. Indeed, many cases of aggravated assault are actually unsuccessful murder attempts (FBI, 2004a). In some states, aggravated assault is known as *malicious wounding*, but whatever the label, it is a felony, usually carrying a prison term of up to 20 years.

In 2003, there were slightly more than 850,000 arrests for aggravated assault, a number that shows a continuing decline that began in 1994 (the 2003 rate is 31% below that of 1994; FBI, 2004a). About 35% of aggravated assaults were committed with blunt objects. Hands, fists, and feet were used in 27% of the assaults; firearms in 19%; knives or other cutting instruments in 18%; and the remainder other weapons.

Same-sex aggravated assaults against nonfamily members have not generated much research, perhaps because such cases are a variant on interpersonal violence in general. There is great research interest, however, in domestic violence, which involves aggravated assault of family members or people living as a family unit.

Domestic Violence

Although it has received increasing publicity in the recent years, physical abuse of intimate partners is nothing new. In ancient Rome, husbands were encouraged to punish their wives for domestic misdeeds and were required to do so if the wives committed adultery. In Europe during the Middle Ages, a husband was expected to punish his wife for "misbehavior" lest he himself suffer punishment at the hands of his neighbors. From the late Middle ages to modern times, there was little objection to "wife beating" as long as it did not result in death or disfigurement. It was not until the mid-19th century that physical punishment of wives lost public support in mainstream Western cultures. Even now, however, traditional cultures and subcultures around the world (including some in the United States) perpetuate the notion of disciplining one's wife and of the husband's duty as "man of the house" to keep both his wife and children in line (L. Walker, 2000). In the United States, the tide of public opinion has clearly turned against the use of physical violence toward wives and, to a lesser extent, toward children. Cultural norms are slow to change, however, and domestic violence in the United States is still rampant. According to the Centers for Disease Control and Prevention (CDCP, 2003), nearly 5.3 million intimate partner victimizations occur each year among U.S. women ages 18 and older. This violence results in nearly 2 million injuries and nearly 1,300 deaths.

Because so many unmarried couples are living together, most states have revised their criminal codes to allow prosecution of "family violence" when domestic partners are cohabiting in a family-like setting whether they are married or not. These code revisions mean that prosecution of violence in such situations can occur in the state's version of family (or domestic relations) court, which has the authority to impose special remedies and punishments (such as excluding one partner from the family residence).

Both men and women experience domestic violence. However, women are 2 to 3 times more likely to report an intimate partner pushed, grabbed, or shoved them, and 7 to 14 times more likely to report an intimate partner beat them up, choked them, or tied them down (Tjaden & Thoennes, 2000a). Some of the difference in numbers may be because men are not as likely to report violence against them. Reviewing dozens of studies of physical violence in heterosexual relationships, psychologist John Archer (1995) found that although women sustain more serious and visible injuries than men during domestic disputes, they are just as likely as men to resort to physical aggression during an argument with an intimate partner including slapping, kicking, biting, choking, and using a weapon (Zuger, 1998). This fact has been obscured until recently because it has usually been men who are charged and arrested in domestic violence cases. The picture is changing, however, in states where laws require police to make arrests if they have reason to believe that physical violence occurred between intimate partners regardless of gender. Many women in those states have been shocked to find themselves behind bars (Mundy, 1997).

The Roots of Domestic Violence

People who engage in domestic violence are not necessarily any different from other violent people. Violence toward loved ones stems from the same roots as violence toward strangers and acquaintances: The perpetrators have not developed sufficient control over their emotions and behavior. However, research has suggested that battering and even killing a spouse or intimate partner is associated with varying combinations of experiences, personality characteristics, and situational factors. Individual factors include:

1. Young age
2. Low self-esteem
3. Low income
4. Low academic achievement
5. Involvement in aggressive or delinquent behavior as a young person
6. Alcohol and drug use
7. Witnessing or experiencing violence as a child
8. Lack of social networks and social isolation
9. Unemployment (Walker, L., 2000; Berkowitz, 1993)

Relationship factors also contribute to interpersonal domestic violence. These include (1) a high degree of marital conflict and instability, (2) belief in strict gender roles in a relationship that is characterized by male dominance in the family coupled with female emotional dependence and insecurity, (3) desire for power and control by one of the partners (usually the man), and (4) frequent anger and hostility toward a partner (Heise & Garcia-Moreno, 2002; Kantor & Jasinski, 1998).

For many, the assault and battery of a spouse or partner is part of a more general pattern of physical violence toward others (including nonrelations and former partners) or at least part of a history of bad temper and poor impulse control. For example, Lorena Bobbitt, a woman who was acquitted of malicious wounding after cutting off her husband's penis, was arrested several years later for beating her mother (Ross, 2005). Her allegedly abusive husband, John Bobbitt, was subsequently convicted of beating a girlfriend after he and Lorena were divorced. Similarly, a 46 year-old Maryland man was arrested for assaulting his wife but was released after she refused to testify against him (Shapira, 2004). Within hours, he stabbed and slashed her to death and was on his way to murder her boyfriend when police intercepted him (Pan, 1997). This man's history of assaults and armed robbery spanned 30 years. In short, people who are not predisposed to be violent in general are unlikely to beat up a spouse or a child (Holtzworth-Monroe, 2000).

Results of the 1985 National Family Violence Survey (Straus & Gelles, 1990) provided data on domestic violence in relation to men's occupations (blue collar vs. white collar), alcohol consumption, and attitudes about the acceptability of hitting a spouse or partner. Men who drank often were more likely to have hit their wives than were men who used alcohol infrequently, regardless of their occupational level and attitudes toward assaulting partners. The highest rate of domestic violence—among blue-collar binge drinkers who approved of wife assaults—was eight times greater than among white-collar men who drank little and did not approve of domestic assault (Straus & Gelles, 1990). There is also a high rate of fatal domestic violence involving men who have ready access to guns including male police officers. When these men become involved in domestic disputes, arguments that might otherwise end in bruises and hurt feelings can escalate into murder. In fact, firearms were the major weapon type used in intimate partner homicides from 1981 to 1998 (Paulozzi, Saltzman, Thompson, & Holmgreen, 2001).

Domestic violence also tends to be associated with high levels of economic and situational stress. Vulnerability factors include marital instability, poor family functioning, and marital conflict that leads to arguments and then to violence, as the partner who is most inclined to react violently feels pushed to the breaking point (Heise & Garcia-Moreno, 2002; Straus & Gelles, 1990). As we show later, assaults against children can be evoked in the same way.

Domestic violence against a partner is different from, say, assault and battery on the street because the victim and offender remain together afterward in a conflict-filled situation that sets the stage for continued violence. Why do abused partners stay in such situations? Theories abound ranging from those that focus on economic and emotional dependence and "battered spouse syndrome" (a variation on PTSD) to learned helplessness and depression (e.g., Ewing, 1987; Grant, 1995; L. Walker, 2000). Many victims tolerate domestic violence because they too have witnessed it among adults in their own childhood homes and may have experienced physical abuse early in life. These people may have come to expect that violence is a normal part of adult relationships. Some chronic victims of domestic violence display alcohol problems, personality disorder (often dependent personality disorder), low self-esteem, and may meet *DSM–IV–TR* criteria for depression. Some victims who tolerate a continuing pattern of domestic abuse appear to have weighed the costs and benefits and concluded that they have more to gain by staying or perhaps more to lose by leaving. The special tragedy of these cases is that successive generations of new perpetrators and new victims—as well as society at large—will continue to suffer because neither partner is willing or able to leave the situation.

There may be hope on the horizon, however. Data published in 2000 (Bureau of Justice Statistics, 2000) indicate that the rate of domestic violence, including murders, is declining. For example, between 1976 and 1998, the number of men murdered by spouses and girlfriends dropped by almost two thirds. The number of Black females killed by spouses, boyfriends, or ex-boyfriends decreased by 45%. Overall, murders of female partners by male partners decreased 14% (Bureau of Justice Statistics, 2000). These decreases have been attributed to a variety of factors including legal and social programs for female victims of domestic violence that resulted in better anger management and coping skills among men and a greater tendency for women to leave violent relationships (Butterfield, 2000).

Stalking

When abused men and women seek to escape violent spouses or partners, they may become victims of stalking. Stalking began to appear in state criminal codes in the early 1990s as legislators focused increasing attention on problems associated with domestic violence (Tjaden, 1997). **Stalking** is a course of conduct directed at a specific person that involves repeated physical or visual proximity; nonconsensual communication; or verbal, written, or implied threats sufficient to cause harm (Tjaden, 1997). Even more specific definitions are found in criminal codes. For instance, the Virginia statute defines stalking as "conduct directed at another person with the intent to place, or with the knowledge that the conduct places, another person in reasonable fear of death, sexual assault, or bodily injury" (Virginia Code Section 18.2–60.3). Estimates indicate that more than one million women and 371,000 men are stalked by intimate partners each year (Tjaden & Thoennes, 2000b).

A survey (Tjaden, 1997) of more than 8,000 women and 8,000 men sponsored by the National Institute of Justice and the Centers for Disease Control and Prevention found that 80% of stalking victims are women and that 87% of male stalkers act alone to target a former or current spouse, wife, or girlfriend. Of stalking by intimate partners, 60% starts before their relationship ends, and 80% of women stalked by a former husband or boyfriends have been physically assaulted by them during that relationship; 31% had been sexually assaulted (Tjaden, 1997). When women engage in stalking, it is more likely to be aimed at a stranger or acquaintance, and they often are assisted by a girlfriend or other accomplice.

Stalkers have been categorized in several ways (Dietz, 1991; R. M. Holmes, 1993; McAnaney, Curliss, & Abeyta-Price, 1993), the most general of which describes them as erotomanic, love obsessional, or simple obsessional (Wallace, 1998). Most stalkers, including those whose victims are current or former domestic partners, are the simple-obsessional type. As the name implies, they are obsessed with knowing about the whereabouts and activities of their victims. *Erotomanic stalkers* falsely believe their victims—usually of higher status, of the opposite gender, and often a celebrity—are in love with them (Dietz, 1991). Margaret Ray, the woman who stalked David Letterman for several years, fits this category (Bruni, 1988). *Love-obsessional stalkers* are also usually delusional. They believe that if they can only get the victim's attention, the victim will fall in love with them. John Hinckley, who sought to attract actress Jodi Foster's attention by shooting President Ronald Reagan, exemplifies the love-obsessional stalker (Johnson, K., 2003).

Given the obsessional nature of most stalking behaviors, it should not be surprising that stalkers tend to repeat their crimes. A total of 80% of stalkers violate orders that they refrain from contact with the victim (Tjaden, 1997). In many states, the first offense is a misdemeanor, but repeat acts are felonies. Virtually all statutes provide for increased penalties with each offense.

Physical and Sexual Abuse of Children

There were an estimate number of 826,000 cases of confirmed child physical abuse in 1999 (National Committee to Prevent Child Abuse, 1999). There were an estimated 1,400 child fatalities reported in 2002[2]; 79% of victims were abused and/or murdered by one of their parents (U.S. Department of Health and Human Services, 2002). Overall, girls are somewhat more likely than boys to be the victims of abuse (52% vs. 47%, respectively), but girls are three times more likely than boys to be victims of sexual abuse. Further, girls over the age of 12 are more than twice as likely to be killed as boys (U.S. Department of Health and Human Services, 1997).

Although some people who batter and kill their children suffer mental disorders, most are relatively normal individuals whose abusive actions occur when they are angry or frustrated. Later, these people are usually aware of the role their anger played in the incident, and they regret their actions (Dietrich, Berkowitz, Kadushin, & McGloin, 1990). Many of the same situational stressors and personal characteristics associated with violence toward a spouse or other intimate partner—persistent conflict, money problems, poor impulse control, a bad temper, abuse of alcohol, and having been abused as a child—can also set the stage for child abuse. The incidence of child abuse is highest in households where single parents live in poverty, with annual incomes below $15,000 (U.S. Department of Health and Human Services, 1995b).

---

[2]This figure is probably an underestimate because many child deaths attributed to noncriminal causes might actually have resulted from abuse. For example, in August 1998, Pennsylvania authorities charged a 69-year-old woman with murdering 8 of her 10 children over a 19-year period beginning in 1949. Their deaths had previously been unexplained or attributed to sudden infant death syndrome.

One study (Kadushin & Martin, 1981) found that 68% of adults who had been reported to authorities for beating their children were unemployed, short of money, coping with illness, and having problems with their partners at the time. Many said that in these stressful circumstances, it was a child's trivial misdeed that triggered their violent outburst (Kadushin & Martin, 1981). One woman described becoming so angry at her children's refusal to clean off the dinner table that when one child played with his food, "I put the knife to him. … I pressed it in him. I was so damn mad" (Kadushin & Martin, 1981, p. 228). In other words, abusive parents are likely to have such poor impulse control that situational factors can unleash aggressive impulses. The danger of losing control is such that parent-training programs usually advise adults not to use any form of physical punishment when they are angry.

Some data has suggested that mothers are considerably more likely than fathers to be the perpetrators of child abuse (Daley & Wilson, 1996; Fagan, 1977), but male offenders are responsible for three fourths of the child abuse incidents reported to police including 92% of sexual assaults and 68 % of physical assaults (U.S. Department of Health & Human Services, 1995b).

Although child abuse can occur in any kind of family, it would appear that the safest environment for children is in a home in which their biological parents are married and living together. The second safest is one in which the children are living with a divorced parent who has remarried. The most dangerous environment is a home where an unmarried mother is cohabiting with a live-in boyfriend who is not the children's father (Fagan, 1997).

Child Sexual Abuse. An estimated 89,000 cases of child sexual abuse were substantiated in 2000 (U.S. Department of Health and Human Services, Substance Abuse and Mental Health Services Administration, 2000). Of all confirmed cases, 96% of child sexual abuse involve adults who are members of the child's family or are persons known to or trusted by the child. Further, 84% of all confirmed cases of child sexual abuse occur in the child's own home (U.S. Department of Justice, 2000). Most victims of child sexual abuse are females, and the percentage of female victims increase with age. That is, 69% of victims of sexual abuse under the age of 6 were female compared with 73% of victims under 12 and 95% at age 19 (U.S. Department of Justice, 2000).

Developing technology has enabled sexual crimes against children. A 2000 survey (Finklehor et al., 2000) found that 19% of children who use the Internet received unwanted sexual solicitation in the past year. Sexual predators "meet" boys and girls in online "chat" rooms, and some of these virtual hookups lead to real-life meetings that are charged as abductions.

Hate Crimes

In June of 1998, three White men—John William King, 23; Shawn Berry, 24; and Lawrence Russell Brewer, 31—offered a ride to James Byrd, Jr., a Black man whom they saw walking down a back road near the small town of Jasper, Texas (Fox, 1999). Instead of taking him home, they drove Byrd to a wooded area where they beat him. Then they killed him by chaining him to the back of their truck and dragging him for several miles. King had been Brewer's cell mate at a Texas state penitentiary from 1995 to 1997 where King was serving time for burglary. Brewer helped King join the Confederate Knights of America, a White supremacist prison gang that "protected" its members from Black and Hispanic inmates and gangs. It appeared that the Byrd killing was an effort by King to attract members to a hate group he was founding in Jasper. Four months later in Laramie Wyoming, Russell Henderson, 21, and Aaron McKinney, 22, abducted, robbed, and viciously beat Matthew Shepard, a 21 year-old University of Wyoming student who was known to be gay (Black, 1999). They left him tied to a fence in a remote area, and although Shepard was found and taken to a hospital, he died of his injuries a few days later.

These cases exemplify **hate crimes**, also known as *bias-motivated crimes*, which are criminal offenses caused by hatred based on a victim's race/ethnicity, religion, sexual orientation, handicap, or national origin (FBI, 2004). Hate crimes are defined not by what only is done but by their motivation, by the offender's bias against the victim. Thus, hate crimes can include murder and nonnegligent manslaughter; forcible rape; aggravated assault; simple assault; intimidation; robbery, burglary; larceny and motor vehicle theft; arson; and destruction, damage, or vandalism of property.

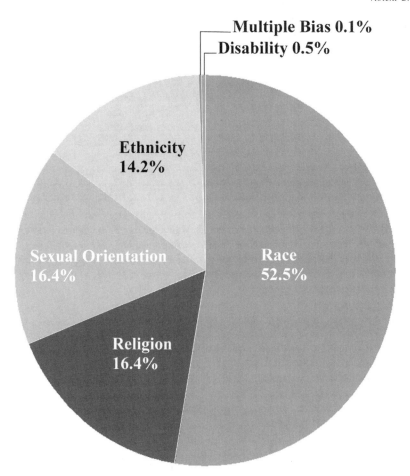

Multiple Bias 0.1%
Disability 0.5%

Ethnicity
14.2%

Sexual Orientation
16.4%

Race
52.5%

Religion
16.4%

FIGURE 10.1 *Hate Crime Victims by Categories.* **From** *Crime in the United States—2003*, **by Federal Bureau of Investigation, 2004, Washington DC: Government Printing Office.**

Hate crimes can target one person or an entire population. Recent efforts at "ethnic cleansing" in Kosovo and Bosnia and at genocide in Rwanda have their counterparts in the ancient Romans' persecution of Christians and in Hitler's attempt to exterminate Jews, Gypsies, and other "inferior" groups. In fact, it can be argued that hate crimes have shaped world history (Hamm, 1996). In the United States, most hate crimes are driven by ethnic and religious biases, although crimes against homosexuals are recently resurgent as well (see Figure 10.1). The first victims of hate crimes in North America were American Indians. They were terrorized, persecuted, uprooted, displaced, and even murdered first by European colonists and then in a more systematic way by the U.S. government as its domain expanded from sea to shining sea (e.g., D. Brown, 1988; Stannard, 1993). The tradition of hate crime in the United States has continued over the past 200 years in the form of lynchings of Blacks; firebombing and vandalism designed to drive Black, Asian, or other minority families from predominantly White neighborhoods; assaults and bombings aimed at homosexuals and their businesses; and desecration of Jewish synagogues and cemeteries with swastikas and other Nazi symbols. There has also been such a surge in anti-Muslim hate crimes since the September 11, 2001, terrorist attacks, although incidents against Jews is more than 10 times greater than those against Muslims (FBI, 2004). Of all religious groups, Jewish people are most likely to be targets of hate crimes.

Even before the Byrd and Shepard murders in 1998, hate crimes in the United States had been getting increasing public scrutiny, largely as a result of several other sensational incidents over the previous 15 years.

The 1984 shooting death in Denver, Colorado, of controversial radio talk show host Alan Berg focused national attention on the activities of a previously unknown cadre of White supremacists who killed Berg because of his "liberal" views toward Blacks and homosexuals (Hillard, 2004). Two years later, three Black men were attacked, and one was killed simply for being in Howard Beach, a predominantly White New York City neighborhood (Hillard, 2004). As bad as these incidents were, it was the bombings of numerous Black churches in the Southern United States in 1995 and 1996 that brought public awareness and concern over bias-motivated crimes to a head. Political and religious leaders realized that the disproportionate number of Black churches being burned indicated that the nation was experiencing a serious wave of hate crimes. The resulting 298 federal arson investigations lead to the arrest of more than 120 suspects and to many convictions (Fletcher, 1996).

About 63% of hate crimes reported in 2003 were perpetrated against persons (FBI, 2004a); the remainder were against property. Intimidation was the most frequent person-oriented crime (almost 50%) followed by simple assault and aggravated assault. Of hate crimes directed against property, destruction, damage, or vandalism were the most frequently reported offenses (FBI, 2004a). The largest percentage of hate crimes are based on victims' ethnicity or religion (see Fig. 10.1).

Hate crimes comprise a relatively small part of the total crime picture in the United States, but their effects extend far beyond their immediate victims. Hate crimes engender fear and anger in virtually every member of the ethnic, religious, or other group targeted by the perpetrators. Further, as seen in the Middle East, South Asia, and various urban centers in the United States, hate crimes tend to create endless cycles of retaliation and counterretaliation between opposing groups.

Characteristics of Hate Crime Offenders

In 2003, 62% of hate-crime offenders were White, and 18% were Black (FBI, 2004a). Very few hate crime offenders know their victims. In 85% of the 452 hate crimes reported to the Boston police in 1996, for example, offenders and victims were strangers to each other (FBI, 1997). About half of all hate crimes are committed by people under the age of 20, which is double the percentage of young people involved in other types of crimes (Bureau of Justice Statistics, 1999). Between 17% and 26% of hate crimes are committed by people under 18 (Bishop & Slowikowski, 1995).

Hate criminals' acts are often impulsive and associated with the disinhibitory effects of alcohol or other drugs. Most perpetrators are thrill seekers who randomly target members of minority groups for harassment and violence; a few (about 2%) are "mission offenders" who believe it is their sacred duty to help rid the world of evil (Levin & McDevitt, 1993). Behind the bullying facade of most hate criminals lies intense insecurity and low-self esteem. Many hate crime offenders are fundamentalist Christians (typically involved in anti-Jewish and antihomosexual acts), fundamentalist Jews (often charged with anti-Muslim acts), and White supremacists (who perpetrate crimes against Black Americans, Jews, homosexuals, and almost anyone else they perceive to be different and therefore inferior). The FBI keeps an especially close watch on "skinheads," a hate group whose members target Blacks and homosexuals. Skinheads generally range in age from 15 to 25, express devotion to "White pride," patriotism, and the rights of the working class. They first appeared in the United States in 1980 but originated in England in the 1970s as part of a movement that included punk rockers, neo-Nazis, and right-wing political protesters (F. E. Hagan, 1997).

What Causes Hate Crimes?

Most hate crimes stem from and are fueled by stereotypes and prejudice. Psychologists define stereotypes as beliefs about other people's attributes based on their membership in some group defined by ethnicity, religion, gender, sexual orientation, age, handicap, or some other identifying factor. *Stereotypes* create the false impression that all members of some defined group share certain, usually negative, characteristics. *Prejudice* involves holding an unjustifiable, usually negative, attitude toward members of a stereotyped group. Literally meaning prejudgment, prejudice results when a judgment about a person is based not on their actual behavior or characteristics but solely on their membership in a stereotyped group.

Prejudice has many sources including resentment brought on by social inequalities, dogmatic religious teachings, the desire to conform to the views of prejudiced peers and elders, and fear and hatred of anyone who is perceived as different (Aronson, 2004; Brehm & Kassin, 2005). Perpetrators of hate crimes typically engage in scapegoating, which in the context of hate crimes means blaming members of a certain group for personal or societal problems. Scapegoating leads some prejudiced people to take out their frustrations on those whom they perceive to be at fault for whatever they are unhappy about. It is no wonder then that hate crimes are especially likely when economic times are tough, when unemployment is high, and when certain ethnic groups are perceived to be getting more than their fair share of resources or enjoying "too much" in the way of economic power or privileges. Many cases of anti-Asian crimes, for example, are motivated by envy of many Asian people's academic and economic success.

Some researchers have argued that the increase in hate crimes seen in the United States during the early 1990s was provoked by an economic recession as well as strong foreign competition for jobs and global markets. During the presidential election campaign in 1992, Americans were inundated with a continuous stream of political messages designed to create fear and resentment of immigrants. At the same time, a surge of immigration was making the U.S. population more ethnically diverse than ever, and many people were uncomfortable with that situation (Dees & Corcoran, 1996). Public debate was raging over the appropriate role of the federal government; some felt that it was doing too much for "them" (meaning immigrants) and not enough for "us" (the White working class). Institutions of every kind were being bashed. "Shock radio" and other populist talk-show hosts were attracting a growing national audience, and the tone of discourse on social and political issues grew increasingly insular, angry, and hateful. Worse, the violence portrayed on television and in movies had helped desensitize viewers to the horrors of acting out angry impulses, thus creating a perfect climate for hate crimes.

Hate crimes also correlate with external events. For example, when Japanese products were beginning to cut heavily into the sales of U.S.-made automobiles and electronic equipment, there was an increase in hate crimes against Japanese people in the United States. Similarly, hate crimes against Arab Americans increased during the 1990 Gulf War, after the Oklahoma City bombing when an initial outpouring of anti-Arab-American sentiment was fueled by the (incorrect) assumption that Arabs were responsible for the blast, and after the September 11, 2001 terrorist attacks on the United States.

Once a climate of hatred is created, hate crimes tend to occur sporadically as impulse, opportunity, and victim availability allow. However, if a single high-profile trigger incident occurs—such the March 1991 police beating of Los Angeles motorist Rodney King—it can set off a wave of hate crimes, sometimes leading to a cycle of retaliatory and counterretaliatory crimes or even civil disorder. As in the King case, the wave of hate crimes begun by an incident in one city can spread to many other cities as well.

Hate crimes illustrate the intertwining of many of the roots of crime we have discussed throughout this book. Individual psychology; social, political, and cultural influences; ethnic profiling; perpetrators' beliefs that they are enforcing the social norm; and economic stressors and conditions can all combine to trigger acts against a hated group. Nowhere is this combination more obvious than in relation to hate crimes against homosexuals.

Fear and dislike of homosexuals is rampant in the United States. For example, a survey of 500 young men in the San Francisco Bay area found that half of them admitted to having committed some form of antigay aggression including name calling, threats, or physical violence (H. B. Franklin, 1998). These men gave one or more of four reasons for their aggression. The first is self defense. Some claimed that all homosexuals are sexual predators and that aggression against them was justified to protect oneself from predation. (This was the claim made by Matthew Shepard's killers; they said they had attacked to "teach him to stay away from them"). A second reason involved ideology. Some assailants viewed themselves as enforcers of the social norm who punish homosexuals for their moral transgressions. A third reason was thrill seeking. Some assailants have claimed to have assaulted gays or lesbians to relieve boredom, "have fun," or feel strong. Finally, some men reported having committed antihomosexual assaults to prove their toughness and heterosexuality to their friends (H. B. Franklin, 1998).

The Politics of Hate Crimes

As the problem of hate crime steadily moved up the political agendas of government leaders during the 1980s, the U.S. Congress enacted the 1990 Hate Crime Statistics Act, which required the FBI's UCR Program to develop a hate crime data collection system. In September 1994, this law was expanded so that the *UCR* would include crimes motivated by hatred of a victim's mental or physical disabilities. Data collection on disability-related crimes began in January 1997.

In 1993, the U.S. Supreme Court held unanimously that although it is unconstitutional to prohibit hate speech on the basis of its content, it is constitutional to impose harsher-than-usual punishment for crimes that were motivated by bias against a victim's ethnicity or other personal characteristics. The Court's ruling meant that although the government cannot infringe on a person's freedom of expression, states can increase penalties for crimes that are based on bias against victims' personal attributes (Biskupic, 1998; S. E. Martin, 1995).

With the exception of Wyoming (where the Shepard murder occurred), Arkansas, Georgia, Hawaii, Indiana, Kansas, Kentucky, New Mexico, and South Carolina, most states have some form of hate-crime laws. All but two of these laws (in Texas and Utah) identify one or more protected victim characteristics. Of these, 20 mention race, religion, or ethnicity; 11 mention sexual orientation; 11 cover gender; and 12 include other categories such as mental or physical disability (Lyman, 1998). After the Shepard and Byrd murders, however, civil rights groups began new campaigns to enact or strengthen state hate crime laws and to demand new federal legislation that would increase penalties for bias-motivated crimes.

The success of these campaigns is by no means certain, however. For example, the Byrd murder resulted in the death penalty for two of his killers and a life sentence for a third but only because it occurred in the course of an abduction (which made it a capital offense in Texas). The state could have invoked its hate crime statute but did not do so because, according to some observers, the prosecutors would have suffered severe criticism and political damage in their conservative jurisdiction (Lyman, 1998). Indeed, efforts to amend the Texas hate crime law to specifically name the groups it covers was defeated in May 1999 because the proposed amendment mentioned homosexuals as a protected group (Duggan, 1999b). Fear of being seen as "soft" on homosexuality has stalled similar legislation in other states. There are other reasons why many legal scholars and judges (including the late Supreme Court Chief Justice William Rehnquist) have been against new hate crime legislation (K. Potter, 1998). They have argued that simply adding more anticrime laws does not deter crime, that criminal laws should not create special classes of victims, and that federal laws should not be enacted that could supersede state law.

Sex Crimes

A junior high school principal admits to having sex with male students over a 2-year period. Scores of female U.S. Air Force Academy cadets report being sexually assaulted by male cadets. A stepfather repeatedly molests his stepdaughter who is in her early teens. A mother makes her children watch while she has sex with her boyfriend and then makes the children participate. An 84-year-old woman is raped in her home by the man who had just completed a prison term for raping her several years earlier. An 11-year-old boy is arrested for repeatedly raping a 5-year-old girl. New prisoners are sized up and targeted for gang-rape initiation into prison society. As these examples illustrate, sex crimes take many forms, and the victims can be male or female, young or old. Here, we examine several types of rape and child molestation, the most serious forms of sex crime.

Forcible Rape

The only sex crime reported in the *UCR* is **forcible rape**, which is defined as "the carnal knowledge [sexual intercourse] of a female forcibly and against her will" (FBI, 2004a).[3] In 2003, there were more than 93,400 reports of forcible or attempted rape in the U.S. (FBI, 2004a).

Almost 38% of the forcible rapes reported in 2003 took place in the most populous Southern states; 25% occurred in the Midwest, 24% in the West, and 13% in the Northeast. Forcible rapes are most likely to occur in July, are least likely in February (FBI, 2003) and tend to occur between 6:00 p.m. and midnight and more on weekends than on weekdays (Perkins & Klaus, 1996). More than one-third of forcible rapes by acquain-

---

[3]The *UCR* definition excludes *statutory rape* in which force is not used but rape is presumed based on the age difference between victim and offender or merely on the young age of the victim.

tances take place in or near the victim's home, whereas more than half of rapes perpetrated by strangers occur in parking lots, alleys, or other public areas (R. Bachman, 1994). Weapons are used in 28% of rapes by strangers but in only 8% of acquaintance rapes (Dobrin, Wierseman, Colin, & McDowall, 1996). Firearms are used in only 6% of all rapes (Perkins & Klaus, 1996).

Date Rape. From a legal standpoint, **date rape**, also known as acquaintance rape, is no different from any other type of forcible rape; it simply refers to unwanted sexual intercourse in the context of a dating relationship (Shotland, 1992). Thus, there is no law concerning date rape *per se*, but if the victim can prove that she did not consent to sex, her attacker will be just as likely to be convicted of rape as if he were a stranger. Men, too, are sometimes raped by female acquaintances, but the methods differ from those of date rape by men. Female victims report being coerced for sexual intercourse through detainment, persistent touching, lies, and being held down, whereas male victims report engaging in unwanted sexual behavior as a result of blackmail or threats with weapons (Waldner-Haugrud & Magruder, 1995).

The most common feature of date rape is the tendency for both parties to have been drinking heavily (Allison & Wrightsman, 1993) and to blame each other for what occurred. In one survey (Stormo, Lang, & Stritzke, 1997), 742 undergraduates were asked to assign blame for rapes in which both offender and victim were intoxicated to varying degrees. In general, women blamed the victim more than the offender for date rape. When each member of the pair was described as equally intoxicated, the victim was perceived to be more blameworthy; only when the victim was more intoxicated than the assailant did the assailant receive the bulk of the blame (Stormo, Lang, & Stritzke, 1997). On college campuses, certain bars and party venues present higher risks for date rape (Boswell & Spade, 1996). The problem has become so common that both men and women at some schools are offered special educational programs about the dangers of date rape and how to avoid it.

Who Rapes? According to 2003 data, 64% of rapists are White, 33% are Black, and the rest represent other ethnic groups (FBI, 2004a). In the vast majority of cases, rapists attack members of their own ethnic group. Rapists tend to be younger than other sexual offenders. Of them, 46% are under age 25, 31% under 21, 16% are under 18, and 6% under the age of 15 (FBI, 2004a).The number of rapes perpetrated by males under the age of 15 has doubled from 3% to 6% between 1961 and 1995, and the number of rapes involving offenders under the age of 10 has more than tripled over the last 25 years (FBI, 1996). Young rapists tend to be extremely violent and dangerous (Miethe & McCorkle, 1998).

A number of studies have outlined the characteristics of adolescent rapists (e.g., Davis & Leitenberg, 1987; Fehrenbach et al., 1993; Knight & Prentky, 1987). About 10% of these rapists have reported being sexually abused by family members (Fehrenbach, P. A., Smith, W., Monastersky, C., & Deisher, R. W., 1986), and 20% have reported exposure to physical abuse and severe family dysfunction such as parental alcoholism or suicide (Hsu & Starzynki, 1990). The most common characteristics shared by adolescent sexual offenders, however, is a deficiency in social skills and social support. Many report that they have no friends, feel powerless, and lack motivation for school or work (Groth, 1977; Groth & Loredo, 1981). If they have had contact with mental health professionals, they are commonly given a diagnosis of conduct disorder (Prentky & Knight, 1986). Like many other violent young offenders, adolescent rapists may have neurological and cognitive deficits (Prentky & Quinsey, 1988) that may help account for their failure to succeed in school (Fehrenbach, Smith, Monastersky, & Deisher, 1986; Prentky & Quinsey, 1988).

Other developmental factors associated with violent adolescent sex offenders include (a) parenting that downplayed nurturing in favor of toughness and failed to encourage the development of empathy for the suffering of others, (b) learning of negative attitudes toward women, (c) reinforcement of myths that women "like it rough" and enjoy being "taken" against their will, and (d) failure to learn how to meet emotional needs in socially acceptable ways (Finkelhor, & Araji, 1986). Some gang rapes—in which a victim is attacked by several individuals—are motivated by desire of young males to prove their manhood, often giving the sexually uninitiated the courage to do what they would not have done alone (Finkelhor & Araji, 1986).

Acquaintance rapists share some characteristics with other rapists. Their propensity for rape may be amplified by the woman's acquiescence to her male partner's dominating role in other aspects of their relationship and by the man's misunderstanding of the woman's (possibly mixed) signals regarding her willingness to have sex (Lundberg-Love & Geffner, 1989; Muehlenhard & Linton, 1987).

Many rapists display symptoms of mental disorder. A significant percentage of incarcerated rapists exhibit psychotic tendencies (Reiss & Roth, 1993; Yarvis, 1995), and 40% to 80% of convicted rapists receive a diagnosis of antisocial personality disorder (Prentky & Quinsey, 1988). Many rapists also display sexual disorders and may have engaged in noncontact sexual crimes such as exhibitionism and voyeurism prior to committing rape (Fehrenbach et al., 1986; Groth, 1977; O'Brien, 1989; Rosenberg & Knight, 1988).

It has long been suggested that the psychological problems of many rapists are traceable to their own experiences as victims of sexual abuse as children. A study (Kruttschnitt, 1980) of the family backgrounds, school and dating history, and emotional experiences of rapists, nonseual offenders, and nonoffenders found that the only clear predictor of sexual as opposed to nonsexual offenses was childhood sexual abuse.

Who is Raped?   Victims of rape are typically young, unmarried, economically disadvantaged women. Men account for less than 10% of officially reported rapes, although most rapes of men occur in prisons where they tend to go unreported. More than half of all rape victims are under 18 years of age. Girls under 12 are victims in about 12% of all reported rapes, and among these, 20% are victimized by their fathers (Brown, Esbensen, & Geis, 1995). Those at highest risk for being raped are Black women, 16 to 19 years old, living in the center of large cities, with annual family incomes of less than $7,500. At lowest risk for rape are White women, 50 years or older, living in rural areas, with annual family incomes of $50,000 to $75,000 (Perkins & Klaus, 1996).

Victims who use alcohol and/or marijuana may increase their vulnerability to rape, especially if it clouds their judgment about letting themselves be drawn into sexual situations. In one study (L. Smith, 1997b), urine samples taken shortly after rape incidents from a random sample of 410 victims from all over the United States showed that nearly 15% had been smoking marijuana, and about 35% had been drinking alcohol; only 1% had been given Rohypnol® (L. Smith, 1997), a so-called date-rape drug.

The significant correlation between the sexual victimization of males and their subsequent role as sexual offenders has been attributed to the special impact of sexual abuse on men. The aftereffects of sexual assaults on men include confusion about sexual orientation (most male rape is perpetrated by other males), mistrust of adult men, PTSD, intimacy problems in romantic relationships (including difficulties in sexual functioning), mood disorders, and suicidal thoughts and impulses (Coxell & King, 1996; Isely & Gehrenbeck-Shim, 1997). Women, too, experience severe post-rape problems, but some researchers have suggested that female rape victims are less traumatized than male victims because women are less likely to have been subjected to violent physical force (the rape of males is generally extremely violent) and perhaps because it does not involve same-sex contact (e.g., Coxell & King, 1996).

Why Rape?   In ancient times, rape was a common means of establishing males' ownership of women. It was not until the advent of the dowry (payment for a woman's hand in marriage) that the premarital loss of a woman's virginity was seen as having a negative impact on her "market value"; and it was not until then that the rape of unmarried women (only) began to bring criminal penalties (Groth, 1977). Rape as ownership is also seen in its association with warfare (Mezey, 1994). Conquering soldiers throughout recorded history have used rape to signify their possession of "women of the enemy" whom they view as the spoils of war.[4]

Whether it occurs during war or in peacetime, rape appears to associated with a number of evolutionary, social, cultural, learning, and individual psychological factors. Evolutionary psychologists have suggested that rape serves an adaptive function for men, providing a way to perpetuate their own genes by impregnating as many women as possible. Learning theory suggests that parents, the media, and other socializing agents in many cultures teach boys gender roles that emphasize the importance of being masculine, aggressive, forceful, dominant, and disrespectful toward women. Men exposed to such influences may easily come to believe that dominating women sexually and against their will shows that they have ideal masculine traits—sometimes called "machismo" (Brownmiller, 1975). One study (O'Donohue, McKay, & Schewe, 1996) of undergraduate

---

[4]This tradition was seen in the civil war in the former Yugoslavia when Serbian army officers raped Bosnian women, not only to possess them but in an attempt at genocide—hoping to impregnate their victims with Serbian children. In 1999, the same charges were made against Serbian forces involved in ousting ethnic Albanians from Kosovo.

males revealed, for example, that "hypermasculine" personality traits are especially likely to be associated with coercive sexual behavior. Other research has shown that men who hold the most traditional and rigid views about the dominance of men and the inferiority of women in society—and who are callous toward the victims of sexual aggression—are more likely to justify or condone rape and to admit to using force and aggressive tactics in their sexual encounters. In one study (Mosher & Anderson, 1987), 75% of 175 male college sophomores admitted to having given their dates alcohol or other drugs to increase their inclination to have sex. Further, 69% used verbal manipulation; 40% tried anger; 13% threatened to use force; and 20% actually used force (Mosher & Anderson, 1987).

A. Nicholas Groth (1979/1984) has identified three types of forcible rape: anger rape, power rape, and sadistic rape (Groth & Birnbaum). Research with 500 convicted sex offenders in the Connecticut Department of Corrections led Groth to conclude that although both aggression and sexuality are involved in every forcible rape, sexuality is secondary to the expression of aggression—the main motivation for rape.[5] Groth's work has been instrumental in the acceptance of rape as a crime of violence rather than an aberrant sexual act (Siegal, 2000).

Anger rape occurs when sexuality serves as a means of discharging rage. The incident may occur on the spur of the moment, and the main goal is to hurt the victim; sex may be an afterthought. The victims of anger rape are usually beaten as well as raped and are the least likely of all rape victims to be blamed in some way for the attack.

Those who engage in *power rape* are not trying to hurt their victims but to conquer them, to be in control. They are not driven by a desire for sexual gratification but for power. Rape enhances self-esteem by proving their manhood. Because power rapes usually involve little or no physical violence, the victim may come to feel that she was somehow at fault for the incident, and if family and friends share this perception, she may receive less support from them. This may especially be the case in some cases of date rape.

Sadistic rape is most often the act of the serial rapist or serial rapist/killer. These offenders torment their victims by degrading them sexually, causing maximum shame and humiliation. This type of rape is particularly traumatic for the victim, often requiring long-term psychiatric care.

Groth found that about 55% of his research sample were power rapists, 40% were anger rapists, and 5% were sadistic rapists.

Child Molestation

A crisis of huge proportions has rocked the American Catholic Church of late. Almost 11,000 cases of child sexual molestation by priests have been reported according to the Church's own studies (The National Review Board for the Protection of Children and Young People, 2004). The reports of widespread sexual abuse of children by people connected with the church put the spotlight on one of the more tragic types of crimes against children—sexual molestation. Most child molesters can be diagnosed as manifesting **pedophilia**, meaning that according to *DSM–IV–TR* criteria, they must be at least 16 years old and have recurrent, intense, sexually arousing fantasies and urges involving sexual contact with children at least 5 years younger than they are (American Psychiatric Association, 2000a). The prevalence of pedophilia is tragically high. Estimates are that as many as 10% to15% of children and adolescents—twice as many girls as boys—are sexually victimized at least once (Mrazek, 1984). The vast majority of pedophiles are male, and their offenses include undressing and looking at a child; exposing themselves to a child; masturbating in the presence of a child; touching and fondling a child; and engaging in oral, anal, or vaginal sex with a child.

Child molesters can be found in all socioeconomic classes, age groups, and occupations. All too often, they work as teachers, ministers, coaches, probation officers, or in other jobs that put them in close contact with children. They use this relationship to encourage trusting children to comply with their sexual demands; 70% to 95% of their victims are acquaintances or family members. Many pedophiles are married men with children (of course Catholic priests are a notable exception). Although they do not usually identify themselves as homosexuals, many of their victims are boys (Lesieur & Welch, 1991).

---

[5]Although this tends to be true overall, younger rapists tend to be more driven by sexual desire as is evident by their choice of young, attractive victims (Felson & Krohn, 1990).

Persons engaging in pedophilic acts can be charged with a variety of crimes depending on the specifics of the acts and the applicable state laws. In all states, sexual penetration constitutes rape; most states consider fondling and touching to be aggravated sexual battery, whereas oral or anal sexual acts qualify as forcible sodomy.

Types of Pedophiles   The simplest classification system for pedophiles defines them as either exclusive (i.e., sexually attracted only to children) or nonexclusive (i.e., sometimes also attracted to adults; American Psychiatric Association, 2000a).

Other systems distinguish among situational molesters, preference molesters, and child rapists (Lanyon, 1986). Situational molesters have a history of normal sexual development and interests and are primarily interested in adult relationships. However, in certain situations and while under stress, they are overcome by an impulse to engage in sexual behaviors with a child. They usually feel great remorse afterward. Pedophilia is more central to the sexuality of preference molesters who have a clear preference for children, usually boys, over adults. If these men have a relationship or marriage with an adult female, it is likely to be part of an effort to be near the woman's children or to divert suspicion about their true sexual interests. These people usually see nothing wrong with their behavior; indeed, they may feel that society is to blame for failing recognize their preferences as just another form of legitimate sexual expression. The child rapist is a violent abuser whose sexual behavior is motivated by power-seeking and expressions of hostility (Lanyon, 1986).

Yet another classification system includes four pedophile subtypes known as physiological, cognitive, affective, and developmentally related (Hall, Shondrick, & Hirschman, 1993). The *physiological* type tends to attack multiple victims but does not engage in physical or sexual violence. The *cognitive* type carefully plans his actions, which are likely to involve rape, whereas the *affective* type is said to lack emotional control and to engage in opportunistic, unplanned, and often violent sex. The *developmentally related* type is most common in men with a long history of personality and adjustment difficulties, family and interpersonal conflicts, and personal experience of victimization during childhood.

Research on pedophiles has suggested that regardless of which classification system is used, most of these men are weak, immature individuals who take pleasure in dominating and controlling others. They tend to have strong needs for immediate sexual gratification and poor impulse control (Groth, 1978; Serin, Malcolm, Khanna, & Barbaree, 1994). They also tend to be lonely, isolated introverts with low self-esteem and a notable lack of success in adult interpersonal relationships (Bumbry & Hansen, 1997; Proulx, McKibben, & Lusignan, 1996). Child molesters are more likely to be depressed than those who commit sex crimes against adults (Hall et al., 1993). They also tend to come from backgrounds that included insecure early attachment and a dysfunctional family life.

Case studies of pedophiles have led to the idea that some of them have experienced so much rejection from their parents and other adults that they turn to children for emotional and physical intimacy. Their feelings of inadequacy, it is said, give rise to faulty cognitions that lead them to perceive a child's emotional responsiveness as a sign of erotic interest (Ivey & Simpson, 1998). It has also been suggested that the sexual abuse that many pedophiles suffered in their own childhood may have led them to become sexual offenders themselves (Bagley, Wood, & Young, 1994; Haywood & Grossman, 1996). Some of the priests found guilty of abusing children had themselves been molested by priests in their churches or teachers in Catholic seminaries.

The Internet: Pedophiles' High-Tech Accomplice.   In August of 1998, police in 12 countries arrested more than 100 suspected pedophiles who were involved in the dissemination of child pornography. Such people are considered dangerous not only because they are in violation of the laws in many lands but also because some of them use the Internet to make arrangements to have sex with children. For example, in 1997, a federal judge in Virginia sentenced a 64-year-old computer consultant to 2 years in prison after he pleaded guilty to crossing state lines to have sex with a 14-year-old girl. He had been arrested through the efforts of an FBI task force targeting pedophiles who use the Internet. He is said to have contacted more than 100 young girls, many as young as 12, and to have met some of them in libraries and other public places. The man also admitted to sexual encounters more than 20 years earlier with his own teenage stepdaughter and with a teenage babysitter (Masters, 1997).

Parents must do their jobs to shield their children against pedophiles lurking on the Internet. Software can help limit youngsters' access to inappropriate Web sites and chat rooms. The FBI has a computer crimes unit that targets Internet stalkers—sexual predators who ensnare young people in chat rooms and try to entice them to meet for a sexual liaison. Conviction of "cyberstalking" carries a maximum 10-year prison term (D. P. Baker, 1999).

Dealing With Repeat and Dangerous Sexual Offenders

Many rapists and other sexual offenders tend to repeat their crimes even if they have received treatment and/or are sent to prison (Hanson, 2000; Proulx, Pellerin, Paradis, & McKibben, 1997). Child molesters in particular tend to commit an increasing number of offenses the longer they are out of prison for a prior offense; in fact, they are 100% more likely than rapists to repeat a sexual crime in the first 25 years after their release from prison (DeAngelis, 1997; Rice & Harris, 1997). Child molesters are especially high risk because more than any other type of sexual offender, they are likely to either deny their crimes or refuse to accept responsibility for them. Many focus on the idea that they cause no physical harm to their victims and are unable to accept that they have caused grave psychological damage (Ivey & Simpson, 1998). They typically blame their young victims for "coming on to them" (Nugent & Kroner, 1996). So although the overall recidivism rate for all sexual offenders is no higher than that of criminals in the general prison population (Hagan & Cho, 1996), the threat posed to potential victims by the presence of child molesters in a community is particularly troubling, especially in view of the long-term effect of child sexual abuse.

In short, child molesters need long-term, intensive supervision in addition to psychological treatment (DeAngelis, 1997). Unfortunately, sex-offender treatment programs are expensive, labor intensive, and in most cases not very effective (Allan, Middleton, & Browne, 1997; Furby & Weinrott, 1980; Marshall & Barbaree, 1988). They might be improved by addressing not only offenders' attraction to children but their lack of empathy, their substance abuse, and other characteristics that motivate repeated sex crimes (T. Ward, Hudson, & McCormack, 1997). Ideally, special treatments will be developed to help sex offenders who were themselves victims of sexual abuse as children (Allan et al., 1997; Marshall, Bryce, & Hudson, 1996) and those who suffer from neurological deficits and learning disabilities (Polaschek, Ward, & Hudson, 1997). Recent research suggests, for example, that group therapy may be effective when used in combination with medications to lower sex drive (Berlin & Kraut, 1996).

Civil Commitment for Sexual Offenders.   Until and unless such programs are in place, most jurisdictions are taking more direct approaches to limiting the dangerousness of sexual offenders. One of these, surgical or chemical castration, is not legal in most U.S. states, but as a result of recent legislation in some states, repeat sexual offenders who have been diagnosed as displaying pedophilia or antisocial personality disorder can be classified as sexually violent predators and committed to a mental institution for life or until they are no longer believed to be dangerous (Sales & Shuman, 1996). The case of Earl Shriner, in the State of Washington, led to passage of the first of these civil commitment laws. Shriner had already served prison terms for the kidnaping and physical and sexual assault of several girls and boys as well as for the murder of a 15-year-old girl. Then, two years after serving a 10-year term for kidnaping and assaulting two 16-year-old girls, he kidnaped a 7-year-old boy, raped him orally and anally, stabbed him in the back, strangled him, and cut off his penis. The boy survived, but the crime so outraged the public that the state enacted its sexually violent predator law (Porterfield, 2000).

The U.S. Supreme Court upheld the constitutionality of sexually violent predator statutes in at least one state (Kansas), and state supreme courts in Oregon and Washington have done the same. However, for a state to civilly commit a sexual offender after his release from prison, there must be a court hearing before a judge (and a jury if the defendant requests one) at which the offender is shown to have a personality disorder or other mental abnormality and to be likely to repeat his crimes. Critics of these laws include psychologists who point out that in many cases, the mental abnormalities that sexual offenders display involve either antisocial personality disorder or pedophilia. The former is, as we noted in chapter 2, not considered serious enough to justify pleas of insanity or incompetence, and the latter is no more than a description in diagnostic terms of the behavior that got the person arrested in the first place (LaFond, 1998). These critics worry that a handful of truly horrible defendants have prompted the creation of laws that could, if applied inappropriately, subject even first-time offenders to life in a mental institution (Winick, 1998). Understandably, proponents are more concerned with the long-term damage pedophiles inflict on their victims and argue that being locked up for life is not too high a price to pay for molesting even one child—and certainly is not excessive if it insures that the offender will not have the opportunity to victimize another.

Sexual Offender Notification Laws.   Most states now have laws allowing—and in some cases, mandating—police to notify the community that a sexual offender has been released from prison and is living in their community.[6] The first such statute, known as Megan's Law, was enacted in New Jersey after 7-year-old Megan Kanka was raped and murdered by her neighbor, a convicted child molester.

Notification laws can help to protect potential victims, but critics point out that they can also make it harder for the released sex criminal to adopt a noncriminal lifestyle if he wants to do so. Notification, they say, invites social ostracization, loss of employment, and eviction for people whose names appear on the sex offender list (Twomey, 1999). True, the shame, humiliation, and other consequences of being publicly identified in this way are stressful and may make it impossible for the offender to ever live a normal life, but proponents of notification laws insist that these consequences pale in comparison to the need to protect children from molestation.

Summary

When discussing violent crimes, we focused on the offenses categorized as such by the FBI—robbery, homicide, rape, and aggravated assault—as well as other categories such as domestic violence and child sexual molestation.

Robbery is associated with romantic notions from the American past. Yet robbery is a violent crime, involving taking or attempting to take something of value from someone with force or threat of violence. Of the several types of robber, the chronic robbers are potentially the most dangerous. Professional or career robbers learn their trade as young men and tend to make a living out of their crime. Most robbers, especially chronic and career robbers, rob for money. Their careers may be marked by periods of earning and burning in which they go on sprees of drinking, doing drugs, and spending money after they take in their ill-gotten gains. Victims of robbers are strangers to their perpetrators about 90% of the time.

There are many types of homicide, but our discussion focused on murder and nonnegligent manslaughter, the intentional killing of others without cause or provocation. Although people tend to be fascinated by bizarre and horrific murders, most murders are more prosaic, everyday encounters between angry spouses and domestic partners, or the settling of scores between drug dealers and rival gangs.

Unlike robbery, in which perpetrators and victims are usually strangers, 51% of murder victims, on average, knew their assailants. You are most likely to be killed by someone you know, not a stranger. Alcohol and drug usage often are connected to homicide. Studies have found as many as 50% of murderers were intoxicated at the time of their crimes.

There are several types of murder, all of which focus on distinct settings, perpetrators, and victims. There are several categories of multiple-victim murders including spree murderers, mass murderers, and serial murderers. Serial murderers fascinate the public and with good reason. Most serial killers come from bizarre pasts and carry out their crimes in distinct ways. Criminal profiling, the use of behavioral sciences and law enforcement resources to track down offenders, got its start with studying the modus operandi of serial murderers (and rapists).

Domestic violence and child abuse are an all-too-common fact in everyday life for many families. These crimes know no class or ethnic boundaries, although they tend to be more prevalent in families challenged by socioeconomic pressures and drug and alcohol use.

---

[6]All 50 states have enacted laws requiring registration of sex offenders with local law enforcement offices. Not all states, however, make this information available to the public.

Hate crimes make up a unique category of crime classification based on the victim and the crime. The FBI keeps data on crimes, be they crimes against persons or their property, which were motivated by racial, ethnic, religious, or sexual bias. Hate crimes are often the result of economic, political, or current events. For instance, hate crimes against Muslims increased after the September 11, 2001 terrorist attacks on the United States.

Rape is the most feared of sex crimes. Although inherently sexual in nature, most rapists are not victimizing women for sex but for the power over their victim that sexual assault provides. There are several methods for categorizing rapists. More than half of rape victims know their accusers. Younger, poorer women are more likely to be raped than older women in a higher earning bracket. Date rape that occurs between acquaintances carries no less a penalty than rape against a stranger, even though some people have that misperception.

The numerous accounts of children having been abused by Catholic priests brought the problem of child molestation to the forefront of the news in recent years. Sexual abuse of children has long-term ramifications for the victim and society, especially when the victim is, as is often the case, a boy. Male victims of sexual molestation often go on to become victimizers themselves, setting in motion an unending chain of abuse and victimization. People who prefer having sex with children, known as pedophiles, are dangerous and hard to cure. They tend to be chronic reoffenders and pose such a danger to society that our legal system allows some of them to be locked up for the rest of their lives, even after serving their prison sentences.

Robbery, murder, aggravated assault, domestic violence, hate crimes, and sex crimes are perpetrated by a relative handful of the most dangerous members of society. The roots of these crimes are usually deep seated psychological, cognitive, and behavioral problems. Few of these criminals are free from mental psychopathology—many display both antisocial personality disorder and substance dependence. Relatively few, too, are likely to overcome these disorders, and fewer still are likely to be rehabilitated enough to adopt more productive, law-abiding lifestyles. Instead, when they are not in prison, these offenders are likely to repeat their offenses, testing the limits of the courts and the social and governmental services available to help them. In other words, most of them will continue to make life more dangerous for the rest of us.

Key Terms

Robbery	*Aggravated assault (malicious wounding)*
Murder	*Stalking*
Terrorism	*Hate crimes*
Criminal profiling	*Forcible Rape*
Battery	*Date rape*
Assault	*Pedophilia*
Simple assault	

Questions for Review

1. What are the four main classification or armed robbers?
2. Name the three categories of multiple-victim murderers.
3. What are the roots of domestic violence, and what kinds of families are most vulnerable?
4. What makes hate crimes different from other crime categories?
5. Discuss the controversy surrounding civil commitment of sexual offenders and sex offender notification laws.

Track It Down

*Criminal Behavio*r Website
www.cassel2e.com
The complete UCRs cited in your text can be viewed here:
www.fbi.gov/ucr/cius_03/pdf/03sec2.pdf
Crime Characteristics—Facts from the Bureau of Justice Statistics
www.ojp.usdoj.gov/bjs/cvict_c.htm
Federal Bureau of Justice Statistics Recidivism Study
www.cor.state.pa.us/stats/lib/stats/BJS%20Recidivism%20Study.pdf
Sex Offenses and Offenders Study from the Bureau of Justice Statistics
www.ojp.usdoj.gov/bjs/pub/pdf/soo.pdf
Child Sexual Abuse Data and Reports
www.prevent-abuse-now.com/stats2.htm
Intimate Partner Violence Fact Sheet
www.cdc.gov/ncipc/factsheets/ipvfacts.htm

11

Economic and Property Crimes

Arson   *Occupational Crime*
Burglary, Larceny, and Auto Theft   *Syndicated Crime*
Fraud

Economic and property crimes (burglary, theft, fraud, white-collar crime, organized crime, and arson) are by far the most common forms of criminal activity, accounting for 90% of all crimes and costing individuals, businesses, and governments hundreds of billions of dollars in direct financial losses each year. The indirect costs cannot be measured in dollars alone. These crimes, and fear of falling victim to them, keep people home at night, raise insurance premiums and taxes, and foster distrust in business and government. In this chapter, we examine economic and property offenses that are *Uniform Crime Reports* (UCR) index crimes–arson, burglary, larceny theft, motor vehicle theft—as well as fraud, occupational, organizational, and syndicated crime, which are categories not covered by the *UCR*.

Arson

Arson is the willful and malicious burning (or attempted burning) of a dwelling, house, public building, motor vehicle, aircraft, or other personal property (FBI, 2004a). There were approximately 71,300 incidents of arson reported in 2003. Of the estimated 16,000 people arrested for arson during 2003, 89% were males; 77% were White, and 21% were Black, and the rest other ethnic groups (FBI, 2004a).

Fixed structures were the targets in 42% of reported arson incidents. Of these, 61% were residential properties, and of these, more than 73% were single-family homes. A total of 33% of arsons were aimed at mobile property, and 95% of these were motor vehicles. The remainder of arsons targeted crops, timber, or other types of property. The average damage cost per arson incident was $11,941, although per incident losses to residences and office structures were much higher (FBI, 2004a).

Motives for Arson

Researchers have identified five primary motives for arson: (1) vandalism, (2) revenge, (3) crime concealment, (4) fraud, and (5) intimidation (Boudreau, Kwan, Faragher, & Denault, 1977).

Of the arsons in 1996, 49% were acts of *vandalism*. Juveniles set most vandalism fires that year as has been the case in previous years; an earlier study (Icove & Estepp, 1987) reported the figure to be as high as 97%.

These fires usually involve more than one youngster and typically occur within a mile of their homes. Many of these juvenile offenders stay at the scene to watch the fire, a tendency that often leads to their arrest.

Revenge fires, which account for about 14% of all arsons, are set to destroy the property of people whom arsonists believe have mistreated them in some way. These fires tend to be set by adult males who already have criminal records. The perpetrator typically drinks alcohol prior to or during the offense (Icove & Estepp, 1987).

Up to about 7% of arson cases are *crime concealment* fires that are set in an effort to destroy evidence of burglary, murder, or other felonies. Sometimes, people who commit suicide also commit arson to hide the cause of their deaths in the hope that their families will find it easier to collect life insurance benefits (Inciardi, 1975).

In more blatant *insurance fraud* fires, people burn down their own homes or businesses to collect property insurance benefits. In some of these cases, the perpetrator engages a professional arsonist to set the fire for a fee. These "torches for hire" are usually 25- to 40-year-old men with prior arrests for burglary, assault, and public drunkenness (Douglas et al., 1992).

A few arsonists are motivated by a desire to frighten people or to alter their behavior in some way. For example, unhappy employees have been known to set a fire to force management to agree to workers' demands. Some arsonists threaten to strike again unless they are paid to desist. *Intimidation-motivated* fires are generally driven by arsonists' economic, social, political, or religious agendas. As we discussed in chapter 10, form of arson may qualify as a hate crime. In still other intimidation-type arson cases, the goal might be to extort money, to terrorize, or to disrupt some activity through sabotage.

Characteristics of Arsonists

Although arson is common, pyromania is rare. Only about one-tenth of 1 percent of arsonists display symptoms of **pyromania**, an impulse control disorder characterized by a continuing pattern of fire setting for pleasure, gratification, and the release of tension (American Psychiatric Association, 2000a; Bradford, 1982; Icove & Estepp, 1987; M. A. Stewart & Culver, 1982). Pyromaniacs do not set fires for monetary gain, for political purposes, to express anger, or to get revenge. It appears, rather, that psychological tension drives them to set a fire and that the tension is released by the excitement of watching the fire and its aftermath. People diagnosed with pyromania not only like to watch fires but may set off false alarms and loiter around fire stations. Some even become firefighters. Firefighters who set fires often do so to be seen as heroes, rushing in to save lives and property, or to earn extra money fighting the very fires they set (U.S. Fire Administration, 2003). In the summer of 2002, two National Forest Service employees were accused of setting two of the largest wildfires in U.S. history, one in Arizona that destroyed more than 432 homes and devastated the economy of nearby communities; it cost an estimated $10 million to control. The fire setter was allegedly motivated by the chance to make $8.00 per hour fighting the fire. Another, in Colorado, destroyed more than 130 homes and threatened the suburb of Denver. This fire cost an estimated $15 million. Prosecutors said the fire setter of this fire was motivated by revenge and the opportunity for financial gain (U.S. Fire Administration, 2003).

To qualify for a diagnosis of pyromania, a person's fire setting must not occur as a result of antisocial personality disorder, conduct disorder, a manic episode, or in association with hallucinations, dementia, mental retardation, or intoxication (see Table 11.1). Most pyromaniacs are poorly adjusted males, often with inadequate social skills and learning difficulties.

Juvenile Arsonists. In 2003, more than 51% of arson arrestees were under the age of 18, and 31% were under the age of 15. Arson has the highest proportion of juvenile arrests for any type of FBI (2004a) index crime. Not all juvenile fire settings are considered arson; many are accidental. Children normally have an interest in fire, and about half of all children engage in fireplay out of curiosity (Kolko, 1985). Several factors are taken into consideration in determining a youngster's criminal intent, including the fire setter's age, the nature and extent of the individual's fire-setting history, and the apparent motive for the fire setting. In addition to vandalism, revenge, or crime concealment, juvenile arson may also be motivated by fascination with fire, efforts to gain peer approval, and even attempts at self-injury (Swaffer & Holing, 1995).

Juvenile fire setters typically develop into arsonists in three stages. The first, seen in children under the age of 7, involves setting fires accidentally or out of curiosity. In the second stage, between the ages of 8 and 12, fire set-

TABLE 11.1 *Diagnostic Criteria for Pyromania*

The features of pyromania are:

(1) Fascination with or curiosity about fire
(2) Experience of tension or arousal before setting the fire
(3) Multiple episodes of deliberate fire setting
(4) Experiences of pleasure or release of tension during and after fire setting;
(5) The fire setting is not done as the result of a delusion or hallucination or committed for economic gain or political purposes

Source: Based on information from American Psychiatric Association. (2000). *Diagnostic and Statistical Manual of Mental Disorders* (4th ed. text revision). Washington, DC: Author.

ting seems to occur as a manifestation of frustration, impulsivity, and aggression and may be symptomatic of con- duct disorder (American Psychiatric Association, 2000a; Hanson, MacKay, Atkinson, & Staley, & 1995; Snyder, 1999). In the third stage, which spans the ages between 13 and 18, the youngster has established a con- tinuing pattern of fire setting aimed at vandalism, revenge, or other aggressive motives (Garry, 1997).

Fire setting in children is a serious matter not only because it can cause significant property damage, per- sonal injury, and loss of life but because there is evidence that as juvenile fire setters mature, they are more likely than other delinquents to engage in more serious antisocial behaviors (Forehand, Wierson, Frame, Kempton, & Armistead, 1991). Youthful repetitive fire setters tend to be socially isolated (Maccoby, 1986), to possess relatively few social skills, to receive diagnoses of CD, and to have been exposed to more family dys- function than other juvenile delinquents (e.g., Barnett & Spitzer, 1994; Kadzin & Kolko, 1986; Kolko, 1989; Wicks-Nelson & Israel, 1997). Indeed, the family backgrounds of juvenile fire setters tends to be similar to those of children with CD in general, a background that typically includes parents with psychological prob- lems and poor marital adjustment (Barnett & Spitzer, 1994; Kazdin & Kolko, 1986; Kolko, 1989).

One study (J. K. Moore, Thompson-Pope, & Whited, 1996) comparing the personalities of 14- to 17-year- old psychiatric inpatients—using profiles from the Minnesota Multiphasic Personality Inventory–Adolescent (MMPI-A™) (Butler, et al., 2004)—found that those with a history of fire setting displayed more severe behav- ior disorder, alienation, depression, and thought disorder and poorer reality testing than boys who had not set fires. Another study (Showers & Pickrell, 1987) compared 186 fire setters to 165 other sex-matched young- sters (aged 4–17) seen in mental health centers or state psychiatric hospitals for children. The results indicate that fire setters were more likely than the other children to show conduct problems such as disobedience and aggressiveness and experienced significantly more neglect and physical abuse at home (Showers & Pickrell, 1987). A third study (Hanson, MacKay, Staley, & Poulton, 1994) showed that compared to other delinquents, antisocial behaviors were seen more often in male juveniles who were repeat fire setters. There is also some evidence that frequent fire setters may have been abused with fire as children, perhaps leading them to believe that using fire is an acceptable method of retaliation (Ritvo, Shanok, & Lewis, 1983).

Adult Arsonists.   The adult fire setter usually manifests a number of behavioral and social problems includ- ing heavy drinking, marital and sexual problems, financial difficulties, occupational problems, and repeated contact with the criminal justice system (Vreeland & Levin, 1980). Several studies have indicated that adult arsonists differ from other types of violent criminals (such as murderers) on several psychological dimensions. In one study (Rasanen, Hakko, & Vaisanen, 1995), for example, 84% of arsonists, as compared to 62% of homicide offenders, had alcohol abuse problems. Arsonists also engaged in more suicidal thinking and made more suicide gestures. The arsonists were four times as likely as the murderers to be suffering from psychosis, three times more likely to be suffering from severe depression, and twice as likely to be mentally retarded. A total of 85% of arsonists had received psychiatric care before committing their crime; they were more often found not guilty by reason of insanity than were murderers (Rasanen et al., 1995). A study (Puri, Baxter, & Cordess, 1995) of the social, demographic, psychiatric, and medical records of male and female fire setters (aged 16–77 years) referred to a British psychiatric service concluded that these people commonly showed psychoactive substance abuse and significantly disturbed interpersonal relationships (85% lived alone). Of the women, 44% had a history of sexual abuse. In fact, female arsonists seem to suffer even more psychopathology than their male counterparts. One study (J. A. Stewart, 1993) found that 92% of female fire setters had received psychiatric diagnoses and that none had set fires for financial gain. Their fire setting tended to be preceded by depression, low-self esteem, poor anger management and, in a few cases, alcohol dependence.

Burglary, Larceny, and Auto Theft

The FBI includes burglary, larceny, motor vehicle theft, and arson as property crimes. We have discussed arson separately. Although violent crimes such as murder, robbery, and rape are committed at a rate of about one every 19 seconds, one of these property crimes is committed every 3 seconds. The criminal's goal is to take property or money, but in contrast to robbery, no force or threat of force is used against the victims. About 41.2% of all reported property crimes in the United States occurred in the South, followed by the West with 25.1%, the Midwest with 21%, and the Northeast with 12.6% (FBI, 2004a).

Burglary

Burglary is the unlawful entry into a structure to commit a felony, usually theft. In some states, forcible burglary is called "breaking and entering with the intent to commit larceny." Figures for 2003 (FBI, 2004a) show that most burglaries, 45%, occurred in the South, whereas 23.6% were in the West, 20.1% in the Midwest, and 11.3% in the Northwest. Burglaries counted for 18% of all property crimes. The largest number of burglaries occurred during July and the lowest number in February. Two out of every three burglaries in 2003 took place in private homes. There were 62% that involved forcible entry, 31% were unlawful entries without force, and the remainder were forcible entry attempts. Of residential burglaries, 62% occurred during the daytime; 58% of the nonresidential burglaries occurred at night. The total dollar loss to burglary in 2003 was approximately $3.5 billion. The average dollar loss per burglary was $1,600 for residential offenses and $1,676 for nonresidential offenses. Of those arrested for burglary during 2003, 86% were males, and of these, 30% were under 18 (an increase of 3% from 1995). Of female offenders, 25% were juveniles. About 70% of arrested burglars were White, 28% Black, and the remainder represented other ethnic races (FBI, 2004a).

Although many burglars steal to get money to support their drug addictions (Cromwell, Olson, & Avary, 1991), the crime is not very lucrative. One study (J. Q. Wilson & Abrahamsen, 1992) found that although burglars estimated their monthly income at over $2,500, the actual figure was only slightly over $200.

Female burglars, who in 2003 comprised only 14% of burglars arrested, generally begin their career later in life than do their male counterparts. They also display more alcoholism and drug addiction; in one study (Decker, Wright, Redfern, & Smith, 1993), 47% considered themselves to be drug addicts or alcoholics, and 72% reported consuming alcohol before committing their crimes. Females often burgle in cooperation with men either as a lookout, driver, or in some other accomplice role, although they are sometimes a full partner in planning and executing the burglary and in the sale of stolen goods (Decker et al., 1993).

As we noted in chapter 10, burglary is often a step along the path to more serious crimes. For example, a significant number of armed robbers came to favor robbery only after having experience at burglary, which they tended to see as taking more time and being less likely to net cash (Wright & Decker, 1997). Indeed, burglary serves as a kind of "kindergarten" for robbers, giving them a chance to get accustomed to committing crimes, taking risks, and evading capture.

Like robbers, some burglars operate only occasionally, but many of them work steadily as professional thieves who take pride in their "craft." One study (Shover, 1972) showed that career thieves tend to consider themselves to have technical competence, personal integrity, financial comfort, and skill at avoiding prison. To reach this status, burglars must (1) develop and practice entry techniques including learning and keeping up to date on how to circumvent security systems and guards, (2) develop a network of accomplices, (3) get inside information about where valuables are kept in residences and offices so as not to waste time searching for them, and (4) cultivate "fences" or buyers who will exchange stolen goods for cash (Cromwell et al., 1991; Shover, 1972). Those aspiring to be professional thieves generally first act as apprentices to more experienced burglars. Their mentors are often siblings or other relatives, or they may be people encountered in juvenile gangs or in prison. Once burglars become professionals, their behavior is reinforced by the deviant culture of other professional burglars.

For each target they consider, professional burglars weigh the risks of capture against the potential benefits and make what, to them, are rational choices about whether to commit their crime and about when, where, and how to do so. Experienced burglars develop proficiency in choosing targets, paying special attention to environmental cues such as fences, gates, and security surveillance warnings that indicate there is something inside worth stealing. They also "case" a potential target by watching it carefully and thoughtfully choosing the time of day and week to maximize the chances of success (MacDonald & Gifford, 1989; M. Taylor & Nee, 1988).

Alan Golder, for example, is a professional "cat burglar" extraordinaire who is currently suspected of having pulled off more than 20 home burglaries in the posh neighborhoods of Greenwich, Connecticut, in 1997. Prior to these "jobs," he had burgled upscale homes in New York, Florida, Texas, and California. In fact, he became known as the "dinner-at-eight bandit" because he stole only when his victims were at home and burglar alarms were turned off, usually at the dinner hour. Golder only stole fine jewels and according to his federal parole officer, has a photographic memory for every piece he has stolen. He also has extraordinary physical agility that allows him to enter and leave houses by scaling trellises and clambering up columns. So thorough is his preparation that he is thought to have memorized every shrub and tree around each mansion he targets. Golder clearly loved his "work," and his competence is grudgingly admired even by those who are trying to find him and put him away for life (Harden, 1998).

Larceny Theft

The UCR defines **larceny theft** as the unlawful taking, carrying, leading, or riding away of property from the possession of another. Larceny theft represents the most common type of crime, comprising the largest portion of FBI crime index offenses reported to law enforcement agencies. In 2003, larceny theft offenses accounted for 67.3% of arrests for property crimes (FBI, 2004a). The largest number of larceny thefts occurred during July and August, and the fewest occurred in February. The Southern states recorded 41.3% of the larceny theft total, followed by the West at 23.9%, the Midwest States at 21.9%, and then the Northeast at 13%. Larceny theft losses to victims nationally in 2003 were $4.9 billion (FBI, 2004a).

There are many varieties of larceny theft including shoplifting, pocket picking, purse snatching, theft from motor vehicles, theft of motor vehicle parts and accessories, bicycle theft, and other thefts for which there is no force, violence, or fraud (see Figure 11.1). However, this crime category does not include embezzlement, confidence games, forgery, and passing worthless checks. As we note following, motor vehicle theft, too, falls into a separate category, although for convenience we mention it here.

A little more than 28% of those arrested for larceny in 2003 were under the age of 18. Females who were arrested for this offense more often than for any other in 1997 comprised 27% of all larceny arrests. Whites accounted for 68.5% of larceny arrests and Blacks 28.8%; the remaining 3% represented other races (FBI, 2004a). Like burglary, larceny offenses are often undertaken to support drug and alcohol addictions. The majority of pathological gamblers, too, have been known to steal money to support their own form of addiction (Blaszczynski & McConaghy, 1994). Larceny is second only to drug offenses as the reason why felons are in state prisons (Beck, 2000).

Auto Theft

Defined as the theft or attempted theft of a motor vehicle, *auto theft* includes the stealing of trucks, buses, motorcycles, motorscooters, and the like. Of all motor vehicles reported stolen in 2003, 73% were automobiles. Auto theft also includes the temporary taking of a vehicle for a "joy ride," also known as unauthorized use. In 2003, 34.5% of auto thefts in the United States occurred in the South, 34.4% in the West, 18.5% in the Midwest, and 12.5% in the Northeast. The highest percentage of vehicles were stolen in January and July and August; the lowest percentage were in February (FBI, 2004a). The estimated value of motor vehicles stolen

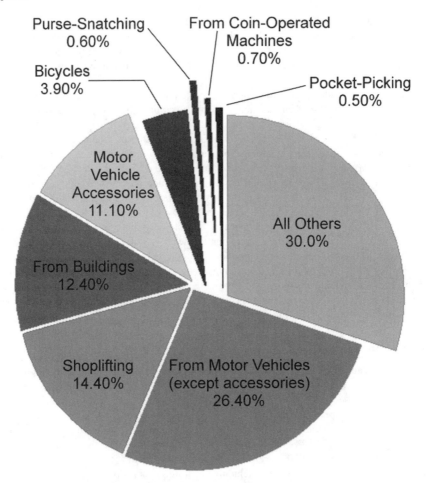

FIGURE 11.1 *Larceny theft distribution by type of theft.* From **Crime in the United States—2003,** by *Federal Bureau of Investigation, 2004, Washington DC: Government Printing Office.*

nationally in 2003 was $8.6 billion. Males accounted for 83.4% of those arrested for auto theft. A little over 60% were White, 35.9% were Black, and the remainder other races. In 2003, 62% of all those arrested for auto theft were under the age of 25, and 29% were under 18 (FBI, 2004a).

Shoplifting

Shoplifting is a common and costly form of larceny theft, comprising more than 14% of all reported larceny theft offenses (FBI, 2004a). However, many incidents are either undiscovered or unreported, so shoplifting is probably far more common than the UCR data indicate. Shoplifting is most common in large shopping malls where widely advertised sales and other intense promotional efforts attract shoplifters as well as customers (Carter, 1995).

Adults and juveniles participate in shoplifting about equally, but this crime occurs in varying patterns over time. Many adults report having engaged in shoplifting occasionally when under the age of 10 and also in their teens (usually the result of peer influence), but most never shoplift or commit other crimes thereafter. Recurrent shoplifting in adolescence, though, can signal the beginning of an adult career in theft. In fact, as with arson, shoplifting that begins in childhood and persists into adolescence is considered a pathway to a lifetime of crime (Kelley, Loeber, Keenan, & DeLamatre, 1997).

TABLE 11.2 *Diagnostic Criteria for Kleptomania*

The features of kleptomania are:

(1) Experience of tension before the theft
(2) Inability to resist compulsion to steal
(3) Theft of items not needed for personal use or monetary value
(4) Experience of pleasure or relief after the theft
(5) The theft is not done in response to a delusion or hallucination or committed to express anger or vengeance.

Source: Based on information from American Psychiatric Association. (2000). *Diagnostic and Statistical Manual of Mental Disorders* (4th ed. text revision). Washington, DC: Author.

Some adults shoplift because they need food, clothing, or other goods for their personal use and cannot afford to purchase them; others shoplift to raise money for living expenses or to support addictions to drugs, alcohol, or gambling (Blaszcynski & McConaghy, 1995). Children and teenagers tend to shoplift as part of a group or on a dare in an effort to obtain peer acceptance. Adolescent shoplifters are strongly influenced by the examples set by shoplifting peers and may fail to see anything wrong with their behavior (Cox, Cox, Anderson, & Moschis, 1993; Lo, 1994). Adolescents tend to shoplift during moderately busy times at locations far from home and to take small amounts of goods mainly for fun and thrills (Lo, 1994).

About 5% of shoplifters steal senselessly and compulsively in a pattern associated with **kleptomania**, an impulse-control disorder meaning "stealing madness" (see Table 11.2). These people usually steal items that are useless to them or that they could easily afford to buy. Often, kleptomaniacs hoard stolen items or secretly return them to the store. Like pyromaniacs, kleptomaniacs say they feel a buildup of tension, experience uncontrollable impulses to steal, and feel pleasure and relief after doing so. Then, because they know that theft is wrong and fear getting caught, they often feel depressed or guilty about their behavior (American Psychiatric Association, 2000a).

The *DSM–IV–TR* lists three types of kleptomania. The *sporadic* type engages in brief stealing sprees separated by long crime-free periods, whereas the *episodic* type's sprees are more extended. *Chronic* kleptomania involves more or less continuous stealing. Whatever the pattern, it may continue for years, even if the stealing results in arrest (American Psychiatric Association, 2000a). Far more women than men are diagnosed with kleptomania, and as many as 80% of women receiving this diagnosis also suffer from depression (Goldman, 1991; McElroy, Pope, Hudson, Keck, & White, 1991; Yates, 1986).

Shoplifters with a history of depression tend to steal when depressed, perhaps because the stimulation and excitement provides relief from depressive symptoms (Goldman, 1991). Research has suggested that elderly shoplifters are increasing in number and that they, too, may steal to relieve depression. Other concurrent disorders include mania, anxiety, eating disorders (particularly bulimia), and substance abuse (Fugure, D'Elia, & Philippe, 1995; Fullerton, Wonderlich, & Gosnell, 1995; Lamontagne, Carpentier, Hetu, & Lacerte-Lamontage, 1994; Lande, 1995; R. H. Moore, 1984).

Fraud

Fraud is defined as the intentional misrepresentation of fact to unlawfully deprive a person of property (U.S. Department of Justice, 1987). It is not recorded as a UCR index crime. All occupational crime, of whatever variety, is based on fraud—usually with the intention of enriching oneself or one's organization at the expense of consumers, investors, stockholders, or taxpayers. But people also commit fraud against other people in situations that have nothing to do with their jobs. For instance, in 1997, a Virginia pharmacist and her live-in boyfriend ransacked mailboxes in a wealthy neighborhood, stealing preapproved credit card applications and opening mail containing the owners' personal financial information. They used this information to order credit cards and then stole them from the mailboxes when they were delivered. They then used the cards to get cash advances from ATM machines. This fraud yielded $317,000 before the pair was caught (Masters, 1998b). In such cases, the victims do not know that anything is amiss until their credit card bills (which are not stolen) arrive.

In other cases, people become willing participants in a scam, sometimes because they trust the perpetrator and sometimes out of ignorance or lack of sophistication. Sadly, even television evangelists have been involved in frauds that net more than $100 million per year from devout, unsuspecting viewers (Friedrichs, 1996). Jim Bakker, for example, defrauded trusting members of his television ministry out of $3.7 million. Sometimes, these evangelists justify their fraudulent fund raising activities with claims of doing "God's work." Several years ago, Oral Roberts told television audiences that God had told him that he would be "called home" (i.e., die) if he did not receive a huge sum of money by a certain date. The money poured in. Like mail thieves, credit-application forgers, and fraudulent home repair companies, dishonest televangelists are just one more breed of criminal who has no regard for the suffering of those they victimize.

Welfare Fraud

State and federal welfare systems provide cash, food stamps, Medicaid benefits, Aid to Families with Dependent Children (AFDC), and other forms of assistance to the poor and disabled. People who cheat these systems by obtaining benefits they do not deserve cost the state and federal government billions of dollars a year. Here are just a few examples:

1. A Pennsylvania resident held 13 different Department of Public Welfare identification cards, and was charged with stealing $22,000 in taxpayer-funded welfare benefits.
2. For 7 years, a couple received AFDC and food stamp benefits they did not need and used the money to build a four-unit apartment house that generated rental income. The wife claimed that her husband had abandoned her and was living in another country when in fact he was with her all the time and was using a post office box to receive his mail.

3. With the more than $100,000 in ill-gotten welfare aid they received for almost 10 years, the owners of a jewelry store hired remodelers to more than triple the size of their 1,200 square foot home.
4. While searching the home of a welfare recipient, welfare fraud investigators recovered over $155,000 cash. Further inquiries revealed that one resident held bank accounts containing $225,000 and was running an operation through which fraudulent Medicaid billings were prepared and submitted en masse. These welfare defendants appear to have stolen several million dollars from the Medicaid system.
5. A couple received welfare despite the fact that both the man and the woman owned businesses and had put down $25,000 to purchase a $200,000 home. At the time of their arrest, the couple had $162,000 in cash and $70,000 in a checking account. These longtime welfare recipients' fleet of cars included a Lexus, Jaguar, BMW, and a vintage Corvette.

California has introduced a sophisticated fingerprinting procedure and other safeguards in an attempt to cut down on the more than $85 million dollars lost annually to people who file for and obtain benefits under more than one name. In 1997, Pennsylvania's aggressive attack on welfare fraud saved $115 million, including recovery of $56.7 million in benefits that already had been paid out.

Fraud Close to Home

It is easy to condemn those who commit fraud, but sometimes, the nearest perpetrator may be in the mirror. All too often, otherwise law-abiding citizens defraud the government, insurance companies, or other entities by cheating on their tax returns; filing inflated claims for loss, damage, or personal injury; or maybe just failing to put money in the parking meter. What is their (or, as the case may be, "our") excuse?

People offer many reasons for cheating on their taxes, among them that the tax code is unfair, that the government wastes tax money anyway, and that "everyone is does it" (Thurman, St. John, & Riggs, 1984). Indeed, most people who cheat on their taxes do not consider it a crime (Levi, 1987) or see it as a stigma to be identified as a tax evader. Some go so far as to suggest that the tax laws are so hard to understand that they encourage a certain amount of fraud born of rebellion (S. Duke, 1983). Many tax cheats know that the government audits only a tiny percentage of the millions of tax returns filed each year, so they play the odds, hoping that the low probability of getting caught will work in their favor in the long run.

Like tax evaders, some of those who seek to defraud their insurance companies are trying to save money, perhaps by understating the number of miles they drive each year to get a reduced rate on car insurance. Others are actually trying to steal money by overstating the size of a loss, sometimes with the help of their attorney and/or physician. On rare occasions, these efforts take on bizarre and macabre dimensions. Several years ago, a Virginia man staged what appeared to be his death in a fiery one-car accident. Although no charred remains were found in the wreckage, he was declared dead. While his family mourned, he collected the death benefits from a large life insurance policy that he had recently purchased on himself in the name of a nonexistent relative. His scam was not discovered until several years later when he applied for employment with what turned out to be a fake social security card.

Less dramatic, but far more common, are cases in which people commit fraud by falsifying information on applications for car loans, household loans, home mortgages, or credit cards so that they can get money or a line of credit for which they would not otherwise have qualified. Many of these individuals intend to repay the loans or pay their credit card charges, but when the time comes, they are not able to do so.

Although common, familiar, and seemingly harmless, cases in which "normal" people underpay taxes, overrepresent insurable losses, misrepresent credit worthiness, or the like are nevertheless fraud, and the perpetrators employ variations of the same tactics used by professional thieves. It is uncomfortable for some people to think about these little crimes in this way, which may be one reason why many people are so forgiving of fraud. Perhaps people are reminded of the biblical injunction: "Let he who is without sin cast the first stone." Whatever the case, many people are involved in crimes of fraud in one way or another—either by perpetrating them or by not taking them seriously when they see others victimized. So in asking why people commit serious fraud, the kind that brings in thousands or even hundreds of thousands of dollars, it might be a good idea for people to look within themselves and, if they have engaged in similar activities on a smaller scale, ask what the "good reasons" were.

Occupational Crime

Criminologist Edwin Sutherland (1940) coined the term "white-collar crime" to distinguish the majority of crimes, which are committed by the poor and the powerless, from those perpetrated by individuals who are gainfully employed and take advantage of their (sometimes powerful) positions. Sutherland's main interest was in conspiracies by corporate executives to violate criminal laws and government regulations, but the concept of white-collar crime—like the range of white collar jobs—has undergone considerable expansion. In fact, most criminologists now prefer the term **occupational crime** to refer to any crime committed in the context of one's occupation or employment (Akers, 1985).

There are two main types of occupational crime—individual and organized—each of which can victimize employers, the public, or both. *Individual occupational crimes* are perpetrated by people acting alone as when an employee brings home office supplies or overcharges customers and keeps the excess. In a more sophisticated variant on individual occupational crime—called "professional occupational crime" "—a doctor, lawyer, or other professional might overcharge or steal assets from a patient or client, submit phony Medicare insurance claims, or commit other offenses.

Organized occupational crime takes place when an organization—through its officers, directors, and employees—commits illegal acts against those outside the organization, be it customers, competitors, employees, or the government.[1] Examples of organized occupational crimes include tax evasion, overcharging consumers, misappropriation of funds, bribery of government officials, investment scams, and securities fraud. Enron is the best—and worst—example of several types of fraudulent activities that have affected employees,

---

[1] Organized occupational crime is not to be confused with the activities of the Mafia and crime syndicates, which we discuss later.

investors, and consumers. In that case, both the individual perpetrators and the organization receive direct benefits from the crimes, leaving the public and employees holding an empty bag.

Much organized occupational crime occurs in legitimate businesses, but there are also companies whose sole purpose is to defraud customers, insurance companies, or the government through phony land or time-share deals, home improvement frauds, travel scams, pyramid selling schemes, and the like. Criminologists refer to this kind of organized occupational crime as *fraudulent business*. Another variant on organized occu-pational crime is *government authority crime* in which government employees and public officials commit crimes made possible by virtue of their positions of power and authority. Typical examples are taking bribes, misappropriating public funds, and stealing public property.

The Cost of Occupational Crime

The total cost of occupational crime is hundreds of times greater than the cost of violent and property crimes, partly because it affects so many victims. For example, very few people will be victims of a violent crime or a property crime, but almost everyone is repeatedly victimized by artificially high interest rates on credit cards, excessive insurance premiums and taxes, and investment losses, all of which are indirectly caused by many varieties of occupational crime. Theft by employees, for example, can raise business costs to the point that the price of consumer goods increase by 10% to 15%; it may even contribute to business failures caused by the financial losses incurred by employers (Friedrichs, 1996). Surprisingly, businesses are reluctant to prosecute thieving employees. In a recent survey conducted by the Association of Certified Fraud Examiners (1999), 84% of companies took no legal action to recover the money stolen by employees, and of those that did, only one in three resulted in a criminal conviction. Employers are far more likely to fire the employee, many of whom are then hired by other companies. These data are especially remarkable given that the average loss by employee theft was $97,000 per case (Association of Certified Fraud Examiners, 1999).

The annual cost of bribery and corruption around the world has been estimated by the World Bank to be at least $1 billion, an amount that excludes embezzlement by employees, but that does include the cost of pay-ing bribes to other businesses to get licenses and contracts (Chartered Institute of Building, 2004). The annual cost of corruption in global development (i.e., construction) projects, such as those financed by the World Bank, is said to be more than $3 billion (Transparency International, 2005). The United States ranks 15th out of 52 countries in terms of business corruption consisting of bribes, kickbacks, fictitious businesses, and ille-gal political contributions (Mukherjee, 1997). In an effort to deter fraud against investors and the market, Congress passed the Sarbanes–Oxley law in 2002, a law that has stringent reporting requirements and holds officers and directors liable for false and misleading financial statements (designed to drive up the price of stock and make the financial picture of the companies look better than they are).

Taxpayers pay dearly for health care providers' gaming the federal reimbursement systems of Medicare and Medicaid. This type of fraud cost fraud costs at least $100 billion per year, mostly as a result of falsification of claims for medical payment reimbursement by health care providers and overcharges for goods and services by pharmaceutical companies and medical equipment suppliers (U.S. Senate Committee on Finance, 2004), a direct loss to the government and taxpayers. Experts estimate that $1 out of every $7 dollars billed to Medicaid or Medicare is fraudulent (Barrett, 2005). Add to that fraud against private health insurers, and the tab is $100 billion annually in fraudulent claims and payouts (Barrett, 2005). The U.S. Government and its citizens lose about $300 billion per year in taxes on unreported income (U.S. Internal Revenue Service, 2005), not to men-tion the billions more that have been lost as a result of criminal fraud in the savings and loan industry and in Wall Street investment scandals. Horrendous as these losses are, the cost of pervasive occupational crime goes beyond money, illness, death, and destruction. It also contributes to widespread mistrust and cynicism about governmental and business leaders. Everyone, it seems, is "on the take."

We consider each main type of occupational crime, beginning with individual occupational crime.

Individual Occupational Crime: Embezzlement

The most common form of individual occupational crime is **embezzlement**, which is the taking of something of value to which one has access based on a position of trust or authority. For example, an employee who has access to the firm's checkbook or the store's cash register might take the opportunity to steal from the company. Sometimes the crime is as simple as taking money from the till. In other cases, it involves more complicated transactions as when an employee in the accounts payable department creates phony vendors and then writes checks to those vendors that the employee endorses and cashes. In still others, the embezzler uses a computer to electronically transfer funds from employer accounts to accounts the employee controls. Here are some examples of various embezzlement schemes:

1. Mary Treadwell, wife of former District of Columbia Mayor Marion Barry, pleaded guilty to embezzling more than $10,000 from city funds. Her plea came just 15 years after she had been convicted, wrongly she claimed, of defrauding the U.S. Department of Housing and Urban Development and the residents of a public housing project that she managed. After serving less than half of her three-year sentence for that conviction, Treadwell got a job with the local parole board and then obtained a position in the D.C. city government that not only paid her $60,000 a year but gave her access to the checkbooks of a neighborhood organization public housing association. She took advantage of this position to write checks to herself, using the money to make mortgage payments and pay credit card bills. When she was arrested, Treadwell claimed that depression and loss of self-esteem as a result of her prior wrongful conviction led to her current offenses (Woodlee, 1998).

2. The scheme concocted by a man who worked as a broker in his family's insurance business was to cash new customers' premium checks without bothering to arrange for the insurance. The plan quickly fell apart when his customers made claims and found that they were not covered. He lost his insurance license and went to jail, and the family business was forced to reimburse his customers for their premiums as well as to pay their claims.

The losses in such cases can be staggering. Maria Umali, an accounting clerk, embezzled $1 million from her employer, a government contracting firm in Northern Virginia; and an Arlington, Virginia, attorney took the same amount from his clients' escrow fund. In another case, a 76-year-old bookkeeper embezzled over $1.3 million from her family's real estate business. The head of the District of Columbia agency for the mentally retarded was found to have embezzled millions of dollars to build a home and a vacation retreat while housing for the agency's clients were in severe disrepair, and suppliers of vital items such as food and mental health services had cut off the agency for nonpayment.

A 2004 survey (Chubb Corporation, 2004) by the Chubb Group of Insurance Corporations estimated that three out of five publicly held companies experience employee theft losses attributed to stealing money or equipment averaging $97,000 (for large companies) to $127,000 (for small companies) per theft scheme. Chubb, which insures companies against employee crime losses, says that employee crime, including embezzlement, is one of the major challenges facing businesses today. However, as noted earlier, most employers do nothing more than fire the embezzlers they catch. This strategy is driven partly by a desire to save the time and money it would cost to pursue each case in court and partly by a recognition that the consequences of prosecution for the embezzler are not likely to be severe. A survey of judges in the Maryland and Virginia jurisdictions surrounding Washington, DC found, for example, that except in the case of professionals (such as attorneys, who tend to receive long prison terms), most first-time embezzlers are given suspended sentences, put on probation, and ordered to repay the money they took. This outcome is even less significant than it sounds, though, because most embezzlers are unable to make restitution, having already spent the stolen money (Locy, 1998). Further, with probation officers overworked by caseloads of drug dealers and violent offenders, embezzlers who fail to make required payments are unlikely to be pursued. Also, even if noncomplying embezzlers are brought before a judge, they are not likely to be made to serve their previously suspended sentences because this would eliminate all hope that the victim will ever be repaid (Locy, 1998).

Individual Occupational Crime: Securities Violations

The world of investing, and especially the world of Wall Street, creates opportunities for individual occupational crime on a scale that can far exceed the aspirations of even the most ambitious embezzler. Consider the case of Michael Milken who in the 1980s was considered the most powerful financier in the world. He was also 1 of 60 people in top Wall Street firms indicted for securities crimes. In 1989, Milken was charged with 98 counts of securities-law violations including insider trading (the use of private information to benefit himself and his clients), manipulating stock prices, and felony fraud. For example, acting on confidential information obtained through his position as a trader in stocks and high-yield ("junk") bonds at the Wall Street firm of Drexel Burnham Lambert, Milken would purchase large quantities of a stock, thus quickly driving up its share prices, and then sell the shares to make astronomical profits for himself and his clients. Milken was sentenced to 10 years in prison. He also paid fines and restitution of more than $1 billion (Crovitz, 1990; J. Gallagher, 1990; R. Thomas, 1990), but even this amount did not cover all the money lost by innocent investors as a result of Milken's fraud and stock manipulation. In 1993, after serving only 2 years of his sentence, Milken was released on early parole in exchange for (a) cooperating with government investigators in their efforts to arrest stock manipulators Milken knew and (b) agreeing not to participate in any securities transactions or Wall Street trading. Shortly after his release, however, Milken was involved in several major business deals including one in which he helped arrange MCI Corporation's investment in Rupert Murdoch's news organization. Instead of being prosecuted for violating the conditions of his parole and returned to prison, the Justice Department accepted a deal whereby Milken paid the U.S. Government the $42 million he had earned in consulting fees on these deals as well as another $5 million in interest (Walsh, 1998). Ironically, Milken had amassed such a huge fortune as a result of his fraudulent activities that he can still live the life of a billionaire.

Milken's arrest was preceded by that of Dennis Levine, another employee of Drexel Burnham Lambert who made more than $12 million in illegal profits from insider trading. Ivan Boesky, a client who benefited from the insider information obtained from Levine and others, was fined $100 million dollars and given a 3-year prison sentence. As part of its involvement in insider trading, Drexel Burnham Lambert pled guilty to stock manipulation charges and agreed to pay $600 million in criminal fines and civil penalties. The company went bankrupt (Pearlstein, 2006).

Professional Occupational Crime

In January of 1998, 11 men were indicted in Federal Court in Alexandria, Virginia, for participating in a scam that defrauded insurance companies of more than $2.7 million dollars in fraudulent medical and legal payments. Members of the ring drove around until they located a motorist whose appearance and automobile suggested maturity, affluence, and paid-up car insurance. Positioning their cars in front of unsuspecting victims, they would suddenly slam on their brakes, causing the targeted motorist to hit them from behind. There were no real injuries in these "accidents," but because the victim was legally at fault, the ring members would ask the victim's insurance company to reimburse them for the medical care that they had supposedly sought.

Physicians who were members of the ring then submitted phony bills for medical services allegedly given to the "injured" drivers. Claiming that these drivers had also sought legal advice, attorney members of the ring filed claims against the insurance company demanding payment not only of the phony medical bills but also of cash awards for their clients' "pain and suffering," lost wages, and other nonexistent damages. The insurance companies paid the bills, unaware that no medical or legal services had actually been rendered and that the doctors and lawyers who sent the bills were themselves part of the fraud ring (Masters, 1998a). In California, the Allstate Insurance Company was defrauded of about $107 million dollars in the same type of scheme associated with about 100 "accidents" taking place between 1992 and 1996.

This type of professional occupational crime adds $200 to $300 to the typical motorists' annual insurance premium, not to mention putting innocent drivers and passengers at risk (M. White, 1998).

Organized Occupational Crime: Legitimate Businesses

Actions by groups of employees that result in false advertising, violations of banking and securities laws, unsafe products, and illegal dumping of environmental wastes are just a few examples of organized occupational crime. Its victims may be individuals or entire industries—and the consequences range from financial loss to serious injury and death.

One of the most notorious examples of organized occupational crime—and, according to some observers, the biggest financial swindle in history—resulted in the collapse of the Bank of Credit and Commerce International (BCCI). BCCI's directors were some of the most well-respected business executives and former politicians in the United States, including the late Clark Clifford, a former Cabinet member. Government investigators discovered that these bank officials (a) accepted bribes in exchange for lending billions of dollars to friends and associates who had no intention of repaying them and (b) used fraudulent accounting methods designed to keep bank examiners and depositors from discovering the truth about these loans (Lohr, 1992). BCCI officers also helped to fund the nefarious activities of Saddam Hussein, Ferdinand Marcos, and leaders of Colombian drug cartels as well as to launder money for dealers in illegal drugs and weapons. Losses to investors in the BCCI case topped $15 billion (Truell & Gurwin, 1992).

Two infamous examples of organized occupational crime that more directly harmed consumers involved the Ford Motor Company and the A.H. Robbins pharmaceutical company. In the Ford case, a group of executives was aware that rear-end collisions could cause gas tank explosions in Ford Pintos manufactured between 1971 and 1976. However, because it would have been so costly to make the design changes necessary to solve this safety problem, the executives refused to do so. More than 50 people died in Pintos as a result of gas tank explosions following rear-end collisions, and Ford paid millions of dollars in damages (Coleman, 1994). Executives of A.H. Robbins sought to protect sales and profits by knowingly misrepresenting the safety of the company's intrauterine birth-control device known as the Dalkon Shield. At least 17 women died, and thousands more were injured by medical complications attributed to the device; Robbins paid out more than $378 million to settle the resulting lawsuits. When Robbins finally filed for bankruptcy, a federal court earmarked $2.5 billion of the company's assets to compensate additional victims (Coleman, 1994).

Some other examples of organized occupational crime that caused huge losses to individuals and financial institutions include:

1. Massive leaks of toxic chemicals from a dumping ground in Love Canal, New York, forced the evacuation and demolition of over 500 homes. Cleaning up the dump cost taxpayers about $200 million.
2. In the late 1980s, there was grossly unethical conduct among savings and loan executives who had financial stakes in companies to which they made loans. Many of these loans exceeded the fair market value of those companies, a fact that came back to haunt the executives when the bottom fell out of the commercial real estate market. This debacle led to the collapse of more than 1,700 lending institutions and to the creation of the Resolution Trust Corporation, a quasi-federal agency whose job it was to oversee the dissolution of the lending organizations and attempt to recoup some of their losses by selling mortgaged properties. The whole affair cost U.S. taxpayers more than $500 billion.

All of these examples involved legitimate businesses that engaged in criminal conduct. Another kind of organized occupational crime is conducted by people involved in illegitimate businesses.

Organized Occupational Crime: Fraudulent Businesses

Not all organized occupational crimes are as massive or sophisticated as in the multibillion dollar cases perpetrated by wealthy and powerful executives. Smaller scale versions can be triggered by a knock at your door where you find a uniformed man who identifies himself as a local building inspector. After looking at the wooden deck at the back of your house, he tells you that its posts are rotten and that he may have to ask you to tear it down if it is not repaired within 30 days. Before leaving, he recommends a company that can do the job for you at a fair price. You call the company and eventually sign a contract to have the deck repaired for $3,500. In fact, your deck was in fine shape, and your visitor was not a building inspector but a "front man" for a dishonest home-improvement business. This is an example of organized occupational crime perpetrated by a fraudulent business.

Other fraudulent businesses entice their customers with schemes for making quick, easy money or acquiring goods at prices "too good to be true." Failing to think critically and to realize that when it seems too good to be true, it probably is, tens of thousands of people are swindled by these companies each year. Land frauds, for example, began in the 1920s and continue to this day. In some of these, people are enticed to visit distant tracts of land via offers of free travel, accommodations, and other gifts and once there, are misled into thinking that the barren plot they can purchase now will be the Las Vegas of the future, worth many times the asking price. Others involve pyramid-type investment and sales schemes, also known as multilevel distributorship scams, which encourage people to purchase franchise dealerships for home cleaning products, cosmetics, health foods, and dietary supplements or even long distance telephone services. These people are assured that they will soon recover their investment and make hundreds of thousands more by not only selling the company's product or service but by recruiting other dealers who will work under them and turn over a percentage of all their sales—as well as of the sales of dealers that they later recruit. If the products or services sell well, and if people buy a franchise early in the company's life, they can indeed make money. As more and more dealers start competing for a fixed pool of customers, however, there is simply not enough income available to make them all rich. Most of those who sign on late in the process are lucky to earn back their original franchise fees. Other blatantly fraudulent businesses operate telemarketing campaigns for bogus health products and penny stocks.

One of most spectacular examples of a fraudulent business came to light in the summer of 1999 when 44-year-old Martin Frankel disappeared from the Connecticut mansion where he ran an unlicensed stock brokerage. In the wake of his departure, investigators found that he had stolen $200 million from large insurance companies in five states. He was arrested four months later, in Hamburg, Germany, but fought extradition to the United States because conviction on fraud charges could put him in jail for life. Instead, he pleaded guilty in a German court to using a falsified passport and failing to pay import duty on $1.6 million in smuggled diamonds. In June of 2000, he was sentenced to serve three years in a German jail, which, as he told reporters, was a lot better than being sent back to the United States. It is unlikely that the insurance companies will ever recover all the money he stole through his fraudulent brokerage (Cowan, 2004).

Government Authority Crime

Groups of employees in federal, state, or local governments have been known to work together to take advantage of their power and access to government funds to defraud the government (and the taxpayers). In 1998, for example, workers at the Virginia Department of Corrections were found to have sold prisoner-made goods to an out-of-state corporation at a price far lower than the Department of Corrections standard. They kept the proceeds for themselves, resulting in millions of dollars in losses to Virginia taxpayers. In this scheme, employees at levels ranging from clerk to manager cooperated in creating and verifying the paper trail necessary to keep their fraud hidden.

Causes of Individual Occupational Crime

Understanding why individuals commit occupational crimes requires attention not only to the offenders' sociocultural background, personality characteristics, and developmental history but also to factors such as the situations in which the offenses take place and the offenders' financial situation (Braithwaite, 1989; Shover & Bryant, 1993). It has been suggested that there are two main types of occupational criminals: those who simply seek money and those who pursue other ego-gratifying goals such as power, control, and influence (Benson & Moore, 1992). The business world provides the perfect venue to use criminal means to satisfy both kinds of goals.

Many of those who engage in individual occupational crime—especially embezzlement—do so out of a simple need for money. These individuals are either impoverished or are living beyond their means and seize the opportunity to make a "quick buck." Most people arrested for embezzlement do not hold positions of high social status and responsibility, but compared to other property offenders, embezzlers are likely to be better educated, to own homes, and to have less prior involvement in the criminal justice system (Wheeler, Wesiberg, Waring, & Bode, 1988).

The percentage of women arrested for individual occupational crime has increased continuously over the last three decades from about 15% in the 1960s to about 43% today. Criminologists believe this change reflects the fact that (a) there are more lower income women than men, and (b) there are more women than men in the work force who are entrusted with company money or who have easy access to it (Albanese, 1995; Coleman, 1995). For example, women are more likely than men to be clerks, cashiers, or secretaries (Steffensmeier,

1995) who have access to and control over company finances and who work in isolation (Locy, 1998). Because men are more likely than women to be managers, they may have access to even larger amounts of company money and may thus be able to steal more money than women can (Daly, 1989). Indeed, losses as a result of manager and executive embezzlement is 16 times greater than those by nonmanagerial employees and four times greater for male than female offenders (Association of Certified Fraud Examiners, 1995).

Individual occupational crimes such as theft, falsification of time cards, padding business expenses, and other fraudulent acts are more common in organizations where workers are treated poorly and are subjected to a hostile work environment. These employees may feel that the opportunity to engage in criminal behavior is a "fringe benefit" to be taken as compensation for working in an oppressive setting. At the same time, managers of such organizations may look the other way because doing so is cheaper than increasing salaries or providing other benefits (Coleman, 1994). The likelihood of individual occupational crime is also elevated in companies where managers fail to monitor employee records and activity. Most offenders are isolated and work alone, especially those involved in embezzlement and other types of employee theft.

Mary Treadwell, the DC government employee mentioned earlier, apparently stole because even though she made enough money to live comfortably, she wanted to live more comfortably. However, why would Michael Milken, who already made millions of dollars a year in legitimate income, risk arrest and imprisonment to bilk investors out of billions more? It probably has less to do with having more money than with the sense of power and control that comes to some people from making money and perhaps from making it illegally.

When individual occupational criminals are caught, the initial reaction from colleagues and employers is often one of surprise. The criminal behavior seems so irrational, so out of character, and so at odds with the offender's professional standing or image that many assume that alcoholism or some other form of mental illness must be responsible (McClintick, 1982). However, although some of these perpetrators may suffer from substance use disorders (Cowles, 1992; Mieth & McCorkle, 1998), most have no special propensity for substance abuse or other mental disorders (Friedrichs, 1996).

So why do they do it? Criminologists and psychologists are by no means sure of the answer, but they have offered a number of theories. Those who take a psychodynamic perspective have suggested that these individuals may commit their crimes out of a desire to be punished for previous acts or impulses about which they already feel guilty (Freud, 1923). If this hypothesis is correct, it could help explain why some occupational offenders engage in such easily detected crimes. The insurance broker we described earlier in this chapter was a depressed loner. Middle-aged and never married, he was estranged from his family. It became apparent to his attorney that he wanted to be convicted and sent to prison. He confided that he felt guilty about not being as successful in his business or personal life as his older brother and that he felt that his mediocrity was a source of shame to the family. He said that he deserved to be in prison for a long time, and he got his wish.

Developmental and cognitive theories focus on occupational criminals' apparent lack of moral development. This emphasis seems especially apropos given that many of these criminals do not perceive that they have done anything wrong. Instead, they engage in massive cognitive distortions in an effort to minimize and morally "neutralize" their crimes. For example, embezzlers often justify their crime by pointing out that they do not get paid enough, that they are merely taking "what they deserve," and that their employer "can afford it." Others maintain the fiction that they are just borrowing the money and that they will repay it later (Creesey, 1973). Health care professionals who defraud insurers and the government often seek to minimize their personal responsibility by claiming to have "made mistakes" or by blaming their crimes on inept employees or confusing paperwork requirements (Jesilow, Pontell, & Geis, 1993). From this perspective, then, individual occupational criminals are like robbers, burglars, and other offenders in that their crimes appear to be motivated by a combination of failure to develop self-control and lack of respect for laws (M. Gottfredson & Hirschi, 1990; Hirschi & Gottfredson, 1987).

Most individual occupational criminals do not show clearly identifiable personality disorders, but they do display traits associated with antisocial personality disorder including cleverness, aloofness, a disregard for the rights of others, and manipulating people for personal gain. They also tend to be risk takers who lack the ability to delay gratification (M. Gottfredson & Hirschi, 1990; Hagan & Kay, 1990; Wheeler, 1992). They may also be narcissistic. For example, biographical accounts of Michael Milken, Charles Keating, and Leona Helmsley (the famous hotel magnate and income tax evader) include mention of several narcissistic personality traits such as obsession with power and control, egocentricity, and a sense of exemption from the rule of law that governs others (Binstein & Bowden, 1993; Pierson, 1989; J. B.Stewart, 1991).[2] Some people involved in individual occupational crime also manifest obsessive–compulsive characteristics including a fixation on maintaining an image of success and on amassing wealth far beyond what they could ever spend (Vise, 1987). Many individual occupational criminals display the same tendency toward recidivism seen in "ordinary" criminals (Weisburd et al., 1993).

In the final analysis, then, white-collar offenders who cheat, defraud, and steal from private employers, the government, and private citizens are not that different from street criminals, at least not in terms of what influences them to commit crimes. Although they are not generally poor and powerless, they are impulsive, irrational, and lacking in self-control. They have little or no empathy for the people they are hurting and no respect for the laws that the rest of the people obey. They appear to be fixed in what Kohlberg (1964) called the preconventional stage of moral development (see chapters 7 and 8), meaning that they would refrain from crime only to avoid punishment; if punishment is seen as unlikely, laws will not deter them. Indeed, the main difference between occupational criminals and street criminals is that the jobs held by the former provide far easier and more lucrative crime opportunities than those available to the latter. Criminologists M. Gottfredson and Hirschi (1990) suggested that "the distinction between crime in the street and crime in the suite" (p. 200) reflects a difference in offenses rather than a difference in offenders.

The Criminal Corporation

What kinds of companies are responsible for organized occupational crime? As we already noted, some exist solely to commit crimes, but the overall profile of the corporate offender is mixed. In some cases, organized occupational crimes are committed by companies whose marginal financial balance sheets lead their executives to resort to crime in hopes of improving their bottom line. It is also the case, however, that large and successful corporations sometimes commit crimes to maintain their economic position in relation to their competitors (Miethe & McCorkle, 1998).

In the red-hot stock market of the late 1990s, though, some companies took corporate crime to a new level. Think of Enron, the global corporate giant that cooked the books, created fictitious shell companies, lied on their publicly filed financial statements, and assured their employees that their Enron stock-funded pension plans were secure—all lies to boost the value of its stock. Further, Enron subsidiaries created false energy crises in the Western states to drive up the prices of the electricity and gas that Enron was selling on the open markets. So widespread was the Enron scheme of corruption and fraud that even its accounting firm, Arthur Anderson, was implicated in helping Enron devise some of its illegal schemes and prepare its false financial reports. For its part in the scheme, Arthur Anderson, a once proud and famous accounting giant, went out of business. Enron went bankrupt, and several of its officers and directors either pled guilty to or were convicted of numerous crimes.

Ironically, the more strictly regulated the industry, the higher the incidence of corporate crime (Coleman, 1995). The tightly regulated pharmaceutical, automobile, and petroleum industries—which manufacture potentially dangerous products or are involved in environmentally hazardous activities—have been the most common corporate violators of federal regulations (Clinard & Yeager, 1980). Within these industries, it is usually employees and managers with specialized knowledge about company practices who are most likely to be involved in corporate crimes.

Not all corporations go the way of Enron and Arthur Anderson. Most continue in business even after they are caught. What allows violators of laws designed to protect the public to continue in business after committing crimes? For one thing, many of their offenses are so-called regulatory crimes, meaning that the Securities and Exchange Commission, the Environmental Protection Agency, or whatever federal agency regulates the business can prosecute violations but have the authority only to assess fines, not mete out prison sentences. So a corporation caught at organized occupational crime may have to pay huge fines, but these will be passed onto the consumer in higher product costs. In fact, fines and damage payments to injured parties are perceived by many corporate executives as just another cost of doing business and ultimately recoverable from its cus-

---

[2]Leona Helmsley is said to have remarked that "only little people pay taxes."

tomers. In cases when there is criminal prosecution, the corporation usually has virtually unlimited resources to not only hire the best lawyers but to wear down the government's legal resources and will to prosecute.

Can the same psychological theories that might explain individual occupational crime also apply to organized occupational crime? The answer is yes and no. Certainly, the decisions that transform a corporation into a criminal organization must be made by individuals, but to understand the causes of organized occupational crimes, one must look beyond these individuals' personal characteristics. The general business setting and climate, the state of the economy, the nature and impact of government regulations, and the specific situation that set the stage for the offense are also important causal factors.

Do certain corporations actually recruit people who are predisposed toward corporate crime or are at least willing to go along with it, or are such people attracted to certain types of corporations (Coleman, 1994)? No one knows for sure, but both factors are probably operating. Some researchers believe that particular corporate cultures promote criminality among its employees in the same sense that living in poverty or being a member of a juvenile gang promotes street crime. Those who support this view say that like street gang members, newer corporate employees learn attitudes and techniques from their more experienced peers and superiors in the organization.

Some organizations are known as *crime-coercive* because they literally compel their employees to commit crimes, whereas others are called *crime facilitative* because they provide conditions that promote criminal conduct (Shover & Bryant, 1993; Szasz, 1986). It has also been suggested that some whole industries—especially those in which competition is most intense—are set up in such a way as to make them **criminogenic**, meaning that they actually breed crime (Clinard & Yeager, 1980). In investment banking and stock trading, for example, employees are constantly under pressure to make more and more money. Those whose personal characteristics make them less likely than others to be law abiding may be the ones most likely to engage in fraudulent or deceptive practices to sell more stocks or bonds. In such an environment, say criminologists, these illegal activities become necessary for individual and corporate survival.

In short, most observers agree that much organized occupational crime would not take place but for (1) a corporate culture that condones, coerces, or facilitates it; (2) a political, economic, and legal system within which it can thrive; and (3) the availability of plenty of individuals who are ready to commit crimes to benefit themselves and their organizations. Indeed, organized occupational crime demonstrates how multifaceted the roots of crime can be.

Still, like other crimes, organized occupational crime depends mainly on individuals within organizations who lack regard both for the law and for the victims who will suffer at their hands. Decades ago, folk singer Woody Guthrie wrote that "some men rob you with a six-gun, some with a fountain pen." Are these corporate criminals any less responsible or reprehensible for the damage they inflict on their victims just because they wear expensive clothes, look respectable, and make substantial donations to worthy causes? Given the relatively anemic efforts made by this society and its law enforcement agencies to severely punish these criminals, the answer, apparently, is yes.

Of the about 40% of all convicted criminals that are sentenced to prison, only 18% of those found guilty of tax fraud, 9% of embezzlers, and 5% of regulatory offenders spend time in jail (Coleman, 1995). Just as employees engaging in organized occupational crime rarely think about their anonymous and far-removed victims, society itself seems to be more tolerant of these crimes than of others because the corporate perpetrators are anonymous and may be perceived as less intent than, say, arsonists on harming individuals. As a result, corporations engaged in crime are often quite shameless. They rationalize and defend their actions as undertaken either in ignorance or in an effort to benefit the public and their investors. Also, because the public and the criminal justice system typically fail to take actions to significantly deter future organizational crime, criminally inclined corporations have little incentive to change their ways unless their crimes cease to be profitable.

Syndicated Crime

"The Mafia," "The Mob," "La Cosa Nostra," and "The Family" are all popular terms for what is commonly called organized crime. We chose to use the term **syndicated crime** (Friedrichs, 1996) to distinguish this form of criminal activity from the organized corporate crime just discussed. Syndicated crime involves a network of individuals and businesses systematically engaged in a variety of criminal enterprises including the sale and distribution of drugs, gambling, extortion, prostitution, loan sharking, and labor racketeering (President's Commission on Organized Crime, 1987).

Crime syndicates are not a new phenomenon; they appeared in the piracy that was rampant in the waters of ancient Greece and Rome. Crime networks were operating, too, in 16th-century London and by the end of the 17th century, had reached the Massachusetts Bay Colony in the New World (McMullan, 1982). The Mafia itself emerged in the 16th century in southern Italy, taking the form of groups, or *cabals*, with names such as *la Camorro, L'unione Siciliana,* and *La Cosa Nostra.* Members of *La Cosa Nostra,* which was part of the Sicilian Mafia, made up a small minority of Italian immigrants who came to the United States at the end of the 19th century (D. A. Smith, 1975). They settled in New York, New Orleans, and in other U.S. cities (Abadinsky, 1985). Members of La Cosa Nostra conducted their first significant criminal activities in the United States in the 1920s after a new federal law made the manufacture and possession of alcohol illegal. At first they mainly supplied alcohol, but soon the organization began to control other illegal activities such as gambling, loan sharking, prostitution, and gun sales. Eventually, they began to infiltrate, take over, or influence many types of legal businesses as well.

There are some differences between organized occupational crime and syndicated crime. First, like other organizations, crime syndicates are set up in a strict hierarchy, but they are open only to a limited membership, usually based on ethnic heritage, who take on specialized roles and obligations and adhere to a vow of loyalty and secrecy about the organization, its membership, and its activities. Second, crime syndicates rely heavily on force, violence, and intimidation as a means of coercing compliance from those within the syndicate and those outside it. Third, as with other business organizations, the growth of crime syndicates is fueled largely by satisfying consumer demands, but these syndicates specialize in meeting demands for goods and services that are illegal. So although legitimate businesses might be engaged in criminal activities in the service of corporate goals, those goals are to make money for themselves and their stockholders. Crime syndicates also aim to make money, but their main goal is to do so through illegal activities; and unlike most corporate executives, the leaders of crime syndicates think nothing of using intimidation and violence to promote their own interests. For example, anyone who threatens to compete with a syndicate may be brutally assaulted or even killed. Crime syndicates will stop at nothing to exert their influence and reap their massive profits.

Fighting Syndicated Crime

In the 1990s, prosecutors in New York were successful in putting several Mafia bosses, including John Gotti, Sr., in prison for life after obtaining convictions on charges of murder, racketeering, and other crimes. In January 1998, New York prosecutors indicted John Gotti, Jr., and 39 other members of the Gambino crime syndicate for extortion, telecommunications (phone card) and construction fraud, labor racketeering, and money laundering. In March 1999, John Jr. pled guilty to extortion and gambling charges in exchange for a government recommendation of 6 years in prison, a $1 million fine, and the return of his home and other property the government had seized. Most of the other indicted members of the Gambino crime syndicate have also pled guilty and are serving prison terms. One of the syndicate's lawyers, Michael Blutrich, was disbarred and is serving a 25-year prison term for his involvement in a money-laundering scheme operating out of a New York striptease bar known as "Scores" (G. B. Smith, 1998).

As a result of the aggressive federal prosecutions that put both John Gotti, Sr., and his son in prison, the Gambino syndicate, once the most influential arm of *La Cosa Nostra* in the United States, has lost a great deal of its power and influence. Syndicated crime is still with us, however, and many believe that it always will be. Its locus of power and the nature of its businesses are changing, though. Some mob watchers believe that the remaining members of *La Cosa Nostra* will engage in "quieter" and "softer" activities such as stock market manipulation and fraudulent sale of prepaid telephone calling cards (Augenstein, 1998).

The fight against syndicated crime will also be made more difficult by the emergence of criminal syndicates run by members of various non-Italian ethnic groups. Among these are the so-called Russian Mafia, also known as "Odessa Malina" and "Prganizatsiya," whose members arrived in large numbers in the United States during the 1970s. They market drugs, weapons, and stolen cars and are involved in extortion, forgery, loan sharking, and racketeering. There are also "Tongs" and "Triads" such as "Wo" and "14 K" whose origins can be traced to 17th-century China. These syndicates, which specialize in gambling, extortion, drug trafficking, robbery, prostitution, murder, and arms dealing, are found mainly in New York and California. Vietnamese gangs such as "Born to Kill" are to be found in most major cities where they are involved in extortion, prostitution, auto theft, arson, gambling, and armed robbery. Closely linked to Chinese organized crime, they are considered to be the most ruthless of Asian crime syndicates. Like the Vietnamese syndicates, Jamaican "posses,"—which formed in Kingston, Jamaica, and carry names such as "Shower Posse" and "Spangler Posse"—came to the United States in the mid-1970s and are especially violent. They, too, operate in most major U.S. cities where their 22,000 members control 30% to 40% of the U.S. crack cocaine trade. They are also involved in gun running, money laundering, fraud, robbery, kidnaping, murder, and auto theft. The Japanese "Yakuza" are located mainly in California and Hawaii. Their origins are in 7th-century Japan, and they have names such as "Yamaguchi" and "Gumi." Specializing in weapons and methamphetamine trafficking to Japan as well as in murder, gambling, and extortion, they have also infiltrated legitimate business activities such as banking and real estate. There are also Colombian crime syndicates, known as the "Medellin" and "Cali" cartels, whose only business is drug trafficking. Their complex organization employs at least 24,000 people, mainly in New York, Miami, Los Angeles, and Houston (Kenney & Finckenauer, 1995). Finally, federal law enforcement agencies have uncovered the existence of organized crime rings, mainly from China and Latin America, whose primary activity is the smuggling of illegal aliens. These groups charge as much as $30,000 to get each alien into the United States and then—by threatening them with exposure and deportation—force these people to engage in drug dealing, prostitution, or unpaid labor for syndicate bosses and their families. Many of them are arrested for criminal activity, but they are usually too frightened to implicate those who run the smuggling and extortion racket that has victimized them (Albanese & Finckenauer, 1997).

However, it is no longer possible to speak of crime syndicates in national terms; they operate across borders all over the world dealing in illegal drugs and other contraband and legal enterprises such as telecommunications, oil and gas, money laundering, cybercrime, and terrorism. The annual gross revenue of crime syndicates across the world is measured in the trillions of dollars. Prosecutorial success in the United States has made inroads in the Mafia in the United States; the growth of the Mafia today is in former Soviet states, China, Pakistan, and Afghanistan. Russia alone is said to have more than 6,000 criminal organizations. Criminologists do not refer to these global syndicates as the Mafia but rather "organized transnational crime" (Broome, 2000).

Federal law enforcement officials are concerned about threats to national security that could arise as a result of crime syndicate involvement in the control of high-tech weaponry including nuclear weapons. This concern focuses especially on the Russian Mafia operating in the United States and in Russia. There is also concern for the health of the international banking system, as ever more sophisticated money laundering schemes are made possible through advanced computer technology (Albanese & Finckenauer, 1997). There is also growing alarm at the number of clandestine drug laboratories producing synthetic drugs such as methamphetamine and PCP (a major activity of the Japanese syndicates). Federal drug agents believe that these laboratories are capable of producing enough illicit drugs to satisfy U.S. consumer demand.

More sophisticated forms of syndicated crime demand more sophisticated methods of detection. If the United States is to be successful in controlling international organized crime, it will need cooperation from foreign governments in surveillance, arrest, and forfeiture of property involved in illegal activities. This is an enormous challenge and one that is difficult to address globally. The U.S. State Department operates a Bureau for International Narcotics and Law Enforcement Affairs designed to get at the roots of transnational crime and money laundering. Legitimate governments cooperate to root out criminal syndicates all over the world. Experts refer to transnational organized crime as the new "evil empire" (Broome, 2000). Criminologists stress that eliminating syndicated crime requires greater attention to eliminating some of the social problems—such as poverty, discrimination, and lack of education—that help create demand for the goods and services of syndicated crime (Albanese & Finckenauer, 1997).

Summary

Although property and economic crimes make up almost 90% of all crime, the public does not express nearly as much concern about these offenses as it does about violent crime. Yet, economic and property crimes, that comprise a substantial majority of all criminal incidents, cost us billions of dollars a year and inflict immeasurable losses of public trust and confidence in government, business, and other social institutions. U.S. jails and prisons are filled not with violent offenders, but with those convicted of property and drug crimes. Many other perpetrators of economic and property crimes are never caught partly, because they include many of us. People are the victims of their own and their neighbor's fraudulent acts against taxing authorities, insurance companies, and credit card companies. Everyone pays for the costs of these crimes in higher prices for goods and services.

Arson, the willful and malicious burning of property, is unique in that the majority or arsonists are minors. Only a few arsonists are diagnosable with pyromania, an impulse-control disorder characterize by setting fires for pleasure, gratification, or the release of tension. Most arsonists set fires to exact revenge, intimidate others, or gain financially through insurance fraud.

Burglary, the unlawful entry into a building to commit larceny, and larceny, the taking of someone's property, make up most property crime. Some burglars make a career of their crimes, but most burglars engage in their crimes to support a drug habit. Auto theft and shoplifting are specific forms of larceny. A shoplifter who, like an arsonist, acts compulsively and steals out of a desire to release tension, is known as a kleptomaniac. Few shoplifters have this disorder.

Fraud takes many forms. Cheating on the government—and thus fellow taxpayers—is common. Businesses and individuals scam the government in many ways—underreporting income, issuing false claims for government reimbursement, lying on applications for benefits— and cost the taxpayers billions of dollars a year.

Occupational and organizational crime takes a huge toll on businesses and consumers. Some individuals use their position to embezzle funds and steal property. Some organizations themselves are involved in fraudulent businesses in whole or in part. As costly as these crimes are, citizens and prosecutors do not seem as concerned about the effect of these crimes as they should be. Somehow, they just do not have the panache of violent crimes.

Crime syndicates have morphed in form from family- or ethnic-centered criminal enterprises to global enterprises that operate all over the world in many countries. Today, syndicates traffic in drugs and weapons, engage in money laundering, support terrorism, and engage in cybercrime. Hot spots for transnational terrorism include Russia and China. The United States takes seriously the threat of transnational criminal syndicates and cooperates with other governments to protect the world from what some call the modern day evil empire.

Key Terms

Arson	*Fraud*
Pyromania	*Occupational crime*
Burglary	*Embezzlement*
Larceny theft	*Criminogenic*
Kleptomania	*Syndicated crime*

Questions for Review

1. Compare and contrast the five types of arson and explain how arson differs from pyromania.
2. What are considered to be the causes of kleptomania?
3. What characteristics do white-collar criminals share with street criminals?
4. What are some differences between organized occupational crime and syndicated crime?
5. What is a criminogenic corporation?

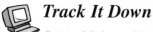

Track It Down

Criminal Behavior Website
www.cassel2e.com
The FBI's Uniform Crime Reports
www.fbi.gov/ucr/cius_03/pdf/03sec1.pdf
Firefighter Arson
www.facts-1.com/usfa_tr-141.pdf
Healthcare Fraud Cases
http://mathiasconsulting.com/taxonomy/view/or/71
The Enron Story
www.aflcio.org/corporateamerica/enron/
The Russian Mafia
http://news.bbc.co.uk/1/hi/special_report/1998/03/98/russian_mafia/70485.stm
Transnational Crime in the 21st Century
www.wjin.net/Pubs/2381.pdf

12

Victims of Crime

We are living in "the age of the victim." Everyone wants to be given special treatment because of something, no matter how ridiculous or trivial that something might be. However, there is nothing trivial about being a victim of crime, and over the last 30 years, crime victims have begun to organize and demand their due from the criminal justice system (Wallace, 1998). In this chapter, we consider crime victims and the suffering they endure as a result of criminal acts. We examine the roles they play in the processes of arrest, trial, sentencing, and sometimes in crime itself.

Who Are Crime Victims?

Generally speaking, a victim is a person who is harmed by the actions of others. Although people tend to think of crime victims mainly as those most directly affected by murderers, robbers, or other offenders, the victims' family and friends are indirectly harmed, too, and can thus be considered victims as well. Accordingly, a typical state statute defines a crime victim as

> A person who has suffered physical, psychological or economic harm as a direct result of the com-
> mission of a felony or of assault and battery, stalking, sexual battery, maiming, or driving while
> intoxicated; a spouse or child of such a person; a parent or legal guardian of such a person who is a
> minor, or a spouse, parent or legal guardian of such a person who is physically or mentally incapac-
> itated or was the victim of a homicide. (Virginia Code Section 19.2–11.01)

Statutes such as this one focus on victims who have legal rights in criminal proceedings, but the concept of crime victim extends far beyond the individuals who are directly or indirectly affected by particular crimes. Crime victims can also include institutions and groups such as neighborhoods wracked by crime, teachers and students at schools where children or staff have been murdered, consumers who must pay higher prices for goods and services because of the impact of shoplifting or fraud, nations illegally attacked by other nations, ethnic groups targeted for genocide, and even natural environments ravaged by violators of pollution laws.

How can you be a victim of crimes that do not harm you directly? If there are burglaries, drive-by shootings, and other forms of violence in your neighborhood and its schools, you are likely to be worried about becoming a victim and take special care to lock your house and car. You may even be less likely to leave your home. If you have children, you may consider educating them at home so as not to risk their falling victim to random gunfire or a killer at school. Perhaps you enjoy riding your bike to school or work, but if rapes and murders are reported on local bike paths, you might give up those rides. For instance, on a clear and sunny Memorial Day in 2005, a bicyclist was riding his bike on one of Virginia's most well-traveled bike paths. At the point where the path winds past a beautiful boating facility, the biker was strangled to death at approximately 4:30 p.m. Word of that stunned bicyclists and joggers who would not have thought of themselves as possible victims in the daylight. Everyone can probably think of other examples of how they have been victimized by crime—even if they have never been attacked or robbed.

The Costs of Victimization

The cost of crime in the United States now exceeds $1 trillion dollars This figure includes the cost of trying and incarcerating perpetrators, loss of productivity of inmates, and direct and indirect victims costs such as medical expenses, lost earnings, victim assistance programs, unrecovered or unreimbursed property damage, pain and suffering, emotional distress, loss of productivity, and loss of enjoyment (D. A. Anderson, 1999). Survivors of violent crimes may also suffer emotional trauma including depression and other symptoms of PTSD such as anxiety, disrupted social relations, nightmares and other sleep disorders, paranoia, confusion, and repeated flashbacks of the traumatic event (Mawby & Walklate, 1994). Victims of sadistic rape are especially prone to experiencing long-term PTSD (Groth, 1979/1984). Lenore Walker (2000) maintains that many victims of domestic violence suffer from PTSD as part of the constellation of symptoms known as "battered woman syndrome." In short, there is no way to quantify the ultimate psychological, emotional, and social costs of crime; and for some victims, the suffering lasts a lifetime.

Victim Statistics

Quantitative data about the prevalence of victimization comes from three sources: (1) the Uniform Crime Reports (UCR), (2) the National Crime Victimization Survey (NCVS), and (3) offender self-report studies.

As we noted in chapter 1, the *UCR* compiles statistics on crime reports submitted by law enforcement agencies. Although it contains some data on victims, its primary focus is the offender. There is a much sharper focus on victims in the NCVS, which is conducted by the Bureau of Justice Statistics in the U.S. Justice Department. Every six months, employees of the U.S. Census Bureau conduct face-to-face or telephone interviews with everyone who is 12 and older in a nationally representative sample. In 2003, the sample was made up of 83,660 households consisting of 149,040 people over the age of 12 (Catalano, 2004). These households remain in the sample for three years. The participants are asked whether anyone in the household was the victim of certain crimes (rape, sexual assault, burglary, and theft of a motor vehicle or other property) and whether or not these crimes were reported to the police. If so, the victims are asked about the emotional, psychological, and financial consequences of the offense and their attitude toward the criminal justice system. These data are valuable, but there is no way to know about the accuracy of NCVS responses. For example, someone might report being victimized by a theft when the missing item was simply lost, or they might not report the item stolen because it was presumed lost. Petty crimes may be forgotten, or respondents might intentionally or unintentionally distort the truth. In particular, those who have been victims of domestic abuse or who see child abuse in their homes may choose not to tell about it (Skogan, 1986).

The offender self-report studies are surveys in which offenders are asked about their victims and the injuries inflicted on them. The most reliable of these surveys are, like the NCVS, conducted by the U.S. Bureau of Justice Statistics. The surveys typically focus on state prison inmates. Like victims, offenders may also distort the truth or misrepresent the facts; in this case, however, the distortions might stem from ignorance or attempts to make themselves look less blameworthy.

In other words, all sources of victim information are flawed in some way, but taken together, they provide the best available picture of victimization in the United States (see Table 12.1 for a summary of this picture.)

TABLE 12.1 *Violent Crime Victims at a Glance*

In 2003, according to Department of Justice and FBI statistics, young people, blacks, and males were most vulnerable to violent crime:

- Except for rape/sexual assault, males had higher rates of victimization than females.
- Most murder victims were male (77 percent).
- Blacks were more likely than persons of other races to be victims.
- Persons age 12 to 19 experienced overall violence at rates higher than rates for persons age 25 or older.

People in lower earning households were more likely to be victims:

- Persons in households earning less than $7,500 were more likely to be victims of robbery and assault.
- Persons earning less than $15,000 suffered the highest rates of aggravated assault.

Unmarried and divorced people are more often victims:

- In 2003, persons who had never married and those who were divorced or separated were victimized at higher rates for robbery and aggravated assault.
- Never married persons were victimized at higher rates than married, widowed, and divorced/separated persons for violent crime overall.

From 1993-1999, the occupations most prone to violence in the workplace were:

- Law enforcement
- Mental health
- Retail sales
- Transportation

Sources: Based on data from Catalano, S.M. (2004). *Criminal Victimization —2003*. Washington, DC: U.S. Department of Justice, Office of Justice Programs, Bureau of Justice Statistics; Federal Bureau of Investigations. (2004). *Crime in the United States—2003*. Washington, DC: Government Printing Office; and Duhart, D. T. (2001). *Violence in the Workplace, 1993–1999*. Washington, DC: U.S. Department of Justice, Office of Justice Programs, Bureau of Justice Statistics.

The Legal Status of Victims

Victims played an important role in the *Code of Hammurabi,* the oldest surviving code of law. Developed in about 2000 B.C. by King Dungi of Sumer (an area that is now part of Iraq), it was adopted by Hammurabi (1792–1750 B.C.), the sixth king of Babylon. The victim's rights provision in Hammurabi's Code decreed that offenders should make their victims as whole as possible. Victims, in turn, were to forgive offenders and not exact vengeance (Wallace, 1998). Much later, Anglo-Saxon law—as codified in the ninth-century handbook of criminal laws, *The Dooms of Alfred*—required a monetary payment, called **wergild**, to a murder victim's family. The exact amount was determined by the victim's social status. If murderers failed to pay *wergild* within a year, they were deemed outlaws and became fair game, literally. Anyone could legally kill them. A version of the *wergild* system is still in use in Saudi Arabia. There, if a murderer's family can pay the sum of money the victim's family demands, the killer can be saved from the death penalty (Schnieder, 1999). Murderers also had to pay fines to the king. It was only when the size of financial penalties began to exceed the resources available to most offenders that attention to victims' rights waned, and they languished in Western society for over a thousand years. Crimes came to be defined as acts against the King or against the peace of the realm; victims or survivors were left out of the process.

In early colonial times in the United States, crimes were prosecuted by victims or their families and friends, not by the state. People could "swear out a warrant," have an alleged offender arrested, and hire an attorney to prosecute the case. Because victims prosecuted, the nature and extent of their injuries and damages were taken into account by judges in pronouncing sentences and establishing penalties. However, concern for victims did not warrant a mention in the U.S. Constitution or the Bill of Rights. Perhaps because of their own experiences with the arbitrary imposition of a British King's law, those who wrote the Constitution were more concerned with protecting the rights of the accused than with the impact of crime on victims. By the 19th century, as increased population and a growing bureaucracy ushered in the precursor of the modern-day criminal justice system, police, prosecutors, and judges became the sole enforcers of law. Prosecutors took over from victims the responsibility for initiating criminal proceedings, and the primary purpose of prosecution focused on holding offenders liable to the government, not to their victims.

Victim Organizations

The situation we just described prevailed until the 1980s when demands by victims groups prompted federal and state governments to take action on their behalf. The rise of this "victim's movement" in the United States was due in large measure to activism by victims' lobbying organizations. One of the first of these appeared in 1978 when Robert and Charlotte Hullinger founded Parents of Murdered Children. However, the most prominent and powerful victims' lobbying organization is Mothers Against Drunk Drivers (MADD). MADD was organized in 1980 by Candy Lighter who lost a child as a result of a drunk driving accident. Although drunk driving is a criminal offense, it is only a misdemeanor if it is a first offense and no one is hurt as a result. MADD was responsible for increasing the rate of prosecution for vehicular manslaughter and second-degree murder when drunk drivers cause deaths. MADD has also been vocal in campaigns to lower, to 0.08%, the blood alcohol level necessary to create a presumption of intoxication.

Throughout the 1980s, victims organizations were frequently featured in the media, and the public became increasingly aware of matters relating to crime victims. Their message—that victims were being ignored or mistreated by the criminal justice system—appealed to voters who were fed up with what they perceived as government "coddling" of criminals at the expense of public safety in general and victims in particular. In other words, victim's rights became, and remain, politically correct.

As the victims' rights movement and the trend toward tougher criminal laws and punishments reinforced each other, the criminal justice process began to change. Victims wanted revenge, and most citizens were in the mood to oblige them. The United States adopted a sharper focus on punishment; the goal of rehabilitating criminals virtually ceased to exist. Prison sentences became longer, thus requiring more prisons—often built with money intended for school construction. As a result, a larger proportion of the population is imprisoned today in the United States than in any other civilized country. The United States is also the only developed country that imposes the death penalty. In addition to encouraging harsher punishment, the victim's movement has helped to pass a number of state and federal laws designed to protect, assist, and/or compensate victims in general and certain categories of victims in particular.

Laws Pertaining to Victims in General

In 1982, Congress passed the Victim and Witness Protection Act (VWPA) aimed at shielding crime victims and witnesses from intimidation by offenders and encouraging notification of victims about offenders' court hearings and trials and about their imminent release from incarceration.[1] That same year, President Reagan appointed a Task Force on Victims of Crime, and in 1984, Congress passed the Victims of Crime Act (VOCA) that established an Office for Victims of Crime (OVC) at the Department of Justice. Using money from federal crime fines, penalties, and bond forfeitures, the OVC gives grants to the states for victim assistance programs (Wallace, 1998). As a result, the 1990s saw an explosion of victim-related activities nationwide. For example, in 1995, the U.S. Department of Justice sponsored the first National Victim Assistance Academy, which provided training to those involved in victim programs. Efforts to protect potential victims were embodied in laws that allow law enforcement agencies to notify citizens when convicted child molesters are about to

---

[1]Most people are familiar with the VWPA as portrayed in movies—when crime witnesses are protected from the mob by being given a new identity and moved to a new location. However, the VWPA's main emphasis is on protecting people who have committed crimes themselves but who are now assisting law enforcement agencies to convict their cohorts in exchange for immunity from prosecution.

be released into a community and in laws requiring HIV testing for sex offenders. Finally, more and more states passed laws requiring that victims be compensated for their pain and suffering using funds from the federal government and state criminal fines. Today, victims routinely file "impact statements" (accounts of how a crime affected them), which judges and juries consider in deciding on punishment for convicted offenders. The federal government, and some states, even give victims the right to make their impact statements orally during sentencing hearings.

Laws Requiring Payment of Money. The VOCA established a Crime Victims Fund that is supplied from fines, costs, and penalties paid by people convicted of federal offenses and from the royalties and other proceeds received from the sale of offenders' books, movie rights, or other products dealing with their stories.[2] The amount of money deposited into the fund varies from year to year, but since the fund's inception in 1985, more than $6 billion has been deposited (Office for Victims of Crime, 2002). Most of the money is used to support state victim compensation funds and victim assistance programs, which themselves are partially supported by fines and penalties associated with state offenses. All 50 states and the District of Columbia have victim compensation programs.

Compensation takes the form of money paid directly to victims to assist with their crime-related expenses such as medical care, mental health counseling, funeral costs, lost wages, and loss of support due to the death or disability of a family member. Maximum awards range from $10,00 to $25,000. As part of the federal government's 1996 Antiterrorism and Effective Death Penalty Act, U.S. states must also provide compensation to citizens who are victims of terrorist acts anywhere in the world. **Victim assistance programs** administered by state and local governments provide counseling, advocacy, and support for victims as they participate in the criminal justice process. In addition, there are approximately 10,000 organizations in the United States that provide services to crime victims, most with support from state and federal governments. These organizations include domestic violence shelters; rape crisis centers; child abuse programs and victim service facilities operating within law enforcement agencies, prosecutor's offices, hospitals, and social service agencies. To receive federal funding in support of their victim assistance programs, states must give priority to programs serving victims of domestic violence, sexual abuse, and child abuse and must also set aside money to help victims of homicide or drunk-driving accidents.

Restitution Laws. Restitution laws—which require offenders to pay their victims for the pain, suffering, and expenses caused by their criminal acts—have been on the federal and state law books since the 1930s, but until the advent of the victims' rights movement, they were used mainly as a way of punishing offenders or as part of a bargain for receiving probation instead of incarceration. Today, the goal of restitution is to make the offender responsible to the victim for the consequences of the offender's actions. The amount of restitution and the payment schedule are determined by a judge in consultation with the probation officer (if the offender is not incarcerated). Some state laws now also require that part of money prisoners earn for their work in jail be turned over to their victims on a regular basis.

From a victim's perspective, the main problem with restitution programs is that they are administered by the courts, which leaves the victim with no direct right to enforce payment. Typically, an offender's nonpayment of restitution comes before the court as a violation of the conditions of probation. When this happens, the offender is at risk for being sent back to prison, but the victim is no better off because the offender is now even less able to make significant restitution payments.

Victim-offender reconciliation programs are designed to help alleviate this problem. Through these programs, victim and offender are brought together by a mediator representing the criminal justice system to agree on a realistic restitution figure and a workable payment schedule. In some jurisdictions, payments are made through and monitored by the victim-offender program itself. Victims' rights groups favor this reconciliation model because it allows victims to participate directly in the restitution process. Criminal justice experts like it too, because it forces offenders to come face to face with their victims and to be directly accountable for the harm they have caused.

---

[2]The fund was made possible by the so-called "Son of Sam" provision, a federal law that prevents criminals from making money as a result of their crimes. Many states have similar laws.

Laws Pertaining to Specific Victim Categories

The 1990s saw the enactment of many new federal and state laws pertaining to specific categories of victims, including victims of domestic violence, sex crimes, hate crimes, and female victims of any violent crime.

Domestic Violence Victims.   After victims of domestic violence brought civil rights lawsuits against law enforcement agencies for not protecting them, many states enacted laws calling for mandatory arrests in response to domestic violence complaints. These laws require investigating officers to arrest all persons who appear to have caused any physical harm. The purpose of mandatory arrest laws is to put the offender in jail for a "cooling-off" period. Many of these laws also require that a court order be issued against the offender that forbids making any contact with the victim (including by simply returning home) until the first court hearing on the case has taken place—usually within 72 hours. These statutes are unique; no other criminal law requires an investigating officer to make an arrest.

Victims of Sexual Offenses.   Some of the earliest statutes pertaining to victims of rape and sexual assault were called **rape shield laws** because they were designed to limit the topics that rape victims can be asked about during their alleged assailant's trial. Congress enacted a rape shield law for victims in federal rape trials—known as the Privacy Protection for Rape Victims Act—in 1978. Similar laws have been passed in many states, and although their specifics vary, they generally provide that testimony about the victim's previous sexual conduct is not permissible unless it is specifically relevant to the establishment of the defendant's guilt or innocence. Thus, a rape victim can be made to testify about aspects of her prior relationship with the offender that may be relevant to determining whether she consented to intercourse and whether there was sexual contact, but she cannot be asked about how many sexual partners she has had in her life or about other aspects of her sexual history.

In many states, feminist victims' rights advocates have helped gain passage of "marital rape" laws, which allow a man to be charged with rape if he forces his wife to have sex after they have been living apart. Even if they are living together, he can be charged with rape if his wife is physically injured during forced sex and with sexual assault if there is no physical injury.

In the 1990s, most states enacted a variety of other laws designed to protect adult and child victims of sexual offenses. For example, nearly every state passed a law requiring that sexual offenders be tested for HIV if their crime involved sexual penetration or other exposure to an offender's bodily fluids. States vary as to whether they require testing before or after conviction. Most states that require testing also require disclosure of the results to the victim or if the victim is a minor, to the parents or guardian. Some states require that the victim receive counseling prior to and after hearing the test results.

All 50 states have laws requiring that when violent sex offenders and child molesters are released from prison, the community in which they live must be notified and/or the offenders must register their presence with the local police. In states that require community notification, information about the offender's presence is distributed via flyers, posters, and newspaper notices. States that have mandatory registration laws allow any member of the public to have access to information about registered offenders in their community. An amendment to the Violent Crime Control and Law Enforcement Act of 1994 established a national computer registry of sex offenders that is open to the public. This amendment—known as Megan's Law in memory of 7-year-old Megan Kanka who was killed by a twice-convicted sex offender living in her New Jersey neighborhood—was enacted to make the states' offender registries fully accessible to all U.S. citizens and law enforcement agencies, not just to residents and law enforcement in the state where the offender resides. When fully operational, the national registry will combine all state offender databases into a single, fully accessible, system.

Hate Crime Victims.   As we noted in chapter 10, many states have adopted hate crime statutes that provide enhanced penalties for offenses motivated by hostility toward people based on their ethnicity, religion, or other personal characteristics. For example, under these laws, defacing a building with graffiti containing ethnic slurs would be subject to a stiffer penalty than other kinds of defacement. The same is true for assaults arising from prejudice and hatred against certain classes of people.

In 1994, President Clinton signed into law a Hate Crimes Sentencing Enhancement Act, which adds years to penalties for federal crimes deemed to have been motivated by bias. A federal hate crimes law has been in existence since 1969, but it covers only crimes related to race, color, national origin, or religious bias. For many years, including in 2005, members of both houses of Congress have proposed expanded hate crimes legislation, the most recent to cover sexual orientation and transgendered persons. Not all states have hate crimes legislation, and of those that do, few have provisions dealing with sexual orientation, gender, or disability.

Hate crime laws have been criticized on a number of grounds. For one thing, criminologists point out that there is no evidence that current hate crime laws have deterred crime. Second, some people believe that by increasing penalties for crimes against members of certain groups, society is placing a higher value on the safety and welfare of those groups. Third, these laws have been challenged by those who claim that they violate First Amendment rights to free speech and expression. Indeed, in a 1992 case in which defendants had been prosecuted for cross burning under a Minnesota law that criminalized the use of Ku Klux Klan crosses and other hate symbols, the U.S. Supreme Court struck down the law as violating the First Amendment (*R.A.V. v. City of St. Paul,* 1992). A year later, however, the Court upheld Wisconsin's hate crime statute when it was enforced against a 19-year-old Black man who—after seeing a Black child being beaten by a White man in the movie *Mississippi Burning*—attacked a White 14-year-old, leaving the victim in a coma for several days (*Wisconsin v. Mitchell,* 1993). The Wisconsin hate crime statute had allowed the defendant's penalty for the attack to be doubled from two to four years. (The Supreme Court reconciled these two apparently conflicting decisions by noting that people cannot be punished for their beliefs, only for their actions that intimidate or harm the person or his property.) Fourth, prosecutors note that it is often difficult or impossible to prove that a crime was motivated by specific bias as opposed to a general disregard for the rights and welfare of other people. For instance, a group of young Black men brutally murdered a middle-aged Asian businessman in a suburb of Washington, DC, in 1998. The area has a long history of Black-on-Asian crime, Black resentment against Asians, and "turf" wars between Black and Asian youths. Was this a hate crime or just a brutal murder? No one heard the perpetrators say anything about hating Asians, so even if they were motivated by hatred, the prosecutor would have no grounds on which to seek enhanced penalties. Finally, judicial experts have faulted efforts to enact federal hate crime legislation because they create new areas in which federal law can supersede state law, thus placing further demands on the federal criminal justice system.

Hate crime legislation in some states has stalled because of disagreement as to which victim categories should be covered. In Texas, for example, a hate crime bill failed because of wrangling over the question of whether enhanced penalties should apply to defendants convicted of killing homosexuals as well as Blacks and other ethnic minorities.

The Role of Victims in the Criminal Justice System

Until recently, victims' participation in the criminal justice system was restricted to testifying about the facts of the crime that affected them. Many victims complained that this limited role made them feel victimized again, this time by the justice system and particularly by prosecutors whose concern for them appears limited to "using" them to get a conviction. Indeed, some victim assistance programs and services provide support for victim witnesses mainly in relation to their upcoming testimony. These programs may actually be based in prosecutors' offices because if victims are not prepared for the adversarial nature of the trial—including cross-examination by a hostile defense attorney—the credibility of their evidence against the defendant might be reduced. Although it is true that prosecutors' support of victim witnesses is often aimed mainly at maximizing the chances of convicting defendants, still, some prosecutors are beginning to take a more public and vocal provictim stance. One of these is Marcia Clark, lead prosecutor in the O.J. Simpson trial who wore a special pin to court to symbolize her personal dedication to the families of the victims in the case.

Beyond such recent changes in philosophy, victims are now allowed to do more than testify at trial. They can file written statements with the court, called **victim impact statements**, and have the **right of allocution**, which allows them to speak at sentencing hearings.

Victim Impact Statements

Victim impact statements are prepared by victims—often with the assistance of prosecutors or other victim assistance personnel—for presentation to the judge or jury before a convicted criminal is sentenced. These statements are intended to describe the physical and emotional consequences of the crime, including property loss and damage, medical and counseling bills, lost wages, and other financial losses. Victims may also suggest a sum of money they wish to receive in restitution by the offender or through victim compensation programs.

Somewhat surprisingly, research has indicated that submitting victim impact statements does not make victims feel any better about their role in the judicial process (R. C. Davis & Smith, 1994). Even more surprisingly, such reports also seem to have limited effect on judges and juries (Erez & Roeger, 1995; Fisher, 1991). There are no indications that victims' statements increase the length of convicted defendants' sentences or result in increased restitution or compensation awards.

Victim Allocution

In the sentencing phase of a criminal trial, the prosecutor and defense attorney each have the right to call witnesses to testify about facts that could have an impact on the type and length of sentence imposed on a convicted defendant. Typically, such testimony comes from people who know the defendant's background and character, and from experts who can testify whether the defendant is likely to commit a similar crime again, and whether he or she is likely or not to be helped by rehabilitative and treatment programs.

Some states now also give victims the right to speak during the sentencing phase. This *allocution* differs from testimony in that a person who testifies does so by answering questions posed by attorneys for the prosecution and the defense. In allocution, the victim presents a prepared statement and is not subject to examination or cross-examination. In death penalty cases, all states allow victims allocution as a part of prosecution efforts to present "aggravating" circumstances that warrant a death sentence. The federal Violent Crime Control Act of 1994 gives victims the right of allocution in federal trials involving sexual abuse or violent crime. When the crime is murder, the victim's family members are allowed to describe the impact of their loss and to emphasize the victim's character and contributions to the community. Judges may set limits on victim allocution, however. In the sentencing phase of the trials of Oklahoma City bombers Timothy McVeigh and Terry Nichols, Judge Richard Matsch tried to strike a balance between the right of victims and their families to speak and his obligation to insure that highly emotional content was kept to a minimum so as to preserve the standard that all trial evidence must serve a legal purpose and not simply serve to inflame jurors' emotions. Thus, Judge Matsch refused to allow videotapes of victims' weddings and ruled that a 9-year-old boy could not testify about the loss of his mother. Even so, the testimony allowed was sufficiently emotional that many jurors wept openly (Collins, 1997). Such testimony was no doubt instrumental in the jury's recommendation of the death penalty for McVeigh, which the judge accepted. Nichols eventually received life in prison, but research confirms what defense attorneys have always believed—that family testimony in capital cases increases the likelihood that the defendant will be sentenced to death (Luginbuhl & Burkhead, 1994).

The Future of Victim's Rights

Recently enacted victims' rights laws and the procedures they allow have gone a long way to protect and compensate victims, but victim advocacy groups argue that these laws have not gone far enough. Efforts to amend the Constitution with a Victims' Rights Amendment have been tried without success. Indeed, the American people and their representatives have historically been cautious about adding provisions to the Constitution that favor even the most deserving of special interest groups. Thus, victim protection and compensation guarantees continue to expand in the form of state and federal laws.

Although victims' rights groups continue to push for more rights and representation in the criminal justice process, judges, prosecutors, and legal scholars have joined defense attorneys in opposing sweeping victims' rights provisions. Why? For one thing, prosecutors and judges feel that current victims' rights laws have already overloaded the criminal justice system with victim-oriented procedures and mechanisms—such as restitution and compensation programs—that restrict their ability to try cases and conduct trials in accordance with their training and expertise. At the same time, legal scholars and defense attorneys worry that expanding victims' rights may ultimately infringe on defendants' rights to a fair trial. Current laws suggest that a workable compromise has emerged, allowing victims' rights to be honored without trampling on the rights of defendants to a fair trial or ignoring society's interest in having the prosecutorial system work for the benefit of us all.

Victimology

The growth of the victim's rights movement helped create a new branch of criminology known as **victimology**, the study of victims and their relationships to offenders and crime (Wallace, 1998). Pioneers in this field included Hans Von Hentig (1948), who anticipated the rise of victimology when he established a typology of victims based on psychological, social, and biological factors. Benjamin Mendelsohn (1974), a practicing attorney and the "father" of victimology, pointed out that in certain types of crime there is often a preexisting relationship between offenders and victims. For instance, more than half all violent crimes in 2003 were committed by someone whom the victim knew. Victims of rape and sexual assaults were the most likely to have known their attackers, followed by murder and robbery victims (Catalano, 2004).

Today, victimologists examine (a) characteristics of individual victims, (b) the relationship between offender and victim, (c) the situation or context in which the victim-offender interaction occurs, and (d) victims' roles in precipitating crime. These researchers have discovered that victims are as varied as criminals and that many victims and offenders share certain characteristics.

Characteristics of Victims

In the first-ever textbook on victims, *The Criminal and His Victim* (1948), Von Hentig pursued his interest in victims' characteristics. Von Hentig noted that crime victims tend to be overrepresented among people who are young, elderly, female, or suffer mental disorders including mental retardation.

The Young. In general, young people are more likely to be the victims of violent crimes. In 2003, persons ages 12 to 24 sustained violent victimization at rates higher than individuals of all other ages. Beginning with the 20 to 24 age category, the rate at which persons were victims declined significantly as the age category increased (Catalano, 2004; FBI, 2004). The risk of being victimized by violent crime is 11 times higher for persons under 25 than for persons over 65: There are 56 versus 5 victimizations per 1,000 persons in each age group. For example, the rate at which people under 25 are robbed is six times higher than for those 65 or older (R. Bachman, 1994; Bureau of Justice Statistics, 2000; Perkins & Klaus, 1996). As we described in chapter 10, young people are also especially vulnerable to physical and sexual abuse by their caregivers.

The Elderly. People over 65 appear to be particularly susceptible to crimes motivated by economic gain, including larceny, burglary, and motor vehicle theft, but they are far less likely than younger people to be murdered, assaulted, or robbed (Bureau of Justice Statistics, 2000). Like young children, the elderly are at elevated risk for abuse and neglect by caregivers. Physical abuse of the elderly commonly consists of assault, the unwarranted administration of drugs, and the improper use of physical restraints, force feeding, and physical punishment. Elder sexual abuse also sometimes occurs and is defined as nonconsensual sexual contact of any kind. Emotional and psychological abuse of the elderly includes verbal assaults, insults, threats, intimidation, humiliation, and harassment. Elder abuse can also take the form of financial exploitation, including unauthorized use of an elder's funds by forging checks, unauthorized cashing of checks, and anything that would be considered larceny theft (U. S. Administration on Aging, 2005).

It is estimated that nearly 500,000 elderly persons experienced abuse and/or neglect in domestic settings (U.S. Administration on Aging, 2005). Exact figures are impossible to obtain, but this estimate probably understates the problem. Indeed, some of those who work with the elderly suggest that for every case of elder abuse that was reported to and substantiated by Adult Protective Services agencies in 1996, at least five others went unreported (U.S. Administration on Aging, 2005). People over the age of 80 are especially likely to be the victims of abuse and neglect. Further, elderly White people are more often abused than are Blacks or other ethnic minorities. Among minority groups, though, Blacks are more likely than others to be abused (U.S. Administration on Aging, 1998). Sadly, it is elderly persons' adult children or spouses who commit approximately 90% of the elder abuse that takes place in private homes (U.S. Administration on Aging, 1998).

In summary, the risk of victimization by violent criminals varies across the life span, increasing through the teenage years, peaking at about age 20, and unless one is victimized by elder abuse, steadily decreases thereafter (Perkins, 1997).

Females. In 2003, males were far more likely to be victims of murder (77% of murder victims were male), robbery, and assault than females. Females were far more likely than males to be victims of sexual assault and, when murdered, to be murdered or assaulted by current or former intimate partners (Catalano, 2004; see chapter 10). Women are also disproportionately represented as victims of elder abuse; although they comprise only 58% of the elderly population, they make up 60% to 76% of those subjected to abuse and neglect. The greatest disparity between men and women was in reported rates of emotional or psychological abuse. Three-fourths of those subjected to this form of abuse were women rather than men.

Race. The rate at which Blacks are victimized by crime is far greater than would be expected from population figures alone. Blacks make up only about 12% of the U.S. population (U.S. Census Bureau, 2001), but they are victimized by crime at higher rates than Whites. Overall, when comparing Whites, Blacks, and all other persons of other races, Blacks had the highest violent crime victimization rate. Hispanics make up 13% of the U.S. population, and those 12 and over experienced 14% of all violent crime in 2003 (Catalano, 2004).

The Poor. In 2003, persons from households with annual incomes of less than $7,500 were robbed and assaulted significantly more often than those from households where annual incomes were above $7,500. Persons from households with annual incomes of less than $35,000 were victimized by burglary more than those whose household incomes were more than $35,000. Urban renters in lower income households were also more likely than higher income suburban or rural homeowners to be burglarized (Catalano, 2004).

The Mentally Disordered. People who suffer from mental disorders, including mental retardation, tend to be especially vulnerable to crime victimization by virtue of their lifestyle, including where they live (many are homeless). People with low levels of intelligence and lower than average ability to function on a day-to-day basis are particularly vulnerable to being defrauded and cheated. Lonely, depressed people too may be victimized by criminals who woo widows, widowers, or "lonely hearts" as part of a plot to marry them for their money and perhaps abuse or even kill them. In the hope of getting attention and affection, wealthy but lonely victims sometimes put themselves in risky situations such as pick-up bars or Internet chat rooms. Some also find themselves ensnared in a criminal plot. In late 1998, a man who came to Virginia to meet a woman he had originally contacted on e-mail was robbed by her and her boyfriend; in 1997, a West Virginia woman was killed by a man she met in cyberspace. The low self-esteem that depressed people often suffer can make them less likely to take action to preserve their safety. They may be more likely than other people to be overwhelmed or surprised by danger.

The Role of Victims in Crime

Because victims' rights groups see victims as blameless, they tend to oppose the scientific examination of the role that victims might play in triggering criminal offenses (Karmen, 2000; Kennedy & Sacco, 1998). Nevertheless, trying to understand crime without including all of its aspects—including victim characteristics and behavior—would be like trying to complete a jigsaw puzzle without having all of the pieces. We consider some of the evidence that researchers have gathered in their studies of victims' roles in certain types of crime. Benjamin Mendlesohn developed a victim classification system that stresses the degree to which society considers victims responsible for their victimization and the nature of the relationship between offenders and victims. His categories include (a) utterly innocent victims such as a child or an unconscious person, (b) victims with minor responsibility as in the case of people who frequent high-crime locales, and (c) victims who are as responsible for what happens to them as those who offend against them, such as someone who helps others commit a crime and is then hurt or killed because of a betrayal during the crime. Other criminologists have focused mainly on classifying victims' roles in facilitating or precipitating criminal offenses. *Facilitation* means being careless or negligent such as leaving doors unlocked or leaving keys in a car. *Precipitation* means behaving in ways that provoke crime such as physically attacking someone who then kills the aggressor (Miethe & McCorkle, 1998).

A large body of victimology research has focused on victims in the total context of the criminal event. This broad, contextual approach has looked at crime in terms of the interaction of victims' characteristics (as outlined by Von Hentig, 1948), their role in precipitating criminal transactions (as described by Mendelsohn), and their lifestyle. The inclusion of victims' lifestyles in this analysis helps illuminate the degree to which certain ways of living place people in high-risk settings. For example, the more time individuals spend in bars and other places where illegal drug sales, fights, and police intervention are common, the more likely they are to be victimized by crime. A recent study of medical examiners' reports filed between 1975 and 1995 found that one-third of all homicide victims were legally drunk at the time of their deaths (Okie, 1999).

Current crime statistics support this *lifestyle exposure* theory. Rates of victimization are highest for young Black males because they tend to associate with other young Black males (who as a group tend to show higher than average rates of criminal behavior), and they tend to spend time in places where criminal offenses often occur (Kennedy & Sacco, 1998). Lifestyle exposure theory is also supported by statistics showing that people who engage in criminal conduct—especially as part of criminal gang activity—are more likely than others to become victims of crime, in part because they are associating with criminals.

Having summarized some of the main victomology models, we show how they apply to victims of specific types of crimes.

Murder. In 2003, of all murders for which the victim-offender relationship were known (55% of murders), 77% knew their assailants, more than in any other category of crime (FBI, 2004). Murder perpetrators and victims share many characteristics including ethnicity, age, and gender (Miethe & Meier, 1994). In 2004, for example, 92% of Black murder victims were slain by Black offenders, and 85% of White murder victims were slain by other Whites (FBI, 2004). Lifestyle exposure theory explains, at least in part, the similarity between murder victims and offenders (L. E. Cohen & Felson, 1979; Hindelang, Gottfredson, & Garofalo, 1978). Offenders and victims may live in the same high-crime neighborhood, frequent the same high-crime places, and engage in high-risk activities such as gambling and drug dealing. In 2003, more than 20% of murders took place in the context of alcoholic brawls, gang killings, and sniper attacks, and 29% of murders in 2003 took place in the context of an argument (FBI, 2004).

To appreciate the importance of the victim's role in some murders, we consider David Luckenbill's (1984) research on a particular type of "homicidal event," which he saw unfolding in five stages:

1. The victim does something to the offender. This something can be as trivial as a verbal comment such as to "get lost."
2. The offender interprets the victim's words or deeds as provocative and insulting.
3. The offender acts to salvage his honor either through verbal or physical retaliation.
4. The victim responds aggressively, signaling to the offender that the interaction may lead to and will only be resolved by violence. Onlookers may incite the parties to further aggression, culminating in violence.
5. Continued violence leads to the victim's death.

Luckenbill (1984) concluded that murder often results from incidents that begin as a rather mundane exchange. At any point in the exchange, either party could have withdrawn from the confrontation. Fatal "road-rage" incidents, for example, usually involve victim precipitation either as the initiator of angry gestures or aggressive driving tactics or in response to those of others. In January 1998, two motorists in Washington, DC, began driving recklessly and at high speed on a congested roadway during the morning rush hour after one driver responded in a hostile manner to the other's tailgating and gesturing. One of the combatants and three innocent people in other cars died in the ensuing multiple vehicle crash. In Florida, an impatient and angry driver shot to death a motorist who was taking too long to find exact change at a highway tollbooth. Witnesses said that before the shooting, the victim and the killer had exchanged hostile hand gestures and then angry insults. Was this victim partially responsible for his own death? It is difficult to answer this question, but with road rage becoming increasingly frequent, campaigns by law enforcement agencies in many states are urging motorists to ignore other drivers' aggressive gestures or driving tactics.

Rape.   Menachim Amir (1971) explored the concept of victim precipitation in a study of over 600 rape cases in which victims had initially agreed to sexual relations and then changed their minds. (In each case, the victim and perpetrator either already knew each other or had just met at a bar and had gone somewhere to have sex.) Amir argued that it was the reversal of consent that precipitated these rapes. Although this view is widely criticized today, it is also the case that had the victim not first consented to sex, she would not have been in the position of fighting off the man. Research on date rape has also highlighted the role of alcohol or other drugs in these crimes. Often, victim and offender are in an intoxicated state that tends to both release inhibitions and cloud judgment (U.S. Department of Health and Human Services, 1992). For women, then, drinking too much, especially in a setting (such as a fraternity house party) where sexual relations are expected to occur, can be a precipitating factor that puts them at risk for sexual assault. Indeed, public perception of "fault" or "blame" in sexual assaults shifts toward the victim in cases in which she is intoxicated or did not offer resistance (Pollard, 1992).

The prevailing attitude among criminologists today is that women should take precautions to avoid rape-risky situations. This view is reflected in programs being offered on college campuses and elsewhere to teach women how to keep themselves out of harm's way—and to teach men to respect women's wishes about sexual activity. However, efforts aimed at helping women avoid precipitating rape—or domestic violence for that matter—are offensive to those who see such efforts as placing more responsibility for crime prevention on victims than on perpetrators and for thus perpetuating males' domination over females in our society (Karmen, 2000; Scully, 1995). Feminists argue that a woman should be allowed to prepare to engage in sex and then change her mind without being assaulted and that anyone, male or female, should feel free to go to virtually anywhere at any time of the day or night without worrying about being raped or robbed or murdered. In the United States today, however, the expectation that these ideals will apply in every situation must be tempered by common sense and caution.

Robbery.   The typical robbery victim is, like the typical robbery offender, a Black man under the age of 25. Victims precipitate robbery mainly by being careless in handling, carrying, or displaying money or other personal property (a factor in about 10% of robbery incidents; Curtis, 1974) and being in high-crime places and/or engaging in high-risk activities such as drug dealing. Working in convenience stores, liquor stores, casinos or other gambling venues, and bars and small motels pose especially high risks for robbery victimization.

Fraud.   People who are excessively acquisitive are especially attractive to criminals. Greed often overcomes these people's common sense, making them vulnerable to fraud and confidence games that promise quick wealth. It is no longer news when such people fall victim to "get-rich-quick" or "tax-avoidance" scams, nor are people surprised to find that many of them are not the helpless elderly but the already wealthy who simply cannot get enough money fast enough.

Domestic Violence.   As we noted in chapter 10, domestic violence includes murder, rape, sexual assault, or aggravated or simple assault committed by a current or former spouse, boyfriend, or girlfriend against an adult. According to the Centers for Disease Control and Prevention (2003), nearly 5.3 million victimizations take place each year in the United States between intimate partners over the age of 18, resulting in nearly 2 million injuries and 1,300 deaths. Intimate partner violence occurs across all populations irrespective of social, economic, religious, or cultural group. However, low-income individuals are disproportionately affected (Heise & Garcia-Moreno, 2002).

There is a high degree of victim participation in domestic violence because, by definition, the parties are living to together in an ongoing intimate relationship. For example, most murders between domestic partners are not the result of a single, sudden blowup but the culmination of increasingly intense conflicts. By studying these escalating "cycles of violence," Lenore Walker (2000) described three distinct phases in the dynamics of the "battering relationship." In the first, or tension-building, phase, the man becomes upset and the woman tries to calm him down. In the second, or battering, phase, the man loses control and assaults the woman. In a third, or respite, phase, the contrite man engages in loving acts and is forgiven by the woman. The intensity of the violence involved in this pattern may increase with each cycle and may sometimes result in murder.

Walker's (2000) model does not address situations—which are more common than most people realize—in which men are the victims of domestic abuse and may die as a result (see chapter 10). A notable example occurred in May of 1998 when *Saturday Night Live* comedian Phil Hartmann was shot to death by his wife as he slept. Unbeknownst to most of their friends, she had been engaging in increasingly abusive outbursts against him; her anger was known to peak when she drank alcohol. After calling the police to report the murder, she shot and killed herself.

Victims of fatal and nonfatal forms of domestic violence are usually participants in relationships characterized by complex dynamics—including social and economic stress, power struggles, unmet dependency needs, and feelings of despair and isolation. In response to claims by women's groups that male-dominated law enforcement organizations were ignoring the plight of victimized women, men who engage in domestic violence are now more likely than ever before to be arrested when the police arrive on the scene of a domestic violence call. In many jurisdictions, however, both men and women are likely to be arrested if there is any evidence that the woman was involved in pushing, shoving, hitting, scratching, or otherwise assaulting the man—regardless of her claim that the man struck the first blow.

Indeed, although most domestic violence offenders are men, women in abusive relationships may find themselves as defendants charged with murder or assault. Some of these women invoke the "abuse excuse" or "battered woman's defense," a justification for the use of harmful or deadly force against an abuser. Several states have enacted laws allowing evidence of long-term abuse to be used in trials and allowing juries to take this evidence into consideration when determining guilt and/or punishment. Virginia's law, for example, says that

> In any criminal prosecution alleging personal injury or death, or the attempt to cause personal injury or death, relevant evidence of repeated physical and psychological abuse of the accused by the victim shall be admissible, subject to the general rules of evidence. (Va. Code Sec. 19.2–270.6).

This defense may be used by male and female defendants who were victims of abuse and, in some states, may be allowed in cases involving gay or lesbian partners.

Child Abuse and Neglect.   Child abuse involves the inflection of physical injuries such as bruises, welts, abrasions, lacerations, cuts, fractures, and burns. Child sexual abuse crimes include "assault and battery with intent to gratify sexual desire," "fondling or touching in an obscene manner," sodomy, and incest. Child neglect involves caregivers failing to provide a child with adequate food, clothing, shelter, and medical attention.

The highest incidence of abuse is reported for children in the middle childhood years, ages 6 to 11. Although boys have a 24% higher risk of physical abuse than girls, girls are sexually abused three times more often than boys. Compared to children living with both parents, children in single-parent families have a 77% greater risk of physical abuse and an 80% greater risk of serious injury or harm, in large part due to the risk of abuse by their mother's boyfriends. The risk of abuse increases with the number of children in a family, and compared to children whose families earn more than $30,000 a year, those in families with annual incomes below $15,000 are more than 18 times more likely to be sexually abused, 22 times more likely to be seriously injured by physical abuse, and 60 times more likely to die from abuse (U.S. Department of Health and Human Services, 1998).

The failure of child welfare agencies and courts to adequately protect children from abusive and neglectful caregivers often compounds the tragedy of child abuse. In one 1998 case in a rural southwestern Virginia town, a judge allowed a woman to retain custody of her baby even though he found her guilty of child abuse. Three months later, she shook her baby to death. In 2000, a Virginia judge ordered a foster family to return a little girl to her mother. Within a week, the child had been murdered by the mother's boyfriend. Worst of all, some authorities do not learn from their mistakes. In 1999, a District of Columbia judge ordered foster parents to send a young child to her mother for a Christmas visit even though the mother had repeatedly abused and neglected her. During the visit, the mother killed the little girl, leaving the judge, social workers, and the mother's attorney blaming everyone but themselves.

The Role of Places in Crime Victimization

Obviously, home can be a dangerous place, especially for those who live with violence-prone people and, most especially, if those people have alcohol problems and if there are guns or other dangerous weapons about. Workplaces and schools, too, can be places where people may be at elevated risk for crime.

The Workplace.   About 1.7 million people a year were victims of violent crime at their workplace for each year from 1993 to 1996. About 900 work-related homicides occurred annually, and workplace violence accounted for 18% of all violent crime during the 7-year period (Duhart, 2001). It is generally the nature of people's work rather than their age, ethnicity, gender, or other characteristics that predict who will be victimized while on the job (Sacco & Kennedy, 1996).

Among the highest risk workplaces are those that involve (a) face-to-face encounters with large numbers of people, (b) handling money, (c) travel, or (d) delivery of passengers or goods (Collins, Cox, & Langan, 1987). Accordingly, among the higher risk workplaces are law enforcement; the U.S. Postal Service; the military (Harlow, 1991); probation departments (Linder & Koehler, 1992); police departments (Mayhew, Elliott, & Dowds, 1989); amusement, recreation, convenience, and fast-food establishments; and urban taxis (R. Block, Felson, & Block, 1984; Rennison, 1999). Law enforcement positions, including police, corrections, and private security officers, represent the highest category of workplace crime, accounting for 11% (Duhart, 2001).

Many workplace victimizations occur as the result of disputes between employees and customers or clients—for example, when a bartender refuses to continue serving a drunken patron, when a teacher disciplines an unruly student, or a police officer intervenes in a domestic dispute (Sacco & Kennedy, 1996). Emergency room medical staff and airline flight attendants suffer an inordinately high rate of assault from patients or air travelers upset over some aspect of the service they are receiving (Salinger, Jesilow, Pontell, & Geis, 1993). Some workplace victims are deliberately targeted—as when an employee who had recently been reprimanded or fired returns to kill the supervisor responsible. In other cases, the victims were simply in the wrong place at the wrong time. The classic example of the latter is the employee who is killed by stray gunfire as an enraged and demented coworker attacks a hated supervisor.

In other words, some jobs are inherently dangerous because they expose workers to high-risk locations, situations, and individuals; those who hold these jobs are thus at higher risk for crime victimization than people in the general population. This was certainly the case in 1997, when a Washington, DC, taxi driver refused to take a passenger into a gang-controlled neighborhood. Unfortunately, and unbeknownst to him, his passenger was a gang member who was infuriated at the driver's reticence and who drew a gun and shot him dead. This fatal incident contained all the elements of a high-risk, victim-offender transaction—an employee working in a dangerous occupation in a crime-ridden location and a violent criminal carrying a weapon, perhaps high on drugs, who was angry and frustrated.

Schools.   Approximately 10 years ago, murders, assaults, and other serious crimes in schools were relatively uncommon (statistically speaking, they are still rare) and occurred mostly in the inner city in relation to gang activity, crack cocaine sales, or both. The at-risk schools installed metal detectors, hired more security guards, and generally became safer. However, recent years have seen an unprecedented amount of violence in schools that had never seen such violence in the past. In the 2001 to 2002 school year, 17 students died in school-related deaths (including accidents and suicides), down from 1999 to 2000 that saw 32 violent deaths in U.S. schools (CDCP, 2004).

Awareness of the significant risk of crime victimization on school property began in the 1980s when a survey by the National Institute of Education (1986) found that 40% of the robberies and 36% of the personal attacks against teenagers occur at school; junior high students were victimized by other students at higher rates than high school students (Rapp, Carrington, & Nicholson, 1986). The survey also illustrated the significant emotional, economic, and social costs of school violence. A third of junior high students in large cities said they avoided certain places at school, such as rest rooms, because they feared being victimized by fellow students. Many students also reported staying home from school because they feared for their safety. More than 100,000 teachers said they had been threatened with physical harm by students. The same report estimated the economic costs of school crime and violence at $200 million annually. For example, burglaries were reported to occur five times more often in schools than in businesses, at an average loss of about $150 per case. In 25% of the schools surveyed, incidents of vandalism occurred at an average rate of once a month.

The results of this survey were somewhat unexpected, and they spurred growing concern about school crime, its impact on students and staff, and its economic and social costs. This concern prompted numerous governmental efforts to intensify their efforts to combat school crime and prompted those who conduct the annual NCVS to include questions about school-related victimization. Eventually, there was a School Crime Supplement to the NCVS. Other surveys, too, helped fill in the school crime picture. For example, the National Adolescent Student Health Survey (American School Health Association, 1989), which contacted more than 11,000 eighth- and 10th-grade students, found that nearly 40% of them had been in a physical fight at school or on a school bus in the past year; 34% had been threatened with physical harm at school; and 13% had been attacked at school. Analyses of the 1993 National Household Education Survey are consistent with these data, showing that half of students in Grades 6 through 12 witnessed some type of crime at school, and about one in eight reported being victimized themselves. As had been the case in earlier surveys, the fear of victimization was significant: 22% of the students reported taking a knife, a gun, or some other weapon to school sometime in the past year "for protection" (Nolin, Davies, & Chandler, 1996). Indeed, surveys consistently show that the main reason students say they carry a weapon to school is for protection (Sheley & Wright, 1993). An average of 5,000 teachers are physically attacked each month, and these attacks are much more likely to result in injury than are assaults on students (Hanke, 1996).

The most recent Youth Risk Behavior Survey by the Centers for Disease Control and Prevention is also consistent with trends identified in earlier surveys. Responses to questionnaires completed by 13,000 students found the following:

- 6% had carried a weapon on school property within 30 days preceding the survey.
- 9% had been threatened or injured with a weapon on school property within 12 months preceding the survey.
- Almost 13% had engaged in a physical fight on school property during the 12 months preceding the survey. (CDCP, 2004)

Although statistically speaking, schools are safer than the streets and children's homes (the most dangerous place of all for children given the high incidence of accidents and child abuse), school crime and violence are widespread. Contrary to popular belief, they are not problems unique to big cities. This point has been dramatically underscored over the past several years, as more than 60 students and teachers were killed by students in locales far removed from inner cities including Bethel, Alaska; Pearl, Mississippi; West Paducah, Kentucky; Jonesboro, Arkansas; Edinboro, Pennsylvania; Springfield, Oregon; Littleton, Colorado; and Red Lake, Minnesota.

Accordingly, fear of death or injury at school is a major preoccupation among virtually all students today. This sad fact is especially tragic given that the prospect of being subjected to crime at school is contrary to everything that schools are supposed to represent: a safe, orderly, child-centered world where learning, sports, and friendships are the norm and where drug dealing, sexual assault, and murder are unthinkable.

Society as a Victim of Crime

Crime negatively affects the attitudes, emotions, and behaviors of whole neighborhoods and communities; of businesses and industries; of schools, students, and teachers; of politicians and educators; and of law-abiding citizens everywhere. Crime also causes a level of fear and dread that although understandable, is usually far out of proportion to the actual threat of danger. What accounts for this misrepresentation? One factor lies in the ways in which crime is reported by the media. Pursuant to the journalistic cliché that "if it bleeds, it leads," news about crimes—especially violent crimes—dominates local and national newscasts to the point that viewers get the false impression that virtually everyone is being victimized (Johnstone, Hawkins, & Michener, 1994). Murder in general, and mass murder in particular, invariably receives breathless media attention. Reporters tend to focus on victims who are sure to elicit the most sympathetic reactions while also heightening people's sense of insecurity: the very young, the elderly, the random victim, the victim killed while helping someone, the victim of a bizarre crime (Chermak, 1995). One analysis of local television newscasts in Washington, DC, found that crime coverage was relentless; when there was a dearth of local crime incidents, news editors imported them from other states (Kurtz, 1998) or presented advice on how to avoid being victimized by crime.

All this media attention tends to make violent crime, which accounts for only 10% of all crime (FBI, 2004), loom larger than it actually is (Riger, Gordon, & LeBailley, 1982). The media's editorial policies can also sensationalize offenses, create "bad guys" (including as-yet-uncharged suspects such as Richard Jewell, the man who turned out not to be responsible for the bombing at the 1994 Atlanta Olympics), and give undue credibility to the reports of victims and law enforcement officials. Finally, media-influenced misperceptions about the prevalence of violent crime can create inappropriately extreme views of what to do about it (Brownstein, 1991; Elias, 1993; Ericson, 1989).

At the same time, a relative lack of media attention leaves most people amazingly unconcerned about the economic and property crimes that do the most harm to the most people, such as fraud, securities violations, embezzlement, and violation of environmental protection laws. As we described in chapter 11, these are crimes that victimize everyone through reduced air and water quality, inflated insurance premiums, excessive credit card interest rates, rising consumer prices, and invasions of everyone's privacy.

Summary

A victim is a person who is harmed by the actions of others. People tend to think of victims as those hurt or killed or whose property is damaged by criminals, but people may be hurt indirectly by crime. Although dollar costs of crime victimization are hard to measure, experts say they run to as much as a trillion dollars a year. This includes the cost of prosecuting and incarcerating criminals, direct costs to individual and business victims, and indirect costs to victims in turns of psychological suffering, lost wages, and lost business productivity.

Data about victims of crime in the United States come from the *UCR*, the NCVS, and offender self-reports. The NCVS is a recurring survey of victims using a large sample of U.S. households that tracks the same population year after year, enabling it to greater show shifts in crime and crime reporting.

Today, victims play a large role in the criminal justice system. Thanks to victims' advocacy groups, state and federal laws have given special status to some victims; strengthened laws dealing with certain types of crime such as child sexual molestation, domestic violence, drunk driving, and hate crime; and provided for meaningful participation in the criminal sentencing process for victims directly harmed by crime. Victims may testify at sentencing and offer impact statements on the psychological and financial costs of their victimization. Victim assistance programs include the requirement that perpetrators pay restitution to their victims.

Criminologists, behavioral scientists who study crime, also study victims, in a discipline known as victimology. Victimology should not be thought of as "blaming the victim." Rather, it is concerned with (1) characteristics of individual victims, (2) relationships between victims and offenders, (3) the situations and contexts within which victimization occurs, and (4) victims' roles in precipitating crime. Victims of some crimes share age, gender, and racial characteristics with their perpetrators because they are living in proximity to or engaging in similar lifestyles with the offenders. Classes of victims about whom data is specially collected include the young, the elderly, women, the poor, the mentally disordered, and racial minority groups. In studying relationships between crime victims and perpetrators, it has been found that most murder and sexual assault/rape victims know their perpetrators, that victims of robbery are least likely to know the offender, that often people's own greed is responsible for their being victims of fraud, and that very young children are the most likely victims of child abuse.

Victimologists study work environments in which crimes are most likely to occur. Not surprisingly, law enforcement tops the list. People working with large numbers of people, and those handling money, delivering passengers or goods, and driving taxis, are more likely to be victims of crimes than those in other work settings. Although school violence is rare, considering the number of schools and children and young people attending, school shootings of late have fostered an awareness that the places where people ought to be safe to learn are sometimes places of heartbreaking tragedy. Virtually all school killings that have been headline news in the past 10 years have taken place in rural or suburban schools, not inner cities.

Studying all elements of a criminal transaction—including the role of victim characteristics and behavior—need not undermine victims' status as wronged individuals. Indeed, doing so is likely to help people better understand and prevent crime.

ey Terms

Wergild

Victim assistance program

Victim-offender reconciliation programs

Victim impact statements

Right of allocution

Rape shield laws

Victimology

uestions for Review

1. What are the three main measures of U.S. crime victimization?
2. What is the legal status of victims in the U.S. criminal justice system today?
3. What are hate crimes, and what is the status of hate crime laws in the United States today?
4. What general characterizations can you make about shared relationships and characteristics between offenders and victims?
5. What are the most dangerous work settings in terms of potential criminal victimization?

 Track It Down

Criminal Behavior Website
www.cassel2e.com
Office for Victims of Crime
www.ojp.usdoj.gov/ovc/
Bureau of Justice Statistics Crime and Victim Statistics
www.ojp.usdoj.gov/bjs/cvict.htm
The School Shooter Threat Assessment
www.fbi.gov/publications/school/school2.pdf
Youth Risk Behavior Surveillance Survey
www.cdc.gov/mmwr/PDF/SS/SS5302.pdf
What You Can Do if You Are a Victim of Crime
www.ojp.usdoj.gov/ovc/publications/factshts/whatyoucando/welcome.html

13

The Punishment of Crime, and the Crime of Punishment

The Goals of Punishment
Sentencing Procedures and Options
Imprisonment

The Death Penalty
Invisible Punishment

"Is there any reason why I should not pronounce sentence at this time?" At the sound of these words, the convicted criminal prepares for the worst and hopes for the best. Will the judge temper justice with mercy, as Shakespeare's Portia begged her father to do? Or will the sentence be harsh, including substantial time in prison? Will the judge have been moved by the defense attorney's (and defendant's) pleas for leniency and "one more chance," or will the sentence reflect the prosecutor's demand to "lock 'em up for life—or at least as long as the law will allow?"

Whatever the decision, sentencing day, a secular judgment day, is the culmination of all the factors and forces we have discussed in this book. Biological, psychological, and social influences brought the convicted person to this day. Police, prosecutor, and jury prevailed over the attempts of the defense attorney to save the defendant from this moment. Now begins the punishment phase of the criminal justice system. In this chapter, we examine the process of punishment, not only as a consequence of crime for the criminal, but as a factor in perpetuating crime in our society.

In the early days of American justice, punishment for criminal behavior took place in public, and consisted of pillory (being placed in restraints and ridiculed on the street), flogging, or execution in a carnival-like atmosphere. With the establishment of the modern criminal justice system, punishment became a more private affair, mainly involving imprisonment, but still often featuring physical pain and humiliation as a means of controlling and disciplining prisoners (D. A. Ward, 1994). It was not until the 1960s, when the law allowed prisoners to sue state officials for cruel and unusual punishment, that a flood of litigation brought to light the horrors perpetrated in many state and federal prisons. Federal courts declared many prison practices were unconstitutional. For example, the entire penitentiary systems in Arkansas and Alabama were dismantled in 1970 (*Holt v. Sarver,* 1970) and 1976, respectively (*Pugh v. Locke,* 1976). Soon, any kind of physical punishment of imprisoned criminals became illegal. Ironically, it was as prison administrators lost the right to inflict physical punishment as a means of controlling convicts that the door was opened for gangs and other aggressive convicts to exert that control. Smarting from the sting of laws limiting their rights to discipline prisoners, prison officials began to ignore prisoners' complaints of abuse at the hands of other prisoners. They said, in essence, "You want to be left alone? We will leave you alone—to fend for yourselves" (R. Johnson, 1996).

New techniques for capital punishment—by electrocution, toxic gas, or lethal injection—were developed with the explicit goal of reducing the public spectacle and physical pain associated with burning, shooting, and hanging (Foucault, 1977).[1] Yet even the new execution methods retain an element of psychological, if not physical, torture. The modern ritual of execution, which we discuss later in this chapter, includes doing whatever is necessary to keep condemned prisoners alive to execute them and to provide drugs and other treatments to restore their mental health to the point that they are competent to be executed. Indeed, in some cases, it may be during preparations for executing a prisoner that the state shows its first obvious interest in the person's physical or mental health.

The Goals of Punishment

The philosophy of punishment in the United States can be set forth in four widely accepted goals:

1. To *isolate* the offender from the public, usually through the process of incarceration.
2. To *rehabilitate* the offender, usually by providing training and therapeutic services, both in prison and in the community.
3. To *deter* future crime in the sentenced defendant (specific deterrence) and in society at large (general deterrence).
4. To exact *retribution* by making defendants "pay their debt" to society for having engaged in criminal conduct.

Juries and judges are typically interested in retribution when they recommend or pass sentences, but they usually have at least one of the other goals of punishment in mind as well. The nature of those other goals is determined partly by how they view the crime, the defendant, and the defendant's role in the crime. Bernard Weiner and his colleagues analyzed the relation between recommended sentences and the attributions that jurors make about the causes of specific crimes (Weiner, Graham, & Reyna, 1997). They classified these causes according to locus, stability, and controllability. *Locus* refers to whether the criminal behavior appeared to have been caused by the criminal's personal characteristics (internal locus) or by factors beyond the criminal's control (external locus). *Stability* refers to whether the cause of the criminal behavior was chronic and permanent or acute and temporary. *Controllability* refers to the degree to which the criminal could have acted to prevent the crime. Thus, if the jury sees a criminal's motive for murder as simply getting the victim's money, the cause of this crime would likely be seen as internal and controllable, and if the defendant has a violent history, this would suggest that the cause of the behavior is stable. However, the same crime and criminal history could be attributed to stable, internal, but uncontrollable causes if the criminal also suffers from longstanding paranoid delusions. Weiner found that a jury's punishment goals varied with the crime under consideration and the causal attributions made about the case. Crimes seen as reflecting internal and controllable causes tend to make jurors focus on the goals of retribution, deterrence, and isolation. Crimes attributed to unstable (temporary) causes tend to lead jurors to focus on the goal of rehabilitation. The emotional responses of jurors also contribute to their choice of punishment goals. Sympathy toward a defendant tends to make the rehabilitative goal most prominent, whereas anger usually brings the retributive goal to the fore (McFatter, 1978).

Over the last 20 years, there has been decreasing emphasis on rehabilitation such that in some states, rehabilitative efforts have virtually disappeared. The change appears due partly to the growing belief that rehabilitation does not work and partly to impatience with its focus on offenders. As we described in chapter 12, the increasingly influential victims' rights movement has helped make jurors less concerned with changing the behavior of convicted criminals and more concerned with making them "pay the price" to those they have harmed and to society in general. Although understandable, this shift in punishment goals may be misguided because, as we show, efforts at rehabilitation can benefit society far more than incarceration alone. We begin

---

[1]Utah still uses firing squads (but gives the defendant the alternative of lethal injection), and four states—Delaware, Montana, New Hampshire, and Washington—still allow hanging, although not in public.

our examination of the punishment process by considering the sentencing recommendations and options open to judges and juries.

Sentencing Procedures and Options

In most states, once jurors have convicted a defendant, they make recommendations to the judge about the length of imprisonment and/or the size of a fine that should be imposed. (They cannot recommend "alternative sanctions" such as probation, a suspended sentence, community confinement, community service, or restitution; these options are decided by judges alone.) After the jury has made its sentencing recommendation, it is discharged and plays no further role in the proceedings. The judge can immediately impose the jury's recommended sentence, but more commonly asks a probation officer to conduct a presentence investigation and file a report with the court. In most states, the defendant, too, has the right to ask for such an investigation.

Bifurcated Trials

Until recently, jurors made their sentencing recommendations at the same time as they deliberated about the defendant's guilt or innocence. In doing so, they had no access to information about the defendant's criminal history because such information would be irrelevant to the defendant's guilt or innocence in the current case and could unduly influence the jury's thinking in the "guilt" phase of their deliberations. Beginning in the early 1990s, federal law and many state laws were amended such that the sentencing stage of jury deliberations was "bifurcated," or separated, from the trial stage. So in jurisdictions where jury work is bifurcated, the jurors first decide only if the defendant is guilty or innocent. If the verdict is guilty, the jurors then attend a sentencing hearing at which evidence is presented to help them decide on what punishment to recommend. At this hearing, the prosecution can tell jurors about the defendant's criminal record and may introduce witnesses who can testify about the defendant's dangerousness. The defendant's attorney will call witnesses to testify on the defendant's behalf, thus softening the impact of the prosecutor's evidence. The defendant, too, is allowed speak—usually to express remorse and plead for mercy—without being cross-examined. Where the law allows it, the defendant's victims have the right to tell the jury how they have been affected; if the law does not allow them to testify, their written victim impact statements may be read by the jury.

In bifurcated trials, judges rarely overturn the sentence recommended by the jury unless it does not conform to what the law allows. The prevailing sentiment, which pleases most prosecutors and victims, is that as representatives of the community and its values, the jury is in the best position to mete out punishment. To help them make a decision that is within the law, jurors are instructed as to the maximum and minimum penalties allowed.

Variations in Sentencing

Because there is a wide range of sentencing possibilities open to judges and juries, defendants convicted of the same crime can receive vastly different punishments in different states or even within the same state. Some see this disparity in sentencing as sentencing inequity, a view that has given rise to some of the most intense criticisms of the U.S. criminal justice system.

Sentencing disparity, or inequity, arises from many factors, including differences in community values, juror demographics, crime details, the perceived role of the victim, and, perhaps of greatest concern, the ethnicity and socioeconomic status of defendants and victims. A high-profile case in Virginia some years back is a case in point. A wealthy young woman was charged with first-degree murder in the death of her boyfriend, a South American polo star who lived with her on her multimillion dollar horse farm. At her trial, the woman pleaded self-defense, claiming that she was in fear for her life at the moment she shot her lover—several times from several feet away while he was eating breakfast, with his back to her. The jury did not accept her claim, but found that the murder was committed in the heat of passion and was not premeditated, presumably because the defendant had presented evidence that the victim had been threatening and abusive. The recommended sentence was 60 days in the county jail and a fine of $2,500 (Masters & Ordonez, 1998). Because the county jail gives one day of "good time" for each day served, she was released in 30 days. During that time, she was given a private cell and telephone, unrestricted visitation privileges, and was allowed to have her meals brought to her from outside. Many well-to-do members of the local community appeared to agree with the verdict and the sentence because, after all, the defendant was a wealthy landowner and the victim was an ethnic minority "gigolo."

This "privileged" defendant's sentence and the manner in which she was allowed to serve it exemplifies the powerful message being sent to potential criminals by the criminal justice system: "If you are rich and powerful and you commit a crime, you may get off with little or no punishment. If not, you are in deep trouble." Elaine Cassel represented women who received 20-year prison sentences for crimes such as writing bad checks and or being with a boyfriend when he made a drug sale to an undercover officer. Each of these women was poor, uneducated, and got no sympathy from the judge or the jury.

In short, the criminal justice system's tendency to discriminate against certain defendants in terms of who gets arrested and prosecuted (see chapter 2) is evident in the sentencing process as well. For example, although Blacks and Whites use drugs at approximately the same rate, Black men are sent to state prisons on drug charges at 14 times the rate of White men (Harrison & Beck, 2005). Further, the number of Blacks serving time for drug offenses increased by 707% between 1985 and 1995 compared to an increase of 306% for Whites (U.S. Sentencing Project, 1998). Finally, as we discuss in more detail later, there is a disproportionate number of Black men on death row.

Largely because of the racial disparity in imprisonment rates for drug offenses, but partly because Black men are more likely than White men to be imprisoned for any crime, Blacks are sent to prison at a rate that is 8.2 times that of Whites; the rate of Hispanics going to prison is about 2½ times that of Whites. In 2001, an estimated 16.6% of adult Black males were current or former State or Federal prisoners—a rate that was twice that of Hispanic males (7.7%) and six times that of White males (2.6%; Bonczar, 2003). Based on current incarceration rates, government statisticians predict that 32.2% of Black males and 17.2% of Hispanic males will go to prison sometime during their lifetime. The chances of White males going to prison is only 5.9%. Disparate numbers hold for women, too. The lifetime chances of going to prison among Black females (5.6%) is nearly as high as for White males. Hispanic females (2.2%) and White females (0.9%) are much less likely to be incarcerated in a prison (Bonczar, 2003).[2]

Sentencing Guidelines

In an effort to reduce the negative effects of sentencing inequity, some states (and some federal laws) now require mandatory sentences and/or follow clearly established sentencing guidelines. **Sentencing guidelines** are recommendations for sentences for particular crimes made to judges by panels of criminal justice experts known as Sentencing Commissions. The guidelines are not made available to jurors, however. The guidelines take into account and quantify factors such as a defendant's prior criminal record, the circumstances and seriousness of the offense, and the average sentences handed down in previous cases involving similar defendants and offenses.

The use of sentencing guidelines is voluntary, and some judges ignore them. Most laws require only that the judge declare for the record that the guidelines were considered and in some states, that reasons be given for not following the guidelines. Accordingly, a judge's failure to heed guidelines in handing down a sentence does not constitute a reason to challenge that sentence. However, state judges who sentence below the guidelines often find themselves with political problems when the time comes for them to reappointed. Federal judges have no such problem, as they have lifetime appointments.

---

[2]Although often used interchangeably, there is a significant distinction between the terms *jail* and *prison*. Jails are run by local authorities and house people sentenced for nonviolent crimes with sentences of less than 12 months, mainly misdemeanors; prisons are state and federal facilities where people serve crimes for felonies. The federal system does not have jails. See chapter 1 for the discussion of felonies versus misdemeanors.

Mandatory Sentences

Mandatory sentences are just that—requirements that judges hand down a particular sentence for a particular crime no matter what the circumstances surrounding that crime. Although few states have established mandatory sentences, they are common in federal criminal statutes. Congress passed these federal laws not so much to correct sentencing inequity (it is not an issue of concern to most voters) but to prevent judges from being too lenient. However, virtually all judges dislike mandatory sentencing laws because they feel these laws take away their power to use their wisdom and discretion in pronouncing sentences.

Mandatory sentencing laws often force judges to impose what they see as unduly harsh punishment. This is particularly true in the case of the "three strikes and you're out" laws passed by many states. As we describe in more detail later, the purpose of these laws is to put those who repeatedly commit serious crimes behind bars for life without the possibility of parole.[3]

Alternatives to Incarceration

As we noted earlier, judges have many sentencing options including (1) incarceration, (2) incarceration that is partly or fully suspended in favor of probation, (3) probation alone, (4) community supervision or confinement, (5) rehabilitation programs, (6) "boot camps," (7) restitution, and (8) fines. Later, we discuss the impact of imprisonment on crime; here we consider the effects of other sentencing options in preventing and controlling crime.

Rehabilitation Programs. Sentences that require convicts to participate in rehabilitation programs are focused on changing the offenders' behavior so that they will be less likely to continue their criminal activities after release. Most of these programs apply psychological theories and research on human learning, cognition, and development to help criminals change their thinking and behavior (e.g., Andrews & Bonta, 1994). These behavior change programs have been quite successful with noncriminal populations, but efforts to use them to rehabilitate criminals have been criticized by criminal justice experts and the public, most of whom believe that "nothing works" (Martinson, 1974).

This pessimism has been challenged by many researchers (Palmer, 1975, 1983; Van Voorhis, 1987) and by meta-analyses that combine and summarize data from many studies. These analyses demonstrate that rehabilitation programs can be effective in changing offenders' behavior (e.g., Andrews & Bonta, 1994; Cullen & Gendreau, 1989) but that some are better than others. The most effective rehabilitation programs are those that follow basic learning principles (Gendreau & Ross, 1987), address the most changeable offender characteristics, and aim at altering factors that are directly associated with criminal behavior. Specifically, it appears best to focus rehabilitation programs on (1) changing the attitudes and thought patterns that engender criminal acts, (2) correcting deficiencies in education and job skills, (3) improving family relationship skills, (4) raising self-esteem, and (5) combating substance abuse and tendencies to spend time with criminal peers (Sherman et al., 1997).

Drug and alcohol treatment programs, particularly those administered in prison settings, can also be effective in reducing recidivism (Eisenberg & Fabelo, 1996; S. S. Martin, Butzin, & Inciardi, 1995; Wexler, Graham, Koronowski, & Lowe, 1995). These programs employ cognitive-behavioral principles not only to help change the way substance-abusing and substance-dependent criminals behave but also the way in which they look at every facet of their lives. The programs are not mandatory, but about 90% of convicts with drug problems choose to participate in them—partly because if they do not, they will probably be denied parole and forced to serve their entire sentences. Given that many of these convicts enter the programs grudgingly, it is all the more remarkable that those who complete them have a 20% lower rate of parole failure (i.e., of being rearrested for using drugs or alcohol or committing other parole violations) than all other inmates including those who entered prison with no record of substance abuse (O'Reilly, 1997).

Probation and Community Supervision. Some convicted criminals have all or part of their prison

---

[3]The imposition of a life sentence under a three strikes law takes place in a separate proceeding after the defendant has been convicted and sentenced for the third time.

sentence suspended and serve instead a probationary period under the supervision of a probation officer who is affiliated with the prison system. The terms and requirements of probation can vary, but typically include attending regular meetings with the probation officer, remaining employed, and refraining from using drugs and alcohol, as confirmed by unannounced urine tests.

Unfortunately, supervised probation does not appear to have a strong effect on crime. This is true partly because the more intense the probation supervision, the greater the likelihood that the offender will be rearrested for technical violations of the law, especially for violations of probation—such as missing a scheduled appointment or failing a drug test. When this happens, offenders typically find themselves in a probation revocation hearing at which a judge decides whether to send them to prison (or back to prison) to serve the sentence that had been suspended when they were put on probation in the first place.

Fines. The limited research on fines and suggests, that in conjunction with probation, they may have a small beneficial effect on recidivism (Gordon & Glaser, 1991).

Boot Camps. Patterned after military basic training camps and usually lasting about three months, boot camps are typically offered to nonviolent offenders as an alternative to incarceration. Analyses of recidivism rates among adult criminals who attend boot camps have shown mixed results. Some states report small deterrent effects (New York Department of Correctional Services, 1993), some find no deterrent effect, (Florida Department of Corrections, 1990), and some show a reverse effect in which attendees are more likely than nonattendees to commit further crimes (Texas Department of Criminal Justice, 1991). The most successful adult boot camps are those that devote more than three hours a day to therapy, counseling, drug treatment, and education and provide some follow-up supervision after participants are released (McKenzie, 1995).

Generally, boot camps for juveniles fail to reduce recidivism and often have the opposite effect such that boot camp "veterans" show higher recidivism rates than offenders who were punished in other ways (Blair, 2000; Bottcher, Isorena, & Belnas, 1996; Peters, 1996). Some criminologists see juvenile boot camps as a poorly thought out alternative that fails to take into account juveniles' response to the harsh control and disrespect that are hallmarks of these programs (Blair, 2000). The state of Maryland suspended its juvenile boot camps in 2000 after reports of widespread physical abuse of residents.

Restitution. As we discussed in chapter 12, most states now require that convicted defendants pay restitution to victims. As desirable as this requirement may be, there is no evidence that it has any deterrent effect on future crime.

Home Confinement and Electronic Monitoring. Several states have employed home confinement (also called house arrest or home detention) as alternatives to incarceration for those convicted of certain lesser offenses. Some courts combine home confinement with other types of punishment such as imprisonment. Martha Stewart, the decorating and media superstar who was convicted in 2004 of lying to federal prosecutors about a stock sale, spent five months in prison after which she was released to home confinement for a five months. (Stewart was also ordered to pay a fine of $30,000 and serve two years probation.) Home-confined offenders must spend extensive periods of time at home unless they are employed, in which case they must still stay home during evenings and weekends. To insure that these offenders comply with the terms of their sentence, electronic monitoring devices may be attached to their ankles or wrists. Another form of electronic monitoring involves computer-generated phone calls to the offender's home, made at random times, to which the offender must respond within a particular period of time.

Compared to incarceration, home confinement and electronic monitoring are cost efficient and relieve prison crowding, but do they deter crime? Data available so far suggests that recidivism rates are low for home-confined, low-risk individuals such as those convicted of driving while intoxicated (Lilly, Ball, Curry, & McMullen, 1993), first-time youthful offenders (Baumer & Mendelsohn, 1992; Baumer, Maxfield, & Mendelsohn, 1993), and some parolees (J. Austin & Hardyman, 1991; Cullen, 1993). These data have not established if the deterrent value of home confinement is significantly different from incarceration or other punishment alternatives (Sherman et al., 1997).

mprisonment

The goals of isolation and retribution, reflecting social and political policies designed to "get tough on crime," have made incarceration in jails or prisons the preferred method for punishing convicted criminals.

Jails are local (city or county) correctional facilities that confine convicts who have been given sentences of a year or less as well as people who fall into a wide variety of other categories. These include (a) defendants who are awaiting trial or sentencing; (b) criminals who have been arrested for violating the conditions of probation, parole, or release on bond; (c) minors being detained pending transfer to juvenile confinement facilities; (d) mentally ill persons awaiting relocation to mental health facilities; and (e) inmates displaced from federal, state, or other confinement facilities because of overcrowding. Local authorities, usually city police or county sheriffs, administer jails.

State prisons are administered by state departments of corrections whose heads are usually appointed by the state's governor.[4] There are also 30 federal prisons that house inmates convicted in federal courts of federal crimes. The Federal Bureau of Prisons administers these facilities, most of which are classified as minimum or medium security. Two maximum-security federal prisons—at Marion, Illinois, and Leavenworth, Kansas—were built to hold the most violent, dangerous, and aggressive inmates, but even these are sometimes not sufficient. There are about 60 "supermax" prisons in 40 states, and construction is underway on an at least 15 more (Human Rights Watch, 1997). In fact, the federal penitentiary system has committed itself to the supermax model for all future construction (Perkinson, 1994). Designed to separate violent inmates from the rest of the prison population and to protect prison guards, prisoners in supermax facilities are in solitary confinement for 23 hours a day. When they leave their cells for solitary exercise, they are shackled. They are not given access to any occupational, educational, or rehabilitative programs.

Although they do what they were designed to do, these new prisons cause considerable concern among criminologists and psychologists because, for one thing, the conditions of extreme isolation prevalent in supermax prisons leave inmates especially vulnerable to abuse by guards. Further, as many as half of these inmates may develop serious mental disorders, especially severe depression or some form of psychosis (Human Rights Watch, 1997). Nonetheless, conditions at supermax facilities are not likely to change. A landmark federal court case challenging the conditions in California's supermax prison system left the system intact, even though the court conceded that these prisons "may press the outer bounds of what most humans can psychologically tolerate" (*Madrid v. Gomez,* 1995, p. 1267). Such outcomes seem to reflect a societal decision to deal with serious crime mainly through harsh punishment and to virtually ignore the goals of altering the causes of crime or rehabilitating and educating criminals (Haney, 1998; Haney & Lynch, 1997). In June 2005, a unanimous U.S. Supreme Court decision (*Wilkinson v. Austin*) expressed some misgivings about the psychological horror of confinement in a supermax prison where, it noted, inmates are deprived of virtual all sensory stimulation and human contact, but like the California federal court case, it did not find supermax confinement, *per se,* in violation of the Eighth Amendment's protection against cruel and unusual punishment as long as a prisoner had some mechanism for challenging the state's finding that only a supermax prison could hold him.

The Prisonization of America

As of June 30, 2004, there were 2,131,180 people in state and federal prisons: 1,348 male inmates per 100,000 men in the United States and 123 female inmates per 100,000 U.S. women (Harrison & Beck, 2005). Black and Hispanic men are far more likely to be incarcerated than White men. At midyear 2004, there were 4,919 Black male prison and jail inmates per 100,000 Black males in the United States compared to 1,717 Hispanic male inmates per 100,000 Hispanic males and 717 White male inmates per 100,000 White males (Harrison & Beck, 2005).

---

[4]Some states and the federal government contract with private companies to run their prisons. At the end of 2003, there were approximately 95,000 prisoners in privately run prisons. Private prisons have been the subject of much debate and litigation. The main criticism is lack of oversight (they are more costly to run than public facilities) and accountability (they are harder to hold responsible for abuse of neglect of prisoners).

The per capita incarceration rate in the United States is six times the world average. It is seven times that of Europe, 14 times that of Japan, and 23 times that of India. There are more prisoners in California alone than in any other country in the world except China and Russia (Currie, 1998). The United States imprisons more people per capita than any country in the world (Mauer, 2003). Further, the incarceration rate is increasing. The jail and prison population is double what it was a decade ago and triple what it was in 1980, despite the fact that the rate of violent crime has been decreasing in the United States since 1992 (FBI, 2004a). On the average, a new jail or prison is built every week in the United States, thus expanding what is already the world's largest penal system (Egan, 1999a). This phenomenon has been referred to as the prisonization of America (Cassel, 2002b).

Why are prison populations rising when violent crime is declining? The answer is that most of the people who are being incarcerated these days are not violent criminals. Only one-fourth of state prison inmates are serving time for a violent offense; most were imprisoned for property crimes, drug law violations, or other offenses (Harrison & Beck, 2005). Further, longer prison terms are being imposed for all types of crime including drug offenses, often as the result of mandatory sentencing guidelines. Finally, in many states, people who might once have been paroled (given early release) are being made to serve their full sentence, and the three strikes laws we discussed earlier are putting convicts in prison, sometimes for life, who might once have received probation (Abramsky, 2002).

Incarceration for Drug Offenses.   The main factor underlying the growth of U.S. prison populations is the growing tendency to incarcerate those who violate drug laws. The number of inmates in federal prisons rose 81% between 1995 and 2003, and more than half of them had been convicted only of a drug crime (Harrison & Beck, 2005). Drug convictions account for one fourth of all state and federal imprisonments combined (Mauer, 2003). However, there are racial disparities in sentences for drug crimes. Blacks are 20% and Hispanics are 40% more likely to receive a prison sentence for a drug crime than are Whites (Bureau of Justice Statistics, 2003b). Regardless of their race, less than 15% of these inmates are being offered drug rehabilitation programs while in prison (ACLU, 2002), meaning that most drug-law violators are likely to continue using drugs and to commit drug-related crimes once they have served their time.

The apparent failure of the current incarceration policy in relation to drug crimes has led some politicians to join many criminologists in asking for a review of that policy. Even Edwin Meese, III, the U.S. Attorney General under President Reagan and one of the architects of punitive federal laws, recently came out in favor of such a review (Egan, 1999a). However, as long as the prison sentence for drug crimes find favor with the American voters, people are likely to see continued reliance on incarceration to punish drug law violations, continued growth in the inmate population, and a continuing need to spend public money on more confinement facilities.

Truth-in-Sentencing and Mandatory Sentencing Laws.   Another factor in driving up prison populations is the passage of truth-in-sentencing and mandatory sentencing laws including three-strikes provisions. Truth-in-sentencing laws generally have abolished parole for good behavior, thus assuring that inmates serve their entire prison terms. Mandatory sentencing laws, too, result in more prisoners remaining behind bars longer without regard to their dangerousness or the costs to society of housing them (Abramsky, 2002). As of March 2004, more than 7,300 prisoners have been sentenced to terms of 25 years to life under California's three-strikes law. The first of the three-strikes statutes—designed to deal with habitual, persistent, and violent offenders—was passed in the state of Washington in 1993. Today, more than half the states have them. Three-strikes laws can be far-reaching or narrowly focused, but the majority of them call for sentences of 25 years to life when one is convicted of a third felony. In some states, all felonies committed need to have been violent crimes. However, in California, the first state to enact three-strikes laws, the second and third felonies can be nonviolent. As of March 2004, after 10 years of three-strikes sentencing in California, more than 7,300 prisoners had been sentenced under its draconian provisions—more than half of them for nonviolent felonies such as petty theft, forgery, and drug possession ("Editorial: Why A3," 2004). With few exceptions, three-strikes laws leave judges no discretion to deviate from the prescribed sentences.

Criminologists and penologists (those who study imprisonment) are calling for review of three-strikes legislation. They point out first that like other mandatory sentencing laws, three-strikes laws usurp the judge's traditional role in fashioning appropriate punishment to it individual crimes and defendants and lock up to many nonviolent criminals at huge taxpayer costs (roughly $31,000 per year per inmate, with costs spiraling upward as the inmate ages and has health problems). In 2005, Santos Reyes was sentenced to 26 years to life for taking the written portion of his brother's driving test for him. Reyes had a prior juvenile burglary conviction (stealing a radio out of a house) and a robbery in which no one was injured. The time between his robbery conviction and his third-strike offense was 13 years (Egelko, 2005).

In 2003, the U.S. Supreme Court struck a blow at three-strikes reformers when it held that California's law was not unconstitutionally cruel and unusual punishment in the case of a man who was sentenced to 50 years to life for his third felony—stealing $153 worth of videotapes (*Lockyear v. Andrade*) and another who was sentenced to 25 years to life for stealing three golf clubs (*Ewing v. California*). Also, in 2004, California voters turned down a referendum that would have softened California's harsh law.

The Effects of Imprisonment

For most prisoners, life within prison walls is at best bleak and tedious, often dangerous and, far from being rehabilitative, may increase the likelihood of further criminal behavior following release. We first consider what life is like behind bars and then look at how and why it encourages crime.

Hans Toch (1977, 1990) has written extensively about the challenges to physical and psychological survival presented by prison life, including (1) lack of physical and mental activity, (2) noise and overcrowding, (3) lack of emotionally supportive relationships, (4) lack of services to facilitate self-improvement, (5) arbitrary enforcement of prison rules and unfair application of discipline, and (6) loss of control over the timing of basic activities such as eating and sleeping. One can get some idea of the extent of these challenges by considering what happened during a crackdown on prisoners by the California Department of Corrections in 1997. Among the new rules imposed on inmates were grooming regulations that made beards, long hair, ponytails, and earrings illegal. Hair length was limited to three inches, with plans to reduce it to two inches later. The prison uniform of blue jeans and denim shirts was replaced with all-white uniforms bearing "CDC Prisoner" in black letters. Packages from home were no longer delivered; family members who wish to send prisoners gifts of food and personal items must purchase them from a state-approved list of vendors who will ship the items to the recipients. Bodybuilding equipment was banned in an effort to prevent convicts from "bulking up" (Claiborne, 1997). One attorney for the California Prison Law Office said that inmates saw the new law as stripping them of the last avenue for any expression of personal identity. "Every minute of their lives is already covered by regulations, so what they do with their bodies is important to them. Basically, their hair is all they have left" (Millard Murphy, as cited in *The Washington Post,* December 21, 1997, p. A3).

The California law that made it legal to get this tough on criminals marked the death knell of the 1975 Federal Inmate Bill of Rights, a law that had given prisoners many of the rights enjoyed by other citizens. In the past 20 years, federal appellate and U.S. Supreme Court decisions have struck down so many provisions of the inmates' rights bill that the concept of humane prison conditions has virtually evaporated. Prisons may now deprive inmates of any right reasonably related to legitimate penal interests. The words *legitimate penal interests* can be defined so broadly as to allow prison officials to use it in support of virtually any deprivation. Indeed, turning away from the Warren Court's legacy of protection of the constitutional rights of the powerless, the Supreme Court now sees virtually no Constitutional limits on prison harshness. Writing for the majority in *Rhodes v. Chapman* (1981), Justice Powell said that "the Constitution does not mandate comfortable prisons, and prisons ... which house persons convicted of serious crimes cannot be free of discomfort" (p. 349). Recent court challenges to the failure of some prison wardens to control violent prisoners and guards or to provide medical care to inmates suffering from serious physical or mental disorders have not changed the Supreme Court's position.

In a 1994 decision arising out of the rape of a prison inmate, the Court ruled that no act or omission, however gross, that resulted in inmate injury would be a violation of the Eighth Amendment unless prison officials actually intended to harm the inmate (*Farmer v. Brennan,* 1994, p. 1980). A 2002 Supreme Court case in which the court did find that the state went too far arose out of an Alabama disciplinary practice of chaining inmates to a stake outside in the boiling hot summer sun for as much as seven hours at a time without water. The guards went so far as to put down water bowls near the inmates and let them watch dogs drink from them. The

Supreme Court found this to be "obvious cruelty" and constitutionally objectionable (*Hope v. Pelzer,* 2002).The harsh conditions imposed by the correctional system can be intensely dehumanizing (Sykes, 1966), leading many prisoners to abandon whatever decent or law-abiding impulses they brought with them and creating such anger and resentment against society that they finish their sentences determined to retaliate with further criminal acts. Several other aspects of prison life also make prisoners more likely to engage in crime both while incarcerated and after being released. These include the availability of drugs, the influence of gangs, and the prevalence of violence and sexual assault.

Drugs.   During one 6-month period in 1997, 9% of the District of Columbia's jail and prison population tested positive for illegal drugs ("Jails Without Walls," 1997). In most state and federal prisons, drugs are easy to obtain, partly because, as the U.S. Justice Department admitted in 1997, a number of correctional officers accept bribes in exchange for allowing drugs to be smuggled in (Suro, 1997). For example, in 2003, a South Carolina state corrections officer was arrested and charged with smuggling marijuana into a prison. Engaging in drug trafficking in prison and from prison is a cooperative effort between prison guards and drug kingpins. One federal prison official described guard bribery as an "occupational hazard" that arises as a function of guards being in such close contact with major drug dealers who have vast sums of cash (Suro, 1997). Some say that marijuana has become the currency of choice for favors in prison, replacing cigarettes (now banned in many correctional facilities).

In the District of Columbia's Lorton Prison in 1996, a prison guard was arrested for murder and conspiracy when he allowed an inmate to enter a cell and kill a fellow inmate. The guard and the murderer had been working together to take over the victim's share of the prison drug trade. A similar case involved drug lord Rayful Edmond, III, who in 1989, began serving a life sentence in the federal prison in Lewisburg, Pennsylvania. Edmond had direct connections with Columbia's cocaine cartel and by 1994 was found to be using his prison cell as a base for making drug deals worth tens of millions of dollars in Washington, DC (Miller, 1998). He told authorities that he made more money selling drugs from prison than he had while on the street. In 1999, Maryland correctional authorities transferred 19 inmates out of a maximum-security prison in an effort to break up a thriving prison business involving drug dealing and liquor sales. The enterprise had relied on guards and employees to ensure its success (Valentine, 1999).[5]

Prison Gangs.   There has always been a "convict code" that tells prisoners to watch out for themselves and not snitch on others (Johnson, 1996). Gang members in prison extend that code by protecting each other, exerting control over guards and nongang inmates, and affiliating to make money in criminal activity (Crime & Justice International Quarterly, 1997; Johnson, 1996). According to a Department of Justice report (J. Moore, 1997), gangs are a major source of violence, corruption, and drug use in adult prisons and juvenile institutions, too. As we noted in chapter 8, prison gangs are usually subsidiaries of street gangs and like street gangs offer their members a sense of identity, belonging, and support as well as money, privilege, power, and protection (Jacobs, 1977). The leaders of prison gangs are usually individuals who have long held high-status positions in street gangs and who still exert considerable influence on the outside.

Gangs began to gain control of some aspects of prison life as the result of a well-intentioned plan that arose in Illinois prisons in the 1970s as numerous gang leaders were being imprisoned there. Prison officials feared they would lose control of their institutions, so they decided to offer gang leaders special privileges and status in exchange for their help in maintaining control over the inmate population. The unfortunate result was an increase in prison gang power and control as well as increased violence stemming from intergang rivalries (Johnson, 1996).

The criminal activities of gangs in prison are often more organized than is the case on the streets. Gang leaders use cellular telephones to facilitate and coordinate gang activity inside and outside the prison, and

---

[5]There are all kinds of entrepreneurs in prison—not just drug dealers. A Long Island investment advisor, Ira Monas, serving time in a New York state prison for fraud, continued his fraud schemes in prison. Using the phone in the common room of the prison, Ira Monas made daily calls to his business connections and controlled the assets of 200 investors and $8.5 million (McFadden, 2001).

access to prison computers allows gang members to acquire personal data on staff including work schedules, credit card numbers, and automobile license plate numbers. Computers also provide access to inventory information including the amount and location of prescription drugs, weapons, and other supplies that have a high market value to prisoner "customers" (Crime and Justice International, 1997). By bribing corrections officers and getting privileged prison work assignments, gang members find it relatively easy to engage in a wide variety of crimes including extortion, intimidation, drug sales, gambling, strong-arm robbery, and homosexual prostitution (R. Johnson, 1996).

One of the most egregious examples of this sort of thing involved Larry Hoover, the leader of a Chicago street gang known as the Gangster Disciples who, along with six fellow members, was found guilty of murder and narcotics conspiracy in May of 1997. When Hoover arrived at an Illinois State maximum security prison to serve his 150- to 200-year sentence, law enforcement officials who had spent 8 years trying to break up the gang thought that its glory days were over. After all, Hoover would never get out of prison and would be cut off from virtually all communication with the outside world. They underestimated him. The Gangster Disciples had more than 30,000 members and annual revenues of at least $100 million, and Hoover used these resources to control the most lucrative drug territory in Chicago—from prison. In fact, Hoover's empire virtually controlled the entire Illinois state prison system. He held jailhouse meetings and issued orders to street Disciples by cell phone. He wore expensive clothes instead of prison garb and dined on food prepared to his specifications. He paid corrections officers to be his bodyguards. He had a key to every door in the prison except the exit door. As criminals entered the prison, his men gave them applications to fill out and if accepted, they were indoctrinated into the gang, given prison assignments, and trained to continue in the gang's business enterprises after their release. He also controlled a prison "board of governors" to keep the inmates in line and an "outside board" to run the street drug trade staffed by teenage "pushers." Hoover required these people to pay him a "tax" equivalent to one day's profit per week, which netted him a weekly income of $200,000 to $300,000. When all this was discovered, he was sentenced to another life term without parole, to be added to his 150-year sentence (Fedarko, 1997).

Violence in Prison. Today, about half all prison violence is linked to gangs (J. Moore, 1997). Gang-related prison violence is usually directed not at guards, but at fellow inmates as part of efforts to enforce threats, discipline members, and protect turf (R. Johnson, 1996). In 1992, for example, a riot broke out at the Leavenworth Federal Prison as a result of rivalry between its two largest gangs, the "DC Blacks" and a gang from Los Angeles (Earley, 1992; Hanna, 1992).

What accounts for the other half of prison violence? It is said that in prison, you are either a perpetrator or a victim, meaning that prisoners must be ready to kill or risk being killed. This maxim reflects the attitude of *convicts* as opposed to *inmates* (Wooden & Parker, 1982). "Inmates" are prisoners who are badly frightened and want their current sentence to be their last prison experience. They want to survive by "doing their time" and staying out of trouble, which they can best accomplish by isolating themselves. More experienced inmates explicitly tell these people that their interests are best served by being uncivil and amoral—that is, by ignoring the suffering of those around them (R. Johnson & Toch, 1988). "Convicts," on the other hand, see prison as a way of life. They have no substantial attachment to the outside world and live by the convict code, which means that they kill snitches whom they see as the most loathsome of inmates, are loyal only to themselves and their friends, and are committed to violence in reaching their goals (M. Silberman, 1995). Convicts usually employ just enough violence to assure that they will not have trouble with their victims in the future. Thus, near-fatal stabbings and beatings are the rule. In other words, convicts' approach to surviving prison is to master the techniques of violence needed in this most violent of social worlds.

The influence of gangs and the prevalence of the convict mentality helps explain why state and federal prisons see so much violence, but the violence in these facilities pales in comparison to what occurs in some formerly state-run correctional facilities that in the interest of cost savings have been turned over to private corporations that run them for profit. For example, the Northeast Ohio Correctional Center (NOCC) in Youngstown, Ohio, is administered by the Corrections Corporation of America (CCA). CCA is the sixth largest prison in the United States behind only the federal government and four states. In one month in 1998, it was the site of more inmate assaults than had taken place in all of Ohio's other prisons in a year (C. W. Thompson, 1998a). CCA officials blame the rate of violence at NOCC on the fact that they receive prisoners who vary greatly in their dangerousness. CCA is the largest private prison. Indeed, the first inmate to die at NOCC was sent there from a facility in the District of Columbia where he had been serving time for parole violations and drug distribution. He was stabbed 15 times and left to die by a prisoner who had come from a maximum-security institution. Several District of Columbia prisoners at NOCC sued CCA, alleging that they were beaten, tear gassed and maced by prison staff on a daily basis. Lawsuits have also been brought by prisoners whose beatings by guards at a privately run facility in Mississippi were captured on videotape (Flinn, 1998).

Reliable data on prison violence is hard to come by, understandable because the governments and corporations do not want the outside world to know what goes on behind prison walls. A recently independent commission made up of people from correctional, political, legal, and civil rights organizations is studying prison violence. The Commission on Safety and Abuse in America's Prisons began holding public hearings in 2005. At its first such hearing in April 2005, wardens and guards described a pervasive culture of violence in today's prisons and jails, where prisoners and guards are involved in raping, murdering, assaulting, and otherwise abusing prisoners. A *New York Times* reporter, Ted Conover, went underground and disguised himself as a prison guard at New York's infamous Sing Sing prison. Conover (2001) cataloged his year of watching prison abuse in the book *Newjack: Guarding Sing Sing.*

Sexual Violence.   Homosexual rape is a fact of prison life. Like heterosexual rape that occurs outside prison walls (see chapter 10), prison rape is an expression of power, anger, and control, not just a sexual act. In fact, rape in prison serves as a special means of domination and debasement. The rapist symbolically emasculates his victim or in prison terms, "robs him of his manhood" (Groth, 1979/1984). Whereas consensual sex in prison tends to be intraracial, most prison rapes are interracial, usually involving Black assailants and White victims (Bowker, 1980; Carroll, 1974; Lockwood, 1980; Wooden & Parker, 1982).

The constant threat of sexual assault is one of the most anxiety-provoking experiences reported by new prisoners and is a major factor in prison suicides (Groth, 1979/1984). Slightly built inmates and those who are imprisoned for molesting children often face threats of gang rape the moment they arrive (Earley, 1992). The rape of child molesters and homosexuals in particular is an expression of contempt for these men and their lifestyles (Groth, 1979/1984).

The policy in most prisons allows inmates who fear (or report) being sexually assaulted to be placed in protective custody in a segregated unit. However, reporting rape is a violation of the convict's code against snitching and, as we noted earlier, being a snitch can be a fatal mistake in spite of protective custody. Yet submitting to sexual assault can also create serious problems. Once word gets out that an inmate has tolerated sexual assault, he becomes fair game for further assaults. Only by successfully refusing sexual advances or retaliating against their assailant later can victims send a message to the convict population that they will not tolerate sexual attacks (Silberman, 1995).

As we discussed in previous chapters, male victims of sexual assault suffer more than pain, shame, and degradation. They are also at higher than average risk for becoming sexual offenders themselves—especially after they are released. Accordingly, sexual violence in prison is something that should concern anyone interested in preventing crime. In fact, the ramifications of all forms of prison violence go far beyond the pain and suffering that prisoners experience. In most cases, prisoners who have been beaten, raped, and tortured will eventually be back in society, and the violence they experienced—and learned to engage in—while imprisoned may generate expressions of violence against everyone else. Yet correctional officers, judges, elected officials, and the general public do not seem to care much about violence in prison. The prevailing attitude is that prisoners "get what they deserve" whether they are imprisoned for violent crime, drug possession, or writing bad checks.

"Prisonized" Prisoners.   A prisoner's primary task is to adapt to life in a "human warehouse with a jungle-like underground" (Toch, 1988). Those who entered prison with the underdeveloped conscience, lack of empathy, and other psychological characteristics typically associated with criminal behavior are not likely to correct these deficiencies behind bars. That kind of personal development requires a disciplined environment, to be sure, but one that is also supportive and nurturing, precisely opposite to what prisons offer (Hoffman, 1982; Nettler, 1984). It is a lack of empathy or concern for others that is most often modeled and rewarded; prisoners are permitted by guards and encouraged by peers to treat other prisoners with indifference or even contempt.

The psychological pain of imprisonment virtually guarantees that prisoners will be released in worse psychological condition than when they were incarcerated. The experience leaves some prisoners with mental disorders they might not otherwise have suffered, and it leaves many others feeling hopeless and helpless. During long years in prison, these inmates gradually become used to being told what to do, to having no control, to making no decisions. In short, they may become less and less able to function independently (R. Johnson, 1996). Further, having developed no new behavioral or occupational skills with which to reshape their lives in a prosocial direction, it is no wonder that they are influenced by criminal peers to return to a life of crime.

The prisoners who are most likely to display good psychological and behavioral functioning despite imprisonment are those serving life terms without the possibility of parole. This fact may seem surprising at first, but a moment's reflection makes it clear that prison is all these people have. "Lifers" tend to see prison as a home, and they take an interest in their surroundings. To the extent allowed by prison restrictions, they take care of their cells and their personal hygiene, they participate in as many activities as possible, and try to develop good relations with the guards (Flanagan, 1988; Johnson, 1996). One 7-year longitudinal study of Canadian lifers offered some insight into their coping skills (Zamble, 1992). For one thing, they ignore the unstructured life of the prison "yard," choosing to spend as much of their time as possible in their cells where they can best control their daily routine. They develop minimal relations with other lifers and maximize their contact with people on the outside. Lifers consistently show improvements in coping skills, indicating psychological growth and increasing maturity. More than other prisoners, lifers seek to improve their behavioral skills and to deal more effectively with their problems. As a result, they suffer decreasing psychological stress over time as reflected in lessening depression and anxiety and better physical health; and although they do not report a decrease in negative emotions such as anger and loneliness, they tend to cope with these emotions better than other prisoners do (Zamble, 1992). In other words, as time goes by, lifers become more acclimated to the deprivations of prison and learn to live a life of compromise with the constraints of the prison environment; they take life behind bars one day at a time (Toch & Adams, 1989). It is ironic, then, that society is least likely to come into contact with the very prisoners who have been affected most positively by their prison experience.

The nonlifers who are rehabilitated in prison are typically those who are the most introspective and self-critical—and who most want to change (Zamble, Porporino, & Kalotay, 1984). Unfortunately, these are all too few. The prison conditions we have described not only stress minds and harden hearts, they teach and encourage the use of criminal skills. As a result, some prisoners become chronic offenders, and some chronic offenders become monsters. When these prisoners are released, society is likely to pay the price in the currency of continuing crime. Of increasing concern, for example, is the number of younger inmates who share cells with older, more violent criminals. Consider the case of John William King who was sentenced to death at the age of 24 for the beating and dragging death of James Byrd in Jasper, Texas in 1998. King was only 20 when he was sent to a Texas penitentiary to serve time for a burglary. His cell mate was Lawrence Brewer, a 28-year-old who already had a long prison record. Brewer befriended King and introduced him to a circle of prisoners affiliated with the Ku Klux Klan. When Brewer got out of prison, he turned up in King's hometown and became his accomplice in the brutal slaying. Those most familiar with the case suggest that both the violent and racist nature of the crime (Byrd was Black) had its roots in King's contacts with Brewer and other violent racists in prison (Duggan, 1999; see chapter 10).

Older Prisoners.   Longer prison sentences, mandatory minimums, and three-strikes law are contributing to the aging of the U.S. prison population. The number of prisoners who are over the age of 50 has risen dramatically from 9,000 in 1986 to 125,000 in 2002 (King & Mauer, 2002). The aging population consists of lifers, new elderly offenders, and chronic reoffenders (see our discussion of Forrest Tucker in chapter 10). The normal affects of aging along with the stress of spending time in prison take a severe mental and physical toll on many of these prisoners. Poor nutrition, inadequate medical care, insufficient exercise and rest, injury from violence, and lack of recreational and social programs can combine to create physical and mental health problems. Accordingly, it is estimated that governments spend an average of $70,000 a year to confine each inmate over 55 years old, a figure three times higher than that for the younger population (Pfeiffer, 2002). Louisiana's Angola State Penitentiary, where prisoners serve the longest sentences in the country, and has the largest prison cemetery in the country. By the time the prisoners die, most have no family and friends to bury them outside the prison; some who do let it be known before their deaths that they want to be buried in Angola's cemetery with their "friends." Angola recently established the first prison hospice to provide palliative care to dying inmates.

Criminologists say that putting aside human rights concerns, incarcerating the elderly makes neither political nor financial sense. Most violence is committed by people in their late teens and early 20s. The older they get, the more likely the prisoners are to be suffering from kidney disease, diabetes, heart disease, and cancer. Admittedly, few receive the best of care for their chronic illnesses, in part because good care is not politically correct and in part because correctional dollars are being squeezed at the other end—bringing in new prisoners. However, prisoners are not allowed to decline treatment—the government has to keep them alive to do its job of making them serve their time.

Women in Prison

At the end of 2004, there were 103,000 women in state and federal prisons, nearly one third of them in Texas, California, and federal prisons (Harrison & Beck, 2005). This number represents an increase of 50% over 1995 figures and an eightfold increase over 1980 when there were only 12,300 women in prison (The Sentencing Project, 2005). There are still far fewer women than men incarcerated in the United States (123 per 100,000 women vs. 1,348 per 100,000 men; Harrison & Beck, 2005), but the population of female prisoners is growing faster. On average, the adult female prison population has grown 10% since 1990 compared to a 6% increase for males (Harrison & Beck, 2005). Convictions for drug offenses account for much of the growth of the female inmate population, although female violent crime is on the rise and so to incarceration for these crimes. Two thirds of the women convicted of violent crimes had killed or injured a relative, intimate, or someone else they knew (a figure twice as high as for male convicts).

Female inmates largely resemble male inmates in terms of age and ethnicity. Most are over 30 and members of an ethnic minority; 38% are Black and 17% Hispanic (Harrision & Beck, 2005). In other words, disparity (or inequity) in sentencing based on ethnicity is prevalent for both genders; women of color are more likely to receive prison sentences—and longer ones—than White women. In 1997, Hispanics (44%) and Blacks (39%) were more likely to be incarcerated for a drug offense than White women (23%).

The rising numbers of female incarcerations reflect a judicial trend toward creating sentencing parity with men. In the past, women would be more likely than men to receive probation for drug and property offenses simply because they were women and many judges did not want to see them serve time. Now, however, the gap between male and female offenders serving time for nonviolent crimes is narrowing (i.e., in 2001, 32% of men vs. 20% of women were sentenced for drug offenses, and 25% of men vs. 19% of women were sentenced for property crimes). However, sentences for female violent offenders still trail those of men (31% vs. 50%; Bureau of Justice Statistics, 2003a). Women are less likely to receive a death sentence, a topic we discuss following.

In a notable exception to the principle of gender equality, feminist criminologists decry the idea of men and women receiving similar sentences for similar crimes. They suggest that the incarceration of women is one more example of male domination of females. Accordingly, several of these criminologists have called for the deinstitutionalization of women prisoners (Chesney-Lind, 1995), arguing that women ought not to be imprisoned at all.

Overall, prison confinement itself tends to be easier for women than for men. This is due partly to the fact that because most women are not convicted of violent crimes, they are usually housed in minimum-security facilities that resemble college dormitories more than prisons. Many female prisoners are allowed to decorate their cells or other personal space with pictures from home and other artifacts. Although, like men, women may have a hard time adjusting to prison life, they are not as often threatened with violence. Sexual coercion is common in women's prisons but without the violent overtones.[6] Women prisoners tend to create "families" in which various individuals take the roles of mother, father (perhaps the one who obtains sex), child, and sibling. They may even conduct "marriages" among themselves (Giallombardo, 1966).

---

[6]Women may also be subject to sexual advances by male guards, but compared to male prisons, the overall risk of sexual assault is not nearly as great.

However, women inmates do suffer more loss of self-esteem than men, and they tend to turn their aggressive impulses against themselves rather than other inmates. Women are more likely than men to mutilate their bodies or attempt suicide, but when they do so, they usually receive medication and psychiatric care, not the harsh discipline typically imposed on male prisoners for similar acts (Sommers & Baskin, 1990). Even though they rarely present a threat to prison order or authority, female inmates are more often given prescription drugs to control their emotions (Morash, Bynum, & Koons, 1998).

As is the case for their male counterparts, few educational or occupational programs are provided to women in prison, which means that they, too, lose the opportunity to gain marketable skills that might help them stay out of trouble when they are released.

Special Problems of Women in Prison. Two-thirds of imprisoned women have at least one child under the age of 18, meaning that there are about 150,000 children in the United States whose mothers are in prison (Thompson, 1998a). Most mothers in prison were living with their children at the time of their arrest and plan to be reunited with them on release. These women report that the most difficult problems they face in prison are worrying about their children and trying to maintain a relationship with them through brief visits, letters, and phone calls. Face-to-face contact is made more difficult by overcrowding in some prisons, which often necessitates moving prisoners to facilities many miles from their families. In 1998, for example, hundreds of female inmates were transferred from prisons in Washington, DC, to institutions in Connecticut, Texas, Florida, and West Virginia. The women were transported on short notice, and most did not get to see their children before they left. For many, interruption of regular meetings with their children took away the only thing that these women had to look forward to.

Prison gynecological services—such as PAP tests, breast examinations, and treatment for sexually transmitted diseases—are often lacking or inadequate (National Commission on Correctional Health Care [NCCHC], 1998). In some jurisdictions, large numbers of women inmates are HIV positive. The figures range as high as 18% in New York State and 41% in the District of Columbia (Bureau of Justice Statistics, 2003a). Giving birth while in prison creates another set of special problems for female inmates and their babies. For one thing, pregnant prisoners receive minimal prenatal care, often leading to difficult births, low birth weight babies, and other difficulties. When labor begins, pregnant inmates are taken to a local hospital,[7] but within 3 days after delivery, the baby is given to family members or local child welfare agencies for placement. The mental health ramifications of this early separation of mother and baby can be enormous, the most significant of which is that the child may not form a secure emotional attachment to the mother (see chapter 7). In fact, mother and child will be strangers to each other if and when they are reunited. Unless these children's surrogate caregivers provide an alternative opportunity for close attachment, they may later develop signs of depression, aggression, and poor school performance (Moses, 1995). They may even follow in their mothers' criminal footsteps—just as their mothers may have followed in the footsteps of their mothers.

In 1992, the Girl Scouts of America partnered with the National Institute of Justice to initiate a program to forge and maintain the mother–daughter bond during a mother's incarceration. Known as "Girl Scouts Beyond Bars," the program is operating in several states including Maryland, Florida, South Carolina, Texas, and Ohio. Girl Scout leaders take girls to visit their mothers in prison, offer programs for mothers and daughters between visits, and help prepare for the reunion on the mother's release (Moses, 1995).

Women in prison also have psychological needs and mental health problems that are different from those of men. Women prisoners are, for example, significantly more likely than men to have suffered physical and sexual abuse as children (43% vs. 12%) and more likely than men to be responsible for children (Morash et al., 1998). In addition, compared to men, women are more concerned with interpersonal relationships and express emotions differently. Accordingly, it has been suggested that the problems of prisonization would be eased if authorities at women's prisons adopted a management style that is less authoritarian and therefore better suited to women inmates (Morash et al., 1998). Further, it would appear that even more than men, women need counseling to help them resolve problems stemming from prior victimization experiences and to cope with the depression and anxiety associated with being separated from their children (NCCHC, 1998).

---

[7]In some cases, the women are placed in shackles while in labor, and some are even shackled during Caesarean sections, episiotomies, or other surgical procedures (N. Siegal, 1999).

In a recent survey of correctional facilities, only a small proportion of administrators had instituted programs and management styles designed specifically for women prisoners, although most were aware that these issues are important (Morash et al., 1998). As is the case with men, the failure of correctional systems to offer the occupational, mental health, and other services that women prisoners need can make it more likely that these women will reoffend when they are released.

Mentally Ill Prisoners

At any given time, one in six prisoners (a rate three times higher than the general population) is suffering from a serious mental disorder such as schizophrenia, bipolar disorder, or major depression (Human Rights Watch, 2004). As we described in chapter 2, mentally ill inmates typically get worse during incarceration due to the stress of prison conditions, the disrupted or inconsistent administration of vital medication, and the punishment they receive when their disorders make it difficult for them to comply with prison rules. If prisoners are to be kept from deteriorating further and helped to regain the stability they will need to function in the community, appropriate mental health treatment should be available to them in prison.

The obligation of correctional authorities to provide treatment for serious mental health conditions has been underscored by Supreme Court decisions (*DeShaney v. Winnebago Department of Social Services,* 1989; *Estelle v. Gamble,* 1976), but federal courts have narrowly defined "serious" as a condition that could "result in further significant injury, ... not routine discomfort that is part of the penalty that criminal offenders pay for their offenses against society" (*McGuckin v. Smith,* 1992, pp. 1059-1060). The same rules apply to prisoners who carried no psychiatric diagnosis when they began their sentences but who become depressed or showed other symptoms of mental disorder as a result of incarceration. The Supreme Court has ruled that "mere depression" or behavioral and emotional problems alone do not qualify as serious mental illnesses mandating treatment, although treatment might be warranted for acute depression, paranoid schizophrenia, "nervous collapse," and suicidal tendencies (*Youngberg v. Romeo,* 1982).

In short, there are no guarantees of treatment beyond the minimal standard required by federal law (see chapter 2), and wardens have considerable discretion about which mental health services they will and will not provide (A. C. Smith, 1999). Typically, guards and wardens will not authorize treatment for prisoners whom they perceive as trying to manipulate them or get special consideration (Cohen, 1994). Further, because most states have no facilities for housing seriously mentally ill prisoners, those prisoners live with the rest of the inmate population where they may be a danger to others and where they are easy targets for cruel and malicious attacks by fellow prisoners. The mentally ill prisoner is less able to comply with the stringent rules of prison life and thus are more prone to disciplinary action. They are referred to as "bugs" by their fellow prisoners (Human Rights Watch, 2004). Some states require them to wear special clothing, ostensibly so that the guards and other correctional personnel can look out for them. In reality, though, this practice makes them an even easier target for the sexual and physical abuse that they are prone to by reason of their condition. If the inmate is mentally retarded, he or she is especially prone to being sexually assaulted in exchange for candy and cigarettes (Human Rights Watch, 2004).

So even though prisons and jails are legally bound to meet a minimum standard of care for mental health services, few actually do so, meaning that only a handful of prisoners who need mental health services actually receive them (Human Rights Watch, 2004). The fault is not entirely that of the criminal justice system. The closure of state mental hospitals that began with the deinstitutionalization movement of the 1960s and the continuing budget cuts for community mental health services means that prisons collectively make up our nation's largest mental health treatment facility, This situation is tragic not only for the prisoners whose disorders go untreated, but also for the rest of society. Comprehensive treatment of mentally disordered prisoners, combined with arrangements for post-release support from local social service agencies, mental health and substance abuse treatment providers, and other community resources, would not only aid in rehabilitating these inmates but would also make communities safer. By failing to provide proper treatment to mentally ill prisoners, the correctional systems are making it more likely that when those prisoners complete their sentences, they will return to the community in a condition that is more disordered and more dangerous than when they were incarcerated.

The Death Penalty

On February 3, 1998, Karla Faye Tucker, 38, was executed in a Texas prison. Fifteen years earlier, she had assisted her boyfriend in the ax murders of two people. Her case attracted far more than the usual protests from death penalty opponents. Then Texas governor (and later President) George W. Bush rejected intense pleas for clemency from dozens of groups and thousands of individuals worldwide. Why did Tucker get so much support when there was so little sympathy expressed for Aileen Wuornos, a Florida woman executed in the same year? The answer is that Wuornos was a hardened, serial murderer whose modus operandi was to ensnare elderly men, take control of their assets, and then kill them. The nation and the world also took little notice when in April of 1998, Joseph John Cannon was executed for killing a mother of eight children when he was 17. He had suffered severe head injuries in a car accident at the age of four and endured a childhood featuring frequent beatings and sexual assaults by a stepfather and grandfather. As a teenager, he had been hospitalized for psychosis and suicide attempts. Also, many across the country celebrated when Oklahoma City federal building bomber Timothy McVeigh died by lethal injection in 2001.

In short, like most people on death row, neither Wuornos, Cannon, nor McVeigh had characteristics that people found attractive or with which most people could identify. Karla Tucker was different. She was White, young, pretty, soft-spoken, and articulate, a model inmate who had become a born-again Christian while in prison. Some who pleaded for her life reasoned that reducing her sentence to life in prison would allow her to be an asset to the prison system, a valuable role model for younger prisoners.

A poll of Texas residents taken after Tucker's execution revealed that support for the death penalty there dropped from 85% to 68% largely as a result of her death (Hentoff, 2000).

A Brief History of the Death Penalty in the United States

America's enthusiastic endorsement of capital punishment is puzzlement to other Western countries, all of which have outlawed the death penalty. This situation is ironic because limiting use of the death penalty was high on the list of improvements that America's founders wanted to make in the English criminal justice system under which they had lived. In the late 1700s, most of the American colonies prescribed execution for about a dozen crimes, including murder, rape, adultery, kidnapping, and blasphemy. This was far fewer than the 200 capital crimes in the English criminal justice system, but the colonies did employ their mother country's grisly methods of execution: burning at the stake or hanging (the latter followed by placing the body in an iron cage called a gibbett to decompose and be eaten by birds). However, evidence of the colonists' reluctance to impose capital punishment could be found in the fact that—unlike those condemned in England—as many as half of the criminals sentenced to death in the colonies received pardons or had their sentences reduced (D. Greenberg, 1974; Hindus, 1980; Mackey, 1982). The Quakers of Pennsylvania are credited with championing the elimination of capital punishment during this era.

The first serious legal challenges to the constitutionality of the death penalty came in the 1960s when, as we noted earlier, prisoners began to sue state correctional systems over conditions that they alleged were cruel and unusual forms of punishment. In particular, attorneys for the National Association for the Advancement of Colored People (NAACP) Legal Defense Fund began to talk about a constitutional challenge to the death penalty based on inequity in its use. They pointed out that 53% of all those executed in the United States between 1930 and 1967 were Black men. Almost all of these executions were in the South, where 90% of the condemned men were Blacks who had been convicted of rape. In 1967, after the U.S. Supreme Court heard this evidence in the case of *Maxwell v. Bishop*, it ordered a moratorium on executions pending a review of how the death penalty was being applied. This order reflected the tenor of the times. By the 1960s, public support for the death penalty had declined, and executions had become rare—there were only seven nationwide in 1967 (Mackey, 1982). In 1964, Oregon became the first state to abolish the death penalty by public referendum. Then, in the 1972 case of *Furman v. Georgia*, the U.S. Supreme Court ruled that the death penalty violated the 8th and 14th Amendments to the Constitution because it was applied in an arbitrary and capricious manner.

However, the Court did *not* rule that capital punishment was inherently cruel and unusual, and this left the door open for states to revise their death penalty laws so that they would be more fairly administered. A total of

33 states enacted new laws, each of which was challenged in lawsuits brought before the Supreme Court; 38 states and the federal government have the death penalty.[8] In 1976, almost 10 years after it had imposed its moratorium on capital punishment, the Court upheld death penalty provisions containing specific guidelines for application (*Gregg v. Georgia,* 1976). The execution of Gary Gilmore by a Utah firing squad in January of 1977 marked the beginning of a resurgence in the use of capital punishment in America. There were 65 executions in 2003 (all men) and 59 in 2004 (Harrison & Beck, 2005). The numbers show a marked decline from the 1999 high of 98 executions. Indeed, there are indications from several fronts that the country's thirst for the death penalty is becoming assuaged. As of April 2005, there were 245 fewer prisoners on death row than at the same time in 2002, continuing a steady decline that began in 2000 (NAACP Legal Defense and Educational Fund, 2005). Some states, including Ohio, imposed moratoriums on executions in the wake of 117 (as of this writing) death row inmates having been exonerated and found to be factually innocent since 1973, largely due to new DNA evidence (Death Penalty Information Center, 2005).[9] The Supreme Court decisions of *Atkins v. Virginia* (2002) and *Roper v. Simmons* (2005), striking down the death penalty for mentally retarded persons and those who committed their offenses as minors, is also slowly but surely reducing the numbers of death row inmates.[10]

For those facing execution, a federal law passed in 1995 set the stage for speedier executions by allowing state and federal appeals of a death sentence to take place concurrently. Previously, a condemned prisoner could appeal to state courts and then pursue three levels of federal appeals. Still, the death penalty is not imposed lightly, nor is it carried out indiscriminately. With the exception of Texas, Virginia, and Florida, most states are slow to carry out death sentences. The appeal process, although now streamlined, is still taken seriously, and it is sometimes successful. The Supreme Court overturned 38 death sentences in 1997 alone (Snell, 1998), and 2 out of Texas on one day in 2005. Further, where capital punishment is allowed, it can only be imposed in cases of aggravated murder—meaning murder committed during the commission of other felonies such as abduction, armed robbery, and rape; murder for hire; murder of a law enforcement officer; multiple murder, and murder arising from drug violations. Similarly, only a limited range of federal crimes carry the death penalty. These include treason and espionage; murder of the President or Vice President, a federal judge or law enforcement agent, a member of Congress, or a Supreme Court Justice; murder during the course of bank robbery or carjacking; murder using a weapon of mass destruction (such as a bomb); murder with a firearm during drug trafficking; and use of the mail to send bombs or other articles with the intent to kill.

Even in these cases, imposition of the death penalty comes only after due deliberation. In all but nine states, the jury that convicts a defendant of a capital crime must, in the trial's sentencing phase, decide whether to recommend the death penalty;[11] and in accordance with a Supreme Court ruling, the jury cannot make its recommendation until it has heard evidence about any aspect of the defendant's background, record, personal character, or the like that would mitigate against execution (*Lockett v. Ohio,* 1978). This evidence—usually presented by the defendant and mental health professionals who have examined the defendant—typically refers to the defendant's remorse, current mental condition, abuse experiences in childhood, potential for rehabilitation, and low risk for future crimes.

Controversy Over the Death Penalty

As the ultimate and most irretrievable form of punishment, the death penalty is the most controversial of all sanctions against crime. The primary arguments in favor of the death penalty are that it deters murder and is

---

[8]There is no death penalty in Alaska, the District of Columbia, Hawaii, Iowa, Maine, Massachusetts, Michigan, Minnesota, North Dakota, Rhode Island, Vermont, West Virginia, or Wisconsin. New York and Kansas courts struck down their states' death penalties in 2004; these states had just reinstated their death penalties in 1994 and 1995, respectively. Their legislatures could enact new laws, although that does not seem likely.

[9]In 1999 alone, eight inmates were exonerated by DNA evidence that had not been available at the time of their convictions.

[10]Removing from death row those who were minors at the time of their crimes requires only a look at prisoner's date of birth and date of the crime. However, *Atkins v. Virginia* requires that the inmate prove that he or she is mentally retarded at the present time, and that requires proof pursuant to the *DSM–IV–TR* criteria (American Psychiatric Association, 2000a).

[11]In two of these, Colorado and Nebraska, the decision is made by a panel of three trial judges, one of whom is the trial court judge. In the other seven, the trial judge alone makes the decision.

cheaper than incarceration. For example, Americans tend to believe that life imprisonment is more expensive than execution (Ellsworth & Gross, 1994). The fact is, however, that the average cost of trying and executing a single defendant ranges from $1.3 million upward to $2 million, whereas the cost per defendant of life imprisonment without parole is estimated at between $750,000 and $1.1 million (Dieter, 2005). In states where inmates spend a decade or more on death row, the cost of execution can reach from $20 to $30 million per execution. According to a recent Gallup poll, 62% of Americans agreed with 80 criminologists that the death penalty does not deter murder (D. Moore, 2004; Radelet & Akers, 1996); and when given the choice of life in prison without parole versus capital punishment, half of the respondents said they would chose life in prison. Without the life without parole option, 7 in 10 still preferred execution for violent crimes (D. Moore, 2004). However, the signs are clear that support for the death penalty has been steadily declining since 2000.

The arguments of those opposed to the death penalty focus not only its lack of cost savings and failure to deter crime but also to what they see as its violation of religious and moral standards and to the injustices associated with it. They worry, for example, that people are being put to death for crimes that they did not commit. These concerns have been made all the more urgent by cases, as we noted previously, in which death row inmates have been released after investigations revealed that they had been wrongly convicted of capital crimes, usually on the basis of circumstantial evidence or faulty eyewitness testimony. In one such case, students at the Northwestern University School of Journalism won the release of Anthony Porter (and obtained a confession by the real perpetrator) who had been on death row in Illinois for 16 years and had come within 48 hours of execution. Porter was the 75th death row inmate freed since 1976, the 10th in Illinois, and the 3rd cleared by Northwestern students (Center on Wrongful Convictions, 2003). The publicity surrounding Porter's case led to an examination of the how the death penalty was used in Ohio. The results showed an appalling lack of concern for due process and fairness. Unable to get the legislature to write greater protections into Ohio's death penalty statute, then Governor George Ryan imposed a moratorium on executions and commuted the capital sentences of all prisoners to life without parole on January 11, 2003, three days before his term ended. That bold move obviously resonated with the legislature and the new governor. Although a new law has been passed, the moratorium remains as of this writing.

Death penalty opponents also see injustice in who receives death sentences—and who is actually executed. The numbers, they say, suggest that the same ethnic discrimination that prompted the Supreme Court's moratorium on executions in 1967—discrimination supposedly eliminated by new laws—remains today. A death sentence is still most likely to be imposed when an Black man kills a White man, often by all-White juries (Ryan, 2003). Rarely will an Black person be sentenced to death for killing another Black person, and the chances that a White man will be put to death for killing a Black man are virtually nil. In fact, prosecutors rarely seek the death penalty in such cases.

There is some research to suggest that executions create a "brutalizing" effect, sending a message that killing is acceptable and thus contributing to increases in violent crime (Thomson, 1999). This evidence is debatable, but just as objective information about the deterrent and economic consequences of capital punishment has not deterred its proponents, a lack of data for a brutalizing effect has not swayed its opponents. Indeed, the views of each side appear to be more strongly related to religious beliefs, moral values, and political convictions than to rational analyses about how best to deal with society's worst criminals (Nietzel, Hasemann, & McCarthy, 1997).

Invisible Punishment

For prisoners not subject to the death penalty or life in prison, the punishment does not necessarily end with the end of their sentence, the completion of probation, and the payment of fines. Increasingly, laws have been enacted that continue to punish ex-convicts for the rest of their lives. We refer to this as "invisible punishment." It is invisible for several reasons: Defendants and even their lawyers may not be aware of these hidden penalties; the penalties work in subtle ways to deprive defendants of rights and opportunities available to most people; the penalties are automatic; and defendants have no recourse from them. Invisible punishment affects not just the offenders but their families, communities, and society at large.

Sex Offenders. As we discussed in chapter 10, serving a sentence for a sex offender considered likely to be a repeat offender may be the beginning of a lifetime struggle to resume life outside bars. The offender may be committed for further treatment using court procedures. In some states, the names, addresses, and social security numbers of all persons convicted of sex crimes of any type, including nonviolent offenses involving, for example, unwanted touching, may be placed on a state's list of sex offenders, published on Web sites, and disseminated throughout the community where the offender lives for the rest of his life. Sex offenders on these lists are routinely barred from holding all kinds of jobs, especially those dealing with children. There have been reports of sex offenders unable to find housing due to the impact of these lists.

Disenfranchisement. In 48 states, persons convicted of felonies lose their right to vote in any type of public election—local, state, or federal. This result is known as **disenfranchisement**. Some states provide a means by which an ex-convict can have the right to vote reinstated, but others do not. There is a growing movement against disenfranchisement, mainly because losing the right to participate in our democracy renders one a second class citizen at best. It severs the commitment a person has to his or her country when rehabilitation requires quite the opposite—that people be committed to being law-abiding members of their society. Lists of convicted felons are also far from accurate. In the 2000 presidential election, there were reports of hundreds of names being erroneously on such lists in several Florida precincts and legitimate voters being turned away from the polls. Later investigation revealed, not surprisingly, that the names erroneously on those lists were almost all Black persons. Because of disparities on prosecution and sentencing in which Blacks are more likely to be convicted of felonies, disenfranchisement falls more heavily on Black men, an estimated 13% of whom are ineligible to vote (Mauer, 2003).

Federally Subsidized Student Loans and State and Federal Entitlement Benefits. Federal and some state laws prohibit persons convicted of any type of drug-related crime, regardless of type of drug or amount, from ever receiving a federally subsidized student loan; from being eligible for public housing benefits; from visiting anyone in a public housing project; and from receiving Medicare, Medicaid, food stamps, and various other welfare benefits. These limitations may last as long as the person lives and affects not just the ex-cons but their families, sometimes in draconian ways. In 2002, the U.S. Supreme Court upheld the federal housing law that allows public housing landlords to evict any person who has as a visitor, house guest, or cotenant any person who has been convicted of a drug crime. In the cases the court heard, elderly and gravely ill people were ejected from their apartments because their children with drug convictions visited them (*Department of Housing and Urban Development v. Rucker, et al.,* 2002).

Social Impacts of Punishment. The prisonization of America appears to have arisen to satisfy society's primary goals in dealing with criminals—isolation and retribution—but with little regard for whether this approach is likely to reduce crime in the long run. As a society, we are ignoring evidence that incarceration is actually likely to increase crime in the long run. For example, research by the Rand Group suggests that spending an additional $1 million a year on treatment for drug offenders would have a far greater impact on reducing serious crime than mandatory prison terms ever will (U.S. Sentencing Project, 1998).

We are also ignoring evidence that imposing more and longer prison terms has done nothing to reduce criminal recidivism. Following their release, about two-thirds of prison inmates will be rearrested for felonies or serious misdemeanors within three years (U.S. Department of Justice, 1997). About 45% of them will be reconvicted, and 40% will be returned to prison. This should not be surprising given the nature of the prison experience and the demise of programs aimed at rehabilitation, education, and vocational training. Indeed, criminal justice experts see the lack of adequate employment opportunities for ex-convicts as the major reason for high recidivism rates. With few marketable skills and training, most ex-convicts have a difficult time getting a decent job at a living wage. With no legitimate income, many of these people simply return to crime (U.S. Department of Justice, 1997). Policymakers have only begun to recently address the problems inherent in prisoner reentry into the community.

However, it is not just the lack of job training and mental health programs that accounts for recidivism. Most ex-convicts have no place to go when they get out of prison except the crime-ridden communities and dysfunctional family systems from whence they came. Even with the best of intentions formed in prison, these people are likely to become criminals again almost by default because they are likely to encounter social pressure to do so and little reason not to do so. In other words, one can argue that current criminal justice policies contribute to and even increase the very crimes they are designed to eliminate because they provide no mechanisms through which criminals are influenced to change their behavior for the better.

Prison is the end of a long road that begins in childhood with the risk factors for crime that we have described in other chapters, so it is a rare prisoner indeed who has the psychological resilience and resources to reform without help while in jail and to become a productive citizen on release. Yet, current criminal justice policies imply that this is precisely what people expect prisoners to do. So although imprisonment removes offenders from society for a time, former felons return to society no better, and in most cases far worse, than when they were incarcerated. To be sure, prisoners pay their debt to society for the crimes they have committed, but society pays a high price, too, not only in terms of the money spent on prisoners and prisons but in terms of the continuing problem of crime.

Prison policies have a huge negative impact on families and some communities. Currently, there are as estimated 1.5 million children who have a parent in prison, including 1 in every 14 Black children (Mumola,2000). These children are growing up not just with the stigma of having a parent in prison, but with the lack of emotional and financial support that will enable them to be successful in their own lives. Communities, especially largely Black communities, may be destabilized by incarceration policies. One study found that in 10% of neighborhoods in Washington, DC, the gender ratio is an estimated 62 men per 100 women (Mauer, 2003).

Society pays a huge fiscal cost as well. Decades of building prisons to house a burgeoning and aging prison population is siphoning off dollars that ought to be spent on health care and education for all citizens. In most states, prisons directly compete with schools for funding, and the prisons are winning (Egan, 1999a). Thus, a commitment to large-scale imprisonment sacrifices the future of all citizens to pay for the past mistakes for the few.

Ultimately, everyone pays a price for crime—and its punishment. Policymakers need to address the larger societal costs, look at punishment policies comprehensively, and make laws that are consistent not just with punishing crime but promoting a healthy society (Mauer, 2003).

Summary

Sentencing day, when punishment for crime is meted out, represents the culmination of the biological, psychological, and social influences that lead the convicted person to stand before the sentencing judge. Over America's 225-year history, the focus of its efforts to punish criminal behavior has shifted from punishment to rehabilitation and back to punishment. Where formerly rehabilitation was the main goal of punishment, it is no longer. Punishment and removal of people from society is the goal of modern corrections. However, it is a policy that may not be in the best interests of society.

Punishment options in use today include imprisonment, execution for capital offenses, probation, fines, and home confinement and electronic monitoring. In most states and federal court, jurors make recommendations for sentences, but judges may alter them somewhat. However, judicial discretion in sentencing has been limited by sentencing guidelines and mandatory sentences.

A term of imprisonment is the main form of punishment in use in the United States today, which incarcerates more people per capita than any country in the world. Its incarceration rates are 8 to 14 times more than European countries and Japan. The U.S. prison population has tripled since 1980 in spite of the fact that violent crime has been on the decline since 1997. The reason for the burgeoning prison population despite decreasing violent crime may be attributed to longer sentences, imprisonment for more offenses including drug possession offenses, people returning to prison for minor parole and probation violations, and recidivism rates fueled in part by the lack of rehabilitation and reentry programs for prisoners when they are released.

Serving time in the United States mainly means serving "hard" time. American prisons are rife with drugs, gang violence, and sexual assaults. Lack of rehabilitation, education, and job programs leave prisoners with little to do except watch television and try to stay out of trouble. A large number of prisoners are mentally ill; many more are aging. These two populations have unique disciplinary and health problems that prisons are ill-equipped to handle. Women prisoners may have somewhat better living conditions than their male counterparts, but their emotional and physical health needs appear to be greater and receive scant attention.

The United States stands alone in civilized countries in its use of the death penalty. The Supreme Court suspended the death penalty for a time, finding fault with some state's applications of it that were inconsistent with the Constitution's protections against cruel and unusual punishment and violative of due process requirements. Many states amended their statutes to comply with new Supreme Court standards. Today, 38 states and the federal government have the death penalty as an option, mostly for various types of murder, but its favor among the public is declining. Too many innocent people on death row have been exonerated by DNA evidence for proponents of the death penalty to continue to claim that innocent people are never executed. The Supreme Court has abolished the death penalty for people who were juveniles at the times their crimes were committed and for condemned persons who are mentally retarded as the time of their executions.

For many convicts, serving time is not the end of their sentence. There are many forms of invisible punishment that may continue to impact on a person long after a sentence has been served. Sex offenders may be hospitalized, monitored, even ostracized for the rest of their lives. Drug offenders may lose their right forever to education loans, public housing, and certain welfare benefits. Almost all offenders will lose, permanently or temporarily, their right to participate in their country's democracy through disenfranchisement—loss of their right to vote.

There are long-term and wide-ranging social effects of this country's imprisonment policies. These effect the children and communities of the offender and society as a whole. Prisons compete with schools for taxpayer dollars, and all too often the prisons are winning. Our laws need to reflect correctional policies that promote the interests of society as a whole and do not just focus on punishment of the offender.

Key Terms

Sentencing guidelines
Mandatory sentences
Disenfranchisement

Questions for Review

1. What sentencing options are available generally in the U.S. criminal justice system?
2. Discuss the prisonization of the United States and what it means for criminal justice policies, defendants, and society at large.
3. What factors have led to a decreasing commitment to and use of the death penalty in the United States today?
4. Discuss the particular challenges faced by mentally ill prisoners.
5. Give five examples of invisible punishment and discuss how these affect families, communities, and the larger society.

Track It Down

Criminal Behavior Website
www.cassel2e.com
Corrections Statistics from the Bureau of Justice Statistics
www.ojp.usdoj.gov/bjs/correct.htm
Death Penalty Information Center
www.deathpenaltyinfo.org/
Committee on Safety and Abuse in America's Prisons
prisoncommission.org/press_release_041905.asp

Human Rights Watch Report: Ill-Equipped: U.S. Prisons and Offenders with Mental Illness
www.hrw.org/reports/2003/usa1003/
The Sentencing Project
www.sentencingproject.org/
Prevalence of Imprisonment in the U.S. Population
www.ojp.usdoj.gov/bjs/pub/ascii/piusp01.txt

14

The Future of Crime

A Review of Risk Factors for Criminal Behavior
Preventing Crime

Obstacles to Crime Prevention
Looking Ahead

In previous chapters, we have defined crime and traced its roots. We have considered how social institutions, including the criminal justice system itself, contribute to crime. We have looked at various types of crime and examined profiles of certain types of criminals. We have explored the role of mental illness in crime. We have also seen that crime is a socially constructed event that develops through the continuing interaction of individual backgrounds and social forces over time. Our explorations make it clear that although we do not understand all the ways in which the individual and social roots of crime influence each other, researchers have discovered enough about risk factors for crime—as well as about factors that militate against criminal behavior—to outline social and psychological programs that have a realistic chance of preventing crime, making it less pervasive and violent, and minimizing its consequences. In this final chapter, we review the major risk factors for crime and then consider some of the programs and policies that offer the best hope of dealing with crime.

A Review of Risk Factors for Criminal Behavior

In the 10th year of his life, Robert Sandifer was prosecuted for eight felonies, including drug possession and armed robbery, in his hometown of Chicago. Because of his young age, he was placed on probation, the maximum penalty allowed by law. Robert had been known to Illinois authorities since the age of 2 when he and his brothers, ages 3 and 5, were taken from their abusive mother by the Department of Children and Family Services and sent to live with his grandmother, three aunts and uncles, and 20 other children. With too little supervision at home and a crime-ridden neighborhood outside, Robert had not quite reached his 3rd birthday when he found himself spending time with gang members. As soon as he was old enough to ride a bike, he was reportedly wielding knives and guns, stealing from stores, setting fires, and selling drugs. One day in 1994, when Robert was 11, a stray bullet from his gun killed a 14-year-old girl. Within days, Robert himself was dead, shot twice in the back of the head, execution style, by fellow gang members who wanted to keep Robert from talking to police about gang activities (Gibbs, 1994).

Stories such as this one are commonplace in the United States nowadays, but, especially when they involve people who are poor and Black, tend to attract only temporary attention and usually only locally. Most Americans just shrug at "that" side of life—perhaps assuming that this sort of thing is to be expected of "poor Black kids in the ghetto." However, the entire nation was riveted in an April 1999 incident when Dylan Klebold and Eric Harris, two White teenagers from affluent suburban families, killed 12 students and a teacher at their high school in Littleton, Colorado, and then killed themselves. For weeks afterward, the Littleton massacre was front-page news and the subject of anguished discussion on television, radio, the Internet, and at dinner tables all over America. What caused these bright young men, who to all appearances had everything going for them, to become so murderously violent? Even the U.S. Congress appropriated money to study the causes of teenage violence and how it can be prevented.

Criminal behavior sometimes does seem senseless, but we hope that reading this book has helped you to recognize how important it is to think about crime as the product of a wide range of individual, family, and societal risk factors that set the stage for it in childhood, adolescence, and adulthood. Let's review what we know about the causes and correlates of crime.

Individual and Peer Group Risk Factors

The major risk factors arising from the characteristics of individual children and their peers include rebelliousness and exposure to deviant peer exemplars.

Rebelliousness.   Young people who feel disconnected from society and its laws, who lack ambition and responsibility, or who actively rebel against society are at higher than average risk for drug abuse, delinquency, and quitting school (Kandel, 1982). The earlier young people drop out of school, begin using drugs, commit crimes, and become sexually active, the greater the likelihood that they will have chronic problems later in life (Elliott, Huizinga, & Morse, 1986). Young people who start to use drugs before the age of 15 are twice as likely to have long-term drug problems than those who wait until after they are 19 (L. N. Robins & Przybeck, 1985). Youngsters who start drinking by the age of 13 are twice as likely to become alcoholics as those who do not start until after 15 (NIAAA, 1998).

Peer Exemplars.   Young people who associate with peers who engage in problem behaviors—violence, delinquency, substance abuse, sexual activity, or quitting school—are much more likely to engage in these behaviors themselves (Farrington, 1991).

Family Risk Factors

Significant family-related risk factors for crime include a family history of dysfunctional or criminal behavior, family management problems, family conflict, and crime-tolerant parental attitudes.

Dysfunctional or Criminal Behavior.   Children raised in a family whose members have a history of addiction to alcohol or other drugs are at increased risk of having alcohol or other drug problems themselves (Kilpatrick et al., 2000; NIAAA, 1998). Children born or raised in a family with a history of criminal activity are at increased risk of becoming delinquent (Farrington, 1991). Children born to teenage mothers are more likely to become teenage parents, and children born to school dropouts are likely to drop out of school themselves (Slavin, 1990).

Family Management Problems.   Poor family management practices include failing to give children clear expectations for behavior, failing to supervise and monitor children, and using excessively harsh or inconsistent punishment. Children exposed to these parenting practices are at higher risk than other children of developing the behavior problems we described in chapter 7 as stepping stones to aggressive, violent, and ultimately, criminal behavior (Farrington, 1991; P. L. Peterson et al., 1994; Thornberry, 1994).

Family Conflict.   Children whose parents are divorced show higher rates of delinquency and substance abuse than other children. However, parental conflict, not divorce per se, contributes most significantly to delinquent behavior (Rutter & Giller, 1983). For instance, domestic violence in the home increases the likelihood that youngsters in that home will engage in violent behavior themselves, especially violent crimes against people (Loeber & Dishion, 1984; Loeber & Stouthaumer-Loeber, 1998).

Parental Attitudes. Children whose parents excuse their law breaking are more likely to become delinquents than are children whose parents are clearly opposed to criminal behavior (Brook et al., 1990; Hawkins & Weis, 1985).

School Risk Factors

The most important school-related risk factors for crime are early signs of antisocial behavior, lack of commitment to school, and academic failure.

Early Signs of Antisocial Behavior. Boys who are persistently aggressive before the third grade or who have trouble controlling their impulses in the classroom are at higher-than-average risk for substance abuse, delinquency, and violent behavior (American Psychological Association, 1993; Loeber, 1988). When a boy's aggressive behavior in the early grades is combined with isolation, withdrawal, or hyperactivity, there is an even greater risk of problem behavior in adolescence (Barkley, 1998; Kellam & Brown, 1982).

Lack of Commitment. Children who are not committed to school or are not motivated to succeed academically are at higher than average risk for displaying crime-related problem behaviors (B. D. Gottfredson, 1988; Johnston, 1991).

Academic Failure. Children who have not succeeded academically by the time they finish elementary school are at increased risk for drug abuse, delinquency, violence, teen pregnancy, and dropping out of school. Whether children fail in school because of lack of mental ability, lack of motivation, or other reasons, it appears that the increased risk for problem behaviors stems from the failure experience itself, including its effect on self-esteem (Farrington, 1991).

Community Risk Factors

The main community risk factors for crime include drugs and alcohol, firearms, violence in the media, community disorganization, and economic and social deprivation.

Drugs and Alcohol. The more easily available drugs and alcohol are in the local community, the greater is the risk that substance abuse will occur (Gorsuch & Butler, 1976). Availability of drugs in school is associated with increased risk for substance abuse by children (Gottfredson, 1988).

Firearms. Easy availability of firearms in a community is correlated with higher rates of violent crime (G. R. Alexander, Massey, Gibbs, & Altekruse, 1985). A high prevalence of people carrying guns make it more likely that an exchange of angry words or blows can escalate into deadly gunfire.

Violence in the Media. Pervasive portrayals of violence on television, in movies and video games, and on the Internet can increase community acceptance of violence and aggression as a means of solving problems and can desensitize viewers to the drastic consequences of violent behavior (e.g., Eron & Huesmann, 1987; National Research Council, 1993).

Community Disorganization. Higher rates of drug problems and crime tend to occur in neighborhoods where people feel little or no sense of attachment to their community and where there is inadequate law enforcement and surveillance of public places (C. A. Murray, 1983; J. Wilson & Hernstein, 1985).

Economic and Social Deprivation. Children who live in communities plagued by extreme poverty and high unemployment are more likely to become delinquents, school dropouts, and teenage parents, and are more likely to engage in violence toward others during adolescence and adulthood (Farrington et al., 1990).

Risk Factors and Crime Prevention

Several aspects of risk factors for crime have implications for crime prevention efforts:

1. The effects of risk factors are multiplicative, not additive. The likelihood of engaging in criminal behavior increases geometrically, not arithmetically, as children are exposed to more risk factors. In other words, being exposed to, say, three risk factors creates a likelihood for criminal behavior that is more than three times the effect of one risk factor. Accordingly, prevention programs are best focused on children who are exposed to the highest number of risks.

2. Risk factors appear in multiple domains. Children can encounter risk factors at home, at school, in the community, in relation to peers, and in their own inherited and socially influenced characteristics. Therefore, the most effective crime prevention programs are likely to be those that are comprehensive enough to address all of these domains.

3. Although the number and intensity of risk factors varies across ethnic groups, the factors appear to operate in the same way for all children. Thus, although prevention programs should be sensitive to the different customs, values, and traditions of particular ethnic groups, the principles on which they are based and the developmental targets they aim to address are likely to be the same for all at-risk children and teenagers.

Protective Factors

Understanding the causes of crime and shaping effective crime-prevention programs depends not only on awareness of the risk factors for criminal behavior, but also on recognizing factors that tend to reduce the risk that children will become criminals. The most important of these protective factors include (1) being female; (2) displaying high intelligence; (3) developing strong social bonds with, and a clear commitment to, parents and other family members, teachers, coaches, youth leaders, and nondelinquent friends; and (4) having a resilient temperament that helps one "bounce back" after encountering adverse environmental circumstances.

Strong, positive relationships with other people help to foster a child's commitment to group or societal goals and values. Young people committed to the prosocial goals of peer groups and community organizations are less likely to use drugs, commit crimes, drop out of school, or do other things that would threaten their bond with these groups. When children learn honesty, unselfishness, fair play, and nonviolence from adults and peers with whom they have strong bonds, they will tend to internalize these characteristics and become committed to a noncriminal lifestyle. In short, learning prosocial attitudes and high standards of personal behavior through the teaching and modeling provided by family members, teachers, and other adults can protect children against the development of antisocial behaviors.

Preventing Crime

The concept of crime prevention is widely misunderstood. Politicians debate prevention versus punishment as if the two were mutually exclusive. They are not. Appropriate punishment is one way to prevent future criminal acts in some past offenders. However, in the parlance of prevention science, punishment is **secondary prevention**. The goal of **primary prevention** is to keep crime from happening in the first place so that punishment is not necessary. Primary prevention programs focus on two fronts: (1) reducing community, school, family, and individual risk factors for crime; and (2) promoting protective factors such as strong parent–child attachment, positive attitudes toward school, and avoidance of drugs and alcohol. Primary prevention programs are aimed at children and young people who are at risk for committing crimes for the first time.

Primary Versus Secondary Prevention

Although ultimately more effective than secondary prevention, primary prevention programs have historically been hard to sell to American politicians and the American people. It is a "hard sell" partly because everyone wants to *do something* about crime and the punishment-only approach—embodied in more and longer prison sentences—provides that something. It is there for all to see, and it satisfies those whose main goal is to seek retribution against criminals. In contrast, primary prevention is somewhat akin to digging a garden and planting seeds—it takes a lot of work, it costs time and money, the project must be given continuous attention, and it takes a long time for the results to appear. Further, the results of primary prevention are more subtle than those of secondary prevention. We can easily see the results of punishment in the growing populations of jails and prisons, but the fruits of primary prevention programs are less immediately obvious. Falling crime rates can as easily be attributed to punishment as to prevention. In short, getting people to pay for results they cannot easily see is a difficult task, which is why the prevention side of the punishment and prevention equation has received relatively little support until recently. However, burgeoning prison populations and the costs of housing prisoners for long terms is taking a toll on most state budgets. Interest in prevention is on the rise, albeit fueled by not much more than fiscal concerns.

To be effective, primary prevention programs must address several risk factor domains. For example, the crime-preventing effects of a Head Start Program alone are likely to be nil for children who must live in a gang- and gun-infested neighborhood. Similarly, arresting men who batter their wives can prevent repeat offenses but mainly in settings where unemployment is low and marriage (rather than cohabitation) is common; the same program in a poverty-ridden, inner-city neighborhood may have little effect. Moreover, crime prevention programs at school cannot work without family support, families cannot function optimally without community support, and individuals cannot overcome high risks without the help of communities and families. In short, prevention programs that address only one set of risk factors are unlikely to have much impact. Unfortunately, those that are more comprehensive are also more expensive.

In 1997, a group of distinguished criminologists presented a report to Congress entitled *Preventing Crime: What Works, What Doesn't, What's Promising* (Sherman et al., 1997). Known as the Sherman Report, it contained a detailed analysis of the results of every crime prevention program for which there was quantifiable data—ranging from punishment-oriented secondary prevention efforts to the most comprehensive primary prevention projects. We use that analysis as a framework for considering the results of prevention efforts focused on punishment, innovative policing, community action, school-based programs, and early interventions with children in at-risk family environments.

Prevention Through Punishment

The United States has the largest penal system in the world. It is the only country in the Western world that has the death penalty, and it also has the highest violent crime rate. Obviously, then, punishment is not preventing crime. In fact, as we described in chapter 13, there is reason to believe that punishment through incarceration is actually helping to perpetuate crime.

This is not to say that punishment has no place in criminal justice. It is vital to incarcerate and to keep incarcerated those criminals who pose the greatest continuing threat to public safety and welfare. To this end, there is great value in laws that allow automatic life sentences without parole for criminals convicted of a third violent offense. When criminals who are so violent and incorrigible that society cannot risk allowing them to be free, they should not be free, ever. However, it would appear that the imposition of long prison terms for less violent criminals, such as thieves or drug users, is a waste of effort and taxpayers' money. These criminals are not likely to receive drug rehabilitation treatment or occupational and stress-coping skills training, so most of them are likely to be rearrested and reincarcerated for the same offenses sooner or later.

Given the evidence on recidivism following imprisonment, we believe that punishment via incarceration can only succeed as a crime prevention tool if it is oriented toward rehabilitation, not retribution. This view is in sharp contrast with that of many prison officials such as Ronald Angelone, former director of the Virginia Department of Corrections. Responding to news reports about the harsh conditions at one of his state's supermax prisons, Angelone said, "It's not a nice place. And I designed it not to be a nice place" (Timberg, 1999, p. C4). Making prisoners as miserable as possible for as long as possible might satisfy our desire for revenge against those who have violated society's laws but what of the costs, in resources and continued crime, of attaining that goal? Beating prisoners, standing by as they rape each other, turning over prison management to gangs, withholding medical and psychiatric treatment—none of these everyday prison practices ultimately benefits society or reduces crime (Stern, 1999).

According to the Sherman Report, there are some punishment-oriented prison programs that *do* show some promise for crime prevention. For example, rehabilitation efforts that are structured; focused; use multiple treatment components; focus on the development of social, academic, and employment skills; and use behavioral and cognitive-behavioral methods to reinforce clearly identified prosocial behaviors have been effective in reducing recidivism, as have prison-based drug and alcohol treatment programs (Sherman et al., 1997; L. M. J. Simon, 1998).

Other effective punishment-oriented programs have been set up as alternatives to prison. These include (1) imposing fines paid over a set period of time and (2) drug and alcohol treatment outside of prison, especially those run by "drug courts," that combine rehabilitation and criminal justice control (e.g., Finkelstein, 2000). In drug courts, judges place offenders on intensively supervised probation, enroll them in drug and alcohol treatment programs, and require them to report for frequent (and sometimes unannounced) urine tests that can detect drug use. If participants fail a urine test or miss a treatment appointment, they are given even more intense supervision and treatment. Except in extreme cases, these offenders are not allowed to drop out of the treatment program. Successful graduates of drug court programs are typically presented with plaques and certificates and perhaps enlisted to provide mentoring and supervision for new enrollees (Sherman et al., 1997).

Special Programs for Convicts With Mental Disorders.   In 1999, Andrew Goldstein, a 29-year-old man who had a long history of severe schizophrenic delusions, killed Kendra Webdale, a total stranger to him, by pushing her in front of a New York City subway train. In his written confession he said, "I felt a sensation, like something was entering me … I got the urge to push, shove, or sidekick. As the train was coming, … I pushed the woman who had blonde hair" (Winerip, 1999, p. 45). Goldstein was convicted of murder and has joined the hundreds of thousands of other inmates with mental disorders who are incarcerated in state and federal prisons (Ditton, 1999). Indeed, there are more mentally disordered people in jails and prisons than there are in mental health facilities (Winerip, 1999). Some of these people are dangerous, but as we noted in chapter 13, few of them will receive the treatment they need to improve their psychological condition and to make them less dangerous. On release, mentally ill ex-convicts are likely to be more disordered than when they were locked up, and they are at high risk for reoffending.

To help prevent crime among the mentally ill, the National Association of Mental Health (2004) makes the following recommendations:

1. Change state criminal codes and create special "mental health courts" so that judges can divert nonviolent offenders with severe mental disorders away from incarceration and into appropriate treatment. Mental health courts are now operating in several states. They are criticized, however, for mainly diverting nonviolent and petty offenders (e.g., those charged with loitering, trespassing, and other public nuisance offenses) who, mental health advocates say, should not be in the criminal justice system to start with. To help prevent the small amount of violent crime perpetrated by seriously mentally people (see our discussion in chapter 10), persons who commit assault, for instance, ought to be eligible for mental health courts (R. Bernstein & Seltzer, 2004).
2. Train law enforcement officers to recognize the signs and symptoms of severe mental illness and to respond effectively and appropriately to people who are experiencing psychiatric crises. This initiative has gained considerable momentum. The National Alliance for the Mentally Ill and other advocacy groups provide this type of training across the country.
3. Create divisions or units within probation and parole departments with specific responsibility for coordinating and administering services for people with severe mental disorders. Many states now have programs that provide a structured, monitored, mental-health regimen for parolees and probationers.

Prevention Through Policing

Despite high hopes for them, the following policing-oriented efforts have been shown to be unsuccessful in preventing crime: (1) arresting juveniles for minor offenses rather than waiting until they commit serious crimes, (2) arresting unemployed perpetrators of domestic assault, (3) arresting people who buy drugs on the street, and (4) increasing police street patrols without focusing on specific crime-risk areas (Sherman et al., 1997).

Effective police-related crime prevention programs include (1) increasing patrols of specific street corners that are "hot spots" for crime, (2) arresting serious repeat offenders and drunk drivers, and (3) arresting employed perpetrators of domestic assault (Sherman et al., 1997). There is also reason to believe that the goal of crime prevention is better served when law enforcement officers work to improve relations with citizens in the communities they serve (Sherman et al., 1997). A growing body of research (e.g., Tyler, 1990) shows a strong positive correlation between citizens' perception of the legitimacy of police authority and their willingness to obey the law. This perception of legitimacy, in turn, is affected by how citizens evaluate the way the police treat them. Accordingly, some police departments are providing training programs designed to teach officers how to replace authoritarian communication tactics with the use of more respectful language that does not flaunt the officer's power. For example, instead of bullying a motorist who engages in an angry tirade about being pulled over, officers are trained to let the driver finish, recognize and accept the anger, and then get on with the business of writing a ticket or whatever needs to be done in the situation (P. Davis, 1998b). This approach tends to create citizen respect for law enforcement that, in turn, improves police–citizen relations, an important factor in crime prevention. One of the biggest obstacles to promoting improved relations between police and citizens is, of course, dispelling the perception among citizens—especially minority citizens—that the police are brutal and biased. As we discussed in chapters 2 and 6, it is still all too common for police to physically abuse arrestees and suspects, to manufacture or lie about evidence, and to single out minority group members for traffic stops and questioning. Treating all citizens fairly and in accordance with the law will make everyone safer.

Prevention Through Community Action

The most immediate and proximate community factors contributing to the perpetuation of serious and violent crime are the easy availability of drugs, firearms, and vulnerable victims (Cook & Moore, 1995). Some communities have tried to address the problem of gun availability in high crime areas through gun buy-back programs. These programs have not been effective in preventing crime because they attract guns mainly from areas where crime is not a major problem or from offenders who use the buy-back cash to purchase better guns (Sherman et al., 1997).

Community programs to reduce gang violence have been ineffective, overall. For example, having law enforcement officers engage in nighttime basketball games and other sports activities with young gang members appears only to increase gang cohesion by reinforcing the gang's "us against them" orientation. However, early intervention with young gang members, individual therapy, training in communication and problem-solving and dispute-resolution skills, and various community services, do hold some promise. Take the cases of Tony Pipkin and Tyrone Curtis. Tony and Tyrone were 7 years old when crack cocaine took over the streets of the poor neighborhood where they lived in Washington, DC. They grew up amid appalling urban violence; more than 130 gang-related homicides took place within a half-mile radius of their homes. Tony lived at various times with his mother, his grandmother and, when neither could take care of him, in a residential facility. Tyrone lived in a relatively stable single-parent home, but both boys were at risk for joining a gang. Neither did so. They steered clear of gang members to avoid being drafted for membership, and they stayed home at night so they would not be killed by stray gunfire. These decisions were encouraged and supported by staff members at a nonprofit neighborhood community center where the boys began to go after school. There they found positive male role models who took them on recreational trips, arranged for them to transfer to a high school outside of their dangerous neighborhood, tutored them in their academic work, and saw to it that they graduated, filled out applications for college admission, and helped them obtain funding for college expenses. Both young men entered college in the fall of 1997 (Escobar, 1997a).

Community-based efforts to reduce crime have also included programs aimed at reducing victim vulnerability. For example, agencies in many low-income communities have launched campaigns to promote direct deposits of welfare and Social Security checks. In the decade or so since these programs were instituted, the incidence of robberies and thefts in these communities has been reduced. Robbery and murder might also be less likely in high-crime areas if automatic cash machines were removed (or not placed in isolated locations), but there has as yet been no systematic effort to do so.

In short, the Sherman Report found only a few community-based programs that appear effective in preventing crime (Sherman et al., 1997). Further, a 1998 report by the National Academy of Sciences concluded that federal and local transportation and housing policies of the last 50 years have substantially contributed to serious crime in certain communities by concentrating poor minority citizens in housing complexes that are cut off from mainstream city life. Without adequate mass transportation and retail shopping resources, these communities provide a perfect environment for the operation and dominance of illegitimate enterprises and gangs.

School-Based Prevention

School-based programs found to be effective in preventing crime are those targeted to teach students the behavioral skills they need to stay out of trouble. These include programs that (1) set rules and goals about acceptable behavior and positively reinforce it; (2) are comprehensive enough and last long enough to build and consistently reward competency in interpersonal communication, self-control, stress management, decision making, social problem solving, and other cognitive activity; and (3) teach specific skills that children can use to avoid alcohol and other drugs (Sherman et al., 1997). The Gang Resistance Education and Training (G.R.E.A.T.) Program is a school-based, life-skills competency program that is taught by uniformed police officers to elementary school students (focusing on third and fourth grades). It trains students in four skill areas: personal skills (goal setting, decision making, and anger management), resiliency (message analysis and problem solving), resistance (refusal, recognition of peer pressure, and antigang and violence norms), and social skills (communication, conflict resolution, social responsibly, and empathy and perspective taking). The program consists of 13 classroom components, a summer extracurricular program, and a family component. Project Legal Enrichment and Decision Making (L.E.A.D.) targets fifth-grade students. Criminal prosecutors teach students about the law and help them recognize the social and legal consequences of criminal behavior. Lessons consist of instruction on the criminal justice system; role-playing resistance scenarios related to drug use, gang involvement, truancy, and driving under the influence; and teaching conflict-resolution kills. Students go on field trips to juvenile court and detention centers, exposing them to the actual consequences of criminal conduct.

The following school-based programs have not been shown effective in preventing crime: (1) counseling students about substance use and delinquency, particularly in peer group settings; (2) providing recreational and other activities in the absence of the more comprehensive skill training programs mentioned previously; and (3) instructional programs that disseminate information about the dangers and evils of crime including those that use scare tactics and appeals based on morality. For example, the Drug Abuse Resistance Education (D.A.R.E.) program is the most common school-based effort aimed at reducing student drug use (used in 80% of U.S. schools and in 56 foreign countries), but it has been found to be almost totally ineffective. The National Academy of Science, the Government Accountability Office, the U.S. Surgeon General, and the U.S. Department of Education all have ruled the program to be not only ineffective but sometimes counterproductive (Kanof, 2003). The reason, say researchers, is that it relies on antidrug lectures by uniformed police officers who offer no specific drug-refusal tactics or other communication and behavioral skills that children need to stay away from drugs. Further, D.A.R.E. targets audiences of elementary school children may be too young to benefit from the instruction (Sherman et al., 1997). Researchers say that life-skills programs such as G.R.E.A.T are effective in teaching students the skills to resist drug and alcohol use (Henson, 2003).

Prevention Through Individual and Family Intervention

As we noted in chapters 7 and 8, people who engage in serious criminal behavior tend to come from families in which parents display antisocial behavior, are in constant conflict, reject or inadequately supervise their children, and employ inconsistent discipline (Loeber & Stouthaumer-Loeber, 1998; Tremblay & Craig, 1995). With these findings in mind, researchers in developmental psychology, social work, criminology, and policy analysis have suggested that programs with the greatest overall potential for crime prevention are family-based interventions that target high-risk homes and begin when children are in their infancy (Crowell & Burgess, 1996; Hawkins, Arthur, & Catalano, 1995; Kumpfer, Molgaard, & Spoth, 1996; Tremblay & Craig, 1995; Wasserman & Miller, 1998; Yoshikawa, 1994).

This view is supported by data that has shown that family risk factors exert powerful effects on a child's involvement in crime, suggesting that the more of these risk factors that are addressed—and the earlier they are addressed—the better. Once family risk factors have had a chance to influence a child over many years, the crime-related problems they cause become more intransigent (Wilson & Howell, 1993). So although programs aimed at infants and young children may be the most expensive in the short run, they may also be the most cost effective in the long run, especially when one takes into account the savings associated with reductions in drug and alcohol abuse, teen pregnancy, special education requirements, and institutionalization (Greenwood, 1999). As we described in chapters 7 and 8, these programs employ in-home interventions, mentoring of parents and children, recreational services for parents and children, and "respite" care for the parents of children who need intensive supervision (such as for behavioral or medical problems).

The most successful early childhood programs are those that (1) address more than one or two factors associated with delinquency and focus on multiple problem behaviors, (2) are designed for children of specific ages and at specific stages of development, and (3) last more than a few months and often several years. In particular, a Task Force on Critical Criminal Justice Issues appointed by then U.S. Attorney General Janet Reno (National Institute of Justice, 1997c) recommended (1) home visitation programs for mothers at high risk for abusing, neglecting, or inadequately providing for their children; (2) educational daycare programs—with a home visitation component for at-risk infants and children that assists parents, teaches parenting skills, and provides marital and family therapy; and (3) programs that focus on meeting the basic needs of infants and preschool children and actively recruit and sustain participation of older children.

The report of the Reno Task Force (National Institute of Justice, 1997c) also emphasized the need for intervention in families where there are criminal parents and suggested that the following programs have the best chance of interrupting the all-too-familiar tendency of children in these families to imitate their parents' behavior:

1. Prenatal counseling, perinatal care (including substance abuse treatment) for pregnant offenders, and hands-on parenting classes for offenders with babies and young children.
2. Programs designed to help recently released, or about to be released, prison or jail inmates to improve their interactions with children and spouses.
3. Referral and advocacy for health, nutrition, and related services to help the children of parents who are under juvenile and/or criminal justice system supervision or conditional release.
4. Recruitment of noncriminal extended family members to care for offenders' children, especially in cultural groups in which the extended family has traditionally played a key role in childrearing.

Obstacles to Crime Prevention

If people know the risks and protective factors associated with crime, and if they have data that tells them which crime prevention programs are effective or promising, why haven't we done a better job of preventing crime? In our view, there are several reasons:

1. Victim's revenge: Society emphasizes retribution and against criminals. This emphasis is reflected in the victims' movement, in public opinion polls, as well as in the views of many in the criminal justice system, and it fuels an orientation toward indiscriminately harsh punishments that do not deter recidivism and may even contribute to it.
2. Social disintegration and the growing underclass: Inequity in patterns of arrest, prosecution, and punishment continue to put a disproportionate number of people of color, especially males, behind bars for nonviolent crimes. These patterns are helping to marginalize certain segments of our society such that the (mostly White) rich get richer while the (mostly minority) poor get poorer—and get prison.
3. America's love affair with guns: The United States is a nation of gun owners. Guns are part of America's heritage, traditions, myths, and rights. The Constitution's specific guarantee that its citizens have the right to bear arms is jealously protected, regardless of the harmful role those arms—in the wrong hands—are playing in making America the world's most violent "civilized" society.
4. Crime in the media: The news media perpetuate myths about crime that lead to more crime.

Victims' Revenge

As we described in chapter 13, the criminal justice system now provides many avenues for victims to participate in the process of prosecuting and punishing criminals. However, victims' rights extend far beyond specific cases. New laws to protect certain classes of victims, sometimes at the risk of violating defendants' rights, continue to be popular with the public.

It is worth noting that the victims' rights movement did not arise in the inner-city ghettos where Black and Hispanic children are killed or injured in violent crimes virtually every day. Indeed, although most crime victims are adults, not children, and although Blacks make up the vast majority of crime victims, most victims' rights laws are related to the tragic deaths of young White females—Megan's Law in New Jersey, Stephanie's Law in Kansas, Jillian's Law in Rhode Island, Joan's Law in New Jersey, and Jenna's Law in New York. White female victims are also featured on the around-the-clock cable television. Who can forget Lacy Peterson, the pregnant woman in California whose husband was convicted of her murder in 2004 and whose case became a fixture on cable television? One can't help but notice that the "damsels in distress" are always White (Robinson, 2005). As grieving White parents become the most powerful lobbyists for harsher criminal punishment, legislative attitudes toward punishment are being continually shaped by the agendas of victims groups. These groups are uniformly dedicated to capital punishment, long prison terms, and restraints on convicts' freedom on release.

The pleas of victims' advocates set emotional fire to the political hay made when politicians tell voters that they are doing something about crime. However, the something they are doing is mainly passing harsher laws and authorizing the building of more prisons to house more inmates for longer periods—even though most of these prisoners will not have committed violent crimes and will not be rehabilitated by their incarceration. As we discussed in chapter 13, today the United States locks up more people for longer periods of time for more crimes than any other country in the world. This is exactly what victims' rights advocates want, but this policy of revenge and retribution does little or nothing to prevent crime and, as we noted in chapter 13, it may contribute to crime.

Social Disintegration and the Growing Underclass

In 1968, President Lyndon B. Johnson appointed a panel of experts under the leadership of former Illinois Governor Otto Kerner to probe the causes of rioting that swept urban America in 1967 following the assassinations of Dr. Martin Luther King, Jr., and Senator Robert F. Kennedy. The Kerner Commission, as it came to be known, warned that the United States was moving toward a social schism in which there would be two separate—and unequal—societies, one Black, one White.

A follow-up report issued in 1999 by the Milton S. Eisenhower Foundation warned that in spite of evidence that violent crime rates are decreasing, crime is still higher in the United States than in any industrialized county. The report noted further that the causes of crime remain strongly rooted in social and political problems. One of the most significant of these problems is poverty. In spite of record-low unemployment, low inflation, and a booming national economy, most inner-city minority adults do not hold a job that pays a living wage. The top 1% of Americans have more money than the bottom 90%—the most lopsided wealth inequality of any industrialized nation. Among other problems cited by the follow-up report as contributing to crime in the long run are (1) the easy availability of handguns, (2) gross inequities in the way Whites and non-Whites are treated in the adult and juvenile justice systems, and (3) law enforcement policies that have led to a dramatic increase in incarceration rates for nonviolent property and drug crimes (Milton S. Eisenhower Foundation, 1999).

Sociologists and criminologists have stressed that this kind of social inequality highlighted in the Eisenhower Foundation report stimulates crime (Bursik, 1988; Reiman, 1995). Violent crime rates—including crimes stemming from gang activity—are positively correlated with income inequality in society and with poverty and unemployment (Curry & Spergel, 1988; Menard & Elliott, 1990; Rosenfeld, 1985).

Ethnic differences in economic opportunity, poverty, crime, and arrest and prosecution practices help account for the fact that, today, one in three Black men are in prison, on parole, or on probation, largely for drug-related crimes (Beck, 2000; Human Rights Watch, 2000). In big cities—such as Washington, DC, Baltimore, and Los Angeles—the percentage exceeds half of the adult Black male population (D. Simon & Burns, 1997). The Hispanic prison population is growing as well and for many of the same reasons that operate in the Black community (Beck, 2000). This large-scale imprisonment of minority men further contributes to the social disintegration of their neighborhoods. In inner-city public and low-income housing populated by Blacks, for example, most of the male residents are young adolescents and gang members. Positive adult male role models are virtually absent for the poverty-stricken children who grow up in these neighborhoods. Raised by mothers, grandmothers, or other female family members, most have little reason to expect that their fate will be much different from that of their male elders. Thus, it appears that social inequality and disintegration are not only important causes and results of crime, but are also major obstacles to crime prevention (Chaiken, 2000). The changes that might lessen the social ills that contribute to crime are not likely to come soon, but until the practical and political obstacles in the path of such changes are overcome, the effects of prevention efforts aimed at individuals and families will be limited.

America's Love Affair With Guns

More than half of all the homes in the United States contain at least one firearm. Although many gun owners say they keep a gun at home at least partly for self-protection, studies conducted over the past decade have suggested that the risks of doing so outweigh the potential benefits. For one thing, there is no evidence that having a gun at home offers substantial protection from injury or death during a burglary or other criminal intrusion by strangers. Guns are used infrequently in self-defense, mainly because criminals typically rely on stealth and surprise to achieve their goals, and few victims have time to reach and use their weapons effectively, particularly if it is properly locked away. Second, firearms in a home are usually a greater threat to occupants than to intruders. Two large-scale studies have found that people living in homes where there is a gun face an increased risk of violent death, even after the effects of other risk factors—including depression, alcoholism, illegal drug use, and history of family violence—are statistically controlled. Specifically, homes with guns are almost five times more likely to be the scene of a suicide and almost three times more likely to be the scene of a homicide than comparable homes where there are no firearms (National Institute of Justice, 1996). Often, one member of a gun-owning household ends up killing another, accidentally or on purpose. Gun violence is especially prevalent in public housing projects, where gangs and drug dealing are also rampant (U.S. Department of Housing and Urban Development, 2000).

Gun-related violence and crime in the United States has reached epidemic proportions. Consider this: Guns have claimed the lives of 567,000 U.S. soldiers in all of the country's wars over the past 140 years, but just since 1920, more than a million U.S. civilians have been killed by firearms—32,436 in 1997 alone (Center for Disease Control and Prevention, 1999). Of all deaths among 15- to 19-year-olds, 25% are attributable to guns, and 85% of all homicide victims in that age group are killed by guns (U.S. Department of Justice, 1996b). Teenage boys in general are more likely to die from gunshot wounds than from all natural causes combined (Hoyert, Kochanek, & Murphy, 1999).

Public opinion surveys have suggested that there is support for increased control over the purchase of handguns. Prosecution strategies aimed at getting guns out of the hands of convicted felons are popular in some jurisdictions, but federal and state lawmakers have still not passed stringent gun-control laws largely due to the lobbying efforts of the National Rifle Association (NRA). The NRA is right in saying that "guns don't kill people—people kill people," but so many people are killing people with guns in the United States that mindless opposition to any and all forms of gun control places a major obstacle in the path of crime prevention. Until that obstacle is removed, the Centers for Disease Control and Prevention has proposed treating guns as a public health problem. It recommends approaching the problem as it does other diseases—focusing on education and prevention rather than treatment (Thompson, 1998).

Crime in the Media

Violent crime rates have dropped significantly from their peaks in the early 1990s, but one would never know it from watching the evening news. A comprehensive study of more than 17,000 local news stories broadcast from October through December, 1996, found that the most common topics covered were crime (20%), weather (11%), accidents and disasters (9%), and human interest and health stories (7% each; Carmody, 1998). Why do broadcasters devote so much attention to crime when it is actually rare—at least in comparison to other newsworthy events? The answer is that crime stories attract viewers, and having more viewers allows stations to raise the rates they can charge advertisers.

TV news directors say they are giving the public what they want, and the popularity of tabloid crime and "real-life" television shows such as *Hard Copy, America's Most Wanted, Cops, America's Scariest Police Chases,* and *CSI* suggests that they are probably right. Still, as we noted in chapter 12, this lopsided coverage gives the impression that crime is more prevalent and more violent than it actually is. For example, although violent crime makes up only 10% of all crime, it is involved in virtually 100% of the crime stories and dramas on television.

Media depictions of crime distort public impressions of the nature as well as the frequency of violent crime. Most violent crime is committed by people who are relatives, friends, or acquaintances of victims. Violent crime by and against strangers is relatively uncommon, yet television crime stories—on the news and in crime dramas—tend to focus on cases in which offender and victim do not know each other. Further, few newscasts or crime dramas try to educate the public about the social, economic, and psychological roots of crime or to dispel myths about crime rates and victim-offender relations. In other words, the picture of crime presented in the mass media leads people to think that most crime is random and that therefore not much can be done to prevent it other than to imprison criminals for as long as possible.

Looking Ahead

Current efforts to fight and prevent crime tend to focus on simple, politically correct solutions, but in our view, there are no simple solutions to the problem of crime. It is likely to remain a problem as long as everyone approaches it through punishment alone. Although recent downward trends in some forms of crime are welcome, they are not the beginning of the end of crime. If society does not supplement a punishment-only approach with serious efforts to prevent the crimes of the next generation and to intervene in the criminal careers of those on probation and parole, crime will not go away.

The most important question for dealing with crime is not whether to emphasize stringent law enforcement or community-based crime prevention programs. The question is how to do both—how to create enough prison space to incarcerate the truly violent while also supporting programs to reduce the flood tide of criminals that is created by the biological, psychological, social, and environmental risk factors we have discussed throughout this book.

Some Directions for Future Research

What do we still need to know about crime? A lot. We think the greatest gap in knowledge at the moment relates to exactly how various risk factors contribute to crime and how they interact with each other in doing so. In 1997, the American Psychological Association published a report listing research questions about aggression and violence that, if answered, could lead to better crime prevention programs (S. Martin, 1997).

The report suggests, for example, that future research into the *biological* roots of violence and aggression should include exploration of (1) the roles of hormones such as testosterone (which is involved in aggressiveness) and neurotransmitter systems, especially those using serotonin and dopamine (which appear to be involved in substance abuse, a major risk factor for crime); (2) the mechanisms of nervous system arousability and its relation to sensitivity to punishment and tendencies toward impulsiveness; and (3) inherited predispositions toward aggressiveness and other behavioral risk factors for crime. As we discussed in several chapters in this book (e.g., chapters 4, 7, 8, 9, and 10), current research into the origins of crime is primarily focusing on its biological roots.

Research on the *psychological* roots of violence and aggression should address (1) how parents, peers, community, and culture mold the scripts, beliefs, and attitudes that influence violent behavior in developing children; (2) how scripts and beliefs interact with current situations to trigger violence, especially how some children come to overreact to situations that they mistakenly perceive to be threatening; and (3) the nature and extent of relations among cognitive abilities, ingrained ways of thinking, and inherited temperament. Research into these correlates of crime are bearing fruit in the problem-solving and other cognitively based prevention programs we discussed previously.

Research on *social and environmental* factors in aggression and violence should focus on (1) the specific roles played by inadequate parenting and discipline and by poverty, (2) which protective factors inoculate some children against entering a life of crime and violence and how they do so, (3) the processes through which peers influence each other's aggressiveness, (4) the mechanisms through which the media promote societal violence, and (5) the role of the Internet in promoting both isolation and a medium for transmitting violence (e.g., Kraut et al., 1998). An great deal of research has taken place and is ongoing in this area, and we discussed much of it in chapter 6.

The Road Ahead

We have painted a rather pessimistic picture of the future of crime, but that future is not entirely bleak. Knowledge gleaned from existing research on crime and the promise of even more valuable information flowing from future research provide reasons for cautious optimism about progress in understanding and preventing crime. Indeed, we trust that reading this book has made you more hopeful than cynical. Ideally, you will use what you have learned to become part of the solution to the problem of crime. After all, crime is woven into the fabric of our society, and, like it or not, each of us has something to do with it. Through our elected officials, *we* decide what crime is and how it should be dealt with. The social policies that *we* support or opposes and the beliefs and prejudices that *we* hold all affect crime. Our attitudes on everything from guns to the rights of minority groups to child rearing can contribute to crime or deter it. So can the way we treat our neighbors. A survey of 9,000 residents from all over the city of Chicago found that the level of violence in a neighborhood is influenced more by the cohesiveness of its residents than by its ethnic makeup or socioeconomic level (Kong, 1997). Seemingly small gestures such as offering to watch a neighbor's child, looking out for their homes and possessions, or intervening when one sees their children misbehave creates what researchers call "collective efficacy" (Bandura, 2000).

In short, you can do something about crime even if you do not engage in research on crime or go into law or law enforcement. You can do something about crime through the choices you make about the way you live and the way you think, through the way you raise or influence children, through the extent of your involvement with your community, and though the way in which you respond to the needs of those who are at risk for becoming criminals.

Summary

Criminal behavior, more often than not, may appear to be senseless, but we have shown that crime is the product of a wide range of individual, family, and society risk factors that set the stage for it in childhood, adolescence, and adulthood. In this chapter, we reviewed the major risk factors for crime and examined the programs and policies that offer the best hope of dealing with crime. We categorized risk factors according to the domains in which they operate: (1) individual and peer group, (2) family, (3) school, and (4) community.

Individuals who feel disconnected from society and rebel against it are at higher risk for drug use, juvenile delinquency, becoming sexually active, and dropping out of school. Young people who associate with peers who engage in these behaviors are more likely to do so themselves and to get into trouble with the law by doing so.

Family risk factors for crime include being raised in a family whose members have a history of drug and/or alcohol addiction and criminal offending, and who have high levels of family conflict with low levels of parenting skills. Parents who excuse the law breaking of their children are aiding in the developing of criminality among their offspring.

Risk factors that appear among young people in educational settings include lack of commitment to school, aggressive and hyperactive behavior, and lack of motivation. These behaviors contribute to school failure that in turn is one of the major contributors to crime.

Community risk factors for crime include easy availability of drugs, alcohol, and firearms; pervasive media violence; lack of adequate law enforcement and surveillance of public places; and economic and social deprivation.

The risk factors for crime are multiplicative, not additive. That is, having three or more risk factors for crime may make one far more than three times likely to engage in crime. Risk factors appear in multiple domains. Thus, effective prevention programs need to address all the domains in which people are raised, educated, and socialized.

As a country, the United States is more focused on punishment than prevention. There are many reasons for this—some fiscal, some political. Part of it is a perception problem—taxpayers cannot "see" prevention, but they can see punishment by growing prison numbers. It is hard to convince people that putting money into prevention is better for society as a whole than is pumping unlimited dollars into corrections. Many of the dollars our government spends on prevention are wasted, as a well-respected government-funded study demonstrated. Blending punishment with prevention is a useful strategy for some offenders, and one sees the results of this approach in drug and mental health courts. Policing high-crime areas, community involvement in the lives of children, and school-based prevention programs such as G.R.E.A.T. and L.E.A.D. have promise. Prevention programs that teach life skills to children as well as probationers and parolees offer hope for preventing crime and recidivism. Home-based programs for at-risk families are labor intensive and expensive at the front end when children are young, but studies have shown they pay off enormously in the long run. The most promising prospects for research into crime and its prevention lie in studying biological, cognitive, social, and environmental factors that lead to crime.

Certain social and political factors, some of them unique to the United States, thwart crime prevention efforts. Among these are increasing pressure from victims' groups to increase time served; a growing underclass that, already marginalized, is more often the target for enforcement of nonviolent and drug crimes; America's love affair with firearms; and pervasive media attention to crime that makes violent crime appear to be more prevalent than it is and that also desensitizes the public to violent crime.

We all—in one way or the other—are involved in crime. We elect the legislators who enact the criminal laws, and we pay the taxes that incarcerate criminals. However, we also touch the lives of many people every day who might be deterred from crime by our words and deeds.

Key Terms

Primary prevention

Secondary prevention

Questions for Review

1. What are the four domains of risk factors for crime?
2. Discuss programs that combine prevention with punishment.
3. Explain how home-based family interventions may be an effective crime prevention strategy.
4. What are the main obstacles to crime prevention in the United States today?
5. What can you do to prevent crime?

 ## Track It Down

Criminal Behavior Website
www.cassel2e.com
Preventing Crime: What Works, What Does't, What's Promising
www.ncjrs.org/works/
Drug Courts
ww.ncjrs.org/spotlight/drug_courts/summary.html
The Role of Mental Health Courts in System Reform
www.bazelon.org/issues/criminalization/publications/mentalhealthcourts/
School-Based Crime Prevention Programs
www.ncjrs.org/works/chapter5.htm
The Brady Center to Prevent Gun Violence
www.bradycenter.org/

Glossary

Adoption studies.   A research method that studies twin and nontwin adoptees to determine what characteristics they share with their biological versus their adoptive families.

Aggravated assault (malicious wounding).   An unlawful attack by one person on another for the purpose of inflicting severe bodily injury.

Allen charge.   An instruction from the judge that attempts to avoid a **hung jury** by encouraging the jurors to try harder to reach a verdict.

Amygdala.   The part of the brain that plays an important role in emotion.

Antisocial personality disorder.   A personality disorder in which people are chronically callous and manipulative, ignore laws and social customs, disregard the rights and feelings of others, behave dishonestly and impulsively, fail to learn from punishment, and lack remorse or guilt over crimes or hurting others.

Arousal.   The measurement of heart rate, blood pressure, respiration rate, skin temperature, galvanic skin response (GSR) and other sweat-related measures, urine production, brain wave activity, physical activation, and muscle tension.

Arson.   The willful and malicious burning (or attempted burning)—with or without intent to defraud—of a dwelling house, public building, motor vehicle, aircraft, or other personal property.

Assault.   Attempting an unwanted touching of a person or leading them to believe that they may be.

Attention-deficit/hyperactivity disorder.   When diagnosed in children, a disorder characterized by inattention, impulsivity, failure to stay on task, distractibility, impatience, disorganization, fidgeting, and difficulty getting along with other children.

Battery.   Unwanted touching of another by means of pushing, hitting, punching, kicking, or other bodily contact.

Behaviorism.   The theory that human behavior is shaped not by instincts or the unconscious but almost entirely by the environment and especially by learning.

Bipsychosocial model of mental illness.   The belief that genetic influences; abnormalities in brain structure and functioning; learned ways of thinking, behaving, and feeling; and families and other social systems within which people grow up and live all play a part in whether or not people will manifest a mental disorder.

Bond (bail).   Money paid (known as **bail**), property pledged, and/or conditions placed on the defendant's release from incarceration pending trial.

Burglary.   The unlawful entry into a structure to commit a felony, usually theft.

Capital felony.   An offense that is potentially punishable by death.

Central nervous system.   The part of the nervous system consisting of the brain and spinal cord.

Cerebral cortex.   The part of the brain involved in thinking, planning, and decision making.

Childhood-adolescent-onset offender.   A criminal whose career begins in childhood.

Classical conditioning.   A type of learning that arises when an unconditioned stimulus, paired with a conditioned stimulus, leads to a conditioned response.

Competent to stand trial.   The requirement that a criminal defendant be able to understand the charges, participate in the legal proceedings associated with a trial in a meaningful way, and assist an attorney in preparing a defense

Conduct disorder.   A severe pattern of childhood disruptiveness consisting of serious antisocial behaviors that substantially infringe on the rights of others; are potentially harmful to the child, to others, or to property; and may violate criminal laws.

Crime.   An intentional act or failure to act that is in violation of criminal law, committed without defense or excuse, and penalized as a felony or misdemeanor.

Criminal profiling.   A process in which investigators study the characteristics of a known crime and then work backward to try to determine the characteristics of the person who might be responsible for the crime.

Criminogenic.   A setting or situation that breeds crime.

Critical criminologists.   Behavioral scientists who study the ways in which criminal laws are used as a mechanism of social control.

Date rape.   Also known as acquaintance rape, but legally no different from any other type of forcible rape and referring to unwanted sexual intercourse in the context of a dating relationship.

Defendant.   The party against whom a legal action is brought.

Defense mechanisms.   According to Sigmund Freud, psychological processes that keep threatening memories, thoughts, and impulses out of consciousness.

Deindividuation.   A psychological state in which individual identity merges with that of a group, and people no longer feel personally responsible or accountable for their actions.

Deinstitutionalization.   The 1960s movement that led to the discharge of thousands of patients hospitalized in mental institutions.

Deoxyribonucleic acid, DNA.   The genetic code for the development and functioning of every cell in the human body.

Diathesis-stress model of mental illness.   The belief that people's genetic or biological predisposition ("diathesis") for psychopathology interacts with environmental factors such that a mental disorder will not appear unless traumatic events, deprivations, or other stressors are sufficiently intense to trigger it.

Disenfranchisement.   Convicted felons' loss of the right to vote in state and federal elections.

Double jeopardy.   Being retried for the same criminal offense after having been acquitted, something that is prohibited by the Fifth Amendment of the U.S. Constitution.

Ecology.   The science of relations between organisms and their surroundings.

Ego.   According to Sigmund Freud's theory, the part of the personality that develops as parents, teachers, and others place limits on the expression of id impulses.

Embezzlement.   The taking of something of value to which one has access based on a position of trust or authority.

Endocrine system.   Directed by the pituitary gland in the brain, this system sends hormones throughout the body.

Environmental psychology.   The study of the mutual impact of human behavior and the natural and built environment (e.g., climate, architectural space, and lighting).

Family studies.   Research method that looks at whether shared characteristics or behaviors are greater among family members who are more closely related (e.g., siblings vs. cousins).

Felony.   An offense punishable by commitment to a state or federal penitentiary for a period of one year to life.

Forcible rape.   Forcible sexual intercourse with a female against her will.

Fraud.   The intentional misrepresentation of fact designed to unlawfully deprive a person of property rights.

Groups.   The basic unit of social interaction consisting of two or more people who join together for a common purpose.

Harmless error.   Mistakes made by a judge at a trial that could not have affected the outcome of a case and thus cannot form the basis for an appeal.

Hate crimes.   Bias-motivated criminal offenses caused by hatred based on a victim's race/ethnicity, religion, sexual orientation, handicap, or national origin.

Hippocampus.   The part of the brain that plays an important role in memory.

Hormones.   Secretions from the glands in the endocrine system that target organs throughout the body.

Hung jury.   A jury that is unable to reach a verdict.

Hypothalamus.   The part of the brain involved in the regulation of hunger, thirst, sex drive, and other motivated behavior.

Id.   According to Sigmund Freud's theory, the unconscious part of the personality where sexual and aggressive instincts reside.

Jury nullification.   When jurors ignore the facts that would allow them to convict a defendant and render a not guilty verdict out of a desire to disregard or protest the law.

Kleptomania.   An impulse control disorder characterized by a buildup of tension, uncontrollable impulses to steal, and feelings of pleasure and relief after doing so.

Larceny theft.   The unlawful taking, carrying, leading, or riding away of property from the possession of another.

Late-onset pathway to crime.   A criminal whose career does not begin until late adolescence or early adulthood.

Learning.   A change in preexisting behavior or mental processes that occurs as a result of experience.

Limbic system.   A group of structures in the brain that include the hippocampus and amygdala that is important for emotion and memory.

Mandatory sentences.   Requirement that judges hand down a particular sentence for a particular crime no matter what the circumstances surrounding that crime

Marxist feminism theory.   Proponents of this theory believe that female criminals are victims of a system designed to exploit them and that much criminal behavior by women stems directly from their victimization by men, especially through physical and sexual abuse and sexual harassment.

Mens rea.   The mental element of culpability meaning that the offender must have had either the express or implied intent to act contrary to law.

Mental disorders.   Conditions that disrupt thinking, feeling, and other psychological processes such that a person behaves in a way that deviates from social expectations and causes significant impairment in occupational, interpersonal, and other important areas of daily functioning.

Misdemeanor.   An offense typically punishable by incarceration for a year or less in a local jail and a fine of up to several thousand dollars.

Monoamine oxidase (MAO).   A brain enzyme that metabolizes serotonin, dopamine, and norepinephrine.

Murder.   The willful, premeditated killing of another person without defense or justification.

Neurotransmitters.   Chemicals released from the brain cells (neurons) that affect other brain cells.

Not guilty by reason of insanity (NGRI).   A jury finding that a defendant was, at the time of the crime, suffering from a serious mental disorder or defect that rendered him unable to understand and appreciate the consequences of his actions and to control his behavior.

Object relations.   Experiences with one's "love objects," the persons to whom people become attached and with whom people seek closeness and intimacy.

Occupational crime (White collar crime).   Any crime committed in the context of one's occupation or employment.

Operant conditioning.   Learning that arises when a certain behavior brings about a desired response from others.

Oppositional defiant disorder.   A childhood disorder characterized by poor emotional control, noncompliance and argumentativeness with parents and teachers, repeated conflicts with peers, and blaming others for problems.

Parens patriae.   The power of a government to act as parents to endangered juveniles.

Pedophilia.   A disorder in which persons, usually male, have recurrent, intense, sexually arousing fantasies and urges involving sexual contact with children at least five years younger than they are.

Peripheral nervous system.   The part of the nervous system that includes the somatic nervous system, which is largely concerned with voluntary control of the muscles, and the autonomic nervous system, which affects motivational, emotional, and other physical reactions.

Personality.   The unique patterns of thinking, feeling, and behaving that are relatively constant throughout one's life and through which one can be compared and contrasted with other people.

Personality disorders.   Consistent, life-long patterns of thinking and acting first appearing in late childhood or early adolescence that deviate substantially from cultural expectations and include actions that cause personal distress and/or discomfort for others and/or problems in interpersonal relationships.

Plaintiff.   The party initiating a legal action.

Primary prevention.   Focus on keeping crime from happening in the first place so that punishment is not necessary.

Psychoactive drugs.   Drugs that affect the brain and create psychological effects.

Psychodynamic theory of crime.   The theory that crime is the product of mostly unconscious psychological and emotional forces.

Psychopathy.   A set of behaviors seen in some criminals consisting of glibness and superficial charm; a grandiose sense of self-worth; need for stimulation and proneness to boredom; pathological lying; a cunning/manipulative style; lack of remorse, guilt, and empathy; poor behavioral control; and criminal versatility.

Psychosexual stages.   According to Sigmund Freud, the five stages of psychological development (oral, anal, phallic, latent, and genital), each of which is focused on the area of the body most associated with pleasure and unconscious conflict at the time.

Psychosocial development.   According to Erik Erikson, the ego develops in eight stages, each of which involves an individual's interactions with others, rather than conflict over internal instincts.

Pyromania.   An impulse control disorder characterized by a continuing pattern of fire setting for pleasure, gratification, and the release of tension.

Rape shield laws.   Laws providing that testimony about a rape victim's previous sexual conduct is not permissible unless it is specifically relevant to the establishment of the defendant's guilt or innocence.

Reactive attachment disorder.   A childhood disorder in which children are unable to form a bond with a caregiver, impairing the development of a sense of self and an ability to develop appropriate social interaction skills.

Restorative justice.   A justice model concerned with repairing the harm done to victims and the community through negotiation, mediation, victim empowerment, and reparation.

Right of allocution.   Victim's rights to make a statement at a sentencing hearing.

Robbery.   The taking or attempting to take anything of value from the care, custody, or control of a person or persons by force of threat or violence and/or by putting the victim in fear.

Secondary prevention.   Focus on punishment of crime as a deterrent factor for future crime.

Sentencing guidelines.   Recommendations for sentences for particular crimes made to judges by panels of criminal justice experts known as Sentencing Commissions.

Simple assault.   A battery without intent to do serious bodily harm.

Social cognition.   The ways in which people perceive, remember, and think about other people.

Social conflict theory.   The belief that capitalist systems insure constant competition between social and political groups wishing to control the government and the economy, with legal and judicial systems that mainly serve the interests of the "power elite."

Social learning.   Learning by watching other people, called models, and vicariously experiencing the consequences of their behavior.

Social psychology.   The branch of psychology that studies how people and groups of people influence the behavior of others.

Sociology. The study of many kinds of groups—from the nuclear family to social, political, and religious institutions—that examines the relationships between individual behavior and membership in these groups.

Stalking. A course of conduct directed at a specific person that involves repeated physical or visual proximity, nonconsensual communication, or verbal, written, or implied threats sufficient to cause harm.

Status offenses. Acts that are legal offenses only if juveniles commit them.

Superego. The part of the personality, acting as the conscience, that develops as individuals adopt the rules, inhibitions, and values of their parents and their culture.

Syndicated crime. A network of individuals and businesses systematically engaged in a variety of criminal enterprises, including the sale and distribution of drugs, gambling, extortion, prostitution, loan-sharking, and racketeering.

Temperament. The biological predisposition to act and respond to the world in particular ways.

Teratogens. Environmental factors and substances including prenatal exposure to drugs and alcohol that adversely affect a developing fetus.

Terrorism. Targeting innocent civilians with violence for political purposes.

Terrorism. The use of illegitimate force to target innocent civilians for political purposes or motives.

Trial de novo. A retrial of misdemeanor charges in a higher court.

Twin studies. A research method that studies twins raised together and raised apart in an effort to try to separate genetic from environmental influences on behavior.

Venire. The group of potential jurors from which a trial jury will be selected.

Victim assistance programs. Administered by state and local governments, they provide counseling, advocacy, and support for victims participating in the criminal justice program.

Victim impact statements. Written statements prepared by victims and provided to the court that describe the physical and emotional consequences of the crime, including property loss and damage, medical and counseling bills, lost wages, and other financial losses.

Victim-offender reconciliation programs. Programs in which victim and offender are brought together by a mediator representing the criminal justice system to agree on a realistic restitution figure and a workable payment schedule.

Victimology. The study of victims and their relationships to offenders and crime.

Voir dire. The process of questioning members of the **venire** in an effort to empanel an impartial jury.

Wergild. Under Anglo-Saxon law, monetary payment the criminal had to make to a murder victim's family.

References

Abadinsky, H. (1985). *Organized crime*. Boston: Allyn & Bacon.

Abraham, H. J. (1994). *The judicial process* (4th ed.). New York: Oxford University Press.

Abrahamsen, D. (1944). *Crime and the human mind*. New York: Columbia University Press.

Abrahamsen, D. (1960). *The psychology of crime*. New York: Columbia University Press.

Abrahamsen, D. (1973). *The murdering mind*. New York: Harper & Row.

Abram, K. M., & Teplin, L. A. (1991). Co-occurring disorders among mentally ill jail detainees: Implications for public policy. *American Psychologist, 46,* 1036–1045.

Abramsky, S. (2002). *Hard time blues: How politics built a prison nation*. New York: St. Martin's Press.

Achenbach, J., & Kovaleski, S. F. (1996, April 7). The profile of a loner. *The Washington Post*, p. A1.

Adams, D. (1991). The Seville statement on violence: Preparing the ground for the construction of peace. Paris: United Nations Educational, Scientific, and Cultural Oranization (UNESCO).

Adamski, A. (1995, January). *Prevalence of computer-related abuse in Poland: Preliminary findings of victimization survey*. Paper presented at the Internet Conference, University of Arkansas at Little Rock.

Addington v. Texas, 441 U.S. 418 (1979).

Adler, A. (1939). *Social interest*. New York: Putnam.

Adler, C. (1992). Violence, gender and social change. *International Social Science Journal, 44,* 267–276.

Adler, F. (1973). Socioeconomic factors influencing jury verdicts. *New York University Review of Law and Social Change, 3,* 1–10.

Adler, F. (1975). *Sisters in crime*. New York: McGraw-Hill.

Adler, S. J. (1994). *The Jury: Trial and error in the American courtroom*. New York: Times Books.

af Klinteberg, B. (1996). The psychopathic personality in a longitudinal perspective. *European Child & Adolescent Psychiatry, 5,* 57–63.

Agnew, R. (1994). The contribution of social-psychological strain theory to the explanation of crime and delinquency. *Advances in Criminological Theory, 6.*

Ahmed, S. W., Bush, P. J., Davidson, F. R., & Iannotti, R. J. (1984, November). *Predicting children's use and intention to use abusable substances*. Paper presented at the annual meeting of the American Public Health Association, Anaheim, CA.

Aichorn, A. (1935). *Wayward youth*. New York: Viking.

Aiello, J.R., & Thompson, D.E. (1980). Personal space, crowding, and spatial behavior in a cultural context. In I. Altman, J.F Wohlwill, & A. Rapaport (Eds.), Human behavior and environment (Vol. 4, pp. 107–178). New York: Plenum.

Ainsworth, M. D. S. (1973). The development of infant-mother attachment. In B. M. Caldwell & H. N. Ricciuti (Eds.), *Review of child development research* (Vol. 3) Chicago: University of Chicago Press.

Ake v. Oklahoma, 470 U.S. 68 (1985).

Akers, R. L. (1985). *Deviant behavior: A social learning approach*. Belmont, CA: Wadsworth.

Albanese, J. S. (1995). *White-collar crime in America*. Englewood Cliffs, NJ: Prentice Hall.

Albanese, J. S. & Finckenauer, J. O. (1997). Domestic and international organized crime. In *Critical criminal justice issues: Task force reports from the American society of criminology*. Washington, DC: U.S. Department of Justice, National Institute of Justice.

Alexander, F. (1935). *Roots of crime*. New York: Knopf.

Alexander, G. R., Massey, R. M., Gibbs, T., & Altekruse, J. M. (1985). Firearm-related fatalities: An epidemiologic assessment of violent death. *American Journal of Public Health, 75,* 165–168.

Alexander, J. (Ed.). (1963). *A brief narration of the case and trial of John Peter Zenger*. Boston: Little, Brown.

Allan, J., Middleton, D., & Browne, K. (1997). Different clients, different needs? Practical issues in community-based treatment for sex offenders. *Criminal Behavior & Mental Health, 7,* 69–84.

Allen v. United States, 164 U.S. 492, 501 (1896).

Allen-Hagen, B. (1993). *Crowding pervasive in juvenile facilities*. Washington, DC: U.S. Department of Justice, Office of Juvenile Justice and Delinquency Prevention.

Allison, J., & Wrightsman, L. (1993). *Rape: The misunderstood crime*. Newbury Park, CA: Sage.

Allnutt, S. H., Bradford, J. M. W., Greenberg, D. M., & Curry, S. (1996). Co-morbidity of alcoholism and the paraphilias. *Journal of Forensic Sciences, 41,* 234–239.

Alm, P., af Klinteberg, B., Humble, K., & Leppert, J. (1996). Psychopathy, platelet MAO activity and criminality among former juvenile delinquents. *Acta Psychiatrica Scandinavica, 94,* 105–111.

Altgeld, J. P. (1890). *Live questions: Including our penal machinery and its victims.* Chicago: Donahue and Henneberry.

American Automobile Association Foundation for Traffic Safety. (1999, August). *Summary of aggressive driving sudy.* Washington, DC: Author.

Anderson, C.A. (1987). Temperature and aggression: Effects on quarterly, yearly, and city rates of violent and nonviolent crime. *Journal of Personality and Social Psychology, 52,* 1161–1173.

American Bar Association. (1989). *ABA criminal justice mental health standards.* Washington, DC: Author.

American Civil Liberties Union. (2002). *Drug policy litigation project.* Washington, DC: Author.

American Civil Liberties Union. (2004, March 3). *ACLU Applauds Governors of South Dakota and Wyoming For Signing Bans on the Death Penalty for Juveniles.* Retrieved January 15, 2005, from http://www.aclu.org/DeathPenalty/DeathPenalty.cfm?ID=15166&c=66

American Psychiatric Association. (1952). *Diagnostic and statistical manual of mental disorders.* Washington, DC: Author.

American Psychiatric Association. (1968). *Diagnostic and statistical manual of mental disorders* (2nd ed.). Washington, DC: Author.

American Psychiatric Association. (1982). APA statement on the insanity defense. *American Journal of Psychiatry, 140,* 681–688.

American Psychiatric Association. (1983). *Statement on prediction of dangerousness.* Washington, DC: Author.

American Psychiatric Association. (1994). *Diagnostic and statistical manual of mental disorders* (4th ed.). Washington, DC: Author.

American Psychiatric Association. (1999, March 19). APA backs bill to help juvenile offenders. *Psychiatric News.* Retrieved June 21, 1999, from http://www.psych.org/pnews/index.html

American Psychiatric Association. (2000a). *Diagnostic and statistical manual of mental disorders* (Vol. 4., text revision). Washington, DC: Author.

American Psychiatric Association. (2000b). *Psychiatric services in jails and prisons* (2nd ed.). Washington DC: Author.

American Psychological Association. (1993). *Violence and youth: Psychology's response.* Washington, DC: Author.

American School Health Association. (1989). *The national adolescent student health survey: A report on the health of America's youth.* Oakland, CA: Society for Public Health Education.

Amir, M. (1971). *Patterns of forcible rape.* Chicago: University of Chicago Press.

Anderson, C. A., Anderson, K. B., & Deuser, W. W. (1996). Examining an affective aggression framework: Weapon and temperature effects on aggressive thoughts, affect, and attitudes. *Personality and Social Psychology Bulletin, 2,* 366–376.

Anderson, C. A., Berkowitz, L., Donnerstein, E., Huesmann, L. R., Johnson, J. D., Linz, D., et al. (2003). The influence of media violence on youth. *Psychological Science in the Public Interest, 4,* 81–110.

Anderson, C. A., & Bushman, B. J. (2001). Effects of violent video games on aggressive behavior, aggressive cognition, aggressive affect, physiological arousal, and prosocial behavior: A meta-analytic review of the scientific literature. *Psychological Science, 12,* 353–359.

Anderson, C. A., Carnagey, N. L., & Eubanks, J. (2003). Exposure to violent media: The effects of songs with violent lyrics on aggressive thoughts and feelings. *Journal of Personality and Social Psychology, 84, 5,* 960–971.

Anderson, C. A., & Dill, K. E. (2000). Video games and aggressive thoughts, feelings, and behavior in the laboratory and in life. *Journal of Personality and Social Psychology, 78,* 722–790.

Anderson, D. A. (1999). The aggregate burden of crime, *Journal of Law & Economics, 42,* 611–642.

Anderson, P. (1997, October 12). Two life terms for Loukaitis. *The Seattle Times,* p. 1.

Andrews, D. A., & Bonta, J. (1994). *The psychology of criminal conduct.* Cincinnati, OH: Anderson Publishing Co.

Andrews, D. A., Zinger, I., Hoge, R. D., Bonta, J., Gendreau, P., & Cullen, F. T. (1990). Does correctional treatment work? A clinically-relevant and psychologically-informed meta-analysis. *Criminology, 28,* 369–404.

Angry 5-year-old took gun to school. (1998, May 11). *Washington Post,* p. A5.

Anno, B. J. (1990). The cost of correctional health care: Results of a national survey. *Journal of Prison and Jail Health, 9*(2), 105–134.

Apodaca, Cooper, and Madden v. Oregon, 406 U.S. 404 (1972).

Applebaum, P. S. (1986). Competence to be executed: Another conundrum for mental health professionals. *Hospital and Community Psychiatry, 37,* 682–684.

Arbuthnot, J., Gordon, D. A., & Jurkovic, G. J. (1987). Personality. In H. C. Quay (Ed.), *Handbook of juvenile delinquency* (pp. 139–183). New York: Wiley.

Archer, J. (1995). Testosterone and aggression. In M. Hillbrand & N. Pilone (Eds.), *The psychobiology of aggression: Engines, measurement, and control* (pp. 3–26).

Aristotle. (1941). *Rhetorica.* New York: Random House.

Arms, R., Russell, G., Sandilands, M. (1979). Effects on the hostility of spectators of viewing aggressive sports. *Social Psychology Quarterly, 42,* 275–279.

Arnett, J. J. (2004). *Adolescence and emerging adulthood: A cultural approach* (2nd ed.). Englewood Cliffs, NJ: Prentice Hall.

Aronow, R. (1980). A therapeutic approach to the acutely overdosed patient. *Journal of Psychedelic Drugs, 12,* 259–268.

Aronson, E. (1995). *The social animal.* New York: Freeman.

Aronson, E. (2004). *The social animal* (9th ed.). New York: Freeman.

Arseneault, L. Tremblay, R. E., Boulerice, B., Séguin, J. R., & Saucier, J. F. (2000). Minor physical anomalies and family adversity as risk factors for violent delinquency in adolescence. *American Journal of Psychiatry, 157,* 917–923. Retrieved January 8, 2005, from http://ajp. psychiatryonline.org/cgi/content/full/157/6/917

Asmussen, K. J. (1992, Fall). Weapon possession in public high schools. *School Safety.*

Assad, G. (1990). *Hallucinations in clinical psychiatry.* New York: Brunner/Mazel.

Association of Certified Fraud Examiners. (1999). Report to the nation: Occupational fraud and abuse. Austin, TX: Author.

Association of Certified Fraud Examiners. (1995). Report to the nation: Occupational fraud and abuse. Austin, TX: Author.

Atkins v. Virginia, 536 U.S. 304 (2003).

Augenstein, N. (1998, June 18). Organized crime going hi-tech. *New York Daily News.* Retrieved May 17, 1999, from http://www.infowar.com/class

Austin, J., & Hardyman, P. (1991). *The use of early parole with electronic monitoring to control prison crowding: Evaluation of the Oklahoma Department of Corrections pre-parole supervised release with electronic monitoring.* Unpublished manuscript, National Institute of Justice.

Austin, R. (1982). Women's liberation and increase in minor, major, and occupational offenses. *Criminology, 20,* 407–430.

Averill, J. (1982). *Anger and aggression: An essay on emotion.* New York: Springer-Verlag.

Aytch, D. M. (1994). Adult attachment status and propensity toward criminal behavior. *Dissertation Abstracts, 55,* 610.

Azar, B. (1997, April). Environment is key to serotonin levels. *American Psychological Association Monitor.* Retrieved April 19, 1999, from http://www.apa.org/monitor/apr97/seroton. html

Babington, C. (1999, April 28). Clinton proposes handgun limits. *Washington Post,* p. A11.

Babor, T. F., Hoffman, M., DelBoca, F. K., Hesselbrock, V., Meyer, R. E., Dolinsky, Z. S., et al. (1992). Types of alcoholics I: Evidence for an empirically-derived typology based on indicators of vulnerability and severity. *Archives of General Psychiatry, 8,* 599–608.

Bachman, J. G., Lloyd, D. J., & O'Malley, P. M. (1981). Smoking, drinking and drug use among American high school students: Correlates and trends, 1975–1979. *American Journal of Public Health, 71,* 59–69.

Bachman, R. (1994). *Violence against women: A national crime victimization survey report.* Washington, DC: Bureau of Justice Statistics.

Bach-y-Rita, G., Lion, J., Climent, C., & Ervin, F. (1971). Episodic dyscontrol: A Study of 130 violent patients. *American Journal of Psychiatry, 127,* 1473–1478.

Bagley, C., Wood, M., & Young, L. (1994). Victim to abuser: Mental health and behavioral sequels of child sexual abuse in a community survey of young adult males. *Child Abuse & Neglect, 18,* 683–697.

Bailey, S. (1996). Adolescents who murder. *Journal of Adolescence, 19,* 19–39.

Bailis, D. S., Darley, J. M., Waxman, T. L., & Robinson, P. H. (1995). Community standards of criminal liability and the insanity defense. *Law and Human Behavior, 19,* 425–446.

Baillargeon, R. (1993). The object concept revisited: New directions in the investigation of infants' physical knowledge. In C. Granrud (Ed.), *Visual perception and cognition in infancy. Carnegie Mellon symposia on cognition.* Hillsdale, NJ: Lawrence Erlbaum Associates, Inc.

Baillargeon, R. (1995). Physical reasoning in infancy. In M. S. Gazzaniga (Ed.), *The cognitive neurosciences* (pp. 181–204). Cambridge, MA: MIT Press.

Baker, D. P. (1997, October 11). In aftermath of deadly day, Mississippi town faces fear. *The Washington Post,* p. A8.

Baker, D. (1998b, February 28). 17-year-old sentenced to die in Florida: Penalty for young "vampire" murderer part of national trend. *The Washington Post,* p. A3.

Baker, D. P. (1998a, January 30). Blast at Alabama abortion clinic kills a policeman, injures a nurse. *The Washington Post,* pp. A1–A6.

Baker, D. P. (1999a, April 30). As execution nears, man's mental illness at issue. *The Washington Post,* pp. B1, B8.

Baker, D. P. (1999b, May 13). Virginia Governor Gilmore stops execution for first time. *The Washington Post,* pp. A1, A15.

Baker, D. P. (1999, December). Stalker's walk. *American Bar Association Journal,* 51–52.

Baker, G., & Adams, W. (1962). Comparison of the delinquencies of boys and girls. *Journal of Criminal Law, Criminology, and Police Science, 53,* 470–475.

Balderian, N. J. (1991). *Abuse causes disabilities: Disabilities and the family.* Culver City, CA: Spectrum.

Baldus, D., Woodworth, G., & Pulaski, C. (1990). *Equal justice and the death penalty: A legal and empirical analysis.* Boston, MA: Northeastern University Press.

Ballew v. Georgia, 435 U.S. 223 (1978).

Bandura, A. (1969). *Principles of behavior modification.* New York: Holt, Rinehart & Winston.

Bandura, A. (1973). *Aggression.* Englewood Cliffs, NJ: Prentice-Hall.

Bandura, A. (1974). Behavior theory and the models of man. *American Psychologist, 29,* 861–862.

Bandura. A. (1977). Self-efficacy: Toward a unifying theory of behavioral change. *Psychological Review, 84,* 191–215.

Bandura, A. (1982). Self-efficacy mechanism in human agency. *American Psychologist, 3,* 344–358.

Bandura, A. (1986). *Social foundations of thought and action: A social cognitive theory.* Englewood Cliffs, NJ: Prentice-Hall.

Bandura, A. (2000). Exercise of human agency through collective efficacy. *Current Directions in Psychological Science, 9,* 75–78.

Bandura, A., Ross, D., & Ross, S. A. (1963). Imitation of film-mediated aggressive models. *Journal of Abnormal and Social Psychology, 66,* 3–11.

Barak, A., Fisher, W. A. (1997). Effects of interactive computer erotica on men's attitudes and behavior toward women: An experimental study. *Computers in Human Behavior, 13,* 353–369.

Barak, G. (1998). *Integrating criminologies.* Boston: Allyn & Bacon.

Barefoot v. Estelle, 463 U.S. 80 (1983).

Barkley, R. A. (1998). *Attention deficit hyperactivity disorder: A handbook for diagnosis and treatment* (2nd ed.). New York: Guilford.

Barkley, R. A., Fischer, M., Edelbrock, C. S., & Smallish, L. (1990). The adolescent outcome of hyperactive children diagnosed by research criteria: An 8-year prospective follow-up study. *American Academy of Child & Adolescent Psychiatry, 29,* 546–557.

Barnes, G. M., Farrell, M. P., & Cairns, A. L. (1986). Parental socialization factors and adolescent drinking behaviors. *Journal of Marriage and the Family, 48,* 27–36.

Barnett, W., & Spitzer, M. (1994). Pathological fire-setting 1951–1991: A review. *Medicine and the Law, 34,* 4–20.

Baron, L., & Straus, M. A. (1987). Four theories of rape: A macrosociological analysis. *Social Problems, 34,* 467–489.

Baron, R. A., & Richardson, D. C. (1994). *Human aggression* (2nd ed.).

Barrett, S. (2005, February 15). Insurance fraud and abuse: A very serious problem. *Quackwatch.* Retrieved June 2, 2005, from http://www.quackwatch.org/02Consumer Protection/insfraud.html

Barry, K. L., Fleming, M. F., & Maxwell, L. B. (1997). Conduct disorder and antisocial personality in adult primary care patients. *Journal of Family Practice, 45,* 151–158.

Basketball debate leads to two deaths. (1997, November 12). *Washington Post,* p. D2.

Bastian, L. (1993). *Criminal Victimization, 1992.* Washington, DC: Bureau of Justice Statistics.

Bastian, L. D., & Taylor, B. M. (1991). *School crime: A national crime victimization survey report.* Washington, DC: Bureau of Justice Statistics.

Bateson v. Kentucky, 476 U.S. 79 (1986).

Baumeister, R. (1995). Self and identity: an introduction. In A. Tesser (Ed.), *Advanced social psychology* (pp. 51-98). New York: McGraw-Hill.

Baumer, T. L., Maxfield, M. G., & Mendelsohn, R. I. (1993). A comparative analysis of three electronically monitored home detention programs. *Justice Quarterly, 10,* 121–142.

Baumer, T. L., & Mendelsohn, R. I. (1992). Electronically monitored home confinement: Does it work? In J. M. Byrne, A. J. Lurigio, and J. Petersilia (Eds.), *Smart sentencing: The emergence of intermediate sanctions.* Newbury Park, CA: Sage.

Baumrind, D. (1973). The development of instrumental competence through socialization. In A. D. Pick (Ed.), *Minnesota symposia on child psychology* (Vol. 7, pp. 3–46). Minneapolis: University of Minnesota Press.

Bauserman, R. (1996). Sexual aggression and pornography: A review of correlational research. *Basic & Applied Social Psychology, 18,* 405–427.

Beck, A. J. (2000). *Prisoners in 1999.* Washington, DC: U.S. Department of Justice, Office of Justice Programs, Bureau of Justice Statistics.

Becker, B. C. (1980, December). Jury nullification: Can a jury be trusted? *Trial, 37,* 58–59.

Beirne, P., & Messesrschmidt, J. (1991). *Criminology.* San Diego: Harcourt Brace.

Bell, P. A. (1992). In defense of the negative affect escape model of heat and aggression. *Psychological Bulletin, 111,* 342–346.

Bell, P. A., Fisher, J. D., Baum, A., & Greene, T. (1996). *Environmental psychology* (4th ed.). Fort Worth, TX: Holt, Rinehart & Winston.

Bell, P. A., Greene, T. C., Fisher, J. D., & Baum, A. (2001). *Environmental psychology* (5th ed.). LOCATION: PUBLISHER.

Bender, L. (1959). Children and adolescents who have killed. *American Journal of Psychiatry, 116,* 510–516.

Benignus, V. A. (1981). Effect of age and body lead burden on CN function in young children: II. EEG Spectra. *Electroencephalography and Clinical Neurophysiology, 52,* 240–248.

Bennett, L A., & Wolin, S. J. (1990). Family culture and alcoholism transmission. In R. L. Collins, K. E. Leonard, & J. S. Seales (Eds.), *Alcohol and the family: Research and clinical perspectives* (pp. 194–219). New York: Guilford.

Benson, M., & Moore, E. (1992). Are white-collar and common offenders the same? An empirical and theoretical critique of a recently proposed general theory of crime. *Journal of Research in Crime and Delinquency, 29,* 251–272.

Benton, D. Hypoglycemia and aggression: A review. *International Journal of Neuroscience, 41,* 163–198.

Berkowitz, L. (1962). *Aggression: A social-psychological analysis.* New York: McGraw-Hill.

Berkowitz, L. (1970). The contagion of violence: A S-R mediational analysis of some effects of observed aggression. In W. J. Arnold & M. M. Page (Eds.), *Nebraska Symposium on Motivation* (Vol. 18, pp. 95–135). Lincoln, NE: University of Nebraska Press.

Berkowitz, L. (1973). Control of aggression. In B. M. Caldwell & Ricciuti (Eds.), *Review of child development research* (Vol. 3, pp. 95–140). Chicago: University of Chicago Press.

Berkowitz, L. (1993). *Aggression: Its causes, consequences, and control.* Philadelphia: Temple University Press.

Berkowitz, L. (1994). Some observations prompted by the Cognitive-neoassociationist view of anger and emotional aggression. In L. R. Huesmann (Ed.), Human aggression: Current perspectives, pp. 35–60. New York: Plenum.

Berlin, F. & Kraut, E. (1986). Pedophilia: Diagnostic Concepts–Treatment and Ethical Considerations. *American Journal of Forensic Psychiatry, VII*(I), 13–29.

Berndt, T. (1982). The features and effects of friendships in early adolescence. *Child Development, 53,* 1447–1469.

Berndt, T., & Perry, T. B. (1986). Children's perceptions of friendships as supportive relationships. *Developmental psychology, 22,* 640–648.

Bernstein, D. A., Clarke-Stewart, A., Roy, E. J., & Wickens, C. D. (1997). *Psychology* (4th ed.). Boston: Houghton Mifflin.

Bernstein, D. A., Clarke-Stewart, A., Roy, E. J., & Wickens, C. D. (2000). *Psychology* (5th ed.). Boston: Houghton Mifflin.

Bernstein, R., & Seltzer, T. (2004). *The role of mental health courts in system reform.* Washington, DC: The Judge David L. Bazelon Center for Mental Health Law. Retrieved from http:// www.bazelon.org/issues/criminalization/publications/ mentalhealthcourts/

Biederman, J. (1986). A family study of patients with attention deficit disorder and normal controls. *Journal of Psychiatric Research, 20,* 263–274.

Biederman, J. Faraone, S.V., & Mick, E. (1999). Clinical correlates of attention deficit hyperactivity disorder in females: Findings from a large group of pediatrically and psychiatrically referred girls. *Journal of American Academy of Child and Adolescent Psychiatry, 38,* 966–975.

Biederman, J., Faraone, S., Milberger, S. Guite, J., Mick, E., & Chen, L. (1996). A prospective 4-year follow-up study of attention deficit hyperactivity and related disorders. *Archives of General Psychiatry, 53,* 437–446.

Biederman, J., Faraone, S., Milberger, S., & Jetton, J. (1996). Is childhood oppositional defiant disorder a precursor to adolescent conduct disorder? Findings from a four-year follow-up study of children with ADHD. *Journal of the American Academy of Child & Adolescent Psychiatry, 35,* 1193–1204.

Biederman, J., Rosenbaum, J. F., Hirshfeld, D. R., Farone, S. V., Bolduc, E. A., Gersten, M., et al. (1990). Psychiatric correlates of behavioral inhibition in young children of parents with and without psychiatric disorders. *Archives of General Psychiatry, 47,* 21–26.

Binstein, M., & Bowden, C. (1993). *Trust me: Charles Keating and the missing billions.* New York: Random House.

Birnbaum, K. (1914). *Die Psychopathischen Verbrecher* (2nd ed.). Leipzig, Germany: Thieme.

Biron, L., Brochu, S., & Desjardins, L. (1995). The issue of drugs and crime among a sample of incarcerated women. *Deviant Behavior, 16,* 25–43.

Bishop, D. M., Frazier, C. E., Lanza-Kaduce, L., & Winner, L. (1996). The transfer of juveniles to criminal court: Does it make a difference? *Crime and Delinquency 42,* 171–191.

Bishop, E., & Slowikowski, J. (1995, August). *Hate crime* (Fact Sheet No. 29). Washington, DC: U.S. Department of Justice, Office of Juvenile Justice and Delinquency Prevention.

Bishop, S. M., & Ingersoll, G. M. (1989). Effects of marital conflict and family structure on the self-concepts of pre-and early adolescents. *Journal of Youth and Adolescence, 18,* 25–38.

Biskupic, J. (1998a, June 12). Court upholds hate crime penalties. *The Washington Post,* p. A1.

Biskupic, J. (1998b, May 19). Insanity hearing allowed for inmate on death row. *The Washington Post,* p. A2.

Biskupic, J. (1999a). Court declines shoplifter's "3 strikes" appeal. *The Washington Post,* p. A6.

Biskupic, J. (1999b, February 8). Increasingly, Jurors turn duty into a powerful protest. *The Washington Post,* pp. A1, A6, A7.

Biskupic, J. (1999c, May 16). Justice O'Connor calls for "concrete action" to fight bias. *The Washington Post,* p. A5.

Bjorkly, S. (1997). Clinical assessment of dangerousness in psychotic patients: Some risk indicators and pitfalls. *Aggression and violent behavior, 2,* 167–178.

BJS Compendium. (2002). *Correctional populations, 2001.*

Black, D. A. (1999). *Partner, child abuse risk factor literature review: National Network of Family Resiliency, National Network for Health.* Retrieved August XX, 2004 from http://www.nnh.org/risk

Black, D. W. (1999). *Bad boys, bad men: Confronting anti-social personality disorder.* New York: Oxford University Press.

Black, R. (1999, Nov 4). McKinney convicted in Shepard murder. Daily Camera. Retrieved May 30, 2006 from http://www.thedailycamera.com/extra/shepard/04agay. html

Blackburn, R. (1968). Personality in relation to extreme aggression in psychiatric offenders. *British Journal of Psychiatry, 114,* 821–828.

Blackburn, R. (1971). Personality types among abnormal homicides. *British Journal of Criminology, 11,* 14–31.

Blackburn, R. (1993). *The psychology of criminal conduct.* Chichester, England: Wiley.

Blackstone, Sir William. (1679). *Commentaries on the laws of England.*

Blair, J. (2000, January 2). Boot camps: An idea whose time came and went. *New York Times Week in Review,* p. 3.

Blair, R. J. R. (1997). Moral reasoning and the child with psychopathic tendencies. *Personality and Individual Differences, 22,* 731–739.

Blair, R. J. R., Jones, L., Clark, F., & Smith, M. (1997). The psychopathic individual: A lack of responsiveness to distress cues? *Psychophysiology, 34,* 192–198.

Blaszczynski, A., & McConaghy, N. (1994). Criminal offenses in Gamblers Anonymous and hospital treated pathological gamblers. *Journal of Gambling Studies, 10*(2), 99–127.

Blatt, S., & Lerner, H. (1983). The psychological assessment of object representation. *Journal of Personality Assessment, 47,* 7–27.

Bleichfeld, B., & Moely, B. (1984). Psychophysiological responses to an infant cry: Comparison of groups of women in different phases of the maternal cycle. *Developmental Psychology, 20,* 1082–1091.

Block, A. A., & Scarpitti, F. (1985). *Poisoning for profit: The Mafia and toxic waste in America.* New York: Morrow.

Block, R., Felson, M., & Block, C. R. (1984). Crime victimization rates for incumbents of 246 occupations. *Sociology and Social Research, 69,* 442–451.

Blum, J. (1998, April 15). Drowsy driver gets five-year sentence. *The Washington Post,* pp. A1, A14.

Blumstein, A. (1995, August). Violence by young people: Why the deadly nexus? *National Institute of Justice Journal,* 2–9.

Blumstein, A., Cohen, J., & Hsieh, P. (1982). *The duration of adult criminal careers. Final report to the national institute of justice.* Washington, DC: National Institute of Justice.

Boehnert, C. (1989). Characteristics of successful and unsuccessful insanity pleas. *Law and Human Behavior, 13,* 31–40.

Bohman, M. (1978). Some genetic aspects of alcoholism and criminality. *Archives of General Psychiatry, 35,* 269–276.

Bonczar, T. P. (2003). *Prevalence of imprisonment in the U.S. population, 1974–2001.* Washington, DC: U.S. Department of Justice, Office of Justice Programs, Bureau of Justice Statistics. Retrieved June 9, 2005, from http://www.ojp.usdoj.gov/bjs/pub/ascii/piusp01. txt

Bonnie, R. (1980). Psychiatry and the death penalty: Emerging problems in Virginia. *Virginia Law Review, 66,* 167–198.

Booth, A., Shelley, G., Mazur, A., Tharp, G., & Kittok, R. (1989). Testosterone, and willing and losing in human competition. *Hormones and Behavior, 23,* 556–571.

Booth, W. (1998a, May 5). Courts death row quandary: How crazy is too crazy to die? *The Washington Post,* p. A3.

Booth, W. (1998b, August 14). Girl's murder focuses light on hidden specter of sibling abuse. *The Washington Post,* p. A3.

Borum, R., & Applebaum, k. (1996). Epilepsy, aggression, and criminal responsibility. *Psychiatric Services, 47,* 762–763.

Boston Globe. (1995, November 28). Hollywood is blamed in token booth attack.

Boston Globe. (1997, August 15). L. I. man turns in son: Says he admitted killing for thrill.

Boswell, A. A., & Spade, J. Z. (1996). Fraternities and collegiate rape culture: Why are some fraternities more dangerous places for women? *Gender & Society, 10,* 133–147.

Bosworth, K., Espelage, D. L., & Simon, T. R. (1999). Factors associated with bullying behavior in middle school students. *The Journal of Early Adolescence, 19,* 341–362.

Bottcher, J., Isorena, T., & Belnas, M. (1996). *Lead: A boot camp and intensive parole program: An impact evaluation: second year findings.* CITY: State of California, Department of Youth Authority, Research Division.

Bouchard, T. J., Jr., & McGue, M. (1981). Familial studies of intelligence: A review. *Science, 212,* 1055–1059.

Boudouris, J., & Turnbull, B. W. (1985). Shock probation in Iowa. *Journal of Offender Counseling Services and Rehabilitation, 9,* 53–67.

Boudreau, J., Kwan, Q., Faragher, W., & Denault, G. (1977). *Arson and arson investigation.* Washington, DC: U.S. Government Printing Office.

Boukydis, D. F. Z., & Burgess, R. L. (1982). Adult physiological response to infant cries: Effects of temperament of infant, parental status, and gender. *Child Development, 53,* 1291–1298.

Bourgois, P. (1996). In search of masculinity: Violence, respect and sexuality among Puerto Rican crack dealers in East Harlem. *British Journal of Criminology, 36,* 412–427.

Bowers, L., Jefferson, D., Strand, J., & Grohmann, J. (1991). *Sexual assaults in Wisconsin, 1990.* Madison: Wisconsin Statistical Analysis Center.

Bowers v. Hardwick, 478 U.S. 186 (1986).

Bowker, Arbitell, & McFerron. (1988). On the relationship between wife beating and child abuse. In K. Yllo & M. Bogard (Eds.), *Perspectives on wife abuse.* Thousand Oaks, CA: Sage.

Bowker, L. H. (1980). *Prison victimization.* New York: Elsevier.

Bowlby, J. (1969). *Attachment and loss: Vol. 1. Attachment.* New York: Basic Books.

Boy's murder confession tossed. (1998, May 8). *Washington Post,* p. A25.

Bradford, J. M. W. (1982). Arson: A clinical study. *Canadian Journal of Psychiatry, 27,* 188–193.

Bradley, P. (2004, December 16). Northern Virginia pain doctor guilty: Jury convicts him on 50 counts. *Richmond Times-Dispatch.* Retrieved January 8, 2005, from http://www.timesdispatch.com/servlet/Satellite? pagename=RTD/MGArticle/RTD_BasicArticle&c= MGArticle&cid=1031779707618

Brady, J. (1983). Arson, urban economy, and organized crime: The case of Boston. *Social Problems, 31,* 1–27.

Braithwaite, J. (1989a). Criminological theory and organizational crime. *Justice Quarterly, 6,* 333–358.

Braithwaite, J. (1989b). *Crime, shame and reintegration.* Cambridge, England: Cambridge University Press.

Brannon, L. (2005). *Gender: Psychological perspectives* (4th ed.). Boston: Allyn & Bacon.

Brantingham, P.L., & Brantingham, P.J. (1981). Notes on the geometry of crime. In P.J. Brantingham & P.L. Brantingham (Eds.), *Environmental criminology.* Beverly Hills, CA.

Bray, R. M., & Noble, A. M. (1978). Authoritarianism and decisions of mock juries: Evidence of jury bias and group polarization. *Journal of Personality and Social Psychology, 36,* 1424–1430.

Breeke, N. J., Enko, P. J., Claret, G., & Seesaw, E. (1991). Of juries and court-appointed experts: The impact of nonadversarial versus adversarial expert testimony. *Law and Human Behavior, 15,* 451–475.

Brehm, J.W. (1966). A theory of psychological reactance. New York: Academic Press.

Brehm, S. S., & Kassin, S. M. (2005). *Social psychology* (6th ed.). Boston: Houghton-Mifflin.

Bremer, J. (1959). *Asexualization.* New York: Macmillan.

Bridges, L. J., & Grolnick, W. S. (1995). The development of emotional self-regulation in infancy and early childhood. In N. Eisenberg (Ed.), *Social development: Review of personality and social psychology.* Thousand Oaks, CA: Sage.

Brier, N. (1989). The relationship between learning disability and delinquency: A review and reappraisal. *Journal of Learning Disabilities, 22,* 546–553.

Brockman, E. S. (1999, March 21). A prisoner of fame and the state of Louisiana. *The New York Times Week in Review,* p. 5.

Brody, J. E. (1999, March 15). Study says early social interaction averts risky teenage behavior. *The New York Times.* Retrieved March 22, 1999, from http://www.nytimes.com/library/national/031599early_intervention.html

Brody, N., & Ehrlichmann, H. (1998). *Personality psychology: The science of individuality.* Upper Saddle River, NJ: Prentice-Hall.

Broidy, L. (1995). Direct supervision and delinquency: Assessing the adequacy of structural proxies. *Journal of Criminal Justice, 23,* 541–554.

Bronfenbrenner, U. (1979). *The ecology of human development.* Cambridge, MA: Harvard University Press.

Bronson, W. C. (1975). Development of behavior with age-mates using the second year of life. In M. Lewis & L. A Rosenblum (Eds.). *The origins of behavior: Friendship and peer relations.* New York: Wiley.

Brook, J. S., Whiteman, M., Cohen, P., & Tanaka, J. S. (1991). Childhood precursors of adolescent drug use: A longitudinal analysis. *Genetic, Social, and General Psychology Monographs, 118,* 195–213.

Brook, J. S., Whiteman, M., Gordon, A. S., & Brook, D. W. (1990). The psychosocial etiology of adolescent drug use: A family interactional approach. *Genetic, Social, and General Psychology Monographs, 116,* 113–267.

Brooke, J. S., Whiteman, M., Hamburg, B. A., & Balka, E. B. (1992). African-American and Puerto Rican drug use: Personality, familial, and other environmental risk factors. *Genetic, Social, and General Psychology Monographs, 118,* 417–438.

Brooks, A. D. (1974). *Law, psychiatry and the mental health system.* Boston: Little, Brown.

Broome, J. (2000, March 9–10). *Transnational crime in the 21st century.* Paper presented at the Transnational Crime Conference, Canberra, Australia. Retrieved June 2, 2005, from http://www.wjin.net/Pubs/2381.pdf

Brown, B.B. (1979, August). Territoriality and residential burglary. Paper presented at the meeting of the American Psychological Association, New York, NY.

Brown, D. (1988). *Bury my heart at Wounded Knee: An Indian history of the American west.* New York: Holt.

Brown, M. P. (1998, January). Juvenile offenders: Should they be tried in adult courts? *USA Today Magazine,* pp. 52–54.

Brown, S. E., Esbensen, F. A., & Geis, G. (1995). *Criminology: Explaining crime and its context* (2nd ed.). Cincinnati, OH: Anderson.

Brownmiller, S. (1975). *Against our will: Men, women, and rape.* New York: Simon & Schuster.

Brownstein, H. H. (1991). The media and the construction of random drug violence. *Social Justice, 18,* 85–103.

Bruni, F. (1998, November 22). Behind the jokes, a life of pain and delusion. *The New York Times,* pp. 41–42.

Bruni, F. (1999, February 21). Behind police brutality: Public assent. *The New York Times Week in Review,* p. 1, 6.

Bruni, F. (1999, November 22). Behind the jokes, a life of pain and delusion. *New York Times.* Retrieved May 30, 2006 from http://query.nytimes.com/gst/fullpage.html?res=9E0CE7DC1130F931A15752C1A96E958260&sec=health&pagewanted=print

Brussel, J. A. (1978). *Casebook of a crime psychiatrist.* New York: Bernard Geis Associates.

Buckner, J. C., & Chesney-Lind, M. (1983). Dramatic cures for juvenile crime: An evaluation of a prison-run delinquency prevention program. *Criminal Justice and Behavior, 10,* 227–247.

Buikhuisen, W. (1982). Aggressive behavior and cognitive disorders. *International Journal of Law and Psychiatry, 5,* 205–217.

Buikhuisen, W. (1987). Cerebral dysfunctions and persistent juvenile delinquency. *Drug Abuse and Alcoholism Newsletter, 9*(2), 1–4.

Bukatko, D., & Daehler, M. (2004). *Child development: A thematic approach* (5th ed.). Boston: Houghton Mifflin.

Bumbry, K. M., & Hansen, D. J. (1997). Intimacy deficits, fear of intimacy, and loneliness among sexual offenders. *Criminal Justice & Behavior, 24,* 315–331.

Bureau of Justice Statistics. (1993a). *Prisons and prisoners.* Washington, DC: U.S. Government Printing Office.

Bureau of Justice Statistics. (1993b). *Survey of state prison inmates, 1991.* Washington, DC: National Institute of Justice.

304 References

Bureau of Justice Statistics. (1997). *A policymaker's guide to hate crimes* (Series: BJA Monograph). Washington, DC: Bureau of Justice Statistics. Redo

Bureau of Justice Statistics. (1998a). *Criminal victimization—1997*. Washington, DC: U.S. Department of Justice, Office of Justice Programs.

Bureau of Justice Statistics. (1998b). *Four in ten criminal offenders report alcohol as a factor in violence.* Washington, DC: U.S. Department of Justice.

Bureau of Justice Statistics. (1999). *Correctional populations in the United States, 1996.* Washington, DC: Author.

Bureau of Justice Statistics. (2000). *Criminal victimization in the United States 1999.* Washington, DC: U.S. Department of Justice, Office of Justice Programs.

Bureau of Justice Statistics. (2002a). *Drug use and crime.* Washington, DC: Office of Justice Programs, U.S. Department of Justice. Retrieved August 3, 2003, from http://www.ojp.usdoj.gov/bjs/dcf/duc.htm

Bureau of Justice Statistics. (2002b). *Recidivism of prisoners released in 1994.* Washington, DC. U.S. Department of Justice, Office of Justice Programs. Retrieved from http://www. cor.state. pa.us/stats/lib/stats/BJS%20Recidivism%20 Study.pdf

Bureau of Justice Statistics. (2003a). *Compendium of Federal Justice Statistics, 2002.* Washington, DC: Bureau of Justice Statistics, Office of Justice Programs, U.S. Department of Justice.

Bureau of Justice Statistics. (2003b). *Criminal offender statistics: Lifetime likelihood of going to state or federal prison.* Retrieved May 26, 2003, from http://www.ojp.usdoj.gov/bjs/crimoff.htm

Bursik, R. (1988). Social disorganization and theories of crime and delinquency: Problems and prospects. *Criminology, 26,* 531–539.

Bursik, R. J., & Webb, J. (1982). Community change and patterns of delinquency. *American Journal of Sociology, 99,* 24–42.

Burton, V., Cullen, F., Evans, T. D., Dunaway, R. G., Kethineni, S., & Payne, G. (1995). The impact of parental controls on delinquency. *Journal of Criminal Justice, 23,* 111–126.

Bushman, B.J., Baumeister, R., & Stack, A.D. (1999). Catharsis, aggression and persuasive influence: Self-fulfilling or self-defeating prophecies?" *Journal of Personality and Social Psychology, 76*(3), 367–377.

Buss, A. H. (1966). *Psychopathology.* New York: Wiley.

Buss, D. M. (1995a). Evolutionary psychology: A new paradigm for psychological science. *Psychological Inquiry, 6,* 1–30.

Buss, D. M. (1995b). The future of evolutionary psychology. *Psychological Inquiry, 6,* 81–87.

Butcher, S. H. (1951). *Aristotle's theory of poetry and fine art.* New York: Dover.

Butcher, J. N., Dahlstrom, W. G., Graham, J. R., Tellegen, A., & Kaemmer, B. (1989). *MMPI–2: Minnesota Multiphasic Personality Inventory–2: Manual for administration and scoring.* Minneapolis: University of Minnesota Press.

Butler, D. R., Ray, A., & Gregory, L. (2000). *America's dumbest criminals from the hit TV show.* New York: Gramercy.

Butcher,J. N., William, C. L., Graham, J. R., Archer, R. P., Tellegen, A., Ben-Porath, Y.S., and Kaemmer, B. (1996/2006). Minnesota Multiphasis Personality Inventory-Adolescent (MMPI-A). Eagan, MN: Pearson Assessments.

Butterfield, F. (1995, November 19). Crime continues to decline, but experts warn of coming storm of juvenile violence. *New York Times,* p. A1.

Butterfield, F. (1998, March 5). By default, jails become mental institutions. *The New York Times.* Retrieved May 6, 1999, from http://www.nami.org/update/ 980305.html

Butterfield, J. (1997, August 17). Study links violence rate to cohesion in community. *The New York Times,* p. A21.

Butterfield, F. (2000, May 18). Study shows racial divide in domestic violence cases. *New York Times.* Retrieved May 18, 2000 from www.nytimes.com

Butts, J. A. (1997). *Delinquency cases waived to criminal court, 1985–1994.* Washington, DC: Office of Juvenile Justice & Delinquency Prevention.

Cacciolla, J. S., Rutherford, M. J., Alterman, A. I., & Snider, E. C. (1994). An examination of the diagnostic criteria for antisocial personality disorder in substance abusers. *Journal of Nervous & Mental Disease, 182,* 517–523.

Cadoret, R. J. (1985). Alcoholism and antisocial personality: Interrelationships, genetic and environmental factors. *Archives of General Psychiatry, 42,* 161–167.

Cadoret, R. J. (1990). Genetics of alcoholism. In R. I. Collins, K E. Leonard, & J. S. Searles (Eds.), *Alcohol and the family: Research and clinical perspectives* (pp. 39–78).

Cairns, R., Cairns, B., Neckerman, J., Ferguson, L., & Gariepy, J. (1989). Growth and aggression: Childhood to early adolescence. *Developmental Psychology, 25,* 320–330.

Calhoun, J.B. (1962). Population density and social pathology. *Scientific American, 206,* 139–148.

Calhoun, G., Jurgens, J., & Chen, F. (1993). The neophyte female delinquent: A review of the literature. *Adolescence, 28,* 461–471.

Callahan, C., & Rivara, F. (1992). Urban high school youth and handguns. *Journal of the American Medical Association, 267,* 3038–3042.

Cambor, R., & Millman, R. B. (1991). Alcohol and drug abuse in adolescents. In M. Lewis (Ed.), *Child and adolescent psychiatry: A comprehensive textbook* (pp. 736–754).

Camp, G. M., & Camp, C. G. (1985). *Prison gangs: Their extent, nature, and impact on prisons.* Washington, DC: U.S. Government Printing Office.

Campbell, A. (1993). *Men, women, and aggression.* New York: Basic Books.

Campbell, A. (1994). *The girls in the gang.* Oxford, England: Basil Blackwell.

Campbell, C., & Robinson, J. (1977). Family and employment status associated with women's criminal behavior. *Psychological Reports, 80,* 307–314.

Campbell, H. (1967). The violent sex offender: A consideration of emasculation in treatment. *Rocky Mountain Medical Journal, 64,* 40–43.

Campbell, S. B. (1990). The socialization and social development of hyperactive children. In M. Lewis & S. M. Miller (Eds.), *Handbook of developmental psychopathology.* New York: Plenum.

Camus, A. (1956). The fall. New York: Vintage Press.

Cantelon, S. (1994). *Family strengthening or high-risk youth* (Fact Sheet No. 8). Washington, DC: Office of Juvenile Justice and Delinquency Prevention.

Cantwell, D. P. (1979). Minimal brain dysfunction in adults: Evidence from studies of psychiatric illness in the families of hyperactive children. In L. Bellak (Ed.), *Psychiatric aspects of minimal brain dysfunction in adults* (pp. 37–44). New York: Grune & Stratton.

Cappella, J. N., & Greene, J.O, (1982). A discrepancy-arousal explanation of mutual influence in expressive behavior in adult and infant-adult interactions. *Communication Monographs, 49,* 89–114.

Capra, F. (1996). *The web of life: A new scientific understanding of living systems.* New York: Anchor Books.

Carlson, V., Cicchetti, D., Barnett, D., & Braunwald, K. (1989). Disorganized/disoriented attachment relationships in maltreated infants. *Developmental Psychology, 25,* 525–531.

Carmody, J. (1998, March 12). Sounds very familiar. *The Washington Post,* p. C5.

Carroll, L. (1974). *Hacks, blacks, and cons: Race relations in a maximum security prison.* Prospect Heights, IL: Waveland Press.

Carroll, L. (1988). Race, ethnicity, and the social order of prison. In R. Johnson & H. Toch (Eds.), *The pains of imprisonment* (pp. 181–203). Prospect Heights, IL: Waveland Press.

Carter, N. (1995). Increased theft as a side effect of sales promotion activities: An exploratory study. *Journal of Business & Psychology, 10,* 57–64.

Casanova, G. M., Domanic, J., McCanne, T., & Milner, J. (1992). Physiological response to non-child-related stressors in mothers at risk for child abuse. *Child Abuse and Neglect, 16,* 31–44.

Caspi, A., Lyman, D., Moffitt, T., & Silvla, P. (1993). Unraveling girls' delinquency: Biological, dispositional, and contextual contributions to adolescent misbehavior. *Developmental Psychology, 29,* 283–289.

Caspi, A., Moffitt, T. E., Silva. P. A., Loeber- Stouthamer, M., Krueger, R. F., & Schmutte, P. S. (1994). Are some people crime-prone? *Criminology, 32,* 163–95.

Cass, S. A., & Kovera, M B. (2001). Research on the effects of child pornography needed. *Monitor on Psychology, 32*(4). Retrieved May 25, 2003, from http://www.apa. org/monitor/apr01/in.html

Cassel, E. (2002a, March 18). The Andrea Yates verdict and sentence: Did the jury do the right thing? *FindLaw's Writ.* Retrieved June 23, 2004, from http://writ.news. findlaw.com/commentary/20020318_cassel.html

Cassel, E. (2002b, April 5). The prisonization of America as a shameful social problem. *Findlaw's Writ.* Retrieved from http:// writ.news. findlaw.com/books/reviews/20020405_cassel.html

Cassel, E. (2002c, February 21). Why the Supreme Court may reverse itself this term, to hold, in a new case, and rule that execution of the mentally retarded is unconstitutional. *Findlaw's Writ.* Retrieved from http://writ.news.findlaw.com/cassel/ 20020221.html

Cassel, E. (2004, February 12). Prosecutor misconduct in two recent high-profile cases: Why it happens and how we can better prevent it. *FindLaw's Writ.* Retrieved June 23, 2004, from http://writ.news.findlaw.com/cassel/ 20040212.html

Cassel, E. (2005, February 3). Did Zoloft make him do it? *Findlaw's Writ.* Retrieved from http://writ.news.findlaw.com/cassel/20050203.html

Castillo, D. N., & Jenkins, E. L. (1994). Industries and occupations at high risk for work-related homicide. *Journal of Occupational Medicine, 36,* 128–129.

Catalano, S. M. (2004). *Criminal victimization, 2003.* Washington, DC: U.S. Department of Justice, Office of Justice Programs, Bureau of Justice Statistics, National Crime Victimization Survey. Retrieved June 3, 2005, from http://www.ojp.usdoj.gov/bjs/pub/ascii/cv03.txt

Cattell, R. B. (1982). *The inheritance of personality and ability: Research methods and findings.* New York: Academic.

Cavior, H., & Howard, L. R. (1973). Facial attractiveness and juvenile delinquency among black offenders and white offenders. *Journal of Abnormal Child Psychology, 1,* 202–213.

Cavior, H., & Schmidt. (1978). Test of the effectiveness of a differential treatment strategy at the Robert F. Kennedy Center. *Criminal Justice and Behavior, 5,* 131–139.

Cazalas, M. (1998, December 12). Faison not guilty by reason of insanity. *The News Herald.* Retrieved April 16, 1999, from http://www.newsherald.com/archive/local/ld121298.htm

Center for Wrongful Convictions. (2003). The Illinois Exonerated: Anthony Porter. Retrieved June 1, 2006 from http://www.law.northwestern.edu/depts/clinic/wrongful/exonerations/porter.htm

Center on Crime, Communities and Culture. (1996). *Mental illness in U.S. jails: Diverting the nonviolent, low-level offender* (Research brief). New York: Author.

Centers for Disease Control. (1999). Firearm mortality. *National Vital Statistics Reports, 47*(19). Retrieved December 7, 1999, from http://www.cdc.gov.nchs/fastats/firearms.htm

Centers for Disease Control and Prevention. (1995, March). CDC surveillance summaries. *Mortality and Morbidity Weekly Report, 44,* SS–1.

Centers for Disease Control and Prevention. (1996). *Youth Risk Behavior Surveillance—United States, 1995.* Atlanta, GA: Author.

Centers for Disease Control and Prevention. (1997). Rates of homicide, suicide, and firearm-related deaths among children: 26 industrialized countries. *MMWR Morbidity and Mortality Weekly Report, 46,* 101–105.

Centers for Disease Control and Prevention. (1998). Youth risk behavior surveillance—United States, 1997. *Mortality and Morbidity Weekly Report, 47,* SS–3.

Centers for Disease Control and Prevention. (2001). *National Vital Statistics Report, 49*(12), p. 16.

Centers for Disease Control and Prevention. (2002, June 28). Youth Risk Behavior Surveillance—United States, 2001. *MMWR Surveillance Summaries, 51*(SSO4), 1–64.

Centers for Disease Control and Prevention. (2003). *Costs of intimate partner violence against women in the United States.* Atlanta, GA: U.S. Department of Health and Human Services.

Centers for Disease Control and Prevention. (2004). Youth risk behavior surveillance—United States, 2003. *Morbidity & Mortality Weekly Report, 53*(SS–2): 1B29. Retrieved June 3, 2005, from http://www.cdc.gov/mmwr/PDF/SS/SS5302.pdf

Centerwall, B. (1989). Exposure to television as a risk factor for violence. *American Journal of Epidemiology, 129,* 643–652.

Chaiken, J. M. (2000, January). Crunching numbers: Crime and incarceration at the end of the millennium. National Institute of Justice Journal. Retrieved March 2, 2000 from, www.ncjrs.org.

Chambliss, W. (1964). A sociological analysis of the law of vagrancy. *Social Problems, 12,* 67–77.

Chartered Institute of Building. (2004, September 29). *World bank finds corruption is costing billions in lost development power.* Retrieved June 2, 2005, from http://www.odiousdebts.org/odiousdebts/index.cfm?DSP'content&ContentID'11519

Chassin, L., Pillow, D., Curran, P., Mollina, B., & Barrera, M. (1993). Relation of parental alcoholism to early adolescent substance use: A test of three mediating mechanisms. *Journal of Abnormal Psychology, 102,* 3–19.

Chatz, T. (1972). Management of male adolescent sex offenders. *International Journal of Offender Therapy, 2,* 109.

Chermak, S. (1995). *Victims in the news.* Boulder, CO: Westview.

Chernicky, D. (1997, October 30). Street claim life of ex-gang member. *Winchester Star,* p. A13.

Chesney-Lind, M. (1987, November). *Girls' crime and womens' place: Toward a feminist model of female delinquency.* Paper presented at the American Society of Criminology meeting, Montreal, Quebec, Canada.

Chesney-Lind, M. (1995). Rethinking women's imprisonment: A critical examination of trends in female incarceration. In B. Price and N. Sokoloff (Eds.), *The criminal justice system and women: Offenders, victims, and workers* (pp. 105–117). New York: McGraw-Hill.

Childhelp USA. (2003). *National child abuse statistics.* Retrieved February 13, 2005, from http://www.childhelpusa.org/abuseinfo_stats.htm

Child poverty surges in area. (1997, May 8). *Washington Post,* p. A1.

Childrens Defense Fund. (2004, August). *Moments in America for children.* Retrieved February 13, 2005, from http://www.childrensdefense.org/data/moments.asp

Christiansen, K. O. (1977). A preliminary study of criminality among twins. In S. Mednick & K. O. Christiansen (Eds.), *Biosocial bases of criminal behavior* (pp. 45–88).

Christianson, S. (2003, February 8). Bad seed or bad science: The story of the Notorious Jukes Family. *New York Times.* Retrieved February 8, 2003, from http://www.nytimes.com (archive no longer available).

Christie, N. (1994). *Crime control as industry: Toward gulags, western style?* (2nd ed.). London: Routledge.

Chubb Corporation. (2004, September 13). *Three in five companies anticipate an employee will steal company funds or equipment this year, Chubb survey finds.* Retrieved June 2, 2005, from http://www.chubb.com/marketing/chubb1802.html

Claiborne, W. (1997, December 21). New look for California inmates. *The Washington Post,* p. A3.

Claiborne, W. (2000, March 2). A life in chaos shaped young shooter. *The Washington Post,* pp. A1, A12.

Clarke-Stewart, K. A. (1980). The father's contribution to child development. In E. A. Pedersen (Ed.), *The father-infant relationship: Observational studies in a family context.* New York: Praeger Special Studies.

Clarke-Stewart, K. A. (1988). Parents' effects on children's development: A decade of progress? *Journal of Applied Developmental Psychology, 9,* 41–84.

Cleary, S., & Luxenburg, J. (1993, October). *Serial murderers: Common background characteristics and their contribution to causation.* Paper presented at the annual meeting of the American Society of Criminology, Miami, FL.

Cleckley, H. (1976). *The mask of sanity.* St. Louis, MO: Mosby. (Original work published 1941)

Clinard, M., & Quinney, R. (1973). *Criminal behavior systems: A typology.* New York: Holt, Rinehart & Winston.

Clinard, M., Quinney, R., & Wildeman. (1994). *Criminal behavior systems: A typology* (3rd ed.). Cincinnati, OH: Anderson Publishing Co.

Clinard, M., & Yeager, P. (1980). *Corporate crime.* New York: Free Press.

Cline, V. (1990). (Privately published monograph). Department of Psychology, University of Utah, Salt Lake City.

Cloninger, C. R. (1987). Neurogenetic adaptive mechanisms in alcoholism. *Science, 236,* 410–416.

Cloninger, C. R., Bohman, M., & Sigvardsson, S. (1981). Inheritance of alcohol abuse: Cross-fostering analysis of adopted men. *Archives of General Psychiatry, 38,* 861–868.

Cloninger, C. R., Christiansen, K. O., Reich, T., & Gottesman, I. (1978). Implications of sex differences in the prevalence of antisocial personality, alcoholism, and criminality for familial transmission. *Archives of General Psychiatry, 35,* 941–951.

Cocozza, J. J. (1992). *Responding to youth with mental disorders in the juvenile justice system.* Seattle, WA: The National Coalition for the Mentally Ill in the Criminal Justice System.

Coe, C. L., & Levin, S. (1983). Biology of aggression. *Bulletin of the American Academy of Psychiatry Law, 11,* 131–148.

Cohen, A. (1999, September 13). Innocent, after proven guilty. *Time,* 26–28.

Cohen, D. (1996). Law, social policy, and violence: The impact of regional cultures. *Journal of Personality and Social Psychology, 70,* 961–978.

Cohen, D. & Nisbett, R. (1994). Self-protection and the culture of honor: Explaining Southern Violence. *Personality and Social Psychology Bulletin, 20,* 551–567.

Cohen, D., Nisbett, R.E., Bowdle, B.F., & Schwartz, N. (1996). Insult, aggression, and the southern culture of honor: An "experimental ethnography." *Journal of Personality and Social Psychology, 70,* 945–960.

Cohen, F. (1994). Offenders with mental disorders in the criminal justice—Correctional process. In B. D. Sales & D. W. Shuman (Eds.), *Law, mental health, and mental disorder* (pp. 397–413). Pacific Grove, CA: Brooks/Cole.

Cohen, L. E., & Felson, M. (1979). Social change and crime rate trends: A routine activity approach. *American Sociological Review, 44,* 588–608.

Cohen, M. (1998). The monetary value of saving a high-risk youth. *Journal of Quantitative Criminology 14,* 5–33.

Cohen, R. (2000, February 22). Capital flaws. *The Washington Post,* p. A19.

Cohen, S. (1977). Angel dust. *Journal of the American Medical Association, 238,* 515–516.

Cohen, S. (1980). Alcoholic hypoglycemia. *Drug Abuse and Alcoholism Newsletter, 9,* 1–4.

Cohn, E.G. (1993). The prediction of police calls for service: The influence of weather and temporal variables on rape and domestic violence. *Journal of Environmental Psychology, 13,* 71–83.

Cohen, S., & Spacapan, S. (1984). The social psychology of noise. In D.M. Jones & A.J. Chapman (Eds.), *Noise and society* (pp. 221–245). Chichester: Wiley.

Cohen, D. & Nisbett, R. (1994). Self-protection and the culture of honor: Explaining Southern Violence. *Personality and Social Psychology Bulletin, 20,* 551–567.

Cohen, D., Nisbett, R.E., Bowdle, B.F., & Schwartz, N. (1996). Insult, aggression, and the southern culture of honor: An "experimental ethnography." Journal of Personality and Social Psychology, 70, 945–960.

Cohn, L. (1995). Risk-perception: Differences between adolescents and adults. *Health Psychology, 14,* 217.

Coid, B., Lewis, S. W., & Reveley, A. M. (1993). A twin study of psychosis and criminality. *British Journal of Psychiatry 162,* 87–92.

Coid, J. (1979). Mania a portu: A critical review of pathological intoxication. *Psychological Medicine, 9,* 709–719.

Coie, J. D., & Jacobs, M. R. (1993). The role of social context in the prevention of conduct disorder. *Development and Psychopathology, 5,* 263–275.

Colb, S. F. (2002). Two Florida murder trials for the killing of Terry King: When prosecutors have doubt. Findlaw.com. Retrieved May 25, 2006 at http://writ.news.findlaw.com/colb/20020910.html#continue

Colburn, D. (1999, January 19). Bizarre case of man who borrowed cars. *The Washington Post/Health,* p. 5.

Cole, D. (1999). *No equal justice: Race and class in the American criminal justice system.* New York: The New Press.

Cole, G. F. (1992). *The American system of criminal justice* (6th ed.). Pacific Grove, CA: Brooks/Cole.

Cole, M., & Cole, S. (1996). *The development of children* (3rd ed.). New York: Freeman.

Coleman, J. W. (1994). *The criminal elite* (3rd ed.). New York: St. Martin's Press.

Coleman, J. W. (1995). Respectable crimes. In J. F. Sheley (Ed.), *Criminology* (pp. 249–269). Belmont, CA: Wadsworth.

Collins, J. (1997, June 16). Day of reckoning. *Time,* 26–29.

Collins, J. & Schlenger, W. (1988). Acute and chronic effects of alcohol use on violence. *Journal of Studies on Alcohol, 4,* 516–521.

Collins, J. J., Cox, B. G., & Langan, P. A. (1987). Job activities and personal crime victimization: Implications for theory. *Social Science Research, 16,* 345–360.

Comer, J. P. (1985). Black violence and public policy. In L. Curtis (Ed.), *American violence and public policy*, pp. 63–86. New Haven, CT: Yale University Press.

Comings, D. E. (1997). Genetic aspects of childhood behavioral disorders. *Child Psychiatry & Human Development, 27,* 139–150.

Comstock, G., & Paik, H. J. (1991). *Television and the American child.* New York: Academic.

Conduit, E. (1995). Angry violence and the influence of films. *Criminal Behavior & Mental Health, 5,* 124–126.

Conger, J. J. (1956). Alcoholism: Theory, problem and challenge: II. Reinforcement theory and the dynamics of alcoholism. *Quarterly Journal of Studies on Alcohol, 101,* 139–152.

Conly, C. (1999). *Coordinating community services for mentally ill offenders: Maryland's community criminal justice treatment program.* Washington, DC: National Institute of Justice, United States Department of Justice, Office of Justice programs.

Connor, D. (1996, January). *Aggressive and antisocial behavior in the broad sense is a huge problem, and we don't know how to talk about it.* Speech presented at the New York Academy of Sciences, New York City.

Connors, E., Lundregan, T., Miller, N., & McEwen, T. (1996). *Convicted by juries, exonerated by science: Case studies in the use of DNA evidence to establish innocence after trial.* Washington, DC: U.S. Department of Justice, National Institute of Justice.

Conover, T. (2001). *Newjack: Guarding Sing Sing.* New York: Vintage.

Cook, P. J., & Moore, M. H. (1995). Gun control. In J. Q. Wilson & J. Petersilia (Eds.), *Crime.* San Francisco: ICS Press.

Cooper, J., Bennett, E. A., & Sukel, H. L. (1996). Complex scientific testimony: How do jurors make decisions? *Law and Human Behavior, 20,* 379–394.

Cooper, R. P., & Werner, P. D. (1990). Predicting violence in newly admitted inmates: A lens model analysis of staff decisions. *Criminal Justice and Behavior, 17,* 431–447.

Cooper v. Oklahoma, 517 U.S. 348 (1966).

Cornell, D. (1990). Prior adjustment of violent juvenile offenders. *Law and Human Behavior, 14,* 569–578.

Cornell, D. G. (1993). Juvenile homicide: A growing national problem. *Behavioral Sciences and the Law, 11,* 389–396.

Cornell, D. (1999). *Psychology of the school shootings* (Testimony presented at the House Judiciary Committee Oversight Hearing to Examine Youth Culture and Violence, March 13, 1999). Retrieved February 27, 2005, from http://www.apa.org/ppo/issues/pcornell.html

Cornell, D. G., Roberts, M., & Oran, G. (1997). The Rey–Osterrieth Complex Figure Test as a neuropsycholgical measure in criminal offenders. *Archives of Clinical Neuropsychology, 12,* 47–56.

Cortes, J., & Gatti, F. (1972). *Delinquency and crime: A biopsychosocial approach.* New York: Semina Press.

Cosmides, L., & Tooby, J. (1994). Beyond intuition and instinct blindness: Toward an evolutionarily rigorous cognitive science. *Cognition, 50,* 41–77.

Cowan, A. L. (2004, December 11). Onetime fugitive gets 17 years for looting insurers. *New York Times,* p. C3.

Cowles, E. L. (1992, November). *Is the boardroom immune? An assessment of drug use on employment-related financial crime.* Paper presented at the Annual Meeting of the American Society of Criminology, New Orleans, LA.

Cox, A. D., Cox, D., Anderson, R. D., & Moschis, G. P. (1993). Social influences on adolescent shoplifting: Theory, evidence, and implications for the retail industry. *Journal of Rehabilitation 69,* 234–246.

Cox, R. P. (1996). An exploration of the demographic and social correlates of criminal behavior among adolescent males. *Journal of Adolescent Health, 19,* 17–24.

Coxell, A., & King, M. B. (1996). Male victims of rape and sexual abuse. *Sexual & Marital Therapy, 11,* 297–308.

Creesey, D. (1973). *Other people's money: A study of the social psychology of embezzlement.* Glencoe, IL: Free Press.

Creesy, D. R. (1969). *Theft of the nation.* New York: Harper & Row.

Crick, N. R., & Dodge, K. A. (1994). A review and reformulation of social-information-processing mechanisms in children's social adjustment. *Psychological Bulletin, 115,* 74–101.

Crick, N. R., & Grotpeter, N. (1995). A review and reformulation of social information-processing mechanisms in children's social adjustment. *Child Development, 66,* 710–722.

Crime and Justice International. (1997, October). *Emerging gangs: An international threat?* Retrieved May 10, 1999, from http://oicj.ascp.uic.edu/spearmint/public/pubs/cji/13/09/130918.cfm

Cromwell, P., Olson, J., & Avary, D. W. (1991). *Breaking and entering: An ethnographic analysis of burglary.* Newbury Park, CA: Sage.

Crovitz, L. G. (1990, May 2). Milken's tragedy: Oh, how the mighty fall before RICO. *Wall Street Journal,* p. A17.

Crow, W. J., & Bull, J. L. (1975). *Robbery deterrence: An applied behavioral science demonstration. Final report.* La Jolla, CA: Western Behavior Sciences Institute.

Crowell, N. A., & Burgess, A. W. (1996). *Understanding violence against women.* Washington, DC: National Academy of Sciences.

Cullen, F. T. (1993). *Control in the community: The limits of reform.* Paper presented at the annual meeting of the International Association of Residential and Community Alternatives, Philadelphia.

Cullen, F. T., & Gendreau, P. (1989). The effectiveness of correctional rehabilitation: Reconsidering the "nothing works" debate. In L. Goodstein & D. Mackenzie (Eds.), *The American prison: Issues in research and policy.* New York: Plenum.

Cummings, S., & Monti, D. (1993). *Gangs: The origin and impact of contemporary youth gangs in the United States.* Albany: State University of New York Press.

Currie, E. (1998). *Crime and punishment in America.* New York: Holt/Metropolitan.

Currie, E., & Sternbach, D. (1987). Confronting crime: An American challenge. New York: Pantheon Books.

Curry, G., & Spergel, I. (1988). Gang homicide, delinquency and the community. *Criminology, 26,* 381–407.

Curtis, L. (1974). Victim-precipitation and violent crimes. *Social Problems, 21,* 594–605.

Dabbs, J., & Morris, R. (1990). Testosterone, social class, and antisocial behavior in a sample of 4,462 men. *Psychological Science, 1,* 209–211.

Dabbs, J. M., Carr, T. S., Frady, R. L., & Riad, J. K. (1995). Testosterone, crime, and misbehavior among 692 male prison inmates. *Personality and Individual Differences, 18,* 627–633.

Dahl, A. A. (1993). The personality disorders: A critical review of family, twin, and adoption studies. *Journal of Personality Disorders, 7,* 86–99.

Dalton, J. (1971). *The premenstrual syndrome.* Springfield, IL: Thomas.

Daley, K. (1989). Gender and varieties of white-collar crime. *Criminology, 27,* 769–793.

Daly, K., & Chesney-Lind, M. (1988). Feminism and criminology. *Justice Quarterly, 5,* 497–538.

Daly, M., & Wilson, M. I. (1996). Violence against stepchildren. *Current Directions in Psychological Science, 5*(3), 77–81.

Daly, M., & Wilson, M. (1997). Crime and conflict: Homicide in evolutionary psychological perspective. *Crime & Justice, 22,* 51–100. Retrieved January 8, 2005, from http://psych.mcmaster.ca/dalywilson/Crime&Conflict.pdf

Damasio, A. R. (2000). A neural basis for sociopathy. *Archives of General Psychiatry, 57,* 128–130.

Damon, W., & Hart, D. (1988). *Self-understanding in childhood and adolescence.* Cambridge, England: Cambridge University Press.

Davidson, R. T. (1974). *Chicano prisoners: The key to San Quentin.* New York: Holt, Rinehart & Winston.

Davis, D., & Beshears, E. (1998, June 19). Boy, 14, shoots himself in head. *The Washington Post,* pp. D1, D4.

Davis, G. E., & Leitenberg, H. (1987). Adolescent sex offenders. *Psychological Bulletin, 101,* 417–427.

Davis, J. H., Au, W. T., Hulbert, L., Chen, X., & Zarnoth, P. (1997). Effects of group size and procedural influence on consensual judgements of quantity: The example of damage awards and mock civil juries. *Journal of Personality and Social Psychology, 73,* 703–718.

Davis, K. D., Kirkpatrick, L. A., Levy, M. B., & OHearn, R. E. (1994). Stalking the elusive love style: Attachment styles, love styles, and relationship development. In R. Erber & R. Gilmore (Eds.), *Theoretical frameworks for personal relationships* (pp. 179–219). Hillsdale, NJ: Lawrence Erlbaum Associates, Inc.

Davis, P. (1995, October 12). If you came this way. Interview on *All Things Considered,* National Public Radio.

Davis, P. (1998a, May 27). Arlington teen guilty of murder plot. *The Washington Post,* p. D3.

Davis, P. (1998b, June 14). For police, the ticket to better relations. *The Washington Post,* pp. B1, B8.

Davis, R. C., & Smith, B. E. (1994). Victim impact statements and victim satisfaction: An unfulfilled promise? *Journal of Criminal Justice, 22,* 1–12.

Dawes, R. M., Faust, D., & Meehl, P. E. (1989). Clinical versus actuarial judgment. *Science, 243,* 1668–1674.

Dawson, J. M., & Langan, P. A. (1994). *Murder in families.* Washington, DC: U.S. Department of Justice.

Dawson, R. (1969). *Sentencing: The decision as to type, length, and conditions of sentence.* Boston: Little, Brown.

Dean, A. L., Nakuj, M. M., Richards, W., & Stringer, S. A. (1986). Effects of parental maltreatment on children's conceptions of interpersonal relationships. *Developmental Psychology, 22,* 617–626.

DeAngelis, T. (1997, June). Trauma at an early age inhibits ability to bond. *American Psychological Association Monitor, XX,* 11.

Death Penalty Information Center. (2005). Innocence and the death penalty. Retrieved June 1, 2006, from http://www.deathpenaltyinfo.org/article.php?did=412&scid=6

Decker, S., Wright, R., Redfern, A., & Smith, D. (1993). A woman's place is in the home: Females and residential burglary. *Justice Quarterly, 10,* 143–163.

Dees, M., & Corcoran, J. (1996). *Gathering storm: The story of America's militia network.* New York: HarperCollins.

DeFrances, C. J., & Steadman, G. W. (1998). *Prosecutors in state courts, 1996.* Washington, DC: Bureau of Justice Statistics.

DeFries, J. C., & Gillis, J. J. (1993). Genetics of reading disability. In R. Plomin & G. E. McClearn (Eds.), *Nature, nurture, & psychology.* Washington, DC: American Psychological Association.

DeFries, J. C., & Plomin, R. (1978). Behavioral genetics. *Annual Reviews in Psychology, 29,* 473–515.

DeFronzo, J. (1984). Climate and crime: Tests of an FBI assumption. *Environment and Behavior, 16,* 185–210.

DeHart, D. D., & Mahoney, J. M. (1994). The serial murderers motivations: An interdisciplinary review. *Omega: Journal of Death & Dying, 29*(1), 29–45.

DeKlyen, M. (1996). Disruptive behavior disorder and intergenerational attachment patterns: A Comparison of clinic-referred and normally functioning preschoolers and their mothers. *Journal of Consulting & Clinical Psychology, 64,* 357–365.

Delville, Y., DeVries, G. J., Schwartz, W. J., & Ferris, C. F. (1998). Flank-marking behavior and the neural distribution of vasopressin innervation in golden hamsters with suprachiasmatic lesions. *Behavioral Neuroscience, 112,* 1486–1501.

Demo, D., & Acock, A. (1988). The impact of divorce on children. In B. Slife (Ed.), *Taking Sides: Clashing views on controversial psychological issues* (pp. 120–128). Guilford, CT: Dushkin Publishing Co.

Denno, D. (1985). Sociological and human developmental explanations of crime: Conflict or consensus? *Criminology, 23,* 711–741.

Denton, K., & Krebs, D. (1990). From the scene to the crime: The effect of alcohol and social context on moral judgment. *Journal of Personality and Social Psychology, 59,* 242–248.

DePanfilils, D., & Brooks, G. (1989). *Child maltreatment and woman abuse: A guide for child protective services intervention.* Washington, DC: National Woman Abuse Prevention Project.

Department of Housing and Urban Development v. Rucker, et al., 535 U.S. 125 (2002).

Dershowitz, A. M. (1994). *The abuse excuse.* Boston: Little, Brown.

Dershowitz, A. M. (1996). *Reasonable doubts: The O. J. Simpson case and the criminal justice system.* New York: Simon & Schuster.

DeShaney v. Winnebago Department of Social Services, 489 U.S. 189 (1989).

Devlin, A. (1996). Criminal classes: Are there links between failure at school and future offending? *Support for Learning, 11*(1), 13–16.

DeVoe, J., Peter, K., Ruddy, S., Miller, A., Planty, M., Snyder, T., et al. (2003). *Indicators of school crime and safety.* Washington, DC: National Center for Education Statistics. Retrieved October 5, 2004, from http://nces. ed.gov/pubsearch/ pubsinfo.asp?pubid= 2004004

Devor, E. J. (1994). A developmental-genetic model of alcoholism Implications for genetic research. *Journal of Consulting and Clinical Psychology, 62,* 1108–1115.

De Vries, R. (1969). Constancy of genetic identity in the years three to six. *Monographs of the Society for Research in Child Development, 34*(X, Serial No. 127).

Diamond, S. (1983). Order in the court: Consistency in criminal court decisions. In J. Scheirer & B. Hammonds (Eds.), *Psychology and the law* (American Psychological Association Master Lecture Series, No. 2). Washington, DC: American Psychological Association.

DiAngelis, T. (1997, April). New research reveals who may molest again. *American Psychological Association Monitor, XX,* 46.

Dieter, R. C. (2005, January 25). Costs of the death penalty and related issues. Testimony before New York State Assembly, Albany, New York. Retrieved June 1, 2006 from http://www.deathpenaltyinfo.org/NY-RCD-Test.pdf

Dietrich, D., Berkowitz, L., Kadushin, A., & McGloin, J. (1990). Some factors influencing abusers' justification of their child abuse. *Child Abuse and Neglect, 14,* 337–345.

Dietz, P. E. (1991). Threatening and otherwise inappropriate letters to Hollywood celebrities. *Journal of Forensic Science, 31,* 185.

DiLalla, D. L., & Gottesman, I. I. (1995). Normal personality characteristics in identical twins discordant for schizophrenia. *Journal of Abnormal Psychology, 104,* 490–499.

Dillehay, R. C., & Nietzel, M. T. (1985). Juror experience and jury verdicts. *Law and Human Behavior, 9,* 179–191.

Dillehay, R. C., & Nietzel, M. T. (1999). Prior jury service. In W. Abbot & J. Batt (Eds.), *A handbook of jury research* (pp. 11.1–11.7). Philadelphia: American Law Institute-American Bar Association.

Ditton, P. M. (1999). *Mental health and treatment of inmates and probationers.* Special Report NJC 174463.

Washington, DC: U.S. Department of Justice, Office of Justice Progerams, Bureau of Justice Statistics.

Ditton, P. M. (1999). Mental health and treatment of inmates and probationers. (Special Report NCJ 174463). Washington, DC: U.S. Department of Justice, Office of Justice Programs, Bureau of Justice Statistics.

Dobrin, A., Wierseman, B., Colin, L., & McDowall, D. (1996). *Statistical handbook on violence in America.* Phoenix, AZ: The Oryx Press.

Dodge, K. A. (1986). A social information processing model of social competence in children. In M. Perlmutter (Ed.), *Minnesota Symposium in Child Psychology* (Vol. 18, pp. 77–125). Hillsdale, NJ: Lawrence Erlbaum Associates, Inc.

Dodge, K. A., Bates, J. E., & Pettit, G. S. (1990). Mechanisms in the cycle of violence. *Science, 250,* 1678–1683.

Dodge, K. A., & Coie, J. D. (1987). Social information-processing factors in reactive and proactive aggression in children's peer groups. *Journal of Personality and Social Psychology, 53,* 389–409.

Dodge, K. A., Pettit, G. S., McClaskey, C. L., & Brown, J. (1986). Social competence in children. *Monographs of the Society for Research in Child Development, 44*(2, Serial No. 213).

Doherty, W. J., & Needle, R. H. (1991). Psychological adjustment and substance use among adolescents before and after parental divorce. *Child development, 62,* 328–337.

Dollard, J., Doob, L., Miller, N., Mowrer, O., & Sears R. (1939). *Frustration and aggression.* New Haven, CT: Yale University Press.

Domino, E. F. (1978). Neurobiology of phencyclidine—An update. In R. C. Peterson & R. C. Stillman (Eds.), *Phencyclidine (PCP) abuse: An appraisal* (NIDA Research Monograph 21) Rockville, MD: National Institute on Drug Abuse.

Donnerstein, E., Linz, D., & Penrod, S. (1987). *Question of pornography: Research findings and implications.* New York: Free Press.

Donnerstein, E., & Wilson, D.W. (1976). Effects of noise and perceived control on ongoing and subsequent aggressive behavior. *Journal of Personality and Social psychology, 34,* 774–781.

Douglas, J. E., Burgess, A. W., Burgess, A. G., & Reseller, R. K. (1992). *Crime classification manual.* New York: Lexington.

Douglas, J. E., Ressler, R. K., Burgess, A. W., & Hartman, C. R. (1986). Criminal profiling from crime scene analysis. *Behavioral Sciences and the Law, 4,* 401–421.

Doyle, J. A. (1995). *The male experience* (3rd ed.). Dubuque, IA: Brown.

Doyle, R. (1996, December). Deaths due to alcohol. *Scientific American.*

Drake, R. E., Bartels, S. J., Teague, G. B., Moordsky, D. L., & Clark, R. E. (1993). Treatment of substance abuse in severely mentally ill patients. *Journal of Nervous and Mental Disorders, 181,* 606–611.

Duffy, B. (1996, April 15). The mad bomber? *U.S. News & World Report,* 29–35.

Dugdale. R. (1910). *The jukes.* New York: Putnam.

Duggan, P. (1999a, February 16). From beloved son to murder suspect. *The Washington Post,* p. A5.

Duggan, P. (1999b, May 16). Texas hate-crime bill dies in bitter legislative standoff. *The Washington Post,* p. A2.

Duggan, P. (2001, January 22). Massive drug sweep divides Texas town: ACLU sues as FBI probes black prosecutions. *The Washington Post,* p. A3.

Duhart, D. T. (2001). *Violence in the workplace, 1993–1999.* Washington, DC: U.S. Department of Justice, Office of Justice Programs, Bureau of Justice Statistics.

Duke, L. (2000, February 26). Jury acquits N.Y. officers. *The Washington Post,* pp. A1, A12.

Duke, S. (1983). Economic crime: Tax offenses. In S. Radish (Ed.), *Encyclopedia of crime and justice* (pp. 683–688). New York: Macmillan and Free Press.

Duncan v. Louisiana, 391 U.S. 145 (1968).

Dunn, J. (1988). Annotation. Sibling influences on childhood development. *Journal of Child Psychology and Psychiatry, 29,* 119–127.

Durham v. United States, 214 F. 2d 862 (1954).

Durkheim, E. (1938/1997). *The rules of sociological method.* In P. Adler & P. Adler (Eds.), *Constructions of deviance: Social power, context, & interaction* (2nd ed., pp. 15–19). Belmont, CA: Wadsworth.

Dusky v. United States, 362 U.S. 401 (1960).

Dweck, C. S., & Licht, B. G. (1980). Learned helplessness and intellectual achievement. In M. E. P. Seligman & J. Garber (Eds.), *Human helplessness: Theory and application.* New York: Academic.

Eagly, A., & Steffan, V. (1986). Gender and aggressive behavior: A meta-analytic review of the social psychological literature. *Psychological Bulletin, 100,* 309–330.

Earley, P. (1992). *The hot house: Life inside Leavenworth penitentiary.* New York: Bantam.

Earls, F. (1994). Oppositional-defiant and conduct disorders. In M. Rutter, E. Taylor, & L. Hersov (Eds.), *Child and adolescent psychiatry: Modern approaches* (3rd ed.). London: Blackwell.

Eck, J. E. (1994). *Drug markets and drug places: A case-control study of the spatial structure of illicit drug dealing.* Unpublished doctoral dissertation, University of Maryland, College Park.

Eck, J. E. (1997). Preventing crime at places. In L. Sherman, D. Gottfredson, D. MacKenzie, J. Eck, P. Reuter, & S. Bushway (Eds.), *Preventing crime: What works, what doesn't, what's promising* (pp. 7-1–7-62). Washington, DC: U.S. Department of Justice.

Edelhertz, H. (1970). *The nature, impact and prosecution of white-collar crime.* Washington, DC: U.S. Government Printing Office.

Editorial: Why A3 strikes needs reform. (September 19, 2004). *San Francisco Chronicle.* Retrieved June 14, 2005, from http://www.sfgate.com/cgi-bin/article.cgi?file=/chronicle/archive/2004/09/19/EDGIJ7ORG11.DTL

Eels, K. (1951). *Intelligence and cultural differences.* Chicago: University of Chicago Press.

Egan, T. (1999a, March 7). Less crime, more criminals. *The New York Times Week in Review,* pp. 1, 16.

Egan, T. (1999b, February 28). War on crack retreats, still taking prisoners. *The New York Times,* pp. 1, 20–21.

Egeland, B., Pianta, R., & Ogawa, J. (1996). Early behavior problems: Pathways to mental disorders in adolescence. *Development & Psychopathology, 8,* 735–749.

Egelko, B. (2005, March 5). Second chance in 3 strikes case. San Francisco Chronicle. Retrieved June 1, 2006, from http://www.sfgate.com/cgi-bin/article.cgi?file=/c/a/2005/03/05/BAG4QBKTSV1.DTL

Egley, A., & Major. A. (2004). *Highlights of the 2002 National Youth Gang Survey.* Washington, DC: Office of Juvenile Justice and Delinquency Prevention, Office of Justice Programs, U.S. Department of Justice.

Ehlers, C. I., & Schuckit, M. A. (1990). EEG fast frequency activity in son of alcoholics. *Biological Psychiatry, 27,* 631–641.

Eichelman, B., Elliott, G., & Barchas, J. (1981). Biochemical, pharmacological, and genetic aspects of aggression. In D. Hamburg & M. B. Trudeau (Eds.), *Biobehavioral aspects of aggression.* New York: Liss.

Eisenberg, M., & Fabelo, T. (1996). Evaluation of the Texas correctional substance abuse treatment initiative: The impact of policy research. *Crime and Delinquency, 42,* 296–308.

Eisenberg, N. (1992). *The caring child.* Cambridge, MA: Harvard University Press.

Elias, R. (1993). *Victims still: The political manipulation of crime victims.* Newbury Park, CA: Sage.

Elicker, J., & Sroufe, L. A. (1993). Predicting peer competence and peer relationships in childhood from early parent-child relationships. In R. Parke & G. Ladd (Eds.), *Family-peer relationships: Modes of linkage.* Hillsdale, NJ: Lawrence Erlbaum Associates, Inc.

Ellickson, P. L., Hays, R D., & Bell, R. M. (1992). Stepping through the drug use sequence: Longitudinal scalogram analysis of initiation and regular use. *Journal of Abnormal Psychology, 101,* 441–451.

Elliott, D., Huizinga, D., & Ageton, S. (1985a). *Explaining delinquency and drug abuse.* Beverly Hills, CA: Sage.

Elliott, D., Huizinga, D., & Ageton, S. S. (1985b). *Multiple problem youth: Delinquency, substance use, and mental health problems.* New York: Springer-Verlag.

Elliott, D. S., Huizinga, D., & Morse, B. (1986). Self-reported violent offending—A descriptive analysis of juvenile violent offenders and their offending careers. *Journal of Interpersonal Violence, 1,* 472–514.

Elliott, R. (1991). Social science data and the APA: The *Lockhart* brief as a case in point. *Law and Human Behavior, 15,* 59–76.

Ellis, L. (1995). Arousal theory and the religiosity-criminality relationship. In P. Cordella & L. Siegel (Eds.), *Readings in contemporary criminological theory* (pp. 65–84). Boston: Northeastern University Press.

Ellison, C., & Sherkat, D. (1993). Conservative Protestants, and support for corporal punishment. *American Sociological Review, 58,* 131–144.

Ellsworth, P. C. (1991). To tell what we know or wait for Godot? *Law and Human Behavior, 15,* 77–90.

Ellsworth, P. C., & Gross, S. (1994). Hardening of the attitudes: Americans' views on the death penalty. *Journal of Social Issues, 50,* 19–52.

Ensminger, M. E. (1990). Sexual activity and problem behaviors among Black, urban adolescents. *Child Development, 61,* 2032–2046.

Ensminger, M. E., Brown, C. H., & Kellam, S. G. (1982). Sex differences in antecedents of substance use among adolescents. *Journal of Social Issues, 38*(2), 25–42.

Epstein, E. E., & McCrady, B. S. (1994). Introduction to the special section: Research on the nature and treatment of alcoholism—Does one inform the other? *Journal of Consulting and Clinical Psychology, 62,* 1091–1095.

Epstein, Y. M., Woolfolk, R. L., & Lehrer, P. M. (1981). Physiological, cognitive, and nonverbal responses to repeated experiences of crowding. *Journal of Applied Social Psychology, 11,* 1–13.

Erez, E., & Roeger, L. (1995). The effect of victim impact statements on sentencing patterns and outcomes: The Australian experience. *Journal of Criminal Justice, 23,* 363–375.

Ericson, R. V. (1989). Mass media, crime, law and justice. *British Journal of Sociology, 31,* 219–249.

Erikson, E. (1946). Ego development and historical change. *The psychoanalytic study of the child* (Vol. 2, pp. 359–396). New York: International Universities Press.

Erikson, E. (1957). The confirmation of the delinquent. *Chicago Review, 10,* 15–23.

Erikson, E. H. (1963). *Childhood and society.* New York: Norton.

Erikson, E. H. (1968). *Identity: Youth and crisis.* New York: Norton.

Eron, L. D. (1982). Parent-child interaction, television violence, and aggression of children. *American Psychologist, 37,* 197–211.

Eron, L., & Huesmann, L. R. (1987). Television as a source of maltreatment of children. *School Psychology Review, 16,* 195–202.

Eron, L., Huesmann, L., Brice, P., Fischer, P., & Mermelstein, R. (1983). Age trends in the development of aggression, sex typing, and related television habits. *Developmental Psychology, 19,* 71–77.

Escobar, G. (1997a, August 24). Graduating with honor from the streets of DC. *The Washington Post,* p. A1, A16.

Escobar, G. (1997b, December 4). Petworths death watch: Northwest community asks, How many women? *The Washington Post,* pp. B1, B6.

Estabrook. A. (1916). *The Jukes in 1915.* Washington, DC: Carnegie Institute of Washington.

Estelle v. Gamble, 429 U.S. 97 (1976).

Evans, G. W., & Jacobs, S.V. (1981). Air pollution and human behavior. *Journal of Social Issues, 37,* 95–125.

Evans, G. W., & Howard, R.B. (1973). Personal space. *Psychological Bulletin, 80,* 334–344.

Ewing, C. P. (1987). *Battered women who kill.* Lexington, KY: DC Heath.

Exner J. (1986). *The Rorschach: A Comprehensive System* (2nd ed.). New York: Wiley.

Eysenck, H. J. (1962). Conditioning and personality. *British Journal of Psychology, 53,* 299–305.

Eysenck, H. J. (1964). *Crime and personality.* Boston: Houghton Mifflin.

Eysenck, H. J. (1967). *The biological basis of personality.* Springfield, IL: Thomas.

Eysenck, H. J. (1987). Arousal and personality: The origins of a theory. In J. Strelau & H. J. Eysenck (Eds.), *Personality dimensions and arousal* (pp. 1–13). New York: Plenum.

Eysenck, H., & Eysenck, S. (1963). On the dual nature of extroversion. *British Journal of Social and Clinical Psychology, 2,* 46–55.

Fagan, J. (1996). *The criminalization of domestic violence: Promises and limits* (Research Report). Washington, DC: National Institute of Justice.

Fagan, P. (1997, September 7). The live-in link with child abuse. *The Washington Post,* p. C4.

Fagot, B. I., & Leinbach, M.D. (1993). Gender-role development in young children: From discrimination to labeling. *Developmental Review, 13,* 205–224.

Farmer v. Brennan, 114 U.S. 1970 (1994).

Farrell, G. (1995). Preventing repeat victimization. In M. Tonry & D. P. Farrington (Ed.), Building a safer society: Strategic approaches to crime prevention. *Crime Justice.* Vol. 19. Chicago, IL: University of Chicago Press.

Farrington, D. P. (1986). Age and crime. In M. Tonry & N. Morris (Eds.), *Crime and Justice Review of Research* (pp. 189–250). Chicago: The University of Chicago Press.

Farrington, D. P. (1987). Early precursors of frequent offending. In J. Q. Wilson & G. C. Loury (Eds.), *From children to citizens: Vol. III. Families, schools, and delinquency prevention.* New York: Springer-Verlag.

Farrington, D. (1991). Childhood aggression and adult violence: Early precursors and later-life outcomes. In D. J. Pepler & K. H. Rubin (Eds.), *The development of childhood aggression* (pp. 5–29). Hillsdale, NJ: Lawrence Erlbaum Associates, Inc.

Farrington, D. (1992, July). *The development of offending and antisocial behavior from childhood to adulthood.* Paper presented at the Congress on Rethinking Delinquency, University of Minho, Braga, Portugal.

Farrington, D. P. (1994a). Childhood, adolescent, and adult features of violent miles. In L. R. Huesmann (Ed.), *Aggressive behavior: Current perspectives* (pp. 215–240).

Farrington, D. P. (1994b). *Psychological explanations of crime.* Aldershot, England: Dartmouth.

Farrington, D. P. (in press). The relationship between low resting heart rate and violence. In A. Raine, D. P. Farrington, P. Brennan, & S. A. Mednick (Eds.), *Biosocial bases of violence.* New York: Plenum.

Farver, J. M., & Branstetter, W. H. (1994). Preschooler's prosocial responses to their peers' distress. *Developmental Psychology, 30,* 334–341.

Fattah, E. A. (1991). *Understanding criminal victimization.* Scarborough, Ontario, Canada: Prentice-Hall Canada.

Faust, D., & Ziskin, J. (1988). The expert witness in psychology and psychiatry. *Science, 242,* 31–35.

Fedarko, K. (1997, May 17). Long arm of the outlaw. *Time, XX,* 42.

Feder, L. (1994). Psychiatric hospitalization history and parole decisions. *Law and Human Behavior, 18,* 395–410.

Federal Bureau of Investigation. (1997). *Crime in the United States: 1996.* Washington, DC: U.S. Government Printing Office.

Federal Bureau of Investigation. (1998). *Crime in the United States: 1997.* Washington, DC: U.S. Government Printing Office.

Federal Bureau of Investigation. (1999). *Crime in the United States: 1998.* Washington, DC: U.S. Government Printing Office.

Federal Bureau of Investigation. (2000). *The School shooter: A threat assessment perspective.* Retrieved May 19, 2005, from http://www.fbi.gov/publications/school/school2.pdf

Federal Bureau of Investigation. (2001). *Crime in the United States: 2000. Uniform Crime Reports.* Washington, DC: Author.

Federal Bureau of Investigation. (2002). *Crime in the United States: 2001. Uniform Crime Reports.* Washington, DC: Author.

Federal Bureau of Investigation. (2003). *Crime in the United States: 2002.* Washington, DC: U.S. Government Printing Office.

Federal Bureau of Investigation. (2004a). *Crime in America—2003.* Washington, DC: Government Printing Office.

Federal Bureau of Investigation. (2004b). *Supplementary homicide reports(1996–2002).* Washington, DC: Author. Retrieved January 8, 2005, from http://www.ojp.usdoj.gov/bjs/homicide/race.htm

Feeney, F. (1986). Robbers as decision makers. In D. Cornish & R. Clarke (Eds.), *The reasoning criminal: Rational choice perspectives on offending* (pp. 53–71). New York: Springer-Verlag.

Feeney, F. (1998). *German and American prosecutions: An approach to statistical comparison.* Washington, DC: Bureau of Justice Statistics.

Fehrenbach, P. A., Smith, W., Monastersky, C., & Deisher, R. W. (1986). Adolescent sexual offenders: Offender and offense characteristics. *American Journal of Orthopsychiatry, 56*(2), 225–233.

Feld, B. (1993). Criminalizing the American juvenile court. In M. Tonry (Ed.), *Crime and justice: A Review of Research* (p. 232). Chicago: University of Chicago Press.

Feldman, D. H. (1994). *Beyond universal in cognitive development* (2nd ed.). Norwood, NJ: Albex.

Feldman, P. (1993). *The psychology of crime: A social science textbook.* New York: Cambridge University Press.

Felson, M. (1994). *Crime in everyday life.* Thousand Oaks, CA: Pine Forge Press.

Felson, R., & Krohn, M. (1990). Motives for rape. *Journal of Research in Crime and Delinquency, 27,* 222–242.

Fendrich, M., Mackesy-Amiti, M. E., Goldstein, P., & Spunt, B. (1995). Substance involvement among juvenile murderers: Comparisons with older offenders based on interviews with prison inmates. *International Journal of the Addictions, 30,* 1363–1382.

Fenton, W., & McGlashan, T. (1991). Natural history of schizophrenia subtypes: I. Longitudinal study of paranoid, hebephrenic, and undifferentiated schizophrenia. *Archives of General Psychiatry, 48,* 969–977.

Ferguson, H. B., Stoddarat, C., & Simeon, J. (1986). Double-blind challenge studies of behavioral and cognitive effects of sucrose-aspartame ingestion in normal children. *Nutrition Reviews Supplement, 44,* 144–158.

Fergusson, D. M., & Horwood, J. L. (1996). The role of adolescent peer affiliations in the continuity between childhood behavioral adjustment and juvenile offending. *Journal of Abnormal Child Psychology, 24,* 202–215.

Fergusson, D., Horwood, L., & Lynskey, M. (1995). The stability of disruptive childhood behavior. *Journal of Abnormal Child Psychology, 23,* 379–396.

Fergusson, D. M., Lynsky, M. T., & Horwood, J. L. (1996). Factors associated with continuity and changes in disruptive behavior patterns between childhood and adolescence. *Journal of Abnormal Child Psychology, 24,* 533–545.

Fernandez, M. E. (1998, June 19). Northeast youth slain while walking dog. *The Washington Post,* pp. D1, D5.

Ferris, C. F. (1996, March/April). The rage of innocents. *The Sciences,* 22–26.

Ferris, C. F., & Grisso. T. (1998). *Understanding aggressive behavior in children.* New York: New York Academy of Sciences.

Fessenden, F. (2000, April 9a). They threaten, seethe and unhinge, then kill in quantity. *New York Times,* pp. 1, 20–21.

Fessenden, F. (2000, April 9b). How youngest killers differ: Peer support. *New York Times,* p. 21

Fineman, K. R. (1995). A model for the qualitative analysis of child and adult fire deviant behavior. *American Journal of Forensic Psychology, 13*(1), 31–60.

Fingerhut, L. A., & Kleinman, J. C. (1990). International and interstate comparisons of homicides among young males. *Journal of the American Medical Association, 263,* 3292–3295.

Finkelhor, D., & Araji, S. (1986). Explanations of pedophilia: A four factor model. *The Journal of Sex Research, 22,* 145–161.

Finkelstein, K. E. (2000, June 23). New York to offer most addicts treatment instead of jail terms. *New York Times,* p. 20.

Finkelhor, D., Mitchell, K., & Wolak, J. (2000). *Online victimizations: A report on the nation's youth.* Washington, DC: Crimes Against Children Research Center.

Finkelhor, D., & Yllo, K. (1985). *License to rape: Sexual abuse of wives.* New York: Holt, Rinehart & Winston.

Finn, P. (1997, September 9). Prison deal reached in Reston slaying. *The Washington Post,* p. B1.

Finn, P., & Melillo, W. (1998, January 28). Kasi challenge may be valid, lawyers say. *The Washington Post,* p. B3.

Finn, P. R., Zeitouni, N. C., & Pihl, R. O. (1990). Effects of alcohol on psychophysiological hyperactivity to non-aversive and aversive stimuli in men at high risk for alcoholism. *Journal of Abnormal Psychology, 99,* 79–85.

Finnegan, W. (1994, January 31). Doubt. *New Yorker.*

Fishbein, D. H. (1990). Biological perspectives in criminology. *Criminology,* 27–72.

Fishbein, D. H. (1992). The psychobiology of female aggression. *Criminal Justice and Behavior, 19,* 19–126.

Fishbein, D. H. (1996a). The biology of antisocial behavior. In J. Conklin (Ed.), *New perspectives in criminology* (pp. 26–38). Boston: Allyn & Bacon.

Fishbein, D. H. (1996b). Selected studies on the biology of antisocial behavior. In J. Conklin (Ed.), *New perspectives in criminology* (pp. 26–38). Needham Heights, MA: Allyn & Bacon.

Fishbein, D. H., Lozovsky, D., & Jaffe, J. H. (1989). Impulsivity, aggression, and neuroendocrine responses to serotonergic stimulation in substance abusers. *Biological Psychiatry, 25,* 1049–66.

Fisher, B. (1991). A neighborhood business area is hurting: Crime, fear of crime, and disorders take their toll. *Crime and Delinquency, 37,* 363–373.

Flanagan, T. J. (1988). Lifers and long-termers: Doing big time. In R. Johnson & H. Toch (Eds.), *The pains of imprisonment* (pp. 115–145). Prospect Heights, IL: Waveland Press.

Flannery, D. J. (1997). *School violence: Risk, preventive intervention, and policy.* Springfield, VA: ERIC Clearinghouse on Urban Education.

Fletcher, M. A. (1996, February 8). U.S. investigates suspicious fires at Southern black churches. *Washington Post,* p. A3.

Fletcher, M A. (1998, June 5). Study finds wide racial disparity in death penalty. *The Washington Post,* p. A24.

Fletcher, M. A. (1998, March 1). Kerner prophecy on race relations came true, report says. *The Washington Post,* p. A6.

Flinn, P. (1998, January 18). The world of privately run prisons. *The Washington Post,* p. B1.

Florida Department of Corrections. (1990). *Florida executive summary: Boot camp: A 25 month review.* Tallahassee: Florida Department of Corrections.

Flynn, E. E. (1992). The graying of America's prison population. *The Prison Journal, 72*(1 & 2), 77–98.

Flynn, E. E. (1995). *Managing elderly offenders* (Report to the National Institute of Justice). Washington, DC: National Institute of Justice.

Flynn, K. (1998, October 23). Persevering woman helps free stranger in '90 murder case. *The New York Times,* pp. A1, A22.

Flynn, K. (1999, February 14). After police killing, many details emerge, but mystery lingers. *The New York Times,* p. 33.

Foley, L. A., & Pigot, M. A. (1997). The influence of forepersons and nonforepersons on mock jury decisions. *American Journal of Forensic Psychology, 15,* 5–17.

Foote, J. (1997). *Expert panel issues report on serious and violent juvenile offenders* (Fact Sheet No. 68). Washington, DC: U.S. Department of Justice, Office of Juvenile Justice and Delinquency Prevention.

Ford v. Wainwright, 477 U.S. 399 (1986).

Forehand, R., Wierson, M., Frame, C. L., Kempton, T., & Armistead, L. (1991). Juvenile firesetting: A unique syndrome or an advanced level of antisocial behavior? *Behavior Research and Therapy, 29,* 125–128.

Former guards indicted. (1998, March 24). *Washington Post,* p. B7.

Forrest, B. (1999, December 12). Risky business. *New York Times Sunday Magazine,* p. 47

Foucault, M. (1977). *Discipline and punish: The birth of the prison.* New York: Pantheon.

Fox, F. (1999, September 17). Justice in Jasper. *Texas Observer.* Retrieved May 30, 2006 from http://www.texasobserver.org/showArticle.asp?ArticleID=275

Fox, J. A. (1996, May 30). *TITLE.* Paper presented at the National Criminal Justice Association Meeting, Washington, DC.

Franklin, B. (1994, August 22). Gender myths still play a role in jury selection. *National Law Journal,* pp. A1, A25.

Franklin, H. B. (1998, February 22). Judgment on our jails. *The Washington Post Book World,* p. 9.

Freed, D. (1992). Federal sentencing in the wake of guidelines: Unacceptable limits on the discretion of sentences. *Yale Law Journal, 101,* 1681–1754.

Freedman, J. L. (2002). *Media violence and its effect on aggression: Assessing the scientific evidence.* Toronto, Ontario, Canada: University of Toronto Press.

Freud, S. (1901). *The psychopathology of everyday life.* New York: Macmillan.

Freud, S. (1953). The transformation of puberty. In J. Strachey (Ed. & Trans.), *The standard edition of the complete psychological works of Sigmund Freud* (Vol. 7). London: Hogarth. (Original work published 1905)

Freud, S. (1923). *The ego and the id.* London: Hogarth.

Freud, S. (1938). *The basic writings of Sigmund Freud.* New York: Modern Library. (Original work published 1906)

Freud, S. (1948). The ego and the id. In *Complete psychological works of Sigmund Freud* (Vol. 19). London: Hogarth.

Friedman, L. M. (1993). *Crime and punishment in American history.* New York: Basic Books.

Friedrichs, D. O. (1996). *Trusted criminals.* Belmont, CA: Wadsworth.

Frodi, A. M., Lamb, M. E., Leavitt, L. A., & Donovan, W. L. (1978). Fathers' and mothers' responses to infant smiles and cries. *Infant Behavior and Development, 1,* 187–198.

Frodi, A., Maccaulay, J., & Thome, P. (1977). Are women always less aggressive than men? A review of the experimental literature. *Psychological Bulletin, 84,* 634–660.

Frost, L. E., & Shepherd, R. E. (1996). Mental health issues in juvenile delinquency proceedings. *Criminal Justice, 11.*

Fugure, R., Delia, A., & Philippe, R. (1995). Considerations on the dynamics of fraud and shoplifting in adult female offenders. *Canadian Journal of Psychiatry, 40,* 150–153.

Fulero, S. M., & Finkel, N. J. (1991). Barring ultimate issue testimony: An insane rule? *Law and Human Behavior, 15,* 495–508.

Fuligni, A., & Eccles, J. (1993). Perceived parent-child relationships and early adolescent's orientation toward peers. *Developmental Psychology, 29,* 622–632.

Fullerton, D. T., Wonderlich, S. A., & Gosnell, B. A. (1995). Clinical characteristics of eating disorder patients who report sexual or physical abuse. *International Journal of Eating Disorders, 17,* 243–249.

Funder, D. C. (1997). *The personality puzzle.* New York: Norton.

Furby, L., & Weinrott, M. (1980). Sex offenders recidivism. A review. *Psychological Bulletin, 105,* 3–30.

Furman v. Georgia, 408 U.S. 238 (1972)

Gabel, S., & Shindledecker, R. (1993). Parental substance abuse and its relationship to severe aggression and antisocial behavior in youth. *American Journal on Addictions, 2,* 48–58.

Gabor, T., Baril, M., Cusson, M., Elie, D., Leblanc, M., & Normandeau, A. (1987). *Armed robbery: Cops, robbers, and victims.* Springfield, IL: Thomas.

Gabrielli, W. D., Jr., Mednick, S. A., Volavka, J., Pollock, V. E., Schulsinger, F., & Itil, T. M. (1982). Electroencephalograms in children of alcoholics. *Psychophysiology, 19,* 404–407.

Gaes, G., Wallace, S., Gilman, E., Klein-Saffran, J., & Supa, S. (2002). The influence of prison gang affiliation on violence and other prison misconduct. *The Prison Journal, 82,* 359–385.

Gaines, P. (1998, February 28). Making a promise to at-risk youths in Washington. *The Washington Post,* p. B3.

Galaway, B., & Hudson, J. (1990). *Criminal justice, restitution, and reconciliation.* Massey, NY: Criminal Justice Press.

Gallagher, J. (1990, 25 June). Good old bad boy. *Time, XX,* 42–43.

Gallagher, W. (1994, September). How we become what we are. *The Atlantic Monthly,* 38–55.

Gamoran, A. (1992). The variable effects of high school tracking. *American Sociological Review, 57,* 812–828.

Ganzer, V., & Sarason, I. (1973). Variables associated with recidivism among juvenile delinquents. *Journal of Consulting and Clinical Psychology, 40,* 1–5.

Garb, H. N. (1989). Clinical judgment, clinical training, and professional experience. *Psychological Bulletin, 105,* 387–396.

Garbarino, J. (1999). *Lost boys: Why our sons turn violent and how we can save them.* New York: Free Press.

Garkinkel, L. F. (1997). *Unique challenges, hopeful responses: A handbook for professionals who work with youth with disabilities in the juvenile justice system.* New York: PACER Center.

Garnefski, N., & Okma, S. (1996). Addiction-risk and aggressive/criminal behavior in adolescence: Influence of family, school and peers. *Journal of Adolescence, 19,* 237–250.

Garrod. A. (1993). *Approaches to moral development: New research and emerging themes.* New York: Teachers College Press.

Garry, E. M. (1997). *Juvenile firesetting and arson.* Washington, DC: Office of Juvenile Justice and Delinquency Prevention.

Geen, R. G. (1990). The influence of the mass media. In R. G. Geen (Ed.), *Mapping Social Psychology Series: Human aggression* (pp. 83–112). Pacific Grove, CA: Brooks/Cole.

Geen, R. G., & McCown, E. J. (1984). Effects of noise and attack on aggression and physiological arousal. *Motivation and Emotion, 8,* 231–241.

Geen, R. G., & Thomas, S. L. (1986). The immediate effects of media violence on behavior. *Journal of Social Issues, 42,* 7–27.

Geen, R. G., & O'Neal, E. C. (1969). Activation of cue-elicited aggression by general arousal. *Journal of Personality and Social Psychology, 11,* 289–292.

Gelberg, L., Linn, L. S., & Leake, B. D. (1988). Mental health, alcohol and drug use, and criminal history among homeless adults. *Hospital and Community Psychiatry, 145,* 191–196.

Gelles, R., & Straus, M. (1979). Determinants of violence in the family: Toward a theoretical integration. In W. R.

Burr, R. Hill, F. I. Nye, & I. L. Reiss (Eds.), *Contemporary theories about the family* (Vol. 1, pp. 549–581). New York: Free Press.

Gelles, R. J., & Cornell, C. P. (1985). *Intimate violence in families.* Newbury Park, CA: Sage.

Gelles, R. J., & Straus, M. A. (1988). *Intimate violence.* New York: Simon & Schuster.

Gelles, R. J., & Straus, M. A. (1990). *Physical violence in American families: Risk factors and adaptations to violence in 8,145 families.* New Brunswick, NJ: Transaction Press.

Gendreau, P., & Ross, R. R. (1979). Effective correctional treatment: Bibliotherapy for cynics. *Crime and Delinquency, 25,* 463–489.

Gendreau, P., & Ross, R. R. (1987). Revivification of rehabilitation: Evidence from the 1980's. *Justice Quarterly, 4,* 349–407.

Gerbner, G., Gross, L., Morgan, M., & Signorielli, N. (1980). The "mainstreaming" of America: Violence profile no. 11. *Journal of Communication, XX,* 10–29

Gerhart, A., & Groer, A. (1997, December 15). A lover's lasting attachment. *The Washington Post,* p. B3.

Giallombardo, R. (1966). *Society of women: A study of women's prison.* New York: Wiley.

Gibbs, N. R. (1994, September 19). Murder in miniature. *Time.* Retrieved June 1, 2006, from http://www.time.com/time/archive/preview/0,10987,981460,00.html

Gibbons, D., & Griswold, M. (1957). Sex differences among juvenile court offenders. *Sociology and Social Research, 42,* 106–110.

Gibbons, D. C. (1992). *Society, crime, and criminal behavior.* Englewood Cliffs, NJ: Prentice-Hall.

Gideon v. Wainwright, 372 U.S. 335 (1963).

Giever, D. (1995, November). *An empirical assessment of the core elements of Gottfredson and Hirschi's general theory of crime.* Paper presented at the American Society of Criminology meeting, Boston.

Gilbert, D.T., & Malone, P.S. (1995). The correspondence bias. *Psychological Bulletin, 117,* 21–38.

Gilliard, D. (1999). *Prison and jail inmates at midyear 1998.* Washington, DC: Bureau of Justice Statistics.

Gilligan, C. (1993). *In a different voice: Psychological theory and women's development.* Cambridge, MA: Harvard University Press.

Gilmore v. Utah, 492 U.S. 1012 (1976).

Ginsburg, B. E., & Carter, B. F. (1987). *Premenstrual syndrome: Ethical and legal implications in a biomedical perspective.* New York: Bantam.

Glaberson, W. (1997, November 11). Unabomber sought revenge, papers show. *The New York Times,* p. A14.

Gleick, E. (1994, December 12). Death of a madman: The final victim. *People, XX,* 126–132.

Glod, M. (1998, June 3). Loudoun judge bans juror background checks. *The Washington Post,* p. B5.

Glueck, S., & Glueck, E. (1934). *Five hundred delinquent women.* New York: Knopf.

Glueck, S. & Glueck, E. (1950). *Unraveling juvenile delinquency.* Cambridge, MA: Harvard University Press.

Glueck, S., & Glueck, E. (1956). *Physique and delinquency.* New York: Harper Bros.

Glueck, S. & Glueck, E. (1968). *Delinquents and nondelinquents in perspective.* Cambridge, MA: Harvard University Press.

Goddard, H. (1920). *Efficiency and levels of intelligence.* Princeton, NJ: Princeton University Press.

Gold, M. (1978). School experiences, self-esteem, and delinquent behavior: A theory for alternative schools. *Crime and Delinquency, 24,* 274–95.

Goldberg, J. (1999, January 31). The don is dead. *The New York Times Magazine,* pp. 25–31, 38, 62, 65–66, 71.

Goldberg, L. R. (1968). Simple models or simple processes? Some research on clinical judgments. *American Psychologist, 23,* 483–496.

Golden, C. J., Hammeke, T. A., & Purisch, A. D. (1979). Luria-Nebraska Neuropsychological Battery. Los Angeles, CA: Western Psychological Services.

Golden, R. (1977). *Disposable children: America's welfare system.* Belmont, CA: Wadsworth.

Goldman, M. J. (1991). Kleptomania: Making sense of the nonsensical. *American Journal of Psychiatry, 148,* 986–995.

Goldstein, A. (1996). *Violence in America: Lessons in understanding the aggression in our lives.* Palo Alto, CA: Davis-Black Publishing.

Goleman, D. (1988, August 23). Sex roles reign powerful as ever in the emotions. *New York Times,* pp. C1, C13.

Goodall, J. (1991). Unusual violence in the overthrow of an alpha male chimpanzee at Gombe. In T. Nishida et al. (Eds.), *Topics in primatology, vol, 1: Human origin.* Tokyo: University of Tokyo Press.

Goodman, J. (2003). Blackout. New York: North Point Press.

Goodstein, L. (1979). Inmate adjustment to prison and the transition to community life. *Journal of Research in Crime and Delinquency, 16,* 246–272.

Goodstein, L., & Harden, B. (1997, June 10). Of birth, death and the prom. *The Washington Post,* p. A3.

Goodwin, D. W. (1985). Alcoholism and genetics: The sins of the fathers. *Archives of General Psychiatry, 42,* 171–174.

Gordon, M. A., & Glaser, D. (1991). The use and effects of financial penalties in municipal courts. *Criminology, 29,* 651–676.

Goranson, R.E. & King, D. (1970). Rioting and daily temperature: Analysis of the U.S. riots in 1967. Toronto: York University Press.

Goreta, M. (1995). A contribution to the theory of psychoanalytic victimology. *Journal of Psychiatry & Law, 23,* 263–281.

Gorsuch, R. L., & Butler, M. C. (1976). Initial drug abuse: A review of predisposing social psychological factors. *Psychological Bulletin, 83,* 120–137.

Gottesman, I. I. (1991). *Schizophrenia genesis: The origins of madness.* New York: Freeman.

Gottfredson, B. D. (1988). *Issues in adolescent drug use.* Unpublished manuscript, U.S. Department of Justice, Johns Hopkins University, Center for Research on Elementary and Middle Schools. Baltimore, MD: Author.

Gottfredson, G. & Gottfredson, D. (1985). *Victimization in schools.* New York: Plenum.

Gottfredson, M. R., & Hirschi, T. (1990a). *A general theory of crime.* Stanford, CA: Stanford University Press.

Gottfredson, M. R. & Hirschi, T. (1990b). The nature of criminality: Low self-control. In M. R. Gottfredson & T. Hirschi (Eds.), *A general theory of crime* (pp. 88–94). Stanford, CA: Stanford University Press.

Gottschalk, E. (1989, 7 August). Churchgoers are the prey as scams rise. *Wall Street Journal,* p. C1.

Gould, S. J. (1995). *Dinosaur in a haystack.* New York: Harmony Books.

Gowen, A. (1998, January 3). Five Maryland teens held without bond after youth is sexually assaulted. *The Washington Post,* p. B2.

Grace, J. (1994, September 12). There are no children here: Chicago's young crime victims. *Time,* 44.

Granklin, K. (1998, August 16). *Psychosocial motivations of hate crime perpetrators.* Paper presented at a meeting of the American Psychological Association, San Francisco, CA.

Grann, D. (2003, January 27). The old man and the gun. *The New Yorker, XX,* 60–69.

Grant, C. A. (1995). Women who kill: The impact of abuse. *Issues in Mental Health Nursing, 16,* 315–326.

Gray, G. (1986). Diet, crime and delinquency: A critique. *Nutrition Reviews Supplement, 44,* 89–94.

Greenberg, A., & Coleman, M. (1976). Depressed 5-hydroxyindole levels associated with hyperactive and aggressive behavior. *Archives of General Psychiatry, 33,* 331–336.

Greenberg, D. (1974). *Crime and law enforcement in the colony of New York, 1691–1776.* Ithaca, NY: Cornell University Press.

Greenberg, M. T., Speltz. J. L., DeKlyen, M., & Endriga, M. C. (1991). Attachment security in preschoolers with and without externalizing problems: A replication. *Developmental Psychopathology, 3,* 413–430.

Greenberger, D. A., & Allen, V. C. (1980). Destruction and complexity: An application of aesthetic theory. *Personality and Social Psychology Bulletin, 6,* 479–483.

Greenfeld, L. A. (1998). *Alcohol and crime: An analysis of national data on the prevalence of alcohol involvement in crime.* Washington, DC: U.S. Department of Justice.

Greenfeld, L. A., Langan, P. A., & Smith, S. K. (1997). *Police use of force.* Washington, DC: Bureau of Justice Statistics and National Institute of Justice.

Greenfeld, L. A., & Snell, T. L. (1999). *Women offenders.* Washington, DC: U.S. Department of Justice, Office of Justice Programs, Bureau of Justice Statistics.

Greenfield, T., & Weisner, C. (1995). Drinking problems and self-reported criminal behavior, arrests and convictions: 1990 US alcohol and 1989 county surveys. *Addiction, 90,* 361–373.

Greenhouse, L. (1989, June 27). Death sentences against retarded and young upheld. *New York Times,* pp. 1, 10.

Greenwood, P. W. (1999). *Costs and benefits of early childhood intervention.* Washington, DC: Office of Juvenile Justice & Delinquency Prevention.

Greenwood, P. W., Rydell, C. P., Abrahamse, A. F., Calukins, J. P., Chiesa, J., Model, K. E., et al. (1994). *Three strikes and you're out: Estimated benefits and costs of California's new mandatory sentencing law.* Santa Monica, CA: RAND.

Gregg v. Georgia, 428 U.S. 153 (1976).

Gregg, V., Gibbs, J. C., & Basinger, K. S. (1994). Patterns of developmental delay in moral judgment by male and female delinquents. *Merrill-Palmer Quarterly, 40,* 538–553.

Gresham, A. C. (1993). The insanity plea: A futile defense for serial killers. *Law & Psychology Review, 17,* 193–208.

Gresswell, D. M., & Holland, C. R. (1994). Multiple murder: A review. *British Journal of Criminology, 34*(1), 1–14.

Griffin, P., Torbet, P., & Szymanski, L. (1998). *Trying juveniles as adults in criminal court: An analysis of state transfer provisions.* Washington, DC: U.S. Department of Justice, Office of Justice Programs, Office of Juvenile Justice and Delinquency Prevention.

Grilo, C. M., Becker, D. F., Walker, M. L., & Levy, K. N. (1995). Psychiatric comorbidity in adolescent inpatients with substance use disorders. *Journal of the American Academy of Child & Adolescent Psychiatry, 34,* 1085–1091.

Grisso, T. (1980). Juvenile's capacities to waive Miranda rights: An empirical analysis. *California Law Review, 68,* 134.

Grisso, T. (1996). Society's retributive response to juvenile violence: A developmental perspective. *Law & Human Behavior, 20,* 229.

Grisso, T. (1997). Juvenile competency to stand trial: Questions in an era of punitive reform. *Criminal Justice, 12.*

Grisso, T., & Siegel, S. K. (1986). Assessment of competency to stand criminal trial. In W. J. Curran, A. L. McGarry, & S. A. Shah (Eds.), *Forensic psychiatry and psychology* (pp. 145–165).

Grisso, T., Steinberg, L., Wollard, J., Cauffman, E., Scott, E., Graham, S., et al. (2003). Juveniles' competence to stand trial: A comparison of adolescents' and adults' capacities as trial defendants. *Law and Human Behavior 27,* 333–363.

Grossman, K. E., & Grossman, K. (1990). The wider concept of attachment in cross-cultural research. *Human Development, 33,* 31–47.

Groth, A. N. (1977). Adolescent sexual offender and his prey. *International Journal of Offender Therapy and Comparative Criminology, 21,* 249–254.

Groth, A. N. (1978). Patterns of sexual assault against children and adolescents. In L. J. Burgess, N. Groth, L. L. Holmstrom, & S. M. Sgroi (Eds.), *Sexual assault of children and adolescents.* Lexington, MA: Heath.

Groth, A. N. (1984). *Men who rape: The psychology of the offender.* New York: Plenum Press. (Original work published 1979)

Groth, A. N., & Loredo, C. M. (1981). Juvenile sexual offenders: Guidelines for assessment. *International Journal of Offender Therapy and Comparative Criminology, 25,* 31–39.

Grubin, D. (1994). Sexual murder. *British Journal of Psychiatry, 165,* 624–629.

Grunson, L. (1994, March 28). A 25-year trial to 5 murder charges, sudden death of her 5 children were slayings, police say. *The New York Times,* pp. B1, B2.

Grunwald, M. (1999, March 16). Coursework in N. Y.: Surviving the police. *The Washington Post,* p. A3.

Guns and jeers used by gang to buy silence. (2005, January 16). *Gainesville (Florida) Sun.* Retrieved February 20, 2005, from http://www.gainesville.com/apps.

Gurr, T. R. (1970). *Why men rebel.* Princeton, NJ: Princeton University Press.

Guttman, A. (1986). *Sport spectators.* New York: Columbia University Press.

Guze, S. B. (1976). *Criminality and psychiatric disorders.* New York: Oxford University Press.

Haapasalo, J., & Trembley, R. E. (1994). Physically aggressive boys from age 6 to 12: Family background, parenting behavior, and prediction of delinquency. *Journal of Consulting and Clinical Psychology, 62,* 1044–1052.

Haddad, J. (1993). Managing the special needs of mentally ill inmates. *American Jails, 7*(1), 62–65.

Hafner, H., & Boker, W. (1973). *Crimes of violence by mentally abnormal offenders* (Trans. H. Marshall). Cambridge, England: Cambridge University Press.

Hagan, F. E. (1997). *Political crime: Ideology and criminality.* Boston: Allyn & Bacon.

Hagan, J. (1989). *Structural criminology.* New Brunswick, NJ: Rutgers University Press.

Hagan, J., & Kay, F. (1990). Gender and delinquency in white-collar families: A power-control perspective. *Crime and Delinquency, 36,* 391–407.

Hagan, M. P., & Cho, M. E. (1996). A comparison of treatment outcomes between adolescent rapists and child sexual offenders. *International Journal of Offender Therapy & Comparative Criminology, 40,* 113–122.

Hale, R. (1994). The role of humiliation and embarrassment in serial murder. *Psychology: A Journal of Human Behavior, 31*(2), 17–23.

Halikakas, J. A., Meller, J., Morse, C., & Lyttle, M. D. (1990). Predicting substance abuse in juvenile offenders: Deficit disorder versus aggressivity. *Child Psychiatry & Human Development, 21,* 49–55.

Hall, E.T. (1963). A system for the notation of proxemic behavior. *American Anthropologist, 65,* 1003–1026.

Hall, E.T. (1966). *The hidden dimension.* New York: Doubleday.

Hall, G. C., Shondrick, D. D., & Hirschman, R. (1993). The role of sexual arousal in sexually aggressive behavior: A meta-analysis. *Journal of Consulting and Clinical Psychology, 61,* 1091–1095.

Hall, G. S. (1904). *Adolescence: Its psychology and its relations to psychology, anthropology, sociology, sex, crime, religion, and education.* New York: Appleton-Century-Crofts.

Haller, E. (1992). High school size and student in discipline: Another aspect of the school consolidation issue. *Educational Evaluation and Policy Analysis, 14,* 145–156.

Hallman, J., Persson, M., & af Klinteberg, B. (2001). Female alcoholism: Differences between female alcoholics with and without a history of additional substance abuse. *Alcohol and Alcoholism, 36,* 564–571.

Halverson, C. F., & Victor, J. B. (1976). Minor physical anomalies and problem behavior in elementary school children. *Child Development, 47,* 281–285.

Hamalainen, M., & Pulkkinen, L. (1996). Problem behavior as a precursor of male criminality. *Development & Psychopathology, 8,* 443–455.

Hamm, M. S. (1996). *Terrorism, hate crime, and anti-government violence: A preliminary review of the research* (Background paper for National Research Council, Commission on Behavioral and Social Sciences and Education, Committee on Law and Justice).

Haney, C. (1998). *Limits to prison pain: Modern psychological theory and rational crime control policy.* Washington, DC: American Psychological Association.

Haney, C., Banks, W., & Zimbardo, P. (1973). Interpersonal dynamics in a stimulated prison. *International Journal of Criminology and Penology, 1,* 69–97.

Haney, C., Hurtado, A., & Vega, L. (1994). "Modern" death qualification: New data on biasing effects. *Law and Human Behavior, 18,* 619–634.

Haney, C., & Lynch, M. (1997). Regulating prisons of the future: A psychological analysis of supermax and solitary confinement. *New York Review of Law and Social Change, 23,* 101–195.

Haney, C., & Zimbardo, P. (1977). The socialization into criminality: On becoming a prisoner and a guard. In J. Tapp & F. Levine (Eds.), *Law, justice, and the individual in society: Psychological and legal issues* (pp. 198–223). New York: Holt, Rinehart & Winston.

Haney, C., & Zimbardo, P. (1998). The past and future of U.S. prison policy: Twenty-five years after the Stanford Prison Experiment. *American Psychologist, 53,* 709–727.

Hanke, P. J. (1996). Putting school crime into perspective: Self-reported school victimizations of high school seniors. *Journal of Criminal Justice, 24,* 207–225.

Hannah, J. (1992, July 7). Inmates restricted after riots in Kansas. *Boston Globe,* p. 3.

Hansen, W. B., Graham, J. W., Shelton, D. R., Flay, B. R., & Johnson, C. A. (1987). The consistency of peer and parent influences on tobacco, alcohol, and marijuana use among young adult adolescents. *Journal of Behavioral Medicine, 17,* 135–154.

Hanson, M., MacKay, S., Atkinson, L., Staley, S. (1995). Firesetting during the preschool period: Assessment and intervention issues. *Canadian Journal of Psychiatry, 40,* 299–303.

Hanson, M., MacKay, S., Staley, S., & Poulton, L. (1994). Delinquent firesetters: A comparative study of delinquency and firesetting histories. *Canadian Journal of Psychiatry, 39,* 230–232.

Hanson, R. K. (2000). Will they do it again? Predicting sex-offense recidivism. *Current Directions in Psychological Science, 9,* 106–109

Haraway, M., & Oneil, J. M. (Eds.). (1999). *What causes men's violence against women.* Thousand Oaks, CA: Sage.

Harburg, E., Davis, D. R., & Caplan, R. (1982). Parent and offspring alcohol use. *Journal of Studies on Alcohol, 43,* 497–516.

Hard, R. D. (1983). Diagnosis of antisocial personality disorder in two prison populations. *American Journal of Psychiatry, 140,* 887–890.

Hardin, B. (1997, October 3). Teen suspect in N. J. slaying engaged in Internet-inspired sex, prosecutor says. *The Washington Post,* p. A4.

Hardin, B. (1998a, March 1). A burglar who comes to dinner. *The Washington Post,* p. A3.

Hardin, B. (1998b, January 22). John Gotti Jr., 39 others are indicted in New York. *The Washington Post,* p. A3.

Hardin, B. (1998c, August 21). New Jersey "prom mom" accepts plea agreement. *The Washington Post,* p. A4.

Hardin, B. (1998d, March 8). Worker kills four at Connecticut lottery. *The Washington Post,* pp. A1, A9.

Hardin, B., & Hedgpeth, D. (2005, March 25). Minnesota killer chafed at life on reservation. *The Washington Post,* pp. A1, A6.

Hardwick, P. J., & Rowton-Lee, M. A. (1996). Adolescent homicide: Towards assessment of risk. *Journal of Adolescence, 19,* 263–276.

Hare, R. D. (1979). Psychopathy and laterality of cerebral function. *Journal of Abnormal Psychology, 88,* 887–890.

Hare, R. D. (1980). A research scale for the assessment of psychopathy in criminal populations. *Personality and Individual Differences, 1,* 111–119.

Hare, R. D. (1981). Psychopathy and violence. In J. Hays, T. Roberts, & K. Solway (Eds.), *Violence and the violent individual.* New York: Jamaica.

Hare, R. D. (1985). *The Psychopathy Checklist.* Vancouver, British Columbia, Canada: University of British Columbia Press.

Hare, R. D. (1991). *The Hare Psychopathy Checklist–Revised.* Toronto, Ontario, Canada: Multi-Health Systems.

Hare, R. D. (1996). Psychopathy: A clinical construct whose time has come. *Criminal Justice & Behavior, 23,* 25–54.

Hare, R. D. (2003). Hare Psychopathy Checklist-Revised, Second Edition (PCL-R, 2nd. Ed.) Toronto, Ontario, Canada: Multi-Health Systems.

Hare, R. D., & Connolly, J. F. (1987). Perceptual asymmetries and information processing in psychopaths. In S. Mednick, T. Moffitt, & S. Stack (Eds.), *The causes of crime: New biological approaches.* Cambridge, England: Cambridge University Press.

Hare, R. D., Forth, A. E., & Stachan, K. E. (1992). Psychopathy and crime across the life span. In R. D. Peters, R. J. McMahon, & V. L. Quinsey (Eds.), *Aggression and violence throughout the life span.* Newbury Park, CA: Sage.

Hare, R. D., Hart, S. D., & Harpur, T. J. (1991). Psychopathy and the *DSM–IV* criteria for antisocial personality disorder. *Journal of Abnormal Psychology, 100,* 391–398.

Hare, R. D., & Jutai, J. (1983). Criminal history of the male psychopath: Some preliminary data. In K. Van Dusen & S. Mednick (Eds.), *Prospective studies of crime and delinquency.* Boston: Kluwer-Nijhoff.

Hare, R. D., & McPherson, L. M. (1984a). Psychopathy and perceptual asymmetry during verbal dichotic listening. *Journal of Abnormal Psychology, 93,* 141–149.

Hare, R. D., & McPherson, L. (1984b). Violent and aggressive behavior by criminal psychopaths. *International Journal of Law and Psychiatry, 7,* 35–50.

Hare, R. D., & Schalling, D. (1978). *Psychopathic behavior: Approaches to research.* New York: Wiley.

Harkins, J.D., Catalano, R. F., Kosterman, R., Abbott, R., & Hill, K. G. (1999). Preventing adolescent health-risk behaviors by strengthening protection during childhood. *Archives of Pediatrics and Adolescent Medicine, 153,* 226–234.

Harlow, C. W. (1987). *Robbery victims.* Washington, DC: Bureau of Justice Statistics.

Harlow, C. W. (1991). *Female victims of violent crime.* Washington, DC: Bureau of Justice Statistics.

Harlow, C. W. (1998). *Profile of jail inmates 1996.* Washington, DC: U.S. Department of Justice, Bureau of Justice Statistics.

Harlowe, H. F. (1959, June). Love in infant monkeys. *Scientific American, XX,* 68–74.

Harries, K.D., & Stadler, S.J. (1988). Heat and violence: New findings from Dallas field data, 1980–1981. *Journal of Applied Social Psychology, 18,* 129–138.

Harris, M. G. (1988). *CHOLAS, Latino girls and gangs.* New York: AMS Press.

Harris, T. (1998). *The silence of the lambs*. New York: St. Martins.

Harrison, P. M., & Beck, A. J. (2005). *Prison and jail inmates at midyear 2004*. Washington, DC: U.S. Department of Justice, Office of Justice Programs, Bureau of Justice Statistics. Retrieved June 9, 2005, from http://www.ojp.usdoj.gov/bjs/pub/ascii/pjim 04.txt

Harry, B., & Balcer, C. (1987). Menstruation and crime: A critical review of the literature from the clinical criminology perspective. *Behavioral Sciences and the Law, 5,* 307–322.

Harter, S. (1996). The personal self in social context. In R. D. Ashmore & L. Jussim (Eds.), *Self and identity: Fundamental issues*. New York: Oxford University Press.

Hartup, W. W. (1974). Aggression in childhood: Developmental perspectives. *American Psychologist, 29,* 336–341.

Haskett, R. F. (1987). Premenstrual dysphoric disorder: Evaluation, pathophysiology and treatment. *Progress in Neuro-Psychopharmacology and Biological Psychiatry, 11,* 129–135.

Hastie, R., Penrod, S. D., & Pennington, N. (1983). *Inside the jury*. Cambridge, MA: Harvard University Press.

Hawkins, J. D., Catalano, R. F. Kosterman, R., Abbott, R., & Hill, K. G. (1999). Preventing adolescent health-risk behaviors by strengthening protection during childhood. *Archives of Pediatrics and Adolescent Medicine, 53,* 226–234.

Hawkins, J. D., Arthur, M. W., & Catalano, R. F. (1995). Preventing substance abuse. In M. Tonry & D. P. Farrington (Eds.), *Building a safer society: Crime and justice* (Vol. 19). Chicago: University of Chicago Press.

Hawkins, J. D., & Lam, T. (1987). Teacher practices, social development, and delinquency. In J. D. Burchard & S. N. Burchard (Eds.), *Prevention of delinquent behavior*. Newbury Park, CA: Sage.

Hawkins, J. D., & Weis, J. G. (1985). The social developmental model: An integrated approach to delinquency prevention. *Journal of Primary Prevention, 6,* 20.

Hayes-Bautista, D. E., Schink, W. O., & Hayes-Bautista, M. (1993). Latinos and the 1992 Los Angeles riots: A behavioral science perspective. *Hispanic Journal of Behavioral Sciences, 15,* 427–448.

Haywood, T. W., & Grossman, L S. (1994). Denial of deviant sexual arousal and psychopathology in child molesters. *Behavior Therapy, 25,* 327–340.

Hazen, C., & Shaver, P. (1994). Attachment as an organizational framework for research on close relationships. *Psychological Inquiry, 5,* 1–22.

Healy, W., & Bonner, A. (1931). *New light on delinquency and its treatment*. New Haven, CT: Yale University Press.

Heath, T. (2000, February 2). Violent profession takes public beating. *Washington Post*, p. B3.

Heavey, C. L., Adelman, H. S., Nelson, P., & Smith, D. C. (1989). Learning problems, anger, perceived control, and misbehavior. *Journal of Learning Disabilities, 22,* 47–50.

Hebb, D. O. (1972). *Textbook of psychology* (3rd ed.). Philadelphia: Saunders.

Heffernan, E. (1972). *Making it in prison: The square, the cool and the life*. New York: Wiley.

Heide, K. M. (1998). *Young killers: The challenge of juvenile homicide*. Thousand Oaks, CA: Sage.

Heilbrun, K. S. (1987). The assessment of competence for execution: An overview. *Behavioral Sciences and the Law, 5,* 383–396.

Heilbrun, K., & Collins, S. (1995). Evaluation of trial competency and mental state at the time of the offense: Report characteristics. *Professional Psychology: Research and Practice, 26,* 61–67.

Heise, L. M., & Garcia-Moreno, C. (2002). *Violence by intimate partners*. World Report on Violence and Health, Geneva, Switzerland: World Health Organization.

Helfgott, J. B. (1997). The relationship between unconscious defensive process and conscious cognitive style in psychopaths. *Criminal Justice & Behavior, 24,* 278–293.

Heller, W., Nitschke, J. B., & Miller, G. A. (1998). Lateralization in emotion and emotional disorders. *Current Directions in Psychological Science, 7,* 26–32.

Hellerstein, D., Frosch, W., & Koenigsberg, H. W. (1987). The clinical significance of command hallucinations. *American Journal of Psychiatry, 144,* 219–221.

Hendin, H. (1994). Fall from power: Suicide of an executive. *Suicide & Life-Threatening Behavior, 24,* 293–301.

Henggeler, S. (1989). *Delinquency in adolescence*. Newbury Park, CA: Sage.

Henry, B., Caspi, A., Moffitt, T., & Silva, P. (1996). Temperamental and familiar predictors of violent and nonviolent criminal convictions: Age 3 to age 18. *Developmental Psychology, 32,* 614–623.

Henson, D. (2003). *Drug abuse resistance education: The effectiveness of DARE*. Retrieved June 21, 2005, from at http://www. alcoholfacts.org/DARE.html

Hentoff, N. (2000, May 15). Meting out justice. *Texas Lawyer*, p. 46.

Heritage Foundation. (1995). *The real root causes of violent crime: The breakdown of marriage, family, and community*. Washington, DC: Author.

Hern, W.M. (1991). Proxemics: The application of theory to conflict arising from antiabortion demonstrations. *Population and Environment: A Journal of Interdisciplinary Studies, 12,* 379–388.

Hertzberg, H. (2003, October 27). Rush in rehab. Talk of the town. *The New Yorker*. Retrieved January 8, 2005, from http://www.newyorker.com/talk/content/?031027 ta_talk_hertzberg

Hesselbrock, V., Meyer, R., & Hesselbrock, M. (1992). Psychopathology and addictive disorders: The specific case of antisocial personality disorder. In C. P. O'Brien

& J. H. Jaffe (Eds.), *Addictive states* (pp. 179–191). New York: Raven.

Hetherington, E. M., Cox, M., & Cox, R. (1982). Effects of divorce on parents and children. In M. Lamb (Ed.), *Nontraditional families*. Hillsdale, NJ: Lawrence Erlbaum Associates, Inc.

Hewitt, B., & Longley, J. (2001, April 9). Sister of mercy. *People Magazine*.

Hiatt, F. (1998, November 1). Cats or kids? *The Washington Post*, p. C7.

Hickey, E. W. (1997). *Serial murderers and their victims* (2nd ed.). Belmont, CA: Wadsworth.

Hill, S. Y. (1992). Absence of paternal sociopathy in the etiology of severe alcoholism: Is there a Type III alcoholism? *Journal of Studies on Alcohol, 53*, 161–169.

Hillard, J. (2004, July 14). Living out loud: Death of a radiohead. Cincinnati CityBeat. Retrieved May 30, 2006 from http://www.citybeat.com/2004-07-14/livingoutloud.shtml

Hindelang, M. J., Gottfredson, M. R., & Garofalo, J. (1978). *Victims of personal crime: An empirical foundation for a theory of personal crime*. Cambridge, MA: Ballinger.

Hindus, M. (1980). *Prison and plantation: Crime, justice, and authority in Massachusetts and South Carolina, 1767–1878*. Chapel Hill: University of North Carolina Press.

Hinshaw, S. P. (1987). On the distinction between attentional deficit/hyperactivity and conduct problems/aggression in child psychopathology. *Psychological Bulletin, 101*, 443–463.

Hippchen, L. (Ed.). (1978). *Biologic-biochemical approaches to treatment of delinquents and criminals*. New York: Von Nostrant Reinhold.

Hiroto, D. S., & Seligman, L. M. E. P. (1975). Generality of learned helplessness in man. *Journal of Personality and Social Psychology, 31*, 311–327.

Hirschi, T. (1969). *Causes of delinquency*. Berkeley: University of California Press.

Hirschi, T. (1995). The family. In J. Q. Wilson & J. Petersilia (Eds.), *Crime*. San Francisco: ICS Press.

Hirschi, T., & Gottfredson, M. (1987). Causes of white-collar crime. *Criminology, 25*, 949–974.

Hirschi, T., & Hindelang, M. (1977). Intelligence and delinquency: A revisionist review. *American Sociological Review, 42*, 471–586.

Hockstader, L. & Whitlock, W. (1999). Israeli court sentences Sheinbein to 24 years. *Washington Post*, p. B1. California Penal Code, 186.22.

Hoffman, M. L. (1982). Development of prosocial motivation: Empathy and guilt. In N. Eisenbert (Ed.), *The development of prosocial behavior* (pp. 281–313). New York: Academic.

Hoffman, M. (1988). Moral development. In M. H. Bornstein & M. E. Lamb (Eds.), *Developmental psychology: An advanced textbook* (2nd ed.). Hillsdale, NJ: Lawrence Erlbaum Associates, Inc.

Hoge, S. K., Bonnie, R. J., Poythress, N. G., & Monahan, J. (2004). Lutz, FL: Psychological Assessment Resources, Inc.

Hollin, C. R. (1989). *Psychology and crime*. London: Routledge.

Holmes, R. M. (1993). Stalking in America: Types and methods of criminal stalkers. *Contemporary Criminal Justice, 9*, 317.

Holmes, R. M., & DeBurger, J. (1988). *Serial murder*. Newbury Park, CA: Sage.

Holmes. S. A. (1999, April 25). Both a victim of racial profiling and a practitioner. *New York Times*, Week in Review, p. 7.

Holmes, S. T., Hickey, E., & Holmes, R. M. (1991). Female serial murderesses: Constructing differentiating typologies. *Journal of Contemporary Criminal Justice, 7*, 245–256.

Holmes, W. C., & Slap, G. B. (1998). Sexual abuse of boys: Definition, prevalence, correlates, sequelae, and management. *Journal of the American Medical Association, 280*, 1855–1862.

Holt v. Sarver, 309 F. Supp. 362 (E.D. Ark. 1970).

Holtzworth-Monroe, A. (2000). A typology of men who are violent toward their female partners: Making sense of the heterogeneity in husband violence. *Current Directions in Psychological Science, 9*, 140–143.

Hooton, E. A. (1939). *The American criminal: An anthropological study*. Cambridge, MA: Harvard University Press.

Hope v. Pelzer, 536 U.S. 730 (2002).

Hops, H., Tildesley, E., Lichtenstein, E., Ary, D., & Sherman, L. (1990). Parent-adolescent problem-solving interactions and drug use. *American Journal of Drug and Alcohol Abuse, 16*, 239–258.

Horney, J. (1978). Menstrual cycles and criminal responsibility. *Law and Human Nature, 2*, 25–36.

Horney, J., Osgood, D. W., & Marshall, I. H. (1996). *Adult patterns of criminal behavior*. Washington, DC: National Institute of Justice.

Horning, D. (1983). Employee theft. In S. Kadish (Ed.), *Encyclopedia of crime and justice* (pp. 698–704). New York: MacMillan and Free Press.

Horowitz, I. A. (1980). Juror selection: A comparison of two methods in several criminal cases. *Journal of Applied Social Psychology, 10*, 86–99.

Horowitz, R., & Schwartz, G. (1974). Honor, normative ambiguity, and gang violence. *American Sociological Review, 39*, 238–251.

Hostages released, fired postal employee surrenders. (1997, December 25). *The Washington Post*, p. A13.

Hotaling, G. T., & Sugarman, D. B. (1986). An analysis of risk markers in husband to wife violence: The current state of knowledge. *Violence and Victims, 1*, 101–124.

Howard, R., Payamal, L. T., & Neo, L. H. (1997). Response modulation deficits in psychopaths: a failure to confirm and a reconsideration of the Patterson-Newman model. *Personality & Individual Differences, 22*, 707–717.

Howell, J. C. (1994). *Gangs* (Fact Sheet No. 12). Washington, DC: Office of Juvenile Justice and Delinquency Prevention.

Howell, J.C., & Decker, S. H. (1999). *The youth gang, drugs, and violence connection.* Washington, DC: U.S. Department of Justice, Office of Justice Programs, Office of Juvenile Justice and Delinquency Prevention.

Hoyert, D. L., Kochanek, K. D. & Murphy, S. L. (1999). Deaths: Final data for 1997. *National Vital Statistics Reports, 47*(19), 1–115.

Hsu, S. S. (1998, June 17). Victim's sister urges clemency. *The Washington Post,* p. B4

Hsu, L., & Starzynski, J. (1990). Adolescent rapists and adolescent child sexual assaulters. *International Journal of Offender Therapy and Comparative Criminology, 34,* 23–30.

Huesmann, L. R., & Eron, L. D. (1986). *Television and the aggressive child: A cross-national comparison.* Hillsdale, NJ: Lawrence Erlbaum Associates, Inc.

Huesmann, L. R., Lagerspetz, K., & Eron, L. D. (1984). Intervening variables in the TV violence-aggression relation: Evidence from two countries. *Developmental Psychology, 20,* 746–775.

Huesmann, L. R., Moise, J. F., & Podolski, C. L. (1997). The effects of media violence on the development of antisocial behavior. In D. M. Stoff, J. Breiling, & J. D. Maser (Eds.), *Handbook of antisocial behavior* (pp. 181–193). New York: Wiley.

Human Rights Watch. (1997). *Cold storage: Super-maximum security confinement in Indiana.* New York: Author.

Human Rights Watch. (2000, May). Punishment and prejudice: Racial disparities in the war on drugs. *Human Rights Watch Report-United States, 12*(2), G1202.

Human Rights Watch. (2004). *Ill-equipped: U.S. prisons and offenders with mental illness.* New York: Author. Retrieved June 15, 2005, from http://www.hrw.org/reports/2003/usa1003/

Humphreys, M. S., Johnstone, E. C., MacMillan, J. F., & Taylor, P. J. (1992). Dangerous behavior preceding first admissions for schizophrenia. *British Journal of Psychiatry, 161,* 501–505.

Hunter, S. (1999, April 28). Literary license to kill: The language of irony is open to misrepresentation. *Washington Post,* pp. C1. 11.

Icove, D. J., & Estepp, M. H. (1987, April). Motive-based offender profiles of arson and fire-related crime. *FBI Law Enforcement Bulletin,* pp. 17–23.

Inciardi, J. A. (1975). *Careers in crime.* Chicago: Rand McNally.

In Colorado, 3 judges rule on penalty in murder case. (1999, April 18). *The New York Times,* p. 26.

Instructions to disregard and the jury: Curative and paradoxical effects. In J. M. Golding & C. M. MacLeod (Eds.), *Intentional forgetting: Interdisciplinary approaches* (pp. 413–434). Mahwah, NJ: Lawrence Erlbaum.

Irwin, J. (1980). *Prisons in turmoil.* Boston: Little, Brown.

Isely, P. J., & Gehrenbeck-Shim, D. (1997). Sexual assault of men in the community. *Journal of Community Psychology, 25,* 159–166.

Ito, T. A., Miller., N., & Pollock, V. E. (1996). Alcohol and aggression: A meta-analysis on the moderating effects of inhibitory cues, triggering events, and self-focused attention. *Psychological Bulletin, 120,* 60–82.

Ivey, G., & Simpson, P. (1998). The psychological life of pedophiles: A phenomenological study. *South African Journal of Psychology, 28*(1), 15–20.

Jackman, T. (2003, May 18). Escape "The Matrix," go directly to jail: Some defendants in slaying cases make reference to hit movie. *The Washington Post,* pp. A1, A10.

Jackson. K. L. (1997). Differences in the background and criminal justice characteristics of young Black, White and Hispanic male federal prison inmates. *Journal of Black Studies, 27,* 494–509.

Jackson, S. (1948/1996). The lottery. In D. Madden (Ed.), A pocketful of prose: Vintage short fiction, Vol II. Ft. Worth, TX: Harcourt-Brace.

Jacobs, J. (1977). The prisoners' rights movement and its impacts. In *Manual of standards for adult correctional institutions* (pp.33–60). College Park, MD: American Correctional Association.

Jacobs, J. (1977). *Stateville: The penitentiary in mass society.* Chicago: University of Chicago Press.

Jails without walls. (1997, September 4). *The Washington Post,* p. A24.

James, R. (1959). Status and competence of jurors. *American Journal of Sociology, 64,* 563–570.

Janik, J. (1992). Dealing with mentally ill offenders. *Law Enforcement Bulletin, 61*(7), 22–26.

Jankowski, M. S. (1991). *Islands in the street: Gangs and American urban society.* Berkeley: University of California Press.

Janoff-Bulman, R., Timko, C., & Carli, L. L. (1985). Cognitive biases in blaming the victim. *Journal of Experimental Social Psychology, 21,* 161–177.

Janssen, E. (1995). Understanding the rapist's mind. *Perspectives in Psychiatric Care, 31*(4), 9–13.

Jaravik, L. F., Klodin, V., & Matsuyama, S. S. (1973). Human aggression and the extra Y chromosome. *American Psychologist, 28,* 674–682.

J. E. B. ex. Rel. T. B., 511 U.S. 127 (1994).

Jesilow, P., Pontell, H. N., & Geis, G. (1993). *Prescription for profit—How doctors defraud Medicaid.* Berkeley: University of California Press.

Jessor, R., & Jessor, S. L. (1977). *Problem behavior and psychosocial development: A longitudinal study of youth.* San Diego: Academic.

Johnson, A. B. (1990). *Out of bedlam: The truth about deinstitutionalization.* New York: Basic Books.

Johnson, C., Webster, B., & Connors, E. (1995). *Prosecuting gangs: A national assessment.* Washington, DC: National Institute of Justice.

Johnson, J. (1994). Witness for the prosecution. *The New Yorker.*

Johnson, K. (2003, December 17). Hinckley allowed unsupervised visits. USA Today. Retrieved May 30, 2006 from http://www.usatoday.com/news/nation/2003-12-17-hinckley-visits_x.htm

Johnson, R. (1990). *Death work: A study of the modern execution process.* Belmont, CA: Wadsworth.

Johnson, R. (1996). *Hard time: Understanding and reforming the prison* (2nd ed.). Belmont, CA: Wadsworth.

Johnson, R., & Toch, J. (1988). Introduction. In R. Johnson & H. Toch (Eds.), *The pains of imprisonment* (pp. 13–21). Prospect Heights, IL: Waveland.

Johnson v. Louisiana, 406 U.S. 356 (1972).

Johnson v. Noot, 323 N.W.2d 724 (Minn. 1982).

Johnston, L. D. (1991). Toward a theory of drug epidemics. In L. Donohew, H. E. Sypher, & W. J. Bukoski (Eds.), *Persuasive communication and drug abuse prevention.* Hillsdale, NJ: Lawrence Erlbaum Associates, Inc.

Johnstone, J. W. C., Hawkins, D. F. Y., & Michener, A. (1994). Homicide reporting in Chicago dailies. *Journalism Quarterly, 71,* 860–872.

Jones, M. C. (1924). A laboratory study of fear: The case of Peter. *Pedagogical Seminary, 31,* 308–315.

Jonsson, P. (2003, June 4). How did Eric Rudolph survive? *Christian Science Monitor.* Retrieved May 30, 2006 from http://www.csmonitor.com/2003/0604/p01s02-usju.html

Josephson, W. (1987). Television violence and children's aggression: Testing the priming, social script, and disinhibition predictions. *Journal of Personality and Social Psychology, 53,* 882–890.

Jurkovic, G., & Prentice, N. (1977). Relations of moral and cognitive development to dimensions of juvenile delinquency. *Journal of Abnormal Psychology, 86,* 414–415.

Kadushin, A., & Martin, J. A. (1981). *Child abuse: An interactional event.* New York: Columbia University Press.

Kagan, J. (1981). *The second year.* Cambridge, MA: Harvard University Press.

Kagan. J. (1984). *The nature of the child.* New York: Basic Books.

Kagan, J. (1989). *Unstable ideas: Temperament, cognition, and self.* Cambridge, MA: Harvard University Press.

Kagan, J., & Snidman, N. (2004). *The long shadow of temperament.* Cambridge, MA: Harvard University Press.

Kagan, J., Snidman, N., Arcus, D., & Reznick, J. (1994). *Galen's prophecy: Temperament in human nature.* New York: Basic Books.

Kahan, D. (1997a, August). Between economics and sociology: The new path of deterrence. *Michigan Law Review.*

Kahan, D. (1997b). Social influence, social meaning, and deterrence. *Virginia Law Review, 83,* 349–395.

Kalven, H., & Zeisel, H. (1966). *The American jury.* Boston: Little, Brown.

Kaminer, W. (1995). *It's all the rage: Crime and culture.* Reading, MA: Addison-Wesley.

Kanapaux, W. (2004). Guilty of mental illness. *Psychiatric Times, XXI*(1). Retrieved March 4, 2005, from http://www.psychiatrictimes.com/p040101a.html

Kandel, D. B. (1982). Epidemiological and psychosocial perspectives on adolescent drug use. *Journal of American Academic Clinical Psychiatry, 21,* 328–347.

Kandel, D. B., & Andrews, K. (1987). Processes of adolescent socialization by parents and peers. *International Journal of Addiction, 22,* 319–342.

Kandel, D., & Davies, M. (1991). Friendship networks, intimacy and illicit drug use in young adulthood: A comparison of two competing theories. *Criminology, 29,* 441–471.

Kandel, D. B., Kessler, R. C., & Marguiles, R. Z. (1978). Antecedents of adolescent initiation into stages of drug use: A developmental analysis. In D. B. Kandel (Ed.), *Longitudinal research on drug use* (pp. 73–98). Washington, DC: Hemisphere.

Kanof, M. (2003). *Youth illicit drug use prevention: DARE long-term evaluations and federal efforts to identify effective programs.* Washington, DC: General Accounting Office.

Kantor, G. K., & Jasinski, J. L. (1998). Dynamics and risk factors in partner violence. In J. L. Jasinski & L. M. Williams (Eds.), *Partner violence: A comprehensive review of 20 years of research.* Thousand Oaks, CA: Sage.

Kaplan, M. F., & Schersching, C. (1981). Juror deliberation: An information integration analysis. In B. Sales (Ed.), *The trial process* (pp. 235–262).

Kappeler, V. E., Blumberg, M., & Potter, G. W. (1996). *The mythology of crime and criminal justice* (2nd ed.). Prospect Heights, IL: Waveland.

Katz, J. (1991). The motivation of the persistent robber. In M. H. Tonry (Ed.), *Crime and justice: A review of the research* (pp. 277–305). Chicago: University of Chicago Press.

Karberg, J. C., & Beck, A. J. (2004). *National prisoner statistics 2003.* Washington, DC: Bureau of Justice Statistics.

Karmen, A. (1990). *Crime victims: An introduction to victimology* (2nd ed.). Pacific Grove, CA: Brooks/Cole.

Karmen, A. (2000). *Crime victims: An introduction to victimology* (4th ed.) Pacific Grove, CA: Brooks/Cole.

Karon, B. P. (1995). Provision of psychotherapy under managed health care: A growing crisis and national nightmare. *Professional Psychology: Research and Practice, 26,* 5–9.

Karr-Morse, R., & Wiley, M. (1997). *Ghosts from the nursery: Tracing the roots of violence.* Boston: Atlantic Monthly Press.

Kassin, S. M., & Studebaker, C. A. (1998). Instructions to disregard and the jury: Curative and paradoxical effects. In J. M. Golding & C. M. MacLeod (Eds.), *Intentional forgetting: Interdisciplinary approaches* (pp.413–434). Hillsdale, NJ: Lawrence Erlbaum Associates, Inc.

Kassin, S. M., & Wrightsman, L. S. (1983). The construction and validation of a juror bias scale. *Journal of Research in Personality, 17,* 423–441.

Katz, J. (1988). *Seductions of crime: Moral and sensual attractions for doing evil.* New York: Basic Books.

Katz, J. (1995). [Review of the book *Burglars on the job: Street life and residential break-ins*]. *Contemporary Sociology, 24,* 798–799.

Katz. R. C., & Marquette, J. (1996). Psychosocial characteristics of young violent offenders: A comparative study. *Criminal Behavior & Mental Health, 6,* 339–348.

Kazdin, A. E., & Kolko, D. J. (1986). Parent psychopathology and family functioning among childhood firesetters. *Journal of Abnormal Child Psychology, 14,* 315–329.

Keeney, B. T., & Heide, K. M. (1994). Gender differences in serial murderers: A preliminary analysis. *Journal of Interpersonal Violence, 9,* 383–398.

Kegley, C. W., Jr. (Ed.). (2003). *The new global terrorism: Characteristics, causes, controls.* Upper Saddle River, NJ: Prentice-Hall.

Kellam, S. G., & Brown, H. (1982). *Social adaptational and psychological antecedents of adolescent psychopathology ten years later.* Baltimore: Johns Hopkins University.

Kellerman, A. (1993, October 7). Gun ownership as a risk factor for homicide in the home. *New England Journal of Medicine, 329*(15).

Kellermann A. (1998). Injuries and deaths due to firearms in the home. *Journal of Trauma, 45,* 263–267.

Kelley, B., Loeber, R., Keenan, K., & DeLamatre, M. (1997, December). Developmental pathways in boy's disruptive and delinquent behavior. In *Juvenile Justice Bulletin.* Washington, DC: Office of Juvenile Justice and Delinquency Prevention.

Kelley, B. T., Thornberry, T. P., & Smith, C. A. (1997). *In the wake of childhood maltreatment.* Washington, DC: Office of Juvenile Justice & Delinquency Prevention.

Kelling, G. (1997, February 9). Restore order and you reduce crime. *The Washington Post,* p. C3.

Kelly, D. (1982). *Creating school failure, youth crime, and deviance.* Los Angeles: Trident Shop.

Kelly, D., & Balch, R. (1971). Social origins and school failure. *Pacific Sociological Review, 14,* 413–430.

Kennedy, L. W., & Sacco, V. F. (1998). *Crime victims in context.* Los Angeles, CA: Roxbury Publishing Co.

Kennedy, R. (1998). *Race, crime, and the law.* New York: Vintage Books.

Kenney, D. J., & Finckenauer, J. O. (1995). *Organized crime in America.* Belmont, CA: Wadsworth.

Keppel, R. D. (1995). Signature murders: A report of several related cases. *Journal of Forensic Sciences, 40,* 670–674.

Kernberg, O. F. (1975). *Borderline conditions and pathological narcissism.* New York: Aronson.

Kernberg, O. F. (1976). *Object relations, theory and clinical psychoanalysis.* New York: Aronson.

Kerr, N. L. (1981). Effects of prior juror experience on juror behavior. *Basic and Applied Social Psychology, 2,* 175–193.

Kerr, N. L., Hymes, R. W., Anderson, A. B., & Weathers, J. E. (1995). Defendant-juror similarity and mock juror judgments. *Law and Human Behavior, 19,* 545–568.

Kesey, K. (1962). *One flew over the cuckoo's nest.* New York: Viking.

Kilpatrick, D. G., Acierno, R., Saunders, B., Resnick, H., Best, C. L., & Schnurr, P. (2000). Risk factors for adolescent substance abuse and dependence: Data from a national sample. *Journal of Consulting and Clinical Psychology, 68,* 19–30.

Kindlon, D. J., Tremblay, R. E., Mezzcappa, E., Earls, F. L., Laruent, D., & Schall, B. (1995). Longitudinal patterns of heart rate and fighting behavior in 9- through 12-year old-boys. *Journal of the American Academy of Child and Adolescent Psychiatry, 34,* 371–77.

King, M. L. (1963). Letter from Birmingham jail. In *To lead or not to lead: Phi Beta Kappa Leadership Development Studies* (pp. 8.27–8.29). Jackson, MS: Phi Theta Kappa

King, R. S., & Mauer, M. (2002). State sentencing and corrections policies in an era of fiscal restraint. Washington, DC: U.S. Sentencing Project.

Kinsley, C., & Svare, B. (1987). Genotype modulates prenatal stress effects on aggression in male and female mice. *Behavioral Neural Biology, 47,* 138–50.

Klahr, D., & Wallace, J. G. (91976). *Cognitive development: An information-processing view.* Hillsdale, NJ: Lawrence Erlbaum Associates, Inc.

Klein, D. C., & Seligman, M. E. P. (1976). Reversal of performance deficits and perceptual deficits in learned helplessness and depression. *Journal of Abnormal Psychology, 85,* 11–26.

Klein, M. (1975). Envy and gratitude. *In Envy and gratitude and other works, 1946–1963* (pp. 176–238). (Original work published 1957)

Klein, M. (1964). *Contributions to psychoanalysis: 1920–1945.* New York: McGraw-Hill.

Klein, M. (1975). *The writings of Melanie Klein.* London: Hogarth.

Klein, M. (1986). Labeling theory and delinquency policy: An empirical test. *Criminal Justice and Behavior, 13,* 47–49.

Klein, M. (1995). *The American street gang: Its nature, prevalence and control.* New York: Oxford University Press.

Klemke, L. W. (1992). *The sociology of shoplifting: Boosters and snitches today.* Westport, CT: Praeger.

Knight, R. A., & Prentky, R. A. (1987). The developmental antecedents and adult adaptations of rapist subtypes. *Criminal Justice and Behavior, 14,* 403–426.

Knox, G. W. (1999). *A national assessment of gangs and security threat groups (STGs) in adult corrections institutions: Results of the 1999 adult corrections survey.* Peotone, IL: National Gang Crime Research Center.

Koch, J. L. (1891). *Die Psychopathischen Minderwertigkeiten*. Ravensburg: Maier.

Kohlberg, L. (1964). The development of moral character. In M. D. Hoffman (Ed.), *Child development*. New York: Sage.

Kohlberg, L. (1976). Moral stages and moralization: The cognitive-developmental approach to moral education. In T. Lickona (Ed.), *Moral development and behavior: Theory, research and social issues* (pp. 31–53.) New York: Holt, Rinehart & Winston.

Kohlberg, L. (1984). *The psychology of moral development: Essays on moral development*. San Francisco: Harper & Row.

Kohlberg, L., Kufmann, P., Scharf, P., & Hickey, J. (1973). *The just community approach in corrections: A manual*. Niantic, CT: Connecticut Department of Corrections.

Kohut, H. (1977). *The restoration of the self*. New York: International Universities Press.

Kolko, D. J. (1989). Fire setting and pyromania. In C. Last & M. Hersen (Eds.), *Handbook of child psychiatric diagnosis*. New York: Wiley.

Kolko, D. J., & Kazdin, A. E. (1994). Children's descriptions of their firesetting incidents: Characteristics and relationship to recidivism. *Journal of the American Academy of Child & Adolescent Psychiatry 33*, 114–122.

Konecni, V. J., Libuser, L., Morton, H., & Ebbesen, E. B. (1975). Effects of a violation of personal space on escape and helping responses. *Journal of Experimental Social Psychology, 11*, 288–299.

Kong, D. (1997, August 15). Study shows cohesiveness curbs neighborhood violence. *The Boston Globe*, p. A12.

Konopka, G. (1966). *The adolescent girl in conflict*. Englewood Cliffs, NJ: Prentice-Hall.

Koop, C. (1987). Report of the Surgeon Generals workshop on pornography and public health. *American Psychologist, 42*, 944–945.

Kotlowitz, A. (1991). *There are no children here*. New York: Anchor Doubleday.

Kovaleski, S. F. (1996). Officials probe Unabomber suspect's failed 1978 relationship. *The Washington Post*, p. A1.

Kovaleski, S. F., & Adams, L. (1996, June 16). A stranger in the family picture. *The Washington Post*, p. A1.

Kozol, H., Boucher, R., & Garofalo, R. (1972). The diagnosis and treatment of dangerousness. *Crime and Delinquency, 18*, 371–392.

Kraepelin, E. (1903–1904). *Psychiatrie: Ein Lehrbuch* (7th ed.). Leipzig, Germany: Barth.

Kramer, R. (1982). Corporate crime: An organizational perspective. In P. Wickman & T. Dailey (Eds.), *White collar and economic crime: A multidisciplinary and crossnational perspective* (pp. 75–94). Lexington, MA: Lexington.

Kratzer, L., & Hodgins, S. (1996). *A typology of offenders: A test of Moffitt's theory among males and females from childhood to age 30*. Paper presented at the meeting of the Life History Research Society, London.

Kratzer, L., & Hodgins, S. (1997). Adult outcomes of child conduct problems: A cohort study. *Journal of Abnormal Child Psychology, 25*, 65–81.

Kraus, R. T. (1995). An enigmatic personality: Case report of a serial killer. *Journal of Orthomolecular medicine, 10*(1), 11–24.

Kraut, R., Patterson, M., Lundmark, V., Kiesler, S., Mukopadhyay, T. Y., & Scherlis, W. (1998). Internet paradox: A social technology that reduces social involvement and psychological well-being? *American Psychologist 53*, 1017–1031.

Krisberg, B., & Onek, D. (1994). *A manual for the comprehensive strategy for serious, violent, and chronic juvenile offenders*. Washington, DC: National Council on Crime and Delinquency.

Krisberg, B., Currie, E., & Onek, D. (1994, November). *Graduated sanctions for serious, violent, and chronic juvenile offenders*. Washington, DC: National Council on Crime and Delinquency.

Krohn, M., Thornberry, T., Collins-Hall, L., & Lizotte, A. (1995). School dropout, delinquent behavior, and drug use. In H. Kaplan (Ed.), *Drugs, crime, and other deviant adaptations: Longitudinal studies*. New York: Plenum.

Kruesi, M. J., Hibbs, E. D., Zahn, T. P., Keysor, C. S., Hamburger, S., Bartko, J. J., et al. (1992). A 2-year prospective follow-up study of children and adolescents with disruptive behavior disorders. *Archives of General Psychiatry, 49*, 429–435.

Krug, E. G., & Powell, K. E. (1998). Firearm-related deaths in the United States and 35 other high-and upper-middle-income countries. *International Journal of Epidemiology, 27*, 5–12.

Kruttschnitt, C. (1980). A sociological, offender-based, study of rape. *Sociological Quarterly, 30*, 305–329.

Kumpfer, K., Molgaard, V., & Spoth, R. (1996). The strengthening families program for the prevention of delinquency and drug use. In R. D. Peters & R. J. McMahon (Eds.), *Preventing childhood disorders, substance abuse and delinquency*. Thousand Oaks, CA: Sage.

Kurtz, H. (1998, May 26). The neighborly newscasts. *The Washington Post*, p. C1.

Kushner, Harvey. (2003). *Encyclopedia of Terrorism*. Thousand Oaks, CA: Sage Publications.

Kwitney, J. (1979). *Vicious circles—The Mafia in the marketplace*. New York: Norton.

Lacayo, R. (1996, April 22). A tale of two brothers. *Time*, 44–51.

Lacquer, W. (1999). *The New Terrorism: Fanaticism and the Arms of Mass Destruction*. Oxford University Press.

LaFond, J. Q. (1998). The costs of enacting a sexual predator law. *Psychology, Public Policy, and Law, 4*, 468–504.

LaFree, G. D. (1989). *Rape and criminal justice: The social construction of sexual assault.* Belmont, CA: Wadsworth.

Lahey, B. B., McBurnett, K., Loeber, R., & Hart, E. L. (1995). Psychobiology of conduct disorder. In G. P. Sholevar (Ed.), *Conduct disorders in children and adolescents: Assessments and interventions* (pp. 27–44). Washington, DC: American Psychiatric Press.

Lamb, H. R., & Shaner, R. (1993). When there are almost no state hospital beds left. Special Section: Policy issues in mental health. *Hospital and Community Psychiatry, 44,* 973–976.

Lamb, M. E. (1976). Parent-infant interaction in 8-month-olds. *Child Psychiatry and Human Development, 7,* 56–63.

Lamb, M. E. (1977). Father-infant and mother-infant interaction in the first year of life. *Child Development, 48,* 167–181.

Lamontagne, Y., Carpentier, N., Hetu, C., & Lacerte-Lamontage, C. (1994). Shoplifting and mental illness. *Canadian Journal of Psychiatry, 39,* 300–302.

Lande, G. (1995). Military shoplifting. *Military Medicine, 160,* 404–407.

Lane, R. (1989). *Roots of violence in black Philadelphia, 1860–1900.* Boston, MA: Harvard University Press.

Langan, P., & Brown, J. (1997). *Felony sentences in state court.* Washington, DC: U.S. Department of Justice, Office of Justice Programs, Bureau of Justice Statistics.

Langan, P. A., & Farrington, D. P. (1998). *Crime and justice in the United States and in England and Wales, 1981–1996.* Washington, DC: Bureau of Justice Statistics.

Lange, J. (1929). *Vebrechen als Schicksal* [Crime and Destiny]. Leipzig, Germany: Georg Thieme Verlag.

Lanyon, R. L. (1986). Theory and treatment in child molestation. *Journal of Consulting and Clinical Psychology, 54,* 176–182.

Laschet, U. (1973). Antiandrogen in the treatment of sex offenders: Mode of action and therapeutic outcome. In J. Zulbin & J. Money (Eds.), *Contemporary sexual behavior.* Baltimore: Johns Hopkins University Press.

Laub, J., & Sampson, R. (1988). Unraveling families and delinquency: A reanalysis of the Gluecks' Data. *Criminology, 26,* 355–380.

Lawrence, R. (1991). Reexamining community corrections models. *Crime and Delinquency, 37,* 436–449.

Lawrence v. Texas, 539 U.S. 1 (2003).

Lawson, G., Peterson, J. S., & Lawson, A. (1983). *Alcoholism and the family: A guide to treatment and prevention.* Rockville, MD: Aspen.

Lazarus, R. S., DeLongis, A., Folkman, S., & Gruen, R. (1985). Stress and adaptational outcomes: The problem of confounded measures. *American Psychologist, 40,* 770–779.

LeBeau, J. (1987). Patterns of stranger and serial rape offending: Factors distinguishing apprehended and at-large offenders. *Journal of Criminal Law and Criminology, 78,* 309–326.

LeBlanc, M., Ouimet, M., & Tremblay, R. (1988). An integrative control theory of delinquent behavior: A validation, 1976–1985. *Psychiatry, 51,* 164–176.

Lee, M., Zimbardo, P. G., & Bertholf, M. (1977, November). Shy murderers. *Psychology Today, 68–70,* 148.

Lefkowitz, B. (1998). *Our guys: The Glen Ridge rape and the secret life of the perfect suburb.* New York: Vintage.

Legault, F., & Strayer, F. F. (1990). The emergence of sex-segregation in preschool peer groups. In F. F. Strayer (Ed.), *Social interaction and behavioral development during early childhood.* Montreal, Quebec, Canada: La Maison D'Ethologie de Montreal.

Legras, A. M. (1932). *Psychese en Criminaliteit bij wellingen.* Utrecht, The Netherlands: Keminken ZOON N. V.

Leinwand, D. (2001, June 16). Ecstasy drug trade turns violent. *USA Today.* Retrieved January 8, 2005, from http://www.usatoday.com/news/nation/2001-05-16-ecstasy-usat.htm

Lengel, A. (1997, December 28). The price of urban violence. *The Washington Post,* pp. B1, B5.

Lengle, A. (2003, February 1). Suit, tie and semiautomatic: FBI, DC Police look for careful part-time bank robber. *The Washington Post,* p. B3.

Leonard, E. (1995). Theoretical criminology and gender. In B. Price & N. Sokoloff (Eds.), *The criminal justice system and women* (2nd ed.). New York: McGraw-Hill.

Leonard, K. E. (1990). Marital functioning among episodic and steady alcoholics. In R. L. Collins, K. E. Leonard, & J. S. Searles (Eds.), *Alcohol and the family: Research and clinical perspectives* (pp. 220–243), New York: Guilford.

Leong, G. B., & Silva, J. A. (1995). Psychiatric-legal analysis of criminal defendants charged with murder: A sample without major mental disorder. *Journal of Forensic Sciences, 40,* 858–861.

Lerner, H. (1986). An object representation approach to Rorschach assessment. In M. Kissen (Ed.), *Assessing object relations phenomena* (pp. 127–142). Madison, CT: International Universities Press.

Lerner, P., & Lerner, H. (1980). Rorschach assessment of primitive defenses in borderline personality structure. In J. Kwawer, H. Lerner, P. Lerner, & A. Sugarman (Eds.), *Borderline phenomena and the Rorschach Test* (pp. 257–274). New York: International Universities Press.

Lesieur, H. R., & Welch, M. (1991). Vice, public disorder, and social control. In J. Sheley (ED.), Criminology: A contemporary handbook (pp. 175–198). Belmont, CA: Wadsworth.

Lester, M. L., & Fishbein, D. H. (1987). Nutrition and neuropsychological development in children. In R. Tarter, D. H. Van Thile, & K. Edwards (Eds.), *Medical neuropsychology: The Impact of disease on behavior.* New York: Plenum.

Levi, M. (1987). *Regulating fraud—White-collar crime and the criminal process*. London: Tavistock.

Levin, B. (1993–1994, Winter). Bias crimes: A theoretical and practical overview. *Stanford Law and Policy Review*.

Levin, J., & McDevitt, J. (1993). *Hate crimes: The rising tide of bigotry and bloodshed*. New York: Plenum.

Levine, S. (1997, September 28). For parents of slaying suspects, an anguishing puzzle. *The Washington Post*, p. B1, B5.

Lewin, K. (1978). *Field theory in social science: Selected theoretical papers*. New York: Harper.

Lewis, A. (1964). *Gideon's trumpet*. New York: Vantage Books.

Lewis, D. O., Moy, E., Jackson, L., Aaronson, R., Restifo, N., Serra, et al. (1985). Biopychosocial characteristics of children who later murder. *American Journal of Psychiatry, 142,* 1161–1167.

Lewis, D., Pinus, J., Feldan, M., Jackson, L., & Bard,, B. (1986). Psychiatric, neurological, and psychoeducational characteristics of 15 death row inmates in the United States. *American Journal of Psychiatry, 143,* 838–845.

Lewis, M., Sullivan, M., & Vasen, M. (1987). Making faces: Age and emotional difference in the posing of emotional expressions. *Developmental Psychology, 23,* 690–697.

Lewontin, R., Rose, S., & Kamin, L. (1984). *Not in our genes: Biology, ideology, and human nature*. New York: Pantheon.

Leyens, J. P., Camino, L., Parke, R. D., & Berkowitz, L. (1975). Effects of movie violence on aggression in a field setting as a function of group dominance and cohesion. *Journal of Personality and Social Psychology, 32,* 346–360.

Lidz, C. W., Mulvey, E. P., & Gardiner, W. (1993). The accuracy of predictions of violence to others. *Journal of the American Medical Association, 269,* 1007–1011.

Lilly, J. R., Ball, R., Curry, G. D., & McMullen, J. (1993). Electronic monitoring of the drunk driver: A seven-year study of the home confinement alternative. *Crime and Delinquency, 39,* 462–484.

Lind, M. (1995, October 23). Jury dismissed. *New Republic*, pp. 10–14.

Linder, R. L., Lerner, S. E., & Burn, R. S. (1981). The experience and effects of PCP abuse. In R. L. Linder, S. E. Lerner, & R. S. Burns (Eds.), *The devils dust: Recognition, management, and prevention of phencyclidine abuse*. Belmont, CA: Wadsworth.

Lindner, C., & Kohler, R. J. (1992). Probation officer victimization: An emerging concern. *Journal of Criminal Justice, 20,* 52–62.

Lingle, J. H., & Ostrom, T. M. (1981). Principles of memory and cognition in attitude formation. In R. E. Petty, T. M. Ostrom, & T. C. Brock (Eds.), *Cognitive responses to persuasion* (pp. 399–420). Hillsdale, NJ: Lawrence Erlbaum Associates, Inc.

Link, B., & Stueve, C. (1994). Psychotic symptoms and the violent/illegal behavior of mental patients compared to community controls. In J. Monahan & H. Steadman (Eds.), *Violence and mental disorder: Developments in risk assessment* (pp. 137–159). Chicago: University of Chicago Press.

Linnoila, M., Virkkunen, M., Scheinin, M., Nuutila, A., Rimon, R., & Goodwin, F. K. (1983). Low cerebrospinal fluid 5-hydroxindoleacetic acid concentration differentiates impulsive from nonimpulsive violent behavior. *Life Sciences, 33,* 2609–2614.

Linz, D. G., Donnerstein, E. I., & Penrod, S. (1988). Effects of long-term exposure to violent and sexually degrading depictions of women. *Journal of Personality & Social Psychology, 55,* 758–768.

Lipsey, M. (1992). Juvenile delinquency treatment: A meta-analytic inquiry into the variability of effects. In T. Cook, et al. (Eds.), *Meta-analysis for explanation: A casebook*. New York: Russell Sage Foundation.

Lipsitt, P., Lelos, D. & McGarry, A. (1971). Competency for trial: A screening instrument. *American Journal of Psychiatry, 128,* 105–109.

Lipton, D., McDonel, E. C., & McFall, R. (1987). Heterosexual perception in rapists. *Journal of Consulting and Clinical Psychology, 55,* 17–21.

Littleton, H. L., & Axsom, D. (2003, November). Rape and seduction scripts for university students: Implications for rape attributions and unacknowledged rape. *Sex Roles: A Journal of Research*. Retrieved January 16, 2005, from http://www.findarticles.com/p/articles/mi_m2294/is_9–10_49/ai_110813268

Litwack, T., & Schlesinger, B. (1999). Assessing and predicting violence: Research, law, and applications. In A. Hess & I. Weiner (Eds.), *Handbook of forensic psychology* (2nd ed., pp. 171–217). New York: Wiley.

Livesley, W. J., Schroeder, M., Jackson, D., & Jang, K. (1994). Categorical distinctions in the study of personality disorder: Implications for classification. *Journal of Abnormal Psychology, 103,* 6–17.

Lizotte, A., & Sheppard, D. (2001, July). Gun use by male juveniles: Research and prevention. *Juvenile Justice Bulletin*.

Lo, L. (1994). Exploring teenage shoplifting behavior: A choice and constraint approach. *Environment & Behavior, 26,* 613–639.

Lochman, J. E. (1987). Self and peer perceptions and attributional biases of aggressive and nonaggressive boys in dyadic interactions. *Journal of Counsulting and Clinical Psychology, 55,* 404–410.

Lochman, J. E., & Dodge, K. A. (1994). Social-cognitive processes of severely violent, moderately aggressive and nonaggressive boys. *Journal of Consulting and Clinical Psychology, 62,* 366–374.

Lochman, J. E., & Lenhart, L. A. (1993). Anger coping intervention for aggressive children: Conceptual models and outcomes effects: Disinhibition disorders in childhood. *Clinical Psychology Review, 10,* 1–42.

Lockett v. Ohio, 438 U.S. 586 (1978).

Lockhart v. McCree, 106 S. Ct. 1758 (1986).

Lockwood, D. (1980). *Prison sexual violence.* New York: Elsevier.

Locy, A. (1998, October 1). Punishing embezzlers is dilemma for judges. *The Washington Post,* pp. A1, A12–A13.

Loeber, R. (1988). Natural histories of conduct problems, delinquency, and associated substance use: Evidence from developmental progressions. In B. B. Lahey & A. E. Kazdin (Eds.), *Advances in Clinical Psychology* (Vol. 11, pp. 73–124). New York: Plenum.

Loeber, R. (1990). Development and risk factors of juvenile antisocial behavior and delinquency. *Clinical Psychology Review, 10,* 1–42.

Loeber, R. (1991). Antisocial behavior: More enduring than changeable? *Journal of the American Academy of Child and Adolescent Psychiatry, 31,* 393–397.

Loeber, R., Burke, J., Mutchka, J., & Lahey, B. (2003). Gun carrying and conduct disorder: A highly combustible combination? Implications for juvenile justice and mental and public health. *Archives of Pediatrics & Adolescent Medicine, 158,* 138–145.

Loeber, R., & Dishion, T. (1983). Early predictors of male delinquency: A review. *Psychological Bulletin, 94,* 68–99.

Loeber, R., & Dishion, T. J. (1984). Boys who fight at home and school: Family conditions influencing cross-setting consistency. *Journal of Consulting and Clinical Psychology, 52,* 759–768.

Loeber, R., Green, S. M., Keenan, K., & Lahey, B. (1995). Which boys will fare worse? Early predictors of the onset of conduct disorder in a six-year longitudinal study. *Journal of the American Academy of Child & Adolescent Psychiatry, 34,* 499–509.

Loeber, R., & Hay, D. F. (1997). Key issues in the development of aggression and violence from childhood to early adulthood. *Annual Review of Psychology, 48,* 371–410.

Loeber, R., Keenan, K., & Zhang, Q. (1997). Boys' experimentation and persistence in developmental pathways toward serious delinquency. *Journal of Child and Family Studies, 6,* 321–357.

Loeber, R., & Stouthamer-Loeber, M. (1986). Family factors as correlates and predictors of juvenile conduct problems and delinquency. In M. Tony & N. Morris (Eds.), *Crime and justice: An annual review of research* (Vol. 7, pp. 29–149). Chicago: University of Chicago Press.

Loeber, R., & Stouthamer-Loeber, M. (1998). Development of juvenile aggression and violence. Some common misconceptions and controversies. *American Psychologist, 53,* 242–259.

Loeber, R., Tremblay, R. E., Gagnon, C., & Charlebois, P. (1989). Continuity and desistance in disruptive boys' early fighting in school. *Development and Psychopathology, 1,* 39–50.

Loehlin, J. C. (1989). Partitioning environmental and genetic contributions to behavioral development. *American Psychologist, 44,* 1285–1292.

Loftus, E. (1993). The reality of repressed memories. *American Psychologist, 48,* 518–537.

Lohr, S. (1992, July 30). Indictment charges Clifford took bribes. *The New York Times,* p. A1.

Loving v. Virginia, 388 U.S. 1 (1967).

Lovinger, C. (1999, April 25). Violence, even before the Internet. *The New York Times Week in Review,* p. 18.

Lowenstein, M., Binder, R. L., & McNiel, D. E. (1990). The relationship between admission symptoms and hospital assaults. *Hospital and Community Psychiatry, 41,* 311–313.

Luckenbill, D. F. (1984). Murder and assault. In R. F. Meier (Ed.), *Major forms of crime.* Beverly Hills, CA: Sage.

Luginbuhl, J., & Burkead, M. (1994). Sources of bias and arbitrariness in the capital trial. *Journal of Social Issues, 50,* 103–124.

Lumet, S. (1957). *Twelve angry men.* Los Angeles, CA: MGM.

Lundberg-Love, P., & Geffner, R. (1989). Date rape: Prevalence, risk factors, and a proposed model. In M. A. Pirog-Good & J. E. Stets (Eds.), *Violence in dating relationships* (pp. 169–184). New York: Praeger.

Lykken, D. T. (1957). A study of anxiety in the sociopathic personality. *Journal of Abnormal and Social Psychology, 55,* 6–10.

Lyman, R. (1998, October 18). Hate laws don't matter, except when they do. *The New York Times Week in Review,* p. 6.

Lynam, D., Moffitt, T., & Stouthamer-Loeber, M. (1993). Explaining the relation between IQ and delinquency: Class, race, test motivation, school failure or self-control. *Journal of Abnormal Psychology, 102,* 187–196.

Maccoby, E. E. (1986). Social groupings in childhood. In D. Olweus, J. Block, & M. Radeke-Yarrow (Eds.), *Development of antisocial and prosocial behavior: Research, theories, and issues.* New York: Academic.

MacDonald, J. M. (1975). *Armed robbery: Offenders and their victims.* Springfield, IL: Thomas.

MacDonald, J., & Gifford, R. (1989). Territorial cues and defensible space theory: The burglar's point of view. *Journal of Environmental Psychology, 9,* 193–205.

MacKenzie, D. L., Brame, R., MacDowell, D., & Souryal, C. (1995). Boot camp prisons and recidivism in eight states. *Criminology, 33,* 327–358.

Mackey, P. E. (1976). *Voices against death: American opposition to capital punishment, 1787–1975.* New York: Burt Franklin.

Mackey, P. E. (1982). *Hanging in the balance: The anti-capital punishment movement in New York State, 1776–1861.* New York: Garland.

Mackie, K., & Hille, B. (1992). Cannabinoids inhibit N-type calcium channels in neuroblastomaglioma cells. *Proceedings of the National Academy of Sciences USA, 89,* 3825–3829.

The mad bomber? (1996, April 15). *U.S. News & World Report, XX,* 29–35.

Madrid v. Gomez, 889 F. Supp. 1146 (N.D. Cal. 1995).

Mahler, M. (1968). *On human symbiosis and the vicissitudes of individuation: Vol I. Infantile psychosis.* New York: International Universities Press.

Mahler, M. (1979). *Selected papers of Margaret S. Mahler.* New York: Aronson.

Mahler, M. S., Pine, F., & Bergman, A. (1975). *The psychological birth of the human infant.* New York: Basic Books.

Malamuth, N. & Check, J. (1981). The effects of media exposure on acceptance of violence against women. A field experiment. *Journal of Research in Personality, 15,* 509–522.

Malatesta, C. Z., Grigoryev, P., Lamb, K., Albin,, M., & Culver, C. (1986). Emotion socialization and expressive development in preterm and full-term infants. *Child Development, 57,* 316–330.

Mann, C. R. (1995). Women of color and the criminal justice system. In B. Price & N. Sokoloff (Eds.), *The criminal justice system and women: Offenders, victims, and workers* (pp. 118–135). New York: McGraw-Hill.

Mannuzza, S., Klein, R. G., Bessler, A., Malloy, P., & LaPadula, M. (1993). Adult outcome of hyperactive boys: Educational achievement, occupational rank, and psychiatric status. *Archives of General Psychiatry, 50,* 565–576.

Mannuzza, S., Klein, R. G., Bessler, A., Malloy, P., & LaPadula, M. (1998). Adult psychiatric status of hyperactive boys grown up. *American Journal of Psychiatry, 155,* 493–498.

"Manslaughter, not murder black and white, and gray. *Time,* June 4, 1998. Retrieved May 30, 2006 from http://www.time.com/time/archive/preview/0,10987,966384,00.html

Marcia, J. E. (1980). Identity in adolescence. In J. Adelson (Ed.), *Handbook of adolescent psychology.* New York: Wiley.

Margolin, J. (1977). Psychological perspectives in terrorism. In Y. Alexander & S. M. Finger (Eds.), *Terrorism: Interdisciplinary perspectives.* New York: John Jay.

Marlatt, G. A. (1987). Alcohol, the magic elixir: Stress, expectancy, and the transformation of emotional states. In E. Gottheil, K. A. Druly, S. Pashko, & S. P. Weinstein (Eds.), *Stress and addiction* (pp. 302–322). New York: Bruner/Mazel.

Marrs-Simon, P. A. (1988). Analysis of sexual disparity of violent behavior in PCP intoxication. *Veterinary and Human Toxicology, 30*(1), 53–55.

Marshall, P. (1993). Allergy and depression: A neurochemical threshold model of the relation between the illnesses. *Psychological Bulletin, 113,* 23–39.

Marshall, W., & Barbaree, H. (1988). The long-term evaluation of a behavioral treatment program for child molesters. *Behavioral Research Therapy, 26,* 499–511.

Marshall, W., & Hambley, L. (1996). Intimacy and loneliness, and their relationship to rape myth acceptance and hostility toward women among rapists. *Journal of Interpersonal Violence, 11,* 586–592.

Marshall, W. L., Bryce, P., & Hudson, S. M. (1996). The enhancement of intimacy and the reduction of loneliness among child molesters. *Journal of Family Violence, 11,* 219–235.

Martell, D. A. (1991). Homeless mentally disordered offenders and violent crimes: Preliminary research findings. *Law and Human Behavior, 15,* 333–346.

Martin, G. B., & Clark, R. D. (1987). Distress crying in neonates: Species and peer specificity. *Developmental Psychology, 18,* 3–9.

Martin, S. E. (1995). A cross-burning is not just an arson: Police social construction of hate crimes in Baltimore County. *Criminology, 33,* 303–326.

Martin, S. (1997, April). APA among those calling for more violence research. *American Psychological Association Monitor, XX,* 18.

Martin, S. E., & Sherman, L. W. (1986). Selective apprehension: A police strategy for repeat offenders. *Criminology, 24,* 155–173.

Martin, S. S., Butzin, C. A., & Inciardi, J. (1995). Assessment of a multistage therapeutic community for drug involved offenders. *Journal of Psychoactive Drugs, 27,* 109–116.

Martinez, R. (1996). Latinos and lethal violence: The impact of poverty and inequality. *Social Problems, 43,* 131–146.

Martinson, R. (1974). What works? Questions and answers about prison reform. *The Public Interest, 10,* 22–24.

Marwick, C. (1996). Childhood aggression needs definition therapy. *Journal of the American Medical Association, 275,* 157.

Marx, G. (May 14, 1997). Violent teens fuel sentencing debate. *Chicago Tribune,* pp. 1, 5.

Masters, B. A. (1997, October 18). Internet user gets 2 years for having sex with girl. *The Washington Post,* pp. B1, B5.

Masters, B. A. (1998a, January 14). 11 accused of causing wrecks to defraud insurers. *The Washington Post,* p. B8.

Masters, B. A. (1998b, March 7). Two plead guilty in credit scam. *The Washington Post,* p. D7.

Masters, B. A. (1998c, May 28). Welfare mother's success story has tragic end. *The Washington Post,* pp. A1, A19.

Masters, B. A., & Melillo, W. (1997, October 16). Emotional debate preceded Kasi death sentence, juror says. *The Washington Post,* p. A1.

Masters, B. A., & Ordonez, J. (1998, May 14). Heiress gets 60 days in polo player's slaying. *The Washington Post,* pp. A1, A20.

Mattes, J. A., & Fink, M. (1987). A family study of patients with temper outbursts. *Journal of Psychiatric Research, 21,* 249–255.

Matthews, T. (1992, February 3). Secrets of a serial killer. *Newsweek, XX,* 45–48.

Matza, D. (1964). *Delinquency and drift.* New York: Wiley.

Mauer, M. (1992). Americans behind bars: A comparison of international rates of incarceration. In W. Churchill & J. J. Vander Wall (Eds.), *Cages of steel: The politics of imprisonment in the United States* (pp. 22–37). Washington, DC: Maisonneuve Press.

Mauer, M. (1995). The international use of incarceration. *Prison Journal, 75,* 113–123.

Mauer, M. (2003). *Comparative international rates of incarceration: An examination of causes and trends.* Paper presented to the U.S. Commission on Civil Rights. Retrieved June 15, 2005, form http://law.wustl.edu/Students/Courses/Schlanger/Fall2004/Prison Seminar/SectionA.pdf

Maughan, B., & Yule, W. (1994). Reading and other learning disabilities. In M. Rutter, E. Taylor, & L. Hersov (Eds.), *Child and adolescent psychiatry: Modern approaches.* Cambridge, MA: Blackwell Scientific.

Mauro, R. (1991). Tipping the scales toward death: The biasing effects of death qualification. In P. Suedfeld & P. Tetlock (Eds.), *Psychology and social policy.* New York: Hemisphere.

Mawbray, R. I., & Walklate, S. (1994). *Critical victimology: International perspectives.* London: Sage.

Maxwell v. Bishop, 398 F2d. 138 (8th Cir. 1968), vacated and remanded 398 U.S. 262 (1970).

Mayhew, P., Elliott, D., & Dowds, L. (1989). *The 1988 British crime survey: A home office research and planning unit report.* London: HMSO Books.

McAnaney, K. G., Curliss, L. A., & Abeyta-Price, C. E. (1993). From imprudence to crime: Anti-stalking laws. *Notre Dame Law Review, 68,* 819.

McBunett, K., Lahey, B. B., Capasso, K., & Loeber, R. (1996). Aggressive symptoms and salivary cortisol in clinic-referred boys with conduct disorder. *Annals of the New York Academy of Sciences, 794,* 169–179.

McCardle, L. & Fihbein, D. H. (1989). The self-reported effects of PCP on human aggression. *Addictive Behaviors, 4,* 465–472.

McClintick, D. (1982). *Indecent exposure.* New York: Del.

McCord, J. (1979). Some child-rearing antecedents of criminal behavior in adult men. *Journal of Personality and Social Psychology, 37,* 1477–1486.

McCord, W., & McCord, J. (1964). *The psychopath: An essay on the criminal mind.* New York: Van Nostrand Reinhold.

McDermott, P. A. (1996). A nationwide study of developmental and gender prevalence for psychopathology in childhood and adolescence. *Journal of Abnormal Child Psychology, 24,* 53–66.

McElroy, S. L., Pope, H. G., Hudson, J. I., Keck, P. E., & White, K. L. (1991). Kleptomania: A report of 20 cases. *American Journal of Psychiatry, 148,* 652–665.

McFadden, R. D. (1997, April 22). Two are held in senseless killings of 2 pizza deliverers. *The Washington Post,* pp. A1, A3.

McFadden, R. D. (2001, February 27). Long Island man accused of running investment fraud from prison. *New York Times.*

McFarland, B. H., & Blair, G. (1995). Delivering comprehensive services to homeless mentally ill offenders. *Psychiatric Services, 46,* 179–180.

McFatter, R. (1978). Sentencing strategies and justice: Effect of punishment philosophy on sentencing decisions. *Journal of Personal & Social Psychology, 36,* 1490–1500.

McGuckin v. Smith, 974 F2d. 1050 (9th Cir., 1992).

McGuffin, P., Riley B., & Plomin, R. (2001, February 16). Genomics and behavior: Toward behavioral genomics. *Science, 291,* 1232–1249. Retrieved January 8, 2005, from http://www.sciencemag.org/cgi/content/full/291/5507/1232

McKay, M., Chapman, J., & Long, N. (1996). Causal attributions for criminal offending and sexual arousal: Comparison of child sex offenders with other offenders. *British Journal of Clinical Psychology, 35,* 63–75.

McKelvey, B. (1977). *American prisons: A history of good intentions.* Montclair, NJ: Patterson Smith.

McKenzie, C. (1995). A study of serial murder. *International Journal of Offender Therapy & Comparative Criminology, 39,* 3–10.

McKlesky v. Kemp, 107 S. Ct. 1756 (1987).

McMullan, J. L. (1982). Criminal organization in sixteenth and seventeenth century London. *Social Problems, 29,* 311–323.

McNeil, D. E. (1994). Hallucinations and violence. In J. Monahan & H. J. Steadman (Eds.), *Violence and mental disorder: Developments in risk assessment* (pp. 183–202). Chicago: University of Chicago Press.

Mead, M. (1958). Adolescence in primitive and modern society. In Maccoby, Newcomb, & Hartley (Eds.), *Readings in social psychology.* New York: Norton.

Mednick, S., Gabrielli, W., & Hutchings, B. (1984). Genetic influences in criminal convictions: Evidence from an adoption cohort. *Science, 224,* 891–894.

Mednick, S. A., Gabriellli, W. F., Jr., & Hutchings, B. (1987). Genetic factors in the etiology of criminal behavior. In S. A. Mednick, T. E. Moffitt, & S. A. Stack (Eds.), *The causes of crime: New biological approaches* (pp. 74–91). New York: Cambridge University Press.

Mednick, S., Moffit, T., & Stack, S. (1987). *The causes of crime: New biological approaches.* Cambridge, England: Cambridge University Press.

Mednick, S., Pollock, V., Volavka, J., & Gabrielli, W. (1982). Biology and violence. In M. Wolfgang & N. Weiner (Eds.), *Criminal violence.* Beverly Hills, CA: Sage.

Mednick, S., Volavka, J., Gabrielli, W., & Itil, T. (1981). EEG a predictor of antisocial behavior. *Criminology, 19,* 219–231.

Meese, E. (1986). *Final report of the attorney generals commission on pornography.* Washington, DC: U.S. Department of Justice.

Megargee, E. I. (1966). Undercontrolled and overcontrolled personality types in extreme antisocial aggression. *Psychological Monographs, 80,* No. 3.

Meierhoeffer, B. S. (1992). *The general effect of mandatory minimum prison terms.* Washington, DC: Federal Judicial Center.

Melillo, W., & Geshears, E. (1998, August 1). Man charged in mother's death. *The Washington Post,* p. B3.

Melillo, W., & Smith, L. (1997, October 9). Man abused boy for weeks, court told. *The Washington Post,* p. D4.

Melloni, R. H., Delville, Y., & Ferris, C. E. (1995). Vaso suppression/serotonin interactions in the anterior hypothalamus control aggressive behavior in golden hamsters [Abstract]. *Society for Neuroscience Abstracts,* 1695.

Meloy, J. R. (1992). *The psychopathic mind: Origins, dynamics, and treatment.* Northvale, NJ: Aronson.

Melton, G. B., Petrila, J., Poythress, N. G., & Slobogin, C. (1987). *Psychological evaluations for the courts.* New York: Guilford.

Menard, S., & Elliott, D. (1990). Self-reported offending, maturational reform, and the Easterlin hypothesis. *Journal of Quantitative Criminology, 6,* 237–268.

Mendelsohn, B. (1956). *The victimology.* Cited in S. Shafer, *The victim and his criminal: A study of functional responsibility.* New York: Random House.

Mendelsohn, B. (1974). The origin of the doctrine of victimology. In I. Drapkin & E. Viano (Eds.), *Victimology.* Lexington, MA: Lexington.

Menninger, K. (1966). *The crime of punishment.* New York: Viking.

Merikangas, K. R. (1990). The genetic epidemiology of alcoholism. *Psychological Medicine, 20,* 11–22.

Messerschmidt, J. (1986). *Capitalism, patriarchy and crime.* Totowa, NJ: Rowman and Littlefield.

Messerschmidt, J. (1993). *Masculinities and crime: Critique and reconceptualization of theory.* Lanham, MD: Rowand & Littlefield.

Messner, S., & Tardiff, K. (1986). Economic inequality and levels of homicide: An analysis of urban neighborhoods. *Criminology, 24,* 297–317.

Metzner, J. L., et al. (1998). Treatment in jails and prisons. In R. M. Wittstein (Ed.), *Treatment of offenders with mental disorders.* New York: Guilford.

Mezey, G. (1994). Rape in war. *Journal of Forensic Psychiatry, 5,* 583–598.

Michaels, D., Zoloth, S. R., Alcabes, P., Braslow, C. A., & Safyer, S. (1992). Homelessness and indicators of mental illness among inmates in New York City's correctional system. *Hospital and Community Psychiatry, 43,* 150–155.

Michalson, L., & Lewis, M. (1985). What do children know about emotions and when do they know it? In M. Lewis & C. Saarhi (Eds.), *The socialization of emotions.* New York: Plenum.

Miethe, T. D., & McCorkle, R. C. (1998). *Crime profiles: The anatomy of dangerous personal, places, and situations.* Los Angeles: Roxbury Publishing Co.

Miethe, T. D., & Meier, R. F. (1994). *Crime and its social context: Toward an integrated theory of offenders, victims, and situations.* Albany: State University of New York Press.

Milavsky, J. R., Kessler, R., Sipp, H., Rubens, W. S., Pearl, D., Bouthilet, L., et al. (Eds.). (1982). *Television and behavior: Ten years of scientific progress and implications for the eighties* (Vol. 2, Technical Reviews, DHHS Publication No. ADM 81–1186). Washington, DC: U.S. Government Printing Office.

Miller, A. (1984). *For your own good.* New York: Farrar, Straus & Giroux.

Miller, B. (1988, April 15). Hinckley loses appeal on leave. *The Washington Post,* p. B3.

Miller, B. (1997a, December 13). DC man pleads guilty to killing child in his care. *The Washington Post,* pp. B1, B7.

Miller, B. (1997b, December 19). Two families mourn as girls' killer is sentenced. *The Washington Post,* p. C2.

Miller, B. (1998a, June 3). Drug kingpin's mother freed. *The Washington Post,* p. B1.

Miller, B. (1998b, April 15). Hinckley loses appeal on leave. *The Washington Post,* p. B3.

Miller, B. (1998c, January 18). Man accused of killing DC officer ready to present cognac defense. *The Washington Post,* p. B10.

Miller, B. (1999, April 23). Weston's mind-set details. *The Washington Post,* pp. A1, A14.

Miller, J. G., & Bersoff, D. M. (1992). Culture and moral judgment: How are conflicts between justice and interpersonal responsibilities resolved? *Journal of Personality and Social Psychology, 62,* 541–554.

Miller, N. (1996, October 18). *Judicial waiver and its alternatives: A legal fact sheet.* Washington, DC: Institute for Law and Justice.

Miller, T. R., Cohen, M. A., & Wiersema, B. (1996). *Victim costs and consequences: A new look.* Washington, DC: National Institute of Justice, U.S. Department of Justice.

Miller, W. B. (1975). *Violence by youth gangs and youth groups as a crime problem in major American cities.* Washington, DC: National Institute for Juvenile Justice and Delinquency Prevention, Office of Juvenile Justice and Delinquency Prevention, U.S. Department of Justice, U.S. Government Printing Office.

Miller, W. R., & Brown, S. A. (1997). Why psychologists should treat alcohol and drug problems. *American Psychologist, 52,* 1269–1279.

Millman, R. B., & Sbriglio, R. (1986). Patterns of use and psychopathology in chronic marijuana users. *Psychiatric Clinics of North America, 9,* 533–545.

Milloy, C. (1997, September 13). A future held in check by a past. *The Washington Post,* pp. B1, B7.

Milton S. Eisenhower Foundation. (1999). *To establish justice, to insure domestic tranquility: A thirty year update of the National Commission on the Causes and Prevention of Violence.* Washington, DC: Author.

Mitchell, A. (1994). *Domestic/dating violence: An information and resource handbook.* Seattle, WA: Metropolitan King County Counsel.

MNSBC News. (2003, May 21). *Three charged in Illinois hazing incident.* Retrieved May 22, 2003, from http://www.msnbc.com/news

Modestin, J., & Ammann, R. (1996). Mental disorder and criminality: Male schizophrenia. *Schizophrenia Bulletin, 22,* 69–82.

Modestin, J., Berger, A., & Amman, R. (1996). Mental disorder and criminality: Male alcoholism. *Journal of Nervous & Mental Disease, 184,* 393–402.

Moffitt, T. E. (1993). Life-course-persistent and adolescent-limited antisocial behavior. *Psychological Review, 100,* 674–701.

Moffitt, T. E. (2001). *Sex differences in antisocial behaviour: Conduct disorder, delinquency, and violence in the Dunedin study.* Cambridge, England: Cambridge University Press.

Moffitt, T. E., Caspi, A., Dickson, N., Silva, P., & Stanton, W. (1996). Childhood-onset versus adolescent-onset antisocial conduct problems in males: Natural history from ages 3 to 18 years. *Development and Psychopathology, 8,* 399–424.

Moffitt, T. E., Caspi, A., Harrington, H., & Milne, B. (2002). Males on the life-course persistent and adolescence-limited antisocial pathways: Follow-up at 26 years. *Development & Psychopathology, 14,* 179–206.

Moffiitt, T., Gabrielli, W., Mednick, S., & Schulsinger, F. (1981). Socioeconomic status, IQ, and delinquency. *Journal of Abnormal Psychology, 90,* 152–156.

Moffitt, T. E., & Lynam, D. R. (1994). The neuropsychology of conduct disorder and delinquency. Implications for understanding antisocial behavior. In D. Fowles, P. Sutker, & S. Goodman (Eds.), *Psychopathy and antisocial personality: A developmental perspective* (pp. 233–262). New York: Springer.

Moffitt, T., & Silva, P. (1988). Self-reported delinquency, neuropsychological deficit, and history of attention deficit disorder. *Journal of Abnormal Child Psychology, 16,* 553–569.

Molden, S. O., & Gottesman, I. I. (1997). At issue: Genes, experience, and chance in schizophrenia—positioning for the 21st century. *Schizophrenia Bulletin, 23,* 547–561.

Molidor, C. (1996). Female gang members: A profile of aggression and victimization. *Social Work, 41,* 251–257.

Monahan, J. (1996). Mental Illness and violent crime. In *NIJ Research Preview.* Rockville, MD: National Institute of Justice.

Monahan, J. (1997). Clinical and actuarial predictions of violence. In D. Faigman, D. Kaye, M. Saks, & J. Sanders (Eds.), *Modern scientific evidence: The law and science of expert testimony* (Vol. I, pp. 300–318). St. Paul, MN: West.

Monahan, J. (1998). *Study funds substance abuse linked to violence in mentally ill.* Retrieved May DAY, YEAR, from http://ness.sys.Virginia.edu/macarthur/Prmac598.html

Monahan, J., & Steadman, H. J. (1996). Violent storms and violent people: How meteorology can inform risk communication in mental health law. *American Psychologist, 51,* 931–938.

Monahan, J., & Walker, L. (1990). *Social science and law: Cases and materials* (2nd ed.). Westbury, NY: The Foundation Press.

Monroe, R. R. (1978). *Brain dysfunction in aggressive criminals.* Lexington, MA: Heath.

Moore, D. (2004, June 2). *Public divided between death penalty and life in prison without parole.* Gallup News Service. Retrieved June 15, 2005, from http://www.deathpenaltyinfo.org/article.php?scid'23&did'1029

Moore, J. (1991). *Going down to the barrio: Home boys and home girls in change.* Philadelphia: Temple University Press.

Moore, J. (1997). *Highlights of the 1995 National Youth Gang Survey.* Washington, DC: Office of Juvenile Justice and Delinquency Prevention.

Moore, J., & Terrett, C. P. (1999). *Highlights of the 1997 National Youth Gang Survey* (Office of Juvenile Justice and Delinquency Prevention Fact Sheet No. 97). Washington, DC: Office of Juvenile Justice and Delinquency Prevention.

Moore, J. K., Jr., Thompson-Pope, S. K., & Whited, R. M. (1996). MMPI–A profiles of adolescent boys with a history of firesetting. *Journal of Personality Assessment, 67,* 116–126.

Moore, R. H. (1984). Shoplifting in middle America: Patterns and motivational correlates. *International Journal of Offender Therapy and Comparative Criminology, 28,* 53–64.

Moran, G., Cutler, B. L., & Loftus, E. F. (1990). Jury selection in major controlled substance trials: The need for extended voir dire. *Forensic Reports, 3,* 331–348.

Morash, M., Bynum, T. S., & Koons, B. A. (1998). *Women offenders: Programming needs and promising approaches.* Washington, DC: National Institute of Justice.

Moses, M. C. (1995). *Keeping incarcerated mothers and their daughters together: Girl Scouts beyond bars.* Washington, DC: National Institute of Justice.

Mosher, D., & Anderson, R. (1987). Macho personality, sexual aggression and reactions to guided imagery of realistic rape. *Journal of Research in Personality, 20,* 77–94.

Mrazek, F. J. (1984). Sexual abuse of children. In B. Lahey & A. E. Kazdin (Eds.), *Advances in child clinical psychology* (pp. 199–215). New York: Plenum Press.

Muehlenhard, C. L., & Linton, M. A. (1987). Date rape and sexual aggression in dating situations: Incidence and risk factors. *Journal of Counseling Psychology, 34,* 186–196.

Mueller, C. W., Donnerstein, E., & Hallam, J. (1983). Violent films and prosocial behavior. *Personality and Social Psychology Bulletin, 9,* 83–89.

Mukherjee, S. (1997, September 26). Corruption drives up trade costs. *Puget Sound Business Journal.* Retrieved June 2, 2005, from http://www.bizjournals.com/seattle/stories/1997/09/29/smallb8.html

Mullen, B. (1986). Atrocity as a function of lynch composition: A self-attention perspective. *Personality and Social Psychology Bulletin, 12,* 187–197.

Mulvey, E. P. (1994). Assessing the evidence of a link between mental illness and violence. *Hospital and Community Psychiatry, 45,* 663.

Mumola, C. J. (1999). *Substance abuse and treatment, state and federal prisoners, 1997.* Washington, DC: U.S. Department of Justice, Office of Justice Programs, Bureau of Justice Statistics.

Mumola, C. J. (2000). *Incarcerated parents and their children.* Washington, DC: Bureau of Justice Statistics, Office of Justice Programs, U.S. Department of Justice.

Mundy, L. (1997, October 26). Zero tolerance. *The Washington Post Magazine,* pp. 20–26.

Murray, H. E. (1943). *Thematic Apperception Test manual.* Cambridge, MA: Harvard University Press.

Murray. C. A. (1983). The physical environment and community control of crime. In J. Q. Wilson (Ed.), *Crime and public policy* (pp. 107–122). San Francisco: Institute for Contemporary Studies.

Murray, C. B., Kaiser, R., & Taylor, S. (1997). The O. J. Simpson verdict: Predictors of beliefs about innocence or guilty. *Journal of Social Issues, 53,* 455–475.

Musty, R. E., & Kaback, L. (1995). Relationship between motivation and depression in chronic marijuana users. *Life Sciences, 56,* 2151–2155.

Muuss, R. (1988). *Theories of adolescence.* New York: Random House.

Myers, D. G. (1996). *Social psychology* (5th ed.). New York: McGraw-Hill.

Myers, M.G., Stewart, D. G., & Brown, S. A. (1998). Progression from conduct disorder to antisocial personality disorder following treatment for adolescent substance abuse. *American Journal of Psychiatry, 155,* 479–485.

NAACP Legal Defense and Educational Fund. (2005). *Death row USA spring 2005.* New York: Author. Retrieved June 15, 2005, from http://www.naacpldf.org/content/pdf/pubs/drusa/DRUSA_Spring_2005.pdf

Nacci, P. L., & Kane, T. R. (1982). *Sexual aggression in prison.* Washington, DC: U.S. Federal Prison System.

Nachshon, I., & Denno, D. (1987). Violent behavior and cerebral hemisphere function. In A. Mednick, T. Moffitt, & S. Stack (Eds.), *The causes of crime: New biological approaches.* Cambridge, England: Cambridge University Press.

Nagan, D., & Land, K. (1993). Age, criminal careers, and population heterogeneity. *Criminology, 31,* 327–62.

Nagin, D. S., Farrington, D. P., & Moffit, T. E. (1995). Life-course trajectories of different types of offenders. *Criminology, 33,* 111–139.

National Alliance for the Mentally Ill. (1999a, March 12). *NAMI applauds NBC news program "Back to Bedlam."* Retrieved May 6, 1999, from http://www.nami.org/pressroom/990312.html

National Alliance for the Mentally Ill. (1999b, April 23). *New report highlights growing housing crisis for people with severe mental illness and other disabilities.* Retrieved May 6, 1999, from http://www.nami.org/update/990423.html

National Association of Mental Health, 2004). Mind Rights Guide 5: Mental health and the courts. Accessed June 1, 2006, from http://www.mind.org. uk/Information/Booklets/Rights+guide/Mind+rights+guide+5.htm

National Center for Justice. (1999). *1998 annual report on cocaine use among arrestees: Arrestees Drug Abuse Monitoring Program (ADAM).* Washington, DC: Author.

National Coalition for Jail Reform. (1984). *Removing the chronically mentally ill from jail: Case studies of collaboration between local criminal justice and mental health systems.* Rockville, MD: U.S. Department of Health and Human Services, National Institute of Mental Health.

National Commission Against Drunk Driving. (1999). *Youth and alcohol.* Retrieved June 1, 2003, from http://www.silcom.com/~sbadp/prevention/teenalc.htm

National Commission on Correctional Health Care. (1998). *Women's health care in correctional settings.* Chicago, IL: Author.

National Commission on the Causes and Prevention of Violence. (1970). *The rule of law: An alternative to violence.* Nashville, TN: Aurora.

National Committee to Prevent Child Abuse. (1999). *Current trends in child abuse reporting and fatalities: The results of the 1998 fifty state survey.* Chicago, IL: Author. Retrieved from http://www.childabuse.org/50data97.html

National Conference on State Legislatures. (1996). *A legislator's guide to comprehensive juvenile justice interventions for youth at risk.* Washington, DC: Author.

National Drug Intelligence Center. (1999). *National drug threat assessment 1999.* Washington, DC: Author.

National Drug Intelligence Center. (2001). *National drug threat assessment 2001 (the domestic perspective).* Washington, DC: U.S. Department of Justice.

National Education Goals Panel. (1989). *Data for the National Education Goals Report: Vol. 1. National data.* Washington, DC: National Education Goals Panel.

National Gang Crime Research Center. (1997). *The facts about gang life in America today: A national study of over 4,000 gang members.* Peotone, IL: Author. Retrieved February 27, 2005, from http://www.ngcrc.com/ngcrc/page9.htm

National Human Genome Research Institute. (2003, April 14). International consortium completes human genome project. Retrieved May 25, 2006 at http://www.genome.gov/11006929

National Institute of Education. (1986). *Violent schools-safe schools: The Safe School Study report to Congress.*

Washington, DC: U.S. Department of Health, Education and Welfare.

National Institute of Justice. (1991). *Understanding and preventing violence.* Washington, DC: Government Printing Office.

National Institute of Justice. (1994). *Breaking the cycle.* Washington, DC: Author.

National Institute of Justice. (1996a). *Understanding and preventing violence: A public perspective.* Washington, DC: U.S. Department of Justice, Office of Justice Programs.

National Institute of Justice. (1996b). *Youth violence, guns, and illicit drug markets.* Rockville, MD: Aspen Systems.

National Institute of Justice. (1997a). *Critical criminal justice issues: Task force reports from the American society of criminology.* Washington, DC: U.S. Department of Justice, National Institute of Justice.

National Institute of Justice. (1997b). *1996 Drug use forecasting: Annual report on adult and juvenile arrestees.* Washington, DC: Government Printing Office.

National Institute of Justice. (1997c). *Task force reports from the American society of criminology.* Washington, DC: U.S. Department of Justice, National Institute of Justice.

National Institute on Alcohol Abuse and Alcoholism. (1998). *Alcohol and health: Eighth special report to Congress.* Rockville, MD: Author.

National Institute on Drug Abuse. (1988). *Methamphetamine abuse and addiction.* Washington, DC: National Institutes of Health.

National Institute on Drug Abuse. (2001). *Monitoring the future national results on adolescent drug use: Overview of key findings, 2000.* Washington, DC: Author.

National Institute on Drug Abuse. (2004). *Monitoring the future national results on adolescent drug use: Overview of key findings, 2003.* Washington, DC. Author.

National Mental Health Association. (1993). *All systems failure.* Alexandria, VA: Author.

National Mental Health Association. (1999). *Children with emotional disorders in the juvenile justice system.* Retrieved June 21, 1999, from http//www.nmha.org/children/justjuv/factsheet.cfm

National Research Council. (1993a). *Losing generations: Adolescents in high-risk settings.* Washington, DC: Panel on High Risk Youth, Committee on Behavioral and Social Sciences and Education, National Research Council, National Academy Press.

National Research Council. (1993b). *Understanding child abuse and neglect.* Washington, DC: National Academy of Sciences.

National Review Board for the Protection of Children and Young People. (2004). *A report on the crisis in the Catholic Church in the United States.* New York: United States Conference of Catholic Bishops. Retrieved June 1, 2005, from http://www.4law.co.il/comer27204.htm

National School Safety Center. (1998). *Checklist of characteristics of youth who have caused school-associated violent deaths.* Retrieved May 6, 1999, from http://www.corrections.com/news/Feature/sidebar.html

Needleman, H. (1996). Bone lead levels and delinquent behavior. *Journal of the American Medical Association, 275,* 363–369.

Nelson, J. (Ed.). (2000). *Police brutality: An anthology.* New York: W. W. Norton.

Nelson, M. B. (1994). *The stronger women get, the more men love football: Sexism and the American culture of sports.* New York: Harcourt Brace.

Nemeth, C., & Sosis, R. M. (1973). A simulated jury: Characteristics of the defendant and the jurors. *Journal of Social Psychology, 90,* 221–229.

Nettler, G. (1984). *Explaining crime.* New York: McGraw-Hill.

Newcorn, J. H., McKay, K., Loeber, R., Bonafida, M., Sharma, V., & Halperin, J. (1996, October). *Emotionality and serotonergic function in aggressive and non-aggressive ADHD children.* Paper presented at the meeting of the American Academy of Child and Adolescent Psychiatry, Philadelphia.

New York Department of Correctional Services. (1993). *The fifth annual report to the legislature on shock incarceration and shock parole supervision.* Albany, New York: Department of Correctional Services and Division of Parole.

New York State Organized Crime Task Force. (1988). *Corruption and racketeering in the New York City construction industry.* Ithaca, NY: ILR Press.

Nicholson, R. A., Norwood, S., & Enyart, C. (1991). Characteristics and outcomes of insanity acquittees in Oklahoma. *Psychological Bulletin, 109,* 355–370.

Nietzel, M. T., Bernstein, D. A., Kramer, G. P., & Milich, R. (2003). *Introduction to clinical psychology.* (6th ed.). Upper Saddle River, NJ: Prentice Hall.

Nietzel, M. T., & Dillehay, R. C. (1986). *Psychological consultation in the courtroom.* New York: Persimmon Press.

Nietzel, M., & Hartung, C. (1993). Psychological research on the police. *Law and Human Behavior, 17,* 151–155.

Nietzel, M. T., Hasemann, D. M., & Lynam, D. R. (1997). Behavioral perspectives on violent behavior. In V. B. Van Hasselt & M. Hersen (Eds.), *Handbook of psychological approaches with violent criminal offenders: Contemporary strategies and issues.* New York: Plenum.

Nietzel, M. T., Hasemann, D., & McCarthy, D. M. (1997). Psychology and capital litigation: Research contributions to courtroom consultation. Unpublished manuscript.

Nietzel, M. T., McCarthy, D. M., & Harris, M. (1999). Juries: The current state of the empirical literature. In R. Roesch & S. Hart (Eds.), *Psychology and law: The state of the discipline* (pp. 23–52). New York: Plenum.

Nietzel, M., Speltz, M., McCauley, E., & Bernstein, D. A. (1998). *Abnormal psychology.* Boston: Allyn & Bacon.

Nieves, E. (2001, January 9). Heroin, an old nemesis, makes an encore. *The New York Times,* p. A9.

Nigg, J. T., & Goldsmith, H. H. (1994). Genetics of personality disorders: Perspectives from personality and psychopathology research. *Psychological Bulletin, 115,* 346–380.

Nolin, M. J., Davies, E., & Chandler, K. (1996, August). Student victimization at school. *Journal of School Health, 66*(6), 216–221.

North American Securities Administration Association. (1990, July 13). *Report to Congress, Subcommittee on Investment Fraud.*

Nugent, P. M., & Kroner, D. G. (1996). Denial, response styles, and admittance of offenses among child molesters and rapists. *Journal of Interpersonal Violence, 11,* 475–486.

Nun-Dinis, M., & Weisner, C. (1977). *The American Journal of Drug and Alcohol Abuse, 23,* 129–141.

Oakes, J. (1985). *Keeping track: How schools structure inequality.* New Haven, CT: Yale University Press.

O'Brien, M. J. (1989). *Characteristics of male adolescent sibling incest offenders: Preliminary findings.* Orwell, VT: Safer Society Press.

O'Connor v. Donaldson, 422 U.S. 563 (1975).

O'Donohue, W., McKay, J., & Schewe, P. (1996). Rape: The roles of outcome expectancies and hypermasculinity. *Sexual Abuse: Journal of Research & Treatment, 8,* 133–141.

Office for Victims of Crime. (2002, January). *Victims of crime act crime victims' fund* (OVC Fact Sheet). Retrieved June 3, 2005, from http://www.ojp.usdoj.gov/ovc/publications/factshts/vocacvf/fs000281.pdf

Office of Juvenile Justice & Delinquency Prevention. (1994a, December). *Violent families and youth violence.* Washington, DC: U.S. Government Printing Office.

Office of Juvenile Justice and Delinquency Prevention. (1994b). *Violent families and youth violence fact sheet.* Washington, DC: Author.

Office of Juvenile Justice & Delinquency Prevention. (1995). *Guide for implementing the comprehensive strategy for serious, violent, and chronic juvenile offenders.* Washington, DC: Author.

Office of Juvenile Justice & Delinquency Prevention. (1996). *Balanced and restorative justice. Program summary.* Washington, D.C.: U.S. Department of Justice, Office of Justice Programs

Office of Juvenile Justice and Delinquency Prevention. (1996a). *Female offenders in the juvenile justice system— Statistics summary.* Washington, DC: U.S. Government Printing Office.

Office of Juvenile Justice & Delinquency Prevention. (1996b). *In the wake of childhood maltreatment.* Washington, DC: U.S. Government Printing Office.

Office of Juvenile Justice & Delinquency Prevention. (1996c). *Report to Congress: Title V incentive grants for local delinquency prevention programs* (Appendix, p. 3). Washington, DC: U.S. Department of Justice.

Office of Juvenile Justice & Delinquency Prevention. (1996d, July). The violent juvenile offender. *Policy Perspective, 5.*

Office of Juvenile Justice & Delinquency Prevention. (1997, January). *Adolescent motherhood: Implications for the juvenile justice system.* Washington, DC: U.S. Government Printing Office.

Office of Juvenile Justice & Delinquency Prevention. (1998a). *Balanced and restorative justice: Program summary.* Washington, DC: U.S. Department of Justice, Office of Justice Programs.

Office of Juvenile Justice & Delinquency Prevention. (1998b). *Guide for implementing the comprehensive strategy for serious, violent, and chronic juvenile offenders.* Washington, DC: Author.

Office of Juvenile Justice & Delinquency Prevention. (1999a). *Juvenile and offenders and victims: 1999 national report.* Washington, DC: U.S. Department of Justice, Office of Justice Programs.

Office of Juvenile Justice & Delinquency Prevention. (1999b). *Report to Congress on juvenile violence research.* Washington, DC: Author. Retrieved February 27, 2005, from http://ojjdp.ncjrs.org/pubs/jvr/contents.html

Office of National Drug Control Policy. (1995). *Drug facts—1994.* Rockville, MD: Bureau of Justice Statistics.

Office of National Drug Control Policy. (2002). *The President's national drug control strategy.* Washington, DC: Author.

O'Hanlon, A. (1998, June 21). Time out for Alan. *The Washington Post Magazine,* pp. 9–23.

Okie, S. (1999, June 1). Alcohol linked to deaths from accidents, murders. *Washington Post Health,* p. 5.

Okin, R. L. (1995). Testing the limits of deinstitutionalization. *Psychiatric Services, 46,* 569–574.

Oliver, M. B. (1994). Portrayals of crime, rate, and aggression in "reality-based" police shows: A contingent analysis. *Journal of Broadcasting & Electronic Media, 38,* 179–192.

Oliver, W. (1994). *The violent social world of Black men.* New York: Lexington.

Oltman, J., & Friedman, S. (1967). Parental deprivation in psychiatric conditions. *Diseases of the Nervous System, 28,* 298–303.

Olweus, D. (1980). Familial and temperamental determinants of aggressive behavior in adolescent boys: A causal analysis. *Developmental Psychology, 16,* 644–660.

Olweus, D. A. (1988). Circulating testosterone levels and aggression in adolescent males: A causal analysis. *Psychosomatic Medicine, 50,* 261–272.

O'Reilly, B. (1997, August 24). The best place to stop drug abuse. *Parade Magazine, XX,* 22–23.

Orne, M. & Holland, C. (1968). On the ecological validity of laboratory deceptions. *International Journal of Psychiatry, 6,* 282–293.

Ouimet, M., & LeBlanc, M. (1996). The role of life experiences in the continuation of the adult criminal career. *Criminal Behavior and Mental Health, 6,* 73–97.

Owen, R. O., Fischer, E. P., Booth, B. M., & Cuffel, B. J. (1996). Medication noncompliance and substance abuse among patients with schizophrenia. *Psychiatric Services, 47,* 853–858.

Pagonis, W. (1999, April 21). Law students witness execution firsthand. *Northern Virginia Daily,* p. 2.

Paik, H., & Comstock, G. (1994). The effects of television violence on antisocial behavior: A meta-analysis. *Communication Research, 21,* 516–546.

Paikoff, R. L., & Brooks-Gunn, J. (1991). Do parent-child relationships change during puberty? *Psychological Bulletin, 110,* 47–66.

Pail, H., & Comstock, G. (1994). The effects of television violence on antisocial behavior: A meta-analysis. *Communication Research, 21,* 516–546.

Palmer, T. (1975). Martinson revisited. *Journal of Research in Crime and Delinquency, 12,* 133–152.

Palmer, T. (1983). The "effectiveness" issue today: An overview. *Federal Probation, 46,* 3–10.

Palmero, G. B. (1994). Murder-suicide: An extended suicide. *International Journal of Offender Therapy & Comparative Criminology, 38,* 205–216.

Pan. P. (1997, October 21). Freed man accused of killing wife. *The Washington Post,* pp. D1, D5.

Pan, P. (1998, March 29). Tougher youth laws examined. *The Washington Post,* pp. B1, B10.

Pan, P., & Thomas-Lester, A. (1997, October 9). Bicyclist guns down motorist: Man becomes enraged after she bumped him, Maryland witnesses say. *The Washington Post,* p. A1.

Pan, P., & Vogel, S. T. (1997, October 10). Cyclist had history of outbursts: Court records show assault charges in District, Maryland. *The Washington Post,* pp. A1, A26.

Paradis, C. M., Horn, L., Lazar, R. M, & Schwartz, D. W. (1994). Brain dysfunction and violent behavior in a man with a congenital subarachnoid cyst. *Hospital & Community Psychiatry, 45,* 714–716.

Parke, R.D., Berkowitz, L., Leyens, J.P., West, S.G., & Sebastian, J. (1977). Some effects of violent and nonviolent movies on the behavior of juvenile delinquents. In L. Berkowitz (Ed.), *Advances in experimental social psychology,* Vol. 10. New York: Academic Press.

Parke, R. D., & Slaby, R. G. (1983). The development of aggression. In P. H. Mussen (Series Ed.) & E. M. Heatherington (Vol. Ed.), *Handbook of child psychology: Vol. 4. Socialization, personality, and social development* (4th ed., pp. 547–641). New York: Wiley.

Parker, S. (1999, April 25). Ex-prisoner's dilemma: Questions for Susan McDougal. *The New York Times Sunday Magazine,* p. 16.

Parsons, O. A., Butters, N., & Nathan, P. E. (Eds). (1987).

Paternoster, R. (1991). *Capital punishment in America.* New York: Lexington.

Paternoster, R., & Brame, R. (2003). *An empirical analysis of Maryland's death sentencing system with respect to the influence of race and legal jurisdiction.* Retrieved May 26, 2003, from http://www.urhome.umd.edu/newsdesk/pdf/finalrep.pdf

Patterson, G. R. (1976). The aggressive child: Victim and architect of a coercive system. In L. A. Hamerlynck, L. C. Handy, & E. J. Mash (Eds.), *Behavior modification and families.* New York: Brunner/Mazel.

Patterson, G. R. (1986). Performance models for antisocial boys. *American Psychologist, 41,* 432–444.

Patterson, G. R., DeBaryshe, B. D., & Ramsey, E. (1989). A developmental perspective on antisocial behavior. *American Psychologist, 44,* 329–445.

Patterson, G. R., & Dishion, T. J. (1985). Contributions of families and peers to delinquency. *Criminology, 23,* 63–77.

Patterson, G. R., Reid, J. B., & Dishion, T. J. (1992). *A social interactional approach: IV. Antisocial boys.* Eugene, OR: Castalia.

Paulhus, D. L., & Martin, C. L. (1986). Predicting adult temperament from minor physical anomalies. *Journal of Personality and Social Psychology, 50,* 1235–1239.

Paulozzi, L. J., Saltzman, L. A., Thompson, M. J., & Holmgreen, P. (2001). Surveillance for homicide among intimate partners: United States, 1981–1988. *CDC Surveillance Summaries 2001, 50*(SS–3), 1–16.

Paulus, P. B. (1988). *Prison crowding: A psychological perspective.* New York: Springer-Verlag.

Paveza, G. J. (1988). Risk factors in father-daughter child sexual abuse: A case-control study. *Journal of Interpersonal Violence, 3,* 290–306.

Payne v. Tennessee, 498 U.S. 29 (1991).

Pearlstein, (2006, May 26). Convictions drive home the point again. *Washington Post,* p. D1.

People v. Decina, 157 N.Y. S.2d 558 (1956).

Perkins, C. A. (1997). *Age patterns of victims of serious violent crime.* Washington, DC: U.S. Department of Justice.

Perkins, C., & Klaus, P. (1996). *Criminal victimization, 1994.* Washington, DC: Bureau of Justice Statistics.

Perkinson, R. (1994). Shackled justice: Florence federal penitentiary and the new politics of punishment. *Social Justice, 21,* 117–132.

Perlin, M. (1994). *The jurisprudence of the insanity defense.* Durham: Carolina Academic Press.

Perry, B., Pollard, R., Blakley, T., Baker, W., & Vigilante, D. (1995). Childhood trauma, the neurobiology of adaptation and "use-dependent" development of the brain: How "states" become "traits." *Infant Mental Health Journal, 16,* 271–289.

Perry, D. G., Perry, L. C., & Rasmussen, P. (1986). Cognitive social learning mediators of aggression. *Child Development, 57,* 700–711.

Peters, M. (1996). *Evaluation of the impact of boot camps for juvenile offenders: Mobile interim report.*

Washington, DC: U.S. Department of Justice, Office of Juvenile Justice and Delinquency Prevention.

Peters, K. D., & Kochanek, K. D. (1998, November 10). Deaths: Final data for 1996. *National Vital Statistics Reports, 47,* 9.

Peterson, B. S. (1995). Neuroimaging in child and adolescent neuropsychiatric disorders. *Journal of the American Academy of Child and Adolescent Psychiatry, 34,* 1560–1576.

Peterson, P. L., Hawkins, J. D., Abbott, R. D., & Catalano, R. F. (1994). Disentangling the effects of parental drinking, family management, and parental alcohol norms on current drinking by Black and White adolescents. *Journal of Research on Adolescents, 4,* 203–227.

Peterson-Badali, M., & Abramovitch, R. (1993). Grade related changes in young people's reasoning about plea bargains. *Law & Human Behavior, 17,* 537.

Petrill, S. A., Plomin, R., Berg, S., Johansson, B., Pederson, N. L., Ahern, F., et al. (1998). The genetic and environmental relationship between general and specific cognitive abilities in twins age 80 and older. *Psychological Science, 9,* 183–189.

Pettigrew, J., & Burcham, J. (1997). Effects of childhood sexual abuse in adult female psychiatric patients. *Australian & New Zealand Journal of Psychiatry, 31,* 208–213.

Pfeiffer, S. (2002, August). One Strike Against the Elderly: Growing Old in Prison," Medill News Service,

Phillips, D. (1986). National experiments on the effects of mass media violence on fatal aggression: Strengths and weaknesses of a new approach. In L. Berkowitz (Ed.), *Advances in experimental social psychology* (Vol., 19, pp. 207–250). Orlando, FL: Academic Press.

Piaget, J. (1965). *The moral judgment of the child.* London: Kegan Paul. (Original work published 1932)

Piaget, J. (1952). *The origins of intelligence in children.* New York: International University Press.

Pianta, R. C., Egeland, B., & Erickson, M. F. (1989). The antecedents of Maltreatment: Results of the mother-child interaction. In C. Cicchetti & V. Carlson (Eds.), *Child maltreatment: Theory and research on the causes and consequences of child abuse and neglect* (pp. 203–253). New York: Cambridge University Press.

Pierson, R. (1989). *The queen of mean: The unauthorized biography of Leona Helmsley.* New York: Bantam.

Pihl, R. O. (1982). Hair element content of violent criminals. *Canadian Journal of Psychiatry, 27,* 533.

Pihl, R. O., & Peterson, J. B. (1991). Attention-deficit hyperactivity disorders, childhood conduct disorder and alcoholism: Is there an association? *Alcohol Health Research World, 15,* 52–56.

Pillmann, F., Rohde, A., Ullrich, S., Draba, S., Sannemüüller, U., & Marneros, A. (1999). Violence, criminal behavior, and the EEG: Significance of left hemispheric focal abnormalities. *Journal of Neuropsychiatry and Clinical Neurosciences* (Vol. 11, pp. 454–457).

Pinel, J. P. J. (1997). *Biopsychology* (3rd ed.). Boston: Allyn & Bacon.

Pinel, P. (1801). *Traite medico-philsophique sur lalilenation mentale.* Paris: Richard, Caille & Ravier.

Plomin, R. (1994). Nature, nurture and social development. *Social Development, 3,* 37–53.

Plomin, R., DeFries, J. C., & McClearn, G. E. (1990). *Behavior genetics: A primer.* New York: Freeman.

Plomin, R., Nitz, K., & Rowe, D. C. (1990). Behavioral genetics and aggressive behavior in childhood. In M. Lewis & S. M. Miller (Eds.), *Handbook of developmental psychopathology* (pp. 119–133). New York: Plenum.

Polaschek, D. L., Ward, T., & Hudson, S. M. (1997). Rape and rapists: Theory and treatment. *Clinical Psychology Review, 17,* 117–144.

Pollard, P. (1992). Judgments about victims and attackers in depicted rapes: A review. *British Journal of Social Psychology, 31,* 307–326.

Pollock, P. H. (1995). A case of spree serial murder with suggested diagnostic opinions. *International Journal of Offender Therapy & Comparative Criminology, 39,* 258–268.

Polycarpou, L. (1999, May 2). The Littleton I know isn't Anytown, it's Notown. *Washington Post,* pp. B1, e.

Porter, B. (1983). Mind hunters. *Psychology Today, 17,* 44–52.

Porter, J. E., & Rourke, P. B. (1985). Socioemotional functioning of learning-disabled children: A subtype analysis of personality patterns. In P. B. Rourke (Ed.), *Neuropsychology of learning disabilities: Essentials of subtype analysis.* New York: Guilford.

Porterfield, E. (2000, April 17). Sex predator law still stirs debate. *Seattle Post-Intelligencer.* Retrieved May 30, 2006 from http://seattlepi.nwsource.com/local/pred171.shtml

Postal clerk slays co-worker, wounds 2, then kills himself. (1997, December 20). *Washington Post,* p. A3.

Postal worker surrenders after freeing hostages unharmed. (1995, December 25). *The New York Times,* p. A1.

Potter, K. (1998, October 18). To fight hate, don't over-legislate. *The Washington Post,* p. C2.

Potter, W. J., Vaughan, M. W., Warren, R., Howley, K., Land, A., & Hagemeyer, J. C. (1995). How real is the portrayal of aggression in television entertainment programming? *Journal of Broadcasting and Electronic Media, 39,* 496–516.

Power, T. G., & Parke, R. D. (1983). Patterns of mother and father play with their 8-month-old infant: A multiple analysis approach. *Infant Behavior and Development, 6,* 453–459.

Pratt, T. C., Blevins, K. R., Daigle, L. E., Cullen, F. T., & Unnever, J. D. (2002). The relationship of ADHD to crime and delinquency: A meta-analysis. *International Journal of Police Science and Management, 4,* 344–360.

Prentice-Dunn, S., & Rogers. R. (1989). Deindividuation and the self-regulation of behavior. In P.B. Paulus (Ed.),

Psychology of group influence (2nd ed.), Mahwah, NJ: Lawrence Erlbaum Associates.

Prentky, R., & Knight, R. (1986). Impulsivity in the lifestyles and criminal behavior of sexual offenders. *Criminal Justice and Behavior, 13,* 141–164.

Prentky, R., & Quinsey, V. L. (1988). *Human sexual aggression: Current perspectives.* New York: New York Academy of Science.

President's Commission on Organized Crime. (1987). *The impact: Organized crime today.* Washington, DC: U.S. Government Printing Office.

Pressley, S.A. (1997, July 5). The Big Easy makes serious effort to solve sobering crime problem. *The Washington Post.* P. A3.

Pressley, S. A. (1998, June 13). Down a dark road to murder. *The Washington Post,* pp. A1, A9.

Prichard, J. C. (1845). *A treatise on insanity* (Trans. D. Davis). New York: Hafner.

Prinz, R. J., Roberts, W. A., & Hantman, E. (1980). Dietary correlates of hyperactive behavior in children. *Journal of Consulting and Clinical Psychology, 48,* 165–167.

Probing the mind of a killer. (1996, April 15). *Newsweek,* 30–40.

Proulx, J., McKibben, A., & Lusignan, R. (1996). Relationships between affective components and sexual behaviors in sexual aggressors. *Sexual Abuse: Journal of Research & Treatment, 8,* 279–289.

Proulx, J., Pellerin, B., Paradis, Y., & McKibben, A. (1997). Static and dynamic predictors of recidivism in sexual aggressors. *Sexual Abuse: Journal of Research & Treatment, 9,* 7–27.

Pugh v. Locke, 406 F. Supp. 318 (M.D. Alab. 1976).

Puri, B. K., Baxter, R., & Cordess, C. C. (1995). Characteristics of fire-setters: A study and proposed multiaxial psychiatric classification. *British Journal of Psychiatry, 166,* 393–396.

Putnam, F. W. (1988). The switch process in multiple personality disorder and other state-change disorders. *Dissociation, 1,* 24–32.

Puzzanchera, C., Stahl, A., Finnegan, T., Tierney, N., & Snyder, H. (2003). *Juvenile court statistics 2000.* Washington, DC: Office of Juvenile Justice and Delinquency Prevention. Retrieved October 5, 2004, from http://ojjdp.ncjrs.org/ojstatbb/court/qa06301. asp?qaDate=20030811

Quay, H. C. (1965). Psychopathic personality as pathological stimulus-seeking. *American Journal of Psychiatry, 122,* 180–183.

Radalet, M., & Akers, R. (1996). *Deterrence and the death penalty: The views of the experts.* Retrieved June 15, 2005, from http://sun.soci.niu.edu/~critcrim/dp/dppapers/mike.deterence

Raine, A. (1990). Interhemispheric transfer in schizophrenics, depresseds and normals with schizoid tendencies. *Journal of Abnormal Psychology, 98,* 35–41.

Raine, A. (1993). *The psychopathology of crime: Criminal behavior as a clinical disorder.* San Diego, CA: Academic.

Raine, A. (2002). Biosocial studies of antisocial and violent behavior in children and adults: A review. *Journal of Abnormal Child Psychology, XX.* Retrieved January 8, 2005, from http://www.findarticles.com/p/articles/mi_m0902/is_4_30/ai_89146368

Raine, A., Brennan, P., & Mednick, S. (1994). Birth complications combined with early maternal rejection at age 1 predispose to violent crime at age 18 years. *Archives of General Psychiatry, 51,* 984–988.

Raine, A., & Jones, F. (1987). Attention, autonomic arousal, and personality in behaviorally disordered children. *Journal of Abnormal Child Psychology, 15,* 583–599.

Raine, A., Buchsbaum, M. S., & LaCasse, L. (1997). Brain abnormalities in murderers indicated by positron emission tomography. *Biological Psychiatry, 42,* 495–508.

Raine, A., Lencz, T., Bihrle, S., LaCasse, L., & Colletti, P. (2000). Reduced prefrontal gray matter volume and reduced autonomic activity in antisocial personality disorder. *Archives of General Psychiatry, 57,* 119–127.

Raine, A., Venables, P. H., & Mednick, S. A. (1997). Low resting heart age at age 3 years predisposes to aggression at age 11: Findings from the Mauritius Joint Child Health Project. *Journal of the American Academy of Child and Adolescent Psychiatry, 36,* 1457–1464.

Raine, A., Venebles, P. H., & Williams, M. (1990). Relationships between central and autonomic measures of arousal at age 15 years and criminality at age 24 years. *Archives of General Psychiatry, 47,* 1003–1007.

Rand, M. (1998). *Criminal victimization 1997, changes 1996–1997 with trends 1993–1997.* Washington, DC: U.S. Department of Justice, Bureau of Justice Statistics.

Rapp, J. A., Carrington, F., & Nicholson, G. (1986). *School crime and violence: Victim's rights.* Malibu, CA: Pepperdine University Press.

Rasanen, P., Hakko, H., & Vaisanen, E. (1995). The mental state of arsonists as determined by forensic psychiatric evaluations. *Bulletin of the American Academy of Psychiatry & the Law, 23,* 547–553.

Rasmussen, K., & Levander, S. (1996). Crime and violence among psychiatric patients in a maximum-security psychiatric hospital. *Criminal Justice & Behavior, 23,* 455–471.

Rassell, M. E., & Mitchell, L. (1990). *Shortchanging education: How the U.S. spends on grades K–12.* Washington, DC: Economic Policy Institute.

R.A.V. v. City of St. Paul, 112 S. Ct. 2538 (1992).

Ray, A., Harris, M., & Butler, D. R. (1997). *World's dumbest criminals.* New York: Rutledge Hill Press.

Ray, D. W., Wandersman, A., Ellisor, J., & Huntington, D. E. (1982). The effects of high density in a juvenile correctional institution. *Basic and Applied Social Psychology, 3,* 95–108.

Reddick, A. J. (1987). *Issue paper: Youth gangs in Florida.* CITY: Committee on Youth, Florida House of Representatives.

Redding, R. E. (2000). *Recidivism rates in juvenile versus criminal court* (Juvenile Justice Fact Sheet). Charlottesville: Institute of Law, Psychiatry, & Public

Policy, University of Virginia. Retrieved October 25, 2004, from http://www.ilppp.virginia.edu/Publications_and_Reports/RecidRates.html

Redl, F., & Toch, H. (1979). The psychoanalytic perspective. In H. Toch (Ed.), *Psychology of crime and criminal justice* (pp. 193–195). New York: Holt, Rinehart & Winston.

Reid, R. T., & Kavanaugh, K. B. (1987). Abusive parents' perceptions of child problem behaviors: An example of parental bias. *Journal of Abnormal Child Psychology, 15,* 457–466.

Reifman, A.S., Larrick, R.P., & Fein, S. (1991). Temper and temperature on the diamond: The heat-aggression relationship in major league baseball. *Personality and Social Psychology Bulletin, 17,* 580–585.

Reiman, J. (1995). *The rich get richer and the poor get prison* (4th ed.). Boston: Allyn & Bacon.

Reisman, J. M. (1976). *A history of clinical psychology.* New York: Irvington.

Reiss, A., & Roth, J. (1993). *Understanding and preventing violence.* Washington, DC: National Academy Press.

Reitan, D. (1993). Halstead-Reitan Neuropsychological Tests Battery (HRNTB). Tucson, AR: Neuropsychology Press.

Rembar, C. (1980). *The law of the land.* New York: Simon & Schuster.

Rennison, C. M. (1999). *Criminal victimization 1998.* Washington, DC: Bureau of Justice Statistics.

Reno, J. (1999, April 15). [Speech to National Press Club, Washington, DC]. Retrieved April 16, 1999, from http://www.doj.gov

Research Institute on Addictions. (1997). *Effect of parental drinking on adolescents.* Buffalo: New York State Office of Alcoholism and Substance Abuse Services.

Resnick, M. D., Bearman, P. S., Blum, R. W., Bauman, K. E., Harris, K. M., & Jones, J. (1997). Protecting adolescents from harm: Findings from the National Longitudinal Study on Adolescent Health. *Journal of the American Medical Association, 278,* 823–832.

Ressler, R. K., & Schachtman, T. (1992). *Whoever fights monsters.* New York: St. Martin's Press.

Ressler, R. K., Burgess, A. W., & Douglas. J. E. (1988). *Sexual homicide: Patterns and motives.* Lexington, MA: Lexington.

Reuter, P. (1993). The cartage industry in New York. In M. Tonry & A. J. Reiss (Eds.), *Beyond the law—Crime in complex organizations* (pp. 149–202). Chicago: University of Chicago Press.

Rey, J. M., Bashir, M. R., Schwarz, M., Richards, I. N., Plapp, J. M., & Stewart, G. W. (1988). Oppositional disorder: Fact or fiction? *Journal of the American Academy of Child and Adolescent Psychiatry, 27,* 157–162.

Rhodes, R. P. (1984). *Organized crime—Crime control vs. civil liberties.* New York: Random House.

Rhodes v. Chapman, 101 S. Ct. 2392 (1981).

Rice, M. E. (1997). Violent offender research and implications for the criminal justice system. *American Psychologist, 52,* 414–423.

Rice, M. E., & Harris, G. T. (1996). Predicting the recidivism of mentally disordered firesetters. *Journal of Interpersonal Violence, 11,* 364–375.

Rice, M. E., & Harris, G. T. (1997). Cross-validation and extension of the Violence Risk Appraisal Guide for child molesters and rapists. *Law & Human Behavior, 21,* 231–241.

A riddle wrapped in a mystery inside an enigma. (1994, December 7). *The New Yorker,* p. 45.

Rider, A. O. (1980). The firesetter: A psychological profile. *FBI Law Enforcement Bulletin, 49,* 1–23.

Riger, S., Gordon, M. Y., & LeBailley, R. (1982). Coping with urban crime: Women's use of precautionary behaviors. *American Journal of Community Psychology, 10,* 369–386.

Rimer, S. (1996, December 4). Expanded inquiry is ordered in death of killer. New York Times. Retrieved May 30, 2006 from http://query.nytimes.com/gst/fullpage.html?sec=health&res=9504EFDB1E3CF937A35751C1A960958260&n=Top%2fReference%2fTimes%20Topics%2fSubjects%2fA%2fAbortion

Rimland, B., & Larson, G. E. (1983). Hair mineral analysis and behavior: An analysis of 51 studies. *Journal of Learning Disabilities, 16,* 279–285.

Ritvo, E., Shanok, S. S., & Lewis, D. O. (1983). Firesetting and nonfiresetting delinquents. *Child Psychiatry and Human Development, 13,* 259–267.

Roberts, C. F., Sargent, E. L., & Chan, A. S. (1993). Verdict selection processes in insanity cases: Juror construals and the effects of guilty but mentally ill instructions. *Law and Human Behavior, 17,* 261–275.

Robey, A., Rosenwal, R., Small, J., & Lee, R. (1964). The runaway girl: A reaction to family stress. *American Journal of Orthopsychiatry, 34,* 763–767.

Robins, L. N. (1966). *Deviant children grown up: A sociological and psychiatric study of sociopathic personality.* Baltimore: Williams & Wilkins.

Robins, L. N. (1991). Conduct disorder. *Journal of Child Psychology and Psychiatry, 32,* 193–212.

Robins, L. N., Helzer, J. E., & Weissman, M. M. (1984). Lifetime prevalence of specific psychiatric disorders in three sites. *Archives of General Psychiatry, 41,* 949–958.

Robins, L. N., & Przybeck, T. (1985). Age of onset of drug use as a factor in drug and other disorders. In C. L. Jones & R. J. Battjes (Eds.), *Etiology of drug abuse: Implications for prevention* (NIDA Research Monograph No. 56, DHHS Publication No. ADM 85–1335, pp. 178–192). Washington, DC: U.S. Government Printing Office.

Robins, L. N., Tipp, J., & Przybeck, T. (1991). Antisocial personality. In L. N. Robins & D. A. Regier (Eds.), *Psychiatric disorders in America* (pp. 258–290). New York: Free Press.

Robins, R. W., Gosling, S. D., & Craik, K. H. (1999). An empirical analysis of trends in psychology. *American Psychologist, 54,* 117–128.

Robinson, E. (2005, June 10). (White) women we love. *The Washington Post,* p. A23. Retrieved from http://www.washingtonpost.com/wp-dyn/ content/article/2005/06/09/AR2005060901729.html

Rochin v. California, 342 U.S. 165, 168 (1952).

Rodin, J., & Baum, A. (1978). Crowding and helplessness: Potential consequences of density and loss of control. In A. Baum & Y. Epstein (Eds.), *Human response to crowding* (pp. 389–401). Mahwah, NJ: Erlbaum.

Roesch, R., & Golding, S. L. (1987). Defining and assessing competence to stand trial. In I. Weiner & A. Hess (Eds.), *Handbook of forensic psychology* (pp. 378–394). New York: Wiley.

Rogers, A. G. (1987). *Gender differences in moral reasoning: A validity study of two moral orientations.* Unpublished doctoral dissertation, Washington University, St. Louis, MO.

Rogers, R., Gillis, J. R., Dickens, S. E., & Bagby, R. M. (1991). Standardized assessment of malingering: Validation of the structured interview of reported symptoms. *Psychological Assessment: A Journal of Clinical and Consulting Psychology, 3,* 89–96.

Rohde, D. (1999, November 7). Jurors and courts assailed in subway killing mistrial. *The New York Times,* p. 32.

Roid, G. (2003). Stanford-Binet Intelligence Scales, Fifth Edition (SB5). Toronto, Ontario, Canada: Thomson-Nelson.

Romano, L. (1998a, August 12). Two Arkansas boys convicted of killings. *The Washington Post,* p. A3.

Romano, L. (1998b, June 21). Year after guilty verdict, jurors visit bombsite. *The Washington Post,* pp. A 1, A17.

Roper v. Simmons 543 U.S. ____ (2005). NOTE: Page not yet assigned by Court.

Rosenberg, R., & Knight, R. A. (1988). Determining male sexual offender subtypes using cluster analysis. *Journal of Quantitative Criminology, 4,* 383–410.

Rosenfeld, R. (1985). Urban crime rates: Effects of inequality, welfare dependency, region and race. In J. Bryne & R. Sampson (Eds.), *The social ecology of crime* (pp. 975–991). New York: Springer-Verlag.

Rosenthal, R., & Jacobsen, L. (1968). *Pygmalion in the classroom.* New York: Holt.

Ross, E. (2005, July 21). The Dworkin-MacKinnon cultural revolution. Menswear.com. Retrieved May 30, 2006 from http://www.mensnewsdaily.com/archive/r/ross-eric/2005/ross072105.htm

Rossman, S. B., & Morley, E. (1996, August). Introduction. *Education and Urban Society, 28,* 395–411.

Rothbart, M. D., & Mauro, J. A. (1990). Questionnaire measures of infant temperament. In J. W. Fagen & J. Colombo (Eds.), *Individual differences in infancy: Reliability, stability and prediction* (pp. 411–429). Hillsdale, NJ: Lawrence Erlbaum Associates, Inc.

Rothbart, M. K., & Ahadi, S. A. (1994). Temperament and the development of personality. *Journal of Abnormal Psychology, 103,* 55–66.

Rotter, J. (1954). *Social learning and clinical psychology.* Englewood Cliffs, NJ: Prentice Hall.

Rotton, J. (1990). Individuals under stress. In C.E. Kimble (Ed.), *Social psychology: Living with people.* New York: W.C. Brown.

Rotton, J., & Frey, J. (1985). Air pollution, weather, and violent crimes: Concomitant time-series analysis of archival data. *Journal of Personality and Social Psychology, 49,* 1207–1220.

Rotton, J. (1986). Determinism redux: Climate and cultural correlates of violence. *Enviornment and Behavior, 18,* 346–368.

Rourke, B. P. (1988). Socioemotional disturbances of learning disabled children. *Journal of Consulting and Clinical Psychology, 56,* 801–810.

Rowe, D., & Gulley, B. (1992). Sibling effects on substance use and delinquency. *Criminology, 30,* 217–232.

Rowe, D. C., Clapp, M., & Wallis, J. (1987). Physical attractiveness and the personality resemblance of identical twins. *Behavioral Genetics, 17,* 191–201.

Ruane, M. E., & Levine, S. (1988, July 31). Surprise plea ends Aron's second trial. *The Washington Post,* pp. A1, A10.

Ruback, R.B., & Carr, T.S. (1984). Crowding in a women's prison: Attitudinal and behavioral effects. *Journal of Applied Social Psychology, 14,* 315–344.

Rubel, R. J. (1977). *The unruly school.* Lexington, MA: Lexington.

Rubin, K. H., LeMare, L. J., & Lollis, S. (1990). Social withdrawal in children: Developmental pathways to peer rejection. In S. R. Asher & J. D. Coie (Eds.), *Peer rejection in childhood* (pp. 217–252).

Rudovskey, D. (1992). Police abuse: Can the violence be contained? *Harvard Civil Rights-Civil Liberties Law Review, 27,* 465.

Rush, B. (1812). *Medical inquiries and observations upon the diseases of the mind.* Philadelphia: Kimber and Richardson.

Rushton, J. P. (1986). Altruism and aggression: The heritability of individual differences. *Journal of Personality and Social Psychology, 50,* 1192–1198.

Russakoff, D. (1998a, February 7). Five New York police indicted for abusing Haitian man. *The Washington Post,* p. A3.

Russakoff, D. (1998b, June 15). From Megan's law to Jenna's, grief inspires legislation. *The Washington Post,* pp. A1, A10.

Russakoff, D. (1999, May 15). A horrific initiation into a tragic club: As seen in inner cities, violence may harm brains of Columbine's children. *The Washington Post,* pp. A3, A8.

Russell, G. (1983). Psychological issues in sports aggression. In J.H. Goldstein (Ed.), *Sports violence.* New York: Springer-Verlag.

Rutter, M. (1990). Psychosocial resilience and protective mechanisms. In J. Rolf, A. S. Masten, D. Cicchetti, K. H. Neuchterlin, & S. Weintraub (Eds.), *Risk and protective factors in the development of psychopathology* (pp. 181–214).

Rutter, M. (1997). Nature-nurture integration: The example of antisocial behavior. *American Psychologist, 52,* 390–398.

Rutter, M., & Garmezy, N. (1983). *Stress, coping & development in children.* New York: McGraw-Hill.

Rutter, M., & Giller, H. (1983). *Juvenile delinquency: Trends and perspectives.* New York: Penguin.

Rutter, M., Giller, H., & Hagell, A. (1998). *Juvenile crime: A major new review.* Cambridge, England: Cambridge University Press.

Rutter, M., Maughan, B., Mortimore, P., & Ouston, J. (1979). *Fifteen thousand hours: Secondary schools and their effects on children.* Cambridge, MA: Harvard University Press.

Rutter, M., Mayhood, L., & Howlin, P. (1992). Language delay and social development. In P. Fletcher & D. Hall (Eds.), *Specific speech and language disorders in children.* San Diego, CA: Singular Publishing Group.

Rutter, M., Tizard, J., & Whitmore, K. (1970). *Education, health, and behavior.* London: Longman.

Ryan, G. (2003, January 11). [Speech at Northwestern University School of Law]. Retrieved June 15, 2003, from http://www.deathpenaltyinfo.org/article.php?scid'13&did'551

Rydelius, P. A. (1988). The development of antisocial behavior and sudden violent death. *Acta Psychiatrica Scandinavica, 77,* 398–403.

Ryden, M.B., Bossenmaier, M., & McLachlan, C. (1991). Aggressive behavior in cognitively impaired nursing home residents. *Research in Nursing and Health, 14,* 87–95.

Sacco, V. F., & Kennedy, L. W. (1996). *The criminal event.* Belmont, CA: Wadsworth.

Sack, K. (1998, October 4). Fugitive in bombing of clinic may be charged with 3 more. *The New York Times,* p. 18.

Sacks, O. (1990). Murder. In O. Sacks, *The man who mistook his wife for a hat.* New York: Harper Perennial Books.

Sagon, C. (2005, April 13). Twinkies, 75 years and counting. *The Washington Post.* Accessed May 25 at http://www.washingtonpost.com/wpdyn/articles/A46062-2005Apr12.html

Sales, B. D., & Shuman, D. W. (1996). *Law, mental health, and mental disorder.* Pacific Grove, CA: Brooks/Cole.

Salinger, D. J. (1951/1991). *Catcher in the rye.* New York: Little Brown.

Salinger, L. R., Jesilow, P., Pontell, H. N., & Geis, G. (1993). Assaults against airline flight attendants: A victimization study. In H. N. Pontell (Ed.), *Social deviance.* Englewood Cliffs, NJ: Prentice Hall.

Saltzman, L. E. (1992, June 10). Weapon involvement and injury outcomes in family and intimate assaults. *Journal of the American Medical Association, 267*(22), 30–43.

Sampson, R. (1987). Personal violence by strangers: An extension and test of the opportunity model of predatory victimization. *Journal of Criminal Law and Criminology, 78,* 327–356.

Sampson, R., & Laub, J. (1993). *Crime in the making.* Cambridge, MA: Harvard University Press.

Sanchez, R. (1998, May 23). Educators struggle for solutions to crisis of school rampages. *The Washington Post,* p. A12.

Sanchez-Bender, M. (1998, May 24). Gillick's slur violated the spirit of the game. *The Washington Post,* p. D7.

Sandys, M., & Dillehay, R. C. (1995). First-ballot votes, predeliberation dispositions, and final verdicts in jury trial. *Law and Human Behavior, 19,* 175–195.

Sanford v. Kentucky, 109 S. Ct. 2969 (1989).

Satcher, D. (2001). *Youth violence: A report of the surgeon general.* Washington, DC: Department of Health and Human Services.

Satterfield, J. H. (1987). Childhood diagnostic and neurophysiological predictors of teenage arrest rates: An eight-year prospective study. In S. Mednick, T. Moffit, & S. Stack (Eds.), *The causes of crime: New biological approaches.* Cambridge, England: Cambridge University Press.

Satterfield, J., Swanson, J., Schell, A., & Lee, F. (1994). Prediction of antisocial behavior in attention-deficit hyperactivity disorder boys from aggression/defiance scores. *Journal of the American Academy of Child and Adolescent Psychiatry, 33,* 185–190.

Saudino, K. J. (1998). Moving beyond the heritability question: New directions in behavioral genetic studies of personality. *Current Directions in Psychological Science, 6,* 86–89.

Saulny, S. (2003, August 22). Two who helped doctor's killer are released after 29 months. New York Times. Retrieved May 30, 2006 from http://query.nytimes.com/gst/fullpage.html?sec=health&res=9C03E4D91639F931A1575BC0A9659C8B63&n=Top%2fReference%2fTimes%20Topics%2fPeople%2fS%2fSlepian%2c%20Barnett%20A%2e

Savage, D. (2002, October 17). Court looks at race bias on juries. *The Los Angeles Times.* Retrieved May 26, 2003, from http://new.blackvoices.com/news/bv_supreme-court021017,0,7178920.story?coll=bv_news_black_headlines

Savitz, L. D. (1972). Introduction. In G. Lombroso-Ferrero (Ed.), *Criminal man.* Montclair, NJ: Patterson Smith.

Schachter, S., & Latane, B. (1964). Crime, cognition and the autonomic nervous system. In M. R. Jones (Ed.), *Nebraska symposium on motivation.* Lincoln: University of Nebraska Press.

Schafer, S. (1968). *The victim and his criminal.* New York: Random House.

Schauss, A. G., & Simonsen, C. E. (1979). A critical analysis of the diets of chronic juvenile offenders (Part I). *Journal of Orthomolecular Psychiatry, 8,* 149–157.

Scherer, K. R., Wallbott, H.G., & Summerfield, A. B. (Eds.). (1986). *Experiencing emotions: A cross-cultural study*. Cambridge, England: Cambridge University Press.

Schettino, A. P., & Borden, R. J. (1976). Sex differences in response to naturalistic crowding: Affective reactions to group size and density. *Personality and Social Psychology Bulletin, 2,* 67–70.

Schiraldi, V., Holman, B., & Beatty, P. (2000). *Poor prescription: The costs of imprisoning drug offenders in the United States.* Washington, DC: Justice Policy Institute.

Schlosser, E. (1997, September). A grief like no other. *The Atlantic Monthly.*

Schneider, A. (1985). *Deterrence and juvenile crime: Results from a National policy experiment.* New York: Springer-Verlag.

Schneider, H. (1999, December 6). Saudis raising blood money to stop killer's execution. *Washington Post,* p. A22.

Schoenthaler, S. J. (1982). The effect of sugar on the treatment and control of antisocial behavior: A double-blind study of an incarcerated juvenile population. *International Journal for Biosocial Research, 3,* 1–9.

Schott, R., & Quattrocchi, M. R. (1994, March). *Predicting the present: Expert testimony and civil commitment.* Paper presented at the annual meeting of the American Association of Psychology and Law, Santa Fe, NM.

Schretlen, D., Wilkins, S. S., Van Gorp, W. G., & Bobholz, J. H. (1992). Cross-validation of a psychological test battery to detect faked insanity. *Psychological Assessment, 4,* 77–83.

Schuckit, M. A., Goodwin, D., W., & Winojur, G. (1972). Biological vulnerability to alcoholism. *American Journal of Psychiatry, 128,* 1132–1136.

Schuckit, M. A., & Morrissey, M. A. (1978). Propoxyphene and phencyclidine (PCP) use in adolescents. *Journal of Clinical Psychiatry, 39,* 7–13.

Schwartz, I. (1989). *Justice for juveniles: Rethinking the best interests of the child.* Lexington, MA: Lexington.

Schwartz, M., & DeKeseredy, W. (1991). Left realist criminology: Strengths, weaknesses and the feminist critique. *Crime, Law and Social Change, 15,* 51–72.

Schwendinger, J., & Schwendinger, H. (1983). *Rape and inequality.* Beverly Hills, CA: Sage.

Scriviner, E. (1994). Police brutality. In M. Costanzo & S. Oscamp (Eds.), *Violence and the law.* Thousand Oaks, CA: Sage.

Scully, D. (1995). Rape is the problem. In B. R. Price & N. J. Sokoloff (Eds.), *The criminal justice system and women* (2nd ed., pp. 197–215). New York: McGraw-Hill.

Scully, D., & Marolla, J. (1997). Convicted rapist's vocabulary of motive: Excuses and justifications. In P. Adler & P. Adler (Eds.), *Constructions of deviance: Social power, context, & interaction* (2nd ed., pp. 271–286). Belmont, CA: Wadsworth.

Seguin, J., Pihl, R., Harden, P., Tremblay, R., & Boulerice, B. (1995). Cognitive and neuropsychological characteristics of physically aggressive boys. *Journal of Abnormal Psychology, 104,* 614–624.

Seifert, K. L. (2000). *Lifespan development.* Boston: Houghton Mifflin.

Seigel, R. K. (1978). Phencyclidine, criminal behavior, and the defense of diminished capacity. In R. C. Peterson & R. C. Stillman (Ed.), *Phencyclidine (PCP) abuse: An appraisal* (NIDA Research Monograph 21). Rockville, MD: National Institute on Drug Abuse.

Seligman, M. E. P. (1975). *Helplessness: On depression, development, and death.* San Francisco: Freeman.

Seligman, M. E. P. (1991). *Learned optimism.* New York: Knopf.

Seligman, M. E. P., & Maier, S. F. (1967). Failure to escape traumatic shock. *Journal of Experimental Psychology, 74,* 1–9.

Seltzer, T. (in press). Mental Health Courts: A misguided attempt to address the criminal justice system's unfair treatment of people with mental illness. *Journal of Psychology, Public Policy & Law.*

Seltzer, T. (2005). Mental Health Courts: A misguided attempt to address the criminal justice system's unfair treatment of people with mental illness. *Psychology, Public Policy & Law, 11*(4), 570–586.

Serin, R. C., Malcolm, P. B., Khanna, A., & Barbaree, H. E. (1994). Psychopathy and deviant sexual arousal in incarcerated sexual offenders. *Journal of Interpersonal Violence, 9,* 3–11.

Shahinfar, A., Kupersmidt, J. B., & Matza L. S. (2001). The relation between exposure to violence and social information processing among incarcerated adolescents. *Journal of Abnormal Psychology 110,* 136–141.

Shapira, I. (2004, August 28). Bobbitt held after fight at Las Vegas home. *Washington Post,* p. A9.

Shaver, K. (1998, March 20). Experts differ on the meaning of Aron's responses to ink blots. *The Washington Post,* p. C4.

Shaver, K., & Pan. P. (1998, May 14). Father charged in Maryland infant's 1987 death. *The Washington Post,* pp. D1, D8.

Shaver, P. R., & Clark, C. L. (1994). The psychodynamics of adult romantic attachment. In J. M. Masling & R. F. Bornstein (Eds.), *Empirical perspectives on object relations theory* (pp. 105–156). Washington, DC: American Psychological Association.

Shaver, P. R., & Hazen, C. (1994). Attachment. In A. L. Weber & J. H. Harvey (Eds.), *Perspectives on close relationships.* Boston: Allyn & Bacon.

Sheffrin, S., & Triest, R. (1992). Can brute deterrence backfire? Perceptions and attitudes in taxpayer compliance. *Tax Compliance and Enforcement, 193,* 212–213.

Shelden, R., Horvath, J., & Tracy, S. (1989). Do status offenders get worse? Some clarifications on escalation. *Crime and Delinquency, 35,* 202–216.

Sheldon, W. H. (1942). *The varieties of temperament: A psychology of constitutional differences.* New York: Harper & Brothers.

Sheldon, W. H. (1949). *Varieties of delinquent youth.* New York: Harper & Brothers.

Sheley, J. F. (1979). *Understanding crime: Concepts, issues, decisions.* Belmont, CA: Wadsworth.

Sheley, J. F., McGee, Z. T., & Wright, J. D. (1992). Gun-related violence in and around inner city schools. *American Journal of the Disabled Child, 146,* 667–682.

Sheley, J. F., & Wright, J. D. (1993, December). *Gun acquisition and possession in selected juvenile samples* (Office of Juvenile Justice & Delinquency Prevention research in brief). Washington, DC: U.S. Department of Justice, National Institute of Justice.

Shelley, M. (1994). *Frankenstein.* New York: Dover. (Original work published 1816)

Shen, F. (1997, October 9). Unlikely pair had little but trouble in common. *The Washington Post,* A1, A18–A19.

Shepherd, R. E., & Zaremba, B. A. (1995). When a disabled juvenile confesses to a crime: Should it be admissible? *Criminal Justice, 9,* 31.

Sher, K. J., Walitzer, J. S., Wood, P. K., & Brent, E. F. (1991). Characteristics of children of alcoholics: Putative risk factors, substance use and abuse, and psychopathology. *Journal of Abnormal Psychology, 100,* 427–488.

Sherman, L. W. (1993). Defiance, deterrence, and irrelevance: A theory of the criminal sanction. *Journal of Research in Crime and Delinquency, 30,* 445–473.

Sherman, L. (1999, December 16). Violence in America. *Online News Hour.* Retrieved August 29, 2004, from http://www.pbs.org/newshour/bb/law/july-dec99/violence_12–16.html

Sherman, L. W., Gottfredson, D., MacKenzie, D., Eck, J., Reuter, P., & Bushway, S. (1997). *Preventing crime: What works, what doesn't, what's promising.* Washington, DC: U.S. Department of Justice, Office of Justice Programs, National Institute of Justice.

Sherman, L., & Rogan, D. P. (1995). Deterrent effects of police raids on crack houses: A randomized, controlled experiment. *Justice Quarterly, 12,* 755–781.

Sherman, L., Schmidt, J. D., & Velke, R. J. (1992). *High crime taverns: A RECAP project in problem-oriented policing. Final report to the National Institute of Justice.* Washington, DC: Crime Control Institute.

Shields, J. (1962). *Monozygotic twins.* Oxford, England: Oxford University Press.

"Shooting Suspect Was Dismissed by Xerox." (1999, November 17). *Honolulu Advertiser.* Retrieved May 30, 2006 from http://the.honoluluadvertiser.com/1999/Nov/17/localnews7.html

Shore, S. (1997, July 6). Mother on trial in son's death: Injuries self-inflicted, she claims. *Richmond Times-Dispatch,* p. A1.

Shotland, R. L. (1992). The theory of the causes of courtship rape: Part 2. *Journal of Social Issues, 48*(1), 127–143.

Shover, N. (1972). Structures and careers in burglary. *Journal of Criminal Law, Criminology and Police Science, 63,* 540–549.

Shover, N., & Bryant, K. M. (1993). Theoretical explanations of corporate crime. In M. B. Blankenship (Ed.), *Understanding corporate criminality* (pp. 141–176). New York: Carland Publishing Co.

Showers, J., & Pickrell, E. (1987). Child firesetters: A study of three populations. *Hospital & Community Psychiatry, 38,* 495–501.

Shweder, R. A., & Bourne, E. J. (1984). Does the concept of person vary cross-culturally? In R. A. Shweder & R. A. LeVine (Eds.), *Culture theory: Essays on mind, self, and emotion.* Cambridge: Cambridge University Press.

Sickmund, M. (2002). *Juveniles in corrections.* Washington, DC: Office of Juvenile Justice and Delinquency Prevention. Retrieved October 5, 2004, from http://ojjdp.ncjrs.org/ojstatbb/corrections/qa08 201. asp?qaDate=20021030

Siegal, N. (1999, April 11). Inmates are again shackled in childbirth, critics say. *The New York Times,* pp. 23–24.

Siegel, L. J. (1998). *Criminology* (6th ed.). Belmont, CA: Thompson/West Publishing Co.

Siegel, L. J. (2000). *Criminology* (7th ed.). St. Paul, MN: West.

Siegel, L. J. (2003). *Criminology* (8th ed.). Belmont, CA: Thomson/Wadsworth.

Siegel, L., & Senna J. (1997). *Juvenile delinquency: Theory, practice and law.* St Paul, MN: West.

Siegel, L., & Senna. J. (2000). *Juvenile delinquency: Theory, patterns, and typologies* (7th ed.). Belmont, CA: Wadsworth.

Siegel, L., & Welsh, B. (2006). *Juvenile delinquency: Theory, practice, and law* (9th ed.). Florence, KY: Thomson Wadsworth.

Siegler, R. S. (1996). *Emerging minds: The process of change in children's thinking.* New York: Oxford University Press.

Siever, L. J., & Davis, K. L. (1991). A psychobiological perspective on the personality disorders. *American Journal of Psychiatry, 148,* 1647–1658.

Signorielli, N. (1990). Television's mean and dangerous world: A continuation of the cultural indicators perspective. In N. Signorielli & M. Morgan (Eds.), *Cultivation analysis: New directions in media effects research* (pp. 85–106). Newbury Park, CA: Sage.

Silberman, C. (1979). *Criminal violence, criminal justice.* New York: Random House.

Silberman, M. (1995). *A world of violence: Corrections in America.* Belmont, CA: Wadsworth.

Silver, E., Cirincione, C., & Steadman, H. J. (1994). Demythologizing inaccurate perceptions of the insanity defense. *Law and Human Behavior, 18,* 63–70.

Silver, L. B. (1992). Psychological and family problems associated with learning disabilities: Assessment and intervention. *Journal of the American Academy of Child and Adolescent Psychiatry, 28,* 319–325.

Simmons, R., & Taylor. J. (1992). A psychosocial model of fan violence. *International Journal of Sport Psychology, 23,* 207–226.

Simon, D., & Burns, E. (1997, September 7). Too much is not enough. *The Washington Post,* pp. C1, C4.

Simon, D., & Burns, E. (1998). *The corner: A year in the life of an inner city neighborhood.* New York: Broadway Books.

Simon, L. M. J. (1998). Does criminal offender treatment work? *Applied and Preventive Psychology, 7,* 137–159.

Simon, R. J. (1967). *The jury and the defense of insanity.* Boston: Little, Brown.

Simon, R. (1975). *The contemporary woman and crime.* New York: McGraw-Hill.

Simpson, S. (1989). Feminist theory, crime and justice. *Criminology, 27,* 605–632.

Singer, M., Anglin, T., Song, L., & Lunghofer, L. (1995). Adolescents' exposure to violence and associated symptoms of psychological trauma. *Journal of the American Medical Association, 273,* 477–482.

Singer, M., Miller, D., Slovak, K., & Frierson, R. (1997). *Mental health consequences of children's exposure to violence.* Cleveland, OH: Case Western Reserve University, Mandel School of Applied Social Sciences.

Singer, S. (1981). Homogeneous victim-offender populations: A review and some research implications. *Journal of Criminal Law and Criminology, 72,* 779–788.

Singer, J. L., & Singer, D. G. (1980). Television viewing, family style and aggressive behavior in preschool children. In M. Green (Ed.), *Violence and the family: Psychiatric, sociological, and historical implications.* Boulder, CO: Westview Press.

Singer, J. L., & Singer, D. G. (1983) Psychologists look at television: Cognitive, developmental, personality and social polity implications. *American Psychologist, 38,* 826–834.

Sipress, A. (1999, November 18). Road rage death wasn't all that surprising. *Milwaukee Journal Sentinel.* Retrieved May 26, 2006 from http://www.findarticles.com/p/articles/mi_qn4196/is_19991118/ai_n1055 2063

Sivard, R. (1989). *World military and social expenditures 1989.* Washington, DC: World Priorities.

Skinner, B. F. (1938). The behavior of organisms. New York: Appleton.

Skogan, W. G. (1986). Methodological issues in the study of victimization. In E. A. Fattah (Ed.), *From crime policy to victim policy: Reorienting the justice system* (pp. 80–116). New York: St. Martin's Press.

Slavin, R. E. (1990). Achievement effects of ability grouping in secondary schools: A best-evidence synthesis. *Review of Educational Research, 60,* 471–499.

Slawson, J. (1926). *The delinquent boys.* Boston: Budget Press.

Sleek, S. (1998, August). The basis for aggression may start in the womb. *American Psychological Association Monitor, XX.* Retrieved March 11, 1999, from http://www.apa.org/monitor/aug98/somb.html

Slevin, P. (1998, March 23). A new way to see the future: School with high-powered backers aims to help troubled DC teens. *The Washington Post,* pp. B1, B8.

Slobogin, C. (1985). The guilty but mentally ill verdict: An idea whose time should not have come. *George Washington Law Review, 53,* 494–527.

Smith, A. C. (1999, September 28). Care of mentally ill prisoners questioned. *St. Petersburg Times,* pp. 1, 8.

Smith, A. M., Gacono, C. B., & Kaufman, L. (1997). A Rorschach comparison of psychopathic and nonpsychopathic conduct disordered adolescents. *Journal of Clinical Psychology, 53,* 289–300.

Smith, C.A. & Ellsworth, P.C. (1987). Patterns of appraisal and emotion related to taking an exam. *Journal of Personality and Social Psychology, 52,* 475–488.

Smith, D. A. (1975). *The Mafia mystique.* New York: Basic Books.

Smith, D. E., & Wesson, D. R. (1980). PCP Abuse: Diagnostic and pharmacological treatment approaches. *Journal of Psychedelic Drugs, 12,* 293–29.

Smith, G. B. (1998, December 3). Plea deal for Jr. Gotti. *New York Daily News.* Retrieved May 17, 1999, from http://www.mostnewyork.com

Smith, G. T., Goldman, M., Greenbaum, P. E., & Christiansen, B. A. (1995). Expectancy for social facilitation from drinking: The divergent paths of high-expectancy and low-expectancy adolescents. *Journal of Abnormal Psychology, 104,* 32–40.

Smith, L. (1997a, December 9). Former Lorena Bobbitt is back in court. *The Washington Post,* p. B3.

Smith, L. (1997b, October 24). Man convicted in attack using date-rape bill. *The Washington Post,* p. B7.

Smith, P. Z. (1993). *Felony defendants in large urban counties, 1990.* Washington, DC: Bureau of Justice Statistics.

Smith, V. L., & Kassin, S. M. (1993). Effects of the dynamite charge on the deliberations of deadlocked juries. *Law and Human Behavior, 17,* 625–644.

Smoking in pregnancy tied to disruptive behavior. (1997, August 5). *Washington Post,* p. 5.

Snarey, J. R. (1985). Cross-cultural universality of social moral development: A critical review of Kohlbergian research. *Psychological Bulletin, 97,* 202–232.

Snell, T. (1994a). *Women in prison.* Washington, DC: U.S. Department of Justice, Office of Justice Programs, Bureau of Justice Statistics. Retrieved February 13, 2005, from http://www.ojp.usdoj.gov/bjs/pub/ascii/wopris.txt

Snell, T. (1994b). *Women in prison: Survey of state prison inmates, 1991.* Washington, DC: U.S. Department of Justice, Office of Justice Programs, Bureau of Justice Statistics.

Snell, T. L. (1998). *Capital punishment 1997.* Washington, DC: Bureau of Justice Statistics.

Snowling, M. J. (1991). Developmental reading disorders. *Journal of Child Psychology and Psychiatry, 32,* 49–77.

Snyder, H. (1988). *Court careers of juvenile offenders.* Washington, DC: U.S. Department of Justice, Office of Juvenile Justice & Delinquency Prevention.

Snyder, H. N. (1999). *Juvenile arson, 1997.* Washington, DC: U.S. Department of Justice, Office of Juvenile Justice & Delinquency Prevention.

Snyder, H. (2004, September). Juvenile arrests 2002. *Juvenile Justice Bulletin.* Retrieved February 27, 2005, from http://www.ncjrs.org/html/ojjdp/204608/ contents.html

Snyder, H., & Sickmund, M. (1999). *Juvenile offenders and victims: A national report.* Washington, DC: National Center for Juvenile Justice, Office of Juvenile Justice & Delinquency Prevention.

Soderstrom, C. A., Dischinger, P. C., Kerns, T. J., & Trifilli, A. L. (1995). Marijuana and other drug use among automobile and motorcycle drivers treated at a trauma center. *Accident Analysis and Prevention, 27,* 131–135.

Solomon, J., & King, P. (1993, July 19). Waging war in the workplace. *Newsweek, XX,* 30–34.

Sommer, R. (1999). Applying environmental psychology. In D.A. Bernstein & A.M. Stec (Eds.), The psychology of everyday life. Boston: Houghton Miflin.

Sommers, I., & Baskin, D. (1990). The prescription of psychiatric medications in prison: Psychiatric versus labeling perspectives. *Justice Quarterly, 7,* 739–755.

Sommers, I., & Baskin, D. (1994). Factors related to female adolescent initiation into violent street crime. *Youth and Society, 25,* 468–489.

Southwick, C. H. (1967). An experimental study of intra-group agonistic Behavior in rhesus monkeys (Macaca mulatta). *Behavior, 28,* 182–209.

Span, P., & Kastor, E. (1998, June 19). Schizophrenic lawyer's triumph turns into tragedy. *The Washington Post,* pp. A1, A18.

Spelman, W. (1995). Criminal careers of public places. In J. E. Eck & D. Weisburd (Eds.), *Crime and place.* Monsey, NY: Criminal Justice Press and Police Executive Research Forum.

Spelman, W., & Eck, J. E. (1989). Sitting ducks, ravenous wolves, and helping hands: New approaches to urban policing. *Public Affairs Comment, 35*(2), 1–9.

Speltz, M., DeKlyen, M., Greenberg, M., & Dryden, M. (1995). Clinical referral for oppositional defiant disorder: Relative significance of attachment and behavioral variables. *Journal of Abnormal Child Psychology, 23,* 487–507.

Spencer-Wendel, S. (2005, May 22). Nathaniel Brazill would have graduated from high school this week. Instead, he is growing up in prison. *Palm Beach Post.* Retrieved May 25, 2006, at http://www.usatoday.com/news/nation/2006-05-18-tate-sentencing_x.htm?csp=34

Spergel, I. A. (1995). *The youth gang problem: A community approach.* New York: Oxford University Press.

Spergel, I. A., & Curry. G. D. (1987). *Gangs, schools, and communities.* Chicago: University of Chicago, School of Social Service Administration.

Stahl, A., Finnegan, T., & Kang, W. (2002). *Easy access to juvenile court statistics: 1985–2000.* Washington, DC: Office of Juvenile Justice & Delinquency Prevention.

Stalenheim, E., von Knorring, L., & Oreland, L. (1997). Platelet monoamine oxidase activity as a biological marker in a Swedish forensic psychiatric population. *Psychiatry Research, 69,* 79–87.

Stanford v. Kentucky, 492 U.S. 316 (1989).

Stannard, D. E. (1993). *American holocaust: The conquest of the new world.* New York: Oxford University Press.

Stasser, G., Kerr, N. L., & Bray, R. M. (1982). The social psychology of jury deliberations: Structure, process, and product. In N. Kerr & R. Bray (Eds.), *The psychology of the courtroom* (pp. 221–256). New York: Academic.

Stattin, H., & Klackenberg-Larsson, I. (1993). Early language and intelligence development and their relationship to future criminal behavior. *Journal of Abnormal Psychology 102,* 369–378.

Steadman, H. J. (1979). *Beating a rap? Defendants found incompetent to stand trial.* Chicago: University of Chicago Press.

Steadman, H. J. (1993). *Reforming the insanity defense: An evaluation of pre- and post- Hinckley reforms.* New York: Guilford.

Steadman, H. J., Barisiak, S., Dvoskin, J., & Holohean, E. J. (1987). A survey of mental disability among state prison inmates. *Hospital and Community Psychiatry, 28,* 1086.

Steadman, H. J., McCarty, D. W., & Morrissey, J. P. (1989). *The mentally ill in jail: Planning for essential services.* New York: Guilford.

Steadman, H. J., Monahan, J., Applebaum, P., Grisso, T., Mulvey, E., Roth, L., et al. (1994). Designing a new generation of risk assessment research. In J. Monahan & H. Steadman (Eds.), *Violence and mental disorder: Developments in risk assessment* (pp. 297–318). Chicago: University of Chicago Press.

Steadman, H. J., Mulvey, E. P., Monahan, J., Robbins, P. C., Appelbaum, P. S., Grisso, T., et al. (1998). Violence by people discharged from acute psychiatric inpatient facilities and by others in the same neighborhoods. *Archives of General Psychiatry, 55,* 393–401.

Steadman, H. J., & Veysey, B. M. (1997). *Providing services for jail inmates with mental disorders: Research in Brief.* Washington, DC: U.S. Department of Justice, National Institute of Justice.

Steffensmeier, D. (1995). Trends in female crime: Its still a man's world. In B. R. Price & N. J. Sokoloff (Eds.), *The criminal justice system and women: Offenders, victims and workers* (2nd ed., pp. 9–104). New York: McGraw-Hill.

Steffensmeier, D., & Allan, E. (1996). Gender and crime: Toward a gendered theory of female offending. *Annual Review of Sociology, 22,* 459–487.

Steinberg, M., Bancroft, J., & Buchanan, J. (1993). Multiple personality disorder in criminal law. *Bulletin of the American Academy of Psychiatry and the Law, 21,* 345–356.

Steiner, P. (1994). *Delinquency prevention.* Washington, DC: Office of Juvenile Justice & Delinquency Prevention.

Steinglass, P., Bennett, L. A., Wolin, S. J., & Reiss, D. (1987). *The alcoholic family.* New York: Basic Books.

Stepp, L. S. (1999, April 23). Why Johnny can't feel. *Washington Post,* pp. C1, 8.

Stern, V. (1999). *A sin against the future: Imprisonment in the modern world.* Boston: Northeastern University Press.

Stevenson, R. L. (1991). *The strange case of Dr. Jekyll and Mr. Hyde.* New York: Dover. (Original work published 1886)

Stewart, J. A. (1993). Profile of female firesetters: Implications for treatment. *British Journal of Psychiatry, 163,* 248–256.

Stewart, J. B. (1991). *Den of thieves.* New York: Simon & Schuster.

Stewart, M. A., & Culver, K. W. (1982). Children who set fires: The clinical picture and a follow-up. *British Journal of Psychiatry, 140,* 357–363.

Stewart, M. A., & de Blois, C. S. (1983). Father-son resemblances in aggressive and antisocial behavior. *British Journal of Psychiatry, 142,* 78–84.

Stewart, M. A., de Blois, C. S., & Cummings, C. (1980). Psychiatric disorder in the parents of hyperactive boys and those with conduct disorder. *Journal of Child Psychology and Psychiatry, 21,* 283–92.

Stewart v. Martinez-Villareal, 000 S. Ct. 0000 (1998).

Stinchcombe, A. (1964). *Rebellion in high school.* Chicago: Quadrangle Press.

Stinson, F. S., Dufour, M. C., Steffans, R. A., & DeBakey, S. (1993). Alcohol-related mortality in the United States, 1979–1989. *Alcohol Health & Research World, 17,* 251–260.

Stoff, D. M., Breiling, J., & Maser, J. D. (Eds.). (1997). *Handbook of antisocial behavior.* New York: Wiley.

Stokels, D. (1978). A typology of crowding experiences. In A. Baum & Y. Epstein (Eds.), *Human response to crowding* (pp. 219–255). Mahwah, NJ: Erlbaum.

Stone, W. L., & LaGreca, A. M. (1990). The social status of children with learning disabilities: A reexamination. *Journal of Learning Disabilities, 23,* 23–37.

Stormo, K. J., Lang, A. R., & Stritzke, W. G. K. (1997). Attributions about acquaintance rape: The role of alcohol and individual differences. *Journal of Applied Social Psychology, 27,* 297–305.

Storr, A. (1970). *Human aggression and violence.* New York: Bantam.

Stott, D. H. (1980). *Delinquency and human nature.* Baltimore: University Park Press.

Strain, E. (1995). Antisocial personality disorder, misbehavior and drug abuse. *Journal of Nervous and Mental Disease, 163,* 162–165.

Straus, M. (1991). Discipline and deviance: Physical punishment of children and violence and other crime in adulthood. *Social Problems, 38,* 101–123.

Straus, M. A, & Baron, L. (1983). *Sexual stratification, pornography, and rape.* Durham, NH: Family Research Laboratory, University of New Hampshire.

Straus, M., & Gelles, R. (1988). *Intimate violence.* New York: Simon & Schuster.

Straus, M. A., & Gelles, R. J. (1990). *Physical violence in American families: Risk factors and adaptations to violence in 8,145 families.* New Brunswick, NJ: Transaction.

Streib, V. (2004). *The juvenile death penalty today: Death sentences and executions for juvenile crimes January 1, 1973 to June 30, 2004.* Retrieved October 5, 2004, from http://www.law.onu.edu/faculty/streib/documents/Juv DeathJune302004NewTables.pdf

Strodtbeck, F. L., & Hook, L. (1961). The social dimensions of a twelve-man jury table. *Sociometry, 24,* 713–719.

Strodtbeck, F. L., James, R., & Hawkins, C. (1957). Social status in jury deliberations. *American Sociological Review, 22,* 713–719.

Struck, D. (1997, April 20). In DC's simple city, complex rules of life and death. *The Washington Post,* A1, A16–A17.

Study: Boys sex abuse underreported. (1998, December 1). *The New York Times.* Retrieved December 1, 1998, from http://www.nytimes.com/aponline/a/AP-Sexual-Abuse.html

Study: Violence hits 10 percent of public schools.(1998, March 20). *Washington Post,* p. A3.

Substance Abuse and Mental Health Services Administration. (2004). *Substance use, abuse, and dependence among youths who have been in jail or a detention center: The National Survey on Drug Use and Health.* Washington, DC: U.S. Department of Health and Human Services, Substance Abuse and Mental Health Services Administration. Retrieved February 20, 2005, from http://oas.samhsa.gov/2k4/Deta inedYouth/ detainedYouth.pdf

Sue, D., Sue, D. W., & Sue, S. (2006). *Understanding abnormal behavior* (8th ed.).

Suicide is recalled as Maine revisits Megan's Law. (1998, February 17). *Washington Post,* p. A2.

Sullivan, H. S. (1953). *The interpersonal theory of psychiatry.* New York: Norton.

Sullivan, H. S. (1965). *Personal psychopathology.* New York: Norton.

Suomi, S., Higley, D., & Linnoila, M. (1997). *Alcohol, Clinical and Experimental Research, 20,* 643–649.

Superville, D. (1997, August 15). Youths cite rise in drugs. *The Boston Globe,* p. A1.

Surawicz, F. G. (1980). Alcoholic hallucinosis: A missed diagnosis. *Canadian Journal of Psychiatry, 25,* 57–63.

Suro, R. (1997, June 1). Officials wonder if bribery arrests at federal prison are isolated or trend. *The Washington Post,* p. A8.

Susman, E. J., Dorn, L. D., Inoff-Germain, G., Nottelmann, E. D., & Chrousos, G. P. (1997). Cortisol reactivity, distress behavior, and behavioral and psychological problems in young adolescents: A longitudinal perspective. *Journal of Research on Adolescence, 7,* 81–105.

Sutherland, E. H. (1940). White-collar criminality. *American Sociological Review, 5,* 1–12.

Sutherland, E. H. (1983). *White-collar crime: The uncut version.* New Haven, CT: Yale University Press.

Sutherland, E. H., & Cressy. D. R. (1974). *Principles of criminology* (9th ed.). New York: Lippincott.

Swaffer, T., & Hollin, C. R. (1995). Adolescent firesetting: Why do they say they do it? *Journal of Adolescence, 18,* 619–623.

Swaim, R. C., Oetting, E. R., Edwards, R W., & Beauvais, F. (1989). Links from emotional distress to adolescent drug use: A path model. *Journal of Consulting and Clinical Psychology, 57,* 227–231.

Swan, N. (1995, January/February). *Early childhood behavior and temperament predict later substance use.* Washington, DC: National Institute of Drug Abuse.

Swanson, H. L. (1991). Operational definitions and learning disabilities: An overview. *Learning Disability Quarterly, 14,* 242–254.

Swanson, J., Borum, R., Swartz, M., & Monahan, J. (1996). Psychotic symptoms and disorders and the risk of violent behavior in the community. *Criminal Behavior and Mental Health, 6,* 309–329.

Swanson, J. W., Estroff, S. E., Swartz, M. S., Borum, R., Lachicotte, W., Zimmer, C., et al. (1997). Violence and severe mental disorder in clinical and community populations: The effects of psychotic symptoms, comorbidity, and lack of treatment. *Psychiatry* (in press).

Swarns, R. (1997, July 8). Lost in the shadows of history: Shabazz's family troubles. *New York Times,* p.1.

Sykes, G. (1966). *The society of captives: A study of a maximum security prison.* New York: Atheneum.

Sykes, G. (1974). The rise of critical criminology. *Journal of Criminal Law and Criminology, 65,* 211.

Sykes, G., & Matza, D. (1957). Techniques of neutralization: A theory of delinquency. *American Sociological Review, 22,* 664–770.

Szasz, A. (1986). Corporations, organized crime, and the disposal of hazardous waste: An examination of the making of a criminogenic regulatory structure. *Criminology, 24,* 1–28.

Szatmari, O., Offard, D., & Boyle, M. H. (1989). Ontario health study: Prevalence of attention deficit disorders with hyperactivity. *Journal of the American Academy of Child and Adolescent Psychiatry, 32,* 1264–1273.

Talbott, J. A., & Glick, I. D. (1986). The inpatient care of the chronically mentally ill. *Schizophrenia Bulletin, 12,* 129–140.

Tarter, R. E., Alterman,, A. I., & Edwards, K. L. (1985). Vulnerability to alcoholism in men: A behavior-genetic perspective. *Journal of Studies on Alcoholism, 46,* 329–356.

Tarter, R., Blackson, T., Martin, C., Seilhamer, R., Pelham, W., & Loeber, R. (1993). Mutual dissatisfaction between mother and son in substance abuse and normal families: Association with child behavior problems. *American Journal on Addiction, 2,* 1–10.

Tarter, R. E., Kabene, M., Escallier, E. A., Laird, S. B., & Jacob, T. (1990). Temperament deviation and risk for alcoholism. *Alcoholism in Clinical and Experimental Research, 14,* 380–382.

Tarter, R. E., & Vanyukov, M. (1994). Alcoholism: A developmental disorder. *Journal of Consulting and Clinical Psychology, 62,* 1096–1107.

Taylor, M., & Nee, C. (1988). The role of cues in simulated residential burglary: A preliminary investigation. *British Journal of Criminology, 28,* 398–401.

Taylor, P. J. (1993). Schizophrenia and crime: Distinctive patterns in association. In S. Hodgins (Ed.), *Crime and mental disorder* (pp. 63–85).

Taylor, P. J., Garety, P., Buchanan, A., Reed, A., Wessely, S., Ray, K., et al. (1994). Delusions and violence. In J. Monahan & H. J. Steadman (Eds.), *Violence and mental disorder: Developments in risk assessment* (pp. 161–182). Chicago: University of Chicago Press.

Teacher sex case sentence criticized as lenient, disparate. (1997, November 17). *Washington Post,* p. A16.

Tellegen, A., Lykken, D. T., Bouchard, T. J., Jr., Wilcox, K. J., Segal, N. L., & Rich, S. (1988). Personality similarity in twins reared apart and reared together. *Journal of Personality and Social Psychology, 54,* 1031–1039.

Teplin, L. A. (1984). The criminalization of the mentally ill: Speculation in search of data. In L. A. Teplin (Ed.), *Mental health and criminal justice.* Newbury Park, CA: Sage.

Teplin, L. A. (1990). The prevalence of severe mental disorder among male urban jail detainees: Comparison with the epidemiological catchment area program. *American Journal of Public Health, 80,* 663.

Teplin, L. A. (1994). Psychiatric and substance abuse disorders among male urban jail detainees. *American Journal of Public Health, 84,* 290–293.

Teplin, L. A., & Pruett, N. S. (1995). Police as street corner psychiatrists: Managing the mentally ill. *International Journal of Law and Psychiatry, 15,* 139–156.

Tessler, R. C., & Dennis, D. L. (1989). *A synthesis of NIMH-funded research concerning persons who are homeless and mentally ill.* Rockville, MD: National Institute of Mental Health.

Texas Department of Criminal Justice. (1991). *Shock incarceration in Texas: Special incarceration program.* Austin, TX: Author.

Thiele, T. E., Marsh, D. J., Ste. Marie, L., Bernstein, I. L., & Palmiter, R. D. (1998). Ethanol consumption and resistance are inversely related to neuropeptide Y levels. *Nature, 396,* 366–369.

Thomas, A., & Chess, S. (1977). *Temperament and development.* New York: Brunner/Mazel.

Thomas, E. (1996, April 22). Blood brothers. *Newsweek, XX,* 28–39.

Thomas, P. (1995). Gun control will decrease crime. In P. A. Winters (Ed.), *Crime and criminals* (pp. 153–160). San Diego, CA: Greenhaven Press.

Thomas, R. (1990, 4 June). Sit down taxpayers. *Newsweek,* 60.

Thomas-Lester, A. (1998, April 26). On 14th St., good deed was fatal. *The Washington Post.*

Thombs, D. L. (1994). *Introduction to addictive behaviors.* New York: Guilford.

Thompson, B. (1998, March 29). Trigger points. *The Washington Post magazine,* pp. 12–30.

Thompson, C. W. (1998, February 26). DC must stop sending inmates to Ohio prison. *The Washington Post,* p. A8.

Thompson, C. W. (1998, January 7). A painful parting for prisoners: DC 's female inmates confront separation from family as transfers begin. *The Washington Post,* p. B1.

Thompson, R. J., & Kronenberger, W. (1990). Behavior problems in children with learning problems. In H. L. Swanson & B. Keogh (Eds.), *Learning disabilities: Theoretical and research issues.* Hillsdale, NJ: Lawrence Erlbaum Associates, Inc.

Thomson, E. (1999). Effects of an execution on homicides in California. *Homicide Studies, 3*(2), 129–150.

Thornberry, T. P. (1994). *Violent families and youth violence* (Fact Sheet No. 21). Washington, DC: U.S. Department of Justice, Office of Juvenile Justice & Delinquency Prevention.

Thornberry, T., & Burch, J. (1997). *Gang members and delinquent behavior.* Washington, DC: Office of Juvenile Justice & Delinquency Prevention.

Thornberry, T., Farnworth, M., Krohn, M., & Lizotte, A. (n.d.). *Peer influence and the initiation to drug use.* Albany, NY: Hindelang Criminal Justice Research Center.

Thorndike, E. I. (1905). The elements of psychology. New York: Seiler.

Thurman, Q., St. John, C., & Riggs, L. (1984). Neutralization and tax evasion: How effective would a moral appeal be in improving compliance to tax laws? *Law & Policy, 6,* 309–327.

Tibbits, S. (1995, November). *Low birth weight, disadvantaged environment and early onset: A test of Moffitt's interactional hypothesis.* Paper presented at the American Society of Criminology meeting, Boston, MA.

Tiihonen, J., Hakola, P., & Eronen, M. (1995). Homicidal behaviour and mental disorders. *British Journal of Psychiatry, 167,* 821.

Timberg, C. (1999, April 18). The hardest time: At the toughest prison in Virginia, tight controls. *The Washington Post,* pp. C1, C4.

Tjaden, P. (1997). *The crime of stalking: How big is the problem?* Washington, DC: U.S. Department of Justice, National Institute of Justice.

Tjaden, P., & Thoennes, N. (2000a). *Extent, nature, and consequences of intimate partner violence: Findings from the National Violence Against Women Survey* (research report). Washington, DC: U.S. Department of Justice.

Tjaden, P., & Thoennes, N. (2000b). *Full report of the prevalence, incidence, and consequences of violence against women: Findings from the National Violence Against Women Survey.* Washington, DC: U.S. Department of Justice.

Toby, J., Smith, W. R., & Smith, D. R. (1985). *Comparative trends in crime victimization in school and in the community: 1974–1981.* Washington, DC: Bureau of Justice Statistics.

Toch, H. (1977). *Living in prison: The ecology of survival.* New York: Free Press.

Toch, H. (1988). Studying and reducing stress. In R. Johnson & H. Toch (Eds.), *The pains of imprisonment* (pp. 25–44). Prospect Heights, IL: Waveland.

Toch, H. (1990). An anthropologist in the prison. *Contemporary Psychology, 35,* p. 581.

Toch, H., & Adams, K. (1989). *Coping: Maladaptation in prisons.* New Brunswick, NJ: Transaction Publishers.

Tolan, P. H., & Thomas, P. (1995). The implications of age of onset for delinquency risk: II. Longitudinal data. *Journal of Abnormal Child Psychology, 23,* 157–181.

Tonry, M. (1996). *Malign neglect: Race, crime, and punishment in America.* New York: Oxford University Press.

Toobin, J. (1996, September 9). The Marcia Clark verdict. *New Yorker, XX,* 58–71.

Torestad, B., & Magnusson, D. (1996). Basic skills, early problematic behavior and social maladjustment. *Educational Studies, 22,* 165–176.

Torrey, E. F., Stieber, J., Ezekiel, J., Wolf, S. M., Charstein, J., Noble, J. H., et al. (1992). *Criminalizing the seriously mentally ill: The abuse of jails as mental hospitals.* Washington, DC: Public Citizen's Health Research Group and the Alliance for the Mentally Ill.

Tough talk on crime. (1997, September 28). *The Washington Post.*

Transparency International. (2005, March 16). *A world built on bribes.* Retrieved June 2, 2005, from http://www.transparency.org/pressreleases_archive/2005/2005.03.16.gcr_relaunch.html

Travis, A. (2003, January 10). Summit over 35% gun crime rise. *The Guardian.* Retrieved February 3, 2005, from http://www.guardian.co.uk/gun/Story/0,2763,872038,00.html

Trembley, R. E., Boulerice, B., Harden, P. W., McDuff, P., Perusse, D., Pihl, R. O., et al. (1996). Do children in Canada become more aggressive as they approach adolescence? In Human Resources Development Canada & Statistics Canada (Eds.), *Growing up in Canada: National longitudinal survey of children and youth* (pp. 127–137). Ottawa, Ontario, Canada: Statistics Canada.

Trembley, R., & Craig, W. (1995). Developmental crime prevention. In M. Tonry & D. P. Farrington (Eds.), *Building a safer society: Crime and justice* (Vol. 19). Chicago: University of Chicago Press.

Trembley, R. E., Loeber, R., Gagnon, C., Charlebois, P., Larivee, S., & LeBlanc, M. (1991). Disruptive boys with stable and unstable high fighting behavior patterns during junior elementary school. *Journal of Abnormal Child Psychology, 19,* 285–300.

Trickett, P. K., & Putnam, F. (1991, August). *Patterns of symptoms in prepubertal and pubertal sexually abused girls.* Paper presented at the Annual meeting of the American Psychological Association, San Francisco, CA.

Trop v. Dulles, 356 U.S. 86 (1958).

Truell, P., & Gurwin, L. (1992). *False profits: The inside story of BCCI, the world's most corrupt financial empire.* New York: Houghton Mifflin.

Trunnel, E. P. & Turner, C. W. (1988). A comparison of the psychological and hormonal factors in women with and without premenstrual syndrome. *Journal of Abnormal Psychology, 97,* 429–436.

Tucker, N. (2000, February 25). Killer of boxer, not guilty. *The Washington Post,* pp. B1, B4.

Tupin, J. P., Mahar, D., & Smith, D. (1973). Two types of violent offenders with psychosocial descriptors. *Diseases of the Nervous System, 34,* 356–363.

Turkheimer, E., & Gottesman, I. I. (1991). Individual differences and the canalization of human behavior. *Developmental Psychology, 27,* 18–22.

Twomey, S. (1999, May 15). For Virginia's must-see web site, the jury is still out. *The Washington Post,* pp. A1, A12.

Tyler, T. (1990). *Why people obey the law.* New Haven, CT: Yale University Press.

Umbreit, M. S. (1998). Restorative justice through victim-offender mediation: A multi-site assessment. *Western Criminology Review 1*(1).

United States v. Brawner, 471 F.2d 969 (1972).

United States v. Lyons, 731 F.2d 243 (5th Cir. 1984).

United States v. Pollard, 171 F. Supp. 476 (E.D. Mich. 1950).

U.S. Administration on Aging. (1998). *The national elder abuse incidence study: Final report, September 1998.* Washington, DC: U.S. Department of Health and Human Services, The Administration on Aging.

U.S. Administration on Aging. (2005). *Elder abuse prevalence and incidence.* Washington, DC: U.S. Department of Health and Human Services, U.S. Administration on Aging. Retrieved June 3, 2005, from http://www.elder-abusecenter.org/pdf/publication/FinalStatistics050331.pdf

U.S. Air Force. (2003). *The report of the working group concerning the deterrence of and response to incidents of sexual assault at the U.S. Air Force Academy.* Washington, DC: Headquarters, United States Air Forces. Retrieved August 3, 2003, from http://www.af.mil/usafa_report/usafa_report.pdf

USA Today. (May 20, 2006). Florida teen gets 30 years for gun possession. Retrieved May 25, 2006 at http://www.usatoday.com/news/nation/2006-05-18-tate-sentencing_x.htm?csp=34

U. S. Attorney General's Commission Report on Pornography, Final Report. (1986). Washington, D.C.: Government Printing Office.

U.S. Census Bureau. (2001). *Census 2000.* Retrieved June 3, 2005, from http://www.census.gov/popest/datasets.html# mrd

U.S. Department of Health and Human Services. (1992). *Youth and alcohol: Dangerous and deadly circumstances.* Washington, DC: Office of the Inspector General.

U.S. Department of Health and Human Services. (1995a). *A nation's shame: Fatal child abuse and neglect in the United States: A report of the U.S. Advisory Board on Child Abuse and Neglect.* Washington, DC: U.S. Advisory Board on Child Abuse and Neglect.

U.S. Department of Health and Human Services. (1995b). *Third national incidence study of child abuse and neglect: Final report.* Washington, DC: National Center on Child Abuse and Neglect.

U.S. Department of Health & Human Services. (1996). *The 1995 U.S. public health survey on drug abuse.* Washington, DC: U.S. Government Printing Office.

U.S. Department of Health and Human Services. (1997). *National Household Survey on Drug Abuse—1997.* Washington, DC: U.S. Department of Health and Human Services, Substance Abuse and Mental Health Services Administration.

U.S. Department of Health and Human Services. (1998). *Child maltreatment 1996: Reports from the states to the national child abuse and neglect data system.* Washington, DC: U.S. Government Printing Office.

U. S. Department of Health and Human Services. Substance Abuse and Mental Health Services Administration. (2000). *National Household Survey on Drug AbuseB1999: Volume I. Summary of National Findings.* Washington, D.C.: U. S. Government Printing Office.

U.S. Department of Health and Human Services. (2002). *Child maltreatment 2002.* Washington, DC: U.S. Department of Health and Human Services Children's Bureau.

U.S. Department of Health and Human Services. (2003). Risk and protective factors for child abuse and neglect. In *Emerging practices in the prevention of child abuse and neglect.* Washington, DC: U.S. Department of Health and Human Services, Administration for Children and Families, Administration on Children, Youth and Families, Children's Bureau, Office on Child Abuse and Neglect. Retrieved February 13, 2005, from http://nccanch.acf.hhs.gov/topics/prevention/emerging/riskprotectivefactors.cfm

U.S. Department of Health and Human Services, National Center on Child Abuse and Neglect. (1997). *Child maltreatment 1995: Reports from the states to the national child abuse and neglect data system.* Washington, DC: U.S. Government Printing Office.

U.S. Department of Health and Human Services, Substance Abuse and Mental Health Services Administration. (1998). *National household survey on drug abuse.* Washington, DC: Author.

U.S. Department of Health and Human Services, Substance Abuse and Mental Health Services Administration. (2000). *National Household Survey on Drug Abuse—1999: Volume I. Summary of national findings.* Washington, DC: U.S. Government Printing Office.

U.S. Department of Housing and Urban Development. (2000, April). *Gun-related violence in public housing communities* (recent research reports). Washington, DC: Author.

U.S. Department of Justice. (1987). *White collar crime.* Washington, DC: Bureau of Justice Statistics, Office of Justice Programs Reports.

U.S. Department of Justice. (1993). *Performance measures for the criminal justice system.* Washington, DC: Bureau of Justice Statistics.

U.S. Department of Justice. (1994). *Women in prison.* Washington, DC: Bureau of Justice Statistics.

U.S. Department of Justice. (1995a). *Childhood victimization and risk for alcohol and drug arrests.* Washington, DC: National Institute of Justice.

U.S. Department of Justice. (1995b). *Victims of childhood sexual abuse: Later criminal consequences.* Washington, DC: National Institute of Justice.

U.S. Department of Justice. (1996a). *Child victimizers: Violent offenders and their victims.* Washington, DC: Bureau of Justice Statistics.

U.S. Department of Justice. (1996b). *Reducing youth gun violence: An overview of programs and initiatives.* Washington, DC: Office of Juvenile Justice and Delinquency Prevention.

U.S. Department of Justice. (1996c). *Understanding and preventing violence: A public perspective.* Washington, DC: National Institute of Justice.

U.S. Department of Justice. (1997a). *Felony sentences in state courts.*

U.S. Department of Justice. (1997b). *Lifetime likelihood of going to state or federal prison.* Washington, DC: Bureau of Justice Statistics.

U.S. Department of Justice. (2000). *Juvenile offenders and victims: 1999 National Report.* Washington, DC: U.S. Department of Justice, Office of Juvenile Justice & Delinquency Prevention.

U.S. Fire Administration. (2003). *Firefighter arson: Special report.* Washington, DC: Federal Emergency Management Administration. Retrieved June 1, 2005, from http://www.facts-1.com/usfa_tr-141.pdf

U.S. Internal Revenue Service. (2005, March 29). *New IRS study provides preliminary tax gap estimate.* Wash-ington, DC: Author. Retrieved June 2, 2005, from http://www.irs.gov/newsroom/article/0,,id'137247,00.html

U.S. Riot Commission. (1968). *Report of the National Advisory Commission on Civil Disorders.* New York: Bantam Books.

U.S. Senate Committee on Finance. (2004, August 18). *GAO finds insufficient Medicaid oversight.* Retrieved June 2, 2005, from http://finance.senate.gov/press/Gpress/2004/prg081804a.pdf

U.S. Sentencing Commission. (1995). *Special report to the Congress: Cocaine and federal sentencing policy.* Washington, DC: Author.

U.S. Sentencing Project. (1997). *Losing the vote: The impact of felony disenfranchisement laws in the United States.* Retrieved April 14, 1999, from http://www.sentencingproject.org

U.S. Sentencing Project. (1998). *National inmate population of two million projected by 2000.* Retrieved April 14, 1999, from http://www.sentencingproject.org

Ustad, K. L., Rogers, R., Sewell, K. W., & Guarnaccia, C. A. (1996). Restoration of competency to stand trial: Assessment with the Georgia court competency test and the competency screening test. *Law and Human Behavior, 20,* 131–146.

Valentine, P. W. (1999, February 14). 19 inmates moved in bid to bust drug ring. *The Washington Post,* pp. C1, C4.

Valzelli, L. (1978). Clinical pharmacology of serotonin. In W. B. Essman (Ed.), *Serotonin in health and disease: Vol. 4. Physiological regulation and pharmacological action* (pp. 295–339). New York: Spectrum.

Valzelli, L. (1981). *Psychobiology of aggression and violence.* New York: Raven.

Van den Boom, D. C. (1989). Neonatal irritability and the development of attachment. In G. A. Kohnstam, J. E. Bates, & M. K. Rothbart (Eds.), *Temperament in childhood* (pp. 299–318). Chichester, England: Wiley.

Van der Molen, J. H. W. (2004). Violence and suffering in television news: Toward a broader conception of harmful television content for children. *Pediatrics, 113,* 1771–1775.

Van Slambrouck, P. (1998, April 27). Execution and a convict's mental state. *The Christian Science Monitor,* p. 3.

Van Voorhis, P. (1987). Correctional effectiveness: The high cost of ignoring success. *Federal Probation, 51,*(1), 56–62.

Vedder, C., & Somerville, D. (1970). *The delinquent girl.* Springfield, IL: Thomas.

Verhulst, F. C., Eussen, M. L., Berden, G. F., Sanders-Woudstra, J., & Van Der Ende, J. (1993). Pathways of problem behaviors from childhood to adolescence. *Journal of the American Academy of Child and Adolescent Psychiatry, 32,* 388–396.

Viano, E. C. (1992). The news media and crime victims: The right to know versus the right to privacy. In E. C. Viano (Ed.), *Critical issues in victimology: International perspectives* (pp. 24–34). New York: Springier.

Vick, K. (1997, October 30). Aron released from mental hospital to home detention. *The Washington Post,* p. B1.

Viemero, V. (1996). Factors in childhood that predict later criminal behavior. *Aggressive Behavior, 22,* 87–97.

Villani, V. S. (2001). Impact of media on children and adolescents: A 10-year review of the research. *Journal of the American Academy of Child and Adolescent Psychiatry, 40,* 392–401.

Vingerhoets, G,, Berckmoes, C., & Stroobant, N. (2003). Cerebral hemodynamics during discrimination of prosodic and semantic emotion in speech studied by transcranial Doppler ultrasonography. *Neuropsychology, 17,* 93–99.

Violence Policy Center. (1998). *Who dies: A look at firearm deaths and injury in America-Revised Edition.* Retrieved April 28, 1999 from http://www.vpc.org/studies/who.htm.

Virkkunen, M., Eggert, M., Rawlings, R., & Linnoila, M. (1996). A prospective follow-up study of alcoholic violent offenders and fire setters. *Archives of General Psychiatry, 53,* 534–529.

Virkkunen, M., & Narvanen, S. (1987). Plasma insulin, tryptophan and serotonin levels during the glucose tolerance test among habitually violent and impulsive offender. *Neuropsychobiology, 17,* 19–23.

Vise, D. A. (1987, March 2). One of the markets best and brightest is caught. *The Washington Post,* pp. A6–A7.

Visher, C. A. (1987). Juror decision making the importance of evidence. *Law and Human Behavior, 11,* 1–17.

Vito, G. (1984). Developments in shock probation: A review of research findings and policy implications. *Federal Probation, 48,* 22–27.

Voeller, K. (1986). Right-hemisphere deficit syndrome in children. *American Journal of Psychiatry, 143,* 1004–1009.

Vogel, S. (1997a, December 19). Baltimore man charged in death of daughter, 7 months. *The Washington Post,* p. C4.

Vogel, S. (1997b, November 6). Boy had to drink whiskey concoction. *The Washington Post,* p. B11.

Vogel, S. (1997c, December 13). Mentally ill Montgomery man absolved in slaying of parents. *The Washington Post,* p. B7.

Vogel, S., & Levine, S. (1997, July 11). Father of dead toddler described use of physical force, police say. *The Washington Post,* pp. D1, D6.

Vold, G., Bernard, T., & Snipes, J. (1998). *Theoretical criminology* (4th ed.). New York: Oxford University Press.

Von Drehele, D., Kenworthy, T., & Jeter, J. (1998, July 26). A descent into fear and rage ended at the Capitol. *The Washington Post,* pp. A1, A22–A23.

Von Hinting, H. (1948). *The criminal and his victim.* New Haven, CT: Yale University Press.

Vreeland, R. G., & Levin, B. M. (1980). Psychological aspects of firesetting. In D. Canter (Ed.), *Fires and human behavior.* Chichester, England: Wiley.

Vrij, A., van der Steen, J., & Koppelaar, L. (1994). Aggression of police officers as a function of temperature. *Journal of Community & Applied Social Psychology, 4,* 365–370.

Waldner-Haugrud, L. K., & Magruder, B. (1995). Male and female sexual victimization in dating relationships: Gender differences in coercion techniques and outcomes. *Violence & Victims, 10,* 203–215.

Walker, L. (2000). *The battered woman syndrome* (2nd ed.). New York: Springer.

Walker, S. (1998). *Popular justice: A history of American criminal justice* (2nd ed.). New York: Oxford University Press.

Wallace, H. (1998). *Victimology: Legal, psychological, and social perspectives.* Boston: Allyn & Bacon.

Wallerstein, J. S., Corbin, S. B., & Lewis, J. M. (1988). Children of divorce: A ten-year study. In E. M. Hetherington & J. Arasteh (Eds.), *Impact of divorce, single parenting, and stepparenting on children.* Hillsdale, NJ: Lawrence Erlbaum Associates, Inc.

Wallerstein J. S., & Kelly, J. B. (1980). *Surviving the breakup: How children and parents cope with divorce.* New York: Basic Books.

Walsh, S. (1998, February 27). Milken to pay U.S. $47 million to settle charge of violating ban. *The Washington Post,* p. G1.

Walter, J. (2000, April 25). In Spokane, long, fearful hunt ends. *Washington Post,* p. A3.

Walters, R., & Brown, M. (1963). Studies of reinforcement of aggression: Transfer of responses to an interpersonal situation. *Child Development, 34,* 563–571.

Ward, D. A. (1994). Alcatraz and Marion: Confinement in super maximum security. In J. R. Roberts (Ed.), *Escaping prison myths: Selected topics in the history of federal corrections* (pp. 81–93). Washington, DC: The American University Press.

Ward, T., Hudson, S. M., & Marshall, W. L. (1996). Attachment style in sex offenders: A preliminary study. *Journal of Sex Research, 33,* 17–26.

Ward, T., Husdon, S. M., & McCormack, J. (1997). The assessment of rapists. *Behavior Change, 14,* 39–54.

Ward T., McCormack, J., & Hudson, S. M. (1997). Sexual offenders perceptions of their intimate relationships. *Sexual Abuse: Journal of Research & Treatment, 9,* 57–74.

Wartner, U., Grossman, K., Fremmer-Bombik, E., & Seuss, G. (1994). Attachment patterns at age six in south Germany: Predictability from infancy and implications for preschool behavior. *Child Development, 65,* 1014–1027.

Washington Post (1998, May 24). Truck driver blocking lane is slain at Florida tollbooth. P. A23.

Wasserman, G. A., & Miller, L. S. (1997). Antisocial behavior. In R. Loeber & D. P. Farrington (Eds.), *Report of OJJDP study group on serious, chronic, and violent juvenile offenders.* Washington, DC: Office of Juvenile Justice & Delinquency Prevention.

Watson, J. B. (1925). *Behaviorism.* New York: Norton.

Watson, J. B., & Rayner, R. (1920). Conditioned emotional reaction. *Journal of Experimental Psychology, 3,* 1–14.

Waxman, S. (2003, July 23). Sons of the father: While Saddam ran Iraq, Uday and Qusay ran amok. *Washington Post,* p. C1.

Webster-Stratton, C. (1985). Comparison of abusive and nonabusive families with conduct-disordered children. *American Journal of Orthopsychiatry, 55,* 59–69.

Webster-Stratton, C. (1998). Preventing conduct problems in head start children: Strengthening parenting competencies. *Journal of Consulting and Clinical Psychology, 66,* 715–730.

Weeks, R., & Widom, C. S. (1998). *Early childhood victimization among incarcerated adult male felons.* Washington, DC: National Institute of Justice.

Weiler, B. L., & Widom, C. S. (1996). Psychopathy and violent behavior in abused and neglected young adults. *Criminal Behaviour & Mental Health, 6,* 253–271.

Weinberg, R. A., Scarr, S., & Waldman, I. D. (1992). The Minnesota transracial adoption study: A follow-up of

IQ test performance at adolescence. *Intelligence, 16,* 117–135.

Weiner, B., Graham, S., & Reyna, C. (1997). An attributional examination of retributive versus utilitarian philosophies of punishment. *Social Justice Research, 10,* 431–452.

Weisburd, D. (1997). *Reorienting crime prevention research and policy: From the causes of criminality to the context of crime.* Rockville, MD: National Criminal Justice Reference Service.

Weisburd, D., Green, L., & Ross, D. (1994). Crime in street level drug markets: A spatial analysis. *Criminologie, 27,* 49–67.

Weisburd, D., Waring, E., Chayet, E., Dickman, D., Fischer, D, & Plant, R. M. (1993). *White collar crime and criminal careers.* Washington, D. C.: National Institute of Justice.

Weisburd, D., Wheeler, S., Waring, E., & Bode, N. (1991). *Crimes of the middle class: White collar offenders in federal courts.* New Haven, CT: Yale University Press.

Weisheit, R., & Mahan, S. (1988). *Women, crime and criminal justice.* Cincinnati, OH: Anderson Publishing.

Weisheit, R., & Wells, L. Ed. (1999). *Youth gangs in rural America.* Washington, DC National Institute of Justice, U.S. Department of Justice.

Weiss, G., & Hechtman, L. (1993). *Hyperactive children grown up* (2nd ed.). New York: Guilford.

Weiss, J., Lamberti, J., & Blackburn, N. (1960). The sudden murderers. *Archives of General Psychiatry, 2,* 670–678.

Weiss, R. (2002, September 30). On Ecstasy, consensus is elusive. *The Washington Post,* p. A7.

Wechsler, D. (1995). Wechsler Adult Intelligence Scale-Third Edition (WAIS-III). San Antonio, TX: Harcourt Assessment, Inc.

Wener, R., Frazier, F. W., & Farbstein, J. (1987, June). Building better jails. *Psychology Today, 21,* 40–44, 48–49.

Wessely, S. (1997). The epidemiology of crime, violence, and schizophrenia. *British Journal of Psychiatry, 170,* 8–11.

Wessely, S., Buchanan, A., Reed, A., Cutting, J., Everitt, B;, Garety, P., et al. (1993). Acting on delusions: I. Prevalence. *British Journal of Psychiatry, 163,* 69–76.

West, D. J., & Farrington, D. P. (1977). Who becomes delinquent? In D. J. West & E. P. Farrington (Eds.), *The delinquent way of life.* London: Heinemann.

Wetter, M., Baer, R., Berry, D., Smith, G., & Larsen, L. (1992). Sensitivity of MMPI–2 validity scales to random responding and malingering. *Psychological Assessment, 4,* 369–374.

Wexler, B. E. (1980). Cerebral laterality and psychiatry: A review of the literature. *American Journal of Psychiatry, 137,* 279–291.

Wexler, H. (1995, November). *Attention deficit disorder, drugs and crime: The dangerous mixture.* Paper presented at the American Society of Criminology meeting. Boston, MA.

Wexler, H. K., Graham, W. F., Koronowski,, R., & Lowe. L. (1995). *Evaluation of amity in-prison and post-release substance abuse treatment programs.* Washington, DC: National Institute of Drug Abuse.

Wheeler, S. (1992). The problem of white-collar motivation. In K. Schlegel & D. Weisburd (Eds.), *White-collar crime reconsidered* (pp. 108–123). Boston: Northeastern University Press.

Wheeler, S., Weisberg, D., Waring, E., & Bode, N. (1988). White collar crimes and criminals. *American Criminal Law Review, 25,* 331–357.

White House Conference on Children. (1990). *Learning into the 21st century.* Washington, DC: Author.

White House Office of National Drug Control Policy. (1997). *The president's drug control strategy.* Washington, DC: Author.

White, H. R. (1991). Marijuana use and delinquency: A test of the independent cause hypothesis. *Journal of Drug Issues, 21,* 231–256.

White, H. R., Padina, R., & LaGrange, R. (1987). Longitudinal predictors of serious substance use and delinquency. *Criminology, 25,* 715–740.

White, J., Moffitt, T. E., Earls, F., Robins, L., & Silva, P. (1990). How early can we tell? Preschool predictors of conduct disorder. *Criminology, 28,* 507–533.

White, M. (1998, February 24). Allstate accuses 45 of insurance fraud. *The Washington Post,* p. D5.

Wicks-Nelson, R., & Israel, A. C. (1997). *Behavior disorders of childhood* (3rd ed.). Upper Saddle River, NJ: Prentice Hall.

Widiger, T., & Trull, T. (1994). Personality disorders and violence. In J. Monaham & H. Steadman (Eds.), *Violence and mental disorder: Developments in risk assessment* (pp. 203–226). Chicago: University of Chicago Press.

Widom, C. S. (1989). The cycle of violence. *Science, 244,* 160–166.

Widom, C. S. (2000, January). Childhood victimization: Early adversity, later psychopathology. *National Institute of Justice Journal, 242,* 1–8. Retrieved May 4, 2000 at www.ncjrs.org

Widom, C. S., & Maxfield, M. G. (2001). *An update on the cycle of violence. National Institute of Justice Research in Brief.* Washington, DC: National Institute of Justice. Retreived February 13, 2005, from http://www.childrensrights.org/PDF/policy/cycle_violence.pdf

Wiehn, P. J. (1988). Mentally ill offenders: Prison's first casualties. In R. Johnson & H. Toch (Eds.), *The pains of imprisonment* (pp. 221–237). Prospect Heights, IL: Waveland.

Wiener, R. L., Habert, K., Shkodriani, G., & Staebler, C. (1991). The social psychology of jury nullification: Predicting when jurors disobey the law. *Journal of Applied Social Psychology, 21,* 1379–1401.

Wilens, T. E., Biederman, J., Spencer, T. J., & Frances, R. J. (1994). Comorbidity of attention deficit hyperactivity and psychoactive substance use disorders. *Hospital and Community Psychiatry, 45,* 421–435.

Wilgoren, D. (1997, December 29). Vandals deface Islamic symbol. *The Washington Post*, p. C1.

Williams v. Florida, 399 U.S. 78 (1970).

Williamson, S., Hare, R. D., & Wong, S. (1987). Violence: Criminal psychopaths and their victims. *Canadian Journal of Behavioral Science, 19*, 454–462.

Wills, T. A., McNamara, G., Vaccaro, D., & Hirky, A. E. (1996). Escalated substance abuse: A longitudinal groping analysis from early to middle adolescence. *Journal of Consulting and Clinical Psychology, 55*, 685–690.

Wilson, B. J., Kunkel, D., Linz, D., Potter, J., Donnerstein, E., Smith, S. L., et al. (1997). Violence in television programming overall: University of California, Santa Barbara study. In M. Seawall (Ed.), *National television violence study* (Vol. 1, pp. 3–184). Thousand Oaks, CA: Sage.

Wilson, D. J. (2000). *Drug use, testing, and treatment in jails.* Washington, DC: Bureau of Justice Statistics, U.S. Department of Justice.

Wilson, E. O. (1975). *Sociobiology.* Cambridge, MA: Harvard University Press.

Wilson, J. Q., & Abrahamsen, A. (1992). Does crime pay? *Justice Quarterly, 9*, 359–377.

Wilson, J., & Herrnstein, R. (1985). *Crime and human nature.* New York: Simon & Schuster.

Wilson, J. J., & Howell, J. C. (1993).
. Washington, DC: U.S. Department of Justice, Office of Justice Programs, Office of Juvenile Justice & Delinquency Prevention.

Wilson, J. Q., & Kelling, G. (1982, March). Broken windows. *Atlantic Monthly, XX*, 31–32.

Wilson, W. H., Ellinwood, E. H., Mathew,, R. J., & Johnson, K. (1994). Effects of marijuana on performance of a computerized cognitive-neuromotor test battery. *Psychiatry Research, 51*, 115–125.

Windle, M. (2004). *Alcohol use among adolescents and young adults.* Washington, DC: National Institute on Alcohol Abuse and Addiction.

Windle, R. C., & Windel, M. (1995). Longitudinal patterns of physical aggression: Associations with adult social, psychiatric, and personality functioning and testosterone levels. *Development and Psychopathology, 7*, 563–585.

Winerip, M. (1999, May 23). Bedlam on the streets. *The New York Times Sunday Magazine*, pp. 42–49, 56, 66, 70.

Winick, B. J. (1998). Sex offender law in the 1990s: A therapeutic jurisprudence analysis. *Psychology, Public Policy, and Law, 4*, 505–570.

Winters, C. (1997, Summer). Learning disabilities, crime, delinquency, and special education placement. *Adolescence, XX*. Retrieved January 30, 2005, from http://www.findarticles.com/p/articles/mi_m2248/is_n126_v32/ai_19619412

Wisconsin v. Mitchell, 113 S. Ct. 2194 (1993).

Wish, E. (1990). U.S. drug policy in the 1990s: Insights from new data on arrestees. *International Journal of Addictions, 25*, 1–15.

Wolf, J. (1997, November 3). Lawyers say CIA defendant has brain lesions. *Reuters News Service.*

Wolfe, D. A., Jaffe, P., Wilson, S. K., & Zak, L. (1985). Children of battered women: The relation of child behavior to family violence and maternal stress. *Journal of Consulting and Clinical Psychology, 53*, 657–665.

Wolfgang, M. (1958). *Patterns in criminal homicide.* Philadelphia: University of Pennsylvania Press.

Wolfgang, M. E. (1972). Cesare Lombroso. In H. Mannheim (Ed.), *Pioneer in Criminology* (2nd ed.). Montclair, NJ: Patterson Smith.

Wolfgang, M. (1995). Transitions of crime in the aging process. *Current Perspectives on Aging and the Life Cycle, 4*, 141–153.

Wolfgang, M., Figlio, R., & Sellin, T. (1972). *Delinquency in a birth cohort.* Chicago: University of Chicago Press.

Woodard, E. H. (1998). *Media in the home 2000: The fourth annual survey of parents and children* (Survey Series No. 7). Philadelphia: The Annenberg Public Policy Center of the University of Pennsylvania.

Woodard, E. H., IV, & Gridina, N. (2000). *Media in the home 2000: The fifth annual survey of parents and children.* Retrieved May 19, 2003, from http://www.appcpenn.org/mediainhome/survey/survey7.pdf

Wooden, W. S., & Parker, J. (1982). *Men behind bars: Sexual exploitation in prison.* New York: Plenum.

Woodlee, Y. (1998, January 31). Treadwell is ordered to prison. *The Washington Post*, p. B4.

Wrangham, R., & Peterson, D. (1996). *Demonic males: Apes and the origins of human violence.* Boston: Houghton Mifflin.

Wren, C. S. (1999, May 9). For heroin's new users, a long hard fall. *The New York Times*, pp. 27–28.

Wright, R. (1994). *The moral animal: Evolutionary psychology and everyday life.* New York: Vintage.

Wright, R. (1995, March 13). The biology of violence. *The New Yorker*, pp. 68–77.

Wright, R. T., & Decker, S. H. (1997). *Armed robbers in action: Stickups and street culture.* Boston, MA: Northeastern University Press.

Wrightsman, L. S., Nietzel, M. T., & Fortune, W. H. (1998). *Psychology and the legal system* (4th ed.). Pacific Grove, CA: Brooks/Cole.

Wulf, S. (1997, September 1). A time bomb explodes: The serenity of a small, close-knit New Hampshire town is shattered when the local crank becomes the demon next door. *Time Magazine.*

Wunderlich, R. (1978). Neuroallergy as a contributing factor to social misfits: Diagnosis and treatment. In L. Hippchen (Ed.), *Ecologic-biochemical approaches to treatment of delinquents and criminals* (pp. 229–254). New York: Von Nostrant Reinhold.

Wynn, K. (1992). Addition and subtraction by human infants. *Nature, 358*, 749–750.

Yablonsky, L. (1996). *The violent gang.* Baltimore: Penguin.

Yamagata, E. P., & Jones, M. A. (2000). *And justice for some.* Washington, DC: Building Blocks for Youth Initiative. Retrieved October 5, 2004, from http://www. buildingblocksforyouth.org/justicefor-some/jfs.html

Yardley, J., & Herszenhorn. D. M. (1998, September 27). Before dying, daughter, 7, tells 911 of policeman's rampage. *The New York Times,* p. 33.

Yarvis, R. M. (1994). Patterns of substance abuse and intoxication among murderers. *Bulletin of the American Academy of Psychiatry & the Law, 22,* 133–144.

Yarvis, R. M. (1995). Diagnostic patterns among three violent offender types. *Bulletin of the American Academy of Psychiatry & The Law, 23,* 411–419.

Yates, E. (1986). The influence of psychosocial factors on nonsensical shoplifting. *International Journal of Offender Therapy and Comparative Criminology, 30,* 203–211.

Yeudall, L. T. (1978). *The neuropsychology of aggression.* Clarence M. Hincks Memorial Lectures, Edmonton, Alberta, Canada.

Yeudall, L., Fromm-Auch, D., & Davies, P. (1982). Neuropsychological impairment of persistent delinquency. *Journal of Nervous and Mental Diseases, 170,* 257–265.

Yoshikawa, H. (1994). Prevention as cumulative protection: Effects of early family support and education on chronic delinquency and its risks. *Psychological Bulletin, 115,* 28–54.

Young, A.S., Forquer, S.L., Tran, A., Starzynski, M., & Shatkin, J. (2000). Identifying clinical competencies that support rehabilitation and empowerment in individuals with severe mental illness. *Journal of Behavioral Health Services Research, 27,* 321–333.

Youngberg v. Romeo, 457 U.S. 307 (1982).

Zahn-Wexler, C., & Radke-Yarrow, M. (1982). The development of altruism: Alternative research strategies. In N. Eisenberg (Ed.), *The development of prosocial behavior.* New York: Academic.

Zaidi, L. Y., Knutson, J. F., & Mehm, J. G. (1989). Transgenerational patterns of abusive parenting: Analog and clinical tests. *Aggressive Behavior, 15,* 137–152.

Zamble, E. (1992). Behavior and adaptation in long-term prison inmates: Descriptive longitudinal results. *Criminal Justice and Behavior, 19,* 409–425.

Zamble, E., Porporino, F., & Kalotay, J. (1984). *An analysis of coping behavior in prison inmates* (Programs branch user report). Ministry of the Solicitor General of Canada:.

Zawitz, M. W., Klaus, P. A., Bachman, R., Bastian, L. D., DeBerry, M. M., Rand, M. R., et al. (1993). *Highlights from 20 years of surveying crime victims: The National crime victimization survey, 1973–92.* Washington, DC: Bureau of Justice Statistics.

Zebrowitz, L. A., & McDonald, S. M. (1991). The impact of litigants' baby-facedness and attractiveness on adjudications in small claims courts. *Law and Human Behavior, 15,* 603–624.

Zehr, H. (1990). *Changing lenses.* Scottsdale, PA: Herald Press.

Zika, S., & Chamberlain, K. (1987). Relation of hassles and personality to subjective well-being. *Journal of Personality and Social Psychology, 53,* 155–163.

Zillman, D. (1989). Aggression and sex: Independent and joint operations. In H. L. Wagner & A.S. R. Manstead (Eds.), *Handbook of psychophysiology: Emotion and social behavior.* Chichester: Wiley.

Zillman, D., Baron, R.A., & Tamborini, R. (1981). Social costs of smoking: Effects of tobacco smoke on hostile behavior. *Journal of Applied Social Psychology, 11,* 548–561.

Zimbardo, P. (1969). The human choice: Individuation, reason, and order versus deindividuation, impulse, and chaos. In W. Arnold & D. Levie (Eds.), *Nebraska symposium on motivation* (pp. 287–293).

Ziskin, J., & Faust, D. (1988). *Coping with psychiatric and psychological testimony* (4th ed.). Marina Del Rey, CA: Lay & Psychology Press.

Zlutnick, S., & Altman, I. (1972). Crowding and human behavior. In J. Wohlwill & D. Carson (Eds.), *Environment and the social sciences: Perspectives and applications* (pp. 44–58). Washington, DC: American Psychological Association.

Zucker, R. A. (1987). The four alcoholisms: A developmental account of the etiologic process. In P. C. Rivers (Ed.), *Nebraska Symposium on Motivation, 1986: Vol. 34. Alcohol and addictive behaviors.* Lincoln: University of Nebraska Press.

Zucker, R. A., & Fitzgerald, H. E. (1991). Early developmental factors and risk for alcohol problems. *Alcohol Health Research World, 15,* 18–24.

Zuger, A. (1998, July 28). A fistful of hostility is found in women. *The New York Times.* Retrieved from http://www.nytimes.com/library/national/ science/072898sci-aggression.html

Zuniga, J. (2004, July 18). Teenage cook shot by gunman Huberty in 1984 now a San Diego police officer. *San Diego Union-Tribune.* Retrieved May 30, 2006 from http://www.signonsandiego.com/uniontrib/20040718/news_1m18massacre.html

Author Index

Note: Page numbers followed by n refer to footnotes.

Subject Index

Note: Page numbers in italics refer to figures; those in boldface refer to tables; those followed by n refer to footnotes.